LIVING ZOROASTRIANISM

URBAN PARSIS SPEAK ABOUT THEIR RELIGION

LIVING ZOROASTRIANISM

**URBAN PARSIS SPEAK
ABOUT THEIR RELIGION**

Philip G. Kreyenbroek

in collaboration with

Shehnaz Neville Munshi

CURZON

First Published in 2001
by Curzon Press
Richmond, Surrey
http://www.curzonpress.co.uk

© 2001 Philip G. Kreyenbroek

Typeset in Palatino by LaserScript Ltd, Mitcham, Surrey
Printed and bound in Great Britain by
TJ International, Padstow, Cornwall

British Library Cataloguing in Publication Data
A catalogue record of this book is available from the British Library

Library of Congress Cataloguing in Publication Data
A catalogue record for this book has been requested

ISBN 0–7007–1328–X

Contents

Contents

PART 3: CONCLUSIONS

Preface

The Parsis are a small group of Iranian descent who have preserved their communal, cultural and religious identity in India for the last ten centuries at least. This book is primarily concerned with the religion of this community, a branch of the ancient faith known as Zoroastrianism. It aims to elucidate the contemporary realities of Parsi religious life on the basis of narrative interviews, a method that is increasingly used in other fields of research and whose value for the study of religion is gradually being discovered. Like all other methods, qualitative research has its inherent limitations. It seems particularly appropriate in this case, however, because it helps to fill some of the more glaring lacunas in our knowledge of modern Parsi religion by throwing light on its subjective and devotional sides. Few adequate descriptions seem to exist of the way in which Parsis understand and practise their religion, and although a considerable amount is known about the classical Zoroastrian tradition as it developed in the Iranian homeland until the 9th or 10th century CE, it cannot be taken for granted that the connection between this ancient tradition and modern Indian realities is simple and straightforward.

An important reason for the scarcity of our information on modern Indian Zoroastrianism is that the interest of most Western academics and some modern Parsis has so far been focused predominantly on the ancient scriptural tradition. This classical tradition, in which doctrine and religious teaching play a major role, is in fact often held to represent the norm for all forms of the religion. That implies that contemporary beliefs, attitudes and practices for which no obvious foundation can be found in the scriptural tradition tend to be dismissed as mistaken or corrupt. A strong preoccupation with classical theology, in other words, has led to an academic understanding of Zoroastrianism which tends to be used as a prescriptive definition of that religion – a state of affairs that has not encouraged the study of the religious lives of modern Parsis as valid expressions of Zoroastrianism.

It is of course true that in some religions the contemporary tradition is strongly influenced by an 'official' form of the faith, which is based on an authoritative interpretation of a canon of sacred texts and is often upheld by a learned priesthood. In such cases, change generally results from interaction between the views of theologians representing official religion, and the needs and perceptions of ordinary believers. Where the daily realities of the latter make a traditional view seem outdated, the former usually adapt their teachings. On the other hand, official religion can act as a brake when developments threaten to happen too fast or be too radical, thus preventing a situation where modern beliefs are obviously at variance with earlier teachings. Where this is the case, the role of official religion in the development of contemporary religious traditions is obvious and important.

Zoroastrianism, on the other hand, differs from most other great religions in that its academic theology virtually stopped evolving some centuries after the Islamic conquest of Iran (7th century CE). As Islam consolidated its hegemony in the centuries that followed, Zoroastrian communities gradually became too marginal and poor to support the substantial group of scholar priests who until then had kept the intellectual and theological traditions of the faith alive. The remaining priestly scholars, it seems, began to devote their energies to writing down as much as they could of the ancient learned tradition, which until then had largely been transmitted orally. Later generations of priests, both in Iran and India, continued to study some of the knowledge contained in these writings, but few further attempts were apparently made to formulate an authoritative Zoroastrian system of doctrines in the light of the conditions of the times. For a long time, it seems, the religious life of Zoroastrian communities was such that this caused few problems. For the Parsis this changed in the early 19th century, when confrontations with Christianity and challenges posed by Western religious concepts and attitudes had the effect of calling into question the validity of traditional religion generally, and priestly learning in particular. The 19th century further saw many Parsis receiving a Western-type education and witnessed the rise of a powerful Parsi merchant class. All this led some Parsis to seek to define their theology, and contributed to the emergence of a series of religious movements springing from a sense of disenchantment with traditional Parsi religion. These movements, some of which still play a role in the life of the community today, generally aim to rediscover or redefine the teachings of Zoroastrianism, and in some cases the deeper meaning of ritual, with a view to establishing a reconstructed, authentic form of the religion.

One of the reasons why these developments have not so far led to the emergence of a unified 'reformed' Zoroastrianism is clearly to be sought in the profound dissimilarities between the teachings of the movements themselves. A further reason may be that a very different understanding of the nature and function of religion – emphasising orthopraxy, faith, and a devotional life that is not strongly based on intellectual beliefs – is deeply ingrained in the community, and most of its members have presumably been reluctant to rethink their religious lives deeply enough to accept a form of religion based on unfamiliar assumptions. However, the activities of the religious movements did have the effect of introducing to the community a theoretical conception of Zoroastrianism as a religion largely based on the authority of the classical tradition, intelligible teachings, and personal belief.

The relationship between the classical and modern traditions among Indian Zoroastrians is therefore a complex one. The Parsi tradition is of course ultimately based on classical Zoroastrianism; in the course of time it seems to have developed along its own lines in many respects, and it is now again influenced by the ideal of an authoritative, 'true' form of the religion which is closely associated with ancient teaching. However, as we saw, there is no consensus as to the precise character of this ideal form of Zoroastrianism and its impact on the religious lives of many Parsis is demonstrably minimal.

Clearly, these factors contribute to the difficulty of studying modern Parsi Zoroastrianism. As was noted earlier, few Western scholars have so far paid much attention to this form of the religion. The Parsis' own writings on religious questions are heterogeneous; apart from some esoteric works, their publications are usually influenced to some extent by Western-inspired definitions of religious concepts. If the views advanced in these works had achieved the status of a new orthodoxy, or even contributed to the emergence of a consensus on Zoroastrian teaching, they could presumably have served as a legitimate basis for research on Parsi religion. Since this is plainly not the case, however, it would seem that modern Parsi religion cannot be adequately understood on the basis of written sources alone, whether classical or modern. The traditional, deductive or prescriptive method of research, which accepts an authoritative form of a religion as a norm in the light of which other forms or aspects of the faith can be understood, therefore seems problematic in this case. As an alternative an inductive, descriptive approach is employed here, studying the evidence of personal testimonies with a view to arriving at a more general understanding. Although they cannot yield statistically significant data, in-depth interviews illustrate the way in which individuals understand and practise their religion. Thus they offer information which has so far been lacking, and further enable one to analyse the similarities and differences, the essential coherence or fundamental heterogeneity of the various practices, views and attitudes they describe or reflect. The evidence of a collection of narrative interviews may therefore contribute towards a tentative description of the realities of modern Parsi religious life.

Because of all this, a project was organised by the present writer in 1994 to collect and study a series of narrative interviews with Indian-based Parsis. These were to be conducted by a member of the community,

Mrs Shehnaz Neville Munshi, who is both interested in and knowledge-able about the traditions of her faith and her community. Mrs Munshi was given a brief but intensive training in interviewing techniques, with emphasis on the need to be non-judgmental, to regard all pertinent answers as valid, and to avoid asking leading questions. A list of queries was drawn up in collaboration with Mrs Munshi and other Parsis. The list contained questions about the informant's personal history, and current views and practices in the sphere of religion; further questions concerned festivals and religious occasions, visits to fire temples and pilgrimages, the Zoroastrian laws of purity, illnesses and cures, death and the afterlife, and beliefs and observances of non-Zoroastrian origin. It was emphasised, however, that these questions were no more than a guideline to keep an interview going if necessary, that there was no need to work through the entire list, and that informants should in any case be free to respond to the questions as briefly or elaborately they wished. The main aim of the interviews was not to obtain answers to specific questions, but rather to allow people to discuss those aspects of religion that were closest to their heart and to express their personal under-standing of their faith. In practice this approach proved very satisfactory. During most interviews the speaker's personal preoccupations and interests quickly came to light and determined the further course of the discussion; not infrequently, moreover, issues came up that could not have been anticipated and were not covered by questions on the list. An additional advantage of this method of interviewing is that it avoids the danger of forcing informants into the straight-jacket of the interviewer's preconceived ideas, as can happen with more structured interviews.

It may be relevant to mention in this context that Mrs Munshi is an active member of 'Zoroastrian Studies', a Bombay-based organisation which generously put its resources at the writer's disposal throughout the period of research. 'Zoroastrian Studies' is not uncontroversial in the community, being known for its outspoken Neo-traditionalist teachings. It should be stressed, however, that all parties concerned were clearly aware of the need for objectivity in carrying out research of this type, and considerable care was taken to ensure that Neo-traditionalist views should neither influence the choice of informants nor obtrude during the interviews themselves. In a few cases where Mrs Munshi's remarks did reflect her personal views, attention is drawn to this in the text.

It became clear at an early stage that the religious culture of Parsi laymen in big cities differed significantly from that of rural communities, and the evidence further suggested that working priests have a distinctive sub-culture, or at least many characteristic traditions of their own. It was therefore decided to study these groups in a later publication focusing on more traditional aspects of Parsi life. The present work contains thirty interviews with Parsis from an urban background.

Only one interviewee is a working priest and one other a priest's wife; in both cases the interviews were included because they seemed particularly relevant in the context of this book.

The selection of interviewees was guided by two more or less contradictory considerations. On the one hand a book of this type should ideally leave the reader with a mental image of Parsi religious life which would accord with that of ordinary community members; on the other hand it should throw light on views, tendencies and movements which influence the majority but are too radical or extreme to be shared by it.

All possible efforts have been made to publish a range of interviews reflecting the main groups, trends and movements which play a role in Parsi religious life today. However, some points should be noted. First of all, the impossibility of holding an in-depth interview on religion with someone who is wholly uninterested in the subject caused an important section of the community to be left unrepresented here. On the opposite side of the scale, beliefs and practices of non-Zoroastrian origin (e.g. those associated with devotion to a Baba or Guru), which in moderate form can be incorporated into a religious life that is essentially Zoroastrian, may in some cases become so predominant that neither Parsi public opinion nor common sense would accept them as expressions of Zoroastrianism. Finally, the interest of the book would hardly be enhanced by including a large number of testimonies remarkable only for being ordinary. The selection of interviews published here therefore does not reflect the whole range of Parsis' views about religion, nor can the frequency of opinions expressed there be taken to represent the currency of such views in the community as a whole. Chapters 3 and 10 aim to provide a context in which the data of the interviews can be better understood.

The book is divided into three main parts: (1) The Background, (2) Interviews, and (3) Conclusions. Chapter 1 offers a brief description of classical Zoroastrianism and its history, concentrating on aspects which are relevant to the main subject of the book. The second Chapter is based on a series of interviews the present writer had with Mrs Munshi and was written in collaboration with her. It contains a survey of what are called, for want of a more adequate term, 'common Parsi observances'; while the few existing sources on Parsi observance tend to concentrate on high priestly rituals, Mrs Munshi described a wide range of ordinary family or community ceremonies which may or may not require the services of a priest but are clearly felt to have religious connotations. Chapter 3 deals with aspects of the social and public life of the Parsi community – its institutions, religious factions, and public debates – with particular reference to Bombay.

The interviews themselves have been grouped under six headings indicating views or attitudes that seem more or less characteristic of the speakers: Traditionalists; Neo-traditionalists; Modernist Views; Eclecticism in Religious Lives; Esoteric Beliefs; and Religion as Cultural Heritage. This division is in many ways an arbitrary one, aimed at making the material more accessible by imposing some sort of order. Hardly any of the categories concerned are clear-cut, nor can personal realities usually be brought under one heading only. For an analysis of various types of Parsi religiosity the reader is referred to Ch. 10, which seeks to interpret the evidence of the interviews.

When the interviews were held contributors were asked whether they wished to be identified in the published work, and a majority replied in the affirmative. Given a researcher's obligation to protect his informants' interests, however, and the fact that statements which seem harmless at one time may involve individuals in unforeseen controversies or disputes later, it was decided to be guided by caution. Those who chose to be identified are therefore named in the list on p. xv but not, generally, in the interviews themselves. Exceptions are made for some informants who are well known in the community for reasons connected with religion (e.g. as religious teachers or because they are prominently associated with religious charities), since their opinions are in any case widely known, and it seemed that the public has a legitimate interest in their views. On the other hand, informants who are chiefly known for other reasons (such as members of socially prominent families) are generally not identified in the interviews even if they play an active role in community affairs.

The interviews were held either in English or Gujarati; recordings of the English interviews were transcribed fully or in part by the present writer, those in Gujarati were translated by Mrs Munshi. It soon became clear that it was impossible to publish a full transcript of most interviews; on average these lasted 90 minutes, and were thus too long for such treatment. Moreover, descriptions of occasions such as weddings and Navjotes tended to become repetitive. The published accounts therefore give a summary of passages which gain little from a full transcription, whilst the speakers' own words are reproduced where this seems important. The summaries inevitably reflect the present writer's interpretation of what was said.

Where the informant's own words are given it was sought to stay as close to the spoken text as possible. Evident slips of the tongue, repetitions, or obvious mistakes in English were omitted or corrected. In some cases long and detailed descriptions which were not relevant to the speaker's main argument were summarised ('my cousin, the daughter of my maternal aunt, who always dressed in red,' might become 'a relative'). Parsi English was treated as a legitimate form of the language and transcribed as spoken. A few typical speech habits (such as the use of 'only' to emphasise the preceding word or phrase), seemed likely to confuse or distract the non-Indian reader and were not retained in the transcript.

The transcription of Gujarati and Iranian terms presented some difficulties. Academic systems for transcribing these languages exist, but in a book of this type they have the disadvantage of being unnecessarily complicated and giving the text a pedantic look. Most Parsis, moreover, are unfamiliar with these systems. For some non-English words they use standard spellings (which do not always meet rigourous criteria of consistency), while in other cases a range of different spellings is found. Where standard Parsi spellings exist these are generally adopted here; for other words a method of transcription is used that is intended to facilitate an adequate pronunciation without marking distinctions that have no meaning unless one is familiar with the languages concerned. No diacritical signs are used; 'a' represents either the first or the second vowel sound of *apart* in Southern English; 'u' is used for the vowels of *book* or *lose*; 'e' for those of French *été, mère,* or *de*; 'i' for those of *tin* or *bean*; 'o' for those of French *beau* or English *on*. In the few cases where longer phrases or sentences in Gujarati are reproduced, such a transcription would be insufficient and diacritics are used, notably *ṭ, ḍ, ṇ, ś* for retroflex consonants, macrons (ā, ū) to indicate long vowels, and a *tilde* (ã, ũ) for nasalised vowels.

Another minor problem was posed by the case endings of some Gujarati words. Nouns ending in *-o* or *-u*, for example, change their ending to *-a* in some circumstances. When speaking English some Parsis call an oil-lamp a *divo* (the *casus rectus*), while others say *diva* (the oblique case); for the plural, *divas* is generally used in English. The plural in *-as* is therefore used here, while in cases where usage varies singulars are given in the *rectus* form. Words of Indian origin that are spelled as English words (e.g. Agiary), are given corresponding plurals (Agiaries).

While the work on this book was in progress, the official name of the metropolis changed from Bombay to Mumbai. As the city is generally referred to in the interviews as Bombay and is still known to most Westerners by that name, the change has not been adopted here.

———

My thanks are due first and foremost to Shehnaz Munshi, who has probably done a greater share of the work than I have, and without whose constant advice, interviewing skills and knowledge of the community the project would have been unlikely to succeed. I am very grateful also to Khojeste Mistree and Firoza Punthakey Mistree for their friendship, their constant support, expert advice, and lavish hospitality. Sarah Stewart, of the School of Oriental and African Studies, London, helped to shape and organise the project and remained involved later. The indefatigable office staff of 'Zoroastrian Studies', notably Shernaz

Panthaky, Jeannie Bharucha and Katy Neemuchwalla, helped in various ways, as did Stefanie Brinkmann, Oliver Henze, Albert de Jong, Susanne Fee Karalus, Mieke Kreyenbroek, Farhad Munshi and Alan V. Williams. Dastur Dr Firoze M. Kotwal enlightened me about various points of ritual.

The project whose results are published here was funded by generous grants from the British Academy and the Spalding Trust. I am grateful to the School of Oriental and African Studies, University of London, for offering me a sabbatical year, which enabled me to complete the first phase of the research before taking up a new post in Göttingen.

The warmth and helpfulness of the contributors made this a most enjoyable experience, and I am grateful to all of them. May the book be worthy of all the effort, knowledge and sincerity they gave to it.

Philip G. Kreyenbroek

The Informants

The names listed here are those of informants who indicated that they wished to be identified; the wishes of those who preferred not to be named have of course been respected.

Aibara, Ervad Yazdi N.
Amroliwala, Mr Phiroze
Antia, Mr Burjor H.
Bana, Mr Sarosh H.
Bharucha, Dr Jeannie B.
Chothia, Mr Rustom C.
Cooper-Vosburgh, Mrs Dinaz
Coyaji, Dr Kurus
Coyaji, Dr Jeroo K.
Dadrawala, Mr Noshir H.
Dalal, Mr Bahadurshah
Dalal-Paghdiwala, Mrs Freny F.
Doctor, Mr Adi F.
Godrej, Mrs Pheroza J.
Khan, Mrs Shirin J.
Khurody, Ms Khursheed
Master-Moos, Dr Meher
Mehta, Mrs Pervin R.
Mistree, Mr Khojeste P.
Mobedji, Mrs Jaloo R.
Moolla, Mrs Dolet D.
Mulla, Mr Noshir D.
Nusservanjee, Mrs Nergish J.
Pithavala, Mr Behram D.
Ranina, Mr Homi
Tamboly, Mr Dinshaw K.

Abbreviations

Ar.	Arabic
Av.	Avestan
A.V.	*Ashem Vohu*
BCE	Before Common Era
CE	Common Era
d.	died
Eng.	English
Guj.	Gujarati
id.	*idem*
Ind.	Indian
Ir.	Iranian
lit.	literally
n.	note
OInd.	Old Indian
OIr	Old Iranian
Pers.	Persian
Phl.	Pahlavi
PK	Philip G. Kreyenbroek
q.v.	*quo vide*
Rs.	Rupees
Skt.	Sanskrit
SM	Shehnaz N. Munshi
s.o.	someone
SS	Sarah R.A. Stewart
s.v.	*sub voce*
Vend.	*Vendidad*
Y.	*Yasna*
Y.A.V.	*Yatha Ahu Vairyo*
Yt.	*Yasht*
ZS	'Zoroastrian Studies'

Part One

The Background

Chapter One

Classical Zoroastrianism

As with other religions, many people's thoughts on the subject of Zoroastrianism are inspired or influenced by a mental image of that faith which is largely based on interpretations of the ancient religious texts. Although, as stated in the Preface, relations between this 'classical' form of Zoroastrianism and modern Parsi religion are complex, some knowledge of the former is indispensable for an adequate understanding of the latter. Apart from questions of doctrine (on which see Ch. 3, 10), the ancient tradition continues to determine or affect Parsi religious life in many ways. Priestly rituals and various other observances are continuations of ancient practice; many of the community's symbols, concepts and images derive from classical Zoroastrianism, even if some of these are now interpreted in novel ways; furthermore, an awareness of the glories of ancient Zoroastrian empires and civilisations contributes to many Parsis' sense of pride in their religious and communal identity.

It seems appropriate, therefore, briefly to discuss aspects of the teachings, observances and history of classical Zoroastrianism. In doing so, however, some reservations must be made. Specialists in the field of ancient Iranian religion disagree on many points, and the sources represent a priestly tradition which tells us little about the religious lives of ordinary believers. The account given here is based on interpretations of the sources which seem plausible to the present writer. To what extent the scriptural tradition reflects the realities of early Zoroastrian communities remains a matter for debate and conjecture.

Zarathustra and his reform

The term 'Zoroastrianism' derives from *Zoroastèr*, the Greek version of the Iranian name *Zarathushtra*, which in the West is usually spelled 'Zarathustra'. Zoroastrians regard Zarathustra as the founder of their religion and as a prophet who was in direct contact with God. Since

Zarathustra lived in the pre-historic period, i.e. before his people began to use writing, we can only speculate as to his date and place. Many scholars believe that Zarathustra lived at a time when the Iranian peoples were engaged in the great migration which eventually brought them from the Central Asian steppes to their later homelands in Iran, Afghanistan, Tajikistan, Northern Iraq and parts of Eastern Anatolia. The most likely date seems to be around 1000 BCE.

It can be inferred from the Zoroastrian tradition that the early Iranian tribes already had a well-developed religious tradition, most aspects of which they shared with their sister-tribes, the ancestors of the northern Indians. The appearance of Zarathustra, however, seems to have coincided with a partial departure from the established tradition, which warrants the assumption that Zarathustra's activities did indeed trigger developments leading to the rise of a new cult which used his name to identify itself. There is evidence to suggest that Zarathustra was a priest who was well versed in the religious traditions of his people. It seems that his novel understanding of religious truth, based perhaps upon visionary experiences occurring in the course of his priestly duties, caused his followers to regard themselves as distinct from the adherents of the older faith. Although this new religion retained many of the traditional beliefs and practices of its precursor, it was based on a wholly original view of the rationale and purpose of existence. Furthermore, it rejected the worship of the *daevas*, a group of divine beings who may have represented the 'might-is-right' ethos popular among a conquering migrant people, in contradistinction to the strictly 'moral' character of another group of gods, the *ahuras*, whose worship Zarathustra endorsed. The word *daeva*, which until then meant 'gods', came to mean 'devils' in the language of the Zoroastrians.

Good and evil supernatural beings

The rejection of the *daevas* is a central element of Zarathustra's teaching. In fact, one of the most prominent new elements of Zarathustra's message was his representation of evil as an autonomous power: not a mere negation of, or departure from, right, but its active and intentional opponent. The forces of evil are headed by Angra Mainyu ('Evil Intention', later Ahriman), the personified, diabolical opponent of 'Beneficent Intention' (Av. Spenta Mainyu) and indeed of God, the good Creator whose name is Ahura Mazda ('Lord Wisdom', later Ohrmazd, Hormazd).

In later Zoroastrianism Spenta Mainyu was identified with Ahura Mazda himself,[1] but earlier he was seen as a separate Being, who formed part of the group of Ahura Mazda's immediate helpers, the seven Amesha Spentas ('Beneficent Immortals'). The Amesha Spentas are powerful divine beings but, as is shown in the following diagram, each also represents a mental quality or concept which man can cultivate or prepare for in his own life; furthermore each Amesha Spenta has a special connection with one of the seven 'creations', the essential elements of the good material world.

Avestan Name	Parsi Name	'Creation'	English meaning of the name
Ahura Mazda (Spenta Mainyu)[2]	Hormazd[3] (Spenta Mainyu)	Man	Lord Wisdom (Beneficent Intention)
Asha Vahishta	Ardibehesht	Fire	Best Righteousness
Vohu Manah	Bahman	Cattle	Good Thought
Khshathra Vairya	Shehrevar	Metal, Sky	The Power that must be chosen
Spenta Armaiti	Aspandad, Aspandarmad	Earth	Beneficent Devotion
Haurvatat	Khordad	Water	Wholeness
Ameretat	Amardad	Plants	Immortality

Besides Ahura Mazda and the Amesha Spentas, the Zoroastrian tradition recognises a number of other divine beings (Av. *Yazata*, Phl. *Yazad*). Each good divinity is held to have an evil opponent.

The Cosmic Battle and the role of Man

Classical Zoroastrianism sees the world as an arena, limited in time and place, in which the forces of good and evil can do battle until evil will have been defeated for ever. All parts of creation belong either to Ahura Mazda or to Angra Mainyu, which means that most 'creations' cannot help being either good or bad. The exception is Man, a good 'creation' who is nevertheless uniquely capable of moral choice. Man, therefore, must choose between good and evil, and his choice will determine the cosmic battle.[4] Humans are therefore expected to strengthen the forces of good by joining them, and by leading a life of Good Thoughts, Good Words and Good Deeds.

At some later stage fatalist ideas entered the tradition, which in a sense cut across Zarathustra's 'moral' world-view based on individual choice,[5] and some attempts were made to achieve a synthesis between the two. It seems probable, however, that beliefs and attitudes based on a dualist world-view continued to play an important role in pre-modern Zoroastrianism.

5

The fate of the soul after death and the End of Time

The right or wrong choice, and in fact every good or wicked thought, word or act, will have consequences after death. Zarathustra may have been the first prophet to teach that recompense will come after this life, with the righteous rejoicing in heaven while the wicked repent in hell. The fate of the soul is determined on the fourth morning after death, when it must cross the 'Chinvad Bridge' to the hereafter. At the Bridge a judgement takes place: some accounts speak of a trial by three divine beings, while others say that the soul will be met by its alter ego, a beautiful young girl if the person has been good, and an unpleasant hag if it has not. Depending on the outcome of the Judgement, the soul goes to heaven or hell, or to purgatory in case of an even balance between good and bad.

Another concept which may have originated with Zarathustra is that of the End of Time. Limited, dynamic time is said to have been created by Ahura Mazda so that evil could be defeated, which would have been impossible had the universe remained in a static, timeless condition. It follows that, once this has been achieved, time as we know it no longer serves a purpose and will come to an end. The process will be set in motion by the appearance of a Saviour (Saoshyant), who will be miraculously born of a virgin mother who bathes in a lake where Zarathustra's semen is preserved. There will be a physical resurrection of the dead, whose last unexpiated sins will be cleansed by a stream of molten metal. This will be followed by a final battle between the opposing forces, and the defeat of Evil. After this, time will end and all humans will exist forever in blissful harmony.

The sacred and religious texts of Zoroastrianism

The corpus of the ancient sacred texts of the Zoroastrians is known as the Avesta. The Zoroastrian tradition claims that the entire Avesta was revealed to Zarathustra by Ahura Mazda. Western scholarship, on the other hand, believes that the various texts making up the Avesta are not all of the same origin, but together constitute what is left of a broad range of sacred texts of various kinds which were handed down orally from generation to generation until they were committed to writing at some time during the Sasanian period (see further below). Only the *Gathas* are widely thought to be the words of Zarathustra.[6] The language of the Avesta, known as Avestan, is an ancient tongue once spoken in Eastern Iran, which continued to be used as the sacred language of Zoroastrianism even when the centre of Zoroastrian civilisation shifted to Persia in the west of the Iranian territories (see below). It is known that a great many Avestan texts have been lost, the present corpus representing about a third of the original. Important parts of the Avesta are the following:

The *Yasna,* a group of texts which constitute the liturgy of the central ritual of Zoroastrianism, which is known by the same name (see below). At the heart of this liturgy – surrounded as it were by the protective power of other texts – are the *Gathas,* the holy 'Songs' of Zarathustra. They represent a very ancient type of sacral poetry which Zarathustra evidently mastered as part of his priestly training, and are extremely difficult to understand.

The *Yashts* are hymns to individual divine beings. Although the texts continued to evolve in oral transmission at least until the Achaemenian period (see below), the core of some Yashts appears to be very old, probably pre-Zoroastrian in origin.

The *Vendidad* consists of texts discussing various topics, which originally appear to have belonged to a scholarly priestly tradition rather than a liturgical one. In the course of time, however, texts belonging to the *Yasna* and *Vendidad* were combined to form the liturgy of a new night ritual, which came to be known as the 'Vendidad'.

The name *Khordeh Avesta* ('little Avesta') is used for a collection of texts which are widely used as prayers (on these see further below).

The Pahlavi Texts represent a later stage in the history of Zoroastrianism; the term Pahlavi is used for Middle Persian, the official language of the Sasanian Empire and the immediate ancestor of modern Persian. As Avestan became less and less easy to understand for later generations, the ancient texts were translated into local vernaculars, and exegetical comments were added. Such translations-cum-commentaries are known as *Zand* (whence the expression 'Zend-Avesta'). The *Zand* forms the core of an extensive religious literature in Pahlavi. Most Pahlavi texts were written down in their final form during the 9th or 10th century CE.

The word *Pazand* is used for a late form of Middle Persian which is written in the Avestan, as opposed to the Pahlavi, alphabet. Some ritual formulae and prayers are preserved in Pazand.

Some Zoroastrian religious texts, mostly of a didactic or practical nature, exist in modern Persian. The considerable corpus of early Gujarati literature which may have a bearing on Zoroastrianism has so far hardly been explored.

Prayer, sudreh and kusti

The traditional Zoroastrian concept of prayer may seem complex to a outsider. The ancient Iranians believed that the Avesta had been directly revealed to Zarathustra by Ahura Mazda. The words of the Avesta were therefore regarded as having a power of their own, which became effective when the texts were correctly recited. Prayer was held to strengthen the divine beings, benefit the world generally, and bring merit to the person who prayed or instructed a priest to pray on his behalf. One of the chief functions of prayer, therefore, was to strengthen the forces of Good, but praying for personal benefit was also known. Even for such purposes, however, the ancient Iranians probably addressed divine beings primarily by reciting established Avestan texts and prayers, rather than by asking for boons in their own words.

Some Avestan texts have probably always been used specifically as prayers; these include the great prayers *Yatha Ahu Vairyo* and *Ashem Vohu*; the *Niyayesh* (prayers) to Meher (Mithra), the Sun, the Moon, the Waters and Fire; the prayers for each watch[7] of the day; the *Sarosh Baj* (a prayer invoking the Yazad Sarosh), and several others. However, many other Avestan texts could also be recited as prayers, and a great many prayers exist which consist of combinations of sacred texts. To give a complete list of such prayers would lie beyond the scope of this book.[8]

Sudreh and kusti. At the ceremony in which a young Zoroastrian is initiated as a full member of the community,[9] he or she is invested with the *sudreh* and *kusti*. The *sudreh* ('sacred shirt') is a muslin upper garment worn under one's other clothes; the *kusti* or 'sacred cord' is tied around the waist. *Sudreh* and *kusti* are regarded as emblems of one's Zoroastrian identity and should always be worn. On various occasions (e.g. before praying, before meals, and after answering calls of nature), one must wash the face and exposed parts of the body and untie and retie the *kusti*, while reciting a few short prayers (this procedure is known as the *padyab-kusti*).

Laws of Purity, Towers of Silence

The concept of purity is most important in Zoroastrianism. Man must keep himself pure both in the moral and the physical sense, and great emphasis is laid on the need to keep the good 'creations' unsullied. Substances issuing from the body were held to be particularly polluting. Great care had to be taken in disposing of hair and nails after they have been cut. Menstruating women generally observed a period of seclusion when they avoided contact with other members of the household and with household objects.

The dead body of a Zoroastrian was regarded as extremely impure, and should not defile any of the sacred 'elements', such as Earth or Fire. Classical Zoroastrianism therefore rejected burial or cremation. As rock and hard stone were thought to be impenetrable and not susceptible to serious pollution, Zoroastrians disposed of their dead by laying them on a stony or rocky surface in the open air, where the bones would soon be stripped clean by animals and birds. At some stage special structures were introduced for this purpose: round roofless 'amphitheatres' inside which there were rows for male, female and children's bodies. These are known in Persian as *dakhme* (Guj. *dokhme*), and in English as 'Towers of Silence'.

Fire temples and priests

The early Iranians worshipped in the open, preferably on mountain tops; a temple cult probably developed in the Achaemenian period. Temple complexes normally contained an area devoted to the performance of rituals, but the temple was essentially thought of as the house of a sacred fire. Zoroastrian places of worship are therefore known in English as 'fire temples'.[10] To a Zoroastrian, fire represents the purity of the divine and Zoroastrians normally face a fire (or another source of light) when praying, both in the fire temple and at home.

In the course of time several categories of sacred fires came to be distinguished. The purification rites for a fire of the highest order, an *Atash Behram*,[11] are very elaborate indeed, and a fire of this rank is most expensive to maintain. Ordinary fire temples normally house an *Atash Adaran*, a fire of the second grade, which requires simpler purification rites and whose maintenance is less costly. From a ritual point of view fires of the third category, *Atash-e Dadgah*, are essentially hearth fires; unlike the other fires they can be kept in a private house, and tended by laymen provided these are in a state of purity.[12] When they are housed in a fire temple, a short consecration ceremony is normally performed.[13] All fires must be fed at the commencement of each of the five watches of the day; the ceremony of offering fuel to a sacred fire (*boy dadan*) is a solemn ritual.[14]

From time immemorial the Iranians distinguished between priestly and lay families. Only a man[15] of priestly family could act as a priest. Little is known about the organisation of the priesthood in the early days of the faith or even under the Achaemenians, but the Sasanian Empire knew an elaborate and highly diversified professional priesthood which played an important role in the administration of the state, and in academic as well as purely religious affairs. After the fall of the Sasanian Empire, the priesthood lost its state backing and in the course of time the Zoroastrian community could no longer maintain such a complex system of priestly ranks and functions (see further Ch. 3).

Rituals

It is perhaps in the sphere of priestly rituals – i.e. ceremonies which require the services of one or more priests – that the greatest degree of continuity can be found in the Zoroastrian tradition. A number of such ceremonies (the 'inner rituals') take place in the fire temple area, or in a place especially consecrated for this purpose (*Dar-e Meher*); the person on whose behalf the ritual is performed may or may not be present. Others (the 'outer rituals') can be performed by priests outside the fire temple, e.g. in private homes. The list of rituals given below is far from exhaustive, referring mainly to ceremonies which are mentioned in the interviews.[16] The descriptions given here represent modern Indian practice, which may differ from the earlier tradition on points of detail.

The *Yasna* (Guj. *Ijashne*) ceremony is the central priestly act of worship. It is a long and complex rite, which must be performed in a consecrated area especially designated for ritual purposes, usually within a fire temple. In modern practice the *Yasna* is celebrated by two priests in the early-morning watch of the day. It is preceded by elaborate preparatory rites and comprises various ritual acts, such as the blessing and tasting of a special kind of bread (*dron, darun*), the consecration of a liquid (*haoma, hom*), and acts of homage to Fire and Water. These acts are accompanied by recitation of the *Yasna* liturgy (on which see above).[17]

The *Vendidad*, which is thought to be of relatively late origin, is unusual in that it is performed at night. Its liturgy consists of alternate recitations of texts from the *Yasna* and *Vendidad*.[18]

The word *baj* has various meanings in Zoroastrian priestly parlance.[19] The ceremony of that name is a relatively short one, in which *drons*, fruit, and animal products such as an egg and clarified butter, are consecrated while liturgical texts are recited. The officiating priest eats a little of the consecrated *dron*, and the blessed food can later be distributed to friends, or given to the priest. *Baj* ceremonies are usually celebrated in a *Dar-e Mehr* but may be performed elsewhere, provided the place has been scrupulously cleaned.

The *Nirangdin* is a very elaborate and complex ritual, requiring a retreat of nine nights on the part of the two priests intending to participate, followed by another eight days of preparatory rituals.[20] These rites are intended to ensure that the priests have the highest possible ritual power. The purpose of the service is to consecrate bulls' urine,[21] thus transforming it into *nirang*, one of the most potent purificatory substances known to Zoroastrianism. After elaborate cleansing of all the implements used, the actual ceremony begins at midnight and takes about eight hours to complete.

The *Afrinagan* can be performed in private houses. It is normally celebrated by two or more priests, who recite prayers over a tray of food in the presence of a fire which is fed during the recitation. These services can be performed on many occasions; it is customary to have *Afrinagans* performed, together with other ceremonies, on the first three days after a death, but also to celebrate happy occasions.[22] The term *jashan* (celebration) is generally used as a synonym of *Afrinagan*.[23]

The *Fareshta* consists of *Afrinagan* and *Baj* services recited for 33 divine Beings individually. Normally several priests are employed for this lengthy ritual, which is usually performed in thanksgiving when a goal is achieved or a wish has been granted.[24]

The term *Satum* refers to a prayer which is recited over a tray containing food that is offered to, or prepared in honour of the *fravashi* (an eternal aspect or part of the soul) of one or more dead loved ones.[25]

The *Farokhshi* is also a service for the *fravashis* of the dead. It is recited by a priest over flowers, fruit, milk and sometimes other items, in front of a fire. The liturgy is that of the *Satum*, combined with parts of the Hymn to the Fravashis (*Farvardin Yasht*).[26]

Funerary ceremonies fall into two categories: those relating to the preparation of the body and its removal to the Towers of Silence, and prayers and rituals for the soul of the deceased.[27]

Purification ceremonies have always been of great importance in Zoroastrianism. On such occasions as the initiation ceremony (Navjote), weddings, the end of the forty-day period after childbirth, and traditionally during the last ten days of the year,[28] people underwent a form of purification known as *nahn*, which is described in Ch. 2.[29]

The Calendar and the watches of the day

At some stage, perhaps under the Achaemenian king Artaxerxes II (404–358 BCE),[30] a common Zoroastrian calendar was introduced, which enabled priests of various Zoroastrian communities throughout the Empire to worship certain divinities on the same day, and thus contributed to the unification of the Zoroastrian 'Church'. This was done by devoting each day of the month, and every month of the year, to a particular divinity. To the 360 days thus named, five more (the 'Gatha days', see Ch. 2) were later added.[31] For purposes of prayer and ritual the day is divided into five watches (Phl. *gah*, Guj. *geh*). Traditionally, Zoroastrians pray at each change of *gah*, and many rituals may only be performed in one particular watch.[32]

Feasts

The seven holiest feasts of classical Zoroastrianism were the New Year (which Parsis call *Navroz*), and six festivals known as *Gahambar*,[33] which took place at fixed points in the religious year. It was a duty to celebrate these seven feasts, each of which was dedicated to one of the Amesha Spentas.[34] (The modern Parsi community no longer celebrates these festivals, and the term *Gahambar* is now used for festive communal meals.)

In many cases, the 'name day' of a Yazata, when the day and the month were both dedicated to that divinity, was celebrated as a festival.[35]

History

As we saw earlier Zoroastrianism probably originated somewhere on the Central Asian steppe or to the East of modern Iran around 1000 BCE. It seems likely that the faith developed among Eastern Iranian peoples for several centuries, and then spread slowly to more western parts of the Iranian realm.

The Achaemenians (559–331 BCE). There are strong indications that the first great Emperors of Iran, the Western Iranian Achaemenians, were already Zoroastrians. The Emperors' adherence to the faith probably did much to promote its further expansion throughout the Iranian realm. From a relatively obscure East-Iranian cult Zoroastrianism thus became the dominant religion of a world Empire.

This new prominence of the Zoroastrian religion in Iran must have had a profound influence on its further development. The ideology of the Achaemenian Empire was based, it seems, on the view that the state prospered because the Emperor enjoyed divine approval. Church and State must have been closely connected, and it can be assumed that the priesthood developed from a caste of locally based 'parish-priests' to an ecclesiastic structure capable of playing a leading role in the administration of an Empire. Furthermore the Iranians, who had hitherto worshipped God in the open, seem to have been sufficiently impressed by the great temples of the surrounding cultures to adopt a temple cult as part of Zoroastrianism (see above).

Alexander the Great and the Seleucids. The non-Iranian Alexander the Great (known in the Zoroastrian tradition as 'Alexander the Accursed') defeated the great Persian Empire in 331 BCE, and a new international culture developed as a result of his conquests. Under Alexander's successors, the Seleucids, Hellenism became the dominant culture in the Middle East and a form of religion based on the Greek tradition came to play an important role there. Zoroastrianism must therefore have lost some of its previous prestige and status, but the structure of religious life in Iran was such that the new cultural and religious impulses probably affected Zoroastrian communities only superficially; some Iranians adopted Hellenist culture and perhaps enriched it with elements of their own heritage, but most people continued to practise their traditional religion and to rely on their priests for guidance in many areas.

The Parthians or Arsacids (mid-3rd century BCE-226 CE). In the course of time the Iranian religious tradition began to reassert itself as a dominant cultural force. The Parthians, who ruled large parts of the Iranian realm as successors to the Seleucids, were Zoroastrians and presumably strengthened the image of Zoroastrianism as the 'natural' religion of the Iranians.

The Sasanians (226–651 CE). This renaissance of Zoroastrianism as a symbol of Iranian culture and nationhood reached its zenith under the Sasanian kings. Like the Achaemenians, the Sasanians were Persians (i.e. from the south-western part of Iran), and they clearly regarded themselves as the true and rightful heirs of that earlier dynasty. Early

Sasanian propaganda represents righteousness in the religious sphere as the chief legitimation of the new dynasty, and Church and State once more came to be very closely linked.

In the process of setting the country to rights the new establishment laid great emphasis on the need for its subjects to be 'good' Zoroastrians, which implied adherence to the religious authority of the state-backed priesthood. The distinction between 'good' and 'bad' Zoroastrians seems to have played a more prominent role in Sasanian religious thought than was the case before, which presumably led to a greater interest in the concept of 'orthodoxy'. Contacts with early Byzantine Christianity, which was much preoccupied with similar questions, may have furthered this process. Other developments which characterised the history of Zoroastrianism in Sasanian times include the rise of the priesthood to enormous influence and status, vigorous intellectual activity in various spheres connected with religion, and the development of an alphabet adequate to render the sounds of Avestan. When this had been achieved the ancient sacred texts were written down, presumably for the first time, and a written Zoroastrian 'canon' came into existence. Although writing thus began to play a role in Zoroastrianism in the Sasanian era, the tradition continued to be primarily an oral one: it was not until well into the post-Sasanian era that the priesthood systematically began to write down parts of an intellectual tradition that in many ways represents the achievements of the Sasanian era.

The Islamic Conquest (mid-7th century CE). As with the Achaemenians, an era when state ideology and religious teaching reinforced one another and Zoroastrianism received full backing from the Court, came to an abrupt end when Iran was overrun by alien conquerors. In the 630s and 640s CE, the newly Islamised Arabs mounted a succession of campaigns against the Sasanian Empire, which they subjected without much difficulty. The last Sasanian king, Yazdegird III, fled the country and is thought to have died in exile in 651. Although the introduction of the new faith did not lead to instant mass conversions – in fact it took several centuries until Islam could be said fully to have supplanted Zoroastrianism – the culture which the conquerors brought with them rapidly developed into a highly fertile civilisation which became dominant in the entire Middle East, and Zoroastrianism was slowly relegated to a marginal position.[36]

This newly marginal status naturally affected the economic position of the Zoroastrians, which in turn led to the impoverishment of their intellectual and religious traditions. Whilst the community continued to need the services of ritual priests, it could no longer support the group of scholar-priests who until then had memorised, studied and developed the learned tradition, most of which had existed in oral form only. As these scholars realised that change was inevitable, they wrote down what they could of their ancient heritage. Most of the extant Pahlavi texts are the result of this ambitious endeavour. Although some of the ancient knowledge had thus been salvaged, standards of priestly learning inevitably declined in the centuries that followed.

The migration to India. At some stage, perhaps in the eighth or in the mid-tenth century,[37] a group of Zoroastrians from the north-eastern part of Iran decided to preserve their religion by fleeing from Muslim dominion. They found their way to India, where they became the ancestors of the community whose lives and ideas are discussed in this book.

Notes

1 See latterly Kreyenbroek 1993.
2 Since there was apparently a firm tradition that there were seven Amesha Spentas, when Spenta Mainyu came to be identified with Ahura Mazda the latter was generally counted as a member of the group.
3 Or 'Hormajd'. Iranian z is realised by many Gujarati speakers as /ʤ/ (as in Eng. *just*). The transcription z is generally preferred here.
4 Zoroastrian teaching is confident that Evil will eventually be overcome, but support from men will presumably hasten the process.
5 Such ideas are often associated with a form of Zoroastrianism known as Zurvanism, which taught that both Hormazd and Ahriman were the children of Zurvan, the God of Time. The status of Zurvanite ideas in pre-Islamic Zoroastrian theology is currently debated by scholars.
6 Some scholars would make the same claim for another group of texts, the *Yasna Haptanghaiti,* whereas others think it unlikely that Zarathustra was the author of the *Gathas.*
7 Phl. *gah,* Guj. *geh,* see further p. 11; for a list of these watches see Appendix.
8 For references to prayers which are mentioned in the interviews, see Index.
9 In India this ceremony is known as the Navjote (on which see below, p. 27f.).
10 In Parsi English the Guj. word 'Agiary' is often used for ordinary fire temples.
11 For an elaborate account of the purification ceremonies needed for fires of the first two categories see Modi 1922: 199–229.
12 See Boyce 1979: 110.
13 See Modi 1922: 229–30.
14 For a description of the ceremony of *boy dadan* in fire temples of different grades see Modi 1922: 219–23.
15 There are indications that women could, theoretically at least, fulfil certain priestly functions (see Kotwal and Kreyenbroek 1992: 39–47; 1995: 121–5). The texts suggest that the male priestly establishment was uncomfortable with this as early as the Sasanian period, and very little is known about the role women may actually have played in such matters.
16 For references see Index; for full descriptions of priestly rituals see Modi 1922.
17 For an elaborate description of the rite see Kotwal and Boyd 1991.
18 See Modi 1922: 330–2.
19 For a survey of the various meanings of the word see Modi 1922: 333, Boyce and Kotwal 1971.
20 Information I owe to Dastur Dr F.M. Kotwal; see also Modi 1922: 241–5.
21 Including, in India, that of the *varasyo,* a purely white bull which has itself been consecrated and is usually kept in the precinct of a fire temple for this purpose.

22 See Modi 1922: 354–84.

23 It can also be used in India to refer to a combination of *Yasna, Afrinagan, Baj, Farokhshi* and *Satum* services, which may be performed on the anniversary of a death, to celebrate the anniversary of the foundation of a fire temple, and on special days in the religious year. See Modi 1922: 428–37.

24 For references see Index. Some Parsis have the *Fareshta* performed as part of the ceremonies of the first year after a death.

25 For a fuller description see Modi 1922: 402–3. Describing the Indian practice of his time, Modi draws attention to the fact that the *Satum* can be recited on occasions which are not obviously connected with death. On solemn occasions the *Satum* is normally performed by priests, but some modern Parsi laymen also do it as part of their regular devotions.

26 See Modi 1922: 384. On the *fravashi* see also below, p. 41 n. 16.

27 For a survey of all ceremonies relating to death see Modi 1922: 48ff. On the part of the laity in Parsi funerals see below, p. 37f.

28 On all these occasions see further Ch. 2, below.

29 See also Modi 1922: 87–96. Two more elaborate purification rituals, the *Bareshnum* and the *Riman* are now seldom performed for the Parsi laity. On these ceremonies see Modi 1922: 97–157.

30 See Boyce 1982: 243–50. Professor Boyce herself is now inclined to doubt the accuracy of this account (private communication 1994), but it still seems plausible to the present writer.

31 This may have happened under the early Sasanians, see Boyce 1979: 104.

32 A survey of the Zoroastrian months, days, and watches is given in the Appendix.

33 On the traditional observances for a *Gahambar* see Modi 1922: 419–28.

34 One *Gahamabar*, which may originally have been dedicated to Spenta Mainyu, was later observed in honour of Ahura Mazda, cf. above, n. 2.

35 For current Parsi practice see below, p. 22f.; on such feasts in the modern Iranian Zoroastrian tradition see Boyce 1977: 84–5.

36 On the interaction between Zoroastrians and Muslims in this period see Choksy 1997.

37 See also below, p. 44f.

Chapter Two

Common Parsi Observances

BASED ON AN ACCOUNT
BY SHEHNAZ N. MUNSHI

In the interviews informants regularly refer to ordinary family or communal observances with religious connotations, many of which may be unfamiliar to readers. In a series of interviews conducted in Bombay in December 1994, Mrs Shehnaz N. Munshi described a range of such ceremonies and practices. The present chapter is based on this account and on later additions by Mrs Munshi. It aims to offer a survey of traditional 'common' observances[1] which are known to, though not necessarily observed by, many modern urban Parsis. In practice religious traditions vary from family to family, some households may observe many of the customs described here while others may barely be aware of some of them. The interviews themselves will give some idea of these variations.

EVERYDAY OBSERVANCES

Daily observances

As soon as one gets out of bed the traditional custom is to pray an *Ashem Vohu* followed by three recitations of the formula *Shekaste shekaste Shaytan* (defeated, defeated is Satan), while rubbing ash or *taro* (unconsecrated bull's urine) on one's hands. This is no longer widely observed, however; most religious Parsis start the day by doing their *kusti* (the untying and retying of the sacred cord while reciting certain prayers) in a way which differs slightly from the normal procedure.[2] This is known as the *vasidi kusti* (*kusti* of pollution), probably because the body is felt to be impure after sleep.

Immediately after that some Parsis face the rising sun, bow to it in respect and rub their hands over their face where the sunlight falls on it. Then most people have a bath, after which they perform the full *padyab kusti*, a ritual ablution of the hands and face[3] followed by the *kusti* ritual proper.[4] Those who have the opportunity may also say their daily *faraziyat* (obligatory prayers)[5] in the morning.[6] Parsis who keep a separate hearth fire for religious purposes usually face this when praying; others may face an oil-lamp (*divo*), which is either kept burning perpetually or lit after the morning bath.

The *loban* (incense) ceremony is a characteristic feature of Parsi devotional life. A small incense burner containing some ash from the hearth-fire or the fire temple and some burning incense or sandalwood, is taken around the house. As many *Ashem Vohu* prayers as possible should be recited while this is done. In traditional families the *loban* is done after the house has been swept and the traditional chalk designs (*rangoli*) have been made on the threshold.

In most households there are no special observances during the afternoon watch, as people are generally at work. In families of working priests the *faraziyat* prayers are said, and some other Parsis also do this. Immediately after sunset the *loban* is done again in many houses, and the evening *faraziyat* are recited.[7] In some households the threshold is wetted before the evening *loban*.

Customs to do with meals

Traditionally Parsis were enjoined to keep silence while eating, reciting the first half of a prayer (the *jamvani baj* or 'protective formula for eating') before beginning their meal and not speaking again until the meal was finished, when they recited the second half of the prayer. This practice, known as 'eating in *baj*' is now obsolete, although it was observed by some families within living memory.

It is customary to keep a little food on one's plate to give to a dog (one's own, a neighbour's or even a stray); this is known as the 'dog's morsel'.[8]

Before drinking liquor traditional Parsis sprinkle some of it on the ground, apparently as an offering to the Amesha Spenta Aspandarmad, the guardian of the earth.

Visiting the fire temple

Immediately before a visit to an Agiary one normally has a bath, although this is not always possible as working people may go in their lunch break or after work. The head must be covered and before entering one washes the exposed parts of the body and does the *kusti* in the outer precincts of the fire temple. Some people first pay their respects to the well in the compound of the fire temple. One may then light an oil lamp; this is optional, however, and many people only do it on special days.

Apart from prayer, an offering of sandalwood to the fire is essential. The wood, which comes in various sizes and prices, is placed on a tray on the threshold of the fire chamber; it will form part of the *boy*, the solemn offering of wood to the fire which is made in each of the five watches of the day. In many fire temples there are wooden boxes with separate compartments for each *geh*, so that those who wish their offering to be given in a particular watch can put it in the appropriate compartment. On the sandalwood tray there is usually a smaller tray with the holy ash of the fire, and one puts some of this on one's forehead.[9] When offering sandalwood it is customary to leave some money in the tray for the priest. On special occasions a *machi* ('throne') may be offered, a construction built with six (in Udwada nine) pieces of sandalwood; after the *machi* has been offered to the fire with an accompanying *Baj* ceremony, the priest recites prayers for the welfare of the family. Garlands (*toran*), usually made of flowers but sometimes of solid silver, may also be offered and hung in the fire temple.

It is customary to greet the pictures of Zarathustra and other venerable men in the fire temple before going to greet the fire. Prayers are said facing the sacred fire. Those who visit the fire temple regularly may just offer sandalwood, recite a short prayer and leave, while others may pray longer.

OBSERVANCES ON FESTIVE OCCASIONS

Whenever a special event like a birthday, Navjote, or wedding is celebrated, the 'festive tray' (*saganni ses*) plays a role in the proceedings. The tray normally contains the following items: an oil lamp; a silver cone representing the mythical Mt Hara; a rose-water sprinkler; wet vermilion powder (*kumkum*) in a silver container; sugar crystals or *batasa* (a white, sweet confection); betel leaves; betel nut; unshelled almonds; turmeric sticks; dried dates; rice; curds; salt; flowers; and a coconut.[10]

The Sagan

This festive salutation is performed on many happy occasions, such as birthdays, Navjotes and weddings. The *ses* is prepared; the person performing the ritual does the *kusti*, lights a *divo* and offers frankincense to the fire which is placed next to the *ses*. The recipient is made to stand on a small wooden platform (*patlo*), facing east. *Kumkum* marks are made, usually first on both feet (though some regard this as un-Zoroastrian), and then on the forehead. A few grains of rice are stuck on the *kumkum* mark on the forehead, and the recipient is made to hold some items from the *ses*. He (or she)[11] is then handed the coconut, a garland is placed round his neck and rice is showered over him.

18

The Achu Michu

This is a welcoming ceremony, which is done on festive occasions such as Navjotes, birthdays and weddings, or when someone returns after a long absence. The *achu michu* tray contains betel leaves, betel nut, dried dates, unshelled almonds, turmeric sticks, rice, an egg, a coconut and a beaker of water. First the egg, then the smaller items (held together in a betel leaf), and finally the coconut is passed around the recipient's head seven times and then thrown away to the right of his feet. Finally, water from the beaker is poured over some grains of rice remaining in the tray. The tray itself is then held above the recipient's head and passed around it seven times.

The Ovarna

The aim of this ceremony is to remove evil; it is done to wish someone well and protect him. It consists of showering rice over the recipient and cracking one's knuckles on one's temples. The *ovarna* is always done after the *achu michu*, but it may also be performed separately.

The bath with milk and flowers

In traditional households a child's birthday begins with a ceremonial bath. (This may also be done for an adult, or on other festive occasions.) A female member of the household puts some warm milk sprinkled with *kumkum*, rice, some flower petals and rose water in the bathroom. The recipient pours this over his body before having a bath.

Suraj vadhavani rit

This is a ceremony to greet the rising sun, which can be performed on any auspicious occasion. Four small bowls containing milk, sweet curds, semolina, and sweet vermicelli (*sev*), are put on a tray which also holds fresh flowers and all the usual items of the *ses*. A *divo* is lit and the tray is put on a *patlo* in a place from where one can see the sun. Three, five or seven ladies take part; they do their *kusti* and gather around the tray. Each lady in turn takes something from the contents of the *ses* and throws it towards the sun as a symbolic offering. The tray is then lifted from the *patlo*, held in the direction of the sun, and again lowered onto the *patlo*. Finally *loban* is offered and the blessings of the sun are invoked.

POPULAR OBSERVANCES

The Mushkil Asan

This popular ceremony connected with the Yazad Behram[12] is usually performed on Fridays – though Tuesdays are preferred in some villages – and on Behram *roj*. Generally on those days a number of items (chickpeas, dry coconut, dates, sugar candy, flowers and fresh lime juice) are placed on a silver tray, people recite their normal prayers and light a *divo* in honour of Behram. The full performance of the rite, however, entails the recitation of the traditional story of *Mushkil Asan*, which illustrates the help which this Being can give. When Behram *roj* falls on a Friday the day is considered particularly auspicious and the story is usually recited as part of the ceremony.

The Ardibeheshtni Chavi

This is a divining ritual, intended to ask the Amesha Spenta Ardibehesht (or in some cases Behram) for information that is otherwise unobtainable. First the participants do their *kusti* and a fire is lit in a fire vase. Then a copy of the *Khordeh Avesta* is opened, and an iron key (*chavi*) is inserted between the pages of the *Yasht* to Ardibehesht (or Behram), in such a way that one end of the key juts out and can be held between the right index fingers of the two participants, i.e. the person who needs the information and the one conducting the ritual. A *kusti* is wound around the book 21 times so that the key is securely fastened. Then the following formula is recited in Gujarati: 'Ardibehesht (Behram) Yazad, please tell the truth. Has XX done such-and-such a thing? If this is true, then make the book turn and fall.' If the statement is true, it is believed that the book will turn around, so that the key slips between the fingers that hold it and the book falls.

Songs and performances by Goyans

The *Atashnu Git* ('Song of the Fire') used to occupy a special place in the devotional life of the Parsis. It is normally recited by *goyans* (professional singers) on such occasions as weddings or Navjotes, and takes about two hours to perform. The song is said to have been composed on the occasion of the foundation of the Navsari Atash Behram. It is full of praise and worship for the Yazad Ardibehesht, and blessings are invoked upon the family which has invited the *goyans*.

Singing plays an important part in traditional Parsi culture; there are special songs for some occasions, and others which can be sung at various functions.[13] The song *Sakhi suraj bhale ugya re* ('Hail to the glorious rising sun') used to be particularly popular; it was played early in the morning on many auspicious days, while members of the household were preparing the house for the celebration.

Moving into a new house

When the foundations of a new house are laid, many families have the liturgy of the *Vendidad* recited at the site, and gold and silver coins, sandalwood, *loban*, and sometimes a copy of the family tree are buried there. Before the move garlands are traditionally put over all the doors of the new house and chalk designs are made on the threshold. The same is done in the old house, where a *divo* is lit before leaving. In a corner of the new house, or in the kitchen, an earthen pot filled with water is placed on a heap of wheat. Such items as betel leaves, betel nut, areca nut and a turmeric stick are put into the pot, which is covered with a piece of red cloth. A coconut is placed on top and the pot is garlanded and decorated with *kumkum* marks. A *divo* is lit and *loban* is offered to the fire. A portrait of Zarathustra is placed near the pot and also garlanded. An egg is passed seven times over the threshold of the main door and then smashed on the ground. The ceremony is usually performed by the *doyenne* of the family in the presence of the other family members. A *Jashan* is always performed when an observant family moves into a new house.

Going on a long journey

When someone leaves home for a considerable period of time a *sagan* is usually done. At the time of leaving the person is made to dip his hand in a beaker of water left standing on the threshold, and it is customary to throw some coins into it. This is thought to ensure a safe and prosperous return. A *Jashan* is generally also performed.

Observances connected with the phases of the moon

The Full and New Moon are regarded as auspicious. On these occasions it is customary to cook *dhandar patyo*,[14] to make special chalk designs and to garland the doors. A day when there is no moon is inauspicious. Traditional Parsis recite the *Mah Bokhtar Niyayesh* (the prayer to the Moon) on all three occasions (Full Moon, New Moon and moonless nights). On the Full Moon of the Hindu month of Ashvini many Parsis cook another special dish called *dudh pak pauva*.

SPECIAL DAYS OF THE RELIGIOUS YEAR

Hamkara Days

These are the days of each month which are devoted to Hormazd, Ardibehesht, Adar, Sarosh and Behram. Many Parsis visit the fire temple on those days, and in some families there are special observances either on all *hamkara* days or on the *roj* of the family's favourite Yazad (Behram, the Yazad of victory and success, is especially popular). Many people decorate the house with garlands and make special chalk designs on the threshold. Where there is no permanent hearth fire or *divo*, incense sticks are often lit. Some families prepare a *ses*, on which they put a *divo* and garland. They then do their *kusti*, light the *divo* and burn incense near the tray. Others put fruits of the season and a beaker of milk and water on the prayer table near the pictures of the ancestors, and pray there. Festive dishes may be cooked, while typically 'non-festive' ones are avoided.

Meher, Fravardin and Ashishvang *roj*, though not *hamkara* days, are also regarded as special by many religious Parsis, who may visit the fire temple on these days.

Parabs

In some cases, when the day dedicated to a Yazad comes in the month dedicated to the same Being, it is regarded as a feast day in the Yazad's honour. Such days are known as *parab*; in English people sometimes speak of the 'birthday' of a Yazad, or of the Yazad's 'element' (such as fire or water). Some *parabs* are more widely celebrated than others; the following survey lists the most important of these occasions and the observances associated with them:

Fravardin mahino,[15] *Fravardin roj (Farvardiyannu parab).* This is the *parab* dedicated to the *fravashis* of the dead.[16] Many Parsis visit the Towers of Silence on that day or on any other day of this month. Priests are often commissioned to recite prayers for the dead at the Towers of Silence; relatives of the deceased usually attend these prayers, offer their respects to the *fravashis*, and pray at the little fire sanctuary in the Tower precinct.[17] A *Hama Anjuman Jashan* (a *Jashan* sponsored by the entire community) is performed in the Tower precinct. Special arrangements are made near the Tower area on this day to cope with the traffic.

Meher mahino Meher roj (Mehragan). This day, which is dedicated to Mithra (Guj. Meher), is celebrated as a major festival by Iranian Zoroastrians but is not normally observed as a *parab* by Parsis. Still, many Parsis visit a fire temple on that day. The Aslaji Agiary in Bombay in particular draws many visitors then, as there is a widespread belief that the Aslaji fire will grant special boons. A possible reason for this relative popularity of the day of Mithra, an ancient divinity about whom Parsis know little,[18] is the perceived connection between that Yazad and Shah Faridun, a mythical Iranian king who is venerated by many and thought to have magical powers.[19]

Ava mahino Ava roj (Avanu parab). This is the very popular 'birthday of the Waters', when hundreds of Parsis go to the sea shores of Bombay – elsewhere they may go to a local river – and many people also go to the fire temple. Prayers are usually offered, especially the short *Ardvisur Niyayesh*, which is dedicated to the Yazad of the Waters. In Bombay many people go to the sea after work but before sunset, as the prayers have to be recited before the sun goes down. They usually bring *dalni poris* (a flat round pastry made of sweet lentils), some of which are offered to the sea while the others are eaten on the beach. Many Parsis also visit the Bhikha Behram Well in Bombay, where some offer a net made of flowers to the Waters. Pregnant women in particular often go there to pray.[20] Mrs Munshi said:

There are places like the Ratan Tata Institute which makes all the Parsi goodies, like *dalni poris,* and some Parsi ladies make them in their own homes. There is one lady who makes huge *poris*, enough for 20 people, you have to order them 15 days in advance. While offering the *dalni poris* some people draw on the sand the same kind of design you do for the *Adar roj parab*.[21] Then you put down the tray with all the things in it, and if you have brought five *poris* you offer two to the sea and have a picnic with the other three. Some people, especially in villages, bring an incense burner and they draw patterns in the sand, offer *loban* and perhaps even light a *divo*. Then you do your *kusti* and make your offering to the Water. In Bombay you do not normally do all this, for the water and the beaches are too dirty.

It is an occasion to enjoy, to be together; you really feel good that so many people have come out. No matter what their differences, they all realise, 'We have to do this, it is part of our religious duty and we do it.' Some people carry the sea water back home in a bottle, and sprinkle it on their threshold. But in Bombay the sea is so polluted, I do not think that many people still do it. Some people even offer milk to the sea; they bring milk in a bottle and offer it, and bring back sea water and sprinkle it all over their homes... You see many devout Parsis reciting the *Ava Niyayesh*[22] on the beach, along the seashore.

The longest queues on that day you will see at the Bhikha Behram Well... On this day you have to queue to light your little *divo* near the well. Alongside the well there is an iron mesh, on which some people hang huge garlands of flowers, or they have a net made of flowers, which is symbolically offered to the Waters. Such nets can also be offered to one's own well if there is one.

Adar mahino Adar roj (Atashnu parab). Preparations for the 'birthday of the Fire' generally start in the afternoon watch of the preceding day (the Uziran *geh* of Daepadar *roj*). In many families a vigil is kept throughout the night of Daepadar *roj* up to the dawn of Adar *roj*, to ensure that the fire does not go out. Mrs Munshi said:

> In some homes the entire kitchen is whitewashed for this *parab*, in which case the preparations obviously start even earlier. Most people start preparations on Daepadar *roj* by having a bath, preparing a *ses* (on which, together with the usual items, they often put a mango, which is not done on other occasions), and cleaning and washing the kitchen, and particularly the place where the fire stands – whether this is a separate hearth fire or a gas stove. Designs are made with *kumkum* and *kharaptu*[23] on the wall just above the fire... and chalk designs are made on the platform where the fire stands. All the laws of purity have to be observed during these preparations. There are flowers in the house and thick pieces of sandalwood are kept ready to keep the fire burning through the night. When the preparations are over those present do their *kusti* and in traditional households everybody recites the *Atash Niyayesh* [prayer to the Fire].

Many people whose only source of fire in the kitchen is a gas-stove do not cook at all during this *parab*, to give the fire a rest. Those who do use their stove (e.g. because they have a separate hearth fire), usually prepare traditional festive dishes. A visit to the fire temple is customary to celebrate the *parab*, and many people go to an Atash Behram instead of their own Agiary; it is usual to light a *divo* and to offer more sandalwood than normally. Many weddings and Navjotes are performed on this day. In the villages, priests go to all Zoroastrian houses and recite the *Atash Niyayesh* in the course of the month of Adar.

Bahman mahino Bahman roj. This *parab* is dedicated to Bahman, who has special links with animals. Some Parsis refrain from eating meat on this day; others extend this to the days of the Yazads associated with Bahman (Mohor, Gosh, and Ram),[24] or to the whole month of Bahman. Special dishes are eaten on this day, including a special type of *khichri*. In Navsari, dogs were traditionally fed on this occasion.

Dae mahino

Although there is no *parab* for Dae, the Creator, the month dedicated to him is very important. *Jashans* are performed throughout the month in fire temples, business premises, and private houses, and many *Gahambars* are held during this month.

Jamshedi Navroz

This is the 'New Year' festival celebrated on 21 March.[25] For a time this was an official Zoroastrian holiday in Bombay, but it is now an optional one only. Nevertheless, many Parsis take the day off and visit the fire temple or have a *Jashan* done in their homes, as this is considered a particularly auspicious day. Parents usually buy new clothes for their children and many people have a festive meal or go out with friends, often to see a Parsi Gujarati play.

The Muktad days

Until a few years ago the Muktad Festival, which is dedicated to the *fravashis* of the dead and begins on the tenth day before the New Year (Aspandarmad *mahino* Ashishvang *roj*), lasted for 18 days.[26] Because of the current shortage of priests and the high cost of services, however, it has been reduced to ten days in most fire temples, although some still celebrate the full 18 days.[27] During Muktad marble tables are set up in the fire temples, on which vases with flowers are placed. On each table there is also a small tray with a consecrated *shyav*[28] and *dron*, a single piece of fruit and a coconut. A *divo* is kept burning continuously on each table. There are private tables with a single vase for one individual *fravashi* or for the members of one family, and *Anjuman* (community) tables, which are for shared use and have flower vases for many people. The ceremonies for the *Anjuman* table are done collectively, those for the private tables separately. For the first year after death those who can afford it usually have a separate table.

Fresh flowers are put in the vases every morning. Many boys and men voluntarily offer their services to the neighbourhood fire temple during Muktad, going there as early as 3.30 a.m. to wash and clean the vases and other utensils and set up the tables. When this is done the actual performance of the rituals begins,[29] which is normally attended by the relatives of the deceased.

Muktad is a busy time for most Parsis: the laity tends to spend much time in prayer, and as the full-time priests cannot cope with the work, part-time priests lend a hand. Nevertheless the performance of the ceremonies is often hasty, which sometimes offends those who commissioned them. Some people therefore set up Muktad tables in their own homes and even have the services performed there, which requires scrupulous observance of all the laws of purity.

A full description of the priestly rituals for the Muktad would lie beyond the scope of this chapter.[30] A ceremony in which the laity have an active role to play is the *Satum*, which involves the preparation of a meal, either in the fire temple by a *gorani* (a woman whose job it is to cook food for religious occasions), or at home by the relatives of the deceased. This food is usually consecrated by a priest, who recites Avestan prayers and symbolically offers the meal to the departed, while sandalwood and incense are offered to a fire.[31] However, this ceremony may also be performed by the laity without the assistance of priests.

In fire temples where Muktad is observed for ten days, the *fravashis* are bid farewell on the last *Gatha* day, the last day of the year. A coconut is broken near the table, the flowers are removed and the vases turned upside down to signify the end of Muktad. In the Ushahin *geh* of that day (the last watch of the night before the New Year), prayers are recited and the *fravashis* are bidden farewell.[32] Where the ceremonies are still held for the full 18 days the farewell ceremony is done in the Ushahin *geh* of Khordadsal.[33]

In private homes an extra *divo* may be lit and kept burning throughout the Muktad period.

The Gatha days

The last five days of the year are known as the 'Gatha days' because each is named after one of the five *Gathas*. The appropriate *Gatha* is to be recited on each day. Some people in Bombay visit seven fire temples at this time, including the four Atash Behrams; others go on a pilgrimage to Udwada, Navsar or Surat.

Pateti (Papeti)

The last 'Gatha day'[34] is known as *Pateti*, which in popular speech has become *Papeti*. The word *patet* means 'repentance' and there may be some ancient connection with repenting the wrongs one has done in the past year. However, Parsis have little awareness of this and regard the occasion as a joyous part of the New Year celebrations.

New Year (Navroz)

The first day of the (Shehenshahi) Parsi year[35] is an official holiday in some states in India, and all Parsi establishments are closed. The Atash Behrams are crowded; in Bombay many people visit all four Atash Behrams, which are situated in the same area. Since this is Hormazd *roj*, many people recite the *Hormazd Yasht*. The day is celebrated in style by most families; formerly there were music bands which could be hired to play popular songs in front of the house, and people played Parsi songs on the gramophone. Towards the end of the day many people go to see a Parsi play.

The Kadmis spend their New Year in a less exuberant atmosphere than the Shehenshahis. The Fasli New Year, coinciding with *Jamshedi Navroz*, is a very joyful occasion.

26

Khordadsal

This day, Fravardin *mahino* Khordad *roj* (the sixth day of the first month), is celebrated as the birthday of the Prophet Zarathustra. Pictures of the Prophet are decorated with garlands. Many people go to the fire temple and generally offer more sandalwood than on ordinary days. In fire temples where Muktad is observed for 18 days, the *shyav* is offered to the *fravashis* in the watch before this day begins.[36]

Other special days

Salgireh days. Every fire temple has its own 'birthday', the anniversary of the 'enthronement' of its fire.[37] A *Jashan* is normally performed for the fire on behalf of the Trustees of the Agiary, and sometimes the Anjuman (the community) has a separate *Jashan* done.

Birthdays are considered to be very special in most Zoroastrian households, and have strong religious connotations. Many Parsis celebrate their birthday twice, once according to the Zoroastrian calendar (the '*roj* birthday'), and once according to the Gregorian one. Generally a *sagan* is performed, there is a festive *ses*, children are given a 'bath with milk and flowers' (see above), new clothes are worn, and special dishes are cooked. Even those who do not often visit the fire temple may do so on their birthday.

RITES OF PASSAGE

To Westerners, who tend to differentiate sharply between 'religious' and 'secular' spheres of life, some of the customs described under this heading – and in this Chapter generally – may seem to belong to the latter category. To many Parsis, on the other hand, the concepts of 'tradition' and 'religion' are closely linked. The customs described here are held to belong exclusively to the Parsi tradition, and many of those interviewed seemed to perceive no essential difference between these traditions and others whose 'religious' element seems more prominent. Many features of these ceremonies, moreover, are felt to be highly symbolic and to reflect religious ideas.

Navjote

This is a child's initiation as a full member of the community, for which he or she (hereafter 'he') must learn the basic *kusti* prayers. The Navjote is generally performed well before the child reaches puberty, often at the age of seven or nine. The ceremony, which must be done before sunset, takes place in a special area designated for festive occasions (*baug*), or in a fire temple.

Before the ceremony a *ses* is prepared, and a bag with clothes and things the child will need during and after the ceremony is got ready. The most important of these is the *sudreh* ('sacred shirt'), which together with the *kusti* is worn as a badge of one's Zoroastrian identity.[38]

In the morning the child has a bath with milk and flowers. He is made to wear a cap, a complete set of new clothes, and in some families a loose, smock-like garment made of embroidered silk cloth (*jhabhlu*). A *sagan* is done, the child is garlanded and given a coconut to carry, and a procession is formed to go to the place where the ceremony will be held. The mother carries a large tray containing a big silver cone, the usual items of the festive *ses*, and a watch for a boy or a sari for a girl.[39]

Before the preparatory purification ceremony (*nahn*) begins, a short version of the *achu michu* is done: an egg and some wetted rice are passed around the child's head. For the *nahn*,[40] which is normally administered by a priest who does not take part in the ceremony proper, the child is made to recite the first part of the *jamvani baj* (cf. above; this is known as 'taking the *baj*'), and to chew a pomegranate leaf. He is then given a small quantity of *nirang* (consecrated bull's urine) to sip, while reciting a prayer known as the *nirang pivani baj* ('formula for drinking *nirang*'). After this he is made to recite the final parts of the *jamvani baj* (thus 'completing the *baj*'). He then steps inside the bathing area, where he is given a ceremonial ablution with *nirang*, followed by one with milk and rose-petals, and then with water. [41]

The child then comes out with his upper torso bare, wearing a *pichori* (a piece of white cotton worn over the shoulders), loose trousers, slippers and a new prayer cap (the prayer cap he wore before the *nahan* cannot be worn again). Before the child steps onto the stage where the ceremony will be performed, the full *achu michu* is done. He then sits down on the stage and the ceremony begins. The child says some prayers and the priest recites blessings and solemnly invests him with the *sudreh* and *kusti*.[42] Finally the *Tandorosti* (a prayer for health and well-being) is recited, and the priest throws rice over the child throughout the recitation. This concludes the formal part of the ceremony. The women of the family then gather around the child and dress him in new clothes especially made for the occasion.

After a Navjote the child is usually taken to a fire temple, where a *machi* may be offered. Later there is usually a big celebration, which ends with a traditional Parsi meal served on banana leaves. Some families have a *Jashan* or a *Fareshta* ceremony done, vows to do this have often been made beforehand. Furthermore, the parents may take the child on a pilgrimage to the Atash Behram at Udwada.

The rice which is showered over the child, and also the flowers, coconut and other contents of the *ses*, are collected and kept for seven days. On the eighth day – the *varovar* – a *sagan* is done for the child and the family visits the fire temple. In the evening they go to the seashore and the items are thrown into the sea together with some fresh flowers.

Puberty

When an adolescent wears clothes associated with adulthood for the first time – a sari in the case of girls, a high 'Parsi cap' (*pheta* or *paghri*) for boys – there may be a *sagan* and a celebration. This is done more often for girls than boys.

When a girl has her first period a little celebration is performed in some households; this was done more widely in earlier days. Since the girl is in an impure state it is impossible to do a *sagan*, but festive food is often prepared and the girl is given a separate set of things to use during menstruation.

Weddings

A wedding is an important event in a traditional Parsi household. The festivities go on for four days and a range of ceremonies may be performed as part of the proceedings, which culminate in the actual marriage service. In modern times few people perform all of these but most families observe some; the most common ceremonies are the *adravanu*, the *madav-saro* and the *divo-adarni rit* (on which see below).

Engagement ceremonies

The rupiya pehervani kriya. If the wedding is scheduled to take place shortly after the *adravanu* (see below), this ceremony is not necessary. If a longer period of betrothal is expected the *rupiya pehervani kriya* is often done, which essentially consists of an exchange of gifts of money between the families.[43] An auspicious day is chosen and a party of women from the boy's family visits the home of the girl. There a *sagan* is done for the bride and the women give her some money and others gifts; a welcoming *sagan* is then performed for the visitors. Later a party of women from the girl's side pays a visit to the home of the boy, bringing money and other gifts in return. A *sagan* is done for the groom, followed by *sagans* for each of the guests, and festive food is served later. After this ceremony the couple may go out together in public, as an acknowledgement that they are engaged.

The adravanu. This is usually the first of the wedding ceremonies, but it may be done up to a year before the marriage instead of the *rupiya pehervani kriya*. The ceremony consists in an exchange of rings; in most cases a pair of silver rings is exchanged first, followed by the actual (gold or diamond) engagement rings. In English some Parsis call this the 'engagement' ceremony. *Sagans* and exchanges of gifts form part of the proceedings.

The dahi machli tray. On the day of the *adravanu* there is also an exchange of gifts of sweet yoghurt (*dahi*) and fish (*machli*; either a real fish or a fish-shaped sweet). Fish is considered to be an auspicious food and the yoghurt symbolises sweetness.

The sakar tapkani ses. Traditionally this ceremony entailed sending the bride's horoscope to the groom's house on a tray (*ses*) which also contained sugar crystals, dry *kumkum* in a container, and a garland. Horoscopes are now no longer sent, but a tray with the other items is still taken to the boy's house on the day of the *adravanu*.

The first day of the wedding celebrations[44]

The madav-saro. This ceremony is performed on the first day of the celebrations, usually in both the bride's and the groom's house. Essentially it consists in the ceremonial planting of a mango sapling in a pot.[45] Apart from the family priest there are five protagonists: the male head of the family and four *sohvasans* (married women who are not widows).

Near the threshold of the main entrance of the house a rectangle is drawn on the wall with *kumkum* and *kharaptu*. Chalk designs are made where the pot for the plant is to be placed. Before the ceremony begins all participants do the *kusti*. The pot is placed on the chalk designs and the sapling is held in place by the head of the family and the four *sohvasans*. Various items, such as dry dates, turmeric sticks, unshelled almonds, betel leaves and nuts, an egg, and a coconut,[46] are passed around the plant. They are then put into the earth; a packet containing shavings of gold and silver and a small ruby or pearl is also buried, together with a few grains of wheat and rice, and a bit of curd. The five protagonists plant the sapling while the priest and the other participants continuously recite the *Yatha Ahu Vairyo*. A small square piece of *malmal* cloth, smeared with turmeric to symbolise sunlight and good fortune, is thrown over the plant, and the four *sohvasans* do the *ovarna* over it. An incense burner is placed near the plant and the participants put *loban* in it and pray for the couple.

The suprani rit ('ceremony of the winnowing fans'). This is traditionally done in the house of both parties immediately after the *madav-saro*. Four decorated winnowing fans are used. Each of these contains grains of rice or wheat, betel nut, betel leaf, areca nut, unshelled almonds, sugar biscuits, and a piece of dried coconut. A brass pestle and mortar are placed on chalk designs and four married women sit around this, each holding a winnowing fan. They throw pieces of turmeric from the fans into the mortar and begin to winnow the contents of the fans. This is done seven times, after which the fans are exchanged; this is done in such a way that each fan changes hands four times. Subsequently the women pound the turmeric sticks in the mortar; the powder is later used for the *pithi chorvani rit* (see below). The other women sing traditional songs throughout the ritual.

Preparing the coconuts. At this stage the coconuts which the bride and groom will carry to the wedding hall are prepared by a *sohvasan.* Each coconut is decorated with *kumkum* marks or a *swastik,* and a cotton thread is passed around it seven times, while a *Yatha Ahu Vairyo* is recited each time.

A tribute to the waters. On the same day *dalni poris* are prepared and taken to the sea by a group of five or seven women on a silver tray which also holds the usual ceremonial items (such as betel nuts, almonds, etc.); the ceremony is traditionally performed by members of both families. The women do their *kusti* and offer the contents of the *ses* to the Waters. Each woman then puts *loban* in an incense burner and asks the Waters to bless the couple. Afterwards seven or nine *dalni poris* are sent to the other family.

The pithi chorvani rit ('ceremony of applying pithi powder'). This can be done several times during the first three days of the celebrations, although most people do it only once. The turmeric which was pounded during the *suprani rit* is mixed with a fragrant yellow powder called *pithi,* and rose water or milk is added to make a paste. The bride stands on the *patlo* and a *sagan* is done for her. She is then covered with a white sheet decorated with *swastik* marks, and *pithi* is smeared on her hands, feet and face. Still covered by the sheet, she is made to sit cross-legged on the *patlo.* The men lift up the *patlo* with the girl sitting on it, and carry it around while singing songs. Then the *patlo* is set down again and the bride is asked questions about the price of gold, rice, dal, and other commodities in the year to come. Her predictions are supposed to come true.[47] Then the sheet is removed and the bride is made to stand on the *patlo* while one of the (female) protagonists holds one end of a ball of cotton thread over her head. The cotton thread is passed from her head to her big toe seven times, so that it forms a long garland. This garland is then made into a necklace, which the bride wears until after the wedding ceremony.

A ceremony to remove evil. After the *pithi chorvani rit* another ceremony is done, apparently in order to remove evil: a dry cake of cow dung is taken and a raw egg is placed in its centre. An inverted saucer-shaped vessel is put on this, an unroasted pappadum is put on top of that, and the whole thing is tied up with string. The bride or groom (the partner in whose house the ceremony is done) smashes it with the right foot.

The second day

The divo-adarni ceremony. On the second day of the wedding celebrations an exchange of gifts takes place between the families, and all the things that have been bought for the couple are taken to the groom's house. Among other things the bride is given a new sari; before she is dressed in this, her future mother-in-law wets the inner corner of the sari, puts some grains of rice on it and ties a knot in the sari to hold the rice (this is done as a sign of welcome). A *divo* is lit in both houses; when the women of each family visit the house of the other they put a silver coin in the *divo*. This is known as *divo-adarni*, 'honouring the *divo*'.

On this day the groom's parents usually give the bride a *rial* (a necklace with a silver coin and green glass beads strung either side of it) to signify her acceptance into the family.

The third day

The khichrini rit. On the third day the bride, groom, and the women who participate in the celebrations in either house, eat some *khichri* (yellow rice) with sugar, *ghee* and pappadums for lunch, to symbolise the good things in store for the couple. The day is also known as *khichrini ritno divas* or 'day of the *khichri* ceremony'.

The varadhni rit. This is the main ceremony of the third day. Five or seven wheaten cakes (*varadhvara*) are sent by the bride's family to the groom's house. Five *sohvasans* take part in the proceedings, each of whom brings an earthen pot filled with water. The women wait at the threshold of the groom's house, where they are welcomed and showered with rice. Each pot is then placed on a heap of wheat or rice, and decorated. A number of items (such as areca nut, a date, betel nut, and a rupee) are placed in the pots. Each pot is covered with a shallow earthen vessel containing things like *sev*, a wheaten cake, and a pappadum. An incense-burner is kept ready alongside; the *doyenne* of the family offers incense to the fire and prays that the life of the couple will be filled with good things.

The varadhpattarni Baj. This is a religious ceremony, to extend an 'auspicious invitation' (*varadhpattar*) to the *fravashis* of the dead and to Ram, the Yazad of Joy. A *Baj* ceremony is dedicated to Ram Yazad, and a *Satum* is performed for the *fravashis*. In both ceremonies, which take place in the fire temple, food is consecrated which is later taken home and eaten by both families.[48]

The ukardi lutvani ramat. This is a game connected with the consecrated food. Some of this is put on a tray, while another tray functions as a dummy. Both trays are hidden and the boys of the family have to find the full tray. Meanwhile the women have equipped themselves with pots of water, which they throw over the boy who finds the tray, while the other boys try to snatch it from him. When the game is finished the *doyenne* of the family offers *loban* near the *madav-saro* plant.

The fourth day

The wedding proper. Parsi weddings generally take place after sunset, whereas Iranian Zoroastrians perform the ceremony in the morning. Tradition has it that this is because of a promise the Parsis made to the local ruler, Jadi Rana, on arrival in India. The bride and groom may – separately – visit the fire temple in the morning of their wedding day. Before the actual ceremony both undergo the *nahn*. The groom is generally the first to be ready; he comes up to the stage where the wedding will take place, but does not yet step onto it. He climbs the steps leading to the stage, where his mother-in-law does the *achu michu* for him; he then steps down again and sits slightly apart from the guests, flanked by the priests. He is given a ring, and one of his new sisters-in-law brings a silver pot with water, into which he dips his hand as a sign that he is now part of the bride's family. The sister-in-law receives a present. The groom then waits for the bride to appear. When she arrives her mother-in-law does an *achu michu* for her and her father-in-law traditionally gives her a pair of earrings.

Before the religious ceremony takes place on the stage, the bride and groom and the priests do their *kusti* and the marriage certificate is signed. They then come onto the stage, where a *divo* and an incense-burner are burning and where the priests, witnesses and close relatives are standing. The couple sit facing each other, with a white sheet between them. They hold hands under the sheet but are not allowed to see each other's face.[49] The priest then winds a cotton thread three times around the clasped hands of the couple. The thread is then wound seven times around their chairs, creating a separate area for the couple; the priests chant one *Yatha Ahu Vairyo* each time the thread is passed around the chairs. After the seventh *Yatha Ahu Vairyo* the bride and the groom throw the rice at each other over the sheet, which is then removed. (The first partner to throw the rice is said to have won the race of love.) The bride's chair is now placed alongside the groom's and both sit facing east, with the seven threads still encircling them. The incense burner is brought to the couple and they bow to the fire before the benediction begins.

The Ashirvad. The *Ashirvad* ('benediction') is then recited by two priests who stand before the couple, while rice is continually thrown over the latter. The witnesses are asked whether they have done everything necessary, and the couple are asked three times if the marriage accords with their wishes. The ritual ends with a short benediction. In the past a second *Ashirvad* was normally recited in Sanskrit, but this is rarely done now; the same is true of another traditional custom, that of repeating the *Ashirvad* in the watch before dawn (the *pachli ratni lagan* or 'wedding ceremony of the last night'). After the *Ashirvad* the groom's father gives presents of money to the priests, and the chief officiating priest is given a shawl. The groom's sister-in-law comes onto the stage and washes his feet. This used to be done with milk, but now only a few drops of milk are put on the tip of the groom's shoes, which are generally too expensive to expose to a fuller treatment. [50]

A visit to the fire temple and celebrations. Immediately after the wedding ceremony the couple visit a fire temple. In the meantime the festivities, consisting of a traditional meal accompanied by music, are already going on and the couple join in on their return.

Subsequent ceremonies connected with the wedding

The varovar. On the eighth day after the wedding the *varovar* is performed: the sapling planted during the *madav-saro* ceremony, and various items which played a role during the wedding ceremonies (such as flowers, coconuts, rice, etc.), are offered to the sea. This is also the day of the couple's first visit to the bride's father's house, where they have a celebratory dinner. When they go home the couple are given a small silver pot covered with red cloth, on which a coconut is placed.

At some stage after the wedding, many couples make a pilgrimage to the Atash Behram at Udwada. A *machi* may be offered by either family after the wedding.

The Randel bharvani rit. This custom may be of Hindu origin,[51] and is slowly dying out. It is still observed in some villages of Gujarat, however, and in Navsari some women still do it professionally. On a wooden bench placed in a corner of the house four heaps are made of different types of grain and pulse: husked rice, unhusked rice, wheat, and *tuvar dal*.[52] Some money is put in the heaps of *tuvar dal* and unhusked rice. On each heap one places a silver pot. Two pots are filled with well water and two with river water, and the pots also contain betel leaves, betel and areca nut, and some money. The mouths of the pots are covered with a red cloth. The women performing the ceremony, who have to be in a state of purity, do their *kusti*, put incense on the fire and ask blessings for the recipient. The pots are kept standing for four or seven days, the water being changed regularly, and finally the contents of the pots and the heaps of grain are offered to the Waters.

Pregnancy, birth and the first baby[53]

The panchmasyu. This is a festive ceremony which is held on an auspicious day after the completion of the fourth month of pregnancy. The prospective parents (hereafter 'the boy' and 'the girl') are invited to the girl's parents' house, where a *sagan* is done for her. She is given a new set of clothes to wear, and five or seven *pendas* (a white, round sweet) and other festive items are placed in the loose front part (*pallu, pallav*) of her sari. The *pallu* is later emptied, either in another room in the same house or in the house of her in-laws.

The agharni. This ceremony may be held when seven or nine months of pregnancy near completion; it is performed by five or seven *sohvasans* and usually takes place on a Thursday (which counts as auspicious), or a Sunday (when people are free). The first part of the ceremony takes place in the boy's house; the mother-to-be steps onto the wooden platform, the *sagan* is done and she is dressed in a new sari while standing on the platform. Her *pallu* is filled with seven (or nine) handfuls of wheat, a coconut and all the items of the *ses*, and a cone-shaped *larvo* (a sweet especially made for the occasion). She must hold all this securely in her *pallu*. Blessings are showered upon her and her mother-in-law gives her a piece of jewellery. After this all the women go to the house of the girl's parents, taking seven or nine *larvas* and a *ses*. On arrival the *achu michu* and *ovarna* are done before the girl enters the house. She is again made to stand on a platform, where the contents of her *pallu* are emptied into a winnowing fan or into the *pallu* of one of the other women, and filled anew by the girl's mother or another senior *sohvasan*. The party then returns to the boy's house, where the *achu michu* and *ovarna* are done and the contents of the *pallu* are once again emptied. The women from the girl's family now come to the boy's house to perform a *sagan* for him and give him a present. The *larvo* is broken up and eaten; the tip of the confection may be given to a newly married family member in the hope that she too may soon have a child.

The last weeks before confinement. The first delivery is regarded as the responsibility of the mother's parents, and she spends the last days or weeks of her pregnancy in their house.

The chatthi. This ceremony is done on the sixth day after the birth, generally at night. A divine being (*Chatthimai* or *Vehmai*) is believed to write the child's destiny during that night, and a blank sheet of paper, red ink, and a quill are put in place for this purpose. The paper should later be carefully kept. Those present do the *kusti*, the *loban* is performed and a *divo* is lit. The ceremony is conducted by the maternal grandmother (or the *doyenne* of the mother's family), who must be in a state of ritual purity. A corner of a room is thoroughly cleaned and a *patlo* is put in place; on the *patlo* there is a tray with the usual items for the *sagan*, a garland, and a set of new clothes which the child will wear on its first visit to the fire temple. On the day of the *chatthi* some people cook only vegetarian food, and the mother generally abstains from eating meat or fish.

Return to normal life. For the first forty days after the birth, the mother is considered to be ritually impure. After this period she resumes her normal life, although she may remain with her parents for some time. Many Parsi women – as well as their mothers, who have constantly been in physical contact with them, and sometimes their husbands – undergo a *nahn* at this stage. The child is then taken to the fire temple for the first time.

The return home. The ceremony to welcome the child to the father's house is known as *vadhavo*. It is held when the mother is ready to return home, usually some months after the birth. Gifts for mother and child from the father's family are taken to the maternal grandparents' house; a traditional gift is a silver rattle, which every family keeps as an heirloom. The presents are brought on a large silver tray, which also contains the usual items for the *sagan,* by a party of women from the father's family. The *achu michu* is done for these women before they enter the house. The mother and child are then made to sit on a chair, a *sagan* is done, the gifts are offered, sweets are distributed and there is singing and merriment. In return the maternal grandparents traditionally do the *jori pori*: they give the mother a Gujarati-style cradle (*jori*), a set of clothes, a small piece of jewellery and anything else she may need for the baby, and some gifts for her mother-in-law. All these gifts are taken to the father's house, where the party is received with celebrations.

The besna. When the baby begins to sit up the *besna* ('sitting') ceremony is done. The usual items for the *sagan* are placed on a tray together with small white *pendas*. A *divo* is lit, the *patlo* is placed on a chalk design, and the child is dressed in new clothes and garlanded. A little wall of *pendas* is built on the *patlo* and the child is made to sit on it. The mother or grandmother then takes a coconut and taps it first on the child's bottom and then six times on the floor; the seventh time she smashes the coconut. The child is then showered with rice and made to eat a little of the sweet.

The pagladu. When the child is learning to walk some families do the *pagladu* ceremony. On an auspicious day the house is decorated and a *ses* is prepared. *Larvas* have been made beforehand, two of them in the shape of a foot. The child is made to sit or stand on the *patlo* and a *sagan* is done. A coconut is passed around the child seven times and smashed near its feet. Then rice is thrown over it, it is given a piece of *larvo*, and there is a celebration.

The gorni bharvani rit. This is a village ceremony which is not normally done in Bombay. It takes place when the child begins to eat solids. The women of the house take a pot containing such items as areca nut, betel nut, betel leaf, almonds, and rice, which they fill with water from seven wells. When the pot is taken back to the house the women call out that those who are unclean should stay out of the way. On arrival at the house the pot is placed on chalk designs and *loban* is offered. Then seven children are called and given *dhandar* to eat; the child for whom the *gorni* is done is also made to eat this and is fed a piece of jaggery (*gor,* whence *gorni*).

The first birthday. This is an important event. A *Jashan* or an act of charity may be performed on the child's behalf and traditionally the grandparents give it an heirloom. Celebrations naturally form an important part of the proceedings. At some stage after the first birthday many families offer a *machi* at the fire temple.

Death

When a traditional Parsi dies in Bombay,[54] the Towers of Silence are notified and a hearse is sent to take the body to one of the *banglis* (buildings for funerary purposes) situated in the area of the Towers.

The sachkar. The *bangli* has facilities for the final bath. The body is first rubbed with *gomez* (unconsecrated cow's urine), and then washed with water by the members of the family or by two attendants from the Towers of Silence. It is dressed in old white pyjamas and an old *sudreh*. The *kusti* is tied round the waist, usually by a male family member, while prayers are said. Then the two *nasesalars* (professionals who handle the body) take charge; they are dressed in white clothes with white gloves and white shoes and socks. After doing their *kusti* they enter the *bangli* in *paivand* (i.e. each holding one end of a cord). They place the body on three stone slabs in a demarcated area of the main hall of the *bangli*, and the subsequent funerary rites take place there. The *nasesalars,* who are in *paivand* throughout the ritual, further prepare and lay out the body. After doing the *padyab-kusti* and taking the *baj* of Sarosh,[55] they draw a furrow around it with a long iron nail while reciting three *Yatha Ahu Vairyos*. At this point the first *sagdid* ('dog's gaze') is done: an attendant brings a dog to look at the body, perhaps to verify that the person is indeed dead.[56] Only when this has been done can fire be brought into the room. A *divo* burns near the head of the deceased, and it is kept burning in the *bangli* during the first four days even after the body has been removed. In the house a *divo* is kept burning near the bed, or in a place that was especially dear to the deceased.

In some cases the body is taken into the Tower soon after the *sachkar*, but if there is a delay it is kept lying in state; a continuous vigil is maintained and prayers are recited even through the night.[57]

The geh-sarna and the removal of the body into the Tower. The main part of the funerary ceremony is known as *Geh-sarna* ('chanting the *Gathas*'). Before it begins the *nasesalars,* keeping *paivand,* bring in an iron bier and place it on the floor near the body. They draw another furrow, which encircles the bier, and recite a short prayer (the *Dasturi*). While the priests perform the *Geh-sarna* the two *nasesalars* line the bier with strips of torn *sudrehs* provided by the deceased's family. A cordon is formed around the bier with a long cord made from such strips of material.

Two priests who are in a state of ritual purity then enter the room in *paivand*. They stand in the doorway, facing the body but as far away from it as possible, and begin to recite the *Ahunavaiti Gatha*. At a certain point in the recitation[58] they pause and avert their faces, as do the mourners; at this time the body is lifted onto the bier. Another *sagdid* is done at this stage. When the body has been laid on the bier the *nasesalars* indicate this by making a noise, and the recitation of prayers is resumed.

The sezdo (last respects). When the *Geh-sarna* is over the male mourners, in *paivand*, pay their respects to the deceased.[59] Still maintaining *paivand*, they then leave the room and wait outside to accompany the body on its last journey. The women then pay their respects, after which the face is covered. The *nasesalars* are now joined by two other officials, the *khandiyas* (corpse-bearers), who help them carry the body to the Tower of Silence. The priests and the male mourners accompany the body in a silent procession, in *paivand*. Nowadays women may join the procession, but formerly this was not customary.

Just outside the Tower, the bier is set down on a marble slab and the face is uncovered for the last time. The final *sagdid* is performed and the mourners pay their last respects. The face is then covered again and the body is taken into the Tower by the *nasesalars*, with the head facing east. The mourners wait near the *sagri* (a small building containing a fire which faces the door of the Tower). When the body has been laid to rest the *nasesalars* clap their hands and the mourners complete their prayers. As a means of purification the mourners are given a few drops of *gomez* to rub on their hands, and they wash the exposed parts of their bodies with water. They do their *kusti* and pay their respects to the fire of the *sagri*. After the removal of the body a metal container filled with flowers is kept next to the *divo* in the *bangli* for the first three days. Milk is fed to the dogs twice a day during this period.

The ceremonies for Sarosh. For three days after the *Geh-sarna* a combination of prayers and rituals takes place which are dedicated to the Yazad Sarosh, who is believed to take care of the soul between the moment of death and the Judgment on the morning of the fourth day. This is known as the *Saroshnu patru* ('invitation to Sarosh').

The afternoon Uthamna. The first *Uthamna* ceremony is done on the afternoon of the third day after death. It is performed by four priests, either at the Tower or in a fire temple. A carpet is spread out for the purpose, which is surrounded by vases with sweet-smelling flowers. Then a white sheet is laid in the centre of the carpet, on which a fire-vase is placed with four *divas* on either side. The fire is lit and, after doing their *kusti*, the priests recite prayers while standing on the carpet. When the final prayer is being recited an attendant offers flowers and rose-water to those present.

The Uthamna of the fourth morning (pachli-ratnu Uthamnu). Traditionally the early morning *Uthamna* of the fourth day was attended only by close relatives and friends. Nowadays, however, there is a tendency to omit the afternoon *Uthamna*, in which case all mourners come to the early morning ceremony. In the very early hours of the fourth day (*c.* 12.45 a.m.), four *Baj* ceremonies are performed at the fire temple for the Yazads Rashne, Ashtad, Ram, Ardafravash[60] and Sarosh; a *dron*, fruits, and a *shyav* are consecrated and then taken to the *bangli*, where the *Uthamna* is performed. The rituals include an *Afrinagan* ceremony for Dahm (the Yazad who guards the soul against attacks from the powers of evil on its way to the Chinvad Bridge), which is performed over the consecrated *dron*, fruits and *shyav*. Towards the end of the ceremony one of the priests stands up and places the *divo*, which had been standing on a tripod, on the floor. The flowers which were standing by the *divo* are scattered and the water is spilled. Those present partake of the consecrated food and go home. The *shyav* is normally given to the priest. After the *Uthamna* a *machi* is offered to the small *sagri* fire at the Towers of Silence.

The jorani kriya. Ceremonies for the surviving spouse can be done together with those for the deceased; a double set of ceremonies is then performed.

Further funerary ceremonies. On the fourth (*chaharom*), tenth (*dasmu*), or thirtieth (*masiso*) day after death a *Vendidad* may be performed; alternatively this can be done on the first death anniversary.

When the rituals of the first four days are over, *Baj*, *Afrinagan* and *Farokhshi* ceremonies may be performed in the fire temple. It is also customary to perform three *Satums* daily, in the early morning, mid-morning and late afternoon. Such rituals are optional, however; some people have them done for the first ten days or the first month, while others continue to have daily ceremonies performed for a year, and again on the death anniversary in the following years. On important days, such as those mentioned above, family and friends of the deceased usually attend the rituals and charities may be announced. Every month of the first year, ceremonies or special prayers may be held on the *roj* of the death and on Fravardin *roj*. On *Fravardiyannu parab* prayers may be recited at the Towers of Silence.

THE LAWS OF PURITY

Menstruation. The traditional complete segregation of menstruating women is now observed very rarely, especially in urban communities. Some women still keep a separate set of clothes for those days, including a *sudreh* and *kusti*, and in some cases these are kept in a separate cupboard. Generally women *in menses* do not touch such objects as prayer books and *divas*. If a form of segregation is observed at all, this is only done inside the house so as to preserve the purity of the home. The woman sits in a corner and avoids all contact with people and things; whatever she needs is handed to her by a member of the family. She either sleeps on a bed consisting of an iron frame around which strips of material are wound to form a mattress (the 'mattress' being removed and washed when the bed is no longer needed), or on the floor. After menstruation it is customary for a woman to take a ritual bath.

Death and funerals. When returning from a visit to the Towers Parsis are held to be ritually unclean. If possible, observant Parsis go home to have a bath, and try not to touch anything until they are clean again; the clothes they wore to the Towers are washed (many people have special clothes for this purpose). The *kusti* is done when leaving the Towers and again on arrival home, where a family member may be waiting at the door with water for the *padyab* ablutions.

Hair and nails. Hair and nails are considered very polluting when they have been cut. Most Parsis have a bath immediately after a haircut or a shave. Some remove their *kusti* when going out to have a haircut; others wear a special *kusti* for the purpose, to avoid the risk of wearing a polluted *kusti* when visiting a Fire Temple. When brushing or combing one's hair, loose hairs are wrapped in a tissue before they are thrown away. Nails should be cut in the bathroom before one's bath, and the parings are thrown into the toilet and flushed down straight away. Traditionally nail parings were collected and buried in the ground, but this is not possible in Bombay.

———

It may be said in conclusion that Mrs Munshi's long and lively account of Parsi customs and observances strikingly illustrates the way in which the Zoroastrian religion has traditionally informed the life of its adherents in India, and continues to shape the religious lives of many. Not only do several of the observances described here reflect the ancient teachings of the Good Religion in an eloquently symbolic manner, but the Parsi tradition clearly offers believers a way to express and experience the spiritual world-view inherent in their faith through a system of practical and often beautiful ritual or customary actions, which can form an intrinsic part of daily life in many spheres. Although the orthopractic side of religion described here no longer plays as central a part in Parsi religious life as may once have been the case, its importance should by no means be underestimated. Mrs Munshi's account, illustrating some of the inner coherence, beauty and symbolism of Parsi lay observance, is perhaps especially important at a time when Parsis' views on these traditions are very divided, and their knowledge of them undoubtedly diminishing.

Notes

1 For descriptions of high priestly rituals the reader is referred to Modi 1922, Kotwal and Boyd 1991, and to the brief overview above, p. 9f.

2 For this *kusti* an *Ashem Vohu* is recited first; then the *kusti* is untied without the *Kem-na Mazda* prayer; on retying it one recites the usual prayers (cf. below, n. 4)

3 See Modi 1922: 92f.

4 i.e. reciting *Kem-na Mazda* while untying the *kusti*, *Hormazd Khodae* when retying it, and ending with *Jasa-me Avanghe Mazda*.

5 Apart from the *kusti* prayers, these comprise the *Sarosh Baj*, the prayer for the *geh* (watch), and the *Khorshed* and *Meher Niyayesh*; the latter two prayers are always recited together and known collectively as the *Khorshed Meher Niyayesh*.

6 On special days (see p. 22f.), many Parsis go to the fire temple instead of praying at home.

7 *viz.* the *kusti* prayers, the prayer for the *Aiwisruthrem geh*, the *Cheragno Namaskar*, the *Sarosh Yasht Vadi* and the *Atash Niyayesh*.

8 See also Modi (1922: 404), who connects this custom particularly with the *Satum* (on which see above, p. 10f.). For its Iranian Zoroastrian counterpart see Boyce 1977: 143-4. ˙

9 Some Parsis even smear ash on their neck and ears or swallow some for internal purification. However, most community members would regard such practices as excessive.

10 Of the betel leaves, betel nuts, almonds, turmeric sticks and dried dates, the total number of items should be seven or nine. Some households add a fish made of silver, as fish are considered to be auspicious.

11 Except where this could give rise to misunderstanding, 'he' will be used here for the sake of convenience.

12 *Mushkil Asan* ('problem solver') seems originally to have been an epithet of Behram; in the story as it is told among Parsis, however, he has become a separate figure who is Behram's companion.

13 See also Russell 1989.

14 A dish of rice and sweet dal which is associated with happy occasions.

15 The Gujarati words *mahino* (month) and *roj* (day) are generally used in such contexts.

16 The ancient Iranian concept of the *fravashi* was a complex one; it was an element of a person's spiritual being that existed before his life on earth, and is capable of intervening in the affairs of this world after his death. In modern Parsi usage the word generally refers to the eternal souls of the dead, though some think of the *fravashi* as an invisible, ideal counterpart of the self that can be contacted by the spiritually advanced. For further references see Index.

17 The Iranis of Bombay (i.e. those whose families came from Iran over the last 150 years) venerate the *fravashis* on their (Kadmi) New Year's Day.

18 Some traces of a communal memory of Meher's original position in Zoroastrianism are implied by the following remark by Mrs Munshi: 'If someone annoyed my grandmother she used to say, "You will have to go to the Court of Meher [and answer for this]." So people know that Meher is an important Yazata.'

19 Mrs Munshi said, 'There is a popular little book called *Afsun-e Shah Faridunni Nirang* [the title of a prayer to Shah Faridun, PGK]. There is one line which, if you recite it 125,000 times within forty days, will assure that you are looked after in your life. I know this because my husband recited this when he was passing through a very bad time; he had no one who could support him financially, and he needed a job but he was officially too young to work. He

recited this prayer and somehow, immediately on the second day, there was a call and he got a job. So he has immense faith in Shah Faridun... I think there is some connection between Meher and Shah Faridun because in the Aslaji fire temple, which has this special connection with Meher *roj*, there are innumerable pictures both of Kookadaru and of Shah Faridun. So I think that Meher has developed over the years because of this association.' It may be relevant to note that Ervad Yazdi Aibara also connects Meher with Shah Faridun (see Interview). His father, Ervad Nadarsha Aibara, who was the initiator of the Kookadaru cult (see below, p. 50), taught that several ancient Kings of Iran who are mentioned in the *Shahname* (and, under older names, in the Avesta), deserve special veneration. The association may therefore have originated with him.

20 Some women recite the *Ardvisur Niyayesh* for 40 days during pregnancy.
21 See below, under Adar *mahino* Adar *roj*.
22 Another term for *Ardvisur Niyayesh*.
23 i.e. a paste made of turmeric powder and wheat flour.
24 These days are referred to in Gujarati as the *annaroja*.
25 The first day of spring coincides with the first day of the year (Fravardin *mahino* Hormazd *roj*) in the Fasli calendar, but not in those of the Shehenshahis and Kadmis (see below, p. 47). The latter therefore celebrate two separate 'New Year' festivals, Jamshedi Navroz and Navroz proper, on which see p. 26.
26 For a full discussion of the development of this observance see Modi 1922: 440.
27 This period includes the so-called *Gatha* days, the last five days of the year, and ends the day after Khordadsal (on these days see, pp. 26, 27).
28 A set of white muslin clothes, see Modi 1922: 81. On the Iranian equivalent see Boyce 1977: 154 n. 32.
29 *viz.* the *Afrinagan, Farokhshi* and *Satum*.
30 For such a description see Modi 1922: 437f.
31 See Modi 1922: 402-4.
32 In some fire temples where the Muktad tables are removed after ten days, the rituals nevertheless continue for the full 18 days.
33 In Navsari Khordadsal was traditionally called *valavo*, 'the day of bidding farewell (to the *fravashis*)'. A variety of sweets were prepared and offered to the *fravashis* on large trays of plated silver. The sweets were taken to the homes of friends and distributed among them on the next day (Amardad *roj*), which is known as *Amardadsal*. Dastur Dr. F.M. Kotwal informs me that the custom is still observed by some families in Navsari.
34 Named *Vahishtoishti Gatha*.
35 For the difference between this festival and Jamshedi Navroz see above, n. 25.
36 i.e. in the Ushahin *geh* of Aspandad *roj*, so that the *shyav* is already laid out when Khordadsal begins (information I owe to Dastur Dr F.M. Kotwal). During the first Muktad after a death, a *shyav* is also offered on New Year's Day.
37 i.e. of the day when the fire was 'enthroned' in the fire temple after its ritual consecration had been completed.
38 See above, p. 7f.
39 The girl will wear this when she first wears a sari, see p. 29.
40 i.e. ceremony in which *nirang* is administered for both external and internal purification.
41 For a detailed description of the *nahn* ceremony see Modi 1922: 90f.

42 Both the *kusti* and the *sudreh* used for this occasion are special. The *kusti* must be woven from 72 strands, whereas fewer strands may be used for ordinary *kustis*. The *sudreh* for the Navjote is stitched by hand and has a button on the collar above the *girehban* (a pocket on the front of the *sudreh*, on which see Modi 1922: 173); there is a buttonhole on the other side of the garment, so that it can be closed at the neck; furthermore it has longer sleeves and is a bit larger than ordinary *sudrehs*.

43 The amount must always be uneven, e.g. Rs. 51, 101, 501 etc.

44 The *adravanu* is often done in the morning of this day. The day always begins with a *sagan* for the bride and the groom in their respective homes.

45 This is the case in modern Indian cities. In villages the sapling is traditionally planted in the courtyard of the house. Village wedding celebrations used to be performed under a canopy (Guj. *mandap*, whence *madav*).

46 Each of these items represents a quality or concept (e.g. strength or fertility) which, it is hoped, will play a role in the marriage.

47 A similar ceremony is sometimes done for the groom.

48 Some people also have these ceremonies performed on the wedding day itself.

49 This part of the ceremony is called *hathevaro*, 'the joining of hands'.

50 For further traditions and games associated with weddings see Modi 1922: 40f.

51 The word *randel*, which may have been the name of a divinity venerated by the Indian Rajputs, suggests that the ceremony was originally dedicated to that Hindu deity. However, the Kurdish Yezidis, who like the Parsis are of Iranian origin, have a very similar ceremony, see Kreyenbroek 1995: 16.

52 A kind of pulse.

53 Many of the observances described here are traditionally done for the first child only.

54 Some Parsis prefer other forms of disposal of the body, which are not discussed here.

55 i.e. they recite part of the prayer text of that name before beginning their task, and the rest when the work is completed (cf. pp. 17, 28); for details see Modi 1922: 61 n. 1.

56 For details see Modi 1922: 56f.

57 Funerals can only take place in two daytime watches, the Havan and the Uziran *geh*, and never at night.

58 When they reach Y. 31.4.

59 All mourners are dressed in white.

60 i.e. the *fravashis*.

Chapter Three

The Parsis
in India

THE HISTORICAL BACKGROUND

A detailed survey of the history of the Parsis in India would lie far beyond the scope of the present work, and no more can be done than to offer a brief sketch of some of the main developments and events so as to enable to reader to understand references in the interviews. A description of the earliest phases of Parsi history would in any case be a hazardous undertaking, since very few reliable sources are available at present. Even on the question of the time of the Zoroastrians' arrival in Gujarat (NW India), there are several theories but so far no consensus. Most Parsis accept an eighth-century date, whereas some Western scholars hold that the Parsis first came to India in the mid-tenth century. Our information on early Parsi history mainly derives from a single source, the *Qisse-ye Sanjan,* which was written down in 1600 CE, presumably on the basis of oral tradition. Chronicles of this kind usually represent history as the community has remembered it for centuries, stressing events that seemed important to generations of Parsis but paying scant attention to factual details which were of lesser interest. The *Qisse-ye Sanjan* is therefore most valuable as a guide to the collective memory of the Parsis of an early age and as the basis of modern Parsis' understanding of their own past, but not always reliable as a historical document in the Western sense. The *Qisse* tells of the arrival of the Zoroastrians in India and the conditions imposed on them by the local ruler, Jadi Rana, and describes the eventful history of the Parsis' oldest Behram fire (Atash Behram), which was guarded against desecration at all costs, at times hidden, and taken from place to place. After many vicissitudes the fire was installed in Udwada in 1742.[1]

It can be assumed that the Indian caste system made it relatively easy for the Parsis to survive as a separate group with its own identity, traditions, and religion.[2] Priests, it seems, long continued to provide leadership to the community and were held in high esteem. In the course of time the Parsis' numbers increased and they settled in various parts of Gujarat; eventually the priests divided this area into five districts (*panthak*), each with its own hereditary priesthood. This division still plays a role in religious affairs today; membership of some lineages entails certain privileges, and every priest knows to which group he belongs.

The meagre evidence at our disposal suggests that, in the early centuries, the Parsis lived modest but reasonably prosperous lives as farmers and small traders. In the course of the 16th century, Surat, an important trading port both for the Indian Moghul Empire and for European companies, attracted increasing numbers of Parsis, who soon found a niche for themselves as agents for European merchants.[3] This was the beginning of a development which was to affect the entire Parsi community in the following centuries: an increasing number of laymen became wealthy and socially prominent and in time their outlook and attitudes changed accordingly. This trend became especially significant when the Portuguese ceded Bombay, then a modest commercial port, to the British in 1661. The new masters intended to turn the town into a major trading centre, and the enterprising Parsis were encouraged to settle there.[4] Parsis began to flock to Bombay, which gradually became the social and cultural centre of Zoroastrian life in India. Bombay had no long-established Parsi community, and new social structures developed in an atmosphere where priestly authority, and perhaps traditional views, probably did not carry as much weight as elsewhere.[5]

Later, in the days of British India, the Parsi merchant families were proud and often spectacularly wealthy subjects of the Raj, generally Western-educated and modern in outlook. The progressive views of this élite, propagated in combination with their proverbial generosity and charity, made themselves felt throughout the community. All this predictably had implications for the way in which religion was understood. Although there is evidence of some thought on doctrine and belief in the course of the preceding centuries,[6] it seems likely that the vast majority of Parsis in those days were content to follow the traditions of their ancestors and the directions of their priests, without paying much attention to questions of doctrine. As the Parsis acquired Western ideas and adopted elements of Western culture it seems that a Western – or Protestant – definition of the nature of religion began to affect their understanding of their own faith.[7] Traditional views of Zoroastrianism as a way of life were challenged by a definition of religion mainly as a divine message relayed by a Prophet and correctly or wrongly interpreted by his followers. Such discrepancies posed problems which were particularly hard to solve for Zoroastrians, since the 'Western' view seems to correspond to a large extent to that of their ancient texts, whereas the 'traditional' position reflects the understanding of many generations of their immediate ancestors. Another factor which played a role here was the 'discovery' of the Avesta by the French Orientalist A.H. Anquetil Duperron in the 18th century and the subsequent study of its language and contents in the West. These academic efforts on the part of outsiders eventually made the Parsis more aware of their sacred texts as potential sources of information, whereas until then they had probably thought of these mainly as divinely revealed words whose comprehension was beyond human understanding.[8]

Tensions in the community came to a head in the first half of the 19th century, when British missionaries, notably the Rev. John Wilson, began to attack the Zoroastrian religion. Wilson had read an early translation of the Avesta at a time when few Parsis may have known that such a thing existed, and attacked a form of Zoroastrianism which could be deduced from his reading but which did not seem familiar to the Parsis of his day. When Zoroastrian priests sought to refute his views they achieved little more than an exposure of their own inadequacy as theologians in a Western sense.[9] While a majority of Parsis may until then have assumed that a profound and true understanding of the teachings of the faith existed in priestly circles, after this incident many became more sceptical. Priestly authority diminished, and the newly sophisticated and wealthy sections of the laity began to search for novel ways of understanding the religion.

In the 19th century, the Parsi community was thus both divided in its views, and challenged from outside. Together these factors seem to have resulted in a sense of crisis, and this in turn contributed to the development of the range of religious movements or schools which will be discussed below. For the community as a whole the 19th century thus marked the transition from a stable self-image based on centuries of traditional life, to a state of affairs where many aspects of Parsi religious and social life were constantly called into question. In the context of 19th century prosperity this may have been seen as positive: an ancient community was on the way to finding its roots again. After more than a century and a half, however, these problems still show no sign of being resolved, and they now inspire mostly pessimistic feelings. Meanwhile the British Raj has given way to the Republic of India, where Parsis have no special status; the community is no longer as affluent as it once was; and many enterprising and progressive Parsis have emigrated to the West, leaving behind a community whose sense of pride and identity seems to some extent to have been eroded.

GROUPS AND RELIGIOUS MOVEMENTS

Shehenshahis, Kadmis and Faslis

As a result of contacts with Iran connected with the *Rivayat* correspondence,[10] the Indian Parsis became aware that their calendar was a month behind that of their brethren in the mother country.[11] In the mid-18th century,[12] this led to disputes and the Parsis divided into two groups (often referred to as 'sects'). The majority group, or 'Shehenshahis',[13] adhered to the traditional Indian calendar while the 'Kadmis'[14] observed the Iranian one. Although no doctrinal differences exist,[15] there were serious tensions between the groups in the 18th and 19th centuries, one of which resulted in the execution of Homaji (see below). In the early 20th century another calendar was proposed, which had its New Year on the traditional date of 21 March, and intercalated one day every four years; those who follow this calendar are known as Faslis.[16] Even more recently a very small group adopted a modified version of the Fasli calendar, and called themselves *Khalis Faslis*.

Traditionalists and Neo-traditionalists

The term 'Traditionalists' is found mostly in publications by Westerners; the Parsis themselves generally say 'orthodox'.[17] The term is used here for those who emphatically adhere to the ancient, traditional ways of their forefathers, most prominently in matters of observance.

In the community, Traditionalists and Neo-traditionalists are seen as one group. The designation 'Neo-traditionalists' is a new coinage, denoting those whose 'orthodox' views in matters of doctrine and ritual derive to a significant extent from the study of the classical religious tradition of Zoroastrianism, partly on the basis of Western academic works. While Traditionalists usually come from a traditional background, Neo-traditionalist views are often adopted after a personal search for religious truth. Neo-traditionalists are generally more preoccupied with doctrinal questions than Traditionalists, and many actively advocate a belief in dualism.[18]

Reformists and Modernists

The Reformist movement, it seems, sprang directly from the clash between traditional Zoroastrianism and Western Protestantism in the 19th century. Many Reformists accepted the Western academic view that only the *Gathas* can be ascribed to Zarathustra,[19] and drew the conclusion that only these texts were valid sources of religious authority. They stressed that Zoroastrianism is a monotheistic faith aiming to teach a system of ethics, and rejected what they saw as an excessive preoccupation with ritual. Instead of the traditional, unintelligible prayers in Avestan, many Reformists demanded translations as a basis for worship and prayer; they emphasised personal responsibility and many felt one could do without priests.[20] In the latter half of the 19th century the Reformists founded societies, schools, debating clubs, and political associations,[21] thus translating their ambitions into effective social action. In course of the 20th century this movement lost its original drive and coherence, at least in India.[22] Some who might once have been Reformists apparently began to feel they could do without religion altogether and regarded their Parsi identity as a purely ethnic one, while others (here termed 'modernists') combine non-traditional views on the religion with some nostalgic feelings for old traditions, and with a modern lifestyle that finds its main inspiration in Western ideas and attitudes.

Theosophists

Theosophy was introduced to India by Mme Helena Blavatsky and Captain H.S. Olcott in the 1880s,[23] and met with a strong response, presumably from Parsis who had become dissatisfied with traditional Zoroastrianism without being prepared to accept the Reformists' views.[24] Soon there was a flourishing branch of the Theosophical Society in Bombay, with many Parsi members. Typical elements of Parsi theosophist religion are a belief in reincarnation, the hidden powers of ritual, and the occult meaning of the Zoroastrian religious texts.[25] The dualist element in Zoroastrian teaching was praised by Olcott,[26] though in the present anti-dualist climate such views do not seem to be prominent among Theosophists. Many Parsis who are strongly influenced by Theosophy are vegetarians or feel they ought to be. At the time of writing, the movement as such seems less influential among Indian Parsis than it once was. As in the case of the Reformists, it is perhaps true to say that some of its ideas have come to be regarded as acceptable ways to interpret Zoroastrianism, which can be adhered to eclectically without the need to accept the whole system of teachings. Many elements that were once characteristic of Theosophy among Parsis, moreover, are also found in the 'indigenous' Parsi movement of Ilm-e Khshnoom.

The Dasatir, Ilm-e Khshnoom and the Pundolites

The Ilm-e Khshnoom movement began in 1902, when Behramshah N. Shroff broke his 30–year silence and started divulging his revelations (see further below). The way of thinking that facilitated the acceptance of such teachings in the community would seem to go further back, however. As early as the 17th century we hear of the existence in India of groups of Zoroastrian mystics;[27] the best known among these is Azar Kaivan,[28] an Iranian Zoroastrian who settled in Patna in the late 16th century. His disciples practised yoga-like austerities and apparently believed in a theosophical-cum-mystical interpretation of Zoroastrian teaching. Ideas which may be connected with the beliefs of these groups are found in the *Dasatir*. This work, which was written in an artificial pseudo-language believed to be ancient, was in fact probably composed in the 16th century in a Persian Sufi milieu.[29] The *Dasatir* claims to contain the sayings of fourteen successive Prophets: from a figure named Mahabad, who is said to have lived in remote prehistory, to the 'Fifth Sasan', who flourished just before the Islamic conquest. These Prophets never died, but had withdrawn from the world and preserved the true teachings of Iran, the extant Avesta containing no more than parables intended for the uninitiated. The *Dasatir* teaches that there is one Divine Being, and a chain of lower 'intelligences'. It advocates spiritual progress through fasting and meditation, and teaches reincarnation. A 'translation' of this work was published in India in 1818, and the *Dasatir* was widely accepted by Parsis as a genuine sacred text; in fact two of the priests who sought to refute the Rev. Wilson's views on Zoroastrianism invoked it as their authority,[30] and in 1869 the learned Dastur Erachji S. Meherjirana listed the work as one of his sources together with such canonical texts as the *Vendidad* and the *Yasna*.[31] H.S. Olcott taught that the authority of the *Dasatir* was equal to that of the *Gathas*,[32] which suggests that Parsis represented this work to him as part of the Zoroastrian canon.

The success of Theosophy, together with the apparent popularity and status of the *Dasatir*, indicates that esoteric teachings were welcomed by many Parsis around the turn of the century. This is confirmed by the response to the message of Behramshah N. Shroff (1858–1927),[33] a simple man of poor priestly background. At the age of 17, it is told, on a journey to Peshawar he met a caravan of people who outwardly appeared to be Muslims but secretly wore the *kusti*. These travellers took him to Iran, to a miraculous place on Mt Demavand where he was enlightened by 'Masters' who explained to him the true esoteric meaning of the Avesta. After his return to Surat he remained silent for 30 years, and then started preaching in 1902.[34] Teachings originating with, or ascribed to Behramshah Shroff form the basis of the small but active movement known as Ilm-e Khshnoom.[35] At the time of writing more than one leader claims to be Shroff's true spiritual heir. Khsnoomist teachings are too complicated to sum up adequately here.[36] The movement attaches great importance to ritual and prayer, which endears it to some priests and puts Khsnoomists in the 'orthodox' camp together with Traditionalists, Neo-traditionalists and

Theosophists. Many followers of the movement expect a saviour figure, Shah Behram Varjavand,[37] to appear around the year 2000 CE, an expectation which is shared by many other Parsis.

The Pundolites form a relatively small occultist movement which for a time was very active in India. They are followers of Minocher Nusservanji Pundol (d. 1975), who, like B.N. Shroff, claimed to have been taken to Mt Demavand and received instruction from a Master. Orthopraxy, a belief in reincarnation and astrology, and speculations about the coming of Shah Behram Varjavand play an important role in the beliefs of this group.

Parsi Cults and Venerated Figures

There are indications that cults of 'Babas' (human objects of devotion), are attracting increasing numbers of Parsi followers. Most Babas are not Parsis,[38] but acts of devotion addressed to some human figures of Parsi origin also play a role in the religious life of the community.

Kookadaru. A much revered figure is Dasturji Jamshed Sorabji Kookadaru,[39] to whom miraculous powers are ascribed. It is said that when the Anjuman Atash Behram was to be consecrated in 1897, Kookadaru had pledged an amount of money he did not possess, but that he miraculously obtained this sum. The late Ervad Nadarsha Aibara claimed to receive messages from Kookadaru and prescribed prayers on the basis of that guidance.[40] Ervad Aibara had a large following, and devotion to Kookadaru is still so great that his picture is seen side by side with that of Zarathustra in many Parsi homes and shops.

Homaji. Many Shehenshahis have ceremonies performed on Dae *mahino* Govad *roj*, the death anniversary of Homaji. This figure, whose full name was Homaji Jamshedji, was a business man from Bharuch (Broach). In his day there were severe tensions between Shehenshahis and Kadmis (see above). A pregnant Kadmi woman was hurt in a communal fight and lost her child. Homaji was identified as the culprit, and eventually executed in 1783.[41] As it is felt that Homaji died for his religion, many Shehenshahis have ceremonies performed for him every year.[42]

The two Jal Babas. In December 1994 Mrs Munshi said:

A curious practice has developed over the last year or so: every Monday in the Aiwisruthrim *geh*, Parsis go to the Banaji Atash Behram to pray to a being called Jal Baba. Nobody knows who Jal Baba is, or what he does, or why he is important, but many Parsis believe in this sort of thing; when someone says that prayer in a particular place at a particular time does wonders, then many will go there. They normally do a *hambandagi*, [i.e.] they recite a short prayer aloud together, and it is believed that the spirit of Jal Baba comes to bless them.

In the course of 1995 there was a new development: a physical Jal Baba started coming to the Aslaji Agiary on Fridays, and rapidly acquired a relatively large following.

The Nagrani. A lady of Parsi origin, who is known as the Nagrani or 'Snake Queen' because she apparently handles these animals, gives regular audiences to her devotees in Bombay. These are attended by large crowds, comprising both Parsis and others. The Nagrani's followers wear the Zoroastrian prayer cap, a tie, and a cobra badge. At the beginning of her audiences, it seems, four Parsi priests do their *kusti*. Most of the Nagrani's devotees come from the underprivileged classes. The cult is strongly condemned by many Parsis.

On the role of cults in the community. Such cults affect the life of the community in various ways. Ideas deriving from the teachings of Kookadaru as expounded by Ervad N. Aibara, for example, are often better known to Parsis than elements of the 'classical' Zoroastrian tradition.[43] The frequent discussions about the acceptability of various cults, moreover, can be seen as attempts by ordinary believers to define their religion (the same is true of the debates on 'marrying out' and conversion, see further below). At one end of the spectrum one finds those who reject any such cults; the other extreme is formed by Parsis who see no harm in seeking supernatural help wherever it may be found. An important dividing line seems to lie between cults of Zoroastrian figures and those of alien ones; many who strongly reject worship of Sai Baba or the Virgin Mary may find it acceptable, and indeed natural, to venerate Kookadaru or Homaji.

SOME ASPECTS OF MODERN SOCIAL AND COMMUNAL LIFE

Numbers

Although most Parsis believe that their numbers are dwindling, the results of a 1991 census[44] show that – for the first time since the 1950s – the Parsi community in India increased slightly between 1981 and 1991.[45] There were 76,382 Zoroastrians in India in that year; 53,794 (70%) of these lived in Bombay, and 60,501 (79%) in the state of Maharashtra as a whole. The Maharashtrian city of Pune (Poona) has the second largest Parsi population in India. Of the remaining Parsis, a majority live in the state of Gujarat, where Navsari and Surat have relatively large communities.

Charities

Parsi charities play an important role in the social and religious life of the community. An enormous range of communal facilities and institutions owes its existence to private charity: from the Atash Behrams and the Towers of Silence, via hospitals and subsidised housing, to a social security system[46] and projects to improve the conditions of rural communities.[47] Parsis are understandably proud of this proof of the generosity of their community, which is widely regarded as an expression of the ethics of their religion.

A number of charitable Trusts are governed by their own Board of Trustees, while others are administered by the Bombay Parsi Punchayat,[48] which also has considerable assets of its own. Trustees of such institutions, and particularly those of the Bombay Punchayet, therefore have a great deal of influence in many spheres, including religion. Trustees are generally elected because they are felt to have a certain eminence, either as highly successful professional people or as members of wealthy families. Those who combine a high eligibility with a readiness to serve may sit on the Boards of a number of Trusts, and consequently have considerable power in the community.[49]

Fire Temples

The status of a Zoroastrian fire temple is determined by that of the fire it houses. As was described in detail in Ch. 1, there are three 'grades' of consecrated fires, the Dadgah fire, which is basically a hearth-fire; the Adaran fire, which is found in most ordinary fire temples (Agiaries); and the very august Atash Behram.

There are eight Atash Behrams in India: one in Udwada (the Iranshah), one in Navsari, four in Bombay (Dadyseth, Wadiaji, Banaji, and Anjuman),[50] and two in Surat (Mody and Vakil). The latter is a Kadmi fire, as are the Dadyseth and Banaji Atash Behrams in Bombay; the others belong to the Shehenshahi community. At the time of writing there are probably just over a hundred Agiaries in the whole of India, forty of which are situated in Bombay.

Priests

Parsi priesthood is hereditary, in the sense that only boys born into priestly families can be initiated as priests. Many such boys nowadays have no intention of becoming full-time priests. Some simply do not train as priests, but others undergo the first initiation, the *Navar*. This entitles one to perform some rituals and to use the title *Ervad*. To rank as a full-fledged priest one must go on to the second initiation, the *Martab*, thus obtaining the higher rank of *Mobed* and the right to perform all rituals. The highest priestly rank is that of *Dastur* or 'High Priest', a title that is often (though not necessarily) linked to the function of chief priest of an Atash Behram. There are currently eight Dasturs in India. Two are based at Udwada, where they share the guardianship of the Atash Behram,[51] the Anjuman and Wadiaji Atash Behrams in Bombay each have their own Dastur, as have the Navsari Atash Behram and the Shehenshahi Atash Behram of Surat. The 'High Priest of the Deccan', a Dastur resident in Pune, does not serve an Atash Behram, and in 1996 the Anjuman (Community Council) of Bangalore, which has no Atash Behram, appointed its own Dastur. It is virtually impossible to estimate the numbers of other working Zoroastrian priests in India, but a recent educated guess put this figure at around 300.[52]

The current lack of enthusiasm for the priesthood poses severe problems for the long-time future of the community, but it is understandable. Until a few centuries ago priests played a leading role in the local communities and were looked up to with all the reverence people of Indian culture tend to feel for religious learning and virtues. Then, especially in the last 150 years, a more critical view came to prevail. Just as many people's idea of religion came to be influenced by Protestantism, so their expectations of the priesthood began to be modelled on the role of European clergymen, which Parsi priests had not been trained to fulfil. The ensuing serious loss of social status had economic consequences;[53] financially, no Parsi priest in India can now hope to compete with laymen in employment requiring a similar amount of training. As a result few gifted youngsters who have other options are prepared to enter the profession. If unchecked, this development could lead to a further deterioration of the reputation of the priesthood.

Efforts to remedy this state of affairs usually take the form of increased pay-offers in a few individual cases.[54] They seldom address the underlying problem, namely that large sections of the Parsi community now require clear and well-founded information on the teachings of their religion, which the average priest cannot offer. Apart from the normal school curriculum, the two training colleges for priests (Madressa)[55] teach their pupils prayers and rituals, some Avestan and Pahlavi, ancient Iranian history as found in the scriptural tradition and the *Shahname*,[56] and a few hours of elementary religious instruction.[57] None of this equips a priest for the demands made on a religious leader by a sophisticated modern community.

As far as can be ascertained, at the time of writing the only organisation aiming to fill this lacuna in priests' knowledge of Zoroastrian doctrine and other relevant subjects is the Athravan Educational Trust (AET). The Trust was founded in 1986 by a group of community leaders of traditionalist and neo-traditionalist leanings,[58] and was backed soon afterwards by the enlightened industrialist Naoroji P. Godrej. The Trust's first project was a three-year educational programme for the priesthood, offering a course of studies including theology, rituals, psychology, sociology and history.[59] In its early years the Trust encountered much opposition, not least from priests who objected to the Neo-traditionalist element in the organisation.

Parsi discourse and community debates

Such definitions and attitudes contributing to religious change as can be inferred from the interviews will be discussed in another chapter, but it may be appropriate to note a few relevant points of a more general nature here. It should be stressed first of all that preaching does not play a role in Zoroastrianism, and that there is neither a well-defined forum (such as a Council) where the validity of various views on religion could be debated and assessed, nor a priesthood well-versed in theology, or indeed an accepted body of doctrines that could form the basis for such discussions. At the time of writing developments with religious implications mainly seem to occur as a result of community discourse generally, and of public debates in the press.

Given that no effective religious authority exists to counteract such developments, ideas and attitudes originating in the surrounding culture may come to be accepted into the Parsi tradition relatively easily.[60] While this could theoretically lead to a disintegration of the tradition, it seems that the impact of such trends is at least partly counteracted by the discourse of this small and closely-knit community. By assimilating, disregarding or resisting new developments, it seems, community discourse prevents indiscriminate acceptance of alien features, and helps to integrate those which are found acceptable into the Parsi tradition.

As the interviews show, for example,[61] it is widely known that reincarnation does not play an obvious role in classical Zoroastrian teaching, but those Parsis who do believe in it state their conviction confidently, apparently without feeling that this impairs their standing as Zoroastrians. The belief in reincarnation – which is of course common in India, is taught by various 'esoteric' Parsi movements and has been adopted by many Parsis outside those groups – could therefore be said to have become part of the range of beliefs which it is acceptable for a Parsi to hold. Explanations for the absence of references to reincarnation in the Avesta have become part of Parsi discourse.[62]

The fact that some Parsis venerate or pray to the Virgin Mary is apparently felt to be too peripheral to provoke a strong reaction in the community; the very fact that it is ignored may help to keep it outside the sphere of recognised Parsi observance. On the other hand there is strong censure in the community of those Parsis who participate in the cult of (non-Zoroastrian) 'Babas', an apparently recent phenomenon which is regarded as significant enough to threaten the mental image most Parsis have of their religion.[63] It remains to be seen if this negative but strong interest in Baba cults is to be interpreted as an indication that these cults are forever beyond the pale, or rather as the first step in a process of semi-acceptance.

Elements of non-Zoroastrian origin which seem to have been accepted without much resistance belong for the most part to the sphere of private belief and practice. Issues which affect the community as a whole are liable to provoke a great deal of debate and controversy. The forum for such battles is usually the Press. In a community not noted for its interest in reading, journalists have been accused of deliberately exacerbating controversies in order to boost sales. The Parsi press mirrors the divisions in the community into an 'orthodox' and a 'liberal' camp: *The Bombay Samachar*, a Parsi-owned Gujarati daily with a small English section, favours 'modernist' views, while the *Jam-e-Jamshed*, which has a similar format, is generally more traditional in its opinions.[64] Controversies often concern the question of who may be recognised as a genuine Parsi and is thus entitled to make use of community facilities;[65] issues which have figured in such debates[66] include re-admission of lapsed Zoroastrians, the conversion of outsiders, and the status of Parsis who have 'married out' and their children.[67] Assumptions underlying the various views on these topics will be discussed in Ch. 10.

Notes

1 See Boyce 1979: 188; Kulke 1974: 31.
2 See Writer 1996.
3 See Kulke 1974: 32f.
4 As early as 1673 a piece of land on Malabar Hill was made over to the Parsis for the construction of Towers of Silence in an appropriate spot, which was then well away from the town (see Kulke 1974: 34). Malabar Hill is now one of the most coveted and expensive areas of Bombay, a city where land prices are anyhow among the highest in the world.
5 Witness the need for a Punchayet, on which see below, n. 48.
6 During the 1570s, the Zoroastrian Dastur Meherji Rana explained the tenets of his religion with considerable success at the court of the Emperor Akbar (see, with references, Kulke 1974: 31). The Emperor later devised a new religion, which comprised elements deriving from Zoroastrianism and Islamic mysticism. The late 16th and early 17th century saw the activities of the Zoroastrian mystic Azar Kayvan (on whom see Corbin 1989) and his disciples, who seem to have attempted to combine Zoroastrianism with elements of Sufi and Hindu thought (Duchesne-Guillemin 1962: 371). It is not known to what extent such movements influenced the majority of Parsis, or are to be regarded as symptoms of a more general quest among Zoroastrians for a deeper understanding of religious truth. The *Rivayats* (a series of epistles dating from the 15th to the 18th century which contain questions on religion

55

asked by Parsis and the replies of the priests of Iran), suggest that religion was then still understood largely in terms of ritual and observance.

7 For an account of this process see Stausberg 1997.

8 For a more detailed account see Boyce 1979: 194–5.

9 For a fuller description see Boyce 1979: 196–7; on Wilson's activities see also Kulke 1974: 93–4; for an analysis of his arguments see Stausberg 1997, Hinnells 1997: 68.

10 See above, n. 6.

11 Since the Zoroastrian calendar has 365 days whereas the solar cycle takes 365 and a quarter days to complete, it seems that intercalations of one month had taken place from time to time in earlier days. In India a month may have been intercalated unilaterally in the 12th century CE, which resulted in a discrepancy between the calendars of the two communities.

12 Boyce (1979: 189): 1746; Kulke (1974: 21): 1730.

13 Or 'Shenshais'; various spellings are found. The term appears to be connected with the Persian word for 'great king', although this etymology has been challenged (see Boyce 1979: 190). According to Kulke (1974: 21), the Shehenshahis form 93 per cent of the Indian Parsis.

14 Or 'Qadmis', from Arabo-Persian *qadim* 'ancient'.

15 On differences in observance see above, p. 26.

16 i.e. 'seasonalists', as their calendar celebrates the ancient festivals in the season to which they may originally have belonged. The Shehenshahis now celebrate their New Year in August, the Kadmis in September. See further Boyce 1979: 212.

17 For references see Index.

18 For an exposition of Neo-traditionalist ideas see Mistree 1982, and cf. the interview with Mr Mistree.

19 See also below, p. 306.

20 For passages from older Reformist sources see Boyce 1984: 139–43.

21 See Boyce 1979: 200–02.

22 Such a movement, though not called by this name, is very much alive among Zoroastrians living in the West, but its views now seem to evoke little response in the mother country.

23 See Kulke 1974: 99; Boyce 1979: 204; Hinnells 1998: 72.

24 On the existence of an older form of Zoroastrian theosophy see further below.

25 For passages from older Theosophist sources see Boyce 1984: 136, 155–6.

26 See Boyce 1979: 204.

27 In the *Dabestan al-Mazaheb,* see Duchesne-Guillemin 1962: 370f.

28 On this figure see Modi 1932; Corbin 1989.

29 See Duchesne-Guillemin 1962: 371; on the *Dasatir* see further Boyce 1979: 197–8.

30 Boyce 1979: 197.

31 See Kotwal and Boyd 1982: 1–2.

32 See Boyce 1979: 204.

33 On Shroff see Hinnells 1988; cf. Boyce 1979: 205; according to Kulke (1974: 22) he was born in 1857.

34 See Boyce 1979: 205.

35 The term originally seems to have meant 'science of dedications', referring to ritual dedicatory formulae which according to Shroff had great mystical significance; since the word from which *khshnoom* is derived basically means 'satisfaction', the name is sometimes translated as 'science of satisfaction'.

36 For a clearer survey of Khshoomist ideas see the interviews with Dr M. Master-Moos and Mr A. Doctor.

37 Beliefs about the coming of Bahram Varzavand (Guj. Behram Varjavand) seem to have been prominent in Zoroastrian communities in Iran in the first centuries after the Arab conquest; they are now combined with the ancient prophecy that a saviour will appear 3000 years after Zarathustra.

38 Meher Baba was a Zoroastrian and is presumably still revered by some Parsis, but as no reference was made to him by any of our informants his cult is not discussed separately here.

39 His real name was Jamshedji S. Madan. For references to Kookadaru in the interviews see Index.

40 cf. the interview with Ervad Yazdi Aibara.

41 See Menant 1898: 67.

42 Generally a *Baj*, in some cases an *Ijashne* or even a *Vendidad* (see above, p. 10).

43 Witness, for example, the venerations for Faridun, on which see above, p. 41 n. 19.

44 Reported in *Parsiana*, July-August 1995.

45 The results of the census are, however, widely regarded with scepticism in the community.

46 See Bulsara in Boyce 1979: 208.

47 See the interview with Mr Tamboly.

48 Alternative spellings of last word of the title are 'Panchayat' and 'Panchayet'. For the history of this institution, which began as an organisation established by laymen to administer and rule the Parsi community in Bombay but now mainly concerns itself with the administration of public Parsi funds and charitable Trusts, see Kulke 1974: 61–7, 69–77.

49 I am indebted for this information to Mr K.P. Mistree (oral communication, 10 September 1995).

50 For the foundation dates of the Bombay Atash Behrams see Kulke 1974: 21, n. 27.

51 One of these Dasturs, Dasturji Dr H.K. Mirza, lives in Bombay and takes an active part in the religious affairs of that city.

52 K.P. Mistree, oral communication, 10 September 1995.

53 See also Kulke 1974: 77–8.

54 At the time of writing the Athornan Mandal (a priestly organisation formed to 'to safeguard and protect the tradition of the religion and chastise any priest who commits anti-religious acts') and the Indian branch of the World Zoroastrian Organisation (for references to which see Index) together operate a scheme to encourage prospective priests. They offer financial assistance to Madressa graduates to enable them to continue their secular education, with the *proviso* that they have to work as full-time priests for a number of years after completing their studies.

55 The Athornan Boarding Madressa at Dadar (Bombay) and the M.F. Cama Athornan Institute at Andheri (a Bombay suburb). The Sir J.J. Madressa at Dhobi Talao (Bombay) is not a training school for priests but offers classes in Avestan and Pahlavi to all who wish to learn. Information I owe to Mrs S.N. Munshi.

56 This is a New Persian source, written by a Muslim but largely based on the ancient myths of Iran. As it offers the most accessible account of these mythical stories it is widely accepted by many Parsis as a part of their tradition.

57 Information I owe to Dastur Dr. F.M. Kotwal, the erstwhile Principal of the Andheri Madressa.

58 *viz.* Dastur Dr F.M. Kotwal, Mr Homi Ranina, and members of 'Zoroastrian Studies'.

59 The Trust has also held Seminars on religion, funded publications, and set up a medical insurance scheme for priests. Information I owe to Mr K.P. Mistree (oral communication, 15 September 1995).

60 See H. Langstaff's findings quoted in Hinnells 1997: 87, and cf. Maneck 1994.

61 For references to the topics discussed here see Index.

62 The explanation that the Avesta is silent on the subject because Parsis have reached a spiritual level that makes further incarnation unnecessary is scoffed at by sceptics, but appears to be widely known (for references see Index).

63 The view that adherence to one religion implies that one should not participate in observances originating in others, may itself have been influenced by Western definitions. In 1819, when British influence on the Parsi community was gaining strength, the Punchayet forbade Parsi women to take part in Hindu and Muslim observances (Menant 1898: 251–3). This suggests that such practices had been common before Western views on religion made them seem un-Zoroastrian.

64 The *Jam-e-Jamshed* is said to have a wider readership among Parsis, whilst the readership of the *Samachar* apparently includes relatively large numbers of non-Parsi Gujarati-speakers. At times of controversy many Parsis buy both publications. Other periodicals playing a role in such debates include the magazine *Parsiana*, perhaps best described as 'middle of the road', and the ultra-conservative periodical *Deen Parast* (see the interview with its Editor, Noshir Dadrawalla). The former is widely read by Parsis throughout the world, the latter mainly by those who share its views.

65 See also Hinnells 1997: 88.

66 A list of instances could be given. Since the community is still traumatised by the memory of some of these controversies, however, and as it would be virtually impossible to give an account doing absolute justice to all parties involved, it seems best to refrain from doing so here. For brief references to two such cases see the Index, under Shah, Wadia.

67 There is much debate, for example, about the current unofficial practice of accepting children of Parsi fathers but not those of Parsi mothers, and about the right of a child of mixed parentage to be initiated as a priest.

Part Two

The Interviews

Chapter Four

Traditionalists

MRS O

Mrs O was born in 1948 in a Gujarati village; her father was a farmer and the family were *Behdins*. There were many children and Mrs O was partly raised by her maternal grandmother in Navsari. She married into the priestly class and has two sons. The account gives examples of the differences in outlook and atmosphere between lay and priestly families, and clearly represents a 'traditionalist' point of view. The interview was conducted in Gujarati.

Mrs Munshi first asks Mrs O where she was born.

> In the village of Ramkuva, we were six sisters and one brother. I was born at 4.30 a.m., and as it was the morning of Hormazd *roj*, my mother used to celebrate my birthday on that day. But after my marriage B. [her husband] said that 4.30 a.m. still belongs to the previous *roj*, so since then I have celebrated my birthday a day earlier.[1]

Mrs O was taught her prayers at primary school – a Parsi school where it was obligatory to wear a Parsi cap, an hour was devoted to religion each day, and on *hamkara* days pupils were taken to the fire temple before classes began. The prayers she learned included the Navjote prayers (*Yatha Ahu Vairyo, Ashem Vohu, Kem-Na Mazda, Hormazd Khodae*), and later the *Khorshed Meher Niyayesh*. A book, the *Navjot Shikshak* ('Navjote Teacher') was used to elucidate questions on religion. The meanings of the prayers were not taught, and the pupils would not have thought of asking. 'We just said yes to whatever we were told to do.' *Monajats* (devotional songs) were not taught, nor were moral religious stories told, but school prizes tended to consist of books telling stories from the *Shahname*. Religion was also taught in the secondary school which Mrs O attended, but students gradually lost interest as they grew older. Mrs O's religious education was reinforced at home. Her grandmother, an observant Zoroastrian, was very strict and refused to serve dinner until the children had said their prayers:

> Our grandmother would tell us to get up early in the morning and recite *Ashem Vohu*, then we did our *kusti* before attending to the daily routine. My grandmother sent to the Fire Temple for *nirang* every day [for ritual cleansing] – no, not *nirang, taro*.[2] And she recited the *Shekaste, shekaste Shaytan* daily.[3] If sometimes there was no *taro*, she took ash in her hand and made us do the same. However, she did not make us do it [the *Shekaste* ritual] regularly and I do not remember it very well; after my grandmother died no one did it and we have forgotten now. But we always had to say our prayers before going to bed.

What did you pray at night?
When we were small, Grandma used to make us recite our prayers but when I grew up I recited the *Aiwisruthrim geh*, *Atash Niyayesh*, and *Mah Bokhtar Niyayesh* [which do not form part of the basic Navjote prayers] from the book, and as I began to understand things better I gradually started praying more, of my own accord.

Did your grandmother keep the fire burning for twenty-four hours?
Yes, and she kept the kitchen absolutely clean. Since the fire was in the kitchen, the kitchen door was always kept half-shut so that servants would not go in. No matter how ill she was, she would clean the kitchen and the fireplace herself, she never asked anyone else to do it.[4]

Did she also keep a divo burning?
No, she was not rich enough to keep a *divo* as well as the fire, but she definitely had a *divo* on every Behram *roj*. She had a lot of faith in Homaji, whose *roj* is Govad *roj*, and she lighted a *divo* for him on that day; she also did it on birthdays.[5]

What about loban?
In the morning, after the sweeping was done and the chalk patterns were made, my grandmother usually did *loban* herself; she did not allow us to do it for fear that we might drop the incense burner. When she was too old to carry on we started doing it. *Loban* was not done at night, but it was customary to bow before the light in the evenings when the lamps were lit. A small garland, which was brought specially by the flower seller, would be put on the lamp.

Do you come from a Behdin or an Athornan family?
We are *Behdins* and we lived in Malesar, where there are no Mobeds [priests],[6] only *Behdins*, and only Shehenshahis. I did not know there was a Kadmi group till I was quite old.

Do you remember what happened on important parabs?
My grandmother sent us to the neighbourhood Agiary.

Not to the Atash Behram?
The Atash Behram was in Mota Faliya, which is quite far from Malesar where we lived, and we went there only on Navroz and Pateti. We only visited the Atash Behram on very festive occasions, and then we went happily, wearing new clothes.

But you were describing how your grandmother celebrated the parabs.
On the *parab* for Fire the fire was kept burning throughout the day, my grandmother lit the *divo*, a box of sandalwood was placed by the fireplace and sandalwood was offered in each *geh*. She would recite prayers and make us pray too. On Daepadar *roj* we cleaned the kitchen, washed the platform, and wiped it with a clean cloth. And on the wall over the fireplace Grandma made us write the words *Dadar Hormazdni Madad Hojoji* [May the Creator Ohrmazd aid us] with *kharaptu* and *kumkum*. She made us draw a ladle and thongs and put chalk designs on the platform of the fireplace. Then she lit the *divo* and put coconut, betel leaves, flowers and all those things in the silver tray, and recited the *Atash Niyayesh*, and made all of us recite it. The fire was kept burning for the entire Adar *roj*, Grandma got up in the night to feed the fire and keep it going; on other days she put the fire to sleep by covering it with ash. In the morning the fire was used for cooking.

Did you cook on the same fire on Adar roj?
Yes, we had no other means of cooking, so we had no choice.

And what about the Ava rojnu parab [the birthday of the Waters]?
On Ava *roj* a bus was hired especially for all the Parsis of the Malesar neighbourhood, and we all went to pay our respects to Ava Yazad. Our exams were over by then so we used to enjoy it a lot, and we always looked forward to going on the bus to Ava Yazad. We would go to the harbour, where there was a lot of water; there were also two buses from Mota Faliya, and two from Malesar, and a big *Jashan* was performed under a *shamiana* [awning, open tent] by many priests. Money for the *Jashan* came from the laity. Parsis sold food, ice-cream and other things, and there was a programme of entertainment, conducted by one Homi Katrak. We always went as far into the water as possible, and offered flowers, sugar candy, etc. Nowadays the waters have receded very far, but the *Jashan* is still done where the sea used to be.

Did you also perform a ritual near the wells in your own neighbourhood?
We did not have a well, although most Parsi houses did. But there was one in a compound nearby, so on *parab* days or other auspicious days

Grandma told us to offer flowers, sugar candy, etc. The people of the neighbourhood used to make a net of flowers to offer to the well. The water in the well near us was considered to be very efficacious. Whenever the *Baj* ritual had to be done for anyone in the neighbourhood water was drawn from this well early in the morning; Grandma would give her own rope and pot. As I said, most people had wells, and on *Avanu parab* everyone cleaned their wells and lit a *divo* there, and we understood that we had to say our prayers there.

Did you celebrate the Farvardiyannu parab [the feast of the Fravashis]?
In Navsari people went to *Doongerwadi* [the Tower of Silence] on that day. We did not go there, as we were small and Grandma sent us to the fire temple instead. Otherwise I do not remember much about the *Farvardiyannu parab*.

Did you celebrate any other parab in your house?
On Meher *mahino* Meher *roj* Grandma would tell us to get a garland of roses for the portrait of Zarathustra in our house.[7] On all *parabs* and *Gahambars* she sent us to the fire temple to light a *divo*. She used to recite her own prayers and told us to do the same, but we did not know what to pray.

Mrs O's grandmother used to pray and have rituals done for Homaji every Govad *roj*, but Mrs O does not know why she had so much faith in Homaji. Bahman *mahino* was observed by the whole family,[8] and Bahman *mahino* Bahman *roj* must have been colourful:

On Bahman *mahino* Bahman *roj* we had to feed *khichri* to the dog and grass to the cow,[9] that is what grandmother told us to do. On that day all the boys from Malesar and Mota Faliya went from one Parsi house to another, in their own neighbourhood and elsewhere. They sang songs and collected *dal*, rice, and other ingredients for making *khichri*. Some people gave them some money, others gave wood for the fire. Then they made the *khichri*, fed some to the dogs first and ate the rest themselves, with a lot of fun and laughter. Everyone contributed willingly, and people looked out for the boys if they were late.

Mrs O also has vivid memories of her Navjote:

My Navjote was done when I was seven years old. It was on my uncle's second or third death anniversary,[10] on Adar *mahino* Behram *roj*. I remember it was a Friday. My aunt had it done [i.e. paid for it], my sister's Navjote and mine together. My aunt and uncle were bringing my sister up and were very fond of her. Mine was performed by Cawasdaru Raoji, whom I liked very much, he looked so benign. Whenever we saw Cawasdaru we felt we were in the presence of a great man. He prayed in a divine voice.

So my Navjote took place in my own neighbourhood, in my Aunt's house. As the day was Adar *mahino* Behram *roj* and it was a Friday, there were lots of Navjotes being done in the neighbourhood. My uncle was in such a hurry that I was given the *nahn* in broad daylight, at 4 o'clock in the afternoon. The *nahn* was done by a priest from Cawasdaru's [i.e. under his direction], but then Cawasdaru himself just did not come. He had so many Navjotes to do – it seemed an endless wait! After the Navjote we had to go to the *Adarian* [i.e. Agiary] next door to pay our respects, and Cawasdaru had tied my *kusti* so loosely that it slipped off as I walked, and my mother quickly put it back on again. After paying our respects to the *Adarian* I went to visit my grandmother in Vandari Mohalla [a part of the town] to ask for her blessing, and then went back to my Auntie's in Agiary Mohalla.

Do you remember who stitched the sudreh?
My aunt had made everything, as she was from a priestly family. She also made the dress for my Navjote.

Mrs O cannot remember what prayers she was made to recite on the occasion, or whether a *machi* was offered. She did not go to Udwada afterwards, nor was she taken to an Atash Behram in Navsari:

There was no family-member to take us! My father did not pay much attention to us. He spent a lot of his money on his friends and on drink. We grew up in poverty, and my two eldest sisters were taken to Bombay by my aunt ....

How were the laws of purity observed in your mother's and grandmother's house?
We had to segregate ourselves during menstruation. In our village my mother had a bed with an iron frame, around which thick bands of cotton webbing were wrapped. For the housework Father used to hire a servant. In Navsari also, from the time we were small, we were made to sit separately, and Grandma had an iron bed. We had to wrap the webbing around it ourselves. When our period was over we had to remove the cotton webbing, wash it, fold it, and put it away for the next month.

Did you go to school on those days?
Yes we did. Grandma handed us all the books and when we returned from school we handed them back to her. She sprinkled them with water, put them back on the table and handed us other books we might need. So Grandma made us follow the laws of purity as much as possible. When she died we went to live at our *fuiji's* [paternal aunt's], and she said, 'I am not going to take all that trouble over you, I

don't care whether you observe these laws or not.' We were young and ignorant and we thought that our *fuiji* was a great lady and that Grandma had been cruel to make us go through all that. But Grandma loved us so much, and took such good care of us. She was very strict as far as the laws of purity were concerned. For four days we could not use water to bathe [in the ordinary way] and we were not allowed to touch any wood.[11] Our plates were made of tin or of pure glass.[12] Everything was kept separate. Even the bathroom door was of iron. She would not even give us water directly. There was a small basin behind the toilet-*cum*-bathroom, which was connected to that room, so if she poured water into the basin we got it through the connecting pipe and filled up our bucket.[13] If we needed water to drink we could not just hold the glass in our hands and ask for water. Grandma used to be very angry if we did that. She made us put it down and only then did she give us water. She always told us not to use too much water during menstruation, it was like rationing.

Did you mind?
No, everyone in our neighbourhood followed these laws so we did not think we had a choice. It was an exclusively Parsi neighbourhood, everyone followed the laws of purity and if someone needed something they would ask another woman, 'Dhunmai, please come, I need some oil'. So people would help each other. These laws were followed by Parsis even at school.

Were you allowed to do your kusti and say your kusti prayers at such times?
Grandma said we should not do it. Our *sudreh* and *kusti*, even our slippers, everything had to be changed [i.e. special articles of clothing had to be used]. Afterwards those things were put away in a steel trunk, to be used again the next month.

Apart from school, were you allowed to go anywhere? Could you wander about in your neighbourhood?
Nowhere! We just had to sit in a corner. Only school was allowed because that was compulsory. We had to observe the laws of purity very strictly. Once, on a very hot summer's night when my grandmother was asleep, I quietly got out of bed and went to sleep in my own bed, saying to myself that I would sneak back to the iron bed before Grandma woke up.[14] But she woke up before me, and when she found me my own bed she made such a fuss that the whole neighbourhood gathered around, and she told them all about my 'wicked' deed!

What happened when your period was over?
Before we had our bath Grandma made us remove the cotton webbing from the iron bed and pour water over it. Then we went into the

bathroom and had our bath. Grandma then sprinkled *taro* over the area, and had it cleaned with water. It was very tiresome having to wash the thick cotton webbing, and to put it back on the bed the following month. Gradually people began to fix sheets of iron over their beds. I asked Grandma to do this also.

Is there anything else you would like to add concerning the laws of purity?
Well, we were not allowed to go anywhere. Once we were invited to a wedding, for four days, and it was just when my period was due. Sure enough, it began at an awkward time, and I knew I would not be pure in time for the wedding. So I decided to brazen it out and not to say anything to Grandma. I was pure again two days before the actual wedding ceremony, though. But Grandma kept wondering how I had missed a period.

Did you not feel guilty, taking part in the rituals in a impure state?
I was in the courtyard for most of the time, playing and singing, and there were not many rituals being done. If there was a ritual I did not take part in it. We did not have to go to the fire temple or anything and as I said, two days before the wedding I was pure again. There was a Navjote at the same time as the wedding. I was invited to that and I went. I was young and innocent at the time and did not realise what I was doing. Of course when my grandmother died and we went to live with my aunt we had total freedom in that respect. We were very happy. Once, on Dussera day [a Hindu festival] I was having my period but taking advantage of my aunt's views, I was getting ready to go to the Dussera fair. However, I was stopped by my sister's sister-in-law. (These sisters-in-law were strict believers in the laws of purity and observed them scrupulously.) She said that she would not go to the fair if I went. Eventually I gave in and did not go, but I was not mature enough to understand why it would have been improper for me to go. When my aunt died we went to live with my mother in the village and there of course we had to observe all the purity laws. That continued after I got married.

About the communal festivals known as *Gahambar*, Mrs O says:

In Navsari *Gahambars* were held very often. When the *Gahambar* in memory of Sir J.J. [Jamsetjee Jejeebhoy] was held, someone would go round from Baug to Baug, inviting people to attend. The *Gahambar* was for men and children, not for women. It was generally done in the afternoon, and rice, *dal* and *kachumbar* [salad] were served. Once a year there was a *Sheri* [*Gahambar* for women], to which women only were invited. All the women from Malesar went. It was held on a day in the month of Dae; it was held in turns for the people from Vandari Mohalla, Vachha Mohalla and Malesar Mohalla, on different days, at

Jamshed Baug. People could contribute to the cost if they wished, but it was not compulsory. Each *mohalla* [city quarter] has its own fund for the *Gahambar* of their *mohalla*. They have *Gahambars* in Navsari even now.

Jashans could be performed on these occasions, and during the big *Gahambars* of Malesar the priests were served meals separately near the entrance of the main hall of Jamshed Baug. On Farvardin *mahino,* Ashishvang *roj, Jashans* were performed in Mota Faliya and Malesar. The Borkharivalas from Malesar used to hold a *Gahambar* where *val* [a kind of pulse] would be served, since it was the time of the new crop. A *Jashan* was done in the evening, and people were given *val ne rotli* [*val* and bread]. They also took this to elderly people who could not come.

When people sat down for the *Gahambar* meal they were first served fruit which had been consecrated during the *Jashan,* and then *val* and bread. As funds increased a side-dish was sometimes served, or *val ne khariya* [*val* and trotters].

Mrs Munshi then asked Mrs O whether she remembered any occasion when her family offered animal sacrifice to the nearby shrine of Jivan Mama, to placate the demoness who is thought to cause smallpox. Although the shrine is originally a Hindu one, the cult seems to have been incorporated into Parsi observance. Mrs O says:

I do not remember it all, but I have some memories to do with smallpox. When I was eight my elder sister got the disease, then my younger sister, and then I. My elder sister and I had it very badly; it would seem to get better and then erupt again. Some people said that perhaps the shadow of a menstruating woman had fallen on us; others told my grandmother to rub a certain kind of stones together and apply the paste to our bodies. All kinds of treatment were tried, and after we were cured Grandma gave us new clothes to wear and took us somewhere. I think she had made a vow to a deity, but I do not remember where she took us.

Was anything done in the house?
Larvas were made and some ceremony was performed. Grandma also did something at Shitla Mata's temple [a Hindu shrine].

Did your grandmother or your parents believe in Babas or shrines belonging to other religions?
My grandmother was very strict about that sort of thing; she did not believe in it.[15] But my *fuiji* is a great believer in Sai Baba.

The one who married a priest?
Yes. She used to bring ash and photographs of Sai Baba and gave one to my mother also. My mother did not do anything elaborate but she

did keep his picture. I don't know if my mother ever went to Shirdi [Sai Baba's ashram], but my aunt went there every month, and her husband was completely crazy about Sai Baba. He died in an accident in a train while returning from one of his trips to Shirdi.

In Navsari there used to be a shrine dedicated to Gomat Pir,[16] and people had a lot of faith in that. My grandmother and maternal uncle seemed to go there often, and I went there myself once or twice, but when I grew older and began to understand things better I stopped going.

Did your grandmother fast, or have any non-Zoroastrian beliefs?
No, she did not believe in any other form of religion. But when my mother had any problems, the servant from my *fuiji*'s house would advise her to do all sorts of things. On Mondays something was done for Shankar. And my mother used to get together with this maid and follow her instructions, like making *larvas* from jaggery, recite some story on Mondays, and so on. Still, all this gradually stopped.

Both Mrs O's mother and grandmother used to do the *Mushkil Asan* ceremony every Friday. Mrs Munshi then asks Mrs O about her marriage:

Was yours a marriage of your own choice or was it an arranged marriage? Were objections raised because, coming from a lay family, you married a priest?
My mother was against marrying into a priestly family, simply because we might not be able strictly to observe all the laws of purity. So my mother was not keen.

Mrs O goes on to explain that her sister and her future sister-in-law had been classmates and fixed it up between them, taking into account the possible difficulties.

My sister asked my sister-in-law whether I would be required to wear a scarf and keep my head covered all the time, and my sister-in-law said that this was not obligatory. I had no idea what would be expected of me, and I had quite a few dresses made. On the other hand I had only the two saris I had been given for the wedding rituals. I had no ordinary saris, and I had only one headscarf. But as soon as we reached Nagpur, where we went to live after the wedding, B asked me to wear a sari, since our house was to be in the compound of the fire temple in Nagpur.

As far as the wedding itself was concerned, B's relatives knew a lot about rituals, whereas my mother had no such knowledge – she just did whatever she was told to do.[17]

Mrs O's own family did not have many rituals performed. The wedding took place in the village of Vyara, which was more convenient than

Navsari for various relatives. From the start Mrs O's husband was very particular about her attire. As she had been trained 'always to be submissive and obedient', she did as she was told. After the wedding the couple went to Navsari to visit the Atash Behram; the next day they went to Udwada and then on to Nagpur, where her husband was the *panthaki* ('parish priest'). Mrs O describes her life there in the following terms:

> As I now belonged to a priestly family I had to keep my head covered constantly, since that was the custom at Nagpur. And I absolutely had to wear a sari. For a priest in Nagpur there was no way he could avoid wearing the clothes priests were supposed to wear. So from then on I got into the habit of keeping my head covered. I did not know all this before I was married. B did not say anything when I wore dresses for the first few days, but then he said he would not stay with me if I did not wear saris. I told him I had no saris, and my sister-in-law also pointed that out to him. In any case, she came to the rescue and we went to the bazaar and bought some ordinary saris. Inside the house I had to wear long gowns, short dresses were simply not allowed. I gradually got used to all this.

> *What did you have to do as a priest's wife?*
> My in-laws were very good to me and I was never made to feel that I was an outsider living in their house. My mind was at ease, there were no tensions. I watched my sister-in-law and gradually learned my duties around the house. At Nagpur I had to help with making things like *drons*,[18] for the *Dron* or *Baj* ritual was performed every day. I had never done this until then, although I had seen it done as a child in Navsari. (In Navsari such ceremonies are done at home, usually as prayers for the dead. A lady used to come to my grandmother's house to make the *drons* on our charcoal fire,[19] so I had seen how it was done.) When I came to Nagpur I learned the exact way of making *drons* from an aunt who used to come over to our house for the purpose.

Mrs O goes on to describe the exact procedure, and says that her husband himself makes the *drons* for special rituals, or for members of his own family, taking great care to observe all rules of purity. Most of the ritual food, however, used to be prepared by the women of the house, who got up around 4.30 a.m. every morning. This was particularly onerous during pregnancy, and the conversation moves on to the birth of Mrs O's first child. When she was pregnant, the *panchmasyu* was performed by her sister-in-law according to written instructions from an older sister-in-law, since no elderly relatives were available to direct the procedures. Mrs O's *agharni* (which is generally done in the seventh month) was done when she was already nine months pregnant, and she went to her mother's house in Navsari at that time. She had her baby in the Parsi Lying-in Hospital in Navsari, where she stayed for forty days, then the *nahn* was administered by her husband and she returned to Nagpur within the week. Her second child was born in a hospital in Nagpur, which had a special Parsi section. The traditional ceremonies for young children – such as the *chatthi, besna* and *pagladu*[20] – were done for both children by Mrs O's sister-in-law according to her elder sister's instructions (the *gorni* was not done because no one could be found who could give instructions.)[21] Mrs O herself was too busy to deal with such things. About babies, Mrs O further says:

> It was very difficult to manage things with them, especially during my periods. When I was breastfeeding, B would give them a bath, gently set them down on a newspaper on the floor, and hand them back to me wrapped in the paper.[22]

The children were named according to the *rasi* system, which determines the child's initials on the basis of its horoscope. Asked about the details of her devotional life Mrs O says:

> As soon as I get up I have a bath and recite the *Hoshbam* prayer, no matter how much work I have ahead of me. I have now also begun to recite the *Ushahin geh*. Then I start my household chores. We are so used to these things that they have become automatic: as soon as one leaves the toilet one does one's *kusti* ... . I was already used to these things from childhood and I continued to observe them. Still, living in a fire temple compound did mean that things were followed rather more strictly. I always used to pray in the Havan *geh*, and then someone told me to pray the *faraziyat* in the Aiwisruthrim *geh* as well, so I did that. Then gradually I began to pray in the Uziran *geh* also. Then, recently, B was away from home and I had more time than normally, and I said to myself, 'Why not pray in the Ushahin *geh* too?' Since then I have been reciting prayers in all five *gehs*. Now that I have got into the habit I try to keep it up. As soon as I wake up I recite the *Ushahin geh, Hoshbam, Mah Bokhtar* and *Atash Niyayesh*, then I start the household work. Since everyone is used to my prayer times now no one disturbs me. At first they used to make fun of me. Even B said, 'You are praying so much, you'll go nuts.'
>
> I also have this idea about not putting clothes I have worn outside back into the cupboard [so I go out as little as possible]. When I have been out to shop I must have touched someone who was menstruating, or come into contact with some impure person, so how can I put those clothes back in my cupboard? And, since B insists on my wearing saris, it means that each time three pieces of clothing have to be washed – sari, blouse and petticoat. So I rarely go out and spend my whole day in prayer.

Asked whether she has a favourite *Yazata*, Mrs O says:

> When I was young I did not even know what a *hamkara* was. I went to
> the fire temple regularly, and one day a friend asked me if I had come
> because it was a *hamkara* day. I had no idea! My grandmother thought
> that Behram *roj* was special, so I knew that, and also about Hormazd
> *roj*. It was only later that I learned that Hormazd, Ardibehesht,
> Behram and Sarosh *roj* are important days. But I consider all days
> equally important. My mother was very fond of Ram *roj*; Ram is to do
> with joy and with weddings; she chose that day for our wedding ...

Mrs Munshi then asks what Mrs O feels about her husband's profession
and about the fact that their children have also been trained as priests:

> I like it very much indeed. When I first went to Nagpur and saw him
> [her husband] giving the *boy* I was very happy; it feels very good [to
> see him serve the fire] and he prays in a melodious voice, which is
> very soothing. I got a lot of knowledge about our religion from him.
> As a *Behdin* I knew very little; even the way I did my *kusti* was wrong
> ... B taught me how to do it properly. So I was very proud to learn all
> this. I never had the slightest doubt about marrying a priest, neither
> before nor after.

*You pray so much. What do you feel about these prayers? Do you pray
because you know it is a good thing to do, or do you feel at peace, or is it just
force of habit?*
Well, it has become a habit now but it also gives me strength. If
anything untoward is about to happen you can feel it inside. But the
strength of prayers gives you the confidence that nothing will really go
wrong. I often tell B that nothing bad is going to happen. One does not
feel frightened about adverse circumstances, because one has this
inner strength.

Are the laws of purity observed even by the men in your house?
In Navsari my father did not have any idea of such matters. Of course
he had a bath after a haircut, but when he came in in the afternoon
after a shave I am not so sure [if he took the trouble to have a bath]! I
learned more about these things after my marriage. My grandmother
had taught me not to cut my nails after a bath. If we did that, we
would create *nasu* and would have to take a bath again. So I knew
about these minor points. But in B's house the observances were
followed more strictly. When he shaved he sat on an iron stool without
touching anything, and he had a bath immediately afterwards. The
children have also been brought up to do this. My son now wears a
beard because every time he shaved, B was worried that he might
touch something in the house [before he had purified himself]. My

sister's and sister-in-law's children follow these rules when they come to our house, I do not know what they do at home.

The family observes several *parabs*, keeps a vegetrarian diet throughout Bahman *mahino*, and goes to the Towers of Silence on the *parab* of Farvardiyan. Mrs O always recites the entire *Farvardin Yasht* at this time, which takes a hour and a half. The family has no hearth fire but on Adar *mahino*, Adar *roj*, Mrs O lights a *divo* and keeps a fire burning continuously in a big vessel, taking its ashes to the fire temple. During the month of Avan (though not necessarily on Ava *mahino*, Ava *roj*, when there is usually a lot of work in the fire temple), *dalni poris* are taken to the sea. Mrs O feels that the Waters, and in particular the Bhikha Behram Well in Bombay, have helped her and her family:

> After B had problems of a legal nature, we have begun to visit the Bhika Behram Well at least once a month. Five years ago when B had trouble with his Trustees here, someone told us to go to the Bhikha Behram Well and ask for help, and to take a vow that we would go there once every month if our problems were solved.

So the Well helped you?
Yes, I am sure it did. Whenever we are faced with trouble [now], we automatically know what is to be done, and how. I was not in the habit of reciting the *Ava Yasht*, but after our troubles started I began to recite it everyday. (It was the beginning of Ava *mahino* when the problems erupted.)

Do you go to the Well in a particular geh?
You can go in the Havan or the Uziran *geh*. We usually go in the Uziran, sometimes later in the Havan *geh*, at 10.30 or 11 a.m.

Do you recite anything in particular when you go to the Well?
I usually recite the *Ava Yasht*, but if there is not enough time I pray the *Ava Niyayesh*. I have already said my prayers at home by that time.

Do you offer a net of flowers every month?
No, I take flowers and sugar candy.

And what about the well here in your own fire temple?
Yes, people have a lot of faith in this well also. So I recite the *Ava Niyayesh* there every day in the evening, in the Uziran *geh*.

Mrs O then goes on to describe her grandmother's death and funeral. Many family members were present at the death, and all kept praying the *Ashem Vohu* all night. In order to save her relatives trouble and expense the old lady had kept a pile of sandalwood and incense in a trunk for the various funerary services. Funerary ceremonies were done at home and in the fire temple for a full year. Immediately after the death, ceremonies were performed at home in Navsari. The last bath was administered by women from the neighbourhood, who always come when there has been a death since the immediate family is usually not in a fit state to cope. The body was carried to the Tower by professional pallbearers and only accompanied by men (women not being allowed to attend the ceremonies at the Tower in Navsari). All the later ceremonies were also observed with great care, with the neighbours advising about correct procedure whenever the family was at a loss. A *Vendidad* ceremony was performed in Navsari 25 years after her grandmother died.

About her experience of the power of prayer, Mrs O says:

> Recently, when we had a lot of problems with the Trustees, an old priest who is a friend of B's gave us the *nirang* of Behram to recite. It was to be recited after praying the *Haptan Yasht Vadi*, and after finishing the recitation we had to recite '*Ya Farman Kam*', which is one of the 101 Names of God, 303 times. I had tremendous faith in this prayer formula and it did us a lot of good. My mother had an old book of *nirangs*. My sister had problems with her pregnancies, she had had a lot of miscarriages, and in this book there was a *nirang* [prayer formula] against miscarriages; it had to be written with saffron water. So my mother made the saffron water and with it she wrote down the *nirang*, and tied it on my sister's waist. The words were written in Avestan, she copied them exactly as they were written [in the book], and tied it on her waist according to the instructions. Of course [my sister] was also having medical treatment, but we felt that the *nirang* did help her.

Have you ever given nirangs to anyone?
No, I don't know enough to do that.

Could you describe the Behram Yasht Nirang in more detail?
A part of the Behram Yasht, the 16th section, has to be recited eight or nine times, and we recite it that way.

Even now?
Yes, we continue to recite it although the specific problem for which it was given no longer exists.

Mrs Munshi then asks Mrs O what traditional songs she knows, and Mrs O recalls a few, including one *monajat* which her grandmother made her recite[23] daily after she had finished her prayers. The conversation returns to the subject of Mrs O's sons training for the priesthood, and Mrs Munshi asks if Mrs O would be happy for them to become full-time priests. Mrs O replies:

> I would be very happy and proud if my sons learned the prayers and rituals and became full-time priests. I would have no objection, and I

am very happy now to see them take part in rituals and prayers. I encourage them to carry on doing it. M [her son] is now learning to do the *Baj*, and I am eager to see that they learn fast. But he makes conditions, only as a joke of course, saying that he'll learn the *Baj* if we give him this and that.

Is it difficult and different, being a priest?
Yes, it is different. Everything has to be done with great care and very precisely. A lot of practice is needed to learn to do his. I have no objections if they learn this art and become sincere and dedicated priests.

MR BURJOR H. ANTIA

Burjor H. Antia (1946) is a well-known lawyer who plays a prominent role in the community, being a Trustee of some fifteen charitable Trusts. Although Mr Antia moves in circles where modernist ideas tend to predominate, his views are strongly traditionalist. The present writer attended the interview.

In the course of a short sketch of his career, Mr Antia says that he comes from a priestly family, and himself studied at the M.F. Cama Athornan Institute[24] for eight years, which inculcated in him the traditions and principles of the Zoroastrian religion. He feels that his present position in life is due to his religious training. Later Mr Antia studied science and eventually he took up law, graduating in 1958. Mr Antia now combines a prominent position in the world of business with an active role in social and community work. He concludes, 'In short, I am following the principle of our Prophet Zarathustra to make others happy in every day and every minute of their lives.'

Asked about his childhood, Mr Antia says that, coming from a priestly family, he was steeped not only in the moral principles of Zoroastrianism but also in the daily practices and customs.

So from my childhood I lived with these and, looking back at the events that have happened, I can say that our *tarikats*, our traditions, our customs and usages are part of our religion and they cannot be ignored. If you ignore this then you will be in peril. *Tarikats* are nothing but a path, a rule, rules to know the religion; without *tarikats* you cannot perform our religion. For example, what are our *tarikats* which I observed from my childhood? That in the morning when you get up, first you have to do *Shekaste shekaste Shaytan*, then take the *taro*, and then you have to do the *kusti*. And then whenever you go to the toilet you have to perform the *kusti*. All these are *tarikats*. Before taking your food you have to pray to God, do your *kusti*, before you go to bed you have to do your *kusti*. All these are the real *tarikats* which I went through, and I still believe after forty, fifty years, that they are worth following for all time to come, until my dying day.

About his early training at the Cama Athornan Institute Mr Antia says:

During the Muktads we were to go and pray every day. Similarly on *hamkaras*, the four or five *hamkaras* of the month. At the Cama Athornan Institute we went to the Agiary in Andheri on those days, to pray before the Fire. Then there were *Jashans*, Mehragan, Jashn-e Sadeh. There was another *Jashan* that was being performed on a hill, we also took part in that.[25]

Mr Antia heard many religious stories from his uncle, who was always most insistent that the ways of the forefathers should continue to be observed. About prayer, Mr Antia says:

My Uncle Khurshedji used to pray *Yatha Ahu Vairyo* when he left the house and when he entered it again. So the thing that was impressed upon my mind and on that of my brothers is that one must always recite *Yatha* and *Ashem*, they are very powerful and vibrant prayers. And when you want to succeed you must always go with the recitation of these words, [in order] not to get harmed in any way. Another very powerful prayer, we have been told, is the *Yenghe Hatam* prayer. I was told this as a child. Our prayers are very vibrant, and I can give an illustration of this. After becoming *Navar* I was performing prayers, reciting prayers during the Muktad days. So one of these days I was performing the *Satum* prayers at my uncle's house at Surat, it was at about four or five o'clock, when I personally experienced that when I was praying, the *thali* [tray] on which all the things were put, started trembling. So I have experienced myself the power of prayers. I have heard stories that the vibration of prayers can break glass – it has happened in some laboratories – but I have experienced the trembling of my *thali* when I was praying. And today also, when somebody is reciting very nicely and I am present, I get the vibration straightaway. Recently, two years ago, when a Dasturji was praying the *Uthamna* ceremony so nicely, I immediately got the vibrations – the body gets some sort of energy … I felt good and mentally elevated.

And then I started praying – somebody told me, and I wanted to do it because Hindus do it, and others also, and I thought, 'Why not? Our Parsi community should [also] have [it]'. So I started praying *Khshnaothra Ahurahe Mazdao* [a dedication to Ahura Mazda] 100 times, 50 times. [I do it] whenever I've got time. And I found the mental peace by reciting this word. This is what I do now – following it up, because I have read many books on prayer, vibrations, meditation. So I wanted to see why in our religion there are no such things. But I myself have experienced it: our prayers are very powerful, [the prayers] that we were taught by our elders, our uncles, our father and mother. My mother was a very religious lady, she was more religious than a priest. We were taught by her in a very nice atmosphere: washing the hands, keeping the clothes clean – she was more orthodox than a priest, though she was from a layman's family.

At a later stage in the interview the discussion comes back to Mr Antia's experiences during prayer and rituals:

I always feel the power, vigour, the vibrations from any such activities appertaining to our Zoroastrian religion. I feel it when I pray before the sea, even when I pray before the *kuva* [well], and at the Banaji Atash Behram well I have always felt it. I feel I am getting some power from outside and going within; it clarifies, it signifies, it ignites my soul, and also the brain.

As Mr Antia's family was a priestly one, his mother and sister observed the laws of menstruation, and 'sat separate' at such times. Mr Antia and his brothers used to cook on those days, and Mr Antia is still glad that he has learned to cook so that he can cope in emergencies. He firmly believes that the details of Zoroastrian ritual and observance have a scientific foundation, apart from being hallowed by the practice of countless generations. Mr Antia's Navjote was performed at home by his father, a qualified priest. Several of the *parabs*, such as those for the Waters and Fire, were observed in his family. Mr Antia's wedding was a traditional one, performed at the Dadyseth Atash Behram in the morning (according to the Iranian tradition), and followed by a visit to Udwada, where a *machi* was offered and charitable gifts were made. At all important points in his life Mr Antia has visited the Udwada Atash Behram and offered a *machi*. He regularly fetches water from the sea and sprinkles it on the floor of his house; every Sunday he does *loban* and lights a *divo*.

Asked whether some Yazatas or Amesha Spentas are more important to him than others, Mr Antia says:

This is the latest trend,[26] but in our times all Ameshaspands were equal, and were kept equal. We celebrated all the days; in my life today Hormazd *roj* and Aneran *roj* are the same.[27] Every day I pray the same things. But nowadays the trend is [to celebrate] Ashishvang *roj*. First it was Behram *roj*; when we were children Behram *roj* was powerful. People used to say, 'On Behram *roj* we will go.' But God has made all *roj* equal – don't do like that. I remember that forty, fifty years ago Behram *roj* was celebrated with great fun, now it must have shifted: Meher *roj* has come, and Ashishvang *roj* has also come. Some people follow Ashishvang *roj* and they go to Udwada; there is a big crowd there on Ashishvang *roj*; it is the latest trend. But according to me all *roj* are equal.

Mr Antia does not use prayers for purposes of healing. He does occasionally advise those who are very ill to pray *Ardibehesht Nirang*, which he believes to be very powerful, but he himself has never used it for such purposes.

The discussion goes on to Mr Antia's student days at the M.F. Cama Athornan Institute; he says that he understood the meanings of the prayers quite well, since he was taught Avestan and Pahlavi, and moreover translations were given in the books. Asked whether, after his initial preference for the *Yatha Ahu Vairyo* and *Ashem Vohu*, he later came to prefer other prayers, he replies:

> I would like to say again that all my prayers are good, equally efficacious. I will not play one off against another. I may tell you, in my College days I went to some astrologer in Surat, and he told me only to recite our own prayers, not outside prayers, Hindu etc. He said, 'The *Haftan Yasht* of yours is a very powerful prayer. You pray this and you'll come up in life.' I used to pray *Haftan Yasht*, I don't say no to it, but what I now do, whenever I find time, is, I take the book, [the] *Khordeh Avesta,* and pray from one end to the other, including *Haftan Yasht*. No playing off one against the others ... And nothing particular on certain days. If I find time, as I say, I pray more, but every day I do *Sarosh Baj, Havan Geh, Khorshed Meher* and *Atash Niyayesh*, before coming to the office.
>
> Right from my childhood we were told that the priestly boys are very smart, very intelligent, and why? Because they undergo the *Navar* ceremony, recite prayers, so they are initiated, they are blessed by our Ameshaspends. So that thing was in my mind; I have seen in my profession, [and] in the medical profession, whoever has come up in life, has become an important member of our community, they have always been priests [here Mr Antia gives examples]. The prayers, the training, the blessings of the Ameshaspends and Yazatas, these have influence. I have seen several people, after *Navar* their life has changed.

Mrs Munshi remarks that in spite of this, and of his priestly training, Mr Antia has chosen a secular career. Mr Antia says that he was very good at priestly studies and was about to enroll for a B.A. in Avestan and Pahlavi, but a friend told him he was wasting his life that way, and that is was better to take science and become a doctor. Mr Antia followed his advice, but ended up reading Law. He still likes the idea of being a priest, however – not necessarily a practising ritual priest but rather one who studies and preaches the religion. He feels he is in fact doing this in his own way, as he lectures a great deal and has published several booklets on religious questions.

About the different fire temples Mr Antia feels much the same as about prayers: all are equal. On one occasion he visited all the forty Agiaries in Bombay in one day on Adar *mahino* Adar *roj*; he made a list of the Agiaries and then figured out the quickest route. Later, when a friend from London visited Bombay Mr Antia took him to visit all the eight Indian Atash Behrams in a single day. At present, he says, there are advertisements in the papers offering a bus trip to all forty Bombay Agiaries in one day. At each fire the experience is the same:

> I feel that my spiritual battery is charged. Every Sunday I go to Banaji Atash Behram, because I am Managing Trustee there. So I go to look after the place, but first I pray. If I don't go, I feel uncomfortable. As if I haven't shaved, as if I haven't changed my clothes, something is missing, I find. So I must go to the fire temple. Once my leg was broken and I was at home for six months, but still with a stick I would go. My wife said, 'Why are you going like that, with a taxi, spending money?' But I would not like to miss going – on Sundays, Muktad days and *hamkara* days.

When discussing such features of Parsi religious life as the Mushkil Asan, the *Afsun-e Shah Faridun*,[28] and the Kookadaru or Homaji cults, Mr Antia says that all these things belong to Parsi culture and he respects them, but that they have no special place in his life. 'I believe in our religion, in our Dadar Hormazd, and no one else.' Even his wife, who did believe in some of these things before she married, lost all interest as soon as she came to his house.

Asked about his views on religion in the community and on his own role, Mr Antia says:

> The first things I would like say is that we exist because of the sacrifices of our forefathers. They have left us all these things so it is our bounden duty to make sure that they are protected, nurtured and maintained – our ancestral things, our Agiaries, our Atash Behrams, or any institution, like Parsi hospitals. It is our duty to maintain it, and every Parsi should devote time and money for maintaining our past heritage. Keeping this in mind I give my time and energy to about fifteen Charitable Trusts. The purpose of my being there is the principle of Asha! Asha is righteousness, straightforwardness, uprightness, truthfulness – so all these things should come out in our institutions. Things should be clean, you should be seen to be honest, people should not think otherwise about Trustees.

On the Zoroastrian funerary rites, Mr Antia says:

Our method of disposal and our death ceremonies are the best, and they should be followed and not be discouraged. I've seen death in my family, I have seen the *sachkar* and all the stages of the funeral.[29] In the *sachkar* I have found substance, in the way all the prayers are used. It protects us from the *riman* [pollution]. I may tell you, one day [a high-ranking member of the legal profession] died and I was obliged to attend the cremation. The next day I got two to three degrees temperature. So at that time I realised that our custom of keeping three feet away from the dead body, of having a *pavi*,[30] is of immense significance. Then the *geh-sarna* ceremony is not only soothing for the relatives, but it breaks the relations of the [dead] person with this world. The proof is that you will never hear any stories about souls or ghosts from *Doongerwadi*; against that, in a Christian cemetery or a Hindu cemetery[31] people will come out with stories that 'somebody came' and this and that. So *geh-sarna* is a very powerful ceremony which cuts off the dead man's relations with this world; the soul really departs and goes on. This is our experience, I have seen it and I believe in it.

In Mr Antia's opinion one should observe the Muktad for the departed as long as they are in one's thoughts. He still does it, for example, for his brother who died in 1967. Some people in the community think this is wrong, but Mr Antia consulted Dasturji Kotwal in the matter and had his opinion confirmed.

Mr Antia has set up a public Charitable Trust in memory of his parents, the Antia Trust to Help the Helpless. The beneficiaries are not just humans who are destitute, but also animals and plants. His first cheque every year goes to an animal hospital and he feels that plants also need help. Asked what gave him this idea Mr Antia says:

Many times when I do meditations,[32] the answer comes: 'Your Trust should be wherever there is life.' ... According to our Zoroastrian religion life is everywhere; it is not only in human beings, but also in animals and plants. If you sow a seed you see it growing and the flower comes, you realise that this is also life. I see this clearly in my bungalow at Dahanu,[33] where I grow plants, and the flowers come. It really makes you realise that you should do something for them also. So keeping that in mind I have created my Trust five, seven years ago, in the name of my parents.

Mr Antia has a family connection with village life, as his maternal grandfather settled in the village of Siganpur near Surat after he retired, and Mr Antia spent part of his childhood there. When he visits Surat in the Christmas vacation he still makes it a point to go to Siganpur and offer a *machi* to the village fire temple, which was established by a local family who became rich. This leads to musings on the public spirit and generosity of previous generations, and their superiority to the materialism and self-centredness of modern Parsi youth. Such generosity ensured that the Siganpur fire temple is well-endowed and can afford to pay its priests well. The discussion moves on to the current general shortage of priests and related problems:

I have got a solution, I have repeatedly said it already. First of all, in our community there are so many differences; we are more divided and less united, on any flimsy ground. Religion is one [such ground] of course, and today we concentrate on religion and our institutions. So for example, in Bombay there are forty Agiaries, so what should we do? In the larger interest of the community, and the religion, and the priestly caste, all Trustees should sit down and decide to maintain ten Agiaries out of the present forty. The fires from the other Agiaries should be brought to the nearest [remaining] Agiary, so they will be preserved as separate fires. The problem of the scarcity of priests would be felt less, and we would pay them better since there would be sufficient income from the ten Agiaries. The [empty] properties could be used either for residential or commercial purposes, and our housing problem would be solved .... And we must pay our priest at least Rs. 10,000! Then, in the long term, we must have a policy how we treat our priests. They should be trained properly, they must be enlightened when they preach our religion. Those who are intelligent can then become B.A. and Ph.D. So we'll get a new category of priests. And there should be a scheme to protect them, from [i.e. run by] the community. For our sake, for the community's sake. The community should provide; their salary should be Rs 10,000 at least. Then only there will be a life. Housing should be provided. If we do it that way, sure they will become priests.

Mr Antia then gives examples of such cases and mentions one instance where a man gave up a well-paid job knowing full well that he would not be paid much as a priest. Mr Antia himself belongs to the Bhagaria lineage[34] and therefore has the right to offer *boy* [fuel] at the Navsari Atash Behram. Until now he has never done this, but he would very much like to do it when he has more time.

Asked if he follows any religious practices other than Zoroastrian ones, Mr Antia replies that his social position sometimes obliges him to attend Hindu functions and that he likes to see the holy places of other religions when travelling, but that he would never initiate or actively participate in non-Zoroastrian observances.

I never disrespect other religions, all religions take one to God. God has put me in the Zoroastrian religion so I will follow it till my dying

81

day. That is my principle. God is in the centre and all religions take you there, but I am in the Zoroastrian religion so I follow that line. I am clear in my mind, I have no disrespect, I don't say, 'Zoroastrianism is the best religion in the world,' I would never say such arrogant things. My religion is good for me, other religions are good for them, [let] everyone follow [their own religion], they ultimately lead to God, [who is] in the centre of all.

Asked about his feelings when he underwent the *Bareshnum* ceremony[35] as part of the process of becoming a *Navar*, Mr Antia says that he understood the meaning of the rituals and therefore did not find the proceedings strange. He had several teachers, the most influential being the famous Dasturji Khurshed Dabu,[36] who had explained the deeper meaning of this ceremony in one of his publications. Mr Antia continues to read books on such subjects:

> I never found it meaningless, I never found it humbug. I've always found our prayers and our ceremonies of great significance, including *bareshnum*.

> *So today if you got the chance to give boy, you would not mind going through the purification rituals?*
> No, in fact I may tell you, since the last three, four, five years the idea is storing up in my mind that during the vacation I go around the world and everywhere – why shouldn't I go to Udwada or Navsari and have the *nahn* for nine days [i.e. undergo the *Bareshnum* purification ritual]? Quietly, just pray. When the *Bareshnum* is to be taken, for nine days there is no talk, nothing, and [one sits] in a corner. I must go and pray. One day I am going to do that. But I'll go to Udwada or Navsari, not Bombay. For Bombay is so commercial, you cannot resolve your things.

Asked about his observance of the rules of purity, Mr Antia says that he prays regularly and does his *kusti* at appropriate times, at least at home; at the office there is not enough privacy. As to haircuts, Mr Antia tries to keep the laws of purity as much as possible. He would never go straight to the office after a funeral, but goes home first to have a bath.

> That is a must. I may tell you, once I did not follow it, and I found the answer: I came here and immediately found some problem.[37]

Mrs Munshi then asks if Mr Antia, as a leading member of the community, has a message for the younger generation. Mr Antia begins by expressing his indignation at the way some younger Zoroastrians ridicule ancient customs which are hallowed by tradition, such as the funerary customs and the fire cult, whose greatness and significance they do not understand. He then quotes the philosopher William J. Durant, whom he describes as 'the world's greatest philosopher':

I strongly recommend all our young people and reformists, and whatever their name is, to try to understand and appreciate what the greatest philosopher has said about traditions and institutions generally: 'Intellect is therefore a vital force in history, but it can also be a dissolvent and destructive power. Out of every 100 ideas, 99% or more will probably be inferior to the traditional response which they propose to replace.' This is a very important sentence: 'No one man, however brilliant or well-informed, can come in their lifetime to such fullness of understanding as to safely judge and dismiss the customs and institutions of his society, for these are the wisdom of generations after centuries of experiment in the laboratories of history.' I rely upon the last sentence and repeat that our institutions, the Agiaries, the Dokhmas [Towers of Silence], or our traditions, are not from my generation, they have been followed by my father, my grandfather, and generations after generations since thousands of years. And nowadays I feel rather disgusted that a young generation comes and tries to ridicule it. So this is the first thing I want to say for posterity, that we must respect our religion, religious customs, religious traditions, and we exist today because of them.

One other tradition which I wish to [recommend?] is to marry within our community. It is very important, very crucial. If you want to survive as a community you have to follow this. Nowadays some people don't want to follow this, and as a result you see that the community is dying. These mixed marriages started at the beginning of the century, and people began by saying a father could be Parsi and a mother non-Parsi. At the end of the century you see that they are saying that the children of a Parsi mother who is married to a non-Parsi can also be Parsis. You can do any such damn thing, but you are killing the community!

Mr Antia then sums up his message to posterity as follows:

Follow your religion faithfully, truly. To achieve this there are three requirements. First of all Dedication, to your religion; then Discipline, self-discipline; and Determination to survive. We are passing through a very critical time. What is our population, among 80 crores [800 million] we are not even 80,000, so we are not even 0,001 percent. It is a very critical time. So we can only survive if there is a determination to survive.

MR HOMI P. RANINA

Mr Homi P. Ranina is a prominent lawyer and company director, who spends much of his time and wealth on charitable pursuits. He is a Trustee of a large number of Trusts, a former Trustee of the Bombay Parsi Punchayet, and has been the main contributor to several projects, such as the restoration of a fire temple in Bombay and the construction of the Kookadaru fire temple at Sanjan. Mrs Sarah Stewart was present at the interview.

Asked about his childhood, Mr Ranina says that he grew up in a nuclear family. His father was traditional and very religious, his mother less so. There were often tensions, as his mother felt that keeping a fire and doing *loban* made the house dirty, while his father insisted on keeping a household fire. Mr Ranina had no special religious education, which he says is the rule rather than the exception in Parsi families. He deplores this, however:

> I think the greatest problem we face in the 20th century is that we got too westernised, the Parsis as a community. Somehow this ridiculous feeling crept in that they have to be modern, they have to be liberal, they have to be what they call broad-minded. So all this means that they have to be secular, not bothering about religious customs, traditions and so on. This is very unfortunate; it only happened in this century. It happened because of, I think, wrong leadership, which was given by the elders of the community – the members who were respected by the community, like the industrialists, the businessmen, who became quite powerful, who became quite wealthy in the early part of the 20th century. You know, you must have heard of the Tatas and the Wadias and the Petits.[38] Now these persons were very traditional, e.g. the original Sir Dinshah Petit, he was a baronet, Sir Jamsetjee Jejeebhoy, and ... we have a whole string of baronets in our community. Now the original baronets were very very traditional, but their children obviously had the benefit of going abroad. Most of them went to the West, to England. But as a result of that they became very secular, very broad-minded. Many of them married local British women, and naturally therefore they came home with different ideas, started propagating those ideas of Western secularism, liberalism. These people being the leaders of the community – or being considered the leaders because they were rich and powerful. And at one time they were really leaders because they had established the Atash Behrams and the Agiaries, so they were really looked up to by the laity. And when these people came and started propagating Western ideals, secularism, and trying to show that they were very broad-minded, liberal, then obviously the people down the line

started behaving in the same way. They said, 'If they can do it why cannot we?' This is how it started.

Asked how the religion was explained to him, Mr Ranina says:

My father was not a very educated man, therefore I don't think he really explained anything. His view was that this was time-tested – these customs have passed the test of time; one should accept them. Obviously he himself did not have any fundamental ideas from a basic knowledge of why it was so. So he traditionally followed the customs – customs in the sense that the Parsis do not really have many customs or rituals except for things like wearing the *sudreh* and *kusti*. The only things they would tell us was that, say, smoking is not good in our religion because we worship fire and it means showing disrespect to the fire. That is the explanation given: smoking amounts to disrespect to the fire. So these are the fundamental things which were taught, you know, or things like, say, there was some degree of prejudice against mixed marriages. I think that stemmed mainly from the fact that if you marry outside the community, then it would amount to creating problems for the children; the children would be torn between two different religions, two different cultures, identities. And of course the important fact that if you want to preserve the religion, if you want the children to preserve the religion, then it is much much better to marry within the community, so that there are no problems about religious beliefs.

In his early life, Mr Ranina was not particularly religious. His Navjote was performed, he used to go to the Agiary from time to time, where he recited the usual prayers from a book; furthermore he took part in the funerary rites of his maternal grandparents, but none of this made any special impression on him. But then something happened:

Well, I would say right up to 1982, right up to the time I was 36 years old, I was never religious-minded. I started my practice as a lawyer when I was 24, 25, and right up to the time I was 35 or so, I was never religious, never religious in the sense that I would not go to a fire temple at all, at all … . But after I was 35 years old, I was fairly successful in my profession, so I don't know, for no explicable reason that I can tell you, somehow I thought I should go to a fire temple. I think I went there with a view to thank God. I believed that my success in my profession was entirely due to God, and I thought why should I not go and thank Him for it? Sometime in July, if I remember correctly, of 1982, after I finished my work I had nothing to do and I was in the Colaba area and, I don't know for what reason, I decided to go into Cusrow Baug.[39] I just circled around the fire temple there. So for no explicable reason I just decided to go into Cusrow Baug and then went around the fire temple. I did not enter the fire temple, I just drove around in my car and came out again. And somehow, again for no explicable reason, I went on doing that for several days and then, after maybe seven or eight days, I decided to go in, so I went in. I went in and did the usual, prayed and came out. And then I just went on doing that every day, every day thereafter.

And at that time that fire temple was in a very dilapidated condition, in spite of the fact that there are a lot of fairly affluent people living in the area of Cusrow Baug and Colaba. So I remember some time: I got to know the priest, the *panthaki*, Mr Aibara.[40] Now my father used to know Mr. Aibara, they had known each other from 1975, '76. Now when I started going to the Cusrow Baug Agiary, naturally this *panthaki* was curious, 'Who is this guy who keeps coming here every day?' So one day he asked me and I said who I was, and of course he recognised my father. I had not known who this Aibara was, because my father had not mentioned him to me. So then he and I became good friends and I kept going. And then, late August, Mr Aibara was in a very bad mood and I kept asking 'What is the problem?' He said, 'Look, there are these short-circuits in this Agiary.' You know July and August are the monsoon months, when it rains heavily in Bombay. And water was leaking from the roof and the wiring was bad and loose and there were short-circuits and he kept saying, 'Look, there are people living here, they are so wealthy and affluent and they don't bother to do anything, and one day the Agiary will catch fire', and things like that, because of the neglect. So again I said, 'Fine, if the Agiary needs to be done up, we will start the work.' So after the monsoon was over we got down to it, and I decided to put in the entire amount, whatever was the cost of the electrification; we changed the entire wiring, and we decided to do it. And then of course so many other things had to be done, plastering and painting. Just one thing which comes to my mind is, these Khshnoomists, Mr Adi Doctor[41] and Mr K.N. Dastur, they came to the Agiary, they knew that we are going to renovate the Agiary and that the fire would have to be shifted to the adjoining room, because otherwise the non-Zoroastrians could not enter to renovate the place. Now they came and said, 'Look, you cannot shift the fire', and they gave their own reasons why you cannot not shift the fire, because they said the fire has established a sort of secret aura or boundary around it and if you shift the fire it will break that. Then we said, 'But how do you get things done?' I mean, you have to do it, and of course the Udwada fire has been shifted time and again, the main Iranshah[42] ... [here Mr Ranina gives a detailed and accurate description of the history of the Iranshah fire], and we were only going to take it from one room to another room to allow the work to go on. But these guys created problems, then Aibara called the three high priests, Dasturji Kotwal, JamaspAsa and Mirza, and they said, 'No, you can shift it.' So one day quietly we shifted it, some time in early December, and then the work started and in April 1983, after five months, the work was completed and the fire was shifted back.

Such munificence obviously became known in the community; Mr Ranina was invited to become a Trustee of the fire temple in question, and has remained involved with religious charitable work ever since.

It changed my outlook in the sense that after I started ... once people knew that I was there, a lot of appeals started coming from the poor, for financial help and things like that, so I started giving money to the people and I became a Trustee of a hospital, the Parsee General Hospital, which is the biggest institution we have. So there again, when I find that there are a lot of unpaid bills of the poor patients, I just pay them off, without of course ... they don't even know about it. So I started doing a lot of things like that, spending a lot of money on religious things. I think I can say even today that I spend almost 25 per cent of my income on charitable and religious purposes. Not that I have to do it, but I just do it.

You did it because you felt that it was needed by the community?
Yes, that is right. I felt that it was needed. Apart from that, you see, to me there are two or three important things. One is that, when you start thinking of yourself, of what you are and of what possibly you are going to be, you realise that this is all so superficial! What do you do with money? After all, you cannot have more than two meals a day, you cannot wear more than one set of clothes at a time, I mean, what do you do with money? And I always felt that the best thing you can do with money is to give it to those who need it more than you do. This is basically my philosophy which has developed. After all you are not going to take it with you when you die. So why not just give away whatever you can during your own lifetime, and make people happy?

Do you think you would still have had this philosophy even if you weren't a Zoroastrian?
Yes, I am sure this philosophy is there even among other religions. It is there among the Christians, it is there among Hindus, after all the Hindus also do a lot of charity. I think it is a universal philosophy. But basically it is not what philosophy you follow. It is what comes to you. Sometimes I get the feeling that human beings can be instruments of God. Ideas are put into your mind by this divine power – what to do, how to act. That is the only explanation I can find for my own life, where up to the age of 35 I had no inclination for religion, or knowledge. Then, suddenly, this change came over me and I have a feeling that it was Destiny. I should also tell you that I am a student of

astrology, and have found a lot of truth in it. There are certain things happening in your life because of the movement of the stars. In 1970 or '71 I went to a Hindu astrologer, who told me that from 1980 to 1983 I would be very successful and become very religious and charitable. Now that came true, and I still remember it. I do relate all this to astrology, but apart from that I believe that things happen in your life at the destined time, whether it is success or disaster, religion or not being religious. I have a feeling that there is a Divine Hand which guides the destinies of people. I believe that because it happened in my life: I went into the Agiary for no explicable reason, so how else could one explain that?

Mr Ranina's belief in the role of Destiny has implications for his views on other matters, such as conversion:

I do not subscribe to the theory that people choose for themselves. [For example, there was the question of] Mr Peterson, an American whose Navjote was performed in the United States.[43] There was a lot of discussion of that in the *Bombay Samachar*. I wrote several articles on conversion, and then there was a letter written by J.R.D. Tata, the famous industrialist, where he said that Parsis must now start marrying outside the community, since there had been a lot of inbreeding, and it was necessary to have fresh blood. As I said, J.R.D. Tata was a big man and nobody wrote against that, but I was the only one who started writing a series of articles. Of course I got a lot of flak from the Editor of the *Bombay Samachar*; after every article he would give his comments, and then again I would write. Finally after some three months he gave up. But I was the only one to refute Mr Tata's point of view.[44]

Now one of my points about conversion was this: at the time when Zarathushtra lived there was no other established religion in the world; there were things like witchcraft, sorcery, worship of idols, stones, whatever, things like the God of Thunder and the God of Lightning. People were so ignorant. When Zarathushtra lived, therefore, he gave the Good Religion: one God, Ahura Mazda, and all the rest. He offered them a choice: between right and wrong, good and bad, virtue and vice. Today we have five or six good religions in the world: Christianity, Islam, Hinduism, whatever, and Zoroastrianism. Now if you are a Christian the point you could raise against Peterson's conversion is this: is Christianity a bad religion? And if it is not evil, what is the point of conversion, because the choice Zarathushtra brought was that between good and bad. Are they trying to say that Christianity is a bad religion, something like sorcery, that he wants to change to Zoroastrianism? After all, I am sure that there are lots of things which are common to both religions. For example, Mother Teresa is doing so much good. You can be a very advanced soul following Christianity; you don't have to become a Zoroastrian ... What I say is, you can accept the philosophy of Zarathushtra without leaving your own religion. The second point I made was this: I think if you are a believer in God then there are certain things in this world which are the will of God. You do not decide who your parents are going to be, or your brothers and sisters. You don't decide what religion you are going to be born in. These things are fundamentally the will of God, and if you are a believer you accept that being born into Christianity as the son of Mr and Mrs Peterson, is the will of God.

Although Mr Ranina says he has no particular affinity with Kookadaru, under Dasturji Aibara's influence he had a *Nirangdin* performed in memory of Kookadaru.[45] He is also a Trustee of the Kookadaru Trust, and played a central role in the foundation of a new fire temple in Sanjan – the only fire temple consecrated in India in the 20th century – which was named after Kookadaru.

Well, we had a fairly good thing in the press, there was a lot of response, a lot of Parsis came for the foundation-stone laying ceremony, which was in 1987. And we started collecting donations from the Parsis. We bought a plot of land, land was very cheap, land was not a problem, but then the construction of the Agiary was about two and a half million rupees. We made appeals but we could not collect more than about Rs. 800,000 from the community. Then from this Kookadaru Trust, of which I am a Trustee, we put in about half a million rupees, and the balance was put in by me – about a million rupees – to complete the Agiary. We started in November '87, we completed it in two years, and in January 1990 we consecrated the fire. The fire was consecrated by the five Turel brothers from Surat. Now in Surat they have the Atash Behram and there is a very experienced priest, by the name of Jehangirji Turel, who has performed more than 100 *Nirangdins*. So we requested him and he said fine because it was the first time that he had consecrated – in this century I do not think that a new fire has been consecrated ...

They all came down, the members of the Turel family all came down with their wives, because they had to cook food for the priests while they were performing the rituals, they cannot go out.

Was the temple consecrated in the traditional way?
Yes absolutely, collecting the four fires, including the fire of a corpse.[46] And purifying it. So Jehangirji Turel from Surat and his three or four cousin-brothers, they all came down from Surat, our own priest was Dasturji Aspandiar Dadachanji. So Aspandiar went there and of

89

course Dasturji Kotwal gave them lots of guidance; it was the first time this was done, it was quite exciting .... In January 1990 we installed the fire in the Agiary.

... One of the reasons [for naming the fire temple after Kookadaru] was that a lot of people are in favour of Dasturji Kookadaru, so when we said we are going to set up a fire temple in memory of Dasturji Kookadaru we did get substantial remittances.

Could you say something about your own relationship with Kookadaru?
Well, I have a lot of respect for him, but nothing special. I mean, I have this photograph. I have [photographs of] Lohraspshah and everybody,[47] but ...

The interview ends with Mr Ranina proudly showing Mrs Munshi photographs of the enthronement of the fire in the Kookadaru Agiary.

————

MRS A

Mrs A was born in a small village in 1935. Her father was a practising priest, so ritual purity was important and Mrs A was brought up in a strictly religious atmosphere. The family later moved to Bombay, where Mrs A went to a Parsi school. Her husband also belongs to the priestly class, although he is not a practising priest. Mrs A has two daughters, who were grown up at the time of the interview, and she works with drug addicts. Mrs Sarah Stewart was present at the interview.

At the beginning of the interview, Mrs A describes her family background:

[My father came] from a priestly family. He had done his *Navar* and *Martab* in the younger days, when he was about twelve, thirteen years old. It was a very big family which my grandma raised and his father, my grandfather, died at a young age, so about three brothers became priests, they were ordained priests. The others did not become [priests]. He was practising till last year, right now he is about 86 and not keeping very good health, so ... Still, he keeps on, but he is not practising in the fire temple. Of course, because of his background we were brought up in a really orthodox and strict manner, with very strict discipline, as young children. Children of the priests those days did not wear sleeveless dresses, and did not go out – especially the girls did not go out very often, [not as often] as they liked. Even in school girls who had their periods were not allowed to touch anything, they could not even take books to school.[48] ... I still remember I used to cry a lot because we were not given any books, and if I wanted to study, if there were exams or something, very slyly my sister would give me a book to read – she would hold it and turn the pages. But we were not allowed to touch anything, we were kept very separate.

But your school did not raise any objections?
No, no, at that time, no. Because they understood that we came from the priestly class and because you have a practising priest, we had such restrictions. And at that time everybody was following and respecting those norms . . . . The thing was, we were feeling very much ashamed that everybody would come to know that we were in that state at that time, you know.

What about at home?
At home of course everything was separate, we were even made to sleep separately on a steel bed and we had to keep everything separate, all our eating utensils, glass utensils and everything. And after we'd get over that thing we had to take a bath, a head bath and a *nahn*, which our father would give [i.e. administer].

Each time?
Each time, yes, with *nirang*. We felt very much apart and embarrassed, you know?

So you did not enjoy it?
Enjoy? At that time we did not understand why we were made to be like that! He would tell us, 'It is to be done, it has to be followed according to the rituals of our Zoroastrian law.' So we had to obey.

Did he say why?
No, he did not say why, he said it is the law of Asha. It is a law of piety and we have to do it. Because he was a practising priest. Actually I remember in those days when we were to sit apart he would not allow us to go into the bathroom, because we were in a small house, with one bathroom only. So what he would do is, he would go to the bathroom first, get his things over, his bath and everything, and go, and pull the door. And we would hear that pulling of the door and then I would get up to go to the toilet. Because we were not allowed to touch a toilet door even; somebody had to sort of put us inside, and [we'd be] knocking from outside . . . . It was that much!

Did your mother do this?
My mother also did the same. My mother was pretty young, and I also started [menstruating] you see, so at times two of us would be together, it was very difficult. And I had three sisters, so sometimes two sisters even were in the same boat. It was really a trying time . . .

And your brothers, did they also have to follow laws of purity like haircuts and nails and everything
Yes, yes, they had to follow everything that our Papa would say.

Asked who taught her religion, Mrs A says:

Papa! He used to sit and tell us history, Iranian history, even at night. He was very fond of Iranian history, the stories of Shah Jamshed, Shah Faridun and Zohak,[49] and what happened to the Iranians and how we came away from there, and how our forefathers sort of sacrificed everything for us. And so that is why we must do everything that we are told to do.[50] They could do it [so] why can't we do it? So we understood that, given our history, if Papa said something it would be authentic and we must follow the norms. So we obeyed.

When your father taught you the prayers did he also teach you the meaning, or did you just learn the Avestan by heart?
He gave us short meanings, and he used to tell us you can read it in the prayer books, with explanation in Gujarati. Because we had learnt [to read] Gujarati [in school] ... we were able to read the prayers. And whenever we used to feel puzzled or confused we used to ask him.

How did your family look after the hearth fire, what did you do?
There was always a permanent *ses*, you know – the tray with the *divo* and *afarganiyu* [fire vase]. And he used to light that fire early in the morning and on certain *roj* the *divo* also, not every day though. And he would put the *loban*, do his prayers and then go. And Mummy would do it after she'd had her bath, after finishing the house work and all that. And we before going out also, we were told to do a little *loban*, and pray. Early in the morning we prayed our *kusti* prayers, *Sarosh Baj* and all, early in the morning, and before going out also three *Yatha Ahu Vairyos, Ashem Vohus*, and do the [*Divano*] *Namaskar* and then go.

And in the morning, were you taught to say prayers like Shekaste shekaste Shaytan?
Yes, we were taught before Navjote, for a little while we did that. But we didn't follow it up in our rush to schools and things like that.

Mrs A's Navjote was performed by her father, who also taught her the Navjote prayers. Her first *kusti* was made by her grandmother, a professional *kusti* weaver.[51] After her Navjote she was made to do her *kusti* at all the times prescribed by the religion. She normally obeyed, although the children might be a little lax when their father was not at home. The girls felt awkward doing their *kusti* in the presence of their brothers, as this involves hitching up and rearranging one's clothes, and they usually retired to their own room for this purpose.

Talking about her marriage, Mrs A says that she was the first to defy the tradition that marriages had to be arranged by the parents. She made her own choice, and since her husband's family was also a priestly one her father did not object. The wedding followed the traditional Parsi pattern; since her in-laws knew little about such ceremonies they did whatever Mrs A's father suggested. The *Atashnu Git* was performed by family members, not professional *goyans*.[52] The question of the meaning of rituals then came up again in the discussion:

Did anyone tell you why all this was done?
They said it is a ritual which we have to follow. I didn't mind, it was just for the good and the family wants it to be done, OK, fine.

So there were no questions. Did you ask questions about the religion, since your father was a priest?
I used to, yes.

What sort of questions, and what sort of answers did you get?
Only there was one answer, you see, 'You just don't have to argue about it. Because we are priestly class we have to do certain things, and I know better than you, so you have to do it.' That was the answer that we'd normally get.

Later in the interview, Mrs A discusses the times she was present at a *Nirangdin* ceremony:

What did they do exactly, can you describe it?
We listened to the prayers and certain pots [played a role], and things were done, and they prepared the *hom-ka pani* [Haoma juice],[53] and we were meant to drink it afterwards after the prayers were over. It was a ritual, a long ritual, and all the prayers – but we didn't understand the meaning of ritual. But it was said that it is done for the welfare of the family and the community.[54]

Mrs A spent the first five years of her married life in her husband's parents' house. She found the customs and observances much the same as in her own family, though the atmosphere was less strict:

I didn't find anything different. Being from a priestly family I was acquainted with all the norms, so I didn't find anything different. But the only thing is, my father was very restrictive and my father-in-law and mother-in-law were not.

So there were no laws of purity?
Nahi [No], laws of purity were there, but you can do it as you like. They were not very rigid about it because he was not a practising priest. So whenever I was … in the period, we were allowed to touch

everything and allowed to go everywhere. That type of restriction was not there in my in-laws' family.[55]

Although this freer atmosphere came as a relief to Mrs A, she has tried to bring up her own daughters to observe some of the traditional rules:

> When they started staying separate I would say, 'Please don't touch the cupboard, there are certain saris and certain things which are for going to the fire temple only, don't touch the *ses*, don't touch the prayer corner where we pray.' So they used to feel very offended [and said], 'What is this, all the old things you are trying to apply to us, are we *harijans* [untouchables] that you are trying to tell us not to touch, not to touch all the time?'[56]

During Mrs A's first pregnancy all the usual observances were done, and she prayed the *Ava Yasht* for forty days for an easy delivery. She went to her mother's house for the birth and stayed there for three or four months. For her second child she again went to her parents' house, but the actual birth took place in hospital, where she stayed for the first forty days:

> Of course again at that time I was to go to my father's place so I was made to stay at the hospital for forty days because my father was a practising priest. He said, 'I would not allow you to touch anything, and for forty days to come home and do these things with a child would be very difficult for you, so it is better for you to stay in the hospital.' So that time I stayed in the Parsi General Hospital for forty days. My mother was told to make arrangements right from the very beginning ... and [at the hospital] they said OK. They understood: because my father was a priest.

> *Did your father visit you?*
> Yes, he would come to visit me but he would not touch, he would just stay apart. He would come and see the baby, he even prayed, but not touching anybody. And he guided us on the sixth day to do the naming ceremony, and also the *chatthi*, when they say the baby's luck is being written on a foolscap page ... [57]

> *Was anything done in relation to astrology, horoscopes or anything?*
> Names were also ... my Daddy found it out [deduced the proper initials] from the astrological point of view. *Rasi* we call it, according to the *rasi* of the time and the date and the day.[58]

> *So the names were given according to the birth sign ...*
> It is followed even up to my daughter's delivery also, for my grandson.

As soon as Mrs A came home, the *nahn* was administered by her father and she could move freely in the house. The *besna* and *pagladu* ceremonies were done for the first child but not for the second,[59] who was just taken to the fire temple every month until she was a year old.

Mrs Munshi then asked what happened in the family in case of contagious diseases. No *devis* [Hindu goddesses] were propitiated in Mrs A's family, it was strictly a matter of prayer and cleanliness. With chickenpox the child was not allowed to have a bath, and had to be sponged to be kept clean. After nine days the patient was to be bathed and taken to the fire temple. Mrs A's father prayed every day at such times, and did the *pichi*:[60] praying the *Ardibehesht Yasht Nirang* while passing a white piece of cloth over the patient from head to toe. Mrs A still prays the *Ardibehesht Yasht Nirang* when there is illness in the family.

Mrs Stewart asked if there were practices which her father, as a priest, disapproved of.

> Because he was a priest he would not allow us to follow any other things [alien practices], like following Babas or going to anybody's temples, or any other things – but to follow our own prayers and our own rituals, with good faith.

What about Kali Chowdas and Dhan Teras?[61]
Only *Dhan Teras*. On *Kali Chowdas* we were not allowed out because of people doing some magic, you know, and we might step on it. On *Dhan Teras* Mummy used to prepare a tray, light a *divo*, and put her silver Lakshmi[62] and any of her golden things in milk and sugar. But he [her father] did not object to that, because there is nothing alien to it. It was just done for propitiating, it was a sign of prosperity, it was nothing alien to our religion. My Mummy used to do it in her village also.

Mrs Stewart then asked what Mrs A feels about Ashishvang, the traditional Zoroastrian divinity of prosperity. Mrs Munshi has to explain the question, ending with the words: 'We know only of Lakshmi and most of us don't know that we have our own Yazad of prosperity.' Mrs A knows little about Ashishvang, though she remembers her father saying that Ashishvang played a role in matters of religion, and she vaguely associates Ashishvang with Shah Faridun's *nirang*,[63] which her father taught her when she was small.

Funerary customs are then discussed and Mrs A describes the funeral of her mother. As her mother was a priest's wife, everything had to be done strictly according to the rules. The family stayed at the Towers of Silence for four days, an experience Mrs A describes as peaceful, uplifting and comforting. 'I felt very good about it; it helps sustain the spirit.' A *Vendidad* was done at the fire temple after four days. For ten years the Muktads were done at the fire temple, but now her father does her mother's Muktad prayers himself, at home.

In the morning, Mrs A and her husband first say an *Ashem Vohu* on waking up, then touch the ground in respect, and get up. Then follows a bath, the *kusti* prayers, followed by breakfast. If it is a propitious day, especially on Mrs A's favourite Meher *roj*, they light a *divo*, say some short prayers (*Khorshed Meher* and *Atash Niyayesh*), and go to the fire temple. Her favourite fire temple is Cusrow Baug Agiary, because she lived there in the early years of her marriage, and she can 'see' the children when she goes there. Mrs A works all day, but in the evening she goes to the fire temple if she has time, or prays at home. On auspicious days, such as *hamkara* days, she does the *loban*. This can only be done, however, if all members of the household are pure, which is not always the case with two grown-up daughters living there.

The *parabs* of the Fire and the Waters are observed in the traditional way. 'I feel happy that we can follow at least something of our tradition and I hope our children will also follow that.' Mrs A used to go to the Towers during the month of Farvardin, but she has given it up recently. She does not follow the traditional observances for Bahman *mahino*, Bahman *roj*, but for the last five years she has prayed the *Bahman Yasht* on all Bahman *rojs*. Someone suggested this to her and she decided to do it. Mrs A has never done the full *Mushkil Asan* rites; she has lighted *divas* on the day concerned but never told the story.

As her husband's health was not very good, a *machi* used to be offered at the Wadiaji Atash Behram on his birthday. When Mr A had problems at work friends suggested that the couple should attend Christian Novenas or go to Sai Baba, but Mrs A would have none of this. She prayed fervently and used to have prayer sessions together with the children.

> I used to tell R [her husband], 'Ahura Mazda is great, don't worry, Ahura Mazda is with us. We have done nothing wrong so why should we worry?' But he always used to question, 'But how great, and when will it come?' You need patience, you see, he is very impatient. I said, 'He is great, and He'll show you one fine day how great He is.' And it came off. I have great faith in *Atash Niyayesh*; it keeps your flame of faith burning.

In her work with drug addicts, Mrs A tells her patients that religion and spirituality can play an important part in their recovery. Her Zoroastrian patients she always advises to start saying *Ashem Vohu* or *Sarosh Baj*. 'Sit with you parents and pray! And of course I will also pray for your happy recovery.'

————

DR F

Dr F was born into a priestly family in the early 1940s. She lived in Bombay until she went to do her Ph.D. in Pune, where she now lives and works as an Associate Professor in the University. Her husband, Dr HF, a medical specialist who is also from a priestly family, attended and participated in the interview. The couple has one son, a medical doctor who has been initiated as a priest. Mr Khojeste Mistree and the present writer attended the interview.

Dr F begins by describing her various activities, including voluntary ones, and her family background. Her grandfather was a practising priest, but he had retired by the time Dr F was born so that she did not witness the routine of a working priest's household. Still, the family was a religious one.

> We grew up in a household with strong beliefs. Not that we were given much detailed education about the religion, but what we were basically taught was faith. And even today I don't go in so much for theology, or what I am supposed to believe, but I believe with faith.

What were you taught to believe in?
What we were asked to believe in was basically an ethical way of life more than anything else. Education was the most important value in life, secular education, knowledge. In my house, books, reading, were very much encouraged, to the extent that my father would buy me a book a day if I could get through it, and I could. But I cannot say that we had any religious education as such; one just believed, it was a gut feeling.

Did it give you a feeling of pride that you were Athornans?
It gave us a feeling of pride that we were Zoroastrians. And secondly we were *Athornans*, but that was not stressed.

As a child, Dr F was first taught the *Ashem Vohu* and *Yatha Ahu Vairyo*, followed by the normal *kusti* prayers. She does not remember being given a detailed explanation about the significance of her Navjote which, at the age of six, she mostly saw as a 'jolly good occasion for fun'. She religiously did her *kusti* five times a day during the first few weeks after her Navjote, but then the novelty wore off.

Dr F had one brother, and Mrs Munshi asks if his *Navar* (first initiation into the priesthood) was performed:

> No, his *Navar* was not done. My father felt that the whole process of becoming a *Navar* was so complicated that it would be a unnecessary burden. My father was not a *Navar* himself, and nor was my brother. But H [her husband] and I were very determined from an early stage

of our marriage that our son would become a *Navar*, and we did that in 1980.

When Dr F was a child several traditional customs were observed; no meat was eaten for four days in Bahman *mahino*; there was often a *divo* burning on special days, but no permanent hearth fire. The laws of purity were not followed:

> No, even though this was a Dastur's[64] household, he was no longer practising. And my *fui* [paternal aunt] was a working woman, so there was no ... [i.e. it was too complicated]. During your period you did not touch the fire, or the *divo*, or the portrait of Zarathustra. Except for that, there was nothing else.

There was a big celebration when Dr F first wore a sari; by this time religion meant more to her. The family observed some of the *parabs*, and prayer played a role:

> I did occasionally take a book and pray. I believed very strongly. I did not spend hours on my knees I would say, but I believed very strongly. I never went to an exam without going to an Agiary, that was a must!

> *Did you say any special prayer before you went to an exam?*
> I used to pray the *Mah-Bokhtar Yasht*, but only, to be very honest, because it was the shortest. I just decided that that was all I could manage on the morning of an exam. But I never began an exam paper without five *Yatha Ahu Vairyos* and three *Ashem Vohus*, never!

> *And you believe that really helped you?*
> I believed I could not possibly start an exam without prayers. I don't know [if it had an effect] because I never tried [to do without prayers].

The subject of the Fs' wedding then comes up. This was done in the traditional way, although ceremonies which are often done in the houses of both parties were performed in one house only. Dr F clearly felt that, underneath the fun and games, there was a serious religious element. Her husband, on the other hand, did not feel that the wedding ritual was important, although he did not mind going through it. When describing his family background he says that his paternal grandfather and one of his uncles were practising priests, but that otherwise he had little contact with priestly affairs:

> Dr HF: My grandmother, who did not come from an *Athornan* family, was very religious. Basically my contact with religion was from her. She taught me prayers, Navjote prayers and so on. But beyond that I don't think my contact with religion, from my parents and so on [amounted to much]. Now to us, the theology of religion did not have much meaning. The fact that we were Parsis, that we believed in

cleanliness, that we believed in education – you know, we were taught that Parsis never lied, that sort of thing . . . So it was more social norms rather than real religion. About the Navjote, all I knew was that when you put on the *kusti* you become a Zoroastrian, but beyond that I still don't know the significance.

Now after your marriage, did you continue to practise what you were taught in your youth?
Dr. F: I continued to do whatever I was doing, to visit the Agiary often, which is a practice that I have always followed. And I began to insist that H should come to, on important occasions such as birthdays, New Year, and things like that – and we did the same with our son. Again he is not the type to go often, but we do sometimes go as a family.

As your son grew up, did you or someone else teach him about the religion.
Dr F: It was me, I taught him! Later, when he went to do his *Navar*, he was sent to a Mobed [priest] to learn. That [i.e. the *Navar*] was I think more a fulfilment of H's and my wishes than his.

Why did you feel it was important for him to become a Navar?
We both of us come from generations of priests and we felt that it would give him a firm grounding in our tradition. It was important to us.

Has it made him more religious?
No, he is not more religious. And that was not the aim. My idea was that this is a family tradition of which we are very proud, and we wanted to maintain it. It was a tough year for him, because in the old days the *Navar* used to give up his normal studies, but he had to do school and *Navar* studies at the same time. So it was tough, but eventually the feeling of joy and pride when he finished and achieved this was quite something!

And does he have any inclination to be active as a priest?
Dr F: No, he does not show any inclination. He has been bludgeoned into it several times, but no, he does not show any inclination.

Dr HF: I think basically he just did it because we wanted him to do it. He would not have done it of his own choice. But the thing is, he is one of those individuals who, when he agrees to do some thing, he does it properly. He did not take shortcuts, he learned all the prayers, and he did it properly.

Could you tell me anything about experiences on visits to fire temples?
Dr F: When I go to an Agiary, I go when it is quiet. I feel that I have a genuine hot-line to God. I have conversations.

Does this happen at any fire temple, or with a particular fire?
Dr F: No, any Agiary that is quiet, although I have an Agiary which I visit regularly. And I feel a very personal relationship, as though I don't need an intermediary to talk to God. And I must say He does hear me.

H, have you had any special experiences in your profession, for example that you asked for divine assistance in prayer and you got it?
Dr HF: I don't regularly pray. I am one of those cheats, I pray only when I am depressed, when I need something. If I am in trouble in the operating theatre, having a complicated operation and sweating, that is the time I pray! I think it gives me a tremendous amount of solace. When I am absolutely down and out I feel that prayer really gives me solace. Now as a scientist, I don't know whether it really has a meaning, but when you are in trouble you do something, and this is my outlet. Now many people go to an Agiary, or to some religious leader or a Baba or something. I just don't believe in those things, but I feel that if I need something, prayer is important to me. But then, at other times when everything is fine, I have a tendency to forget God.

Do you say just any prayer, or is there a special one?
Dr HF: Usually I just pray *Ashem Vohu* and *Yatha Ahu Vairyo* and do a *kusti,* that sort of thing.

Do you have any eclectic beliefs,[65] or is it only Zoroastrianism?
Dr F: We have a prayer niche, and somebody gave me a picture of Buddha so I put it there, and I have a picture of Ganesh,[66] so I put it there. But no, basically I only believe in Zarathustra. I don't understand much of the religion, but whatever it is, I am just a staunch Zoroastrian.

As you are both form a priestly background, can you tell us something about what you have seen of the interaction between priests and laity? What do you think the role of priests used to be, and what is it now? Do you think there is a change since your young days?
Dr F: Yes, I think there is a change. My grandfather, who died when I was very small, was an immensely learned man. If he had lived longer he might have taught me a lot, and explained a lot. But since then I found that the priests are ill-educated. They are basically paid very badly, they lead such frustrated, difficult lives. And I feel it is a very important part of our culture that we should look after the priests. But unfortunately, the priests are not in a position to give us any idea about religion.

If you have a problem in the family, do you go to a priest for help? Have you ever gone to a priest for help and got it?
Dr F: No. I asked Khojeste [Mistree] for a prayer once and he gave it to me and it worked. But nothing else.

So do you feel there has been a kind of schism between laity and priests?
Dr F: No, not a schism, but over the years there has been a lack. And that lack cannot be filled by priests who are ill-educated and so desperately poor that their children no longer want to go into this profession.

Mrs Munshi then asks if Dr F has ever experienced a tendency among the laity to avoid social contacts with priests because they are supposed to bring bad luck. Dr F recalls that she once asked her grandmother about an expression suggesting this, and her grandmother indignantly dismissed it, saying, 'Only the *Behdins* say that!'. Dr F finds the Zoroastrian method of disposal of the dead, and the prayers connected with it, very good and beautiful. She observes the annual Muktad prayers, and says a special prayer on Farvardin *mahino* Farvardin *roj*. She used to go to the Towers on that day, but has not done so for a long time. She observes the *parabs* of Water and Fire, and says the appropriate prayers if she has time. Dr F does the *Mushkil Asan* ceremony regularly, although this was not done in her mother's house. Mrs Munshi asks if Dr F has ever experienced special contacts with the dead, such as visions or messages.

Dr F: No. Only sometimes, when you pray for somebody to whom you have been very close you feel that maybe they are listening and maybe they are doing a little to prod something to help you. I feel that rarely, but sometimes very strongly.

Mrs Munshi then asks Dr HF about a story that has gained a certain currency in the community, namely that plants won't grow in Dr HF's office because, as a gynaecologist, he sees many women who are technically in a state of impurity, so that something about them might prevent plants from growing. Dr HF answers that he is not sure that he believes in this at all, and that the story started as a joke between his son and himself.

Asked about stories they were told as children, Dr F says she was not told many stories but remembers some tales from the *Shahname*. Dr HF heard many stories about Behramshah Shroff[67] in his youth, because his eldest uncle was a disciple of Shroff's.

Asked about prayers, Dr F says that when anyone is ill she always prays the *nirang* of the *Vanant Yasht*.[68] When she feels agitated, even when stuck in traffic, she always prays.

Mr Mistree then enters the conversation and asks whether the Fs' son is more like his mother or his father as far as religion is concerned. Dr F say that, as a doctor and a scientist, he is more like his father and pooh-poohs many of the things she tells him. However, she stresses that this may change later in life. Her brother, also a doctor, was not at all religious in his youth but now visits Agiaries regularly and often goes to Udwada. 'So I hope that whatever my son has absorbed by osmosis, it *will* be there in him.' Dr HF objects that visits to an Agiary and to Udwada do not necessarily imply the sort of religiosity he sees in his wife, which seems to him exceptional. About his son he says that father and son, though both very proud of being Zoroastrians, went to the same Christian school and never had much Zoroastrian religious education. As a result, he feels that what is meaningful to both them is the social side of Parsi identity and that neither is very religious. Dr F stresses that her son is immensely proud of being a Parsi, much more so than other people of his age.

Mr Mistree asks how it is that, although Dr F seems to have received very little formal religious education, she has still developed a strong devotional life. Dr F answers as follows:

My mother taught me, 'This is what you pray when you are in trouble'. I pray all the six *nirangs* every day. I may not have a scarf over my head or face Zarathustra,[69] but at some stage, perhaps rushing off to college, every day I pray all the *nirangs* attached to the major prayers.[70] Why the *nirangs*? Because they are short! But I like to pray them. It is a matter of faith. I have always done that, even in my college days. It was not a matter of hours each day, although I go through periods when I do pray a lot. I must say – it is not very nice to admit this, but when my son has an exam, I sit at home and pray. All through that paper! I mean, I don't just sit around and walk around, I sit there and pray.

Dr HF: May I just comment? My maternal grandmother (the *Behdin*) she used to pray a lot. We used to make fun of her that she would go on praying, go on praying. But I have felt that, since her death, when the prayers stopped, I found a change, you know. Things do not go the way they used to go when she was praying. As a scientist I don't even believe in all this, but there is a gut-feeling that there is a difference since she is dead. Maybe there was some power in those prayers that is not there any more.

Dr F: When this house was built – you know we bury certain things under a new house, like a *kusti*, a coin, and things like that[71] – I wanted to put H's grandmother's main prayer book under the house, but H did not want to part with that. But she had a few other prayer books, and I was determined that one of H's grandmother's [prayer] books would be part of the foundations of this house. So I did that, and I really said a special prayer when I put it in: the house is founded on the Avesta in a very literal sense.

Dr F: I really feel that in any great problems that have come, I have always appealed to Behram Yazad, and no matter what, maybe after a period of trials and tribulations, but one comes out of it.

The discussion moves on to the current trend among Parsis to venerate Babas and other gurus. Together the Fs tell a hilarious story about a relative of theirs who goes to the Agiary every day and prays sincerely, but also keeps an extensive 'pantheon' of images of gurus, deities, Babas, dead ancestors and prominent people – including members of the British Royal Family – in his prayer area at home, and never travels without it. All Parsis present feel that such syncretism is 'a very Parsi thing'. Dr F thinks that one reason for this is that Zoroastrianism is not a congregational religion. Dr HF is of the opinion that being a Parsi is now largely a matter of social, rather than religious, identity. He is sure that younger, Westernised people are no longer interested in the religious side. His wife strongly disagrees, observing that one now sees more young people in Agiaries than formerly.

———

MR S

Mr S was born in 1941. He went to High School and College and has a Diploma in Interior Decoration. He works as an interior decorator and is also active in the fields of marketing and public relations. He is a public-spirited man who sits on various committees and does voluntary social work. His wife was present during part of the interview and took part in the discussion at the end. The family's religious life is not untypical of that of many middle class Parsis.

Mr S lives with his wife and two children, and with two of his aunts. He was an only child and speaks highly and with gratitude of his parents' efforts to meet all his needs. He had little formal education in the field of religion, but his mother taught him the basic Zoroastrian prayers (*Yatha Ahu Vairyo* and *Ashem Vohu*), and later sent him to a priest to improve his pronunciation before his Navjote. Mr S remembers his mother reciting the prayers to him while giving him his bath, and explaining the basic teachings of the religion when he was very small. He thinks she told him stories in which Zarathustra played a role, but cannot remember these in detail.

As a child Mr S lived in an extended family, with his paternal grandmother and paternal aunt and uncle. His grandmother was a matriarch, and the two men of the house deferred to her.[72] When Mr S's grandmother died, the two families became more distinct from each other. Mr S is not sure whether a separate hearth-fire was kept burning all the time, but efforts were certainly made to observe the usual Zoroastrian rituals. There was a prayer corner where all religious objects, such as the utensils for the *loban*, were kept. The *loban* ceremony was done in the evening and possibly also in the morning. Mr S's maternal grandmother's place was a huge bungalow. His mother used to go there when she had her period, taking the child with her, because there was a separate room with such commodities as iron beds.[73] Mr S's maternal grandfather was a highly religious man, who always wore a cap, prayed in each *geh* whatever the circumstances, kept a hearth fire burning continuously, and had a separate prayer room in his house. Although he was a layman his general demeanour was like that of a priest. Since some of his own children were less interested in religion, he encouraged his grandchildren to be observant. Mr S attributes his own religious turn of mind to this family atmosphere.

Mr S describes himself as 'one hundred percent religious, with an unshakeable faith in my religion', but he does not pray a great deal and does not know many prayers by heart. A small room in his house serves as a separate prayer room, and he tries to keep a fire going for twenty-four hours. The family is torn between their environmentalist views, which make them disapprove of burning wood unnecessarily, and their religious feelings which demand a fire. On the whole the religious sentiments prevail, largely because of Mr S's very strong sense of gratitude to the Lord Almighty, who has always provided for him. This part of the interview is highly emotional, Mr S breaks down and cries more than once. The only time Mr S, whose English is perfect, uses a pronoun for God in this context, it is 'she'. He goes on to speak of his mother, who always cooked the typical Parsi dishes on special days and made sure he had a bath with milk and flowers on his birthday even after his marriage. Mr S's parents had their local fire temple and visited the Wadiaji and Banaji Atash Behrams very regularly on important days. The great *parabs* were observed according to the Shehenshahi calendar. Recently, however, Mr S's family has come to prefer the Fasli calendar.[74]

Mr S's whole family underwent the *nahn* forty days after the birth of a child, and the purity laws about hair and nails are observed; hair and nails are never cut on Saturdays or Mondays.[75] 'Sometimes maybe it is a little overstressed; it is based on childhood impressions, I have no rationale for it, I have no basis for it.'

Instead of taking *loban* around the house, family members offer *loban* to the fire individually in the prayer room. Coming back to his personal sense of religion, Mr S says:

> On the one hand I don't pray for a long time, but on the other hand I can say that the sincerity of my communication with God is totally complete. I am one of the fortunate few to believe that I can communicate with God, express my sense of gratitude, which I know reaches him. At the same time I have complete satisfaction. Not that you take a prayer book and recite prayers for two hours – in the five or seven minutes that I pray in a day I communicate with God Almighty

totally. Whatever I feel I need to tell Him, I do, and He has taken care to respond on almost anything and everything. For my fifty-four years I have had a two-way communication channel.

Mr S goes on to relate a number of miraculous things which have happened to him. Once he fell off a running train and was unharmed. The first thing he did afterwards was to go to the nearest fire temple, and around this time he began to visit the Banaji Atash Behram every Sunday. He has continued to do this without fail, whatever the circumstances, when he is in Bombay. His family now generally accompany him. On another occasion he was nearly drowned when trying to save a friend, and he firmly believes that God saved him.

Mr S prays in his prayer room for a few minutes in the morning and at night; he performs his *kusti* after his bath, but not on such occasions as leaving the toilet. About prayer he says:

> I shut my eyes, I am closed to the world, although I have not reached that stage where I do not know what is happening around me, but I do not like to be disturbed. No phone calls, nothing at all! My thoughts are only of the Lord Almighty, and maybe during that time I express my happiness with everything that has gone past. I express, maybe, my desires for others. God never lets you down.

Mr S has experienced this divine help in his social work. When one approaches God on behalf of others, without ulterior motives, in his experience there is 'almost one hundred percent success'.

> From these kinds of things you have to believe that there is someone who can see everything, who is witness to all that I am doing and who says, 'Yes this person needs to be looked after, needs to be guided.'

Even when Mr S's prayers were not granted something good has always come from the affair in question, which again points to divine wisdom. 'In any case, when it was important the result has always been favourable.' Mr S touches the ground whenever he leaves the house and again on reaching his destination.[76] 'It is bowing in respect and gratitude, and acknowledging, "Thank you for all you are doing for me".'

Mr S's was a love marriage; the couple had known each other for three years when they married. Mr S's future mother-in-law had reservations because the horoscopes did not match, 'But there again the Lord Almighty was working in his own way.' The *adravanu* ceremony and the *madav-saro* were done. Mrs S had a relative who knew many traditional Parsi songs, which were performed at the wedding. Mr S had heard that in some families bride and groom do not meet during the four days before the wedding but this was not done in his case. One *Ashirvad* was performed,[77] and the couple went to Udwada after the wedding. When his first child was born Mr S had wished for a son and his wish was granted, which again confirmed his faith in God. Mrs S spent the first forty days at her mother's place. As her parents live in cramped quarters they did the best they could as far as the rules of purity were concerned. The *chatthi* and *pagladu* were done for both children. No horoscopes were made.

Mr S believes that all religions are paths towards the same God, and that a follower of any religion can be a good human being. His religiosity has expressed itself through Zoroastrianism, but he feels he would have been the same person had he been born into another faith. Still, if he could choose an identity for another life he would like to be a Zoroastrian again. He respects all religions and thinks it is pointless to seek to convert others to one's own faith. He has no objections to people leaving a religion they do not feel happy with, but feels very strongly that one should be faithful to the religion one has chosen. He has no sympathy, therefore, with Parsis who remain Zoroastrians but also venerate Sai Baba or the Virgin Mary.

Mr S's children's Navjote was performed inside the Atash Behram. He celebrated this event with a certain splendour, and still has some doubts as to whether the money would have been better spent on charity. Quiet charity plays an important part in his religious life.

Mr S regards death from natural causes as part of life, and does not get unduly upset over it. He does feel, however, that the funerary rituals should be observed, and he had *Vendidad* ceremonies performed for both his parents. He observed the Muktads for his parents for a long time, but discontinued them recently because he feels the ceremonies have become too commercialised;[78] he cannot do something that seems to him meaningless.

The discussion moves on to his family life, which is warm and intimate, and where the children at times admonish their father about religious matters. Towards the end of the interview Mr S repeats that, although his own typical prayer is just 'Help me' or 'Help somebody else', he has a deep faith in prayer and in God, 'who will never let you down.'

Mrs S then describes her prayer routine, which the children also follow. They do one *kusti* and one prayer after their bath. 'And our devotion to the religion is total; there is no outside Baba or anything. We find that our religion gives us complete spiritual strength in everything we do.' Her own special prayers are a short version of the *Hom Yasht* for the well-being of the family, and Dastur Kookadaru's[79] prayer to *Shehrevar Ameshaspand*, which brings success in one's working life. She has recently begun to pray *Ava-Ardvisur Niyayesh*, 'a mystic prayer which gives you a little internal strength.' These three prayers she recites every day, along with the *kusti* prayers and the *Sarosh Baj*. She also prays the

Gathas during the *Gatha* days.[80] She confirms her husband's remark that the family now follows the Fasli calendar,[81] largely under her mother's influence. This creates no problems for her husband, whose short prayers need no mention of the *roj*.[82] It could lead to complications for the others,[83] but Mrs S reminds them regularly what day it is. She observes the *parab* for the Fire in the traditional manner, according to the Fasli calendar. For Ava *mahino* Ava *roj* the family goes to the sea but does not offer *dalni poris*. 'It should make sense, what is the sense in putting the *dalni pori* into the water? I have a very logical mind and I won't do things just because they have been done traditionally, unless there is a logic behind it.' Since the family is largely vegetarian there is nothing special about the month of Bahman.

Mrs S has no special experiences of the miraculous power of *nirangs*. One of Mr S's aunts does the *Mushkil Asan* in their house every Friday, but Mrs S does not take part in this. 'I have never done it, and I don't feel the need. I feel that the prayers that I offer are good enough for me.'

MRS N

Mrs N was born in a Gujarati village in 1914. When she was eight years old her family moved to a town with a large Parsi population, where there were Parsi schools and other facilities. She married in 1942 and moved to Bombay, where she lives with her husband and her two children, who are both unmarried. The family owns a shop selling religious articles. The interview took place partly in Gujarati and partly in English.

Mrs N spent her early childhood in an extended family of 36 people. The family was very religious, all women wore the *mathabanu* (headscarf) and in the evenings the entire family gathered for joint prayers. The children – 18 in all – were left relatively free, but as they saw their elders pray constantly they learned the prayers more or less automatically. Those whose Navjote had been done had to wear a cap[84] and bow to the sun at sunrise, do their *kusti*, and say, 'God, please make this day pass in laughter and play. Bless us and keep us all safe.'[85] Even the younger children had to pray five *Yatha Ahu Vairyos* and three *Ashem Vohus* before breakfast. They were always made to pray loudly; since all the children had to do this even the non-Parsi servants had become familiar enough with the Zoroastrian prayers to correct any mistakes. The meaning of the prayers was not discussed. The children were also taught *monajats*, which they sang together before going to bed. Favourite stories included tales from the *Shahname* and stories about King Akbar and Birbal, which are popular among Gujaratis from different religious backgrounds. Mrs N still loves the *Shahname* stories.

The conversation then moves on to the traditional ways of the village. There were only five Parsi families there, the other villagers being Hindus. Mrs N's brother's wedding was attended by various Rajas and Maharajas, who were magnificently entertained. The *madav-saro* was done, there were two *Ashirvads*, and the usual Parsi traditions were observed. As there was no fire temple in the village the couple paid their respects to the fire vase at home. In Mrs N's parents' home religious education was not very strict, the children were generally free to do as they pleased. There were no taboos:

> Nothing at all! Only when a person died you must not laugh much, you must not hurt the people who have lost, to have respect.

Talking about death and funerals, Mrs N recalls the customs in the village. As there was no Tower of Silence the dead were buried in an *aramgah* (cemetery); usually the body was placed in a coffin, but some people expressed a wish to be buried directly in the ground, which was normally respected.[86] The ceremonies for Sarosh were done for one month.[87] Food for the *Satum*[88] was prepared every day, and the ladies of the house had to take a 'head-bath'[89] before entering the kitchen. If no priest was available an uncle recited the prayers over the *Satum* offerings. Later the food was distributed to the children.

Mrs N does not remember how the Muktad days were celebrated, for two of her uncles would go to Surat for the purpose and she did not witness it; she knows that the family had a Muktad table in Surat.[90] Asked about the rules of purity in the village, Mrs N says that menstruating women could not enter the kitchen, 'sat separate', and could not go out. Men could not shave or cut nails for five days, presumably the *Gatha* days. Navjote and birthday celebrations followed the customary pattern.

As far as religion was concerned things did not change much for the children when they moved from the village to the town of Nagpur. They still had to pray regularly in the morning and at night, mostly reading from a prayer book. The family had an ever-burning fire in the house. Observance of the laws of purity was relaxed, however, as her mother did not force the children. When they were impure they did not pray and were not allowed into the kitchen (where the fire was), but wore their normal *sudreh* and *kusti*,[91] and went to school as usual. Mrs N does not believe that any Parsis in Nagpur wore a special *sudreh* and *kusti* at such times.

Astrology played an important role in the choice of a husband for Mrs N. Her sister, whose horoscope had not been compared with her husband's, returned home as a widow after only a few years of marriage and her father therefore insisted that Mrs N should marry a boy who came under Mars.[92] A neighbour happened to know a family who were looking for a girl with the same kind of horoscope. Any remaining hesitations vanished when Mrs N's father died suddenly, because her mother was determined to carry out his wishes. On her father's death-anniversary Mrs N moved to Bombay, where Mr N lived, and she married him six months later. All traditional ceremonies were performed and the couple went to Udwada immediately afterwards. In those days Mrs N's husband did not pray much, but she herself continued her established routine of having a prayer session at about three in the afternoon, after she had finished her work and had a bath. The *parabs* of the Waters and of Fire were celebrated. These customs were discontinued when the family moved house, a few years before the interview.

> I don't do all this in this house, and to tell you the truth the children are not interested. They know what has to be done but they don't have the kind of instinct that we have. It must be my fault, I think, although there was school as well.

For her first delivery Mrs N went to her mother's house in Nagpur and brought the baby back to Bombay when he was five months old. Most of the traditional ceremonies connected with childbirth were not done. The *chatthi* was not allowed in the hospital; Mrs N did not 'sit separate' for forty days because her mother did not believe in it, whilst her mother-in-law felt the same about the *besna* and *pagladu*. The children's horoscopes were made, however, because Mrs N herself is a strong believer in astrology.

The running of the shop, originally shared by three brothers, gradually devolved on Mr N alone; when he suffered from a slipped disc his wife had to take over. From that day onwards she has rarely missed a day. Since the shop sells religious articles Mrs N's gender was a problem; for about eight days each month she could not enter the shop because her touch was considered polluting. To solve this difficulty she had a hysterectomy at the age of 42. When Mrs Munshi asks if she did not think this a very big sacrifice, Mrs N answers, 'Not at all, I loved going to the shop.'

The interview then moves on to her family life when the children were small. The family had daily joint prayer sessions at about 3 p.m., saying a few simple prayers; then at night Mrs N would light the fire and pray, while her small son also sat with a book and pretended to pray. Mrs N taught the children about the religion from a book which covered a wide range of subjects:

> Everything about the Navjote, and the life of Zarathustra, and about our *pehelvans* [heroes] and their lives. How we came to India, and where we settled – all that was in the book. We did not know any ancient history and neither did my son, as he was at St Mary's [a Christian school]. He did not learn anything [there], so he was very interested when I taught him.

What else did you teach them?
Never to tell lies. That they should ask us for anything they might need, and that we would provide it. Not to steal.

On special days Mrs N may pray a bit more than normally, for example the hymn to the Yazad of the day, but she does not often go to the fire temple. Her favourite *Yashts* are those of Hormazd and Ardibehesht. About twice a month she prays the *Behram Yasht*, in which her sister-in-law has great faith but with which she herself has no special affinity.[93]

Later, when disscussing funerals, Mrs N says that she had a *Vendidad* peformed for her mother on the fourth day after her death, and again on her birthday. Both ceremonies were performed at Udwada.

Why in Udwada, any particular reason?
The priests here were reluctant to do it and they did not recite the whole *Vendidad*. They finished by 5.30 or 6 in the morning, whereas there [in Udwada] they continued to pray until 8 or 8.30.

Did you attend any of the ceremonies?
Yes.

Can you describe your feelings at the time?
If you ask me, I don't know the meaning of it all. But I know that it is the *Vendidad* and that it is for the soul of the departed, so one feels happy.

Mrs N approves very much of the Zoroastrian method of disposal of the dead, as the soil is not polluted and no wood is burnt unecessarily.[94] However, she also has a very positive recollection of the *aramgahs* of the village and town of her youth, and she describes the funerary procedures there.

The prayers are all done at home, and then the body is taken there. The priest pray a little. A pit is dug[95] and the crate is lowered into it, and we had to stand and keep reciting the *Yatha Ahu Vairyo*. My best prayer is the *Yatha Ahu Vairyo*. I always recite it, whether I hear of something good or bad.

You were saying that the crate with the body is placed in the grave. Is the grave lined with stones?
Nothing at all. Sometimes people ask to have their body placed directly in the earth, and then that is done.

But is the coffin not lined with stone or anything?
No, nothing at all.

So there is direct contact with the earth?
If you lay the body directly in the earth then there is direct contact. We would take flowers there ... I liked it there very much. Very peaceful!

Moving on to Mrs N's regular visits to the Towers on the *parab* of Farvardiyan, Mrs Munshi asks what Mrs N prays there.

> There it is mostly the priests who pray, we do not pray so much. I must tell you I love to listen to the priests reciting prayers ... [We have] two priests, C and D from Fanasvadi, where the Dadyseth Atash Behram is located.They recite in this melodious voice. C told me that he had two sons and he wanted them to become *Navar*. He asked if I knew of any sponsors.

What is your relationship with C?
All our prayers used to be done at the Wadiaji Atash Behram, Y was our priest. He was then transferred somewhere else so we had no priest. And we went to the Dadyseth fire temple and there C told us he would recite all our family prayers – and he recited them in such a melodious voice that I always listened intently, laying my prayer book aside. So I told my husband that he needed a sponsor for his two sons and asked if we could do it. My husband said yes, so we called C and on Adar *roj*, my mother-in-law's death anniversary, we all went to Udwada and had the *Navar* done for his first son.

In Udwada?
Yes, they are from Udwada and only if the *Navar* is done there can they give *boy* [at the Iranshah]. And then, when his second son was ready we had his *Navar* done in memory of my mother. My brothers and sisters had all come. It was so beautiful!

Are those boys now practising priests?
No, unfortunately not. The youngest goes to pray but they also have secular jobs. The eldest had said long ago that he would not pray or give *boy*. My husband felt very bad about it. They were only ten or eleven when their *Navar* was done, and the eldest joined an Italian firm and went to Rome, so he lost touch with prayers and he told his father that he would not perform any ceremonies. But the younger one does.

Formerly Mrs N's father-in-law sponsored a women's *Gahambar* in Valsad every year in honour of his paternal grandmother. Later, when things got very expensive, this was reduced to once in two years, and when the father-in-law died it was discontinued. However, the family still gives money to a local school every year.

Mrs N has no faith in Babas or other non-Zoroastrian spiritual leaders. From stories her neighbour tells her she has come to the conclusion that Sai Baba must be a good man, 'But that does not mean I should go [to visit him].' For her the Zoroastrian prayers are enough. Whenever she gets some important news, good or bad, she recites the *Yatha Ahu Vairyo*; she did this, for example, when the house where she had previously lived burned down. When people in her family fall ill she puts her hand on the patient's head and recites the *Ardibehesht Yasht Nirang*, but does not do the *pichi*.[96] Her daughter came to believe strongly in the power of prayer when a vulture sat motionless in a tree opposite the family home for days without moving. It finally left, and the daughter told her mother that she had been constantly praying for this. Once, when Mrs N's husband was seriously ill, he recited the *Yatha Ahu Vairyo* all the time and unexpectedly got better.

So you have great faith in the Yatha Ahu Vairyo.
Yes, even now, during the riots[97] my niece's son had a providential escape. His bus was just a little ahead of the bus that was blown up. She came to me and asked me what she should do. I told her to get a *Jashan* done and to tell her son to recite the *Yatha Ahu Vairyo* as soon as he steps out of the house. And not only has she told her son to do it, but her husband now also does it.

MR K

Mr K was born in 1927 in Bombay. He studied Commerce and Economics at College and followed courses in Catering Technology and Applied Nutrition. Until his retirement in 1986 he worked for Indian Airlines in various capacities.

Both Mr K's mother and one of his teachers stressed Mr K's identity as a Zoroastrian and the importance of the traditional way of life. There were daily visits to the Agiary. At home he learned that Zarathustra was the prophet of the Zoroastrians and that they believe in one God, Ahura Mazda, and should reject any other deity. The priest who taught him religion at school told many stories from the *Shahname*, and Mr K remembers that he stressed the moral side of the religion: Good Thoughts, Words and Deeds.

The laws of purity were very strictly observed in his family. His mother used to 'sit separate' during her periods, and food was ordered from a hotel on those days. His sisters went to school, but had to keep completely separate at home during menstruation; as their touch was polluting they had separate items of daily use for those days, and even a drink of water had to be given to them by someone else. Everyone had a bath after a haircut, the hot water being fetched by someone who was not impure; all the clothes that were worn during the haircut were washed. Family members did their *kusti* after leaving the toilet. A kerosene lamp was kept burning during the day; at an earlier stage it was kept burning for twenty-four hours. On *parab* days the family went to the fire temple.

As a small child Mr K was frail and sickly, and his mother made a vow that she would take him to Udwada for his first haircut at the age of seven. This was done: he had the haircut, underwent a *nahn*, and then went to pay homage to the fire.

Mr K's marriage was an arranged one. It was not easy for him to find the right girl, as he was very exacting in the matter of the laws of purity. Eventually, however, a girl from a priestly family was found who was used to these things. Even so there was friction, because his bride refused to comply with Mr K's demand that she should cover her head with a head-scarf[98] as well as her sari; the bride finally compromised by wearing a handkerchief on her head. Mr K's view is that one's wedding takes place only once in a lifetime and that it should be done 'in a completely religious way.' The *madav saro* was done four days before the wedding and the couple was told that they should not meet from that time until the wedding; no reason was given. Mr K had insisted that they should meet on the morning of the wedding day to visit four *Atash Behrams* together, but the bride stayed away. Some days after the wedding the couple went to Udwada. Although Mrs K was from a priestly family she had not been especially trained to be a priest's wife; she had no great knowledge of religious observances and in fact Mr K had to teach her a number of these.

Mr K's daily routine is as follows:

I get up in the morning. First I do my *kusti*, then have a bath, then clean all the utensils, the *sabi* [portrait, probably of Zarathustra] and everything. Then, after lighting a *divo*, I pray *Sarosh Baj*, [the] *geh* [prayer], *Khorshed-Meher* [*Niyayesh*], *Satumno Kardo*. And as far as my prayers to the fire are concerned I do them over there in the *Atashkade* [fire temple][99] or in the Atash Behram: *Atash Niyayesh*, then *Hormazd Yashtni Nirang*, *Ardibehesht Yashtni Nirang* ... I do everything over there, in the fire temple. Every day I must go to a fire temple.

You said earlier that you wash the utensils. Which utensils do you mean?
The glass and the vessel for the milk. For the *Satumno Kardo* you must have milk and flowers. I pray it every day for family members who have died.[100] I drink the milk afterwards, and after a few days I remove the flowers and throw them away on a nearby hill.

Mr K then mentions that, before praying, he also burns sandalwood in a fire vase, after which he does the *loban*. He has five favourite Yazads: Hormazd, Ardibehesht, Adar, Sarosh and Behram. On the *roj* of these Yazads he prays their *Yashts*. He goes to all the four Atash Behrams in Bombay on Adar *mahino* Adar *roj*; on the 'birthday of the Waters' he goes to the seaside or to another source of water, and prays the *Ava Yasht*. He regularly offers a *machi* on his birthday at the Dadyseth Atash Behram.

When an enterprise has been successful, he sometimes offers a *machi* to the fire or to Ahura Mazda. He recounts that once he was planning to go to Iran but found himself in a double bind: the airline would not issue the ticket unless he had a visa, and the Consulate refused to give him a visa without a ticket. No solution seemed possible, but he happened to pass the Wadiaji Atash Behram and prayed to Ahura Mazda, vowing to offer a *machi* if his problem was solved. That very day the airline gave him his ticket and the Consulate opened especially on a Saturday to issue a visa. The *machi* was duly offered. When he was hoping for a promotion he would often vow to have a *machi* performed at all eight Atash Behrams in India, and this usually had the desired effect.

Mr K greatly benefited from reciting the *Ardibehesht Yasht* after an operation. His mother was saved against all expectations after two severe heart attacks, which Mr K attributes to the grace of Ahura Mazda; no special prayers were said at the time, although the family prayed the usual prayers at home.

At one time the *Mushkil Asan* was performed at Mr K's home; later he used to attend the ceremony every Friday at someone else's house. Eventually, however, someone told him that this was a Muslim custom and that Zoroastrians should only venerate Ahura Mazda and His son, the Fire, and he gave it up.[101]

Every year Mr K has the *Farokhshi* performed, and also the *Baj* ceremonies for the Prophet Zarathustra and for Homaji. He attends all these ceremonies. Mrs Munshi asks why he frowns upon the *Mushkil Asan*, which is performed in honour of the Yazad Behram, but has a high ritual celebrated for Homaji, who is not a Yazad. Mr K replies that it is merely a question of paying respect to Homaji, not of worship. In any case, he is 'dead against' non-Zoroastrian cults like that of Sai Baba, and describes his various fights with Zoroastrian priests who promote or observe such cults. He once smashed a picture of Christ in an Agiary. He observes all Shehenshahi, Kadmi, and Khalis Fasli[102] feast days, but no non-Zoroastrian ones.

Mr K is the President of the Jashan Committee of Nargol, his wife's place of origin, where there are some thirty or forty Parsi families. A *Jashan* is held there on every *parab* day – i.e. whenever the dedication of the day coincides with that of the month.[103] This means that several occasions are observed there which pass unnoticed elsewhere, although admittedly few people attend the less well-known functions. Mr K has never missed a funeral when he was in Nargol. In fact he has twice served as a *khandyo* – taking the body to the Tower on foot and taking it inside – as there are no professional corpse-bearers in this small community. Special clothes are kept for such functions, and after the ceremony all those who acted as corpse-bearers have a *nahn*. After this they put on their normal clothes. The cleaning of the Towers is the responsibility of the local Anjuman.[104] Mrs Munshi, who of course has never been inside a Tower, asks whether it is clean there. Mr K says that he was made to take off his glasses so that he cannot be certain, but his general impression is that it was quite clean.

MR T

Mr T was born in 1938 and has lived outside India for a considerable part of his life. He holds a B.Sc. from Bombay University and has held a responsible post in the Indo-Burma Petroleum Company. At the time of the interview he was working as an Engineering Consultant. Mr T plays an active role in Parsi public life; among other functions he holds the post of Honorary Secretary of a local Zoroastrian Association and he is an Honorary Professor in 'Zoroastrian College'.[105] Although Mr T's personal history and some of his views differ from those of most Traditionalists, he clearly has much in common with that group. Mr T's wife was present during the interview and contributed to it at the end.

Mr T had what he calls a 'peculiar religious life'. He was born in Switzerland, where his mother died two days after his birth and where he was brought up by a Christian lady for the first seven years of his life. He thus grew up in a Christian environment. At the age of seven he went to live in Africa with his father and they also lived in Bombay for some time. Then, in 1952, his father died and Mr T went to stay with an uncle in Zanzibar. He went back to India in 1955.

> There I was exposed to religion in a very simple way. I saw for the first time what a fire temple was. I had been in Bombay from 1946 to 1950, and the only religious thing that happened was that my Navjote was performed. And that also was performed in a very hurried way, because we were going back to Africa. My Dad wanted to stay in Bombay, but it was impossible so he decided to return to Africa and I insisted on going with him. It was decided that my Navjote should be performed immediately. So it was very hurriedly performed in the Agiary over here, with no friends, nothing that a normal Navjote would have. After that I came back to India in 1955, when I went to College and did not take much interest in religion. In the mid-1960s one of my friends told me, 'There are religious classes, Sunday classes, going on in our colony,[106] why don't you come and join us?' So I said, 'OK, let us see what it is like, if I like it, fine.' So I went and it was there that I first met Dasturji Kutar.[107] And he taught us religion in a beautiful way. He was a no-nonsense man, he was a good speaker, he could lecture beautifully – I've got some of his lectures on tape also –

and it was through him that I learned something about our religion. Then after his death I did not proceed further until 1970 or 1971, when I had a motorcycle accident and was confined to bed. At that time, having nothing to do, I started reading all sorts of books on all sorts of occult subjects. And then it struck me that instead of reading all these things about others, why not read something about our own religion. And a lot of controversies were going on [in the Parsi community], people were not agreed on any of the important subjects. That is why I decided to take it up and go to it myself. I never joined any group, because all the groups were warring with each other. I just took up the basic books and started going through them one by one. And that is how I have come to the stage where I have my own views on religion. Dasturji Kutar taught us many things, he used to lecture on various subjects; one [series of] lecture[s] was on the *Yatha Ahu Vairyo*, which went on for about twenty, thirty sessions. Then he took a very long lecture for a couple of years on life after death. And in the lectures people used to digress by asking him all sorts of questions. His classes were entirely informal, whoever wanted to take notes took notes. And finally he used to come to the fire temple over here, and we used to meet him in the fire temple and we used to pester him with questions and argue with him. We even used to make him wild at times, you know, by asking very controversial things … Even as I lecture nowadays, I find that some things I could not understand at the time make a lot of sense now. I cannot give you any concrete examples, but quite often as I write I find that something was already taught to us at that time … Most of all, what I gained from the lectures is that they were a sort of stepping stone for me to continue further. They were very general, he was not going very deeply into the subject, he was always speaking to a very illiterate sort of crowd and therefore there was not much of deeper religion that we could learn from him, except leading a good Zoroastrian life. He was a Persian scholar and he used to refer to a lot of Persian quotations from the *Shahname*. He was very inspirational; those who had attended his lectures always wanted to hear him again and again.

What changes did he bring about in your personal life?
He told us a lot about prayers, he used to say that the *faraziyat* prayers[108] should be prayed. Basically we found: these are our duties which we are not doing, so let us start doing them. It was a sort of guilt complex. Actually I was praying even before that. My prayer life started after my Dad died. He died in Zanzibar and we don't have Towers of Silence, we have a graveyard over there. After his demise, although all the ceremonies were performed, after a month or two I started seeing him in my dreams. He came once, after some days I saw

116

him again, and then a third time. And then I asked my maternal uncle, I told him, 'This is what is happening, I keep seeing my Dad.' So he said, 'You do one thing, you pray this prayer for remembering the dead, which we call *Satumno Kardo*.'[109] So I said OK, and I started praying that prayer. And ever since I have not had him enter my dreams.

Mr T had to learn to read Gujarati in order to read the prayer books, but even so he did not understand the meaning of the Avestan words. This did not matter to him, as he was happy that the prayer itself had the desired effect.

The typical thing the Parsis are taught [is]: if you pray this *nirang*, this happens, if you pray that *nirang*, that happens. So you start with a sort of selfish motive, without going into the depth of it. Without praying for the sake of praying, but praying for the sake of either getting something or warding off something. That selfish motive of prayer, that went on in my life for a long, long time. And then afterwards, as I started studying the religion, I found, 'No, you shouldn't be so selfish!' And Dasturji also used to teach us, 'You should not be selfish, you should pray for the love of God, you should pray for the sake of praying.' And then, slowly, over a long period of time, as I started studying more and more of the religion I found that prayer has different meanings for different people.

Nowadays I try to tell people, 'You should not just pray for the sake of getting something. You should be grateful to God for your existence, for the state you are in. Don't just keep crabbing to God about what you don't have.'

Mr T's was an arranged marriage. There was an engagement ceremony on the day when the Navjote of his brother-in-law's children was performed. The wedding followed the traditional pattern; there was no Sanskrit *Ashirvad*. The wedding was performed by Ervad Kutar, who had also done Mr T's Navjote. When the couple moved into their first apartment, a *Jashan* was done because relatives said it was the right thing to do. At that time Mr T himself did not know why one should have such a ceremony performed, but he complied with the others' wishes. During his wife's first pregnancy the *agharni* was done. When the first child was born his wife stayed in hospital for most of the traditional forty days, then she had a *nahn* and went to stay at her mother's place for a time. Mr T's mother-in-law insisted that the names of the children should be chosen according to the *rasi*,[110] and this was done.

I always had a deep respect for elders, and whatever her mother said ... Her mother was a very holy, simple, nice person, and also a very practical person. She was not in favour of too many ceremonies which did not mean much. She said, 'We'll have the bare minimum,' and that sort of thing. When she said that the children should be named as per the *rasi*, I said, 'OK, let's do it as per the *rasi*. Whatever you say we'll do.'

The family does not find it possible to observe many of the purity laws. When they first married the apartment was too small to permit of it. Since they were not able to keep a separate hearth-fire, a *divo* was kept burning for 24 hours, and his wife avoided any contact with it during her periods. Also, when Mr T intended to go to the fire temple on such days he tried to avoid contact with his wife. The whole family observes the rules about hairs and nails. Mr T stresses that he believes in the rules of purity, which should ideally be observed more stringently, but this would not be practical in his case. The family prays together every day:

> That is one thing my maternal uncle taught me in Africa. He used to insist we come back at 6.30 or 7, and then the whole household must pray together. He did a lot to educate the basic instincts in me. He used to pray a lot, and I stayed with him for three years. We had a little prayer room in the house. After my Dad's demise, when I went to stay with them, I was given that prayer room as my study. So we had a little lamp burning for 24 hours, and he used to initiate that evening prayer. We used to do the *kusti* and the evening *Atashno Namaskar* prayer. And from there I was taught that people should pray together. During one of our functions at school there was a big thing about 'The family that prays together stays together,' and we had our own prayers at home. So when my children came to be of an age when they could talk, I started teaching them the prayers, even though they did not understand what they prayed. First the little one use to be on his mother's lap and fall asleep, but we used to sit together every night and pray together. Now we pray separately because we all have different schedules, but for many years we used to sit and pray together. Just simple prayers, the *kusti* prayers. The *Sarosh Baj* was a little too long; we taught it to the boys and told them to pray it on their own. I wanted them to learn more prayers so I said, 'If I pray the *Sarosh Baj* with them they will get tired, and they will not go for it.' So then I started praying the *nirangs* of the *Yashts*: *Hormazd Yasht*, *Ardibehesht Yasht*, then *Sarosh Yasht Vadi*, *Hom Yasht* and *Vanand Yasht*.[111] We used to pray all these. And then we used to pray the *Khudavind Khavind* song,[112] which my mother-in-law introduced. That went on for years, that was our prayer life.

Mr T has devoted a great deal of energy to teaching his children about the religion, teaching them the prayers and explaining various matters of Zoroastrian teaching and observance. Last year a nephew came to

Bombay from abroad, and asked Mr T to prepare his children for their Navjote. He is proud of his success with these children, and is now preparing a children's column to be published in *Jam-e-Jamshed*.[113]

Asked whether he has had any special religious experiences or has a favourite fire temple, Mr T says:

> Yes, I do have a favourite fire temple. I have been visiting this fire temple for years now, because it is close by. And in the fire temple there is an *Adaryan* fire[114] which of course is behind bars, and there is the *Dadgah* fire.[115] Now the *Dadgah* fire was always kept in a terrible state by these people, the priests never used to tend it properly, so whenever I used to go I used to clean it up nicely, remove the old ash, clean the place around it. That is how I got attached to it. And I always say my *Atash Niyayesh*, the prayer to the fire, in front of that fire, not the main fire. The reason being, not that I have disrespect for the main fire, I have terrific respect for all the fires. But everybody who comes prays in front of the main fire and very few people pray in front of this fire. So I say, 'Let me pray in front of the little fire, which is getting less love and attention.'

Asked whether he visits the fire on all important days, Mr T replies:

> I'll be very frank with you. To me every day is fire temple day, I make no difference between a *hamkara* day or Navroz or any other day. But I have made it a point that, in case I cannot visit the temple for some reason or other, I should not get a guilt feeling. Quite often I come late from work and the fire temple closes at nine o'clock, and you just cannot go in after that. In such cases I make it a point not to feel sick about it ... sometimes I phone home and tell the boys to go to the temple and put the sandalwood, sometimes they are not available and the wood does not get offered, that is all!

Do you sometimes offer machis?
Yes I do, and there is a reason. We have a register for *machis* in our Agiary, and some years ago it happened that *machis* were not offered every day. So I said that *machis* should be offered. In the case of an Atash Behram, even if the laity does not do it then the Trustees should see to it, it has to be taken from the Trustees' funds. But in the Adaryan there is no such rule. So I had a bright idea and said, 'On days when there is nobody offering a *machi*, you note it as my *machi*.' And for a number of years, when people were not offering *machis* I filled the gap. That was the only reason, not that we had any business for it ... no favours asked or anything. And today there are so many *machis* being offered that my *machi* does not even come up now. For the last three years I don't remember having paid for a single one.

119

Mr T does not normally light a *divo* in the fire temple area because he keeps three *divas* in his house. His wife does the *loban* in the evenings every day. Mrs T now takes part in the discussion and explains that *loban* is done in the evening mainly to protect the family from evil spirits, which are felt to be powerful at night. On Ava *mahino* Ava *roj* the family goes to the sea to make offerings. Mrs T's mother used to make *dalni poris* every year, but Mrs T herself does not do so. On the eve of the 'Birthday of the Fire' the *loban* ceremony (which involves fire) is done for a longer time at night and the *Atash Niyayesh* is recited. Mrs T says that her neighbour recites nine *Atash Niyayesh* prayers and keeps the hearth fire burning throughout the night; Mr T remarks that the same was done in Africa. On Farvardin *mahino* Farvardin *roj* the family attends a *Jashan*.

Mrs T's favourite Yazad is Behram; she performs the *Mushkil Asan* ceremony every Friday, which is a tradition in her family. She believes the ceremony will ward off evil; even if it is one's fate to encounter difficulties they will be less serious because of it. She tells a story about her nephew's boss, who never prayed and did not even have a prayer book in the house. One day his daughter went missing; Mrs T's nephew told his boss to pray the *Behram Yasht* and *Ava Niyayesh* and lent him his prayer book. The family prayed as directed and the girl was found alive and well within a day or two.

Mr T prays the *faraziyat* and the *Satumno Kardo* in the morning; in the evening he recites the *Atash Niyayesh* in the fire temple when he has looked after the lesser fire there, and the *Behram* and *Ohrmazd Yashts*.

The family makes pilgrimages to Udwada, Navsari and Surat from time to time, on one occasion they visited four Atash Behrams during one trip. Such journeys are made when convenient, and often combined with family visits. Pilgrimages are never made to 'bribe the Lord' (i.e. to have a wish fulfilled), but because Mr and Mrs T wish to do it. Mrs T once took her sons to pay their respects to the four Atash Behrams in Bombay. Since Parsis who come from abroad often do this, she feels that Bombay-based Parsis should not do less. Both parents are very happy that their sons visit the fire temple regularly. As far as religion is concerned, Mr T feels that the family does what it can.

Notes

1 This illustrates the importance Parsis, and particularly Parsi priests, attach to questions of time, and to birthdays. If one is born on the day dedicated to a certain divinity one has a link with that *Yazad*, so it is important to be precise in such matters.
2 The meaning of these and other Gujarati terms is given in the Word List.
3 On this observance see above, p. 16.
4 Since a fire used for religious purposes was burning in the kitchen, purity was felt to be very important. Non-Zoroastrian servants were therefore not

allowed into the kitchen and the grandmother made sure that the place was kept clean.

5 Note that no fundamental difference appears to be perceived between Homaji, a historical figure who is venerated because he is felt to be a martyr, and divine beings.

6 This illustrates the strict division between priestly and lay Zoroastrian families in the traditional Parsi communities of Gujarat.

7 This could be taken to indicate that some Parsis feel that Meher (the great *Yazata* Mithra of classical Zoroastrianism) is important, but are no longer quite sure why, cf. above, p. 23 with n. 18.

8 i.e. they refrained from eating meat in that month.

9 This custom suggests that the link between Bahman and animals was a living reality in people's mind.

10 It is not untypical to have such rites performed on a day which already has a special significance for the family, such as a death anniversary.

11 Wood, being porous, is thought to absorb pollution very easily.

12 It is believed that metal and glass do not absorb pollution.

13 Anything that could be construed as direct contact between a menstruating woman and a source of water, which should be kept free from pollution, was clearly avoided.

14 Note that it was the grandmother's anger that was feared; the notion that such behaviour might be an offence against God clearly did not play a role in the girl's thoughts.

15 Note, however, the earlier description of a visit to a Hindu shrine, and the apparent lack of awareness of any contradiction.

16 Presumably a Sufi saint, certainly not a Parsi. The preference for Parsi institutions was clearly based on considerations of loyalty, not on a belief that Parsi observances were the only effective ones.

17 This seems to illustrate the difference between the priestly and lay ways of life: any member of a working priest's family would have a detailed knowledge of rituals and religious observances, whereas many lay people neither need nor possess such knowledge.

18 On the *dron* or 'sacred bread' see above, p. 10.

19 In Bombay this ceremony is nearly always performed in a fire temple. However, Dastur Dr F.M. Kotwal informs me that it is indeed permissible to do it in a clean place in a private house.

20 See above, pp. 35, 36.

21 It is interesting to note that such domestic ceremonies did not come into the sphere of competence of the children's father, who is a working priest.

22 The direct touch of an 'impure' woman would be polluting for the baby.

23 The text of *monajats* can be recited without singing.

24 A training college for priests, see above, p. 57 n. 55.

25 At this stage of the interview Mr Antia said that he could not recollect much about this service. Later on he remembered that this was the *Shehen Baj*, an ancient rite intended to further the affairs of the (Sasanian) King and his state, which must be performed by old priests while younger priests may only watch.

26 i.e. the tendency to concentrate on the worship of some specific Yazads such as Ashishvang, who is expected to give riches, or Behram, who brings success.

27 i.e. days which are generally held to be auspicious and others which are not.

28 A popular incantation associated with the mythical hero Faridun. For further references see Index

29 See above, p. 37f.

30 The demarcated area in which the body is placed, see above, p. 37.

31 Sic. Presumably a slip of the tongue.

32 It is interesting to note that this staunch and traditional Zoroastrian uses the term 'meditation', which is more readily associated with Hinduism or Buddhism. He presumably uses the term to refer to his Zoroastrian prayers.

33 A wealthy Bombay suburb.

34 One of the five priestly lineages see above, p. 45.

35 A lengthy and demanding purification ceremony, which involves a retreat from the world for nine nights, with a minimum of food and sleep. See also above, p. 15 n. 29.

36 Dastur K. Dabu was also a leading Theosophist (see Hinnells 1997: 76).

37 The implication is that the problem occurred because Mr Antia had gone to the office in a state of impurity, cf. his earlier remarks on getting ill after attending a cremation.

38 Wealthy and prominent Parsi merchant families.

39 A well-known Parsi 'colony' (*baug*), a group of buildings providing affordable housing for Parsis, which are sometimes set in their own grounds. Cusrow Baug has a fire temple serving the community.

40 On Ervad Nadarsha Aibara see above, p. 50, and the interview with Y. Aibara.

41 For Mr Doctor's views on the importance of auras see the interview with him in Ch. 8.

42 The implication is that if it was permissible to relocate the oldest sacred fire in India several times, there could be no valid grounds for the Khshnoomists' objections in the case of a relatively minor fire.

43 The conversion of Mr J. Peterson, which was confirmed by the authority of some U.S.-based Zoroastrian priests when his Navjote was performed, caused a great deal of debate in Parsi circles.

44 On such debates on community issues see pp. 55, 310f. The late J.R.D. Tata was one of the idols of the Parsi community, and it must have taken a certain amount of courage to contradict him in print.

45 On the *Nirangdin* see above, p. 10; on Kookadaru see above, p. 50, and the interview with Y. Aibara.

46 On the consecration of the various categories of fire temples see Modi 1922: 199ff.

47 Lohraspshah is one of the heroes described in the *Shahname* who are much venerated by the followers of Kookadaru. See above, p. 23 with n. 19, and the interviews with Mrs X and Y. Aibara.

48 The language of this passage has been slightly altered. On the rules of purity concerning menstruation see also above, p. 39f. When Mrs A was young such rules were observed more widely and strictly than they are now.

49 Mostly, it seems, tales from the *Shahname*.

50 The argument that one must follow and obey the tradition because previous generations have made great sacrifices to maintain it, is often heard in Parsi circles.

51 Many Parsis believe that the task of *kusti* weaving traditionally devolved on women of the priestly class only. At the time of writing *kusti* weavers may come from priestly or lay families.

52 cf. above, p. 52.

53 The juice of the Haoma plant, which is extracted and consecrated during some of the high rituals.

54 This passage seems to sum up the attitude of many traditionalists with particular clarity.

55 It is interesting to note that in Mrs A's mind the question of observance of the purity laws is chiefly connected with the occupation of the bread-winner. The question of sin, or of God's Will, does not arise in this context. See further below, p. 300f.

56 In other words, observances which had determined part of Mrs A's life seem alien to the next generation, to whom their grandfather's view that something has to be done simply because it is required by tradition is equally unlikely to appeal.

57 See above, p. 35.

58 The *rasi* system determines the initials the child may have on the basis of its horoscope.

59 On these ceremonies, which are often performed for the first child only, see above, p. 36.

60 A system of healing by means of prayer and 'magnetic passes', as described here.

61 These are festivals of Hindu origin, which are observed to some extent by many Parsis. *Kali Chowdas* is associated with magic; on *Dhan Teras* people wash their jewellery in milk.

62 An image of the Hindu goddess of prosperity.

63 A prayer associated with the ancient Iranian hero Faridun, on which see also above, p. 23 with n. 19.

64 The word *dastur* is often used as a respectful title for any priest.

65 i.e. beliefs of non-Zoroastrian origin, held together with more traditional ideas.

66 A Hindu deity.

67 On B.N. Shroff see above, p. 49f.

68 A short formula based upon this *Yasht*, which is often associated with healing.

69 Dr F apparently regards it as desirable to face a portrait of Zarathustra when praying. It may be that she takes it for granted that a flame burns underneath such a picture, as Zoroastrians generally pray facing a fire or another source of light.

70 i.e. short prayer formulas based on the text of the *Yashts*.

71 Asked for more information Dr F mentioned that, in addition to a prayer book and *kusti*, a little gold and silver and the day's newspaper are normally buried under a new house.

72 This is not unusual in traditional Parsi families. Parsi culture is remarkably free from male chauvinism, and the mother or wife of the 'man of the house' is often the most powerful person in the household.

73 On the use of iron beds during menstruation see above, p. 39f.

74 On these calendars see above, p. 47.

75 Although the Zoroastrian calendar has no equivalent to our days of the week, the Hindu calendar does. Parsis must therefore have been familiar with the concept of a seven-day week since they came to India, and many people now observe ceremonies on a certain day of the week: rites for Behram Yazad are widely held to be particularly effective when performed on a Friday, and Mr S's family obviously has strong feelings about Saturdays and Mondays.

76 This is done in some traditional families.

77 See above, p. 33.

78 cf. above, p. 25.

79 On Kookadaru see above, p. 50.

80 On these days see above, p. 26.
81 See above, p. 47.
82 In these prayers there is no need to state the day and *geh*, as may be required in longer prayer sequences.
83 *viz.* because the Fasli calendar is rarely marked on Parsi calendars and is relatively uncommon, so that friends and neighbours are unlikely to remind one of special days.
84 i.e. their head had to be covered.
85 *Khodāyjī ājno dīvas hasto ramto gujārjo. Badhāne sārā rūḍā rākhjo.*
86 To some Parsis this might seem improper, as the dead body directly pollutes the earth. The local community, however, clearly had no such feelings, or the practice would not have been allowed.
87 On these ceremonies see above, p. 38.
88 On the *Satum* see above, p. 10.
89 A bath which includes washing one's hair.
90 i.e. the family had a special table in a fire temple there, see above, p. 25.
91 Some people have special items which are only worn during menstruation.
92 Guj. *mangal.* The astrological system used in the Parsi community clearly differs in many ways from that used in the West, but none of our informants provided detailed information on the subject.
93 It is interesting to note that, although few Parsis understand the meaning of Avestan prayers, many have a strong preference for certain prayers and feel indifferent to others. Nor is this always a question of believing that one prayer is more effective than another; in this case, for example, the only consideration referred to was that of 'liking' the prayer.
94 Note, however, Mrs N's comments on the procedure at the *aramgah*, where the question of pollution does not seem to play a role. It seems fair to infer that Mrs N approves of most or all methods of disposal which are practised by Zoroastrians because she feels they are part of her religious tradition, but that she is not really preoccupied with such things.
95 Mrs N literally says, 'three days before the funeral a pit is dug.' This seems unlikely, however, and may be no more than a slip of the tongue.
96 i.e. she does not make 'passes' over the patient's body while reciting certain prayers, cf. the interview with Mrs A with n. 60.
97 There had been violent communal riots in Bombay a few years before the interview took place.
98 Many traditional Parsi women wear such scarves, which are known as *mathubanu* or *mathabanu.*
99 This term is widely used in Iran, but not among Parsis; here it is probably a conscious 'Iranism'.
100 On performance of the *Satum* ritual by laymen see above, p. 10 with n. 25.
101 This is not untypical; few Parsis are in a position to be certain whether a ritual or observance is originally Zoroastrian, or if it has been borrowed from another religious tradition. In this case the custom is in fact likely to be of Zoroastrian origin, although a very similar observance forms part of the Iranian Muslim tradition.
102 See above, p. 47.
103 On the *parabs* which are widely observed see above, p. 22f. Several occasions when the day and month dedicated to the same Yazad coincide are not generally celebrated by Parsis.
104 The local Zoroastrian 'Association', a body representing the community.
105 See the interview with Dr Master-Moos

106 i.e. in our *Baug* or Parsi housing estate.
107 On Ervad Darabshah Kutar see also the interview with Dr Y.
108 The 'obligatory' or basic prayers, see above, p. 17 with n. 5.
109 The prayer for the *Satum*, on which see above, n. 100.
110 A method of choosing names on the basis of the horoscope, cf. aboveW, n. 58.
111 In other words, Mr T began to pray the shorter *nirangs* instead of the long hymns to various divine beings.
112 One of the *monajats* or devotional songs.
113 On this Parsi newspaper see above, p. 55.
114 A common Parsi term for an *Adaran*, a fire of the second grade, on which see above, p. 9.
115 i.e. a fire of the third grade, see above, p. 9.

Chapter Five

Neo-Traditionalists

MR KHOJESTE MISTREE

Khojeste Mistree was born in India in the late 1940s. He grew up in Pune (Poona), but studied in Britain. After qualifying as a chartered accountant he went on to read for a degree in Oriental Studies at Oxford. He later returned to India, where he began to share his knowledge with the community, who started attending his lectures by the hundreds. As a result of his success he soon became a controversial figure, adored by many but disliked by others. He co-founded 'Zoroastrian Studies', an active centre for teaching and explaining the Zoroastrian religion. Mr Mistree is a prominent exponent of 'Neo-traditionalism'. The present writer attended the interview.

Asked about his home background, Mr Mistree says:

I grew up in Poona, where my mother lived then; she was a very strong-willed person, very secular in her outlook. There is very little of religion really that I can remember from when I was young. We used to go a Fire Temple periodically; sometimes a *Jashan* was performed at our place. I think what I remember above all from those *Jashans* is eating the *chashni* [consecrated food]. I was never given a properly structured framework for the religion. My mother practised the religion in her own eclectic way; perhaps unlike most other Parsis she had to work with many Hindus. She was a doctor working in the slums of Poona. Therefore the earliest memories I have [about religion] are of what happened in Hinduism. For example my mother had one patient who was able to foretell the future, she had another patient who had the ability to predict anything bad that would happen. As I grew up there was another lady who had the amazing ability of producing holy red powder from nowhere. So more than structured religion I think I was exposed to what one might call the

126

paranormal. At a very early age, when I was about eight or nine, I discovered my gift for water divining. At that time, in the fifties, no water diviner in India would have revealed his secrets. It meant that I invented my own technique of how to find water, so one had to deal with things which science could not at that stage explain. This gave me an interest in things occult, in things unusual, which most other children of my age would not be bothered about. It was these sort of things that made me realise that life was not just about eating, going out and being merry – of course I did those things but I felt there was something more to life. I developed a natural instinct of wanting to experience the supernatural. So to me, then, that was the religion; I do not recollect having been told about the meaning of the *Ashem*, the *Yatha Ahu Vairyo* prayers, in fact I would say that I really had no religious input when I was young. I remember my Navjote, which was a big occasion for me, where I was taught my prayers by my grandmother, but the Navjote ceremony itself was not explained in any detail. I was told to do things and, unquestioningly, I did them. I was not at that stage particularly interested to know why it was important for the Navjote to happen, except that it made me feel good that I was being welcomed into the fold. In that sense there was a feeling of recognition. Otherwise all my Navjote memories are those of presents, food, the beautiful strings of lights which one of my mother's patients had hung in our garden.

I liked going to the fire temple and, curiously, often I used to go on my own to the Sir J.J. fire in Poona. I have always had a special feeling for that fire; it was not my mother's fire temple, but somehow I liked to go to it on my own, often on my way back from school. I did not go on a regular basis, just whenever the spirit took me. When I had a water divining job to do I would sometimes go to the fire temple and ask the fire to help me. So there was, if you like, a kind of relationship I developed with this fire at an early age.

Did you say a lot of prayers by then or did you just talk to the fire, experience the fire?
I generally would just experience the fire. I have never been one for excessive prayer and therefore the only prayers I knew in those days were my basic *kusti* prayers, nothing more, not even the *Sarosh Baj*.

Was there a trip to Udwada after the Navjote, were things like that done?
No trip to Udwada then, at least as far as I remember. In fact I think I went to Udwada for the first time when I was perhaps twelve or thirteen years old, many years after my Navjote. Udwada was some 400 kilometres by road from Poona, remember, and my mother, being a doctor, never had a weekend to spare to go there by car.

Did anything interesting happen between the time of your Navjote and the time you went to England, later?
Yes. A very important thing happened during my last years at school. My mother had gone for an evening drive on a Sunday with some other ladies. On the outskirts of Poona a Parsi gentleman hailed the car. He knew one of the occupants of the car, but not my mother. He looked at my mother and he said, 'Madam, I would like to come and talk to you.' My mother invited him, and I remember this man coming, very strong, very well built. He turned out to be a strong man from a circus, by the name of Bahadur Gamadia. (Bahadur died four years ago now.) He was the first Parsi mystic who entered my life. As I was told later, in his meditation he was told to make contact with my mother, and through this contact he would make a spiritual contact with me. So he took me under his wing, and he would come to our house when he was in town. He was able to read one's mind absolutely perfectly; he also had the ability to make things happen, in a sense controlling people's minds. He was also responsible for perhaps opening some of my psychic *chakras*, in terms of making me more sensitive to matters of the world above. And this helped me in my water divining activities, because in a very short time I became a very, very well-known water diviner; as a school-going boy I was earning an income that was liable to tax. Now Bahadurji helped me in my divining work, he would pray when I went on a difficult divining job. But he never revealed to me who his gurus were. Still, from conversations I gathered that they were Sufi saints,[1] some of whom were living and some of whom had died. He would go to the graves of these Sufi *pirs*, and he told me that he sometimes went for two or three days, picking up their vibrations. And through that energy he was able to help me. I just took that for granted. So in that sense I did have a kind of spiritual discipline which the average Parsi boy would not be exposed to. My brother never developed this sort of interest and this sort of liking, it very much seemed to be something that I personally went in for.

Did you discuss this at home?
It all happened quite naturally. I did not have long discussions with my mother because she was always busy. I was closer to my grandmother, who shuttled between Bombay and Poona; when she came to Poona I was with her. But I did not share these things; it was very much a personal, individual quest. But even in those school days I knew that I had to do something which would be different from what my schoolmates would eventually do. Like I felt that I had a certain mission which I had to accomplish in matters of the spirit.

Did Bahadur Gamadia use any of our Zoroastrian prayers?
Nothing that I am aware of. All he said was, 'Continue to be a good Zoroastrian,' whatever that meant.

But he did not tell you what being a good Zoroastrian entailed?
Nothing! I had absolutely no formal education when it comes to religion, and specifically Zoroastrianism. I grew up in a Christian school and I suppose I knew more bits from the Bible than I knew from my own tradition. Yet there was a natural empathy I felt towards being Parsi. To me that was important, being a Parsi and therefore being different from other children.

So afterwards, I believe, you went to Oxford to study accountancy?
No, no, that is not how it worked. In those days, going to England was virtually impossible because of Indian foreign exchange regulations. But some time in the mid-sixties I was invited for a water divining congress in England. The British Society of Dowsers had heard about my work. (I think I was one of the youngest dowsers who made it to that congress.) They invited me to Tunbridge Wells to read a paper on my water divining work in India. I feel I got psychic help from Bahadur Gamadia, so that all the travel arrangements fell into place whilst it was virtually impossible in those days to leave the country as a schoolboy! I first went to Switzerland, where my father lived in those days, and it was the first time I saw my father since my birth. It was kind of strange seeing this man who, I was told, was my father. I remember going to his flat on that Sunday morning; I rang the doorbell and after two or three minutes this man came down in his dressing gown. I looked at him and he looked at me, and I stuck out my hand and said, 'Hi Pop!' I spent a few days with him just before going to the congress. I had practically no money. My father gave me some money, and then I arrived in England. I was not even 18 then, and it was very courageous of my mother to allow me to go to London, especially in those days, when Flower Power was at its height. I got off at the Earls Court Bus Depot, where the bus from the airport dropped us. Now Bahadurji had told me that money would come for me. I was walking down Earls Court Road when a fairly nondescript person came walking towards me from the opposite side. He looked at me and I looked at him, and there was a sort of recognition, I can only tell you, a sort of spiritual recognition. He held out his hand, in which there was an envelope. As if it was normal, I just took the envelope from his hand and he continued walking in the opposite direction and I continued walking ahead. In that envelope was the exact amount of money which I required for the congress; that is how the money came. Then in England I came to realise that this spiritual world, whatever it is, not only existed but that it actually

129

worked for me! How could somebody just walk up to me and give me money for this congress? It was just too coincidental and too unusual.

And no questions arose in your mind, like, 'Should I take this'?
Not at all, it was like meeting somebody normally and shaking hands with a person. But Bahadurji had taught me a certain spiritual exercise and a gesture, which is something I still use from time to time when a situation is very difficult and, for a greater good, it still works.

Some days later I went to Tunbridge Wells and the congress was a great success for me, judging from the audience's response and given that I was about fifty years younger than most other people. I met the cream of British aristocracy; everyone was very polite and, as they had done their dowsing work in the colonies when Britain still had its Raj, they were very happy to share their secrets with me. Because for me water divining was not just like an English tea party; it was helping real people, it was helping farmers, industrialists setting up their factories. In those few days at Tunbridge Wells I had certain dreams, where I felt I was being told to stay on in England longer. When I left India it was basically just going to be a holiday, go to the congress and come back. But something told me I had to stay, and I had to discover something for myself. I went back to London. I had a few introductions to Parsis, whom I contacted. Then, very strongly in my ... I don't want to use the word meditation because I did not have any specific technique of meditation. However, I would just sit quietly, maybe in a park or by the river, and a message would come through, and a clear indication would be given to me. I sat one day in Hyde Park and was told that I had to stay in England for some spiritual work, and so I decided to stay. Everybody in India was horrified because, as I say, I was fourteen, fifteen, and it was in the mid-sixties, in the days of Flower Power. One could have gone totally wild. But my mother had great confidence in me and supported my decision. She said, 'If you want to stay I will support you; I am not going to ask you to return to India, but you must do something that will eventually earn you your bread and butter. If you want to do your other things you must do them concurrently with a formal education.' So I discovered that accountancy was a very good possibility to explore, as you could become an articled clerk. They would then pay me a sort of stipend, which would help me to survive in England. So, to cut a long story short, I had to find an accountancy firm that would give me a job. Now my grandmother's nephew, who lived in London, knew of an accountant who was looking around for an articled clerk. I was called in for an interview, and for some reason our chemistries clicked and he was willing to take me on. But I had to sit for some O level and A level exams in order to serve my period of articleship. So I had to study, I had to work in order to earn a living, and I had to develop my spiritual interests all at the same time. My mother was very supportive, because finances were tough. Everything, clothes, even a thread and needle, was sent from India. There were other Parsi boys doing accountancy who basically came from well-off backgrounds, so I was the only person, I felt, who had to struggle in that sense. But I can safely say that I never went without a meal, money just trickled in. Somebody would come from India; I got a grant of £5 a month from a Parsi gentleman; then the Freemasons decided to adopt me and they gave me £50 a year for three years. Somehow I managed to live on that budget. Ahura Mazda was truly looking after me.

In any case, unlike the other Parsi boys, my interests were more in matters of the spirit. When others went pub-crawling I went to Interfaith meetings or to a spiritual concert. So within months my network began to develop amongst a certain kind of people, people who were in search of something spiritual. This was probably one of the most spiritual periods which England has known; everyone who was interested in such things seemed to drift there, and I had chosen to be part of that world.

Did all that bring you closer to Zoroastrianism?
Well, no. My closeness to Zoroastrianism I have to attribute to two or three major happenings. One was getting to know an English girl. She was maybe ten years older than me, but she was very interested in matters of the spirit. She began to probe and ask questions about my religion, and I could not answer them. She made me turn inwards, to discover my own roots, in fact my own being. So far I had been exposed to everything non-Zoroastrian, and it was this girl who made me focus on Zoroastrianism, which eventually led me to discover the esoteric tradition of the living faith. She used to ask me to chant the Avestan prayers and she would sit meditating, listening to how I prayed. Going into absolute moments of ecstasy! So then I thought, 'If she feels this way there must be something there.' She could not just be feeling this for the sake of feeling it. She in turn knew of a Kabbalist, and I then came into contact with a lovely man, Warren Kenton, who was a Kabbalist in the New Age sense. So I began to study Kabbalah with him, and for years I attended his classes. But at the same time I then began to apply Kabbalah to what I began to experience through the Zoroastrian tradition. Over the years I read a number of books on Zoroastrianism and I found that they seemed to be more or less superficial. What I read there was either very scholarly or I felt that the authors somehow missed the point. They certainly did not give me an answer to my spiritual quest. However, through my Kabbalistic training I began to understand the principles underlying esoteric philosophy.

I began to realise that, in order to be able to understand myself, I had to discover myself as a Zoroastrian. It was rather painful because for every hundred books one could find on New Age spirituality I could hardly find one book on Zoroastrianism, and some of the books I did find were boring and difficult to understand. I then came into contact with more people, who asked more questions. So it was a question of assimilating information very quickly, and then sharing. I got in touch with the Interfaith movement, where I had to talk about Zoroastrianism. Now I could not quite say to these people that Zoroastrianism was about Good Words, Thoughts and Deeds, because these intelligent people would say, 'Surely all religions talk of good thoughts, words and deeds, why do you feel yours is so special?' And suddenly I realised that clearly that was not the answer, that Zoroastrianism had something else to offer the world, but at that stage I did not know what.

So I read whatever I could find on Zoroastrianism, and that meant reading a lot of trash, a lot of popular books. And I then felt that I had to undergo a rigorous formal training in Zoroastrianism. At this stage I was under the spiritual guidance of a Turkish mystic, Bulent Rauf, who had started a very powerful Sufi movement in England called Beshara. In this movement they studied Ibn al-Arabi's *Fusus [al-Hikam]*,[2] which basically talks about the concept of an absolute, transcendent God. And I found it very difficult to understand how this concept of an absolute, transcendent God would fit in with the Zoroastrian paradigm of Ahura Mazda, the Lord of Wisdom. And I remember struggling with the *Fusus* at Beshara, where we would perhaps read only two or three lines a day. I was doing all this while studying to become a chartered accountant. By the time I qualified as an accountant I was well into studying and experiencing Zoroastrianism. My boss, who was a very special man, allowed me to go to Iran for eight weeks when officially I only had two weeks [vacation]. The Iranian experience was very important, as I was able to experience Zoroastrianism at the grass root level. In many ways it was totally different from the Parsi paradigm I was used to. I had a number of religious experiences there which were to change me fundamentally.

When I did well in accountancy my boss offered me a junior partnership, which was unheard of in those days. At the same time all these other things were happening; I met a lot of different people, Buddhist monks but also British aristocrats who were searching for something spiritual. So within this exclusive circle of friends I was seen as a sort of Zoroastrian guru. But the most important thing all of them told me was, 'Khojeste, you have to discover your own roots and share them with us.' In other words the common plank was to discover our mystical roots and bring out a New Age understanding from our different perspectives.

One day a famous Tibetan Buddhist teacher visited London, and I was standing in a long queue outside the building where he was. He told his assistants, 'There is a Zoroastrian outside and I want to talk to him.' And they fetched me from outside. He gave me a scarf, and he was the first person to talk to me about Khshnoomism.[3] He said, 'One of your people went to Iran some sixty years ago. You will now have to do the same thing for your people.' I was completely taken aback. I had begun to read something about Khshnoomism, especially about Shroff. And he said, 'You will have to bring down the light for your people, who have completely veered away from the religion.' Now to me this was important, for here was someone from a completely different tradition, not part of Beshara, not a Sufi, not somebody that I interacted with on a regular basis, picking me up from the road and giving me this message. Of course, Shroff's zoroastrianised Theosophy never appealed to me personally.

Did you not ask yourself, 'Why me?'
No, in these sort of things you never ask, 'Why me?', because in a sense that is arrogance. In the normal world perhaps this false sense of humbleness comes, but the spiritual world, I feel, works differently. If you have to do a job you have to do it; it is not a question of why me or why you. I mean, how can I question divinity? If I am meant to be an agent for God I just have to do it. As time went on, I could see that I was being trained and prepared for a particular mission.

Gradually more and more people came to know me, and I was giving lectures at Universities and so forth. I was then sent to Krishnamurthi's set-up in Hampshire, and I spent a few days with this great philosopher. With Krishnamurthi the experience was rather different because his whole approach was that established religions had failed, and that one had to be conscious of one's own spiritual path through this intellectual paradigm. My philosophical base was being strengthened, but I could not carry the Zoroastrian tag with me, which by that time was becoming very important.

I was also taken to Bertrand Russell by a friend of mine who knew him. This was when Russell was in his late eighties or early nineties, a few years before he died. Somehow he knew what a Parsi was. I was very impressed with him, after all Russell was a free thinker and one of the great, great intellectual giants in philosophy. He had a very squeaky voice and he said [mimics], 'Oh, you're Mister Khojeste Mystery. You're a Parsi from Bombay.' I said, 'Yes, sir, I am a Parsi.' And then he talked to me and I was very impressed with him. Of course he did not believe in formal religion either, but it is curious that these non-religious types have had a greater influence upon me than priests of any religion.

Some years later I was taken to meet to the Archbishop of Canterbury, Dr Ramsey. He was into Interfaith and very keen that the Zoroastrian tradition should be represented in England, and I was asked to represent Zoroastrianism. So occasionally I would go off to these tea parties with the Archbishop of Canterbury.

Now whilst all this was happening, some of the Sufis in England got specifically interested in Zoroastrianism, because for some reason they found the Avestan chants very beautiful. They found it inspirational when I chanted the *Ashem Vohu* or the *Yatha Ahu Vairyo* prayers, as taught to me by Zoroastrian mystics in Iran. And this gave me great pleasure because I felt that spiritually I could communicate with people on the level of sound, rather than in terms of what the *Ashem Vohu* means or what the *Yatha Ahu Vairyo* means. And because of this I was taken by my Turkish teacher to meet Pir Vilayat Khan, who was a big Sufi name in those days, the son of Hazrat Inayat Khan. He gave me a private audience, which I was told was a great honour. And he shut his eyes (we were sitting as we are sitting now), and he said, 'I gather you are going to Iran in the next six weeks. I want you to go to Shahrud, and I want you to meet somebody there.' I said, 'But why Shahrud?' and he said, 'You will see.' And then he said, 'In Shahrud you will be given a book, and you will be given instructions what to do with that book.' He then sort of flattered me, and told me that he saw my vibrations to be very good and what have you. So off I went to Iran, and in those days I used to know some very rich Zoroastrians in Tehran. And in those days if you lived in Tehran you never went to the villages, that was like the boondocks. You just lived this high life in Tehran. So when I told my hosts I was going to Shahrud they really thought I had lost my marbles.

I got to Shahrud by bus at about six thirty in the morning, and I could not imagine why I was there. It is not a Zoroastrian town, it is the back of beyond, six hundred odd miles north-east of Tehran. I remember this pharmacist opening his chemist's shop. He looked at me and I looked at him, and I suddenly had a flash of my old teacher Bahadur Gamadia, who had shown me one or two occult things. This man invited me in and I said, 'Look, I've been given a name in England, and the name was Khanom [Mrs] Azudin, who is supposed to live in Shahrud.' He looked at this name and he said he did not know. So I sat there and I said, 'You know I have been sent from England to meet this person, there must be this person.' So, typically Iranian style, he called other people, but none of them could figure it out. So I really felt very stupid: Pir Vilayat Khan had sent me on a wild goose chase! I was about to get up when a person walked into the store. He looked at me I looked at him, and again there is a little occult practice which one does. And he said, 'You've come from England, you are a Zoroastrian?' I said yes – I was overjoyed. He said, 'You have come to meet Khanom Azudi.' So the others had not been able to figure out that Azudin stood for Azudi! It turned out that this lady was the wife of Iran's Foreign Minister in Mossadeq's time in the 1950s, so she was a very prominent lady. This man called up Khanom Azudi, who could speak English. She said, 'Before you come for dinner tonight, go to the grave of Bayazid Bestami.'[4] So off I went to Bayazid's grave. By then all my meditations and prayers were Zoroastrian. I would never go into Islamic chants, except for *Ya Hu*,[5] that was the only non-Zoroastrian chant I might do, but even there I later discovered that in Avestan *hu* means 'good' and *ya* is a pronoun, so it somehow has a Zoroastrian connection.

What Zoroastrian chants did you do at this time?
Basically the *Ashem Vohu* and *Yatha Ahu Vairyo* prayers, recited in a slow chanting way. Anyway, I went to Bayazid's grave, paid my respects, spent all day there, meditated, reflected, and in the evening I went to see the great Mrs Azudi. She had a very beautiful house, in the middle of nowhere. And at dinner she gave me a book and, surprise of surprises, it was *The Dawn and Twilight of Zoroastrianism* by Zaehner.[6] For two years in England I was trying to find it in antiquarian bookshops and I could not. So she gave me this book and said, 'Read it; I want you to travel right across Iran, and go to Shushtar to discover the place where Mansur al-Hallaj[7] has been.' I nearly freaked out, because Pir Vilayat Khan had also told me in London that, from Shahrud, I would have to go to some faraway place near Basra, where Hallaj had once lived. The name of Hallaj had first entered my horizon when Pir Vilayat Khan mentioned him. I had not known who he was, except that he was a Sufi mystic. So the next day I set off, travelling nearly 36 hours by bus. I arrived close to Shushtar. Now Vilayat Khan had said that I would have to find this site where Hallaj had been. And Massignon,[8] in his book on Hallaj, has a particular story about Hallaj and a fire, where he mentions a place called Tushtar. But there was no Tushtar on the map, only Shushtar. So I had to take my divining rods (whenever I went to Iran, my rods were always with me), and eventually I felt that Shushtar and Tushtar were probably the same place. So this bus dropped me about four in the morning, the sun had just risen. I really began to ask myself if I was going mad. What the hell was I doing travelling to these strange kind of places following the hints people had given me? At which point a jeep drove up to me, and the man asked me what I was doing there so early in the morning. I had to be very circumspect, as Sufis are not well respected in that area. Anyway this guy said, 'I will take you to a very learned man of this area; his name is Mulla Sharif al-Din.' So I was taken to his house,

and I felt a bit nervous because this was the first time I met a high-ranking Muslim cleric in Iran. I looked at him, he looked at me, and I just sheepishly said, 'I am a dervish, and I am looking for Hallaj.' He just laughed and said, 'Never heard of him; you'll have to go to Basra.' Now Basra is in Iraq and there was no way I was going to Iraq. Then as I was leaving his house, feeling despondent, I suddenly saw two beautiful Zoroastrian motifs. So I looked at them and I said, 'This is Zoroastrian.' He was taken aback and he beckoned me again, and he started asking me questions and suddenly he became quite friendly. I told him about wanting to find Hallaj's place, where there was a story about Hallaj entering a Zoroastrian temple. It is said that as he entered, the fire, which according to the story was lit by Zarathustra, went out and the priest started crying. Hallaj then told the priest, 'I am as Zoroastrian as you are,' and he raised his hand and the fire reappeared. I told this to Sharif al-Din and he said, 'There is such a place in the neighbourhood, but there is no way you can go there now.' It was so hot that the tar on the road was melting. People had just stopped work at eight in the morning because of this heat wave, and yours truly wanted to go to find a place where there was a shrine to Hallaj in the desert. So I talked to him, I took out my divining rods – they often help me in strange situations – and he took out two stone tablets and asked me to date them for him. I used my rods and I dated them; they were Zoroastrian. (I still have photographs of these tablets.) He was most impressed and he said, 'OK, I will send my son with you but you will have to go on camelback to go to Hallaj's … temple or wherever he had been.' So off I went on this camel and we went into the desert. Finally Sharif al-Din's son said, 'This is where my father asked me to bring you.' I looked around and there was nothing. I thought, 'Gosh, the heat is getting to me.' The man told me to come away as there was nothing, but I said No. So I took out my rods while sitting on the camel, and did a 360° scan and I got a reading from my dowsing rods. So off I wandered to that particular spot. Sharif al-Din's son just left me, and part of me was saying, 'Khojeste, you are mad. Apart from anything else, how are you going to make the camel stop?' Anyway, the camel went in the direction I wanted, and as we got closer to that place I saw that there was an actual structure... I walked up to the shrine, tape-recorder and all. I sat there for two hours. I cannot tell you how that time passed. For when I became conscious – that is all I can say, I mean I *was* conscious but I felt as if something had hit me – two of the most powerful Zoroastrian *manthras* came through, and I recorded them on my old-fashioned tape recorder, I still have it on a spool. I knew then that my mission was accomplished. That night I took the bus back to Tehran and the next day I flew back to England, met my Turkish teacher and said,

'Mission accomplished. I found what you sent me for.' And he was overjoyed, he hugged and kissed me and said lots of nice things. And I felt that I had achieved something, although not something Zoroastrian.

But did you realise that the chant was Zoroastrian?
Yes, yes, absolutely. I knew that the word was Avestan.

You knew that, even though you heard it for the first time?
I knew that this chant would become the most important key for *me*, for Zoroastrian spiritual work.

Some 18 months later I sailed through my accountancy exams and I remember going to the Earls Court Fair in January to book my sailing boat, which I had always dreamt about. Having qualified as an accountant the world was at my feet, my boss had offered me a junior partnership and, from having survived on seven pounds ten shillings, now one was talking of megabucks. One day Bulent and Warren, who were like my two teachers, called me for supper. They said, 'Khojeste, we have to give you some news.' So I said, 'Oh, oh, now what is going to happen?' I was all set to become an accountant. I was looking at houses in the Hampstead area and everything was sort of working out. Bulent said, 'Khojeste, you'll have to give up accountancy.' I was devastated, having done accountancy, having got this super job, everything was made for me. They said, 'No, you will have to train formally in your religion. You have had all the mystical inputs coming in, but now you must go back to your roots and discover your religion from its source.' And that was perhaps the most difficult decision I had to make in my life: do I give up the high life and go back to being a student? And I said, 'How can I become a student, I am an accountant now, how do I get into a University to study religion with an accountancy background?' And they said, 'That will all be arranged, don't worry. You go and meditate.' They felt sorry for me but on the other hand they were taskmasters. So I thought and worried.

A few weeks later a friend of mine from Beshara came to see me, and was fascinated by my dowsing. And he said, 'My Moral Tutor at Oxford is very interested in water divining. I have spoken to him about you and he wants to meet you. Why don't you come for tea?' So I said OK; it sounded pleasant enough. So off we went, and he had this beautiful house outside Oxford, an old, old country house. He then made me sit down and I jumped from the chair he made me sit down on. I was a bit embarrassed, you have to be very polite in this upper-crust English society. So he said, 'What has happened to you?' So I said, 'Excuse me, sir, but I don't feel too comfortable sitting here, because I am getting these shingles in my body, and I have a feeling

137

that I am sitting on a stream of water.' So he burst out laughing, and he said, 'You are absolutely right, there is water.' He removed the carpet from his living room and there was a wooden lid; he opened the lid and there was a well. So straightway I proved my credentials, in a sense. He asked me to tell him more about water divining, so I was in my element. Now this friend of mine told the Tutor, 'Khojeste would love to study at Oxford University.' (I had told him what my teachers had said.) Now this man was Senior Tutor for Admissions at St Edmund's Hall, Oxford; he said, 'Oxford prides itself in having unusual characters, and I like you. I am willing to give you admission to my College, provided the basic criteria are met.' Without seeing a scrap of paper! I said, 'But, sir, I am an accountant.' He said, 'That is all right; just find someone who can tutor you at Oxford; if you do I am willing to give you a College place.'

So I thought this was very strange, a week ago I didn't know how I could get up to Oxford, and here a Senior Tutor offers me a place. I told Bulent, and he started laughing, and said, 'Do you think we're such fools that we haven't planned this for you?' Then I became more drawn to this: if doors were opening in the way they were, clearly there was something in it. Then I found out that the man at Oxford I had to convince was Zaehner,[9] whose book I had been given in Shahrud.

Mr Mistree goes on to say that Professor Zaehner took a lot of convincing, as he was not in favour of teaching either accountants or those who were themselves believers; nor did he believe in any link between Zoroastrianism and Sufism. However, other Senior Members of the University, apparently miraculously, came to Mr Mistree's aid and smoothed his path. Moreover, financial support was provided in unexpected and providential ways, so that he was able to commence his studies.

Did you feel some kind of compulsion to do all this?
Yes, by then I knew that accountancy was going to be a fall-back, professionally speaking. Look, so much cannot happen, it cannot be coincidence! I have never said this in such detail, but by then it was very clear that, whatever I personally wanted, in terms of megabucks, a Hampstead home and what have you, it would have to be shelved, because I had to go back to being a student. I had to learn about Zoroastrianism intellectually as opposed to what I was picking up spiritually along the way.

Within a comparatively short period of time Professor Zaehner, who was never very congenial to Mr Mistree, died, and Professor Mary Boyce from London University wrote to Mr Mistree to offer help. Mr Mistree went to see her and he immediately realised that she was going to be his teacher.

A way was eventually found for Professor Boyce to supervise Mr Mistree while he remained based at Oxford. He eventually took his degree.

Didn't you find it strange that all these openings came to you from people who had no connection with Zoroastrianism, and yet they encouraged you to follow Zoroastrianism?

This is probably the most unusual development in my life, namely that rather than from Zoroastrian sources I rediscovered my roots through non-Zoroastrian channels. But had it happened in any other way, I would not have been where I am. I would not have been able to do a hundredth of what, perhaps, I have done. What Oxford did for me was to give me a kind of precision of thought. Spending years working under Professor Boyce with her razor-sharp mind and ruthlessness when it came to the written word, all this trained me in a way which I think is incredibly good. I did not have that in my spiritual development when I went through all the Sufi bits – my mind did not have this preciseness which I would like to believe I now have.

So two things happened, a spiritual development and an intellectual one that prepared you. And then you came to India. Did your Masters tell you that you would now have to work full time in the field of religion, or did that come from within you?

Well, that was a bit odd. I used to come to India quite regularly, once or twice a year. People here in India were surprised and curious; here was a man with an English qualification as an accountant – which was seen as the highest there was – studying religion! Many people thought I was daft, or indeed possessed by some force. I basically came back to India for my grandmother. She was getting old and I was very fond of her. I wanted to stay with her and spend time with her. Having come back with an Oxford degree and chartered accountancy, again the world was at my feet in India. But I was very clearly told in my meditation that I was to spend time in India, and wait and see. This was the time when Alan[10] came to India, and we did a slide show [on Zoroastrianism] together, where we had to call in the police because the crowds were so huge; the talk had to be repeated twice. Soon afterwards James Russell[11] came. These two colleagues were kind of instrumental, both had slightly mystical backgrounds which, as academics, they would never disclose to the outside world. They said, 'Khojeste, why don't you stay in India and train a new generation of your own people?' And it felt right at that stage to start an intensive class. For perhaps two years – my intention was to return to England, where I had lived for about seventeen years and which by then was my home. But then after that you know what happened, I just stayed on here ...

139

How did it feel, the initial adulation which gradually diminished?
I never thought I'd be a religious pop-star – I can truly say I know how it feels to be a guru or a pop-star. As you know, when I first came to India, people would have to make an appointment six or seven weeks in advance to see me. I was invited to on average two dinners a night. From what I can remember the whole of Bombay was absolutely agog – here was a young person talking about religion in a clear and understandable way! But in my spiritual training I knew that this adulation would peter out, and that the real work was to actually train people. So yes, it was exciting while it lasted, being the talk of the town, meeting every prominent Zoroastrian there was to meet. It was unusual for someone who had other options to be so involved with religion. Generally, who studied religion in India then? People who were not able to do well in their secular lives. The priesthood was seen as a no-go vocation. And here was I – young, from England, articulate, an accountant. I did not have to do religion, I did not come from a poor background, and yet I was doing all this! I was an enigma to most people. And of course some people thought I was doing this for some ulterior motive, though I have never understood how one could make megabucks teaching Zoroastrianism, since our society is closed. If I did a Rajneesh thing,[12] say, of course we could take off!

So do you have a feeling of 'mission accomplished' as you had in Shahrud, or is there a sense of disappointment after spending two decades working in religion?
I don't know, a bit of both if I am to be brutally honest. There is part of me which feels like a granddad; given the uniqueness of the experiences Ahura Mazda has given me, I feel that, certainly, an element of my mission has been accomplished. I cannot think of any other comparable figure in the community who has been through the sort of experiences I have had. But I'd be dishonest if I denied that I now sometimes have doubts, and sometimes ask myself, 'Is it worth it,' in terms of what I have done, with the terrible amount of pain and anguish and hostility I've had to face, when all I've tried to do is to teach Zoroastrianism to those who seek it. Of course if I had wanted to start a new cult that would not have been difficult, but my Oxford training and my search for knowledge would not allow me to do that. For me, being faithful to the texts is very important; one might think something, but if one cannot find references in classical Zoroastrianism then one questions it.

I am sure that you get strength from what you have learned. Don't you get any messages telling you to carry on?
Yes, otherwise I'd probably kill myself. I realise that the work I set out to do, or that I was, in inverted commas, 'chosen for', is not a nine-to-five office job. It's an unusual job, it is dealing with people's spiritual well-being. And yes, if one succeeds and one actually helps people

and one sees that glint in the person's eye, that they found what I've said good or helpful, then there is a sense of satisfaction.

Could we go back to your personal religious life. What do you feel about going into a fire temple, about prayers?
You see, my training in one sense is mystical, and therefore I do not see myself as religious in the traditional Parsi mode. I do not for instance sit and pray as much as most ZS ['Zoroastrian Studies'] people do. To me religious experience always happens through communicating with the fire. I get messages, I get insights. I often understand something which I've never read, and one month later I may read it in a text, and wonder how I knew about it in the first instance. To me that is immensely satisfying. So as far as my religious life is concerned, it is humdrum, quite pedestrian, being a Parsi and always feeling very comfortable wearing the *sudreh* and *kusti*, taking part in the basic outer rituals. That feeling has been with me since my days in England, as I did not come from a devout religious background. I think now the ritual influence comes through my studies and through Firoza [his wife]; if Firoza wasn't around I would probably be less of a ritualist than I am today. But to me religion is not rituals *per se*, to me the greatest strength of Zoroastrianism is the intellectual paradigm, which I know something about and which I believe I understand both intellectually and, now, emotionally. So for example, take a ceremony like the *Jashan*. I emotionally experience it while the ceremony is being performed, but I derive much greater strength from intellectually understanding what the *Jashan* is all about: the ceremony which, for example, was celebrated at the moment of creation – then my mind begins to think what this moment of Creation may have been, what the force of divinity may have been at that moment. In other words I don't think of the *Jashan* as 'Let's have some *malido* and fruit,'[13] but more as an alchemical process between the physical and spiritual world. So for me the ritual experience comes through the intellectual paradigm. If you were to ask me if it would be conceivable for me to go to a fire temple straight from work, without having a bath, the answer would be yes. In that sense I have a feeling of oneness with Zoroastrians in Iran, where the ritual form has been lost, but the mystical form has been retained.

PK: *How do you integrate the mystical side of your experiences and the study of classical Zoroastrianism, given that the sources tell us little about a mystical element in Zoroastrianism?*
I cannot tell you how I've integrated it, I just feel comfortable with both. I am very glad to have passed through what I call 'the Boyce sausage machine,' to be pulverised by her in order to get my mind to think in a very precise way. I think this was necessary for me because I

was getting too airy-fairy and 'mystical'. But had the mystical side not happened, and had these amazing things not happened, I would not have been at Oxford University. Today I think there is a sort of recognition of both, perhaps with greater emphasis on the intellectual side. Except when we go to Iran – when I see some special old fires there, and have now been permitted to show these fires to other people,[14] that is a very gratifying, very beautiful, very emotional feeling for me. Like when I take Zoroastrians on trips to Iran – from the world above I have now been given the green light to introduce people to what I had experienced twenty-odd years ago. Which in a sense is a confirmation for me that all I've done over the last twenty, twenty-five years must have been right. Otherwise the doors would not have opened for me to become the teacher of a new generation of people, young and old. A very satisfying thing from the intellectual side is the fact that, through the people I've taught, a new genre of children's religious material has begun to see the light of day. I think when history is written about ZS this certainly will be an important component – people will look at the kind of material we have produced, which is faithful to classical Zoroastrianism but uses 20th century teaching methods. To me that is a very important balance.

But there is still that mystical part of me which remains open. It has to be open, otherwise these fires that we see in Iran, these interesting people we meet there – I don't think would happen, that door would be shut. But, having said that, one comes to the reality of Zoroastrianism in a diasporic sense, and that reality is that Zoroastrians follow orthopraxy without having a clear intellectual understanding why they do so. So their observance of rituals is based on need, whilst my emphasis is more on the intellectual strength and beauty of Zoroastrianism, which most of the community seem to be blissfully oblivious of, or which they see in a negative light. Often I am told, 'Khojeste, you intellectualise the religion too much.' But then when you see priests blindly performing the rituals, when you see Zoroastrians who wear the *sudreh* and *kusti* and go to the fire temple every day, but are downright crooked when they come out of the fire temple, then you begin to ask what is more important, the ritual dimension – going to the fire temple and being an absolute crook – or the intellectual conviction, which gives one the ethical strength of promoting harmony in the world, which is what I see as the bedrock of Zoroastrian spirituality.

SM: *In your life, do you feel that any particular Amesha Spenta or Yazata has had a particular role to play, or is that not part of your understanding of Zoroastrianism.*

To me, because I understand the Amesha Spentas as key principles working together in all that I do, whatever I do in life I always reflect on how the seven Amesha Spentas are working in a given action. But if I am asked to name one Immortal, then it would probably be Vohu Manah [Good Thought or Mind].

But that is Vohu Manah as the concept of the Good Mind, I am talking of Bahman as an Amshaspend.[15] *Would you then place him above all the rest?*
No, because as I said, to me all the seven Amesha Spentas work together. To me that is fundamental to Zoroastrianism. I don't think that over a period of my life one Amesha Spenta has predominated over the others – of course, some may have been misfiring more often than not, while some may be working better for me – but to me it is the composite being of the seven Amesha Spentas giving me Zoroastrian insights.

And talking about fires once again, is there any particular fire which you relate to more than to others, which gives you more mystical inputs or messages than the rest?
O, yes, each fire has its own quality. Clearly I've seen a lot of fires over the last twenty-five years. Some fires make me feel very devotional, others give me a sense of peace and tranquillity. Other fires I feel are genuinely unhappy. They talk to me, the fires, or they communicate with me and I communicate with the fires. But if you are saying, looking at a fire, has any miracle happened to me in India, the answer is no. Maybe my whole life is a kind of miracle, so I cannot distinguish the wood from the trees. But, having said that, there are certain fires one feels more comfortable with. On a spiritual level I would say that some fires I have now experienced in Iran would be my spiritual beacons. In India, the Poona fire at the Sir J.J. Agiary is quite special for me, but maybe that is because I grew up in Poona. The Navsari Atash Behram Fire I feel quite close to as well. The Udwada Fire I am not particularly drawn to – that may sound blasphemous, but it is just not my fire. And then, when one presents oneself before the Holy of Holies and opens oneself spiritually, then I believe that the fire gives you a specific message. Moreover, because I do not want to fall into the category of being a creature of habit as far as fires are concerned, I make a point of visiting different fires in Bombay. With certain practical constraints – there are forty-four sacred fires in Bombay and I haven't made it a point of visiting a new fire temple every week, say. But if I have been going to one fire temple quite regularly, I change that on principle. I don't want going to the fire temple to become an unconscious habit. The experience of visiting a fire temple has to be mystical, has to be special. Now, as I am a family man, some days I might take the family because it is a *hamkara* day, and go to a temple where parking is easy. I also go to the fire temple impulsively as I feel the urge.

Asked how he sees the future of 'Zoroastrian Studies', Mr Mistree says that on the one hand he feels that much has been accomplished and he can leave further development in the hands of those he has trained, but on the other hand he still feels very protective about it:

I see religious education as the key to community survival. If the education is absorbed, then I do not think that issues of conversion and marrying out will remain very important, for most people will not want to marry out in the first place. Ironically, I am really not worked up about the issues that the rest of the community seem to think are important. Conversion is not an issue that makes my blood boil one way or the other. What I see as the prime, most important transfusion or input that we can give the community is good religious education. If we can give that, then the business of marrying out, the business of conversion, the business of housing for Parsis, all that I believe would automatically fall into place. Because if we were able to produce Zoroastrians with a vision, who recognised their religious responsibilities, then it goes without saying that if they made a lot of money they would share it in charity, so charitable flats would automatically be built. Religious education would be well funded. In other words, if we were all a hundred percent Zoroastrians we would have very few problems. And the way to get people, if not to be a hundred percent Zoroastrians then at least to be twenty percent Zoroastrians, is through religious education. Not by going to the fire temple every day, not by doing *Jashans* and *Ijashnes* and *Vendidads* every day, but by somehow opening people's minds through the intellectual paradigm of Zoroastrianism as *versus* the other way, which is that of sheer faith and belief.

For example, if one looks at the Khshnoomists, the Theosophists, or the Christian Scientists or the followers of Sai Baba – none of these traditions or cults have a specific, recognised ideology in terms of being scripturally verifiable. Most Parsis believe in Sai Baba but tell me, what is Sai Baba's religious ideology; what is Sai Baba's theological paradigm? There is none, except 'God is One'. That is the only slogan I see with Sai Baba. Does Sai Baba talk about dualism, or why bad things happen to good people. Does Sai Baba talk about the Amesha Spentas, or about the afterlife? The answer is no! So you have Zoroastrians growing up with a faith-based paradigm, which is belief in terms of what you emotionally experience without in any way polishing your mind. And I believe that what is most important is that we have to polish our minds to be able to become better Zoroastrians.

Over the last twenty years, 'Zoroastrian Studies', with its creative teaching methods, has trained hundreds if not thousands of children and young adults. We think that the future of the community lies in creating religious awareness anchored in scholastic studies. Which is what ZS has pioneered!

———

DR JEANNIE BHARUCHA

Dr Jeannie Bharucha (1933) is a medical doctor. She comes from a priestly family but married a layman; she is now a widow with an adopted son. In the course of her life she rediscovered the importance of religion and gave up part of her medical practice to do volunteer work for 'Zoroastrian Studies'; she is now one of the mainstays of that organisation. The present author and his wife attended the interview.

Asked by Mrs Munshi to introduce herself, Dr Bharucha says:

> I practise medicine part-time, but my real love in life is my religion, to practise my religion and to study it. Initially I had a full-time practice till I met Khojeste Mistree, then I got involved with his lectures, took his course for training teachers in the religion, and since then I have never looked back. I have never been sorry for having given up my full-time practice.

Dr Bharucha goes on to say that religion has always been part of her life. She does not think any one figure in her childhood was of special importance in this respect, but the fact that she came from a priestly family probably helped. As a child she lived in a joint family, where her grandmother was the matriarch. All family members were devout and practising Zoroastrians:

> The first thing my grandmother told me is that I was a Zoroastrian and therefore I had to be extra-careful in what I thought, in what I said and what I did, because as a Zoroastrian I had to be more careful that I always spoke good and did good. That is the first thing I remember. From then on it was more a way of life for me, seeing my people practise the religion, seeing my people teaching me the prayers, starting with the *Ashem Vohu* and *Yatha Ahu Vairyo* ... They said that I should pray, the reason I was given was that it was for my own spiritual good; that if I wanted to know God better the prayers would help me. But as a child let me tell you I was not very fond of praying, for somehow praying in a language I did not understand I found boring. But since I had implicit faith in what my people told me I used to pray. I accepted it. And I was told right from the beginning, especially by my father, that God was like a friend to me. That if I had any troubles, God would help me, but then I must listen to what God tells me, and what God tells me is to be good. This is basically when I

was a very small child. I remember that, as a child, I used to be afraid of the dark and I always asked my mother to sit by my bedside till I fell asleep, or to leave the light on. And I remember my father telling me once, when my mother or my aunt could not come, he told me, 'If you are afraid of anything in your life, you have the best protection of all, which even your mother or your aunt or I, no one can give you; that protection comes from Ahura Mazda, you just call upon Him, you just recite the *Yatha Ahu Vairyo* prayer, and you'll be safe, your fears will go!' As a child I always believed implicitly what I was told by grown-ups, and I said, 'OK, I'd like to put it into practice.' And the next time I was afraid, I said the *Yatha Ahu Vairyo* prayer. I must have been five or six years old. And somehow, for whatever reason, psychological reason, I no longer felt afraid. And from that day till this day I have never been afraid of the dark. That strengthened my faith in my religion, and I learned to talk to God in my own way – not necessarily through prayers, but in my own way. If I had done something naughty I would go to Him and say, 'I am very sorry, please forgive me. But please help me, I was in a bad situation (if I had told a lie and knew I would be in trouble for it), please help me!' And somehow I always felt that He saw me through, I always had the strength to face whatever the consequences were.

Dr Bharucha's mother belonged to a well-known priestly family from Navsari, and all the males in her family had been initiated into the priesthood, her father being *Navar* and *Martab*.[16] None of them actually practised as professional priests, however, as they had demanding secular jobs. Still, those family rituals which could be done at home were performed by Dr Bharucha's father. There was a special prayer room for such purposes:

During the Muktads the room would be emptied out completely and the Muktads used to be done at home, all the prayers except for those obligatory prayers done in the Fire Temple complex, like the *Baj* ceremony, the Muktad prayers [i.e. rituals] were done at home by my own people. I used to feel it was a very joyous occasion, I used to help my mother and my aunt to clean out that room, to sweep it and paint one corner with whitewash and so on. I suppose I was more in the way than helping, but it was a lot of fun. Then we would string a white bedsheet across the ceiling and in the corner where the floor and walls had been whitewashed we would put the Muktad ... it was not really a table, it was a tripod. So we would have the table under the canopy of the bedsheet, and I used to help preparing that table, in the sense of washing out the vases, filling them with water, as I was told to do it, saying *Khshnaothra Ahurahe Mazdao* [a prayer formula] and *Ashem Vohu* three times and rinsing it out three times. All that I was taught as a child. Of course I could not do anything without having a bath first and wearing clean clothes and, once my Navjote was done, after doing my *kusti* ritual. Only then would I be allowed to enter that room. And we used to keep that room with white curtains on the windows and doors, and the door was more or less kept shut, so that anybody passing by who was not a Zoroastrian could not come in inadvertently, and look at the Muktad things.

As a child I was very fascinated by this room, I could not understand why, I could not describe why, but there was something like a magnet drawing me to that room. If I were in the house I would sneak up on that room when the Muktads were on. I would just go in quietly and sit on one of the metal chairs (because only metal chairs were provided in that room) and just keep on looking at the flower arrangements and the water, and of course [there was] the fragrance of the sandalwood and the *loban*, looking at the *divo*. Nothing else, I did not pray, I did not do anything but I used to come away feeling very happy. So much so that if I got up in the middle of the night I would go to that room, just sit there for some time, and go back to bed. I was told that during the Muktads the souls of the dear departed come down at that time; they are with us, they are visiting us. And my grandmother told me the reason I felt happy in that room was because I am with people I know, and who know me. I never had any fear of the dead like some people have. I was told that when somebody dies they do not really die, they go into the spiritual world, a world that we cannot see but they can see us. And if we are good and if we ask them to help us, they'll always come down to help us. That we should not grieve because they are not really gone.

Discipline was very strict in Dr Bharucha's family. Her grandmother would go around with a cane in her hand, and if Dr Bharucha was caught coming out of the toilet without doing her *kusti* she could expect 'one whack on the shin, where it hurt the most.' She would know perfectly well that she had offended, but as she regarded God mostly as a friend she would just say, 'Please God forgive me. Please allow me for once not to do my prayers.' She felt that was enough.

I was also told that I should have a bath every day, keep myself clean, not to walk barefoot anywhere no matter what. Because I was told about Good and Evil, in the sense that Good comes from God, and that Evil is a monster to be feared, to be kept away and not to be indulged. That God will not be able to help me if I listen to the Evil One, to Ahriman. And that if I walk barefoot then through the dirt on the floor Ahriman will get into my body and make me do bad things.[17] And basically I was a coward as a child and I just said, 'Forget it, I don't want Ahriman coming into my body!'

And one thing that was always stressed is that as a Zoroastrian I had to speak the truth no matter what the consequences would be. If I have done a wrong I must be brave enough to take the punishment for it. Whatever happens I must not lie. I was told that if I lied, sooner or later I would be punished even more than if I spoke the truth and took the consequences immediately. Not that I never lied, but when I lied I would say to God, 'Please Dadarji [Creator] forgive me this once, don't let Ahriman punish me.' I had my own internal dialogue with God, which to this day I continue in my own way, in a different way, but in my own way.

The laws of purity were strictly observed in Dr Bharucha's family, at least in the house. However, when she had reached puberty she rebelled to a certain extent, and some compromises were found. She was no longer confined to one room during her period, for example, but it was still forbidden for her to touch anything associated with religion, or indeed most things in the house. She could not help herself to food and had to be served by others; she could not touch her parents except when she absolutely had to; nor could she go into the prayer room or into the kitchen, where a hearth fire was kept. She was not allowed to come close to anyone who was praying or doing their *kusti* and she had to use separate school books. She was told that Ahriman had brought this upon her, and she was therefore impure. If she were to pray the words would go to Ahriman who would just destroy them, so she should not pray.

I remember rebelling and telling my parents, 'This is the time when we need protection most because we are already under attack by Ahriman, so why aren't we allowed to pray?' The only answer I got was, 'Mazda knows you are doing it for Him, He will take care of you.' Not a logical answer, I grant you, but still it was an answer.

Asked if she was told that she was under the special protection of one of the Yazads, whom she should venerate particularly, Dr Bharucha says:

No, not that one was to be venerated more than the others. I was told about the Amesha Spentas, I was told about the Yazatas and I was told that each one will help me in different ways; like if I wanted to be successful and pass my exams I should think of Behram Yazad, if I wanted to learn more in my studies I should think of Ava Ardvisur. I was told that if I kept myself clean and pure and was essentially a good girl, then I would always be in the care of Sarosh Yazata, I was also told that on Bahman *mahino* Bahman *roj* ... there was a particular custom that my mother made me practise. Before putting me to bed at night I was given a bath with milk and rose petals. She would then make me wear absolutely clean white clothes. I was told, 'Now think of Bahman Ameshaspand and go to sleep.' Bahman would take care of me, take care of my mind, so that I would wake up the next morning thinking and experiencing only what was good. My mother used to say, 'Bahman Ameshaspand will come in your dreams. But you must go to sleep asking him to come to you and you must go to sleep with good thoughts. For if you harbour anything that is not good, any resentment or anger, then he will not come near you.' I have never heard of anyone else doing this, but this is what I was brought up with and I remember it very vividly.[18]

When Dr Bharucha grew up she began to question much of what she had been told. She noticed that good people were not always rewarded, and discussions in the community about proper Zoroastrian belief and practice made her wonder what was true. Some said that, after a brief spell in heaven or hell, one came back again to earth after death since one life was not enough to become perfect, whereas others denied this. Again, some Parsis advocated vegetarianism and said that meat was impure and evil; others held no such views. Dr Bharucha's family could not give satisfactory answers, and she started attending lectures on Zoroastrianism, like those of the late Dastur Dabu.[19]

Dasturji Dabu, quoting from the *Gathas*, emphatically said that there is reincarnation. And just as I was beginning to believe, 'Yes, there must be reincarnation,' in the same talk Dasturji Unvala[20] stood up and challenged him, challenged him in no uncertain terms. So I was left totally confused! I said, 'Who is right?' So then I said to myself, 'Drop the matter, one person says one thing, one person says something else. If I cannot find the true answer, what Zarathustra has actually told us, then I am not going to accept the matter.' If you had asked me at that time about my beliefs in vegetarianism or reincarnation, I would have said, 'I have no beliefs, I don't believe in reincarnation, I don't believe in resurrection, I believe in nothing! In a sense I believe that there is a heaven and hell, further than that I don't know.' As far as vegetarianism was concerned I compromised. As Bahman *roj* was supposed to be for the animals, that day and all the days of the *hamkars* I would observe a vegetarian diet, and the whole of Bahman month also. So I was trying to play safe, have it both ways, [thinking]: I don't know whether there is or there isn't, at least let me do this much. That is how it was going on. Then I heard some Ilm-e Khshnoom people talking, things that actually seemed ridiculous to my mind, like when they said, 'Zoroastrians are the best people in the world, and you don't reincarnate when you are a Zoroastrian.'[21] And I said, 'What happens if you are a bad Zoroastrian? How can they just go to heaven and stay there? They are still bad. They may be Zoroastrians, but ... ' And then I said, 'As far as I know God, He is a very fair God, a very just God, so how can bad people go to heaven?'

And of course I heard from various sources that all religions are one. Again that would not jell in my mind. 'If all religions are one why do we call God by different names? And why are only Zoroastrians made aware that there is a law of purity to be observed. Why is it that everyone else can go barefoot, why aren't we allowed to do it?' So those were the questions in my mind, and I wasted years not knowing about them. I just basically kept practising the faith out of devotion to Mazda, in my own way. But wherever I had doubts I would leave it, for I did not take anybody's answer as the truth. I must have wasted the better part of my youth in that way. I was well into my thirties when I first heard Khojeste. What he said appealed to my reason; what impressed me most were the references he gave from various scriptures, books I had never even heard of. The way he spoke about the religion was so logical. Some of the references he gave I would enquire into, and I found that he was right. So I made it a point to attend most of his lectures. But when he spoke of Good and Evil, something happened. 'He says that God is not all-powerful, what is he talking about? How can God not be all-powerful?' That set my mind thinking, 'All right, if God is all-powerful, why doesn't he destroy Ahriman? If God is all-powerful, why is there so much evil in this world?' So all this was brewing in my mind, and then Khojeste mentioned that he wanted to teach a batch of students in depth, so they could in turn become teachers. Of course you had to fulfil certain conditions, fill up a form, go for an interview, write an essay ... I immediately jumped at the chance, I went through the whole course, and it completely changed my life.

As a doctor, Dr Bharucha has often experienced the power of prayer, most strikingly on two occasions:

A patient came to me regularly to get B-complex injections. She came one afternoon and I gave her a shot. Suddenly she slid to the floor unconscious. She had no pulse, no blood pressure, and I was absolutely petrified! My immediate reaction was, 'Mazda help! Mazda, Mazda, Mazda!' That was all I could say. I tried all sorts of things but I could not even push an injection into her veins, they just would not take it. I tried cardiac massage, nothing happened. All the time I was saying Mazda's name, I was so panicky that I could not say any prayers, I could only say 'Mazda'. Then, I knew that Sarosh Yazata was the Yazata for souls,[22] so I started saying, 'Please Sarosh Yazata, give her back to me, let her live,' that sort of thing, you know. And, just like that, suddenly my assistant said, 'Madam, come!' I put my stethoscope on her chest, I heard one thud. Nothing more. After some time, another thud! Oh, my God, honestly, it was like making a dead person come alive again. She had come to me at 4.30 in the afternoon, and by the time I heard the first thud it was 7 o'clock. And to this day, inside me – it is my truth, people may say what they like, but me, I know: Mazda answered my prayers; Sarosh Yazata answered my prayers. If it had not been for them I would have lost that patient.

I had a very bad heart case who was also a cancer patient; his heart was very erratic from time to time. One day I got a phone call saying that he had had another attack and I should come over. I went there, and the heart was fibrillating, that is, going so fast you cannot count the beats, and the person more or less passes out. The pulse was very very fast, I gave the usual standard injections and so on, [but] it would not come under control! I was at my wits end; it was going from bad to worse, the patient was beginning to turn blue. And I said, 'What else can I give?' I was talking to Mazda, and something told me to empty out my box of injections, so I emptied it out on the bed. Sorting through the phials, I invariably picked up a particular phial which I knew would not work in this case, which I knew would be wrong to give. So I put it aside, went trough the phials again and picked up the same injection. This happened three times, and then something made me think, 'I am taking Mazda's name and I am picking up this phial.' And I said in my mind, 'Mazda, please take care, please take care of me!' I opened the phial and gave the injection. Within five minutes the heart settled down, the patient recovered. My prayers were answered again. To this day I believe in this: there is nothing that is not possible if one asks for Mazda's help (of course if it is a good thing). That is how my faith got strengthened ...

Dr Bharucha went on to talk about her internal dialogue with Mazda:

I cannot remember any time when I was indifferent to God. He has been with me from the time I was born, the first conscious thought I had. Since then Mazda and I have been sort of, you know ... To this day I talk to him, sometimes I get irritated and say, 'Come on, Mazda, enough is enough!' You know, in that sort of way. I don't feel I am blaspheming, He knows what is in my heart. I can joke about Him, talk about Him but, I don't know, I feel very close to Him.

Dr Bharucha's husband was also very religious, and he made her pray regularly:

You see, right up to the time I got married my prayers were restricted to doing the *kusti*, doing the *Sarosh Baj*, the *Dinno Kalmo*, the *Tandorosti* prayer, and the 101 Names of Ahura Mazda.[23] My excuse was – I knew I was making excuses – 'Where is the time? I've got so much to study, there is no time.' I believed implicitly in prayers, yes, but the motivation to pray ... Basically as I said I used to feel bored praying, and I was always told that one should pray with one's mind on one's prayers and invariably my mind would stray from the prayers. So I used to tell Mazda, whenever I would pray these basic prayers, I would start out saying 'Mazda, I am praying, please take it. I mean every word of what I am reciting.' Not knowing any words, of course, I had that sort of complete faith in the prayers. But I did not like to recite lengthy prayers. And then soon after I got married I got an allergic rash on my skin, which would not go whatever I tried. I tried allopathy, I tried homeopathy, I tried Ayurvedic medicine, it just would not go! So finally I gave up trying anything at all. Now as a student my husband shared his hostel with a man who later became a Mobed, Peshotan Anklesaria, who did a Doctorate in Avestan later on, he was the head of the Madressa in Andheri.[24] So my husband went to see him. In fact I had told my husband, 'I am taking no more treatment, Mazda has to cure me for the treatment is not working. You find out what prayers I should say.' So he asked his friend, and Peshotan Anklesaria told him to tell me daily to recite the *Ardibehesht, Hom* and *Vanant Yashts*. So I took his word for it, and from that day I started reciting, and with the *nirang* of each of these Yashts I did the *pichi*.[25] I would do it on my skin, on my hands and then on my legs. Believe you me, I had stopped all treatment for more than two months before I started the prayers. Then in a month's time my skin began to clear, nothing new appeared and the old lesions began to dry out. By the time two months had passed not even a stain was left on my skin. And that somehow told me that just talking to Mazda, just being close to Mazda, was not enough, I must pray! Since that day I got motivated to pray.

Initially Dr Bharucha only knew a limited number of prayers but as time went on she often felt inspired to start reciting a new prayer. When asked how long it now takes her to pray, Dr Bharucha first giggles and says that it depends, but later in the conversation she mentions needing a minimum of two hours each morning. She cannot pray in a crowd, though, and prefers to pray at home on *parab* days when many Zoroastrians meet and pray together.

When Dr Bharucha's husband was critically ill, she refused to accept that he would not recover. When he did die, she broke down for a minute at first:

I allowed the tears to flow. And as I was crying I thought, 'Why am I crying? This damned Ahriman has already taken a life. I'll not make him happy by crying.'[26] And just like that my tears dried ... But I had that awful hollow feeling inside me, and all I could do was to say, 'Mazda! Please Mazda, now what?' And somehow, after his body was taken into the *Dakhme* [Tower of Silence], that awful feeling just dropped! I told Khojeste at the time, 'I was feeling totally miserable, but now I am feeling at peace.'

So his death did not shake your faith?

No, not at all, in fact it made it stronger! I don't know where I found it within myself, but instead of becoming a broken-down wreck I was able to build my life all over again, and in fact I am stronger today than I was when my husband was alive ...

And today I know that my religion is my backbone. Without it I would collapse. If I did not have Mazda and the spiritual world around me all the time, guiding me, helping me, saving me very often from myself, I would not be able to live. For me, life is synonymous with Mazda!

MS KHURSHEED KHURODY

Ms Khursheed N. Khurody (1966) is a cosmopolitan Parsi lady. She was educated largely in Britain and the U.S., but was living in Bombay with her father and grandmother at the time of the interview. She is well known in the Zoroastrian community for her many talents, both intellectual and artistic.

Mrs Munshi begins the interview by asking Ms Khurody to introduce herself. Ms Khurody says:

I grew up here in Bombay until I was about nine years old, in a relatively international Parsi family. My parents were both educated overseas, though they had returned to India. We did not particularly grow up in an orthodox Parsi setting, using the term orthodox in the sense of 'traditional', though we did observe the main Parsi festivals and holidays in a relatively moderate way, such as a visit to the Agiary for New Year or Papeti, maybe a traditional Parsi lunch on festive days, but not much else. Soon afterwards, at the age of about ten, my younger sister and I were sent off to boarding school for about eleven months in India, and then for ten years in the UK, because our parents were transferred to the Middle East, where proper schooling was not available. This time in England was followed in my case by University in San Francisco; then I went on to Harvard Graduate School in Boston. And when I had just finished that programme I returned to India in June 1997 because my mother was critically ill, and sadly I lost her. Since then I have been here in India, at least temporarily.

Mrs Munshi asks how it is that, after such a long time abroad and so much exposure to Western influences, Ms Khurody still has strong emotional bonds with Zoroastrianism; she wonders whether Ms Khurody's grandparents were influential in this respect. That, however, proves not to have been the case:

My grandparents actually had very little influence, because they followed almost no Zoroastrian practices, except of course social practices which are required if you don't want to be out of place, such as wearing the appropriate sari at weddings and meeting on appropriate feast days. Apart from that, there is certainly no one in my family who followed any of these things. But I think the single largest factor that made me keep a hold on my roots were my visits to Bombay once a year over the past twenty years or so, and visiting Parsi families for one reason or another, relatives and friends – and starting to get a feel for Parsi culture gradually and taking to it primarily because of the warmth. For my sister and myself, who were struggling in an alien country far away almost on our own, the warmth of Parsi households is what drew me to Parsi-ism, if I could coin that term. And from there I started picking up small things, like the daily practice of putting chalk outside [the front door], and I gradually incorporated that in our own home – that was followed by lighting a *divo*, then by more frequent visits the Agiary, popping in to see all Parsis congregate at the time of Muktad prayers. So little by little it grew – mostly because that was the environment that gave loving care, which is what children need, and we lacked that a lot in boarding school. Then it became a matter of curiosity and interest; and then it became an intellectual pursuit, I started reading books, going to classes, learning the symbolism of things properly instead of just practising them blindly. So that is how the whole thing grew.

So the search was entirely your own, it had nothing to do with parental influence or family background?
No, absolutely nothing. The other thing that helped to spark off my journey into Zoroastrianism were the frequent questions [about my religion] – by school-mates, fellow students, professors, teachers. At first I had no idea, I was way out in the English countryside, there wasn't a Zoroastrian in sight, I never met a Zoroastrian in my ten years in England. Then in San Francisco, at that stage I was a little older and I started to meet more Zoroastrian families and I realised that, being a Zoroastrian overseas, I really did not know anything. So I was not much help to either my own community or to those around me, I could not stick up for my own culture because I did not know much about it. And the sense of being slightly ashamed put me into gear. That is how I started my whole journey.

Ms Khurody's Navjote was done together with that of her sister, and each stage of the proceedings was photographed by a well-known professional and later published in the *National Geographic.*

Pains were taken to ensure that everything was done exactly right. I remember we had one High Priest and another senior priest

154

performing our Navjote together, in this very house, according to the old custom of aristocratic Parsi families, where funerals, Navjotes and weddings are always done at home. That was done in our sort of families, old families, it is also done in the M family who live downstairs. When old Mrs M died last year, her funeral was done at home. One of the last Parsi funerals where they walked the body all the way up to *Doongerwadi*.

So the Navjote was done in that tradition, which gave my father a lot of control over the ceremony. There were very few guests, about a hundred is all our living room can accommodate, the reception was held later – and there was pin-drop silence throughout the prayers. My parents prided themselves on that, because they believe it is a religious rite. In a *Baug*[27] frequently everyone is so caught up in the glamour of the food and the music and the noise and everything else that follows afterwards, that they are distracted from the ceremony itself. None of that happened in our home, the ceremony was very quiet and very sacred.

What impression did it make on you, apart from all the excitement – were things explained to you?
Nothing was explained about the meaning of the rituals, but I was told very clearly what to do. There were rose petals and I think a little milk, and we were also taught our [Navjote] prayers extremely well. I did not understand the symbolism of the Navjote, but what was really dinned into us was that this was a very sacred ceremony, and we were urged to keep very quiet and not to fidget. It was impressed upon us that after this ceremony life would change, we'd be adults in our own right and we would carry a moral responsibility as Zoroastrians from that time onwards. That was rather unnerving but it did cause us to take it very seriously.

Did life really change for you as far as religion was concerned?
Not really, definitely not. Like all children we were told to do our *sudreh* and *kusti* regularly, and then when we went back to school it waned. My sister dropped it completely, I did it whenever I felt like it or when I came to India and had to be in a religious setting. You have to have your parents behind you to push you, otherwise I think children tend to drop it. Fortunately as I said I had other reasons to make me take it up again much later at College.

So you are saying that there was a period when wearing the sudreh and kusti and reciting the prayers had no attraction for you, and that later it grew as you began to search for yourself?
It did not have much meaning during my teens, at the time of Secondary School, High School, but towards the end of High School,

when I began to apply for Colleges, it took on a greater meaning. I never gave up *sudrehs*, though, that is something I clung to – largely because it was something sacred, something given to me by my Mummy, something from home. So I always wore *sudrehs* though not always the *kusti*. So in some strange way the *sudreh* did have a hold on me, although I did not have a hold on what it all meant.

At this stage of the interview, Ms Khurody says that another factor to draw her towards Zoroastrianism was her early fascination with the sound of the chanting of Avestan. Ms Khurody is a talented musician and sounds mean much to her. She used to be one of the few children who were able to sit still during rituals, because she was captivated by the sound of the chanting.

So gradually that [the chanting] grew on me much as a concerto or a symphony would grow on me, and drove me to want to be able to sing the prayers in the same way. When I was a child it was never enough to just listen to music, I had to go and fiddle with the piano and work it out for myself, and it is the same with Zoroastrianism, it is not enough just to sit and listen to the prayers, the sound is very captivating and I have to take part in it. That is what I am doing now, learning how to chant them and how to say them.

Ms Khurody also appreciates the sounds of other religious traditions, but only Zoroastrian prayers give her the feeling that they belong to her. The discussion then turns to Ms Khurody's family history. Apart from memories of the many achievements and the impressive charity of her ancestors, there are also family anecdotes. About her maternal grandfather Ms Khurody says:

There are many stories about Grandpa. For example, he was in charge of the Towers of Silence, and I was repeatedly told that – much to the horror of many people – he was one of the first if not *the* first Trustee to physically walk into the Tower and to clean everything up – just for the sake of hygiene he went in there.[28] He was also the first, I think, who had the *nasesalars* and the other pall-bearers to tea,[29] and made sure that their basic needs were taken care of. This was highly respected in his time and I think still is, he was a very forward-looking person, though I am sure also frowned upon by many Parsis who consider it a no-no to be in touch with people who are in touch with the dead.

Discussing the differences between herself, who has kept her emotional bonds with India and with Parsi culture, and her sister, who has become completely assimilated to English culture, Ms Khurody says:

In my case there is a tremendous emotional bond with India. This has kept me in contact with the smell of *sukhad*, which never left my sensibility, or walking into a house where I knew I would be really loved simply because it had chalk outside, that kept me going, and kept me clinging, for I felt more threatened by the alien culture. So I kept holding on to threads, whereas she let go. People tell me that, when we are much older, she may want to come back to her roots. I have not come to that stage of my life, so I don't know.

Mrs Munshi then asks about the observance of the laws of purity in Ms Khurody's youth and nowadays.

Laws of purity, if interpreted as [rules about] childbirth, menstruation, bathrooms – things like that were certainly not followed in my generation, though both my grandmothers followed that when they were young girls. But my sister and I, when we had our periods we were just like any other child, we stayed in the same house and most of the time my parents did not even know. So nothing was done in that sense, ever. Now, though, because of my intellectual grasp of dualism, and my understanding of a very simple system of checks and balances, credits and debits, which is how I see it – everything that is impure feeds the left-hand column and everything that is pure and light feeds the right-side column – so as I have a clear understanding of dualism and a strong sense of the distinction between the right and the left as I see it, I myself do observe the laws of purity. But I am careful not to thrust them on my family, because we are still very young and it is a bit odd for me to be teaching my father and grandmother to observe the rules of purity, it would not go down well, and it is certainly not going to influence them. But on my own and with the servants I do see to it that these things are observed, within intelligent limits, within reason, without having any staunch rules. For example one of the servants lights a *divo* in the morning, when she has her period she hands over to the head maid, if the head maid should also have her period she hands over to me. It is the same with chalk, and I have also introduced another thing, at 6 o'clock in the evening the *afargan*[30] is taken around the house. It began slowly with chalk, it took a year, a year and a half, because my parents felt it was making more work for the servants. But now that is established, and it was followed by the *divo*, which is also well established now, and slowly, over the past couple of years I have started the *afargan* at 6 o'clock. I am a very good diplomat in some things, for I explained to the family that it kept the mosquitoes away, so they look at it from their point of view and I look at it from my theological point of view, and we are happy with things like that. Similarly with menstruation, I observe it myself and I kind of enforce it with the servants and we respect each other's wishes. Fortunately I don't have to impose that on my father. When I tell him that I would rather not go to the Agiary with him, or to his

Company *Jashan* because I have my period, there are time when he scowls at me because he has always seen me as a rational, intelligent young woman who has grown up in the West, and he finds it a little odd that I have gone back to what he thinks is an archaic practice. But still, I do observe them.

There is another interesting thing, my family are ultra-paranoid about tidiness and hygiene at the personal level. I don't think they have paid any attention to the fact that this is actually a very Zoroastrian thing, the sense of Order is very Zoroastrian ... chaos is the opposite to what a Zoroastrian should desire. So that has been established for reasons that really have nothing to do with Zoroastrianism but now, because of my knowledge, I realise how Zoroastrian it is. That helps me to keep to it even more. Now keeping order in the various aspects of my life has a totally new meaning for me.

Having so recently returned to live in India, Ms Khurody still has difficulty with some everyday aspects of Parsi culture, like wearing a sari, speaking Gujarati and eating Parsi food, but she hopes to get used to these things with the help of Parsi friends.

Ms Khurody then describes how she had her first 'very own' *Jashan* performed when her parents came to visit her in her first student's apartment in San Francisco. By that time she was also beginning to feel more confident about explaining Zoroastrian observances to outsiders, such as fellow students and teachers. She goes on to describe her discovery of Zoroastrianism:

I started my study of Zoroastrianism with very basic things, history, social customs. Then I went on to theology, the theory of dualism. Then I moved into slightly more technical things, what the *Gathas* say, and the *Vendidad*, actual textual references. Now I am moving into more complex things, like the significance of rituals and higher rituals – now here what has personally affected me in the last few months is that I have established things for myself, like going to the Agiary more often. I actually make it a point to go when something intellectually fascinating is going on, like the *Nirangdin* and *Ijashne* ceremonies, which are so rare now. I try to attend those things. I took a great interest in the period of Muktad last August, and had my mother's whole Muktad done at home, where for the first time in my life I swept her entire bedroom, bathroom and everything.[31] For a whole ten days I got up very very early, in the wee hours of the morning, to be able to hold this ritual according to the Zoroastrian tradition and as the priests would wish, doing everything they would wish me to do, failing which they would not have agreed to do it in the house.

A lot of that has become something I don't just *do*, but which I now *am*.

158

What about prayers, do you say any special prayers?
I say my *kusti* prayers twice a day normally, in the mornings and in
the evenings. I have also adopted a special *kusti* for the days I am
having my period, and Mummy's *kusti* for the other days. I do say
my *kusti* prayers. And, out of my own interest and my intellectual
love of the logic of Zoroastrianism and its rationalism and dualism,
I have taken all this as my own and wish to use it by becoming
India's first para-mobed.[32] So I work on chapters of prayers, and I
am about to graduate from a course taught by Zoroastrian Studies,
by Jeannie Bharucha, which is an academic course on rituals,
customs, theology, history, etcetera. From there I'll move to the
Madressa[33] and actually physically be taught how to do the
ceremonies. How to tend the fires, how to recite the prayers, how
to coordinate both. Now that I have the intellectual backing and I
know what I am doing, I'd like actually to take part in our rituals
instead of just being an observer.

*That is very interesting, about you becoming the first woman para-mobed. Do
you really see this happening within, say, the next two years?*
Well, I see it happening within the next few months, if I can get my act
together in sheer terms of homework. I do a fair amount of dancing,
am training to dance professionally; I play the piano, which I also
hope to do professionally; I love to write; I am running my Mummy's
business – apart from all these different things if I can give enough
hours to my Zoroastrian studies, as I hope to do, then maybe by the
late summer I'll have finished the course. My goal is to take part and
perform during the next Muktad period; I hope to be able to do the
Satum prayers, and I have started asking around for families who will
employ me to do their prayers next August.

Have you had any response?
Oh yes, I have had people asking me to do Navjotes, and to do *Jashans*,
which I have gladly accepted because a *Jashan* is something I am
technically allowed to do. Some people have said I could do their
Satum prayers, but I haven't yet had the confidence to say yes to a
Navjote. First of all because I am not sure it is within the realm of what
I will be allowed to do, and second because I am not even sure I'll
finish the homework for it, in terms of knowing how to perform the
ceremony. But I am pretty sure I will have finished *Baj*, *Satum* and
Jashans.[34] If I can even do that much, and the basic Muktad prayers,
the *Afrinagan* and *Farokhshi* prayers this summer, that is a quarter or
half the battle won, and then I can take the rest little by little. Since I
am the only girl and there are no formal courses [for girls], I am
structuring my own course.

159

Are you learning the prayers by rote?
No, I will not learn the prayers by rote, for it would take a very very long time. And considering there are a lot of little boys at the Madressa today who read from a book, I think I will do the same, because it is more important for me to master quantity at this point, to master four ceremonies instead of just one. I don't want to be a pianist who plays only Mozart, I want to play a fair repertoire, and the same in Zoroastrianism. I'd like to be able to do the *Farokhshi, Afrinagan, Jashan* all by the summer. If I have to grasp all that on top of what Jeannie is teaching me about the symbolism and meaning of Zoroastrianism, as well as all my other activities, I think learning things by rote comes at the bottom of the list. I don't think there is any sin or crime in looking at the book if I need to.

Have you had any personal experiences where prayer helped you at difficult times in your life?
That is an interesting question. I am not sure I can answer that; I am told that this is because I am still young, that the experience of what personal prayers can do is something that comes with age. Maybe that is true, because I cannot honestly say that at times of stress – exam time or crisis time, or even during the worst time of my life, when I was graduating from Harvard, trying to have a career and watching my Mum die of cancer all at the same time, when nothing really seemed to help – I cannot say that saying prayers all day long was something that really helped me, or even that I went as far as saying prayers all day long, because I didn't have faith enough that that would help me.

But there are people, like Khojeste [Mistree], who say that there are rituals during which you can actually transform and you experience another state of being – the metaphysics, the paranormal, that is something I haven't honestly experienced as yet in my soul. I have experienced a lot intellectually, and it has not just stuck in the brain, it has certainly flowed to the heart in the sense that my prayers and rootedness have given me a strong sense of confidence. I have never toppled [broken down], for instance, and I know that people like me, who are highly emotional, artistic and very highly strung, tend to topple one way or another. I can safely say that this has not happened because of a deep sense of faith, so yes, up to that level I have experienced something deep down in my soul, but no other paranormal transformations.

Mrs Munshi then asks if Ms Khurody is particularly attached to any special fire or fire temple. Ms Khurody answers that she began her explorations of fire temples in much the same spirit as she would approach a new museum, being guided by a sense of atmosphere and beauty. She therefore does like some fire temples better than others, but for aesthetic rather than devotional or spiritual reasons. Ms Khurody says that she has never 'seen something in the fire' that gave her a special feeling about a fire temple. She has, however, had some experiences at Udwada which, she says, may not have meant anything at all but which she feels were supernatural. Once she went there to pray for a man who means much to her; her parents were with her and she had already lit fifteen *divas* on their behalf and her own. When she came to light the sixteenth for her friend, however, she sustained slight burns in exactly the same place where her friend had once spilt hot coffee over her wrist. Some three weeks after that, acquaintances telephoned to ask her to come to Udwada with them; normally Ms Khurody is too busy to accept such invitations, but this time she accepted without hesitation although she did not know why. When she arrived at Udwada a friend of Ms Khurody's friend, about whom he had often spoken to her, walked into the Atash Behram. Because of those experiences the Udwada fire is special to her.

> *Do you have a special affinity with any of the Yazatas or Amesha Spentas?*
> Not at all. The Amesha Spentas and Yazatas are still something very intellectual for me; I haven't yet evolved to a stage or level of being able to feel them, and make them something of the soul – like my friendship with Ahura Mazda, which I feel is very strong. But as far as the Amesha Spentas are concerned I am still very much concerned with the intellectual side, the structure [of the group of Amesha Spentas], their functions in Zoroastrianism, how they are represented during a *Jashan* and how we invoke them at the time of prayers. But it is still very much an intellectual interest, it has not yet filtered through to the personal.

The conversation then turns back to Parsi customs and traditional observances. In that context Ms Khurody mentions her downstairs neighbours, in whose household many of the old customs are still faithfully followed:

> P is for me the archetypal Parsi lady; there is always chalk, and it is exactly proportional to the days of the calendar, very festive on festive days, and very sober for a whole year after her mother's death. They eat exactly the right kind of Parsi food, she won't even step into an Agiary unless she has washed her hair. She does her *divo* two or three times a day, prays for many hours – they are very loving people, and as my father is home so little they have had a huge influence on my sister and me.
>
> A year and a half ago P's mother passed away at the age of ninety. I remember waking up one morning and my Mummy said, 'M Aunty

was very bad last night, she is sinking'. Being very young and never having dealt with death before I kept well away, though my grandmother was down all day long, and I was aware that people were coming in and out of their apartment all any long to be by her bedside as she died. So again I observed all the things going on down there purely from an intellectual viewpoint, but it was amazing for me. At about 3.30 in the afternoon my father took my sister and me out to do some shopping and when we came back we were informed by the watchman that she had passed away. A little later furniture started coming into our house, chairs, dining tables, our entire living room was full because theirs was being emptied. Parsi servants and staff were brought in to clean the floors, a *divo* was lit, a priest was brought in. I remember that the area where they were going to lay her body was scrubbed and a marble slab was put there and the body must have been put on it, though I did not witness that as I did not have the courage to deal with it (I watched from a window while all this was going on and I could see a little). Then the priest started praying.

The following morning at six I got up for my usual walk, only to be confronted by a truckfull of plastic chairs, they were laid out not just in the house but in the entire driveway of the block of flats and part of the road had also been cordoned off for this funeral. At seven, I think, people had started arriving. As I was there, I helped with the proceedings and watched the whole thing with a great deal of interest. The funeral finally happened at 8.30 or 9 if I am not mistaken, because there were other funerals at *Doongerwadi*. Then the priest came, and I sat in the driveway with the men because I was too afraid to see a body. The house was full of women; the prayers could be heard right around the block, there were cars all over. It was a really aristocratic funeral, with all the old Parsi families of Bombay gathered. After the prayers people lined up to see the body, and then the hearse from *Doongerwadi* came, but it was only brought here to bring the pall-bearers,[35] they were not going to take the body in the hearse. So after they took up the body and put the cloth on top of it, they walked out of the house with the entire congregation following. The traffic in the neighbourhood practically came to a standstill to watch this; nobody had seen a Parsi ceremony on the streets for years. They marched all the way to *Doongerwadi*, with all the male mourners and some of the women following.

I remember seeing that procession, and wondering about it.
I see. Then, once the body had been moved out of the flat I had more courage to go into it and I sat with P for a while. She observed the customs extremely strictly; there was not a non-Parsi person allowed anywhere near that household; Parsi servants had been hired as substitutes for the regular ones.

What fascinated me most of all was the *Uthamna* ceremony, which took place on the third day. I think they had a group of twelve Dasturjis, with Dasturji Kotwal at the head. It was an amazing *Uthamna*, with high-quality *loban* – the only way I can describe it is 'sensuous'. It was sensuous for the ears, the sound of twelve priests praying in harmony; it was sensuous because of the sense of smell, the smell of *loban* had spread over the entire building. There was pin-drop silence, since the prayers were at home; there were huge numbers of Parsis all in traditional Parsi dress. All the custom were followed, rose water was sprinkled on everyone's hands by Parsi servants. Everything was done according to the tradition. I remember thinking that I too wanted to have my wedding and my funeral in our own home. Only later I heard that one can only have a funeral on the ground floor and we are on the second floor. But fortunately I can have my wedding here.

The downstairs neighbours' home is almost a second home for Ms Khurody, and she was very much taken aback when she found that Zoroastrian tradition could bar her access to it. One of the family's servants had a baby recently and since she had no relatives to take care of her, Ms Khurody and the other servants fulfilled that function. What she had not reckoned with was that, in the eyes of her neighbour, this made her impure for the first forty days after the birth, and she was not allowed into their house.

I nearly died when she told me that. And religious as I may seem to the community, and interested as I may be in being a para-mobed, rules like this still came as a thunderbolt. It became a great amusement for many Parsis in the community, because they said, 'On the one hand you are going to be a para-mobed, and on the other hand you wear these jeans with holes in them, sneakers, tank-tops with no *sudreh* underneath, you do a number of things that are so very American.' They find that very hard to reconcile. This was probably the first time in my life that I was faced with a hard-and-fast Parsi household rule which I simply had to obey, and it was extremely difficult for me. This is where I slipped back into what I call the Zoroastrian rebellious youth mode. I made every possible attempt to argue, fight, I could not fathom how I could live forty days without my dear neighbours. P finally gave in to the extent that she said I could sit on my own in a separate area of the house and not walk into the main part of the house. Then she said, 'Every time you touch the baby, even if you do not touch the mother, you have to bathe.' The interesting thing is that her husband does not observe any of these customs. So they were torn and I was torn.

I am still stumbling through these forty days, and the way we are doing it now is that B [P's husband] comes up to me to watch television, and on days when my hair is washed and I have not touched the baby I can go down. On days when I have helped with the baby or touched the mother, I do not go down. Interestingly I have now almost pulled through those forty days, observing most of these things. I haven't taken to it kindly, I cannot say that I liked it. There is still a lot of rebelliousness in me.

Mrs Munshi expresses her astonishment that someone who has been so deeply influenced by Zoroastrianism still regularly wears tank-tops without a *sudreh*. Ms Khurody says:

Oh yes, well, that is something that I don't think is going to change. This is something that a lot of older Parsis find fascinating in my case. Because in most families you are either one way or the other. For example X's wife, a young girl my age, a modern girl, but she won't even walk around with her hair uncovered. On the other extreme you have the average young, Anglo-Indian or American-Indian[36] youth who observe anything but Zoroastrianism, who blatantly flout all Zoroastrian rules. And then you have someone like myself, who am very American and English in my thinking, in my clothing, in my approach to things – but curiously also follow quaint practices like not lighting the *divo* for my Mummy on days I have my period, not going downstairs unless I have washed my hear.

But at the same time I cannot see myself wearing a priestly outfit all the time once I am a para-mobed. I love the priestly clothes, I think it is a extremely sexy outfit for a girl, but ...

What about the sudreh, Khursheed?
The *sudreh* and the *kusti* I wear everyday, but as a dancer – I do about four hours of intensive classical ballet training every day, and those hours I can never wear a *sudreh*. And often in summer, in bikinis, swimsuits or short tank-tops I am unable to wear one for practical reasons. But at all other times I wear one, and I wear it during all religious ceremonies. I certainly will wear priestly clothes when I perform ceremonies. I think having a girl's face covered by a *padam*[37] and having only her eyes peep out is very sexy and very appealing. I'll wear that gladly but I am also a modern girl who has had a modern upbringing and who wears miniskirts and backless tops, and I think that will continue. But I'd like to evolve a system for myself and maybe for others, to show that the two can continue in tandem and not clash with each other. It is not easy, as I realised with the baby recently, when as I said I had a huge shock and I still have not got over it.

I must tell you, if I had known about it, I might not have come for the interview till the forty days were over. Just to show you that there are more people like your neighbour.

This is a very fascinating phenomenon for me, because it is really old-world practice of Zoroastrianism, and a direct clash with [the ideas of] a modern young girl – but a modern young girl who *is* interested, that I must say. In the case of a girl who is not interested it is a blatant, overt clash; but for me it is more subtle, in my heart my religion matters so much to me. But at the same time here is a classic example of a young person clashing with the older [system of values]. But how I rebelled, I was actually amazed at how strongly I rebelled about this rule!

———

MR NOSHIR DADRAWALA

Noshir Dadrawala (1961) is a professional consultant to philanthropic organisations, but he is best known in the Zoroastrian community for his journalistic activities. He writes for the weekly *Jam-e-Jamshed* as a special correspondent, and is the General Editor of the very conservative monthly *Deen Parast*. The present writer attended the interview.

Mr Dadrawala begins by telling about his youth in Balsar, where he was born. His parents had married late because his mother belonged to a priestly family and his father was a *Behdin*, which led to fierce opposition to the marriage in his mother's family.

> There was this feeling in the family that if a girl from the *Athornan* marries outside the priestly fold, there is darkness in the family. But I think tempers cooled after ten, fifteen years and finally they got married. I am the product of a late marriage.

Mr Dadrawala lived in Balsar with his maternal grandmother until he was about five years old. The family lived in an area where only Parsi priests lived at that time. Mr Dadrawala remarks with some regret that his grandmother's house is now owned by a Muslim. He has many memories associated with this house; there was an Agiary directly opposite and he remembers the traditional ways of the community, such as doing *loban* in the evenings. His traditional upbringing he attributes mostly to his mother, who was a very 'prayerful' woman. His father did not recite many different prayers, but he had a strong faith in the religion, reciting the *Yatha Ahu Vairyo* even when walking home from his office. He used to tell his son how reciting this prayer had protected him from various dangers:

> I have a very clear memory that he said he was walking in the Fort area [of Bombay] one day, and he was crossing the road, and suddenly felt that someone literally picked him up and threw him aside, and a

car came whizzing by. And when he looked around he said he saw nobody over there. Now fantastic as the story may seem, he made it seem very believable to me. It made a very strong impression on me as a child. He had a strong belief in *Yatha* and *Ashem*, and he used to recite that all the time. I have never seen him hold a book and recite from the Avesta, which is what my mother used to do, but he had implicit faith in the religion. He believed in believing in Zoroastrianism alone, he would not tolerate any other religious beliefs; he was very averse to that kind of thing.

Mr Dadrawala was taught to do his *kusti,* and this was strictly enforced, but otherwise he had no religious training. No explanations were offered, which caused him to lose interest in the religion for a time later in life.

Both Mr Dadrawala's parents died of cancer when he was about seventeen and, being an only child, he felt very alone.

I just had to take the situation as it came. I had tried to be prayerful in their sickness, but I did not have a strong religious base at that time. I was in this state of mind when I was not a firm believer in the religion. I had come to that stage because I was going to College where I was reading Science, and my education was turning me more and more atheistic. I had a number of religious questions to which my parents had no answer because they had no formal religious education. They had faith but as to fundamental questions as to why we were doing certain things, they had no answers. And even the local *panthaki* had no answers, he would just say, 'This is our custom.' To a person who was in the Science field this made no sense; if I asked a logical question I wanted a logical answer. I felt we were just doing this because it was a tradition, and tradition did not mean much to me at that age. I tried to be prayerful, prayed to God to save my parents and things like that, but it just did not work, they died.

One of the consequences of his parents' deaths was that Mr Dadrawala was forced to give up his studies and take a job. By coincidence he found a job microfilming rare books on Zoroastrianism. Whilst doing this he had a certain amount of free time, and he began reading the books he was microfilming.

This was stage-managed by Mazda, things were falling into my lap. I was looking at the meanings of the Avestan texts and things were beginning to unfold. I began to appreciate more and more of the religion, and gradually started attending classes. At that time there were K.N. Dastur's classes which I used to go to, and Meher Moos was giving some classes.[38] Of course I have outgrown all that stuff now. At that stage, when I had no kind of religious knowledge, they did answer my questions. And they did inspire faith in the religion. So

I started getting more and more religious. I found that there is a meaning to everything we do. I realised that fire is not merely a symbol of our religion, there is more to it than that. I started looking at how fires are consecrated,[39] now that is a lot of time to spend on creating a mere symbol! There is something more to it; it is a living and conscious entity before whom you prostrate yourself.[40]

Gradually Mr Dadrawala began to adopt various religious customs, such as having a *divo* and going to the Agiary, and he became increasingly involved with community projects, which led to contacts with religious leaders and to an increased knowledge of the faith.

Talking about the developments in the religion and the community, the first thing Mr Dadrawala mentions is that even in the late 1970s and early 80s there were no books on Zoroastrianism available in Bombay, but such books are available now. Also Zoroastrian youth now seems to be taking a real interest in the religion, which was not the case some fifteen years ago. He feels that many young Zoroastrians are very traditional, which he welcomes. Asked what he means by tradition and why he thinks it important, Mr Dadrawala replies:

Let me put it this way, the *kusti* prayers and the *faraziyat* should be done; regular visits to the fire temple; observing the *tarikats* of the religion, like keeping your head covered (I don't keep my head covered all the time because I have a secular job – perhaps will one day – but I do keep it covered at home), not intermarrying.

Some years ago Mr Dadrawala was himself afflicted by the illness that killed his parents, but he made a complete recovery. He did not recite special prayers for health, but does feel that the illness has brought him closer to God. A *Jashan* was performed when he finished his treatment.

Talking about his journalistic work Mr Dadrawala says:

The mainstay of my work over the last ten, twelve years has been voicing my feelings about intermarriages, conversions, which I have always very strongly opposed. In the less orthodox press you usually find a lot of propaganda for intermarriage going on. I, in my own way and in the light of my own studies, have always opposed it, and I try to argue my case as logically as possible, based on traditional doctrinal line. So that has been the main focus all these years; it has been a battle, upholding the traditional values of the community. Because I feel we as a community in India survived mainly because we never encouraged conversion in India, and until the turn of the century no one even dreamt of intermarriage.

Also, before I forget, there has been this propaganda against *dokhme-nashini* [exposure of the body in a Tower of Silence], which is the traditional disposal of the dead. I think it is one of the best systems even today, it is the most eco-friendly system. It is the best system available in times when people think of ecology and things like that. It does not pollute any elements of nature. It is something that should be preserved, as vigorously as we can! It is eco-friendly, and based on the traditions of the religion.

Mr Dadrawala goes on to say that he regards words like 'orthodox' and even 'fundamentalist' as positive, epithets to be proud of. Asked whether he thinks of the ban on conversions as primarily a 'religious' matter or as a question of tradition, he says:

But I think tradition is part of the religion, so it is a tradition that is part of the religious way of life. Take *dokhme-nashini*, that is a tradition which has its roots in the religion, for if you bury a body you pollute the earth. So it is not merely upholding a tradition, it is upholding our religion, that is how I perceive it.

Mr Dadrawala goes on to describe the circumstances that led to the foundation of *Deen Parast*. During the Roxan Shah affair[41] those who represented the traditional point of view, especially Dastur Dr F.M. Kotwal, were reviled in the liberal press while the more traditionalist *Jam-e-Jamshed* did little to defend them. As a reaction, a number of Dastur Kotwal's sympathisers felt the need to have a separate paper of an entirely traditional stamp. The magazine is 'unashamedly orthodox, and proud to be orthodox. Orthodoxy to me means following the right path.' Asked what he means by 'the right path', Mr Dadrawala says:

The path that has been followed by us these thousands of years. This is a very deep subject; you have to realise how and why our community has survived. You have to look at the groups who went to other countries like China and the Punjab after the fall of the Sasanian Empire – these communities have just disappeared because they have not been orthodox and traditional in the sense we perceive it, and these communities are now completely lost. The only stock that has survived is the one that landed on the shores of Diu [in India], and we have survived because of our traditions, like not converting, not intermarrying, believing in systems like *dokhme-nashini*, and so many other things.

Mr Dadrawala does not believe that the situation of the Zoroastrian religion is deteriorating any faster than it did in the past; the real problem in his view is liberal propaganda. He concedes that intermarriage is on the increase, but denies that there is a decrease in the numbers of Zoroastrians. He claims that those Zoroastrians who migrated to the West have never been counted, and that it is a question of redistribution, rather than diminution, of the community.

An event that deeply moved and influenced Mr Dadrawala was his recent visit to Iran, on a tour led by Khojeste Mistree. Seeing the ancient monuments with his own eyes was a 'high you cannot describe', but the spiritual side of the journey had an even greater impact on him. Visits to various fires in Iran led him to develop a more personal relationship with fires than was the case before:

> I began to empathise with fire, have a different feeling about fire. Before, I was a believer in fire, now I am not just a believer – I have come to empathise with fire. I have a different feeling about fires now, because we have seen some absolutely miraculous things in Yazd.[42] At two places at least we have seen these fires that burn without fuel, and I think there is no logical or scientific explanation as to how it happens. We have just seen these miracles and that is it! It defies logic, it defies science, you just see it and you are stunned. And to narrate a very personal experience, one of the first fires we went to was in the village of Cham. It is a very secret fire … but we were allowed to see it. And the brilliance of this fire that I saw – I mean, spontaneously I began to cry over there, and that's something that has never happened to me in my life. I have been to the Iranshah,[43] I have been to all the Atash Behrams in Bombay, but I have never been moved to tears. In Cham, as everybody could see, I cried like a baby. I was so moved I was sobbing on the bus. Whenever I am in difficulty now my thoughts go to the Cham fire.
>
> Ever since I have come back to India I have moved away from community politics and have concentrated more on religious topics and religious education. Because politicians will come and go, Trustees of the Punchayet[44] will come and go, but what is important is to educate our youth in the values of the religion, and what it has to feel so proud about. Let the community know what it means to be descended from Cyrus the Great. Who Cyrus the Great was, who Darius the Great was.[45] And this has affected even my twelve year old son; he is tremendously impressed by these special fires of Yazd. And he is more religious and learned than I was at twelve. So I think it is wonderful, very positive

Notes

1 i.e. Islamic mystics. On earlier links beween Indian Zoroastrians and Islamic and Hindu mystics see above, p. 55 n. 6. To modern Parsis such connections may seem surprising.
2 A leading Islamic mystic, who died in 1240 CE; the *Fusus al-Hikam* is one of his works.
3 i.e. Ilm-e Khshnoom, on which see above, p. 48f.
4 An early Sufi.

5 An Arabic formula widely used in Sufi practice, meaning 'Oh (Thou who art) He (i.e. God).'

6 A well-known book on Zoroastrianism.

7 A great early Sufi, who was executed for his seemingly extravagant claims in 922 CE.

8 A prominent French Orientalist and author of the best-known study on al-Hallaj.

9 The late Prof. R. C. Zaehner.

10 Dr Alan V. Williams, now of Manchester University.

11 Prof James R. Russell, now of Harvard University.

12 i.e. found a religious movement which was open to all, as 'Bhagwan' Shree Rajneesh did.

13 i.e. food consecrated during the ritual and later eaten by those who have attended it.

14 See the interview with Mr Dadrawala.

15 It is interesting to note that, for Mrs Munshi, the two are distinct.

16 i.e. he was a fully qualified priest; for the terms see above, p. 52.

17 It is interesting to note the association of dirt with evil, and of non-traditional behaviour, such as walking barefoot, with both.

18 The custom may go back to the idea that one can make an Amesha Spenta or Yazata part of one's being by internalising the qualities associated with him or her (on the *Gathic* origin of this belief see Kreyenbroek 1985: 10–30).

19 Dastur Khurshed S. Dabu, High Priest of the Wadiaji Atash Behram (1948–1977), who interpreted Zoroastrianism in the light of Theosophist teachings; for further references see Ch. 8, nn. 30, 80, and the Index.

20 Dr Jamshedji M. Unvala, who was critical of Dastur Dabu's theosophist teachings (see Mistree 1990: 242).

21 This refers to the opinion that the reason why the Zoroastrian scriptures do not appear to teach reincarnation is that Zoroastrians are spiritually so evolved that their souls have no further need of rebirth.

22 The Yazad Sarosh is thought to watch over the soul of the dead for the first three days after death, and subsequently to take it to the Chinvad Bridge, on which see above, p. 6. On Sarosh (Av. Sraosha) see Kreyenbroek 1985.

23 Well-known prayers.

24 The M.F. Cama Athornan Institute, see above, p. 57 n. 55.

25 A ceremony which consists in passing one's hand over a patient, or over a part of one's body, while reciting certain prayers; cf. the interview with Mrs A, above, p. 95 with n. 60.

26 In classical Zoroastrianism crying for the dead was disapproved of as it was held to strengthen the powers of evil.

27 i.e. in one of the more usually venues for Navjotes

28 Traditionally only *khandiyas* are permitted to enter the Towers of Silence (see above, p. 38). That a Trustee of the Towers would go into the Tower to clean it up probably seemed revolutionary to one section of the community, and revolting to another.

29 The professional activities of such functionaries are considered extremely polluting and they are shunned by many other Parsis.

30 i.e. the fire-vase, presumably with *loban*.

31 Rooms that are to be used in connection with ritual purposes may not be cleaned by non-Zoroastrians.

32 i.e. a lay person who performs some of the tasks of a priest.

33 A training college for priests, see above, p. 57 with n. 55.

34 On these rituals see above, p. 9f.
35 Normally a hearse takes the body to the Towers. In this case, however, the procession went there on foot.
36 i.e. Indians who have been deeply influenced by English and American culture.
37 A piece of cloth covering the lower part of the face.
38 Both are prominent representatives of the Ilm-e Khshnoom movement; see the interview with Dr Master-Moos.
39 On this long and laborious process see above, p. 9.
40 For Mr Dadrawala's view of fire as a personal entity see further below.
41 The remark refers to one of the most traumatic incidents in Parsi community life in recent years. In January 1990, Mrs Roxan Darshan Shah, a young woman from an upper-class Parsi family who was married to a non-Zoroastrian, had a fatal car accident. While her family wished her obsequies to be held at the Towers of Silence, members of the traditionalist wing of the community, notably Dastur Dr F.M. Kotwal, argued that she was to be regarded as a lapsed Zoroastrian and therefore not entitled to the use of the Towers. The affair received a great deal of coverage in the Parsi press. On the community debates on the subject of marrying out see below, p. 311f.
42 A town in Iran.
43 The Atash Behram at Udwada.
44 On the Bombay Parsi Punchayet see above, p. 52 with n. 48.
45 Both are early kings of the Achaemenian dynasty, on which see above, p. 12.

Chapter Six

Modernist Views

MRS H

Mrs H (1948) is the wife of one of India's leading industrialists; she has two children. She was a promising painter in her younger years and has a deep interest in the arts.

About her childhood, Mrs H says that her mother saw to it that religion played a role in the children's upbringing.

We were encouraged to go to the Agiary from a very young age. My sibling is eight years younger than I, and it was my responsibility to encourage him to come with me. We used to enjoy going there because the priest in charge of the Agiary always had a twinkle in his eye and was always interested in what we were doing as children, and never pressurised us into doing our *kusti*, or praying, or anything like that. It was a lot of fun, going to the Agiary. That priest lived all his life literally on the bench of that Agiary, I think. He did not teach us our Navjote prayers; that was done by a distant relative of my mother's. Silla Aunty also taught us to read Gujarati, so we could read the prayer book. I feel very grateful to her today – after so many years when I used to fight with her, because she used to come on a Saturday afternoon or a Sunday afternoon, and if we were going to an afternoon show it was my responsibility to tell her to come early. If I forgot to tell her, then I just missed the movie, I had to do my prayers. It is only now when I look back ... She also taught me Parsi cookery, which interests me.

Learning prayers was all by rote, no meanings were taught. I had a small prayer book, I still have it today – of course I know the prayers by heart, but I still refer to the book – and several years ago, when I was in the US for a long time, I found that there were many explanations in that book: about the calendar, and what each day signified, what each month signified, and also the meaning of the *gehs*. We always skipped that part of our prayers as children. So it was only in the 1990s that I saw that it was all there, and that is when I started taking an interest in what the days symbolised, what the calendar meant.

You mean, till then you were just doing it blindly?
By rote, by rote! I was not even doing it with blind faith, I just said the prayers by rote. Now my father has blind faith; he also prays by rote but he has a blind faith. I was doing it for different reasons ... maybe the chanting of the verses gave me some solace without my realising it. I think with children it starts that way, it really does! I thought my son had an inclination towards prayers, because he never rebelled when he was made to learn his prayers. (My daughter did!). I thought he would go on to build on that strength, but he has not. At least not so far, but I never give up!

If I had sat down with a seven-year old, I don't think he would have listened to me. Today I think he probably will listen to me, because he knows he is going away from home and he knows that this is what is going to make him unique. In some of his college applications we have written that what makes his application different from those of other children is that he is a Zoroastrian!

Do you think that sense of uniqueness has helped you?
It definitely has. You know, we hear that all Parsis are followers of this Baba or that Mata,[1] or go to a particular mosque, or fervently attend some Hindu festival. I just look at it this way, that I am unique! And when you look, especially at the last 200 years when we have been an important economic force in India – we have given, we have given expecting nothing in return! That, that form of charity is unique amongst us; I have really not seen it consciously in any other group.

Even though you have travelled so widely, and been in touch with so many people?
Yes, you know it is very special! And I try to practise it in my own life. Because to me, when you give you have to give with love; if you can give with love, *any* charity is charity well done. But if you give grudgingly, or wondering if your name will be on the plaque, you really have to rethink your values. Sometimes you may not even give in terms of money, but just by your presence. If you give with an open palm – even an ordinary citizen from a low economic stratum can give with love – and if you do that, what more can one want? This is what I have learned through my religion, through my parents.

Returning to her religious upbringing, Mrs H says that few of the traditions were observed in her parents' house. When Mrs H wanted to light a *divo*, her mother told her that once she started she would have to light it every day ('you cannot switch your God on and off'), and she accepted that it would be better to give up the idea. As an adult she now feels:

Maybe, when I am driving by [an Atash Behram] and saying my prayers, and I am just thinking of the Atash Behram, maybe that is a better sort of *divo*.

The laws of purity were not followed very strictly when Mrs H was a child, although her mother felt that one should not touch the sandalwood for the fire temple when one was not in a state of purity. Mrs H is skeptical about such views, since one cannot tell who has handled the sandalwood before it came to the Parsi home. She respects other people's attitudes, but her own approach is pragmatic:

I respect it. I would not flaunt it [a non-observance of the laws of purity]. But sometimes, in times of happiness and in times of death, sadness – suppose you have your period and it is your father who has died! Your body might just have reacted to the shock. And so, if you have your period, what are you going to do? Should one insist that such a lady be thrown out of the place, or do you just keep quiet, say your own prayer to God for forgiveness, and carry on? I think I would do the latter. I am not encouraging girls to do that, but everyone has to make their own decisions. Or suppose it is your daughter's Navjote, are you not going to go to the ceremony? On the other hand, I would say, don't go to the fire temple, because that you *can* avoid. These are all very very personal things. Our religion says you have a choice. Exercise it judiciously, and decide according to the occasion.

And did no one explain to you why we have those laws?
Of course they did, of course they did, but as I say, you have a choice. If [another] woman does this, frankly I would not even want to know about it. And if it is a sin, it is between her and her Maker!

Mrs Munshi then asks about *parabs* and other festive occasions. Mrs H answers that some of the *parabs* were observed to some extent, and other festive occasions were and are observed with great enjoyment. The day of the interview happens to be the birthday of her niece, and the family is going to celebrate this in the traditional Parsi way. Since her niece's father is not a Parsi, this leads on to a discussion of the question of 'marrying out', which begins with a remark by Mrs H:

I am sure my sister-in-law has already gone to the Atash Behram – no, to the Agiary. She does not want to go to an Atash Behram where she is not welcome,[2] so she goes to an Agiary.

Since there is this in your family, how is it reconciled? On the one hand one has given up part of the religion ...
[Politely, but with some vehemence.] I don't think my sister-in-law has given up her religion at all!

Not in the sense of practising it, of course, but one forsakes something of the religion when one takes that step, and yet everything about the religion ...
I don't think so! That may be the difference between what you are saying and what I am thinking. I don't believe my sister-in-law has forsaken anything! As a matter of fact both my nieces have had their Navjote done together with my children, and there was a Zoroastrian priest who taught them their prayers. All the children go to the Agiaries. I don't think my sister-in-law has forsaken her religion at all – she has just married out of the community. And I think that seeing how well and diligently my sister-in-law observes her religion, as she was taught it, has also made her husband see the good in his religion.

The dilemma is going to come if these girls – if they marry Zoroastrians I'll be the happiest person. But if they don't – of course I'll be happy at the time of their marriage, but I don't know what sort of Zoroastrianism they will be handing over to their children. Because even though they see their mother practising the religion at home and they take part in all Zoroastrian activities and festivities, and they have this great anchor of Zoroastrian grandparents, uncles, aunts, nieces – still if they marry non-Zoroastrians, I don't know. It is that generation we should think about. In India, at least in Bombay, they'll still see it, we have a strong presence here. But what about those places where there are just four Zoroastrian families, or even forty? Those kids are being reared in a totally different environment, and they are with children of very different backgrounds. They are not even going to *find* a Zoroastrian spouse ...

The interview then returns to Zoroastrian observances. At the time of Mrs H's wedding, her future mother-in-law did not think such things necessary, but her husband's grandmother insisted that the *madav-saro* be done. Mrs H says that she usually does not understand the meaning of rituals. She has recently witnessed the *Nirangdin* ceremony for the first time, and merely found it interesting from an intellectual point of view. About rituals she says:

For me, religion is something very personal, Shehnaz. I respect what, in inverted commas, I call the 'hocus-pocus', and if someone else does it I'll let them do it, but whether in my personal life *I* would be able to do it – as I said that is basically up to me.

Essentially it is like wearing the *sudreh* and *kusti*: so many people don't wear it; so many people wear it and don't show it; so many people wear it and flaunt it. I wear it, I've always worn it.

And what does that mean to you, why do you wear it?
I am a Zoroastrian. Why was I born into this faith? My faith demands
that I wear this, I think it is an integral part of Zoroastrianism. Other
things may or may not be essential – I give it individual thought when
the need arises.

And if it was necessary and it was explained to you why ...
If our religion said that we had to go to the Agiary every Sunday I
would go.

You mean that, the way things are, everything is nebulous?
Yes, sometimes things are very woolly and you have to [find your own
solutions]. Of course nowadays there is a lot of work being done. You
are bringing out this book.[3] Maybe these things were there in Gujarati
and nobody bothered to read it, or it was in such archaic Gujarati that
you could read it but would not understand it.[4] You have to
communicate in language that is understood by the majority of the
people. Even training for the priesthood is now getting easier. It is a
change for the better, definitely for the better I think.

As the H family is a priestly one, Mrs H is hoping that her son will
eventually undergo priestly training. Mrs Munshi then mentions Mrs H's
father, who prays a great deal, and asks what influence he had on his
daughter's life.

> I've never gone to him with any queries on religion, because he prays
> by rote. I have never really asked him much, I keep on telling him,
> 'You pray for us, you pray for all our souls.'
>   I believe that sometimes, when you don't want to face reality, you
> immerse yourself in your prayers. You are never going to solve
> anything by just praying. Work is worship for me. I see my mother
> working – she could easily be praying as well, but then nothing would
> function in that household! So maybe it is good that one of them prays
> and the other works.

Any Zoroastrian stories, myths or legends Mrs H knows she had to learn
from books later in life. She is very glad that more and more publications
now appear in English so that Parsis have access to much of the
information they need.
    Mrs H stayed at home for forty days after the birth of both her
children – the first time because her mother insisted, the second time
because she herself wanted to. She has always made her children wear
the *sudreh* and *kusti* all the time but her daughter, who is studying
abroad, now only wears it when she is back home. Mrs H has dinned
the significance of these symbols into the children when they were
young.

Mrs H goes to the fire temple regularly, sometimes taking the children. When she was young her mother saw to it that prayers for the family's well-being were performed in her favourite Agiary and Mrs H continues this practice, having prayers said even when she herself is not in Bombay.

Mrs H ends every day with prayers. She likes all prayers and she says them all. She has no favourite Yazata or temple fire; she likes the Wadiaji Atash Behram because one hears no traffic noise while praying, and she is attached to one particular Agiary partly because she likes the priests. The family had a bad experience at the Iranshah at Udwada, where a priest insulted her father because his arms were not fully covered. Also, there were masses of beggars outside the Atash Behram, and Mrs H feels that there are better ways of taking care of the poor. She has never returned there and has no wish to do so; she much prefers the Atash Behrams of Navsari and Surat. There is a non-Zoroastrian sanctuary in South India that is special to her, but when she goes there she says her Zoroastrian prayers. If there were a Zoroastrian fire temple in that location, Mrs H says she would visit it every year.

When her husband's firm was celebrating its centenary, the family had thought of trying to assemble 100 priests to hold a *Jashan*.[5] To their amazement, 217 priests came:

> It was really a magical moment, I don't think it can be repeated very easily. It was the numbers, the incredible response, the way the prayers sounded. Basically the *jashan* is between two priests,[6] the rest are on the periphery. In this case we could not hear the voices of the two main priests. We had not anticipated so many people coming, but when all of them, all 217 came ... the prayers had a special vibration. All our prayers have a special vibration I am told, but to hear so many praying! It was not only a visual spectacle, it was also very soothing on the ears. Only I wish they would not pray so fast, as if they had a train to catch, but that is my complaint all the time with priests.

The interview ends with a detailed and animated discussion of the need for a better education for priests, and the crucial importance of the priesthood for Zoroastrian community life – showing that for Mrs H working and planning for the good of the community are indeed essential parts of religious life.

———

DR Y

Dr Y was born in 1942 in Bombay, where she has lived all her life. She is a medical specialist.

Both Dr Y's parents were religious and she went to a Zoroastrian school, where she was taught religion by Ervad Darabshah Kutar. Ervad Kutar taught religion by means of stories, and his classes were so popular that even non-Zoroastrian pupils obtained special permission to attend them. Ervad Kutar stressed that religion is more than ritual alone.

> Ritual and religion are two different things. You may fall prey to rituals, but unless you know the meaning of each ritual you don't practise it, because then you become a slave of religion. He said that religion should be a guidance to you, you should not be a slave to it. A simple story which I still remember and which I told to my own children is that a Zoroastrian gentleman used to go to the fire temple every day, but he would pray in a hurry, he would tie his *kusti* in one minute, a few minutes; he would bow half-heartedly, and then run back to his office. And one day the head-priest called him, 'This is not the way to way to worship your fire and your religion. I will teach you how to pray before God. Now take your *kusti* properly in your hand, see that it does not touch the floor, you have to hold it in this particular manner.' And then the priest asked the gentleman, 'Which prayer was better, your coming here every day in a hurry and walking out, or the way I taught you today? Which prayer had more impact on your mind?' And the gentleman said, 'The first prayer, which I used to do every day.' The head priest was very disappointed and asked him why. He said, 'Whatever I was praying was from my heart and mind, I was really concentrating. And when you taught me these details, all the time in front of my eyes was how to hold, how to do it, how much time should I take. I was not concentrating from my heart of hearts. So my first prayer was more effective.' And [Ervad Kutar] told us, 'This is what I want to convey, when you grow up you may become a very busy person .... you may not have time to go to the fire temple. When sleeping at night, you can fall asleep, pray one or two prayers, pray whilst driving. Your head need not be covered ... ' And we were always taught in our religion, by our parents, that when you pray your head should be covered. But I still follow it, when I am driving I am praying, just before sleeping I pray. My head is not covered but there is full concentration.

Ervad Kutar told many stories from the *Shahname*, and whatever Dr Y learned about religion she learned at this school. In Medical School she felt totally cut off from her religion; her ideas changed and she began to think that all religions were the same.

Dr Y's grandmother never began the day without prayers; she said *Shekaste shekaste Shaytan* as soon as she got out of bed, and rubbed her hands with *taro*. After that she went to the kitchen, fed the hearth-fire with sandalwood and prayed. The children were not allowed into the kitchen, where the hearth fire was, before they had had their bath. When praying they had to stand still in one corner. Dr Y's parents were not quite so religious as her grandmother, but she remembers her father lighting a *divo* every morning and praying for at least half an hour. Her mother normally got up at 5 a.m., much before the others, saw to the fire and prayed. Dr Y notes that one hardly ever sees this nowadays. She tried to have a separate prayer corner with a fire in her own house, but it proved too taxing to observe the necessary rules of purity. Dr Y was taught her prayers by her mother; her grandmother also listened and corrected any mistakes (for a short time there was a priestly instructor). Her parents prayed silently and did not use *taro*; they knew the prayers by heart and did not read them from a book. Dr Y thinks that her grandmother knew the meaning of the prayers, but she herself does not. Dr Y's elder sister and brother were more religious-minded than she was; her brother, who has now died, used to pray continuously and her sister prays at least for an hour a day.

Dr Y's Navjote was performed together with her sister's, when she was six and her sister nine years old. She feels she was too young to understand the purpose of the ceremony, and thinks the difference in age at this time may be one of the reasons why her sister is more religious than she is. Dr Y's grandmother was a strong believer in ritual and tradition. Once out of bed, one was not allowed to sleep on it again until the following night. If her grandchildren tried to have an afternoon nap she was upset and ordered them to wash their face, do their *kusti* and say their prayers. The children also had to do their *kusti* before lunch and dinner, and in the evening when the lamps were lit. The grandmother tried to make the children do this when coming out of the toilet; Dr Y and her siblings found this unacceptable,[7] 'and she gave up,' but other children in the family did observe it. In any case, such rules were strictly observed only when the children were in their grandmother's house but much less so at home. At her grandmother's, a menstruating woman had to sit in a corner, was not allowed to touch anything and could either sleep on the floor with only one sheet and and one pillow, or prepare her own iron bed.[8] Even to go to the toilet Dr Y had to ask her brother to open the door for her at such times. Dr Y used to feel indignant about this treatment, 'as if we were untouchables.' Later Ervad Kutar explained that these rules were intended to afford a woman a much-needed time of rest, and this convinced her. Her grandmother, however, said this was nonsense. According to her it was well known that pickles would spoil, and flowers wither, if they were touched by a menstruating woman,

179

which showed that evil rays emanated from a woman's body at such times. Because of all the restrictions – which included a ban on bicycling – it was obvious to everyone when a girl had her period, and Dr Y recalls the embarrassment this caused. Dr Y's own mother, a working woman, was less strict but still 'carried it too far.' Dr Y herself, living in a small house with two young girls, finds it impossible to follow all the traditional rules of purity, although her mother insists that one can do it if the will is there. She does, however try to keep a special sari for visiting the fire temple.

For Dr Y's wedding her mother invited *goyans* to sing the *Atashnu Git* and religious songs.[9] On the wedding day a *Fareshta* ceremony[10] was performed in the fire temple, which the couple attended. Her mother-in-law, although she belonged to a priestly family, was very modern and allowed her to move freely in the house and to touch everything during her periods. Dr Y's husband is a qualified priest who has undergone the *Navar*, but he no longer practises because he has forgotten much of his training. Her son is *Navar Martab*[11] and enjoys practising from time to time, especially during Muktad.[12] 'I often ask him, "Do you pray properly or do you skip certain words you cannot pronounce?" He says, "No, I take my own time but I pray sincerely".' Her son would rather not accept any money for his priestly serrvices but it is often forced upon him; some of his colleagues, on the other hand, are mainly interested in the financial gains.

Dr Y, herself of *Behdin* origin, married into a priestly family from the same area and social background. At her wedding she refused to participate in such ceremonies as the *pithi chorvani rit*,[13] because she did not understand the purpose of it. The *madav saro* was performed; normally only women whose husbands are alive take part in this, but all the women close to Dr Y were widows, and she proudly tells that she insisted that they should perform the ceremony.

> So I broke another tradition or rule of our Zoroastrian family. Right from childhood, if I did not understand something I had a habit of asking people, so much so that sometimes people got irritated. My father used to say, 'Keep quiet for five minutes.' What does not satisfy my conscience I don't do; even now I don't do it.

During Dr Y's first pregnancy the *panchmasyu* and *agharni* ceremonies were done, but she did not allow sweets to be distributed to an extravagant number of neighbours, and offended her mother-in-law by refusing to accept the gift of a jewel. After her first child was born her parents did the *chatthi* ceremony; Dr Y herself was not involved in this, although she does not object to such rituals as long as they are not wasteful. The names were not chosen in accordance with the traditional *rasi* system, but for personal reasons. Dr Y's first two children were girls, which was fine with her since her father used to say, 'When you have a daughter you get Lakshmi in the house.'[14] Her elder sister, however, hoped that the next child would be a son; she prayed to Ava Yazad for forty days and a son was born. When another sister remained childless, the elder sister insisted that prayer would help. No child was born, however, for:

> ... in between she lost faith in our Zoroastrian religion. She used to say, 'I pray so religiously, but somehow or other I never get anything.' So we used to tell her, 'Don't pray with the idea that you will get something. Prayer is for mental peace, prayer is for thanking God that we [i.e. our circumstances] are better than others.' So we used to console her like that ...

Dr Y loves to pray. She intends to pray more when she retires, and jokes about this with her family. She reads the prayers, although the words are familiar to her by now and she can pray very fast.[15] She does not know the literal meaning of what she prays but she knows the purpose of each prayer, which is enough for her. In the fire temple, Dr Y prays the *geh, Khorshed Meher* and *Atash Niyayesh, Dua Nam-setayeshne, Mah Bokhtar Niyayesh.*[16] If she comes on her day off, she prays longer. She observes the *parab* of Adar *roj,*[17] in the traditional way, but no other *parabs.* Her children pray less than she does, saying that work is true worship. Asked about her opinion of the role of prayer in curing illness, Dr Y says:

> Yes, I have experienced that. When I was in tenth standard, the last year of school, there was a big epidemic of smallpox and I was one of the victims, for I had not been immunised, the secondary immunisation had not been done. So I suffered from smallpox, and the doctors had given up hope completely, my blood reports were very bad and I could not see with my left eye; the ophthalmologist said, 'She might lose her left eye because there is a pox in the eye also.' And at that time my grandmother sat and prayed continuously near my bed, and I certainly feel that her prayers have helped me. She prayed *Ardibehesht Nirang.* My elder sister also has a lot of faith; if one of my children is ill and has a high temperature, 103, 105^0, she comes and says, 'Come, let me pray.' And she prays *Ardibehesht Yashtni Nirang.*[18] And I see that the moment she prays, it may be coincidence but immediately I find that the children are less ill and more cheerful. It works, it works! Even as a doctor – I have seen so many critical cases and when my mind comes to a dead end, if I have done everything and I don't know what more you can do for this dying baby, that time I just stand in a corner and I pray, 'Just give me clarity, if I missed something, please God, help me out!' And suddenly I get an idea, 'Why not give this particular drug, or could it be that I have missed this investigation?'

And I suddenly ask them, 'Do blood tests ... ' There have been many instances, not just one or two! Of course God cannot listen to me every time and grant my prayer, but I have rarely lost a child because I did not do something. I immediately keep on getting ideas, 'Why not try this, why not change the treatment.' When a baby is on a ventilator, or when there is another critical situation, I pray continuously for two or three hours, *Ashem Vohu, Yatha Ahu Vairyo, Kem-na Mazda*, whatever comes to my mind. I don't know much orally, most prayers I have to read from the book, but these are the *kusti* prayers which we know by heart. I keep on praying and I keep on saying, 'You strengthen my arms.' [Here follows a detailed description of a recent case where prayer brought a solution.]

So many times, with diagnosis, I think it is due to prayers, for medical knowledge is becoming so extensive that it is not possible for one doctor to know everything. And I suddenly get an inspiration, 'Why not open this book, or why not wake up this person and find out?' And I get the answer because I get clarity in my mind when I pray.

Dr Y feels, however, that her work has priority over religion.

Suppose if I had a patient's phone call, I would stop my prayer to attend it and then come back and continue. But I have been taught that once your prayer is interrupted, you again [have to] start with *kusti*, which I don't do. Because I feel, how many times should I keep on doing it, people keep on ringing me up. My husband often says, 'Shall I tell them you are praying?' But I tell him, 'No. My work is first and prayer is second.' And if I have done something good, say there is a seriously sick child and I have been with that child for three hours, then if I don't pray I feel my religion is that. I give more importance to work than prayer. My whole thinking has changed.

Dr Y's brother died two years before the interview was held, and because of this she has been going to the fire temple more often than usually. At one time she used to go as often as eight times a month to pray[19] for a recently departed soul, because her mother believed very strongly in this. In the long run this proved incompatible with her duties as a doctor, since one has to wait one's turn before a priest is free to pray for one, and she tended to be late for work. She complains that no consideration is given to the fact that she is a doctor; in fact she feels that people who come after her are often served earlier if they give large tips to priests. Her visits are now limited to three days in the month to pray for her brother (including Behram *roj*, when she particularly likes to pray), the other days she prays at home. Almost every evening before going to her consulting room Dr Y has a bath, lights a *divo*, puts milk and water into place, and prays the *Satum* for all her dead relatives, praying *Cheragno Namaskar, Dinno Kalmo,* and *Tandorosti*; if there is time she adds *Sarosh Yasht Vadi*. When her brother died the whole family was shaken. Over two years have passed since then, but although Dr Y feels it is wrong,[20] none of the family have yet come to terms with his death. Holidays are not planned because there would be too many memories, and even visits to the cinema usually prove painful because of such associations. Dr Y's sister-in law condemns this, saying that the family is trying to pull the soul back by praying and remembering.[21] However, when things get too much for Dr Y she feels she has to pray for her brother. In fact the only thing that gives comfort is prayer. When she prays in the fire temple, she feels her brother is with her, though she does not know whether this is because the living are trying to 'drag the soul back', or because the soul is really there. About life after death Dr Y says:

> We were always taught that in the Zoroastrian religion there is no rebirth, and that is why we pray for the dead. But I always felt that there is rebirth, I don't know for what reason. Sometimes I look at people and we get along very well, but there are also people I just don't like to talk to, I feel that I would waste my time. I always feel that this must be related to past lives. Also I am very much attracted to North India, to the Himalaya mountains, but the South has never attracted me. I always feel that there is something from a past life that attracts me, I may be wrong. I often read in the papers that some child recollected what his previous birth was, so I feel there must be something there.
>
> But we were taught that whatever there is, is in this life. You do good things and you get a reward; you harm somebody and God will definitely make you realise it. It is in this generation – after death your soul progresses; if you have done your duty well then your soul keeps on going further and further. The prayer which we do after death helps the soul to progress. Then you are free of your duties, that is the explanation we are given. But if I don't do my duty well then I might have to come back. But Zoroastrianism says no, you do it here only. So that is always in my mind, but I have never understood why some people, I don't like their faces, I don't like this, I don't like that. What is this?

Dr Y has never got around to performing any form of pilgrimage, although she has long meant to do things like visiting seven fire temples on a single day. She has never been to Udwada on the *parab* of the Fire, although she would like to do this. She goes to Udwada sporadically (unlike her elder sister who goes some five times a month); she had planned a visit recently but her daughter pointed out that this would involve leaving her elderly mother alone for four days, which did not seem a pious thing to do, so she cancelled the trip. In any case, Udwada does not attract her much, perhaps because of some bad experiences with priests from there. When she was small the priest who was to prepare her for her Navjote, and who was from Udwada, showed her and her friends pornographic pictures; later, a priest in Udwada accepted money to do a long ceremony but came out after five minutes, claiming that he had done the entire ritual; another time she caught priests joking and laughing during a service in memory of her father.

Asked for a recent significant experience, Dr Y recounts that her sister-in-law came to Bombay from abroad and asked to be taken to a Hindu Ashram. Dr Y accompanied her there and was struck by the luxurious and worldly feel of the place, which made her appreciate the serene atmosphere of fire temples all the more, in spite of shortcomings like the ones mentioned earlier.

Dr Y likes to go to the Christian *mela* [fair] at Mount Mary Church in Bombay to offer candles, and she has been to see Sai Baba. She learned from her father to keep images of various divinities, prophets and religious leaders in her house. He used to say, 'Be faithful to the religion in which you were born, try to understand the teachings of your own faith, and bow before all the gods before you leave the house.' 'So I do have feelings of respect for other religions also. And many times we are told that Zoroastrianism is the oldest and the best religion, but I always tell people that it is not like that. All religions are the same, they all teach you to be good human beings.' However, Dr Y would like to learn more about the teachings of Zoroastrianism, because she often feels inadequate when trying to teach the religion to her own children.

> Whatever books I have bought [on Zoroastrianism], they only discuss rituals, how to do the *kusti* – or they are about the *Gathas*. I find them very hard to understand. I have not come across a book [on Zoroastrianism] which can enlighten ordinary people, like for example [in] Buddhism, the Eightfold Path, which lay people can understand. And it is because there is too much of detail that there are so many controversies in the religion. If it was simplified more people would accept it.

––––––

MR DINSHAW K. TAMBOLY

Mr Dinshaw K. Tamboly (born 1945) holds degrees in Business Studies from Indian and British Universities. He is a successful businessman but also devotes a large part of his time to community affairs. He is a Member of the Managing Committee of the World Zoroastrian

Organisation (W.Z.O), and Chairman of the Bombay-based W.Z.O. Trust Funds. In this capacity he has led a team which, over the six years preceding the interview, has rehabilitated nearly three hundred impoverished Parsi families in rural India, and also extends help to a large number of urban Parsis. At the time of writing Mr Tamboly was the most recently elected Trustee of the Bombay Parsi Punchayet,[22] an influential and highly prestigious post. He holds several other Trustee-ships.

About his childhood Mr Tamboly says that he comes from a middle class Parsi family. He describes his early years as follows:

> [It was] a very regular, ordinary Parsi type of upbringing. We have never been an overly religious family. My father prays every morning for an hour but I think that is more from force of habit than because he understands the true meaning of the prayers. Whilst we went to the Agiaries and Atash Behrams regularly on festive days, religion was something that was well beyond our comprehension. In fact it still is, very much. While I do believe, very much, in the power of prayer, the Almighty, Ahura Mazda, still what I personally have always felt [to be a pity] is that the prayers have never been made known to us in layman's language. If you read the Bible it is in a language you can understand. I realise that this may be due to the language in which our prayers were first spoken, the very fact that ours is the oldest revealed religion and all that.

> A very important turning point for me was that, in the year 1982 . . . by a strange set of coincidences, I met Khojeste Mistree. He was killing time at the Tata Guest House [in Navsari] and I also had time on my hands (I was not into this welfare work then), and I just spent maybe half an hour to 45 minutes with him. That was the initial turning point in my attitude towards welfare work, and it has got me where I am today. Khojeste told me to read his book, *Zoroastrianism, an Ethnic Perspective* – a book I have not just read once but probably half a dozen times and which I have given to twenty, thirty people. Because it was something that really made me understand what Zoroastrianism is all about. For that I am eternally grateful to Khojeste and to 'Zoroastrian Studies'. At that time the community became something very meaningful to me, until then I was mostly interested in corporations, I had no special interest in the Parsis.

Mr Tamboly goes on to say that his wife, who is his first cousin, was brought up in the family tradition, where social and community work had always been regarded as important. From the time of their marriage in the late 1960s, the couple had always planned to devote time to social work when they were financially secure and could spend time on things other than their careers. These plans took shape in the 1980s when, apart

from his meeting with Mr Mistree, Mr Tamboly and his wife also came
into contact with Mr S. Captain, one of the leading figures in W.Z.O., a
meeting that led to Mr Tamboly's involvement with that organisation.
Then in 1989, Mr Captain came to India and informed Mr Tamboly that a
report had been published on the lamentable socio-economic position of
many Parsis in rural areas of South Gujarat. He invited Mr Tamboly to
come with him to Gujarat to investigate. When it became clear that the
Surat Punchayet did not intend to take active steps to improve things, it
was decided that W.Z.O. would step in. The Surat Punchayet later
decided to join this project and a Committee was formed, 'the Federation
of Parsi Zoroastrian Anjumans of India'. Eventually, however, given the
magnitude of the task and the bureaucratic procedures involved in
committee work, it was decided that things could be better managed by
setting up a Trust – the W.Z.O. Trust, which began with a sum of no more
than £1000. The more Mr Tamboly saw of the conditions of poor rural
Parsis the more convinced he became of the need to help. He got more
money from various sources, and the Trust began its work, which
consisted in such things as offering training in agricultural methods and
improving farming conditions, rather than handing out dole-like gifts of
money. Mr Tamboly stresses the importance of making people self-reliant
rather than dependent on charity. When the beneficiaries of Trust
schemes begin to earn more, they are expected to give back a percentage
of their additional earnings as contributions to the work of the Trust, so
that they themselves become donors. Mr Tamboly goes on to describe the
– spectacular – success of the Trust.

Returning to the topic of his early religious life, Mr Tamboly fondly
describes the traditional devotional life in Navsari, where part of his
family lived and which he visited frequently. At the time of writing he
still tries to attend one traditional *Gahambar* every year. Mrs Munshi asks
what he felt about such traditional festivities as a young man.

> At that time it did not evoke any special feelings; it was just fun time.
> But with hindsight, having come into this area of activity, I believe it is
> a very rich heritage, which we will continue to support and treasure
> all our lives, and will pass on to our children. It is our culture, it is our
> heritage, and it is something we are all very proud of. As a child I
> never looked at it with those eyes. Today I look at it from a different
> angle.

Mr Tamboly's wife, whose Navjote was performed in Navsari, was
taught the meaning of that ceremony, but he himself had no such
instruction. There is an old family tradition that all family members
gather once a year at a place near Udwada, and there are usually
'pilgrimage-cum-picnic' visits to that place. Another family tradition is
that, whenever a child is born, *machis* are offered to the fire.

As to the rules of purity, Mr Tamboly says that one did not have a haircut on Saturdays in his family and, although he cannot defend it rationally, he would still hesitate to do this. His wife was made to observe all the rules of purity in Navsari right up to the time of their marriage (on the other hand her brother's wife, who objected strongly, was allowed to do as she pleased although she lived in the same house). Mrs Munshi asks whether Mr Tamboly himself, who grew up in a less 'orthodox' atmosphere, had disliked such practices:

> No, that never came to mind. First of all we had always been trained to respect age, and secondly we had been taught that whatever our elders do, they do with our best [interests] at heart. There may have been some questions in our minds, but they were not strong enough to be voiced.

All Mr Tamboly's aunts and uncles have now passed away, and elaborate rituals were performed for the sake of their souls.

> The Navsari part of the family were very very orthodox people and we had a *Nirangdin* performed for my father-in-law when he died, and later also for my mother-in-law who had died earlier in 1982. We had the *Hamayasht*[23] performed. It was a beautiful ceremony, as far as I remember it [consisted of] seven *Vendidads* and 144 *Ijashnes*. However, at this point something happened. For lay people like us there are a lot of confusions because we get conflicting advice. In this particular case I had asked Dasturji Kotwal at the Wadiaji Atash Behram, and he had told me that all the ceremonies had to be completed between the New Year and the next *Gatha* days,[24] otherwise the whole ceremony would have to be repeated. I had said, 'It is absolutely fine by us.' Whether we could attend the ceremonies or not, he should just go ahead. At first things went along beautifully but then, as always happens, the tempo slackened, breaks started to occur, and just before the Muktads came [at the end of the year] we found that one or two *Vendidads* and about 20, 24 *Ijashnes* were left. It was something that was way beyond our control. So I went to Dasturji Kotwal and said it was all right as far as we were concerned [to repeat the whole ritual]. But it was very surprising, he said it was all right and the remaining ceremonies could be done after the New Year. When I pressed him further he just told me not to worry.
>
> When a person in such an exalted position, you know [contradicts himself in such matters], when such directions are [inconsistent], it becomes very confusing for the laity.[25] ... It [Avestan] is a very difficult language and we don't get enough things to depend on. When you read the Bible you probably know about Christianity, but in our religion, when you want to learn and this type of signals come out then it is confusing.

187

But do you think things are improving, compared to the time when you were young.
Yes, definitely. In the last twenty years or so awareness of the religion has increased enormously. I remember in my youth, in the 1960s, we were never really bothered about religious matters. In Bombay there were no religious classes in those days. It is fantastic that our children are now taking advantage of such classes. It will ensure continuity of knowledge, and continuity of our religion and rites.

Why did you have those ceremonies performed?
As I told you, Khojeste's book had a very profound effect on me. That is why I went to see Dasturji Kotwal. I wanted to do a *Nirangdin* for my mother-in-law, but Dasturji said that for ladies it was better to do a *Hamayasht*, so we did that.

Apart from this problem, did it give you satisfaction?
Immense satisfaction! I used to make it a point to go visit practically every time the *Ijashnes* were held in the morning, to spend an hour or so there.

Did it give you a sense of fulfilling a religious duty, or of being closer to God?
Mostly being closer to nature, being closer to God. It was not a matter of fulfilling duty for the sake of fulfilling it. You felt that sense of inner peace, of inner calm, of inner satisfaction, that you are at peace with the world.

Have there been any other times when you have felt this sense of oneness with the Creator?
Yes, I feel that I am blessed to have the opportunity to do positive constructive work which I genuinely believe is changing people's lives. That is a source of immense, immense pleasure. I feel we have done something good with our lives, we may not have achieved name and fame like others, but whatever we have done has been well worth the effort ...

What is your mental image of God?
I don't imagine God in any particular form, I have never wondered what God would look like. The way I look at it, when we have fulfilled our destiny on Planet Earth and go up, that is the time when everything is going to be judged at the Bridge. That is what I am always thinking about: 'Am I doing something right?' For many years I have had this habit of analysing what has happened in the day before I go to bed, and try to think about right and wrong decisions I have made that day so that tomorrow I won't make that mistake again. So I do this little bit of soul-searching before retiring at night and that has helped me a lot.

Do you recite any special prayers at night?
No, I just do the *kusti*.

When Mr Tamboly had just come under the influence of Khojeste Mistree's book he kept a vegetarian diet throughout the month of Bahman, but in the long run this proved impossible to keep up. The family keeps most of the *parabs* in the traditional way. The Amesha Spenta Ardibehesht is particularly dear to Mr Tamboly, but he says no special prayers on Ardibehesht *roj*. Mr Tamboly has no special affinity with a particular fire; when he visits Navsari he is sometimes acutely aware that he ought to visit a fire temple more often, but the pressures of ordinary life generally cause such feeling to recede to the background.

Since Mr Tamboly has strong links with Navsari, Mrs Munshi asks him about a phenomenon which is much in evidence in that town, namely the veneration of *dargahs* – small shrines originally associated with Sufism. Mr Tamboly answers that such places are indeed much respected by Navsari Parsis and that his mother-in-law used to take him to such a place when he came to visit her. When she died the practice was discontinued in his family. The custom, he says, is connected with the tendency to think in terms of 'auspicious' and 'inauspicious', and older Parsis have learnt it from their parents. Mr Tamboly does not believe that such practices are in any way detrimental to the religion, or indeed have much to do with it; his mother-in-law, for instance, was a very staunch Zoroastrian. He calls such practices 'additional insurance'.

Mr Tamboly has no affinity whatever with Baba-cults. There is a photograph of Sai Baba in his office because one of his father's erstwhile partners was a devotee, but it has no religious significance for him. A discussion of the work of the Bombay Parsi Punchayet follows. Mr Tamboly stresses again that charity should not lead to dependence. In the course of the discussion Mrs Munshi asks whether the Punchayet could do something against the growing phenomenon of strange cults of Parsi origin such as that of the Nagrani, which she describes as very influential among poor Parsis. Mr Tamboly agrees that the phenomenon is worrying, but doubts if the Punchayet would have the means to address the problem.

Mrs Munshi then remarks that in the course of the interview, Mr Tamboly has repeatedly described his uncles and aunts as 'orthodox', and asks him what he means by that term.

I mean that, because it [the religious tradition] was there, they accepted it, believed in it, and followed it blindly. That generation, the one before ours. My generation was the time when we started asking questions, and did not accept things just because they were told to us. They [the older generation] did not know the answers, so they could not answer us. And that is why I call them orthodox, I don't consider myself to be an orthodox person, or a Reformist, I see myself as a pragmatist. I like to ask questions. There are so many questions one seeks answers to.

At the time of my election to the Punchayet, all sides asked me so many questions [about the religion]. I said, 'Look, you are asking me my views on things about which nobody has been able to give clear guidelines. There are so many questions where one can only ask why. What do my views on religious issues matter, don't judge me on those things – don't bring in religion in the case of a person who does not really understand the religion, although he would like to understand it. Judge me on what I can do for the community.' They all voted for me in the end, but I had to convince them that I was not such a bad guy really.

At the time of his election some Parsis suspected Mr Tamboly of being against disposal of the dead in the Towers of Silence, which he says is not the case at all. About his views on the afterlife, Mr Tamboly says that he has never thought much about such things. 'Why think about the next life when there is so much to do in this one?'

———

MRS E

Mrs E was born in 1946 in Bombay. She is married to a Parsi business-man, has two children, and is director of a school. The family moves in upper class circles. Both Mrs E's mother and the present writer attended the interview. Some discussion about religion took place as soon as the interviewer reached the house, before the recorder was switched on.

Mrs E went to an English missionary school and then to a convent school, and was therefore much exposed to Christianity. However, her paternal grandfather had told her many stories about his life, which always had a religious content. He taught Mrs E that in order to counteract the workings of the devil (whose Zoroastrian name Mrs E cannot remember), all one had to do was to pray *Yatha Ahu Vairyo*.

And to this day, if there is a problem it is always *Yatha Ahu Vairyo*. And I must say it has helped. It has always saved me in the nick of time. I have had some dangerous things happen to me. Like two or three years ago I was walking on a beach in Goa. It was my last evening and it was so beautiful, and I was walking and walking, and it got darker and darker, and suddenly there was this man. I thought, 'Oh my God, now what?' The only thing I had was my prayer, and I kept saying it with a vengeance. The man probably thought, 'What is she saying?' But I kept saying it, and he tried to attack me but something within me made me howl like an animal. And sure enough, he went. So I really believe so deeply in our prayers. If I was a Hindu I'd probably believe in their prayers, but this is what I know. I remember when I was in America, everyone said I should not go to a particular place because there had been so many rapes. But I would sing that Christian hymn, 'The Lord is my Shepherd, I shall not want.' And I really have never feared anything. [Laughs] But now I have begun to think, 'You had better look after yourself, it is not fair!'[26]

The family always went to the Atash Behram on *Pateti* and *Khordadsal*. Mrs E had a strong bond with her paternal grandparents who were observant Zoroastrians, and who inculcated a sense of religious tradition in her.

I loved their traditions. My Mummy had no traditions. Always there would be Granny praying with her beads, and my grandfather always telling us how to pray towards the light. There was a *divo*; they did *loban*. Then I went to this missionary school where they stressed the Christian religion, but I used to pray my own prayers in translation, they allowed you to do that. And I saw my father pray every morning, and he used to do charity, which must have made an impression on me as a child.

But my religious education was practically nothing, it was zero because of the way we were brought up, very Anglicised and all that. But I was very attracted to the religion, I had that feeling for religion. And when I got married, my husband is not at all religious but his family is very religious. My sister-in-law goes to the Atash Behram practically every other day if not every day, and my mother-in-law goes as often as possible, on all the important days. [Mrs E struggles with the word *hamkara*.] You see, everything I know is from books, so the pronunciation is not there, and my husband makes fun of it. You see what he took for granted, for me was an awakening. I was so excited: 'So that is how you do it.' Now I could know these things. So I took to it like a duck to water, I loved it all. But of course I have my own way of doing it. You know how some events in your life make you suddenly believe, like your children not being well. So this happened, and I decided to pray the *Ardibehesht Yasht*. I had learned about it from my mother-in-law. So that stuck, and now I pray the *Ardibehesht Yasht* every day, even if it is the last thing at night. That is the time when I pray, that is the only time I get when I am quiet and ready. On weekends I try to get *Behram Yasht* said, once a week, and I believe in that. And if possible the *Khorshed Yasht* and *Meher Yasht* over the weekend.

There is a very strong search, a very strong longing in me, but unfortunately, as they say, the flesh is weak. I would like to do much more. My in-laws have grown up with all these traditions. My husband has always known all these things, and he does not do them. But for me it is all, 'Oh these are nice things to do.' And I am basically a traditional person. I am an old-fashioned woman.

Mrs E's wedding followed the traditional pattern, with the *madav saro*, although a number of rituals (such as the *suprani rit* and *pithi chorvani rit*) were not done because the family did not know about them. The symbolism of the *madav saro* seemed obvious, but otherwise Mrs E regarded these ceremonies as 'just customs'. Asked if she had both *Ashirvads* done, Mrs E confesses that she does not know. Faced with the choice between a short and a long ceremony she remembers she chose the long one, but she knows little about the technicalities.

Mrs E has always followed the laws of purity to the extent that she would not touch a *divo* when she had her period.

My grandparents looked on every woman who had her period as a sort of witch, or as bad, and this horrified me. Those [were the things we observed], basic, very basic. If I was in any other [social group?], I would be considered really like a foreigner or something. Because Mummy did not believe in it [and did not teach me]; her mother believed in everything but she did not.

Asked about favourite *Yazads*, Mrs E says:

Behram Yazd, I believe very strongly in Behram Yazad. And my mother-in-law believes very much in Ashishvang *roj*, and she believes in Meher *roj*. She believes very much in visiting the Aslaji Agiary.[27] I have been there, but I don't go like she goes on every Meher *roj*. I believe in my religion. I have never really needed to go to a particular Agiary on a particular day. I believe so strongly in Behram Yazad, I put all my eggs in one basket.

In such a traditional background I don't expect there would be scope for things like Sai Baba or anything like that?
Well, she [the mother-in-law] does have pictures. I think that she believes very strongly in Ganesh,[28] but only as an outsider, not as part of her.[29] She says it is lucky, Lakshmi is [also] lucky. I think lots of Parsis believe in that kind of thing. At school the children want to do *puja* and I am the Director of the school, so I allow them the freedom to do that. It makes no difference to me, I respect it but I do not pray. At the most I would say 'Bless us'. I certainly would not pray as I would pray to Behram Yazad.

I have a great respect for Kookadaru, again from my husband's tradition, very much. And I have heard of Jal Baba, the recent Baba.[30] You know, you don't pray to them, you venerate them. If somebody told you that someone was special you would want to give them the kind of respect that is due to them, that is all.

On Ava *mahino* Ava *roj* Mrs E's mother-in-law always sends her a *dalni pori*, and Mrs E takes the children to the seashore, making offerings and saying the appropriate prayers. The 'Birthday of the Fire' is celebrated by scrubbing and decorating the fireplace and saying prayers. Mrs E's mother-in-law is 'into that', and reminds her of such *parabs*. The Hindu custom of washing money in milk on the thirteenth day of the *Divali* festival,[31] which many Parsis observe, also appeals to Mrs E Sr., but her daughter-in-law resolutely refuses to do it. On Bahman *mahino* Bahman *roj* the family eats vegetarian food, at least when Mrs E remembers the day; there is no question of observing this throughout the month. On *hamkara* days there are always garlands in the house and Parsi dishes are cooked.

All the customs for pregnancy and early childhood (such as the *panchmasyu*, *agharni* and *chatthi*) were observed because Mrs E's mother-in-law insisted. The *chatthi* took Mrs E by surprise; she had known nothing about it and had to choose a name for the child quickly. Forty days after the births Mrs E underwent the traditional purification rituals. On the upbringing of her children, Mrs E says:

They have seen me pray, and pray longer at weekends, but I have never forced them into it because you see what happened to my husband. He was forced to spend hours in the Atash Behram, and it really put him off. And I had to slowly bring him round. Now he is coming back. He has come full circle, and he believes very much in prayer, but in his own quiet way. It is not the ritualistic way at all. But he reminds me to do things. About the children I feel I have not done enough. When they were little I used to read them stories from books about our religion, and they would sit and listen. But slowly they decided that it was not that much fun, and they wanted to do other things. There are so many other things to do and I suppose I was too preoccupied. I feel I failed them in a sense, I did not have that much to give, I don't have enough knowledge.

When my husband was young, every Behram *roj* they would all sit and do this ceremony with *chana* [chickpeas] on a sheet [the *Mushkil Asan*],[32] and they would recite the whole story of *Mushkil Asan*. So one day I said to my mother-in-law, 'Why don't we do it so the children can experience it?' So we did it once and the kids enjoyed it, but I haven't demanded it every time, because of course it means effort for her to organise it. So they have learnt a little bit from their grandmother. Basically the whole environment in my mother-in-law's family is very Zoroastrian, Parsi. Every aspect of it, the good and the bad.

As to death, Mrs E says that her mother-in-law, like many Parsis, has a horror of even thinking about it. Mrs E herself has a bath and gives her clothes to the *dhobi* immediately after coming back from any function connected with death. She learned this from her mother-in-law, her parents do not do it even when coming back from a funeral. Mrs E has no strong negative feelings about death, thinking of it as a transition. She observes many traditional customs, such as attending *Jashans* and doing the *Satum.*

> I feel tradition is important. If we have no tradition, slowly nothing will matter, everything will disappear into 'Why do this, why do that?' So I feel these few things are like hooks for you to identify what you are. Sometimes when I am lazy, I say, 'It is not really important.' My father, who was a very orthodox Parsi, has suddenly become [negligent]. I am very disappointed in him, I say, 'Daddy, why haven't you done this, you should have!' It is not that he is old, but he has suddenly very much gone into Hindu philosophy, he reads a lot of that. And he has some very interesting books; I myself have been very attracted to Maharishi Ramana's philosophy. He says, 'First of all find out who you are. Who am I?' That is more important than anything. And I have tried, but I haven't got anywhere.

Mrs Munshi then asks Mrs E about her understanding of Ahriman, the Evil Principle:

> It is funny you should ask. Someone had said something [negative] about my son yesterday, and the first thing I did was, I took an egg, waved it around him, and chucked it away.[33] That again comes from my mother-in-law, my mother would never do something like that. It has nothing to do with the *achu michu*,[34] I just did it because I wanted the *najar* [evil eye] off my son! It is not that I really believe in it, but sometimes desperate people do desperate things.

Mrs E's in-laws are against wearing black and for a long time Mrs E did not wear it, 'But now black has become so fashionable! But I won't wear it on my birthday or on *Papeti*,[35] and try not to wear it on New Year's day.'

Mrs E regrets not knowing any of the traditional Parsi songs, which she liked very much on the few occasions when she has heard them. She feels the lack of traditions: 'We seem to have moved too far away from everything that was part of our culture, become too sophisticated.'

Mrs E's favourite fire temple is the Banaji Atash Behram, and she loves going to Udwada. Such trips are part picnic, part religious observance. The family usually goes along when others are going, and do not go on a special date. On a visit to Navsari, which was undertaken for other purposes, the family also visited the Atash Behram there.

Before the interview began, Mrs E had said that the meaning of some Avestan texts, including the *Behram Yasht*, made no sense to her. The interview, however, revealed Mrs E's love of prayer, and in particular of the *Behram Yasht*. Mrs Munshi asked her about this apparent discrepancy.

> I know! I know the meaning partly, and it makes no sense to me really, but I know it [the *Behram Yasht*][36] stands for victory and power, and those are the things that I am asking God for. In everything we do we need that little push from somewhere else. Now that we discussed that [just before the interview], I can say it to you, otherwise I would not have been able to express that. I don't know, you do so many things without realising exactly why. You do a lot of things intuitively, don't you? Some people do not need religion so much, others need it much more to lean on. I think, maybe Mummy's not stressing religion so much made me want it more.
>
> I do *loban* every evening. I am not quite sure why I do it, apparently it is to drive out evil spirits which hate smoke. This is what I gleaned from somebody ... [laughs] apparently they live especially in corners, so I make sure I take it to all the corners. There are little things like that that we do every day.

About the issue of conversion and marrying out of the community, Mrs E says:

> It is just common sense to me that Zoroaster wanted to convert the people to good, what he felt was the best for everybody. So why would he want to exclude some people, 'No, you are not fit for my religion, you are not fit for my thoughts!' I don't think that anyone with any intelligence or goodness in him could do that, and I really don't see that it should be even an issue. We are supposed to be the charitable religion, and we are being so exclusive and stupid. It makes no sense to me, I am sorry!

Here Mrs E's mother intervenes to say that marriage to a non-Zoroastrian seriously affects the vibrations: 'Maybe they are happy, but we all have our own vibrations, and when you marry outside your community then you mix up the vibrations. That is not a good thing for you, not a good thing for the soul.' Mrs E is not sure how to approach the matter in the case of her son:

> I was thinking, should I tell Y [her son], 'Look, you must not even think about marrying outside the community,' or should I think, 'Well, as long as he gets a really good human being? Isn't that more important than getting a *jabri* [domineering] Parsi wife or something?' But then I thought, 'God, there would be no tradition to hand down!' But then, think of the Jews, they have managed to preserve their

tradition. And take me, for instance, I came from a non-observant background, came into this family and I have taken to it like a duck to water, whereas my husband, who grew up with all these traditions, has no time for them.

But you told me that, now that you are working on him, he is already coming back to the religion. There was already that knowledge of the tradition.
He is coming back to the spiritual path, not to the traditions. He does not believe in traditions, he is not that kind of person. There are certain people who believe in rituals and there are people who do not.

I remember, R [the husband] and I were discussing Y: 'How should we handle him? Should we just tell him that he'll be better off marrying a Parsi, or shall we do what our parents did to us, terrorise him?'

Terrorise?
[Laughs.] It was not even discussed by my father, it was my mother who translated [the family sentiments]. There was this whole thing in the family, you know. There was my grandfather, when his son married an American he said, 'Can you imagine the shame that I feel?' It was very much a part of our upbringing: this was not even to be thought of. I remember when boys who were not Parsis wanted to court me, my mother giving me this terrible picture of my father jumping up and down and killing me almost, and throwing me out. And I think R was the same. When he was abroad, his grandmother would write in every single letter: '*Hasto ramto kumaro avje*' [come back happy, and as a bachelor]. Every single letter ended like that.

What I am trying to see is, in the final analysis what is more important? I feel that eventually the soul has to be pure and good, the other things are extras in a way. How do I know that if he married a wonderful girl who loved the religion, why should she not want to follow our religion? And supposing he married a very sophisticated money-grubbing Parsi woman who did not care for any of this? You cannot be really sure.

MRS V

Mrs V (1948) was born in Bombay but spent most of her childhood in Ootacamund ('Ooty'). At the time of the interview Mrs V, who has been married to an American, was living in Bombay with her 11-year old daughter. She is a free-lance designer, works in a furniture shop, and does charity work. Mrs Sarah Stewart was present at the interview.

The interview begins with a discussion of Mrs V's childhood. She was an only child; her parents lived in Bombay when they were first married but soon afterwards Mrs V's mother moved to Ooty, taking the child with her. The mother was not religious and Mrs V went to a Christian school, so that she was taught very little about Zoroastrianism. At the age of seven Mrs V became seriously ill and was taken to England for treatment. On her return to India her grandmother insisted that her Navjote should be done, as she was not expected to live. Mrs V remembers being taught her prayers by a 'huge Dasturji', who despaired of her lack of interest. She returned to Ooty soon afterwards and since she was the only Parsi at school she soon gave up wearing her *sudreh* and *kusti*. Mrs V continued to fall ill in May of each year, and every year her grandmother sent her a new *kusti*, which her mother generally lost or mislaid. Her only contact with Zoroastrianism was during her holidays in Bombay with her grandmother, who was very religious and always tried to make her speak Gujarati. Her father had a sound knowledge of the religion and occasionally went to the Agiary. He was thus able to guide her in religious matters when asked, but he never forced her to accept the religion.

At the end of her school years Mrs V began to question all forms of religion. After school she returned to Bombay and eventually joined Air India, where she worked as stewardess for fourteen years. In the course of time she became interested in 'the Zoroastrian religion as a religion, rather than as the Parsis were actually practising it.' She started reading books on the subject. She also came into contact with Khojeste Mistree, who was then living in Oxford, and under his influence became interested in various esoteric subjects, such as vibrations and numerology, but she never specifically discussed Zoroastrianism with him at this time. Mrs V was living in England when her father died in 1982, and she could not return in time for the funeral.

I was here for the *Uthamna* prayers,[37] which were in the early morning. And my aunt took me for a walk up, in the [grounds of the] Towers of Silence, to show me where he had been taken. I felt very sad missing my father, though actually I was happy that I had not seen him dead, for purely selfish reasons. I remember when she took me for that walk, at four in the morning, it was the most beautiful sensation I have ever had. The vibrations of peace were very strong, and of holiness, a feeling like when you go into an old church ... I remember feeling very peaceful and slightly confused about my own emotions, not having been there ... but also very happy and wanting to know more about what happened there, because I had never really been there before. And looking out over Bombay in the early morning, it was all very beautiful.

Mrs V then began going to some lectures on Zoroastrianism organised by 'Zoroastrian Studies'.

We got into a lot of arguments, because he kept telling me that the child of a Zoroastrian woman married to a non-Zoroastrian could not be ... [hesitates],[38] and I could not understand this. Anyhow, as it happened, I did marry outside my own faith, I married an American. But before I had done that, I told my Dad that if I should marry a Parsi I would like to have some Dasturji or someone come and teach me, what my prayers meant, and why there were all these rituals ...

Mrs V and her husband lived in the US. She had a daughter in 1983, and returned to Bombay around 1986. In America she was not directly in touch with other Parsis. She read *Parsiana*, but felt alienated because children from mixed marriages were not accepted if the mother was a Parsi, while the children of a male Parsi were more easily recognised as Zoroastrians. A turning point came when her five-year old daughter, having been to a Navjote, showed a great interest in the Zoroastrian religion and insisted that she wanted to have her Navjote done.

And I kept saying, 'You cannot have a Navjote, and you must not tell anyone you are a Parsi because you are not a Parsi. You can say you are a Zoroastrian if you are allowed to do the Navjote, but you are never allowed to say you are a Parsi.' Now that was really difficult to explain to her. I kept saying, 'You are half Indian and half American.' Anyhow, she got more and more interested and more and more keen, so the thought started growing in my mind, and eventually I fished out my prayer book and I gave it to her, and I got a tape for her. It was amazing, she sat listening to that tape all on her own for hours in the afternoon.

What tape was that?
This tape that has been done by the ZS ['Zoroastrian Studies'] people about the Navjote ceremony. She listened to it a lot and for me, just listening to these prayers going through my house, it was a great feeling! Anyhow I started trying to learn my prayers to teach her, which of course was not successful, for I could say the *Ashem Vohu* and that was about it. Eventually I went to my aunt, two of my aunts, and asked them to say the prayers to me. I would recite after them, and I would then come home and teach it to her. We went on like this for the next two or three years, and finally I got a Dasturji for her, for she said I was teaching her wrong. So now I have got a Dasturji for her and she is having her Navjote! Now a lot of people – and I am talking about my family members – have said 'How can you? Why do you make her do what you want, why do you put pressure on her?' And I explain that it is not me. Then they say that an eight-year-old cannot make such a choice. I disagree, because she has! I am not a practising Parsi, but through this child I have become more aware, and learned about it, and it is really interesting.

In fact I had a discussion with a Dasturji in London about this, who came to do a *Jashan* in my friend's house. And before he knew who my daughter was he said, 'I sense this child's eyes boring through me.' Like, her vibrations were very strong. And I said, 'Would you like this child to have a Navjote?' He said, 'Why?' I said, 'She is half American.' He said, 'No, I would not do it, but I would find someone for you.' But even he said that he felt a great presence coming from her. Most people do not believe it, but she has been a great catalyst for me. I do believe that we choose our parents, and I believe she chose me to teach me to go back on that path. Because I suddenly realised that our religion basically is so simple and so pure and so easy. In the sense that it does not tell you a million times, 'Don't do this and don't do that, come and confess ... ' It is so basic, it is very pure, I realise, and I want to know more now, it is a nature religion.

Asked how she would feel if her daughter lost some of her present interest in the religion later on, Mrs V says that she hopes she would understand if her daughter stopped wearing her *sudreh* and *kusti* at boarding school, but:

I hope she would not drop her prayers the way I did. I think saying your prayers is the most important thing, these things like the *sudreh* and *kusti* are more symbolic things, trigger-things to help us, to guide us ... To me the most important thing is that I would like her to say her prayers as far as possible, and to try and live by what she has been taught, like Good Thoughts, Good Words, Good Deeds. Which I have been teaching her from the beginning, from the time she was tiny: what you put out comes back to you. She has been taught that since she was very small, before the religious aspect came into the picture. And I certainly would like to have had a more traditional upbringing. When I see my cousins and my aunts, when they go abroad or when they have their birthday, and I see the traditional *patlo*[39] and the garlands, I love that, and I have always felt I have missed out. Because I do think we sometimes need a little bit of ritual or symbolism to keep us in touch with what is going on. It is not like going to church every Sunday, you know, going to the Agiary is a thing you do by choice ... I would like to try to be more traditional, and one thing I would really like to do – I haven't yet figured out how to go about it – I would really like to have *loban* in my home. It is something my grandmother always did, and the lady downstairs, every morning when I smell it, instantly that memory of my grandmother is triggered off. I'd love to do it, but I don't know what prayers to say, and how to go about it.

Asked what it is that pulled her back to Zoroastrianism in spite of her upbringing, Mrs V says:

Because I just feel it is a very wise and simple religion. I know all religions basically teach you the same things, but what I feel is that, if I could try and follow the basic teaching of Zoroastrianism – which as I said earlier is so simple, there is nothing like Ten Commandments or millions of laws to follow – that would improve me as a person, and my life, and what I can do for other people.

Mrs V goes on to describe how the superficial piety she experienced in her Christian school made her feel disenchanted with Christianity later in life. She feels that all religions have something beautiful in them, and would not hesitate to visit a church when travelling. 'But I am not necessarily saying Our Father any more, just saying my own words.' She feels that Zoroastrianism is less demanding than Christianity. Asked about her feelings concerning the rules of purity in this respect, Mrs V answers:

I must say I am confused about some of those. I don't really agree with outsiders not being allowed into the Agiaries. I understand the point of view but I don't necessarily agree with it. Yes, the inner sanctum should be kept pure, with only Parsis going in, but at some point I feel those outsiders who are interested should be allowed to come in. Like they do in a church or a temple, in many temples they don't allow you into the inner sanctum, in churches you don't go up to the altar. But I do feel that it would be nice if one could have a little more openness there. And this childbirth business,[40] I don't know enough because I did not go through it. If you have your period you cannot go to the Towers of Silence, and you cannot say your prayers. These things are all based on very old traditions and perhaps in those days they were important. I don't think they are important today.

Would you like to learn more about the tradition?
Yes, I wish there was more interaction, where people could sit and discuss rather than be lectured to. You know lots of people told me that they went to these lectures which Mr Mistree had, and people gave lectures, which were interesting ... But I think, if we could have small discussions like this, I don't mean three of us,[41] an open house let us say, twice a month. Whoever wishes to come can come, and things could be discussed: you have more knowledge than I have on this point, please explain it to me. If I don't agree with you don't shout at me and condemn me, but I am open to explanations.

A lot of the young Parsis today are quite lost. A lot who are brought up very traditionally, they go through all the rituals of the Navjote but they haven't a clue what they mean. They say their prayers and think they are very good as Parsis, but actually as to why they do it or what it means, not many people can tell you.

Mrs V remembers filming a traditional Parsi wedding and not knowing anything about the rituals. She would like to learn more, but objects to doing things blindly. She believes, however, in the vibrations of the Zoroastrian prayers, which are very old, and as she does 'a lot of alternative things', such as positive thinking, she realises the importance of vibrations.

> So I do believe that if you say the prayers correctly, out loud I mean, not just in your mind, I feel that they will help you, provided you are saying them – you may not understand each word, but you are saying them with your heart, with meaning and good intentions. Then I think they will benefit you. That is the holistic way of looking at it, it is the vibrations, it is the thought, it is the hearing of the prayer and your faith in that prayer. So yes, I do believe that. But in my prayer-book I have a translation of the prayers, which is very nice, so I can look at it .... I tried to explain to her [her daughter] when she was very young; these prayers were very difficult to explain even with a translation, but she seems quite wise in her own little way, she has understood a lot more. She is ready to tell me that I don't understand, and that I am wrong!

The child has a very happy and open relationship with her religious teacher, and Mrs V is confident that she is well taught. She feels that children should be given a choice in religious matters, such as in the question of doing a Navjote. She rejects the criticisms levelled at her by those who feel that her daughter's Navjote is inappropriate:

> I believe that religion is a very personal thing, I don't think anyone in this world has the right to tell anyone else what religion they should be! I explained to my daughter also: 'If you choose to be a Zoroastrian nobody can deny that to you, but you cannot call yourself a Parsi or a Chinese or whatever it might be, for those are man-made rules. But if you choose to say your prayers according to the Zoroastrian faith, there is nobody who can stop you from saying them. Nobody can tell me or you or anybody what religion they should follow.' It is something I feel very strongly about; I talked to Khojeste [Mistree] about it also. I don't know a lot, but I feel that now with the community dwindling and the faith maybe not being practised as it should, we need to absorb the younger people more, have discussions ... Let us understand what our religion is telling us, what it means, why we are doing this and not doing that ... be a little more open about accepting children of mixed marriages into the faith. I don't understand this whole big *tamasha* [to-do] that is going on, children who can come in from the father's side but not from the mother's side. In most religions in the world, when you think about it, it is the

woman who teaches the child the basics of the religion, any religion, so I don't understand why there is this huge divide on this issue.

Because of her daughter's Navjote Mrs V herself has acquired a *sudreh* and *kusti* again, and invited a priest to come and give her a 'refresher course' in the proper ways of handling these items.

> It is almost like a second initiation for me. And I know one thing, I am certainly going to respect my *sudreh* and *kusti* much more than I did as a child, or than my mother did. It is something much more precious to me today. I am certainly going to use my *sudreh* and *kusti* much more than I used to ... But the most important thing to me is to learn my prayers, and I also want some more knowledge about the religion as it was originally taught, the philosophical side.

Mrs V regrets that she was taught practically nothing about the Zoroastrian tradition. She recalls that when she came home with her child it was her cousin, not her mother, who did the traditional welcoming ceremony, and that she herself grew up without any such customs. She feels religion will give her daughter a much-needed sense of belonging and identity, and she herself has always felt the lack of 'anything traditional or symbolic' in her upbringing. The fact that for the last few years she has put chalk-marks outside her door in the Zoroastrian way gives Mrs V a sense of satisfaction and identity. Memories of the *loban* and other ceremonies in her grandmother's house come up again, and Mrs V describes her love of fire:

> I have always loved fire; it is just the ritual of it, the whole thing of lighting those embers and putting that [hesitates] *sukhad*? ... *loban* and *sukhad* [incense and sandalwood]. And also when I go to an Agiary I always stand for a while, alone, in front of that big fire. As long as I can without disturbing anybody. With my eyes closed, I do not really watch it, but there is a great sense of peace. It is a wonderful feeling. And also, whenever I watch prayers or religious functions I do know that I am transfixed by that *afarganyu* [fire vase], I never take my eyes off it, ever! Always, always staring at it throughout any prayer; it is something very strong in me.

Mrs V's aunt organised a Muktad ceremony for her father the first year after his death, and every year on his death anniversary she put a *divo* in her father's room, with flowers, as a way of remembering him. Otherwise, since she was not taught any traditional mourning rituals, she mourned her father in her own personal way by frequently playing his favourite music.

Since her return to India, Mrs V has made a point of wearing a sari in the special Parsi style. 'That is another thing I do; these are all my small little ways of doing the things that I want to do for identity. Not what someone else would tell me to do or what I feel I should do. I am very much my own person. And that is about it.'

Notes

1 'Mother', a feminine spiritual guide.
2 *viz.* because it may be known that she is married to a non-Zoroastrian.
3 The remark refers to the present book.
4 Mrs H means that until recently she had not seen many publications on Zoroastrianism that were helpful to most Parsis.
5 See above, p. 10.
6 i.e. the ritual is basically performed by two priests.
7 Many Parsis feel embarrassed about this, perhaps because it usually involves loosening one's outer clothes and the process is relatively conspicuous.
8 On the use of an iron bed during menstruation see above, p. 39f.
9 See above, p. 20f.
10 See above, p. 10.
11 i.e. a fully qualified priest.
12 On the need for extra priests at this time see above, p. 25.
13 On this ceremony see above, p. 32.
14 Note the reference to the Hindu goddess of wealth, which illustrates the way in which symbols and idiomatic expressions of Hindu origin are used by Parsis as a matter of course, and may thus imperceptibly influence their views on many things.
15 In other words, Dr Y does not know the Avestan texts by heart but they have become very familiar.
16 A moderately long prayer sequence.
17 The 'birthday of the Fire'.
18 A slightly longer name for the prayer mentioned earlier, which is widely recited in cases of illness.
19 'Praying', as the term is used here, may refer to the act of getting a priest to recite prayers or perform a ritual. The original versions of several interviews show that no fundamental distinction is perceived between purely verbal prayer and rituals accompanied by liturgical formulae. See also below, p. 295.
20 On classical Zoroastrian attitudes to mourning see above, p. 170 n. 26.
21 The appropriate period for keeping up prayers and rituals for the dead is a much-debated issue in Parsi circles (see e.g. the interviews with Mr Antia and Mrs Q).
22 See above, p. 52 with n. 48.
23 A combination of *Vendidad* and *Yasna* (Guj. *Ijashne*) ceremonies.
24 i.e. within one religious year.
25 Dastur Kotwal's decision may have been based on the authority of such sources as the Pahlavi *Dadestan i Denig* (*DD.* 81, see Kreyenbroek 1987b: 188), where it is said that if money for a ceremony is paid to a priest in good faith the merit accrues to the person ordering the ritual in spite of any shortcomings. It is interesting to note, however, that for Mr Tamboly, who relies on priestly authority in religious matters, the apparent contradiction

probably did more to shake his confidence than a further request for money (for more ceremonies) might have done.

26 i.e. you cannot leave all to God.

27 On the custom of visiting this fire temple on Meher *mahino* Meher *roj* see above, p. 22f.

28 A Hindu divinity.

29 In other words, Mrs E's mother-in-law believes that such divinities have power, but her loyalty to Zoroastrianism forbids her to worship them as part of her own religion.

30 See pp. 50, 308f.

31 This festival is known as *Dhan Teras*.

32 See above, p. 20.

33 *viz.* to remove the evil. Mrs E clearly associates the idea of an evil power with superstition.

34 On this ceremony, in which an egg is also passed around the head of the recipient, see above, p. 19.

35 On Pateti or Papeti see above, p. 26.

36 In fact, in classical Zoroastrianism it is the Yazad Behram who stands for these things, the hymn being merely a way of praying to him.

37 i.e. the rituals of the fourth morning after death, on which see above, p. 38f. The actual disposal of the body in the Tower would have taken place a few days earlier.

38 The remark refers to the view of many 'traditional' Parsis that the child of a non-Zoroastrian father and a Zoroastrian mother cannot be regarded as a Zoroastrian. See also above, p. 58 n. 67.

39 A small wooden platform used, among other things, for the *sagan*; see above, p. 18.

40 i.e. the rules of purity affecting a woman during the first forty days after a birth.

41 i.e. Mrs V herself, Mrs Munshi and Mrs Stewart.

Chapter Seven

Eclecticism in Religious Views

MRS X

Mrs X was born in 1935. She holds degrees in English, French and Geography. She has worked as a teacher and later became Principal of her school. She is married with two children, and is interested in 'all contemporary religions and Yoga.'

Mrs X has always lived in Bombay and has no roots in a village. She was taught about the religion by her mother, who was very religious. Her father was not religious at all, but made the children learn their prayers nevertheless. At the age of six or seven Mrs X was taught more prayers by Mrs Nusservanjee.[1] Her Navjote was done when she was six. She did not realise the significance of the *sudreh* and *kusti* at the time; once her *kusti* slipped off at night, and she tells with an embarrassed giggle that she let it hang over a chair all night.[2] About her early religious development Mrs X says:

I had a lot of faith in Zoroaster. To me the Lord Ahura Mazda *was* Zoroaster; I did not know a lot about the Lord Ahura Mazda. My Mummy saw to it that we did go to the Agiary on different *roj*, like Hormajd *roj*, Behram *roj*, Sarosh *roj*, and kneel down and pray to the fire. And respect the Waters, respect Plants, respect Fire – there was no smoking in our house. And apart from that I always felt an awe and a love, for God was something awesome to me. Zoroaster was my God; I did not understand Ahura Mazda as I understand Him today, as the one cosmic, big shining Light. And there was a lot of faith in Behram Yazad, such a lot of faith! Even as a child I remember the *Mushkil Asan*.[3] And I remember my mother had a lot of faith [in this] ... When my Mummy was in her *menses* she would ask me to do it. I was so small that I could hardly reach the table but I could recite the Behram Yazad story with blinding faith. And the *chana* [chickpeas] was not for yourself to eat, it was to be given to the poor in the name of Behram Yazad, the mighty, victorious *Fareshta* [angel] who'll get rid of all the evil. Maybe I was a bit clever, I understood that this was a *Fareshta* who would help. Later, after my marriage, I gave up this practice, but I still believe in it in a way, because when we take the name of Behram Yazad, we always say *Mushkil Asan Sahib* [Lord Problem-solver], that means the *Fareshta* who will get rid of your troubles.

Mrs X was taught to recite all the normal Zoroastrian prayers and could also recite several *monajats* as a child. Later, at school, she was taught by Dasturji Darabshah Kutar,[4] whom she describes as a very inspiring priest. Dastur Kutar told stories from the *Shahname*, and from that time onwards Mrs X began to read books about ancient Iranian mythology. The question of *dakhme-nashini*[5] was also discussed in class; it both frightened and fascinated Mrs X at the time. Later Dastur Kutar died and was succeeded by his brother, whose teaching did not appeal to her, and she lost interest. 'So I firmly believe that it is through stories and love and music that one can learn about religion.' Ava Yazad also fascinated Mrs X; she was born on Ashishvang *roj*, which is connected with Ava Yazad,[6] married on that *roj*, and has a special affinity with it. 'I used to love the Waters, I still love the Waters.' Her mother used to give the children *dalni poris* to offer to the Waters, together with flowers, sugar and coconut on every Ava *roj*.

Later Mrs X studied Yoga and Vedanta with a teacher whom she adored and who greatly respected the Parsis and fire. At about the same time, in the early 1980s, she met Khojeste Mistree,[7] whose teaching had a profound influence on her.

> I think that was the revival, for me and for the children in the school! I don't know why, maybe because Khojeste was young and charismatic. His oratory was very beautiful, in English. He spoke from his heart, sincerely; it was laity talking to laity, there was no priest involved. And then I was taught by Jeannie Bharucha.[8] ... At some stage I had given up wearing my *sudreh* and *kusti*, only because it came in the way of my dressing, for no other reason. It was Jeannie Bharucha who told me, 'Wear the *kusti*!' And I think after I began wearing the *kusti* a lot of my difficulties went away. What I have learned of my Zoroastrian religion is through Khojeste and through Jeannie Bharucha. And mind you, Jeannie did a course with us, not for one or two days, but for *one full year*, every week! And then we introduced it in our school ... and we have not repented a moment.

Asked if she still does Yoga,[9] Mrs X says:

> Yes, I do my Yoga, and it was thus that I found that you can be spiritually inclined and not religiously inclined, or religious and not

spiritually evolved at all.[10] So it was so good to be spiritually evolved
and at the same time religiously evolved. And then I found that, if this
is Yoga, then Zoroaster was the greatest Yogi of them all! I found that
what is Yogic is all in Zoroaster. It is so nice that our religion teaches
about being happy: you be happy and make others happy, you eat and
make others eat, you earn and make others earn. There is no
selfishness. And prayer also ... I'll be honest: if I were to say a small
Hail Mary, I would not hesitate; if I were to say the *Gayatri Mantra* [a
Hindu formula], I would not hesitate. But I would not worship.[11]
Whatever is universal, just say it if you like the meaning of it. I now
have *Vispe Humata* [an Avestan prayer formula], translated into
English. Everyone says it is universal, we don't say it in Avestan, we
say it in English. It is the same as the *Gayatri Mantra*, because the
Gayatri Mantra is also beautiful: 'Lord, bring us from darkness into
light, from hatred into love.' Like St Francis Assisi's prayer, it is the
most beautiful prayer! And to me my *Sarosh Baj* is the best prayer!

Although Mrs X's mother was religious the family did not have 'this
problem of untouchability' (during menstruation) in their house. When
the women had their period they would not touch the *divo* or the table on
which it stood, or go to a Navjote or a fire temple, but they were allowed
to do their *kusti* and say their prayers. Menstruation was regarded as a
natural phenomenon and Mrs X is still glad that this was the case. She is
willing to respect tradition in this matter, but does not believe there is
anything intrinsically evil about menstruation.

When Mrs X was a child the family had a *divo* burning continuously,
later this became inconvenient and incense sticks were used when
required. *Loban* was done at one time but it was stopped a long time ago,
as it became too expensive and in any case family members had no time
for such ceremonies. *Parabs* were not observed. The first time Mrs X went
to Udwada on pilgrimage was when her daughter was born. As a child,
Mrs X used to sit near the fire in the fire temple and look into it, and she
remembers loving the fire. She saw the *Atashnu Git* performed in the
house of a neighbour and liked it. At some stage she gave up praying
because she did not understand the meaning; she read some translations
and explanations but they did not appeal to her. Later, when she took up
Yoga, Mrs X's Swami advised her to 'Go to God with your heart, not with
your intellect ... the vibrations are important.' During her second
pregnancy Mrs X was advised to pray the *Ava Ardvisur Niyayesh*; she
prayed it for forty days and all her wishes for the child were granted:

So today the Water and the Fire are very important; and I have been
reading my *Gathas* for the last 15 years, all the five days.[12] I do my
loban in the morning on certain days, anniversaries. I pray every
morning when I get up; I have a cup of tea and whether I have my

bath or not, I sit down and I pray for twenty minutes. I do my *kusti* prayers, then I do my *Sarosh Baj*, then a small *Atash [Niyayesh]*, then *Ava Ardvisur [Niyayesh]*. And then Dasturji Aibara[13] has given me three prayers, *Airyamanem* prayers, they are extracts from the *Gathas*. I do that, that is all.

Mrs X's marriage was a love-match. Like herself her husband came from a 'medium-religious family, no taboos'. The wedding was a traditional one, with *madav saro, suprani rit*, and *divo-adarni*.[14] Later Mrs X organised all these ceremonies – which she had to learn from a book – for her nieces. Mrs X enjoys rituals of this kind. 'It is just fun. And traditions and customs, I believe, are important.'

Mrs X says that funerary ceremonies used to frighten her as a child:

My first experience was when my 28–year old aunt died … I was eleven or twelve years old at the time and I had never been to a funeral. So we were all taken to the funeral and made to sit in the front row, and that thing [the bier] was so close to us, and at one time everybody said 'Look down, look down', when the body was lifted up.[15] I was a precocious child at that time and I thought, 'Why are they asking me to look down?' So I looked up and saw all the body being lifted. And when they were putting her onto that thing her eyes opened … I still cannot forget that. But I was a child, I did not mind …

The most painful was my brother, he was only 25! He was an Airforce lieutenant and he was going to get married in two months time, and his plane crashed and he died. I think that was the most painful ceremony I ever went to. All the four-day ceremonies were done. And I think we became more religious after his death, we believed more in the Muktads after his death, we were totally involved with ceremonies after his death!

Mrs X had been told about the funerary rituals as a child. The reasons for praying for the soul were not specifically discussed but Mrs X has always felt that they are important, 'whether the soul is reborn or not.'[16] She still performs a special observance on the anniversary of her brother's death: she takes a bath, puts flowers, milk and fruit in place, does her *kusti* and prays *Havan geh* and *Satumno Kardo*, with a *divo* and incense.[17] Her husband does not pray much but does do his *kusti*, and he goes to the Agiary. Her son also does his *kusti*. Her daughter used not to pray, but when she developed health problems Mrs X advised her to start doing so:

I told her, 'Pray! Our prayers definitely have power over difficulties.' I am a great believer in this. I gave her special prayers from one of Khojeste's papers, *Ushta* [the ZS Newsletter], and from that I took the *Ardibehesht Nirang*, and gave it to her. I said, 'This is in English, you do not know Gujarati, now pray with your heart and soul!' And then I made her pray to Meher Yazad. Meher is also very dear to us. I recently found out, because of the Kookadaru cult.[18] (I used to like Kookadaru, but I never used to worship him. But then I did find that there is something there!) And she got better, and now she agrees and she prays.

Mrs X's mother taught her observances like the *chatthi, besna,* and *pagladu,* which she later performed for her children and then for her niece's baby. To Mrs X's regret, however, her own children appear uninterested in marriage although they are in their late twenties and thirties.

My husband and I, we had such a gay time for ten years before we married. These children won't even date. They say, 'Show me, where are the people to date? You don't want us to marry out of the community, so who can we date?' We are a middle class orthodox family, we don't allow our daughters to go out with just anybody and everybody! About that I am a bit orthodox, I am quite strict ... I believe that marriages are destined by God, so why should I make any effort? I am a great fatalist, if He thinks it is the right moment, He will do it, why should I bother? They say birth, marriage and death are all destined, so why should I bother? I think our Parsi boys are ... you know they believe in equality, they trust their wives, they work at home with their wives, never mind if they are called sissies by the Hindus, they help their wives, they are sweet, they pamper their wives like American husbands. But they are not very rich, the good brains are all going abroad, there is a big brain drain amongst the Parsis and those boys are not coming back. But they are not happy, and our girls from here are very wary now, they don't want to go to the States, they know that life is not easy there.

From the undesirable nature of 'marrying out', the conversation moves on to the question of other religions.

Not that I disrespect any religion. To me, now with Yoga, all religion is one. My religion is the best for me because I am born in it, but I think there should be one world religion. It is impossible, but humanity is my religion today. What is the use of being a Zoroastrian who is not charitable, who is wicked, who is aggressive, who is sinful? I think the essence of religion today should be humanity.

Mrs X believes very strongly in charity, and it plays an important role in the religious lives of members of her family. Mrs X's predilection for dogs is discussed. Mrs X loves all animals, and refuses to accept the traditional Zoroastrian idea that such animals as mice are Satanic creatures.

Asked about her belief in Kookadaru, Mrs X says:

In 1985 I went through a very bad health set-back, and I was getting very ill. And my sister who lives at Cusrow Baug said, 'Come on, I'll take you to Dasturji Aibara, he'll give you some prayers.' And, much against my will, I went. I did not like Dasturji Aibara, because he was very strict. And Dasturji said, 'Will you say these prayers?' I said, 'OK, Dasturji', and he gave me a picture of Kookadaru with a picture of an Iranian king. He always used to give Kookadaru with a picture of any Iranian king, Kookadaru and Faridun Padshah, Kookadaru and Lohrasp or Kookadaru and Kaikhusrow Padshah. And I said, 'What am I to do?' He said, 'Wear it over your heart.' I said, 'All the time? It will show from under my dresses.' He said, 'You wear it.' So I came out. First I asked Mrs Nusservanjee to translate these prayers, I wanted to know what was there. So she read them and she said, 'There is nothing bad, they are from the *Gathas,* they are beautiful. What harm is there if you read it every day?' But at the top of the prayer there were the names of Faridun Padshah, Lohrasp, Kaikhusrow, Jamshid and also Kookadaru! So they used to associate the *fravashi*[19] of Kookadaru with all these big Padshahs! And I still read it every day. And I showed Mrs Nusservanjee the picture he had given me; there was Kookadaru, but I said, 'Who is this king with the feather in his cap?' She said, 'Kaikhusrow, the biggest Yogi amongst the Iranian kings. This is symbolic, you will soon meet a Yogi.' And I met my Swami *in one month*! At that time I did not realise, [I thought] it was a coincidence. But she had told me, 'This picture signifies you are going to meet a very great man who will teach you a lot about the *atman* and the soul and spirituality apart from any religion.' And I have learned a lot! I now understand what the *fravashi* is:[20] within us, the Spenta Mainyu, that spark within us, which we say comes from God.

Do you do the Kookadaru Baj[21] *all the time?*
No, but whenever I go to the Aslaji fire temple or Banaji – I love the Banaji Atash Behram, it has a fascination for me.

Do you go there on Mondays?[22]
No, I go when there are no crowds, but I love the Banaji. My Navjote was also at the Banaji Atash Behram. I find some link there, I like it.

Do you go to the Aslaji on Meher mahino Meher roj?[23]
No, but since the last three months I have done it for my daughter's health,[24] and there is an improvement! There are so many people there, what is the harm in offering *sukhad* [sandalwood] and praying? It is good! And there are Parsis praying to the *peepul* tree also, it is a Hindu belief because Shiva is supposed to be in the *peepul* tree. To me, Yoga has taught that Shiva is your superconsciousness! Shiva is not a god, he is your superconsciousness! And what is Ahura Mazda but

210

your superconsciousness, your cosmic consciousness, your light? So Shiva and Ahura Mazda and Cosmic Consciousness is all the same! And what harm is there if a Parsi goes and tends the tree? It is so nice! He is looking after the tree, so indirectly he is doing (it for) Bahman Amesha Spenta Yazad![25] ... We have a cosmopolitan crowd here, somebody will go to Sai Baba and bring me a little statue ... if they bring me little gods – they brought me a Krishna, they brought me an *Om*, they brought a Mother Mary, they brought me Christ, they brought me a Shiva – I am lucky! These big people have come to my door, why should I cast them out? Every one is my friend, I say hello to them every morning, what is wrong with that?

Mrs X observes the *parabs* for the Fire and the Water; as she is normally at school her husband or daughter makes the preparations at home. Mrs X does a ceremony at the school on those days, which has now become a tradition. Mrs X does not eat meat on Bahman *mahino* Bahman *roj* – or on Good Friday.[26] Because of Christian influences on her education she loves Christ and Mother Mary, though not Christianity as such: 'If Zoroaster teaches me happiness, Christ taught me love and forgiveness.' She lights a candle on Good Friday. She remembers being fascinated by the stories of the Bible, which she compares to what 'Zoroastrian Studies' is now teaching in schools.

Mrs X offers a *machi* regularly on the death-anniversaries of her mother and her brother, because her mother used to offer a *machi*, and it is a way of remembering them. For a long time the family did all the traditional birthday ceremonies for the children, including the bath with milk and flowers.[27] Her children still do a *sagan* for her on her birthday. On festive days the family always has traditional Parsi festive dishes. She does not normally pray the *Yashts* because they are too long, preferring the shorter *Niyayesh* prayers. She has prayed the *Sarosh Yasht Vadi* in the past, and has recited the *Gathas* regularly for the last fifteen years. She has visited Sanjan[28] and Udwada, and is planning trips to Navsari and Surat; she longs to see the Surat Atash Behram.

Mrs X hardly observes any Hindu customs. She washes her gold ring in milk at the *Divali* festival, as many Parsis do. On *Kali Chowdas* (the 14th day of *Divali*),[29] she used to take an egg around the house and throw it away, in order to remove evil. Many Parsis in her area still do this. She recounts that when she was a child, on *Kali Chowdas* she once broke open earthen pots in which Hindus had put things for purposes of magic. Her mother was horrified:

> She washed me, she put *taro* on me and she made me do four *kustis* in four different directions. She said, 'If you don't do it tomorrow you'll go mad or you'll die.'[30]

MRS U

Mrs U was born in Rawalpindi in 1926. She moved to Karachi as a child and came to Bombay at the time of the Partition of India and Pakistan in 1947. She graduated from Bombay University and worked as a stenographer for some time. She is married to a well-known art-dealer and has two children. Mrs Sarah Stewart was present at the interview.

The interview begins with a description of Mrs U's childhood in Karachi. She went to a Parsi school, where a Zoroastrian cap was worn (which was not done at home), and prayers were said at Assembly. Some other girls tried to get out of attending religious observances by claiming to have their periods, but not Mrs U:

> I enjoyed all those religious ceremonies, I mean religious prayers and all that. And I still remember that when I was in fourth standard, my aunt had given me a lovely piece to recite at the elocution competition. It was called 'Prayer', something about prayers, and it was called in Gujarati *Bandagi e-j jindagi che* [Prayer is Life itself]. I won a first prize in that; it was seven rupees – in those days that was a lot. The last four lines were in English:
>
> > *Prayer is the soul's sincere desire,*
> > *Uttered or unexpressed,*
> > *It is the notion of a hidden fire*
> > *That trembles in the breast.*
>
> Now these four lines have sort of, [made] a mark on my memory, you know, and I tell everyone to pray. I have great faith in prayers, I tell everyone, people at home and all my friends, that our sincere prayers never go unheard.

At home many of the traditional Parsi observances were done; there was a *divo, loban* was done, and birthdays were celebrated in the traditional way. Mrs U has fond memories of Karachi, where the community spirit was stronger than in Bombay.

> So my childhood days were very happy, and all the Parsi traditions were enjoyed, and I tell you we Parsis there were very much united, not like these Bombay Parsis who are so ... they are all self-centred. On occasions like New Year or on such festivals, [in Bombay] people used to crowd and go to cinemas or go to plays and all that, whilst in Karachi we Parsis used to meet together and do *hamazor*,[31] we used to have *hambandagi* [communal prayers] during the Muktad days. We used to have prayers and do *hamazor*. You know what *hamazor* means, we meet each other and there are flowers. And then, whenever there were any Parsi *Gahambars* we used to go there and enjoy the

Gahambars also. So the Parsis in Karachi were very united, nobody was very poor. There were vast charities. And I remember in Karachi one very nice incident was, we had a neighbour who used to look after all his brother's children and all that, so every night at 7 o'clock, after sunset, we would call all the neighbour's children and we used to sing all the *monajats*, and it was so nice.

All Mrs U remembers about her religious instruction is that Dr Dhalla[32] used to come on Fridays to teach the *kusti* prayers. She remembers being taught the *Khorshed Meher Niyayesh*. As regards the meaning of the prayers, Mrs U says:

We were taught the meaning but I did not understand much. It was so mystical and unclear in my mind that even when I got married my brother in law – he had sort of atheist tendencies – he always used to tell me, 'You are praying so much, do you understand what you are praying?' I said, 'No, I do not understand what I am praying but I have faith, and I pray.' I believe in the power of prayer, and I tell everyone that. I don't understand much about it, but whenever there is any religious thing I try and attend. But now I am getting old and I cannot go on my own, so I miss all that. But I still pray, I get up early, 6 o'clock, I have my bath, and I pray.

When discussing her Zoroastrian schooling, Mrs U contrasts it with her sister's education:

But my sister was just the opposite, because she was brought up in a convent school at Murree, so when she came to Karachi she could not adjust herself to this Parsi school. Till she died a few years ago she always had that Christian influence in her. Of course she used to go to the Agiary, but she always carried this Dominic Xavier – now I respect all religions, I pray to Mother Mary on Sundays, then I pray to Sai Baba on Thursdays, and I respect all religions – it is not that I am bigoted, that only our Zoroastrians [are right]. All religions are the same but ... my sister was very fond of all this Christianity.

Because Mrs U was a sickly child her Navjote was done in a fire temple in Karachi. Her marrriage was an arranged one, and since both families were strict and old-fashioned she had to fight to be allowed to work during her engagement. The four-day ceremonies were done, including the *madav saro*, but neither horoscopes nor religious singing formed part of the proceedings. 'My mother-in-law, though she was very strict, she did not believe in *garbas*[33] and all that.'

About the laws of purity Mrs U says:

My mother was very strict, when we had our period we mustn't touch the *matka* [earthen pot] for drinking-water, and we mustn't go into the kitchen, we mustn't sit on the chair where she prayed, or sit on her bed, and all that. So when I got married and I came here – of course in the beginning I wanted to go and visit my people, my mother. And she would tell me, 'Please, if you are like that, don't sit on my bed, don't touch my chair.'

Your mother would tell you that? What about your in-laws?
My own mother, but here they didn't mind about that.[34]

What about prayers, did you say your prayers and do your kusti when you had your period?
No, not to do it! I still remember, when your seven-day period was over, have a head-wash, throw away all your clothes in the *dhobi*[35] with your bed-sheets, everything in the *dhobi*.

Did you have a separate bed?
No, nothing like that.

No segregation?
No segregation, my in-laws were very reformed like that, they said these are all old-fashioned customs. But they were strict in certain ways, disciplinarian types: [you] must be at home, do all the house work, dusting, cleaning, kitchen – the daughter-in-law must do all the work. They were that orthodox type.

When Mrs U returned home after childbirth, her mother-in-law did not allow her to go out during the first forty days, but she was allowed to touch everything in the house. When the forty days were completed she had a *nahn* at the Agiary. During Mrs U's first pregnancy the *panchmasyu* and the *agharni* were done. When the children were born her mother-in-law did a *sagan* each month, but the *besna* was not performed for her daughter, 'So naturally, when she fell so often and sprained her ankle, people said that is because the *besna* was not done.'

Tradition plays an important role in Mrs U's family life. The whole family follows the traditional rules about haircuts; for cutting nails only her son does this. Mrs U has been forced to discontinue the practice of doing *loban* in the mornings because the house has to be swept first and the sweeper comes too late for it to make sense. However, the family light a fire in the kitchen when they come home, and Mr U prays to it every night. She goes to the Towers of Silence on Farvardin *mahino* Farvardin *roj*, and recites the *Ava Niyayesh* every day in the month of Ava. No meat is eaten on Bahman *mahino* Bahman *roj*, and on the five days associated with it.[36] Elaborate preparations are made for the 'birthday of the Fire':

On Adar *mahino* Adar *roj* we clean up the kitchen two days before, and my fire table also.[37] I clean up everything.

214

Two days before?
Yes, naturally. Then on the Daepadar *roj*,[38] at four o'clock, quarter to four, that is in the Uziran *geh*, I do the *loban* in the kitchen and here also. And I light the fire and pray the *Atash Niyayesh*. But it is said that if you pray five *Atash Niyayesh*, from Daepadar *roj* to Adar *roj*, that is most efficacious. Uziran *geh*: *Atash Niyayesh*; Aiwisruthrim *geh*: *Atash Niyayesh*. Twelve o'clock in the night I get up and light the fire. And I have even taught my neighbours that, so when they see my light at twelve o'clock they also get up. But only on *Atashnu parab*. That is, then Ushahin *geh*, then again in the early morning, next day's Havan [*geh*] it is Adar *mahino* Adar *roj*.

To Mrs U's regret her daughter, who emigrated to Australia, no longer wears the *sudreh* and *kusti*:

And the uncle who took her, the uncle and auntie don't believe in it, they don't believe in our religion, so how do you expect my daughter to wear it?[39] But I always tell her. And now, at this age, she realises and she always writes and tells me, 'Mummy, pray for me, Mummy, go to the *kuva* [the Bhikha Behram Well], and light a *divo*.' I always go there, I light a *divo* whenever I am passing. Or, 'Mummy, pray *Ardibehesht Yashtni Nirang* for me, Mummy, pray this for me.' But my son is just the opposite, he is a strong Zoroastrian ...

When you say your son is a staunch Zoroastrian, what sort of religious instruction did he have, what did you teach him and what was he taught at school?
He went to an English school here, but at home he saw my father-in-law praying every morning, lighting the *divo*, lighting the *agar batti* [incense sticks], and my mother-in-law praying after the bath, and all of us praying, so you know, he has seen this around him, that affects the child. My daughter went away at an early age; she saw us praying and all that, but the place where she went, where uncle and auntie never prayed, you see. So naturally she came under a different type of influence. Whereas my son ...

SS: He did not have any religious instruction outside the house?
Who, my son? No! When they had the Navjote ceremony I remember we used to have the priest coming and teaching them the *kusti* prayers [and nothing else]. But he used to see his grandfather praying and everybody praying, so that is the thing: when you have environment.

Discussing her prayer routine Mrs U says that, although she used to have a bath and do her *kusti* immediately on waking up, now she needs to buy milk very early in the morning, so she has her bath after this; then she does her *kusti* and offers some personal prayers for blessings.[40] She then has tea, after which she 'sits for her prayers':

Ek-so-ek nam [the 101 Names of God] that is a must, then I say my *Sarosh Baj*, then my *Havan geh*, and *Khorshed Meher Niyayesh*. And I feel so empty if I don't pray, I grumble, I say, 'Today you did not give me enough time to pray.' I tell my husband, my son, 'You all got up so early that I had no time to say my prayers, you [should] sleep till I finish my prayers!' My husband jokes and says, 'Now one minute you pray from your red book, one minute from your pink book, then from your green book.' I say, 'Never mind, I get the satisfaction.' If I don't pray, I feel very empty – that something has been left out in me. I mean I must have my prayers.

On *hamkara* days Mrs U goes to the fire temple to pray, and on the anniversary of her mother's death she has a *Baj* service done there. The *Shekaste, shekaste Shaytan* formula[41] she associates with her school-days; she has long meant to ask someone the meaning of it but never got round to doing so. When asked whether she has any favourite Amesha Spentas or Yazatas, Mrs U says:

Behram Yazad, Pak-afsun-e Shah Faridun, and the *Kookadaru Baj* I always do.[42]

You do special prayers?
Yes, special prayers; every day I pray from that pink book ...

The Kookadaruni Nirang?[43]
Yes, and I even get this Kookadaru's *Baj* done. On his date of birth and his date of death. Then *Homaji Baj* and *Jartoshtno Diso*.

Any special reason why you get Kookadaru's Baj done?
You know, you invoke their blessing, you pray to them to bless you, and be thankful for all the mercies that you have received.

But were these stories told to you about Kookadaru, Homaji, the background?
No, I don't know any background, but I have got lots of books I read. Gujarati books, *Karamat-e Khudae*[44] and all that. About our distinct miracles performed by Kookadaru.

You said that Behram was your favourite Yazad, do you do anything special on Behram roj?
Yes, I do. Every Tuesday I do *Behram Yazadno divo*.[45]

Why every Tuesday?
Because I read that if you do it on a Friday ... I used to do that, but I read somewhere that Friday is mostly for the Muslims. So I switched it to Tuesday. I just put sugar, crystalised sugar, *chana*, flowers and a *divo*, and read that story ...

Do you recite the Behram Yasht every day?

Not every day, on Behram *roj*. I like my *Hormazd Yasht*, so whenever there is time I do *Hormazd Yasht*. And now, when people are not keeping in good health I recite *Ardibehesht Yasht*.[46] I don't know much about the religion, but whenever somebody tells me that this is good for this, and this is good for that, I just follow it. I don't ridicule, I don't run down anything.

Did you ever experience that, through prayers, somebody in the family was healed?

Yes, yes, yes! I tell you when my son was very ill I was given that small book of *Pak-afsun-e Shah Faridun*. So for three days, at a certain time only, and on certain days only, you had to say the whole prayer, and recite that long prayer for three days at a fixed time. And I must say that it has healed him.[47] Those were called *Pak-afsun-e Shah Faridun* prayers for good health. It is a very long prayer, I'll show it you you. And sometimes I translate Gujarati prayers, a few lines, and send it to my daughter, who cannot read Gujarati books. I have given her a cassette also, I have given her prayer books. I just say, 'You try and say: *Yatha mari madad ne Sarosh mari panah* [The *Y.A.V.* prayer is my help and Sarosh is my protection].' I just teach everyone that, *Yatha mari madad ne Sarosh mari panah*.

Questions about the afterlife evoke little response. After a brief discussion of her husband's interest in charities, the conversation returns to the subject of prayer and its benefits when troubles come. The following discussion ensues.

But do you feel the same when you pray to Mother Mary or Sai Baba, which is what you said?

I pray to Mother Mary, and to dear Saint Dominic Xavier, I have great faith in Dominic Xavier.

What do you pray?

Just, 'Please help me, please pray for us.' That is all.

And for Sai Baba?

[For] Sai Baba I just light a simple *divo*, I put a little statue, that is all, and I say, 'Sai Baba, please help us.' There was one Australian lady who had come here and she had lost her health when a very young girl, and she wanted to go to Sai Baba's temple here in Bombay, so I took her there. I respect all the religions. But my son does not believe in that.

Do you find when you pray to other religions that your prayers are accepted?

Yes, I feel that! I pray sincerely – first my prayers, first my Zoroastrian prayers and then I say, 'Help me, solve my problems'. And I feel that if you pray sincerely, if you ask God to help you, your prayers never go unheard. I always write that to my daughter: our sincere prayers never go unheard.

Whoever you pray to?
Yes, whoever you pray to. You see, I pray to Saint Dominic Xavier, and I contribute there, and I get the monthly magazine, and every afternoon I just read one or two lines and then I just go off to sleep. But my son says, 'Mummy, you respect everyone, I am just with my Zoroastrian religion.' My son says he will not enter a church or a temple. I say that is wrong!

———

MRS L

Mrs L was born in Bombay in 1935. She holds various academic degrees, and a Licentiate in Music from a British College. She is a professional music teacher of considerable repute and has directed and conducted several performances of Parsi music and songs.

Mrs L has an orthodox family background, although her parents themselves were 'modern'. She spent most of her time at her maternal grandparents' house. Her maternal grandfather was very pious and prayed for long periods during the day and night; his wife prayed in each of the five *gehs*. Her grandfather taught her the Navjote prayers and explained their meaning; she was also taught the devotional song (*monajat*) *Khudavind Khavind*. Mrs. L does not remember the meaning of the prayers but does recollect such general principles as never telling lies, not stealing, and obedience to parents. Her father was transferred to Madras while she was still at school, and she was sent to a Christian convent-school there. She was impressed by the piety of the nuns but never felt drawn towards Christianity.

Mrs L's father was also very strict, and made her do her *kusti* first thing in the morning and last thing at night. Her paternal grandmother regularly performed the *Satum* for the dead.[48]

> She had a long list of relatives for whom she prayed nearly every morning. In her bedroom she had a small niche where she kept a table[49] and a stove and some vessels. And she used to get flowers every day and she and my aunt used to make a sweet dish and put it on a tray, and put incense and sandalwood. They would get up very early in the morning and do this.

Mrs L's grandmother was a very orthodox woman who wore traditional Parsi clothes and kept her head covered all day long. She would allow her young granddaughter into her room most times but her daughter-in-law could not come in when she was menstruating. Since the older lady was orthodox whereas Mrs L's mother did not observe many of the purity laws, Mrs L's father bought two adjoining flats with communicating doors; the younger woman avoided her mother-in-law's flat when she had her period.[50] The only things Mrs L herself had to observe during menstruation was not to touch prayer books, not to go to the fire temple, and not to wear festive clothes. She was allowed to go to school, touch her school books and play the piano, and neither she nor her mother ever 'sat separately' on such days, as these things were not observed on her mother's side of the family. At the end of her period, Mrs L just had a 'head-bath' and her clothes were washed.

Loban was done in the mornings, and for a time also at night; after Mrs L's paternal grandmother died it was only done on religious occasions. On the 'birthday of the Waters' and other important days, sea water was brought to the house and was sprinkled on the thresholds. When ceremonies were done in the fire temple the consecrated food was brought to the house and everyone who was not in an impure state would have some.

Mrs Munshi inquires whether Mrs L asked her parents many questions about the religion. Mrs L says:

> No, unfortunately we were brought up in such a strict way and made to believe whatever the parents said. And to be very honest, I feel that even my parents perhaps did not know much about the religion, about the meaning of each prayer. Although my father used to pray with the book in his hand before he went to the office. And I have rarely seen my mother sit down with a book and pray. She was so busy with so many things. And both my father and my mother believed that work was worship.[51] Their first duty was to their children and they rarely found an hour for themselves to say the prayers.

Mrs L's maternal grandfather used to tell her stories about the heroes of the *Shahname*, and about the early history of the Parsis.

There was an *agharni* for her mother when she was seven months pregnant with Mrs L's younger brother;[52] Mrs L does not remember a *panchmasyu*.[53] Her mother came home from the hospital after twelve days but stayed with her own mother for the rest of the forty days, after which both mother and grandmother had a *nahn* at home. The *besna* and *pagladu* ceremonies were done for the baby.

Mrs L remembers her own aversion to *nirang* (consecrated bull's urine) as a child, otherwise she has positive memories of her Navjote. No *goyans*[54] were invited then, but Mrs L says that she has heard *goyans* sing at weddings. As a young adult Mrs L went to the Agiary whenever she could, and the family had many *Jashans* performed in the house:

We had *Jashans* performed in the house, for good health, for aunts' weddings and all that. And I had this faith that whenever something nice was to take place one must have a *Jashan* performed in the house: sometimes it was done in the house with four Dasturs[55] and sometimes just two Dasturs. They bring their own things, the fruits and so on, they bring their own *afarganyu* [fire vase]. They only took [i.e. lit] the *divo* from the lighted lamp of our house. They light the fire and then they say the prayers. It is done before a wedding or after someone gets well. After we came back from Madras, after a long period of two years, my grandmother said, 'When you come back, get a *Jashan* performed in this house. So any evil thoughts or things that have happened in the house in your absence get washed away.'

And we used to go to the Agiary or the Atash Behram on birthdays, my parents' anniversaries, on New Year's Day – Jamshedi Navroze – and during the Muktad time. And in those early days my father would make it a point that we visited at least three Atash Behrams on New Year's Day. And it was a practice to visit all the relatives on Princess Street and Dhobi Talao.[56]

The conversation moves on to Mrs L's wedding. She married relatively late in life and refused to allow any extravagance in the wedding ceremonies. Mr L was very modern, having lived long in Canada, and was uninterested in rituals. There was a simple engagement ceremony, after which the couple visited the Agiary. Religious ceremonies performed prior to the wedding included the *Baj* in honour of Ram and the *Satum* for the dead.[57] Contrary to custom the wedding itself was performed in the fire temple in the presence of just a few friends; afterwards the couple went to pray to the fire. Earlier they had visited the Dastur who was to marry them, and he explained the meaning of the rituals, gave advice about marriage and lent them a book on the marriage service. Mrs L's favourite Yazad is Behram. When she wanted to get married, an Iranian Dastur advised her to pray the *Behram Yasht* for forty days. Shortly before her marriage, her husband was out of a job, and Mrs L again prayed the *Behram Yasht*. She likes praying, but only does it when a sincere feeling tells her she should; she does not believe in reading long prayers from a book for no particular purpose, but says that when she really wants to pray she can concentrate.

In the month of Bahman, Mrs L says, one is supposed to observe a meatless diet for the whole month. She herself would not mind doing this, but her husband objects and the family now refrains from eating meat on eight days of the month. The family observes the 'birthday of the Fire' in the traditional way, and on *Fravardiyannu parab* a visit is made to the Tower of Silence. Mrs L goes to the sea one day of the month of Ava, but not on Ava *roj*, as the seashores are too crowded then. (Mrs L cannot stand crowds, she went to the Banaji Atash Behram on Mondays[58] for a time but stopped going because she felt claustrophobic.)

At one stage in her life Mrs L devoted much of her time to looking after her mother, who had had a stroke and whose speech was impaired. A devotee of Dastur Aibara[59] advised Mrs L to seek his help. Dastur Aibara gave her prayers, which he told her to pray every day on her mother's behalf:

This is how I got into praying more prayers than I had ever done before .... My father had been very strict about the *kusti* prayers, and I did it. But it was only when I started praying for my mother that I used to pray from the book. I started pronouncing correctly and got to know the prayers much better. The meaning also, which was given side by side,[60] I came to know ... I believe that Dasturji Aibara used to take passages from the *Yashts* and *Niyayesh* and different prayers, and he used to combine them. And for certain sicknesses he gave certain prayers. And he used to write down the name of that person in a whole list of names. I believe that he used to get up every day and say certain prayers for the sick people and mention all those names, for forty days. And after forty days you were supposed to go back to him. And he would either say, 'Continue for the next forty days,' or he would change the prayers. And along with the prayers we were asked to put a glass of water near the photograph of Dasturji Kookadaru, and of Shah Faridun, or another [ancient hero] ... it depended on the type of illness and on the person who needed help. And after the prayer that water was supposed to be taken [i.e. drunk] by the patient. It did help my mother in the sense that she became less nervous, calmer, and she had the strength to be rehabilitated. After she had been totally unable to speak or even utter a sound, she started talking again in a reasonable manner. We did it for a quite few years, every day. And at first there were breaks, you know;[61] but in the course of that time I stopped having my periods so there was no question of a break then. Otherwise we are not supposed to pray during those days ... The photograph, the page of the prayer and the glass were supposed to be kept on a separate shelf. Dasturji Aibara, though he believed in all this staunch purification and all that, said we had to change with the times. He said, 'Today there is no place in a room when five, six children are there, servants may be going in and out, you have no room to yourself. So you can be a little relaxed and allow the servants to come in and clean the room. It is OK .... But you can touch [these things] only after your bath, not during the [rest of the] day, and the prayers must be said before twelve noon.' After my mother died, somehow I stopped saying these prayers for myself (he had given prayers for myself also and for my husband). But recently I started saying them again.

Mrs L's maternal grandfather, who was a pious Zoroastrian and died with the *Yatha Ahu Vairyo* on his lips, was also a Theosophist; his brother had been secretary to Mrs Annie Besant. Most of Mrs L's relatives believe in Theosophy, though her mother did not. Mrs L's father was a Freemason. She herself has become interested in Theosophy:

> When my grandfather died my maternal uncle said, 'He is not dead!' Now the Theosophists believe in reincarnation, many many reincarnations. He told me a few things. That was the first time I got some message about life after this earth. Then I got so interested that I started reading a few books. But I am not a staunch Theosophist, and I have no inclination to join the Freemasons. That comes from your heart, if you want to do it you do it. Theosophy is not specific to any religion, it only believes in the Truth. We are not drawn to anything else; it is just a philosophy of life. It may not coincide with our Zoroastrian thoughts and beliefs; there are many controversies, and I would not like to go into that. My personal view is that I understood simple things of Theosophy, which I would like to follow.
>
> But the greatest thing is, after my marriage I went to Madras and I was very much affected by certain philosophies started by Ramana Maharishi; he was a great philosopher in the South ... I visited that place and I was so much [impressed]; it is again a philosophy, not a religion, [although] there are *artis* [Hindu ceremonies] being performed and *slokas* [Hindu formulas] being said. As I said, I have visited many temples and mosques and I have never been drawn [to other faiths]. I studied in Sophia College, where Parsis refused to send their daughters because at that time one Parsi girl had been converted to Christianity. But my father said, 'I have faith in my child, she will not be affected.' I was never affected. Today so many Christian nuns come to the house and try to propagate the Christian religion, offering pamphlets and this and that ... I say thank you, and read it, and just throw away those pamphlets. It does not give me any incitement. Our own religion has so many things we still have to learn, which I frankly say I don't know. In other temples I say *Yatha* and *Ashem*, as my grandfather taught me, because all religions are alike, all religions lead you to the only Truth.

Mrs L then recounts how she got involved with the 'Zoroastrian Studies' project of recording religious songs.

> I find today's generation more interested in knowing what our religion is giving them than we were in our days, because our parents themselves were not so knowledgeable; they just said, 'Say your prayers,' and sometimes gave you the meaning. There was no, sort of, compulsion. Perhaps there were other families where joint prayers

were being said in the evenings. That was so in my mother's family in her young days; they would all sit together and pray before dinner.

Both Mr and Mrs L set great store by personal cleanliness, and Mrs L says the usual morning prayers. She used to frequent fire temples, partly because her mother thought this a good way of meeting potential husbands, but now she goes less often:

> Now I feel that my devotion is within me; I pray and I feel I am in front of the temple fire. When I close my eyes I think of the Dadyseth Agiary in Fountain (not the Atash Behram), I imagine the fire in front of me. I do a lot of yoga, and when my teacher tells us to close our eyes when we are meditating and says, 'Close your eyes and pray to your God' (because we are a multi-communal group), then when I close my eyes I only see the fire.

The interview closes with a solo performance by Mrs L of a modern musical work inspired by religious themes. After the interview Mrs L wrote to Mrs Munshi to add that she had been deeply inspired by the religious classes of Dastur Navruz D. Minochehrhomji, to which she was introduced shortly after the death of her father in 1960.

MRS Q

Mrs Q was born in 1922 in a small town in Gujarat, but went to school in Bombay. After secondary education she did an undergraduate course in 'home science'. She is married with two children and lives in Bombay; the family is wealthy and has an established position in society. Mrs Q is the founder-director of a Bombay school. In many ways, Mrs Q could be called a traditionalist and she probably regards herself as one; the interview is included in the present chapter because it illustrates with particular clarity how beliefs and practices of non-Zoroastrian origin can come to be adopted by staunch Zoroastrians.

Mrs Q comes from an observant *Behdin* family. For the Christmas holidays the family usually went to stay with Mrs Q's grandparents, who lived next door to an Agiary; one could hear the prayers being chanted from their house. Whenever they went there Mrs Q's mother always had a *Fareshta* ceremony performed, and *chashni*[62] was sent to relatives and friends. Mrs Q's Navjote was done in Bombay by a priest who was a family friend. About her religious beliefs Mrs Q says:

> We all wear *sudreh* and *kusti* and we all believe in the existence of the Almighty, and I was taught that we had to go to the Agiary, or if we cannot go the Agiary at least to send *sukhad* [sandalwood] on

auspicious days, and almost every day. My mother had told me that, and I have taught my children that. My daughter still performs the same ritual; my son of course, as boys are, is less religious-minded, but I am happy to say that my daughter-in-law is also very religious-minded like me, and she also believes in going to the Agiary and sending *sukhad* and having *machi* and everything done. It so happens that today is my granddaughter's *roj* birthday,[63] so my husband has just left for the Agiary. My husband is much more religious-minded, outwardly, than myself. He says his prayers every day. I also used to say my prayers every day, from my childhood until I started work, but with business and work I don't find time. But that does not mean that I do not believe in God. I believe in God far more than I think my husband does; one does not have to sit with a book to show one's religiousness. The very fact that you can communicate with your Creator ... And fortunately I happen to live in a house from where we can see the sea, so every morning we take the name of God and Ava Ardvisur, Mah Bokhtar Yazad, Dadar Yazad and bow my head in homage to the Almighty, the Creator. And every time we meet foreign friends, if we get close enough to talk about religion, I talk about our religion. Because our religion I feel is based on Creation, and what God has created for mankind and humanity. We have no enforced rituals, like the Catholics have to go to church every Sunday and during Lent they have to abstain. We have our Bahman *mahino*[64] – another strange thing is that my husband and I are not so keen on the Bahman *mahino*, we only do the Bahman *mahino* Bahman *roj*, but both my children have observed the full month for years, wherever they are, whether they are in America or the UK or anything. Everybody finds it very strange that we don't do it and yet they do it, so they are very conscious of the fact that we should observe some kind of self-discipline.

As a child Mrs Q was made aware of various traditional practices, such as the *parabs*, but her family did not observe them. Her mother got up at five o'clock every morning to say her prayers, so Mrs Q used to wake up to the sound of her praying. Her parents had a table with photographs of the departed, and after finishing her prayers Mrs Q's mother used to put fresh flowers and some burning incense there and offer a little milk over which prayers had been said; the milk was later given to the dogs in the area.[65] Mrs Q herself also followed this practice for some time. There was no fire burning in her parents' house, but her mother did the *loban* ceremony every morning.

We don't do it [i.e. *loban*] in my home, but both my son and daughter-in-law feel that we should do it, for the simple reason that it is the best pesticide available compared to all the chemicals we use for pest-control.

In Mrs Q's mother's family there was no tradition of 'sitting separately' during menstruation, but Mrs Q had an aunt whose daughters observed all the purity laws and she learned a great deal from them. Later in life Mrs Q kept special clothes for these occasions and washed her *sudreh* and *kusti* every day during menstruation. She feels that present-day pollution illustrates the need for cleanliness and purity.

Mrs Q had been taught the usual prayers, but started praying much more when her mother died suddenly. As she found that she was praying more and more, she began to read books in order to understand what she was praying. She felt 'a great deal of peace of mind after I finished praying,' and used to go to the Agiary more regularly than is possible now because of her age and the problems of transport. Her husband still goes to the Agiary often and has *machis* done for the birthdays of all family members. Mrs Q says that her husband still has ceremonies performed for his parents and his paternal grandfather, although his father died some thirty-eight years, and his mother and grandfather over seventy years before the time of the interview.

> He feels that it is his duty to pray for his dear departed family, and very often we have this argument that, 'Now it is so many years, let the souls rest in peace.' I very often say, 'Please, it is so many years, if the souls had been born again they would have had their life-span and gone also.' But he still insists. Once he said, 'As long as I am alive this has to be done.' So after that we stopped arguing.

Mrs Q's favourite Yazad is Ava Ardvisur (who is connected with the Waters), perhaps because when she was a child, every time the family went to Gujarat her mother used to throw coins and pieces of coconut into the sea when the train passed over a bridge. Mrs Q still makes frequent offerings to the sea and prays to Ava Yazad morning, noon and night. For her this is an 'everyday worship'; she does nothing special on Ava *mahino* Ava *roj*. When Mrs Q begins her day she invokes Sarosh Yazad and Behram and Mushkil Asan[66] with a short formula.

Mrs Q herself and both her children had traditional Parsi weddings. After childbirth she did not go out at all for forty days, and her daughter and daughter-in-law did the same. Ceremonies like the *sagan, pagladu* and *besna* were done for all Mrs Q's children and grandchildren. Her husband's family believed in the *rasi* (astrological) system of naming a child, and Mrs Q's daughter was named in accordance with that system. Since it had been her late mother's wish that her son should be given a certain name regardless of the *rasi*, her wishes were respected. Her daughter does not believe in *rasi* but her daughter-in-law does.

Mrs Q feels it is important to teach children about God, since everyone ultimately depends on Him; she feels that she has been successful in transmitting the faith to her own children. The family observes many traditional customs (see also above); family members have a bath immediately after a haircut; birthdays are celebrated in the traditional way, and chalk designs and garlands mark all festive days.

Mrs Q does her *kusti* after her morning bath, and again last thing at night. Before going to sleep she says 'my prayer, which is between my God and myself', and which includes asking blessings for all family members. There is a thanksgiving *Jashan* in the house at least once a year.

When major problems have been solved, the first thing always is to have a *Fareshta* ceremony done,[67] and then all the charities …

Charities are important to Mrs Q, as she was taught to share whatever God has given her. She still dispenses charity on the death-anniversary of her mother, who died over forty years before the interview. Apart from supporting charitable foundations, she also helps poor Parsi families.

Talking about her feelings concerning the Towers of Silence, Mrs Q says that there was a time when she disliked this institution, but she is now very much in favour of it. The only thing she dislikes is that during a funeral the women have to sit in a place where they can see the body being handled by the corpse-bearers;[68] she feels that it would be an improvement if this could be avoided. She very much believes in the efficacy of the prayers and rituals for the soul of the deceased. Regarding her views on the afterlife, Mrs Q says:

From whatever little I have read about the religion, we feel that we Zoroastrians are of such a high level that we are not reborn,[69] but I don't believe that, I feel we must be reborn. This is just what I personally believe.

Asked about her thoughts on the problem of Good and Evil, Mrs Q says:

I believe that the good and the evil in one's life is a continuation of the past life to this life and into the next life. I suppose the source of Evil must have come down right from the time of Creation, from the time humanity started, because everyone is not born equal, and there is bound to be a gap between the level of goodness and the level of evil, and the level of those evil thoughts which are always trying to bring down the good thoughts. So I always feel that we should pray for good thoughts to combat the source of evil influence in our lives.[70]

And through prayers you think one can achieve that?
Oh yes, definitely, one can certainly get a balanced view and a more calm sense of mind after having prayers, and it certainly does help.

Vows also mean much to Mrs Q. When she was expecting her second child a friend made a vow on her behalf that if the child was a son the family should go to Udwada for a big *machi*. Mrs Q was somewhat taken aback by this, but she honoured the vow. Mrs Q's faith in vows includes those to non-Zoroastrian holy beings. A Catholic South Indian friend of hers once took a vow on her behalf to the effect that, if Mrs Q's daughter would marry, Mrs Q would send a wedding ring to a South Indian Christian shrine; the vow was honoured at the time of her daughter's marriage. On one occasion when her husband had business problems, he vowed that the whole family would go to the same Christian shrine if the difficulties were resolved, and this also happened. Another time, when Mrs Q was in a car with some Hindu friends, the car was caught up in a traffic jam right in front of the Hindu Babulnath temple complex in Bombay; her friends told her that if she prayed to this temple her difficulties would always be resolved. Mrs Q felt doubtful about this, as she did not think one ought to believe in other religions. However, it so happened that some months later she had a problem, and her car was again forced to stop in the same place. Mrs Q therefore asked the deity to solve her problem, and this happened. In view of this, Mrs Q decided that religious denominations did not really matter, and she now sends regular gifts to this temple. In South India Mrs Q has been taken to Hindu and Muslim sanctuaries as well as the Christian shrine mentioned earlier; her daughter often goes there and Mrs Q always sends some money for the sanctuaries of all three faiths. She further supports the Shri Aurobindo temple at Pondicherry. She does not pray to the holy beings in question, except to the Lady of the Christian shrine, to whom she offers prayers daily after her Zoroastrian prayers. This broad-mindedness in religious matters does not mean that she condones wrongful practices within the Zoroastrian sphere, and she roundly condemns the Nagrani cult.[71]

The most important thing in Mrs Q's life, she says, has been the guidance of Ahura Mazda and the teachings of Zarathustra. When she was in the process of founding her school there were several coincidences which indicated to her that God wanted her to do this:

> It was in my destiny to start the school; God had ordained it. I firmly believe that, no matter how much we human beings say that you carry your destiny in your own hand – no! You do carry your destiny in your own hand, but not completely. And the major part is the guidance of Ahura Mazda. Absolutely!

Mrs Q says that she feels there is a great need for a revival of the religion, which leads to a discussion of the question of conversion.

> I believe that we should have a certain amount of purity of our race. But now, looking at it from a practical point of view, I feel that we should take in the children of the girls who marry out of the community, provided the father does not object .... I think basically it

is very necessary for a child to have faith in God, no matter what religion you are born with, whether you are a Zoroastrian, Hindu, Muslim, Christian, Jew, or whatever. The faith in God is necessary for the well-being of the soul. That is what I feel.

———

Notes

1 On Mrs Nusservanjee see the interview on pp. 253–8.
2 Many traditional Zoroastrians consider it essential to wear the *kusti* at all times except when having a bath, as a symbol of the constant protection of the faith against evil.
3 See above, p. 20.
4 On Ervad Kutar see also the interviews with Mr T and Dr Y.
5 i.e. the disposal of the dead in the Towers of Silence.
6 The Yazad Ashishvang, who represents opulence, is regarded as a *hamkara* or associate of the Yazad of the Waters (Ava).
7 See the interview on pp. 126–45.
8 See the interview on pp. 145–53.
9 As a Neo-traditionalist, Mrs Munshi probably perceives a contradiction in Mrs X's enthusiasm for Zoroastrian teaching and her love of Yoga. Mrs X clearly understands the criticism implied in the question and emphatically rejects it.
10 The term 'religious' here apparently means 'following the Zoroastrian tradition', while 'spiritually evolved' refers to progress on the path of Yoga.
11 The term 'worship' here seems to have a connotation of loyalty to a saint or religious group, as opposed to believing in the power, or appreciating the beauty, of certain prayers. This strengthens the impression (see previous note) that for Mrs X there is a distinction between 'religion', which involves loyalty and tradition, and 'spirituality' which has to do with a personal quest for truth.
12 i.e. Mrs X recites the *Gathas* during the five last days of the year, which are known as the *Gatha* days.
13 See the interview with Ervad Y. Aibara.
14 On these ceremonies see above, p. 30.
15 For a description of the proceedings at the Tower see above, p. 37f.
16 The implication seems to be that Mrs X is inclined to believe in reincarnation, but thinks that funerary rituals may be helpful even if the soul is to be reborn.
17 In other words, she performs a *Satum* for her brother (see above, p. 10).
18 cf. above, p. 41 n. 19, p. 50.
19 In the Avesta the *fravashis* are described as parts of the human soul which existed before a person is born and live on after death. While Zoroastrians may not worship a human being, they do pray for the *fravashi* of a revered figure.
20 On the original meaning of the term *fravashi* see previous note. In some forms of modern Zoroastrian teaching the term is understood to denote the divine element within each human being. Spenta Mainyu is the Amesha Spenta representing 'Beneficent Intention', who has been compared to the Christian concept of the Holy Ghost. On Spenta Mainyu see also above, p. 4f.

21 A prayer for the *fravashi* of the late Dastur Kookadaru, on whom see above, n. 18.
22 i.e. at the time when people gather to venerate Jal Baba, see above, p. 50f.
23 On visits to the Aslaji Agiary on this day see above, p. 22.
24 There is of course only one Meher *mahino* Meher *roj* in a year. Mrs X probably means that she visits the Aslaji every Meher *roj*.
25 In classical Zoroastrianism the Amesha Spenta Bahman was thought to look after animals. Mrs X is probably thinking of this connection.
26 This may be connected with the fact that Catholics avoid eating meat on Fridays.
27 See above, p. 19.
28 The place where the first Zoroastrians to come to India are thought to have landed.
29 For references to *Dhan Teras* and *Kali Chowdas* see Index.
30 The mother's reaction illustrates the fact that a Parsi may strongly disapprove of an alien observance without doubting that it could be effective.
31 The term refers to a special way of greeting one another by placing one's flattened right hand between the flattened hands of the other, see Modi 1922: 378–9.
32 On this Karachi High Priest see Hinnells 1997: 70–1; for further references see Index.
33 Russell (1989: 55) defines the *garbo* as 'a Gujarati line or circle dance, in which the participants, who can be both men and women, intone a song with repeated choruses while clapping the hands thrice ... '
34 Clearly, in Mrs U's opinion such things were entirely for the senior woman of the house to decide. There is no suggestion that she thought of breaking the traditional rules as 'sin', or felt any personal responsibility in such matters.
35 i.e. send it to the laundry.
36 See above, p. 24.
37 i.e. the table on which the fire stands.
38 i.e. on the day preceding Adar *roj*.
39 For Mrs U 'believing in our religion' and wearing its outer emblems are obviously closely connected.
40 Guj. *dua-magvi*. Such personal prayers may precede the normal prayer routine.
41 On this formula see above, p. 16.
42 'Behram Yazad' is the name of a divine being; '*Pak-afsun-e Shah Faridun*' is a prayer to Faridun (cf. above, p. 41 n. 19), who in classical Zoroastrianism is regarded as a king or heroic figure rather than a divinity. Kookadaru was a man, not a Yazad (see above, p. 50). To Mrs U, however, all these observances apparently have the same emotional value.
43 A prayer for Kookadaru.
44 i.e. 'God's Miraculous Actions'.
45 i.e. the *Mushkil Asan* ceremony, on which see above, p. 20.
46 This *Yasht* is often recited in cases of illness.
47 Note that there is no suggestion here that Faridun intervened when a prayer associated with him was recited; it was the prayer itself, it seems, or the intention behind it that had the desired effect, cf. below, p. 296.
48 On the *Satum* see above, p. 10 with n. 25.
49 In many Parsi households there is a table, often with photographs of deceased family members on it, which is used especially for such domestic ritual purposes.

50 It is interesting to note that there appear to have been no attempts to determine which approach was 'better'; both were obviously felt to be valid and an effective solution was found to the practical problems posed by the different views and habits of the two women.

51 A frequently heard maxim in Parsi circles, see also the interviews with Mrs H and Dr Y.

52 Many Parsi families perform these ceremonies for the first child only (see above, p. 34f with n. 53), but this custom was evidently not followed here.

53 On these ceremonies see above, p. 34f.

54 Professional singers, see above, p. 20f.

55 i.e. priests; the word 'dastur' can be used as an honorific title for the priesthood generally.

56 Princess Street is now officially named J. Shankersheth Road, but still usually referred to by the old name. Both the H.B. Wadia Atash Behram and the Anjuman Atash Behram are on this road, while others are in the same area, which is known as Dhobi Talao.

57 See above, p. 32.

58 Parsis go there on Mondays to worship Jal Baba, see above, n. 22.

59 See above, p. 50, and cf. the interview with Ervad Y. Aibara.

60 i.e. on the opposite page.

61 Mrs L means that the prayer routine could not be done when she had her period.

62 i.e. food that was blessed during the ritual.

63 i.e. her birthday according to the Zoroastrian calendar, see above, p. 27.

64 i.e. days when many Parsis do not eat meat. The implication is that a form of abstaining is not unknown in Zoroastrianism.

65 On the *Satum* see above, n. 48; on the 'morsel of the dog' in connection with that ceremony see above, p. 17 with n. 8.

66 On the Yazad Behram and Mushkil Asan see above, p. 20 with n. 12.

67 See above, p. 10.

68 For a similar sentiment see the interview with Ms Khurody.

69 This remark seems to refer to the idea that the Avesta does not mention reincarnation because the Zoroastrians represent the highest level of human evolution so that, unlike others, Zoroastrians will not be reborn on this earth, cf. the interview with Dr Bharucha with n. 21.

70 Although Mrs Q does not adhere to any 'esoteric' school of thought, reincarnation plays a central role in her ideas. What is apparently implied is that the 'gap between the level of goodness' of different people is due to the fact that some souls are more advanced than others, having lived through more previous births. On the question of reincarnation see also above, p. 54.

71 On the Nagrani see above, p. 51.

Chapter Eight

Esoteric Beliefs

DR MEHER MASTER-MOOS

Dr Meher Master-Moos (1943) is the author of twelve books and many articles on Law, the Zoroastrian religion, and alternative medicine. She was the first Parsi woman Law graduate at Oxford University, and the first non-European woman to hold an Assistant Professorship in Law in Canada. She is the recipient of many further honours, both in the academic and public spheres. In the Zoroastrian community she is best known as a leading exponent of the Ilm-e Khshnoom movement, being the Founder President of the 'Mazdayasnie Monasterie', the 'All India Shah Behram Baug Society for Scientific and Educational Research', and of 'Zoroastrian College', which she founded at Sanjan (Gujarat) in 1986.

Asked to introduce herself, Dr Moos begins as follows:

Well, at the moment I am running the Zoroastrian College, which was started some years ago. One of its main purposes is to prepare the people of this earth for leading a life in harmony with the Cosmic Laws which are contained in the ancient Avestan tradition, and to prepare people for the advent of the Spiritual Rainidar[1] Shah Behram Varjavand Saheb, when he comes out into public life at the end of this [i.e. 20th] century or at the beginning of next century. So this College is meant for people all over the world, but especially emphasises the very ancient living Zoroastrian tradition, which goes back for many thousands of years, so that people can once again learn how to lead that kind of life, and get away from the Westernisation which has overcome many people in the Parsi community and also a lot of people in the world generally.

Talking about her family background, Dr Moos says that her maternal grandfather was also a scholar and a prolific writer on religious matters, and that he used to read stories from the *Shahname* every night before dinner. When Dr Moos was nine her parents moved from India to Dar es Salam in East Africa. As there was a great deal of Christian influence there, Dr Moos's mother always made sure that the Parsi children had a chance to experience and learn about their own tradition. Both parents were active in the small Parsi community, her father as President of the Anjuman. Regular *Jashans* were held, and Dr Moos's Navjote was the first in East Africa. Every morning, prayers were said and a fire was lit in a fire vase. All this gave the family a very strong sense of their Zoroastrian identity. The importance of rituals, and of the Avestan language, was stressed. 'Survival meant: you must know Avesta[2] and do your rituals.'

After her Senior Cambridge Certificate, Dr Moos went to India for six months and then on to England for further study. Around this time, she began to study the Avesta, copying the whole of Taraporevala's *Divine Songs of Zarathushtra*[3] in an attempt to teach herself the language and meaning of the prayers at the age of fourteen. Dr Moos feels that she always had an intuitive understanding of the religion; she was very upset, for example, when she saw her hosts in England burn rubbish in the garden, which meant they were polluting fire. After finishing her studies in the UK she came to India from 1965–68. She then went to the USA to do her L.L.M. degree. While still in College, she was offered three University appointments; in order to make the right choice she prayed the *Yatha Ahu Vairyo* prayer over and over again, which she feels afforded her direct communication with Ahura Mazda.

Dr Moos's first contact with Ilm-e Khshnoom took place in the period 1965–68, when she was staying with her parents, who had returned to Poona. There her mother convened the 'Poona Spiritual Studies Circle', which held regular lectures on spiritual and religious subjects. Urged by her Parsi friends, she invited Mr Jehangirji Chiniwalla, one of the early teachers of Behramshah N. Shroff's message.[4] Later she went to see him in Bombay every month and recorded lectures he gave especially for this purpose, which she would then play at the 'Spiritual Studies Circle' sessions in Poona. At first Dr Moos herself was not drawn towards Ilm-e Khshnoom:

> I used to bunk those lectures, quite honestly ... I was interested in religion, certainly, but I was not yet ready for Khshnoom, which is esoteric wisdom. You need to have a few knockings before you are ripe for that. You see, religion is a broad term. There are different aspects to religion; there is what you may call religion for everyday life, for everybody, which is routine: you go through it and that is what everybody should follow, simple precepts like Good Thoughts, Good Words, Good Deeds. Then there is the scholarly aspect, the language, the grammar, the linguistics, an intellectual level. Then there is the

spiritual level, the esoteric, occult level, which is to open your inner wisdom, or awareness. So you have to be ready at different levels, you see? Probably at that age I was not yet ripe for that level, but I was very much at the traditional level.

After this initial contact, Dr Moos went to the US, worked in Canada and later in Australia, returned to India and married. In 1973 she went through a traumatic period of conflicts with her husband and mother-in-law, and she began to explore the Zoroastrian teachings about marriage. In studying the Zoroastrian tradition, she found herself puzzled by the severity of the punishments she found there for killing an animal called *udra*, a word usually translated as 'otter'. She could not see why killing an otter should be such a heinous sin, and felt that there had to be a deeper meaning to the text. She asked J. Chiniwalla, who had mentioned the word repeatedly in his lectures, and he gave her his esoteric Gujarati translation and interpretation of the entire *Vendidad*. (Here Dr Moos explains that translations of the Sacred Texts depend on the translator's level of understanding and development, and that Western translations of the Avesta are inevitably influenced by the Christian background of their authors.) Dr Moos studied Chiniwalla's esoteric interpretation of the *Vendidad* chapter by chapter, her mother reading it out for her in Gujarati while she translated it into English. The interpretation of the word *udra* she found there ('a soul rising from the level of the animal kingdom to that of the human kingdom, a creature in a state of spiritual transformation') satisfied her as it made clear why killing such a creature is regarded as a grave sin. Dr Moos explains that souls evolve from the mineral level to the animal, human, *Nim-Yazad* (semi-divine), and finally to the *Yazatic* (divine, angelic) level. The process of transformation from the animal to the human level takes place through birth as an *udra*: the 'split souls' of 100 dogs are merged together in an *udra*, under the influence of the vibrations of light.[5] Dr Moos thinks that the word *udra* may denote a beaver, a dolphin, or possibly a seal.

> Personally, this introduced me for the first time to the depth of Ilm-e Khshnoom, and the depth of spiritual understanding of what is behind all the superficiality of our religious ceremonies and weddings and prayers and so on. I mean you can read the same text from different viewpoints, and the depth of the viewpoint depends on the level of evolution of that individual person ... This provided me with a very strong background of faith, of understanding the depth of our faith, which gave me a lot of courage and stability to face whatever came.

As a result, Dr Moos became very interested in the spiritual dimensions of her religion, not least in the power of the vibrations of *manthras* and rituals:

You gain the strength through the performance of ceremonies. It is the action plus the word plus the thought, all combined, which create the power. So I was put into the direction of performance of ceremonies, especially the *pav-mahal* ceremonies[6] like *Ijeshne* [Yasna] and *Vendidad*. I used to get the *Ijeshne* and *Vendidad* performed every month, three *Ijeshnes* every month and the *Vendidad* as often as possible ... The most powerful ceremony is the *Nirangdin*. I have had two *Nirangdins* performed, one in Surat and one in Bombay, one for my grandfather and one for my grandmother. The *Nirangdin* is a miracle-working ceremony... If you have three *Ijeshnes* performed on three consecutive days, any problem in your life will be solved by the grace of Ahura Mazda. But if you have a *Nirangdin* performed it involves six consecutive *Ijeshne* and midnight *Vendidads*, and the collective power of that ceremony is immense.

Dr Moos recounts that she received the gift of land for the Zoroastrian College at the time when she had the *Nirangdin* ceremony performed for her grandmother, and that the registration of the land in her name, which usually takes years, was completed in a few weeks.[7]

Ever since 1973 Dr Moos has been actively engaged in promoting the esoteric side of Zoroastrianism. On her return from a visit to Israel and Iran (where she was aware that the *Sahebdelan*, or Hidden Spiritual Masters, were watching over her), a manuscript came to her which contained transcripts of some of the late Behramshah Shroff's lectures on the origins of the world and the cosmos. This was one of ten such documents hidden in a trunk which Shroff had ordered to be kept closed for fifty years after his death. About the end of this period the trunk came to light; it was opened by Shroff's grandson's wife, who happened to be an old friend of Dr Moos.[8] Eventually she was given all the documents to translate and publish.

In the course of a discussion about B.N. Shroff's methods of teaching Dr Moos mentions his refusal to leave anything behind, whether samples of his handwriting or photographs. She explains this by saying that such remnants of terrestrial existence hold the soul back in its onward journey – as does burial and also some prayers and rituals which invite the soul back to earth. The aim should be to break the cycle of reincarnation, allowing the soul to go on to higher levels of existence. When the soul reaches the Chinvad Bridge it discards even the ethereal body which it has held on to until then, but it is by no means easy for a soul to reach the Bridge.

When the soul leaves, first it has to go to the North Pole to get out of the electromagnetic circuit of the earth before it can take off into space. Then it goes into space, to the *dahyu* regions,[9] which are vast expanses of ethereal matter, with jungles and mountains. The soul must cross all these regions till it reaches the Chinvad Bridge, which is between the fifth, fourth and third *dahyus*. Very, very few souls – [those] which are given the benefit of having the Mazdayasni Zoroastrian ceremonies performed for them – can manage to make the journey at top speed [so that the soul reaches the Bridge on the fourth morning after death] ... Other souls, ordinary souls, even Parsis' souls if they don't receive this booster force, can take days and months and years, even hundreds of years entangled in these jungles and paths and mountains. All souls have to go through these *dahyu* regions of space, it is how you go that makes the difference. After the Bridge come other levels of the *dahyu* regions, and then you reach the level of the solar system, of the planet Saturn. From Saturn the space-ships take off, carrying souls to different constellations. Saturn is the entry and exit point. The rings of Saturn provide a kind of landing ground for spacecraft coming from other galaxies ... From whatever star souls come, they come into the orbit of the solar system making the landing through the rings of Saturn. There souls enter different crafts – it is like a change of flight – to go to different regions of the interplanetary spaces.

Prayers for the soul go to its 'spiritual bank account', which is kept at the Chinvad Bridge and from which the soul can draw; but the wicked soul is weighed down by its own misdeeds and takes a long time to progress to that point.[10]

Dr Moos goes on to discuss the question of marriage, for which a fundamental understanding of the Aryan Cosmogony is needed. She explains that, first of all, through the power of the vibrations of the *Yatha Ahu Vairyo* prayer, Ahura Mazda created his own *fravashi*,[11] which circled the universe seven times and created seven enormous circles in space, the *dahyus*. By means of vibrations, sounds and light, galaxies of souls were then created. The very high souls were the Amesha Spentas and the Yazatas. All souls were subject to the same Cosmic Law and all had freedom of choice. Some disobeyed the Law and became wicked: even Ahriman and the demons are souls created by Ahura Mazda who did not stay on the right path. In the course of creation those souls who wanted to evolve chose not to remain in the starry regions, but to explore the universe. When these finally came to the earth level a special division of the original soul took place, into a male and a female half. In other words, a soul could enter a male or female mineral, evolve into a male or female plant, and so on to the human level. All souls on planet earth have this quality of halfness. The ultimate aim is for the two halves to become reunited. This fusion of original halves, known as *khaetvadatha*,[12] takes place during the couple's last incarnation as human beings, since only the reunited whole can proceed to the Half-Yazad level. The marriages of earlier incarnations, however, do not necessarily involve the original partners and merely serve to remind people of this ultimate aim.

The Amesha Spentas and Yazads are Ahura Mazda's independent helpers, each with their own task. As far as humans are concerned, the more they worship the divine beings the more help they will receive. Dr Moos tells how, at a time when she was having her period and could not be directly contacted by spiritual beings, Behram Yazad gave a friend of hers a message for her. Atash Behram fires sometimes speak to her:

> So in the beginning of August or the end of July 1984 I was in Udwada and I went to the Atash Behram. Atash Padshah[13] communicates with me and speaks with me, but I was not expecting any communication at all, I was just sitting there saying my prayers. Suddenly Atash Padshah gave me a message that a national calamity on a vast scale will occur very soon. When this book [of mine] on Sarosh Yazad has been released – it will be released when the moon has become full – and then [when] from Full Moon it goes to New Moon and assumes a boat shape, [i.e.] roughly eleven days after the Full Moon, a national calamity will take place. Like a fool, I did not understand the message properly. I thought Bombay would be flooded, that was my mundane, humdrum thinking. But that was not at all what it was about. What happened – August passed, September passed, and it was the Full Moon of October when this book was released (actually on the day of the Full Moon). And from that day, for the moon to wane and reach that position, it was exactly the 31st of October [the day Indira Gandhi was assassinated]. On the night of the 30th of October I was sitting in a taxi and I saw this crescent moon, I thought, 'My God everything is still, like the calm before a storm. The book is out, this is the moon position, something terrible is going to happen.' And sure enough, the next day I was working and somebody came in and said, 'The BBC has given this news.' It's like that, Atash Padshahs talk to you but you must understand what they are saying.

Dr Moos says that earlier, in 1981, her astral body was transported by Sarosh Yazad through the different *dahyu* levels, to be initiated and prepared for a certain work. A few days after that, on 6 June 1981, she had a vision in which she was shown her entire life, both past and future. During this vision B.N. Shroff performed a *Jashan* for her in the mountains and gave her a piece of wood, which first turned into a sword and then into a pen, signifying that her task in life was to fight evil by means of writing. During that vision she was also shown a piece of land by a river, which she took to be in England. Slowly, through the power of her pen, a building arose to which people from all over the world would come for spiritual learning. When the building was completed a community of some seventy people would live there and the whole enterprise would be part of the labour of preparing the world for the advent of Shah Behram Varjavand and the Aquarian Age. After fourteen years Shah Behram Varjavand would come and walk around the building three times, which means that it would be a spiritual centre.

A little later again, in December 1981, Dr Moos was on a train travelling from Bombay to Poona, passing a group of mountains where the Abed Sahebs[14] have an abode (as they also do in the area where Dr Moos lives, where they cleanse the fire temple and look after Dr Moos). While on the train, Dr Moos received a message that something was going to happen and she must be ready. On her return from Poona, in the first week of 1982, an old gentleman, Mr K, walked into her office and offered her a piece of land. His story was that he had been adopted by a clairvoyant Parsi lady, who used to come to him in dreams after she died. She had instructed him to start buying land in the Gujarat area, which is very difficult in India except for farmers. Mr K, however, managed to carry out her instructions. The preceding December, just when Dr Moos had her premonition, his mother's spirit had come to him and told him that the time was now ripe to start a spiritual centre. She instructed him to give some of his land to Dr Moos (whose books he knew, but whom he had never met). When Dr Moos saw the land it was exactly as she had seen it in her earlier vision. She accepted the offer, and the land was transferred and registered with miraculous rapidity.

This was the beginning of Zoroastrian College, to whose promotion much of Dr Moos's time is now devoted. Since Ahriman is aware that the College will hurt him severely, she says, he is working against her with particular energy. The Kookadaru cult – which at one time attracted a great deal of charity money that might otherwise have come to her – she considers to be the result of the Evil One's machinations, and at one time she had ten lawsuits going against the movement's leaders. She claims that the Jal Baba cult was started by others deliberately to attract people to the Banaji Atash Behram, away from the Karani Agiary where Dastur Aibara worked.[15] She herself refused to have anything to do with such ploys; she did not interfere to put a stop to it, but will not take part in the cult herself.

In spite of her hostility to the Kookadaru cult, Dr Moos has a great respect for Dastur Aibara, who once cured her when doctors could do nothing. Once Dastur Aibara was directed by Kookadaru Saheb to attend a book-launch for one of her books, and to sit in a certain place. He later told her that he had seen two spiritual figures standing behind her, B.N. Shroff and another, whose description Dr Moos recognised as that of the late Colonel Dinshaw Ghadiyali, the author of a system of spectro-chromemetry[16] on which she was working at the time. Ervad Aibara insisted, and Dr Moos agrees, that these figures were speaking through her and that she was acting as a medium.

The photography of auras is one of Dr Moos's fields of interest. The light in the aura, she says, is connected with the Amesha Spenta Khordad. Her own aura shows that hers is an advanced soul. Dr Moos was the pioneer of Kirlian photography[17] in India, and now possesses a spectrochromemetry machine. There are only two such machines in the world, both in India; one used to be in the possession of the heirs of Colonel Ghadiyali. Dr Moos promised Col. Ghadiyali's soul in the Udwada Atash Behram that she would make his name famous if she could have it, contacted his family, and was allowed to carry it home without difficulty. Some people, she says, can cure the aura of the soul and even remove the karmic effects of previous lives. A Russian lady who, like the mythical Shah Lohrasp, can communicate with her own *farohar,*[18] managed to take a photograph of it. Dr Moos showed Mrs Munshi a Xerox of the original photograph.

Vibrations play an important role in Dr Moos's thinking. She always wears a headscarf since otherwise the four *chakras* at the top of the head may be harmed by the friction between vibrations of the outer atmosphere and those of the aura. It also keeps hairs from falling on the ground, where they can pick up vibrations of dirt and disease and transmit them to a person for as long as a year. In the old days Zoroastrians had special pits in which they buried hairs, but in modern Bombay the best thing is to wrap them in several layers of paper – not newspapers as they carry photographs, which have vibrations of their own – and throw them away. For a number of years Dr Moos used to play tapes of Avestan *manthras* and harmonious music to the plants in the garden of Zoroastrian College. The plants loved these vibrations and flourished.

Asked about her views on the differences between religions, Dr Moos says:

> Every religion is connected with a different planet, and every soul has to experience different things in a particular life, to learn a particular lesson. For example, Christian souls need to learn the lesson of love, Buddhist souls need to learn the lesson of *dharma*, Muslim souls are warriors, whether they want it or not they have to fight. Mazdayasni Daena means the knowledge of the Laws of Mazda, the Cosmic Laws which are applicable to all souls. Everyone must follow their own path, but they must know the Cosmic Law. There is a vast difference between ritual and awareness of Cosmic Truth. You see, Cosmic Wisdom is above all religion. Religion takes it up to here; when you have reached here, you become aware of the Cosmic Truths.

MR ADI F. DOCTOR

Mr Adi F. Doctor (1937) graduated from Bombay University in two subjects, Commerce, and Iranian Studies (Avestan and Pahlavi). He has worked in a bank for much of his life but is now retired and works as a free-lance journalist. He is very interested in in Western classical music, and is known in the community as an exponent of Ilm-e Khshnoom teaching.

Asked to introduce himself, Mr Doctor says that he comes from a traditional Zoroastrian family. Talking about his education, he says:

> I studied Avestan and Pahlavi ... under Dr Mirza and the late Dr Unvala.[19] Thereafter for some years I lay fallow, as it were, where religious activities were concerned. Then, in 1975, I came across this esoteric side of the Zoroastrian religion which is normally known as Ilm-e Khshnoom. Now this is where the change came about. Because, since I had studied Avesta and Pahlavi I could apply [the Khshnoomic teachings to what I knew already]. There were many things which I did not know at all. I mean I could not understand the rationale behind certain prayers, ceremonies and so forth. These I tried to understand and today I can say that one can justify why these prayers are there, the *Niyayesh, Yashts* and so forth, and the significance lying behind the Avestic words.

Mr Doctor's parents prayed regularly, every morning and evening. His father in particular was 'a stickler' for prayers. This impressed Mr Doctor as a child, and he began looking at prayer books. Mr Doctor's father taught him to pray – although he did not explain the meaning of the prayers – and told bedtime stories which were not necessarily religious but always contained a moral or lesson. Mr Doctor was often ill, and he became aware of the efficacy of prayer because his illnesses were usually treated by means of praying. His mother was very fond of Behram Yazad and taught her son to invoke him when he was at a loss at exams.[20] Mr Doctor continued to do this even in his University days.

> That is how the faith was built up. I did not know anything about the language or anything of that sort, but all I knew was that if I prayed certain things this would help me out in my difficulty ... I had almost a blind faith.

Another figure who was influential in religious matters was Mr Doctor's maternal grandfather. He was a *boyvala* (priest serving a sacred fire) at the Dadyseth Atash Behram.[21] When Mr Doctor was small the family lived directly opposite the Atash Behram and he spent a lot of time there. At the Atash Behram there was an elderly priest who taught him prayers and later performed his Navjote.

Although Mr Doctor's parents believed in strict obedience to rules, owing to practical difficulties the rules of purity were not followed, with the exception of those concerning hair and nails. The family tended to do the *kusti* only off and on, e.g. after a bath or before a meal, but not very regularly. For a long time there was no hearth-fire, but *divas* were lit regularly. Most of the *parabs* were observed in the traditional way; Mr Doctor's father was a good draughtsman and the family particularly enjoyed his drawings of religious symbols on the kitchen wall for the *parab* of the Fire. Birthdays were celebrated in the Parsi manner, with a *sagan* and a visit to the fire temple, where the *Tandorosti* [22] was recited by a priest and a *divo* was lit. Festive Parsi dishes were also prepared. Hindu observances were followed on *Kali Chowdas* and *Dhan Teras*,[23] but otherwise there were no Hindu influences.

Before going to school in the morning, Mr Doctor was taught to do the *kusti*, and pray the *Sarosh Baj*, *Dinno Kalmo* and other prayers. His father went to the Agiari on all days devoted to Yazads connected with fire (Hormazd, Ardibehesht, Adar, Sarosh and Behram *roj*) and on all *parab* days and anniversaries of fire temples. The father spent about half of every Sunday in the fire temple but his son did not normally go with him.

In Mr Doctor's younger days nothing special was done on Behram *roj*, but later his mother got into the habit of performing the *Mushkil Asan*. Mr Doctor, however, regards this as a Muslim practice alien to the spirit of Zoroastrianism[24] and eventually he made his mother give up the practice and recite the *Behram Yasht* instead. Mr Doctor's preoccupation with correct observance led to another change in the family's customs. His mother, being from a priestly family, used to sew the family's *sudrehs* herself. At some stage Mr Doctor discovered that the way she had been taught to do this did not accord with accepted practice, and from then on the family bought their *sudrehs* from a shop.

About his Navjote, Mr Doctor's most striking memory is that his maternal uncle insisted that no photographs should be taken. This is unusual at Navjotes and it was resented by the rest of the family, but no one had the heart to go against the old man's wishes. At that time nobody understood the reason for this, but Mr Doctor says that he knows now, and at a recent Navjote he made the parents do the same thing:

> Now again, I may not be able to convince somebody with empirical evidence, but I'll try and tell you what happens ... The Navjote is being performed, and the priests recite Avesta prayers. Now we very strongly believe that every Avestic word has its own vibrations.[25] These vibrations are very subtle. Other languages such as English only have gross vibrations, because English is a hotch-potch of so many other world languages. Avesta on the other hand is on the other

extreme; it has very subtle vibrations. The Avestan words are meant to be subtle because they have to cross the layers of atmosphere surrounding the earth and the other dimensions ... . All these vibrations must rise across all these dimensions which are around the earth. When I speak in Gujarati or English, the vibrations are so dense that they remain here only. And secondly we all have a personal atmosphere, which surrounds our physical body ... There are nine physical bodies whose names are given in the Avesta ... These nine constituents of every human being are again invisible subtle bodies, so when the Avesta is recited, in my personal atmosphere, along the nine bodies, the Avestic vibrations go forth in them and then they go out .... Now what happens – when a photograph is taken, invariably there is a flash. Electric lights have their own radiation, and they say that if you sit in tube-light radiations for a long time it might affect your health, sometimes it might even lead to cancer. So what happens is that the radiations from the flashbulb vitiate the Avestic vibrations which are created around the children, around the priest and around the congregation. They vitiate the entire atmosphere. The more subtle a thing, the more careful you ought to be that something that is gross and dense should not fall on that, otherwise it gets neutralised. Now as I said there are some people who say, 'Oh, this is all nonsense,' and many people call it mumbo-jumbo. So it all depends on the person, it is up to him or her to believe or not to believe. But I very firmly believe.

The first death Mr Doctor experienced was his grandmother's, when he was about five years old. The funerary rites were performed at home, and he noticed that the knees were bent after the *sachkar*. Mr Doctor mentions that there has been a controversy in the community about bending the knees of the dead.[26]

Because we don't know the reason behind these things we engage in those controversies. But much, much later I came to know why the knees are bent. And that was because, you see the *Nasa Druj* [demon of pollution] which starts emanating from a Zoroastrian corpse gets stronger and stronger as time passes. And it afflicts those in the vicinity also, and the ground on which the body lays also gets polluted. So the scientific reason behind this was that, when they bent the knees a lesser area was occupied [and polluted] ... Unfortunately we have given up that custom.

Mr Doctor was very fond of praying. After taking a degree in Commerce he decided to discover what he was praying, and embarked on the study of Avestan and Pahlavi at one of the Madressas. One of his teachers there stressed the importance of the *tarikat*s (rituals and observances), but others discussed only problems of philology.

241

Ultimately, to cut the whole thing short, I sat all the exams ... And that was when, I can say in retrospect, for the first time my faith in the recitation of prayers was shaken. It was because of the pure study of philology that my recitation of prayers began to be affected. I said to myself, 'Look, the *Aban Yasht* is full of historical [references], but what is there in it for me to pray?' These critical questions started cropping up in my mind, and after that I began to reduce the number of *Niyayeshes* and *Yashts* that I prayed. In a nutshell, I became more materialistic because of the study of Pahlavi. The biggest advantage I had was the pronunciation, that improved, but the drawback was that my faith in the prayers was shaken.

Around that time, Mr Doctor began to feel 'fed-up' with India. The love of Western classical music had come into his life and he thought of emigrating to Austria. He felt he knew all there was to know about the religion, and that it did not have much to offer him. The only points on which he felt strongly were *dakhme-nashini* (disposal of the dead in the Towers), which he favoured and advocated, and interreligious marriages, which he opposed. He started writing in the Parsi Press, always representing the 'orthodox' view. He had a long argument in the press with other authors about reincarnation, which he condemned as 'all humbug'.

Until twenty years ago. That was a sea-change, which I am coming to now. I wanted to leave India, I was fed up with everything, I wanted to marry a *Fräulein* in Germany or Austria.[27] I made two trips there, to Salzburg and Vienna, and then I came back – in retrospect I believe it was in my destiny to return here. The last trip was in 1974. Then, in 1974, I gradually began to take an interest in occultism – not Zoroastrian occultism, I did not know anything about that. I would frequent, religiously, the Strand Bookstore, and I would buy many, many books, nothing to do with religion, just non-fiction. And from time to time I would come across one or two of these kinds of books, on the esoteric side.

While this interest was developing Mr Doctor had regular conversations with another Parsi who was working in the same building, K.N. Dastur, who belonged to Ilm-e Khshnoom and was close to the Chiniwalla brothers.[28]

One day I told him about a book I had come across in Strand Bookstore, where it said you can hear the voices of the dead on the tape-recorder. I said the book was very fascinating and I wanted to try it. He said, 'No, no, don't do that, please don't do that.' I said, 'Why?' He said, 'Look, at this juncture I will not tell you the reason behind it all because it is a long story. But I am just requesting you as a friend, don't do it!' I said, 'OK, I won't do it,' and that was that. Then one day, just out of the blue, I asked him one question and that was the turning point. I asked him, 'Why is it that the Prophet Zarathustra, who is of such a high calibre and all that' – at that time I did not know exactly what that calibre was, but I said, 'Why is that kind of a Prophet saying things like, "Whither do I go, what shall I do,"[29] and all that stuff?' So he just turned red in his face and he said, 'Why are you asking me this question?' Then he said, 'I think now I must tell you something. I will give you one book to read. You read that and let me know how you feel.' So he gave me the book by N. Mama, in English, called *A Mazdayasnan Mystic*, about Behramshah Shroff. Now till then I [only] knew that there had been a lot of mud-slinging against him, particularly in *Jam-e [-Jamshed]*. And the main person who was doing that was Khurshed Dabu.[30] I used to read all those things, and in those days I would just chuckle at such things because I did not know enough. Now that became my turning point. I said, 'I did not know anything about this.' OK, we were told about Demavand[31] and all that, but [now I found that] in Demavand there was another world altogether! Of course, my background was already there in a general sense. I knew that there were certain things like Masters. If I had not known about occultism, I really don't know what my reaction would have been. I feel quite sure that when you are destined to come across these things, it is given to you. So the scales started falling from my eyes. And overnight I, who was such a staunch anti-reincarnationist, I became a very staunch reincarnationist. There was no turning back then. Once I knew who Behramshah Shroff was, I was keen to know what he taught, what he had said. That is how I started getting books ... Something within myself kept telling me, 'This is it, this is what I have been looking for.' What really converted me was that for every question which I asked myself I could get an answer.

Mr Doctor goes on to explain that the basis of the study of Avestan is Sanskrit (rather than Avestan) grammar, which he feels casts some doubt on the correctness of established translations.[32] In studying the Avesta he now uses a combination of philology and Khshnoom, which 'nobody can beat, as you get the advantages of both worlds.' In his opinion, what is important is the *tavil* (exegesis, interpretation), the hidden meaning behind the Avestan words. This approach opened up a new world for him. Mr Doctor explains how Behramshah Shroff was taken from Peshawar to Demavand, where he stayed for three and a half years, being instructed by the Real Masters. Afterwards he remained silent for thirty years because he had been told not to reveal anything until there were certain planetary aspects, which occurred in 1905.[33] Mr Doctor further says that ordinary people cannot apply *tavil* to the texts, because this is only given to specially designated and blessed persons.

As far as Mr Doctor's everyday life is concerned, his conversion to Khshoom made him realise the importance of ceremonies and observances. He says that there are many things[34] which are not, or barely, mentioned in the Avesta but which are nevertheless age-old and integral parts of the Zoroastrian religion and have been handed down in the oral religious tradition. Mr Doctor began to observe all the basic *tarikats* of Zoroastrianism, which incidentally caused his health to improve materially. He also attended various classes on Khshnoom, which taught him a great deal. His journalistic activities also changed; while his earlier articles had been fairly superficial he now began to represent the Khshnoomist view with passion. At one stage a well-known figure who was due to give a lecture on Khshnoom in Gujarati was unable to do so, and recommended Mr Doctor as a substitute. Until then Mr Doctor's Gujarati had been weak and he had never spoken in public, but he was able to do it. He also finds there has been a change in his dealings with other people, as he has become more patient because of the changes in his religious life.

> The one thing I am sorry for is that most of my fellow-Zoroastrians are not aware of the blessings and advantages of following these ancient Zoroastrian proceedings and disciplines ... First, as I said, I wanted to live in Vienna, mainly because of music, I wanted to sell up my things in India. But after this ... the inner sense of rejoicing I get from leading this Khshnoomic [life] – *khshnoom* itself means ecstasy or bliss – you cannot describe in words, you cannot describe it as the so-called worldly happiness. Ordinary men may have plenty of that, but this is something ... inner rejoicing, oh, yes! Beautiful! There is so much in nature, the truths, the mysteries of nature!

Mr Doctor goes on to describe the hidden reasons for various ritual acts, which are all explained by Behramshah Shroff and which make it imperative to follow the traditional ritual directions scrupulously. He goes on to describe Behramshah Shroff's classes. Shroff used to say that the time was not yet ripe to reveal all, and that the Masters had forbidden him to reveal more than would be safe for the people of this time to know.

Asked about the question of Good and Evil, Heaven and Hell, Mr Doctor says that he has discovered that the antithesis one finds in the Avesta between *garo demana* ('the house of song', i.e. heaven) and *drujo demana* ('the house of evil', generally understood to mean 'hell'), is that between paradise and this world: it is on this earth that evil reigns in the form of passions and anger, and the soul can be born here several times in order to be purified.[35]

Mr Doctor mentions the seven 'planes of nature' (*dahyu*).[36] If all ceremonies have been performed for the soul, he says, even the soul of a murderer can progress relatively quickly from this earthly plane to the Chinvad Bridge,[37] but as most modern Zoroastrians do not lead ritually pure lives it usually takes much longer, and the soul remains semi-unconscious and attracted to the earth for a long time.[38] The concept of the Bridge is to be understood metaphorically, as a test or examination to be passed. At the Bridge the law of *karma* is operative. The soul meets the figure of a woman, beautiful or ugly as the case may be, who represents its deeds on earth;[39] no one can intercede for the soul there, all depends on its own past actions. According to Mr Doctor's understanding of one of the funerary prayers,[40] the average time for a Zoroastrian to wait on the threshold of the Chinvat Bridge is 57 years.[41] He believes that there is no point in having a *Nirangdin* performed for a deceased person until at least twelve years have passed since the death. Reincarnation comes much, much later, the minimum period between births being 900–1000 years. For non-Zoroastrians the rules are different, as they are on a lower rung of the developmental ladder.[42]

Asked about his daily routine of religious observance, Mr Doctor indicates that he follows the traditional rules with great precision, cleansing himself with *taro* or lime juice on getting out of bed, and doing his *kusti* whenever tradition requires. As the human body has energy, which in the Avesta is regarded as a form of fire, Mr Doctor compares the *kusti* ritual to offering incense to the temple fire. Apart from the obligatory prayers he recites prayers addressed to the divine beings who are connected with the planets that are affecting him on the day in question. For most of his devotions he follows the Fasli calendar, although he was brought up in the Shehenshahi tradition.[43] As his father used to do, he now prays in the fire temple on Hormazd, Ardibehesht, Sarosh and Adar *roj* of every month – visiting each of Bombay's four Atash Behrams in turn – and also each month on the day of his father's death. He does *loban* every morning after taking a bath, and keeps a perpetual fire burning in his house. As Mr Doctor is unmarried, is often away from home and is in any case too busy to purify himself several times a day before feeding the fire, he has had to invent a special way to keep it burning after feeding it in the morning. He would like to go to Udwada at least once a year but says that one cannot just go to Udwada: the invitation must come from the Fire itself. 'If it does not [invite you], something will crop up to prevent your going, you may not be aware of this, but it is there!' Mr Doctor objects to busloads of Parsis going to Udwada without proper preparations and purifications. 'They are polluting the whole atmosphere.'

MR BEHRAM D. PITHAVALA

Behram D. Pithavala (1905) is the author of many publications on esoteric and occult themes, which have had a certain impact on sections of the community.[44] Mr Pithavala was 96 at the time of the interview, which therefore not only illustrates the thought of a prominent Parsi esotericist, but also offers fascinating glimpses into Parsi life in the early part of the 20th century. The interview was conducted in Gujarati.

Asked about his religious upbringing, Mr Pithavala says that he was born in Navsari, into a religious working-class household. He was taught the prayers at an early age so that he knew all the important prayers by heart at the time of his Navjote. Later, after his matriculation exam, he came into contact with a man called Ardeshir Billimoria, whom he describes as a 'very great astrologer and religious scholar, who was also a Theosophist.' Mr Billimoria published a magazine named *Cherag*; he took Mr Pithavala under his wing and employed him on a salary of 15 Rupees per month.[45] Another influential figure in Mr Pithavala's early life was Munchershah Master, who also played a role in the career of Behramshah Shroff, the founder of Ilm-e Khshnoom.

So there was astrology, Ilm-e Khshnoom and Theosophy. How did those things relate to religion?
Ilm-e Khshnoom *is* a kind of religion; it is the esoteric side of religion. Theosophy is the philosophy of religion. Ardeshir used to organise *Jashans* in Navsari on *parab* days, and Munchershah used to attend those. Ardeshir was not a priest and I was not from an *Athornan* family either, so these functions were held at Noshirwan Lodge.[46] There used to be lectures there too, good speakers were invited. I tried to give lectures but Ardeshir said it was not my forte, so I began to write. My first article appeared in *Cherag*, it was a Gujarati translation of an English article on Hazrat Ali.[47]

Although this suggests that Mr Pithavala was open to non-Zoroastrian teachings and ideas, he was much less tolerant of Parsis who behaved in a manner incompatible with Zoroastrian tradition:

In those days Parsi women used to attend exorcising sessions which were conducted by low-caste local women. They [the exorcists] shook all over their bodies and went into a trance, and then answered questions that were put to them. There was a craze for this sort of thing at the time, and lots of our people were influenced by these alien fashions. A photographer friend and I used to go there and pretend to be ordinary members of the public, but in reality we took photographs of the session, which we threatened to publish in the newspapers if those misguided Parsi women took part in these sessions again. So our people became afraid to attend the sessions.

But why did they go there in the first place?
To find solutions to troubles or cures for illnesses. The exorciser claimed that the person concerned was possessed by something evil, and they used a broomstick to drive it out.

About other communities, Mr Pithavala says:

In those days non-Zoroastrians were known as *durvands*. That is an Avestan word which does not mean a wicked person, as it is commonly translated, but one from whom we have to stay aloof.[48]

Why was that?
In those days there was no problem of inter-caste marriages. We knew that these were different people and we had to stay away from them.

But in your school you must have had people from all castes?
No, it was a Parsi school. Only in the higher classes did we have people from other castes as well. The primary classes were given religious instruction up to the time they had their Navjotes, and then we were examined. We were not taught any meanings of prayers. I used to pray with devotion and remember God with devotion so I had some idea [of the essential meaning of the prayers]. I used to recite the *Gathas* from Kangaji's book, which gave translations, and that convinced me that there is some meaning in this. We do not have books like the Bible or the *Bhagavad Gita*.

So in the course of time Mr Pithavala began to see that meaning could be found in the Zoroastrian tradition; he explains that the sequence of the days of the Zoroastrian calendar,[49] for example, has a deeper significance:

I figured out that there was a system being followed in the thirty days of the calendar. It is divided into four parts, two parts of seven days each and two of eight. Each week is a training period, and each starts with the name of Ahura Mazda. The first period is preliminary: it includes [the days of] Bahman (good thoughts) and Spendarmad (good actions, meditations).

The second begins with Daepadar, followed by Adar which increases our *rae* or inner self, and Ava purifies our inner emotions. Khurshed then gives us the strength to carry on without fearing anyone. Mohor is our inner foundation, it is also called *gao-chithra* – *gao* is light, *chithra* is the soul, our inner strength – the Hindus call it *pran shakti*, 'life-giving energy'. Tir teaches us the right type of charity. Gosh is for abstinence, not only from eating meat but also from bad thoughts. (I have been a vegetarian from the time I was in school.)

Meher gives us spiritual guidance, Sarosh makes our conscience pure, Rashne shows us the way of truth. Behram gives us victory, Ram stands for joy.

In the last week one gets the reward for doing all these meritorious deeds in the previous three weeks. Din is *daena*, our conscience which has been purified by the performance of all these deeds. Ashishvang gives us spiritual wealth. Ashtad teaches us occult sciences. Asman is the time for actual work, not only on the material level, but work in the true sense of the word. Zamyad is a time of warning – after doing all this you might still slip up, so be careful! Mahraspand works, not for your personal salvation only but you must uplift others also. The final stage is reached on [day] Aneran; here your duty is not only to yourself but to others as well.

The first is the preliminary stage, the second the stage of actions, the third represents the result of our actions, and the final stage shows us the path to salvation – we have to look not only to our salvation but also uplift others around us.

As a child Mr Pithavala had no playmates as there were no other boys of his age in their area. He did not like fiction, and his chief interest was in reading books on religion. Mr Pithavala explains this by saying, 'I was naturally attracted to religion because of my past life. We are always attracted to what we did most in our past life.' He was also most interested to hear lectures on religion:

Then there were what were called *bazm-e duniya*[50] – there was *bazm-e duniya Behram, bazme-duniya Adar*. Do you know what that means ?

No, I am afraid not.
Bazm means a meeting. It was like an association, a meeting: *bazm-e ruz-e Behram* meant that every one met on Behram *roj*, and so on. The members would meet and have discussions. There was one Mr Dadachanji who used to come from Bombay and others who came to give lectures. I used to attend these lectures.

Going back to Mr Pithavala's early years, Mrs Munshi asked him about the way the Parsis used to dress then.

Is it true that Parsis in those days dressed almost like Hindus?
No, not in my time, that must have been much earlier. In our time men wore *sudreh* and pyjamas and a *paghri* [Parsi cap]. Women dressed in saris and always covered their heads. We were told that if we slept without covering our head at night, Ahriman would enter our body through the exposed part of the head. To this day I always cover my head, even at night. [51]

Do you remember any stories being told?
Shahname kirtans [sessions] were organised at various places and there were meetings where poems were recited. People used to come from Surat. On Pateti, the last *Gatha* day, Parsis never went to bed in

Navsari, especially young boys, they used to have fun all night. Huge swings were tied across the street from one end of the *mohalla* to the other and everybody had fun there. Around midnight people from all over Navsari gathered in the Atash Behram compound, where there was a very festive atmosphere; people did not go home till four or five in the morning. On our way back from the Atash Behram we used to play pranks on people, knocked on doors and got up to all sorts of mischief.

The New Year was always celebrated with a visit to the Atash Behram. We had an early morning bath and went to the fire temple. My aunt, who had adopted me as her son, was a very pious lady. Ten to fifteen days before the Muktads, the entire house was washed. All of us were made to take a *nahn*. Menstruating women were sent to another house for that time. In several of the dishes made for the Muktads rice was used, which my aunt washed, dried and ground herself – others just ground it without washing. Our *mohalla* did not have fresh water, we had to get it from a village which was some distance away. (I used to carry pots of water on my head.) That water was used for ritual purposes as well as for domestic use. The Muktads were done in the house itself and the priest came and recited prayers three times a day, so the atmosphere was peaceful and soothing. When the Muktads were over, one actually had the feeling that someone had left, you felt the emptiness. We recited small prayers like the *Satumno kardo*, but the priest did most of the prayers [and rituals]. The Muktad ceremonies were always done at home in those days, not in the fire temples.

Mr Pithavala left school at the age of nineteen and went from Navsari to Bombay in search of a job. As time went on he became more and more knowledgeable about astrology and began to publish articles on the subject. This brings the conversation back to Mr Pithavala's early patrons, and Mrs Munshi asks what role Munchershah Master played in promoting the work of Behramshah Shroff. Mr Pithavala replies:

Behramshah Shroff did not get along with his mother, so he left his home in Surat and went to his uncle's place in Peshawar. He used to go out in the evenings for a stroll and on one such evening he had to relieve himself, after which he took some soil from the ground and rubbed his hands with it. A group of figures, the 'Sahebs', were observing all this from a distance. They had a tent there and they beckoned Behramshah Shroff to come to them, and asked him about his background. He told them his story and it seems that they then said they were from Iran and that he should accompany them there. Behramshah Shroff's uncle did not trust them – he thought they were dangerous Pathans,[52] so he did not give Behramshah Shroff permission to go with them. But the Sahebs insisted. Against the false claim that B. Shroff's mother in Surat was gravely ill, the Sahebs stated that she was not only quite well, but was in fact celebrating her birthday that very day and having a great time. The uncle then understood that these men had some power and gave Behramshah Shroff permission to go. He stayed there [in Iran] for nearly two to two and a half years. The Masters took him blindfolded to Mt Demavand, where he was taught the esoteric side of the religion. There were 72 Sahebs living there; their leader was called Murzban Saheb. He has since died, and now their leader is Rashidji.

How do you know all this?
From the followers of Ilm-e-Khshnoom, the followers of Behramshah Shroff... After this Shroff lived in Surat for thirty years waiting for the right time. He also thought that the Parsis of those days might not listen to him and would make fun of him. So he waited. Then Munchershah Master became aware of him. One day Munchershah was giving a talk about the fire, and Shroff suddenly claimed that he knew a lot of things about fire. So Munchershah invited him to come to Bombay where he said he would introduce him to Cama Seth[53] and others. So he came to Bombay. He gave many lectures, and Camaji was also very pleased ... Then he came to Surat where he wanted to build a Fasli *Atashkade*,[54] for which a foundation was in fact laid. But the Sahebs got angry and told him that he should not have done such a thing. So it seems he died soon after that from shock; he fell down, was taken ill and died! The time was not ripe to build a Fasli *Atashkade*, but he tried to override the authority of the Sahebs and build one. He was very much against photography, which he regarded as idolatry.

We know that he had a pleasing personality and that he wore a beard. It was my misfortune that I never met him. A rail ticket from Navsari to Surat only cost four *annas* in those days, but it was not in my destiny.

Mr Pithavala goes on to describe some of his own esoteric interpretations of Zoroastrian terms and concepts, and the refusal of the Dasturs to accept these. He then talks about his efforts to get married: before he met his wife he interviewed nearly 100 girls, but none of their horoscopes matched his. This in turn leads to a discussion on the relationship between astrology and the Zoroastrian religion. Mr Pithavala says that if a planet is afflicted one may counteract the effects of this by reciting the *Yasht* of the Yazad whom the planet represents.

About his esoteric interpretations of religion, Mr Pithavala says they are inspired by 'general reading'. The insights he derives from this he applies to Zoroastrian religious knowledge, many points of which are still obscure. He regards it as significant, for example, that people from various cultures who have had out-of-body experiences all claim that the ethereal body lives for 72 hours after death, which explains why Zoroastrians have the final funerary service on the fourth morning after death. 'So everything fits in beautifully. We have to look for help to other systems. It all fits in with our beliefs.' Similarly, Mr Pithavala says that both the Rosicrucians and Behramshah Shroff have stated that 'the span of this life together with the interlife is 144 years.'

So you believe in reincarnation?
Yes, definitely. Only it is not reincarnation – that means that a human soul is born again as an animal; we believe in rebirth. Zarathustra has given a clear indication of this in *Yasna* 45.7, which means that the sinful person comes back to earth again and again. The pious soul goes to heaven but the sinner has to enter another body and come back because of his sins. Our religion is the only one to teach that there is an 'interlife period', an interval of 57 years between death and rebirth. This has now been corroborated by regression hypnosis.

What do you think the function of the interlife period is?
The soul repents of its misdeeds during that time. It is mentioned in the *Patet Pashemani*, where there is a reference to 57 years: 19 for thoughts, 19 for words, and 19 for actions.

Is the soul reborn as a Zoroastrian after this?
The soul selects where it will go. This is mentioned in *Yasna* 46.1: 'Which land shall I go to?' There is no land on high, 'land' means other planets ... . The soul selects the land, and then the religious community in which it wishes to be born.

So the soul selects, and Ahura Mazda sends it where it wants to go?
It is done together with Meher, Sarosh and Rashne Yazad,[55] the three Lords of *karma*.

Speaking of Yazatas, which one has the greatest influence on your life?
Right now I am very much attached to Aspandarmad, Spenta Armaiti. She gives us wisdom, that is stated in the first three paragraphs of the *Atash Niyayesh*, which are from the *Gathas*.

Has it always been Spandarmad?
No, first it was Bahman.

Do you do anything special for Spendarmad?
There is a sentence which I often repeat: *spentam armaitim vanguhim verene, ha me astu,*[56] 'I remember good Spenta Armaiti, may she be mine.'

Do you celebrate the parabs at home and observe the little ritual acts?
In Bombay this is forgotten now. I used to go to the Agiary but now it is all gone. In Bombay no one does these things any more. In Navsari it

251

used to happen. Yes, I think it is very important ... Our Dasturs do nothing. As far as my family is concerned, I think they should grow up like flowers, especially in matters of religion, no one should be forced.

I myself pray in the morning, after my bath, and again at night, and I also do my *kusti* at each change of *geh*. At 12 noon I remember the Iranshah Fire – I pray that the community will survive and carry on. *Din-e Zarathoshti shad bad.*[57]

Why at noon, particularly?
Because the sun is at its zenith at noon, that is the best time of day, when the strength of evil is somewhat lessened. All great men and souls pray at that time ... Do you know that during the World War, Churchill had fixed a time in the evening? At 9 o'clock every evening, when Big Ben chimed every Englishmen prayed that England would win the war. And it actually happened! [Hitler] went to Russia but he could not come to England. That was the power of the *manthra*.

We also go to the Atash Behram to offer prayers for the dead. Those prayers comfort them, the soul feels lonely in the heavenly world and our good thoughts and prayers comfort them. They are confused. They no longer have their physical body, so they can see what wrongs they have done in their past lives, how they have lost opportunities and so on. So they are comforted by sincere prayers; but not by mechanical prayers performed by priests.

For how long do you continue to have prayers done for the departed in your family?
My son died thirty years ago and I still have prayers done for him

But what about the interlife, has the soul not taken birth already?
No, the soul has not taken birth, that happens after 57 years. And even then the soul can feel the effect of our prayers, so one can continue to pray.

Do you or your family have any eclectic[58] beliefs?
No, certainly not. Also, the laws of purity are followed in this house. My daughter does not come to our house when she is menstruating. After me I don't know what will happen. It is not that my children do it because they are afraid of me, more that there is an understanding [that such things are to be observed in my house].

Do you think it is important?
Most important. When a woman is menstruating it is a process which continues for a number of days. Now even after going to the toilet we have to wash our hands and do our *kusti* every time, so one has to follow the laws of purity even more strictly where there is continuous

impurity. You know the story about Jesus Christ? When Mary Magdalene touched his robe he turned round and said, 'Who touched me? My glory is gone.' That means his aura was affected. It has been proved that even pickles go bad [when a menstruating woman touches them.] So it is all scientifically proved.

Apart from the laws of purity, what else have you passed on to your children?
Nothing in particular. Whatever has been passed on has come from observation.[59] I do not force anything upon them – only if it comes from within [will it have any effect]. Whatever tendencies you have accumulated in your past life, you return to earth with all that. You don't come with a blank slate.

Thank you very much. Is there anything you wish to add for posterity?
The most important problem just now is the loss of *Parsipanu* [Parsi culture and identity] – I call it the P-factor. It is being eroded every day. Another thing is: Rite and Right. If you give up Rite, then Right also goes. Our rituals are very important, if we lose them we lose our identity. So *Parsipanu* should be preserved and rituals should be maintained to some extent. Human nature is such that it needs rituals. There are Parsis who say that the *sudreh* and *kusti* are useless, that rituals are no good, but those same people observe other rituals: they go to Sai Baba, for instance, or do *arti* [a form of Hindu worship], some go to churches. In the villages and in Navsari people used to go to women who went into a trance, and we had a crusade against this practice. Once I was even beaten with a brush those women used for exorcising evil![60]

MRS NERGISH NUSSERVANJEE

Mrs Nergish Nusservanjee was born in 1918 in Bombay; she is married with three children. Mrs Nusservanjee took Sanskrit at school, went to a well-known College for three years, and was later trained by Madame Montessori. She also studied Avestan, and some Pahlavi, at the Sir J.J. Madressa for eight years. Later she came under the influence of the Theosophical movement, which continues to inspire her. She has taught religion and Zoroastrian prayers for thirty years, and still does some teaching. Mrs Nusservanjee's husband and the present writer attended the interview.

Mrs Nusservanjee comes from a simple lay family, where prayer played a central role. She was first taught her prayers by her mother and was later sent to a children's class taught by a priest, where she learned the *kusti* prayers, the *Sarosh Baj* and the *Patet Pashemani*;[61] the children were always made to face a source of light when praying. The meaning of the prayers was not taught and, unlike modern children, Mrs Nusservanjee did not think of asking questions. A hearth fire was kept burning in her parents' house, and the family continues this practice even now, keeping a separate hearth fire in the kitchen. Mrs Nusservanjee's daughter keeps a fire in a separate prayer room.

Mrs Nusservanjee was trained by Madame Montessori and started her career as an infant school teacher; then at some stage the Principal of the school asked her to take a prayer class. Mrs Nusservanjee took her responsibilities seriously and began to study the proper pronunciation of the prayers, learning from books. Later she and her husband joined Dastur Minochehrhomji's[62] class on Sundays; they took their daughter along, as there was a special children's class. When the teacher of that class left, Mrs Nusservanjee took over, attending Dastur Minochehrhomji's classes on another day. She got so interested in questions of religion that she asked Dastur Minochehrhomji to teach her the meaning of the Avestan prayers. He was reluctant to do so, however, and she went on to the Sir J.J. Madressa,[63] where she attended Dastur Mirza's classes.[64] As Mrs Nusservanjee was over fifty years old at the time, Dasturji Mirza was reluctant to accept her as a pupil but she persuaded him, arguing that her knowledge of Sanskrit (a 'sister language' to Avestan) would help her. Originally she was only interested in learning the meaning of the prayers, not in Avestan grammar or in sitting exams, but after a time things became more serious. Subjects taught in the adults' class included the *Rapithvin geh* prayer, the *Tishtar Yasht*, and the *Gathas*. Dastur Minochehrhomji had already paid attention to the recitation of the *Gathas* and explained the meaning of the texts, but in Dastur Mirza's class grammar was very much part of the course. Mrs Nusservanjee came to understand several Avestan texts well but – in common with all Avestan scholars – still finds the *Gathas* very difficult. Pahlavi proved more taxing than expected and Mrs Nusservanjee did not get as far as she did with Avestan. These classes did advance her spiritual search to some extent and she continued for eight years. One day, however, she joined 'this Blavatsky lodge',[65] where she found knowledge of a kind that appealed to her more:

> I wanted an occult meaning of my religion. If you just see the meaning from the prayer book, you still won't be able to understand it. [Dastur] Mirza only taught the grammatical side; that gave me the root, so that I could find out the meaning of each word. But I could get the [real] meaning from the Blavatsky Lodge,[66] hard teaching there, very hard teaching! [Dastur] Dhalla attended the meetings,[67] but he did not teach; other members of the Lodge used to take the Sunday class. They were mostly Parsis, and Jains also. We studied religions, Hinduism,

Christianity, Zoroastrianism, Jainism, Buddhism, all the religions ...
Madame Blavatsky's works are very difficult to understand, but
because I had learned all this about the Zoroastrian religion I used to
understand a little bit. She used to give us the occult meanings. For
example *Tir Yasht*, Tir Yazad.[68] Mirza used to give us the meaning of it,
but just a brush-up only. Just, 'This word means this,' and so on. It was
not so very important, I just continued because I wanted to learn.
Otherwise it was of no use, it just gave me some hints. Dasturji
Minochehrhomji's classes were much the same. Then I started reading
Dastur Pithavala's book,[69] *In Search of Divine Light*, a beautiful,
excellent book. He gave us the occult meaning of each and every thing,
how to tie the *kusti* in the correct way and so on. He is also a
Theosophist. And he is so humble, very sweet. He is my *guru* at
present.

Mrs Nusservanjee now tends to pray only those prayers whose meanings
she understands. She does not have a favourite Yazad since she feels all
divine beings are equally important, all having their role to play.

Some people say that these supreme Powers are residing in us and we
have to develop them. Others say that they are there, individually, in
the universe. I believe in both: they are there also and they are within
us also.[70] They are attributes of God, aren't they?

Asked about her understanding of Evil, Mrs Nusservanjee says:

Before God created the universe He created these two opposite forces.
God created these opposite forces because without each one nothing
could exist.[71] Evil is different from Ahriman, it is in men only! God
has created two opposite forces – I don't say evil. God is not evil, so
He cannot create it. He has created two forces, positive and negative,
good and not-good – I don't say bad, because God is not bad, He
cannot create bad things. You know, in electricity also there are
positive and negative currents. If two currents are positive, no light! In
the same way God created good and not-good. Because of these forces
the world has become manifest.

Evil emerged from men only, because of their selfishness. Because
there is selfishness, selfish love. God has not created evil. At present,
the upper hand is evil now. But Angra Mainyu [Ahriman] is not evil,
Angra Mainyu is a force.

Mrs Nusservanjee observes the Fasli calendar.[72] She associates the *parabs*
with biorhythms. Ava *mahino* Ava *roj*,[73] in her opinion, is not related to
water as we see it, but has to do with currents of God's goodness which
are inside man. One has to be alert to detect these currents in oneself. Mrs
Nusservanjee would not dream of taking *dalni poris* to the Waters on that

day: *poris* should be given to poor people, not to the sea. Mrs Nusservanjee has observed a completely vegetarian diet for two years, but gave it up when she realised how many problems it caused to her non-vegetarian hosts. She keeps a vegetarian diet on Bahman *mahino* Bahman *roj*, except when she forgets. Adar *mahino* Adar *roj*, in her opinion, is the day when the Fire at Udwada was enthroned. On such days she prays and may go to a fire temple, but she does not follow the traditional customs.

> I don't know if it helps me or not, but I do pray. I believe that we must say *Atash Niyayesh* seven times. More is better, not exactly seven!

The conversation then turns to the power of *nirangs*, short prayer formulas used for specific purposes:

> I believe in healing. *Ahmai raeshca*,[74] there are eight blessings in *Ahmai raeshca*. When someone is ill, first I say my *kusti* prayer and then I start, even when the patient is asleep. I practised on my husband also; he did not know, he was asleep. I just pass my hand [over the patient], saying my *Ahmai raeshca* prayer, and *Hazangrem*[75] also, for the health of the soul. *Ahmai raeshca* is for physical health and *Hazangrem* is for the soul. I don't know if it helps me or not, but I have that belief. *Ardibehesht Yasht* also, that is for health. I don't know if I have ever used that, but I have prayed *Ahmai raeshca*.[76]

Neither Mrs Nusservanjee's mother nor her mother-in-law were very strict about the rules of purity. Mrs Nusservanjee was taught that she should use a separate *kusti* during her period but she did not do so, being content to wash her regular *kusti* after those days. Her daughter does not believe in the laws of purity at all, and refused to observe them even when her mother-in-law insisted.

Mrs Nusservanjee does not consider such customs as the *besna* and *pagladu* very necessary,[77] but as they are age-old customs she expects they must do the child some good. She has read that the Navjote should not be performed until a child is seven years and three months old, when 'the soul and the body are joined,' and the child is capable of understanding the meaning of the ceremony. As to the ceremonies for the dead, Dastur Mirza told Mrs Nusservanjee that they should be done for one year, at least for ordinary people; those who spent their entire life in prayer have no need of such rituals. Asked about her ideas concerning the afterlife Mrs Nusservanjee says:

> Yes, [there is] life after death! I have read Leadbeater's[78] book, I read Annie Besant's book,[79] I read Dasturji Bode's book also, and then Dasturji Dabu's[80] book on life after death. There is a life after death! We Zoroastrians, we do not believe that there is life after death.[81] But

we believe, we Zoroastrian Theosophists do believe in it. Dastur Minochehrhomji also used to tell us, 'There is life after death!' What happens depends upon the *karma*, what one has done with [one's] life. To us *karma* is very important. So do your best *karma* in life! In the *Hormazd Yasht* also there is a para, that the man who has not done many good deeds, he is in *Misvanem Gatu*,[82] not here, not there. He has to pass on ... I believe in reincarnation. There are so many reasons, from the *Gathas* also, there are so many paras. It is not Hinduism, it is a fact! Minochehrhomji also believed in reincarnation. He used to tell us, 'You just tell those people [that] in the same class almost always there are some children who are highly intelligent, some who are normal, and some who are very low in intelligence. The very intelligent child must have come into this world for the third of fourth time, the second type less, and the third one must be a new soul.'

Mrs Nusservanjee goes on to explain that the occult significance of the five watches of the day is that each represents a stage in the evolution of the human soul. *Ushahin* [the dawn watch] she associates with an Avestan word for consciousness and with a word *hin* which, she says, means 'without'.[83] The Ushahin *geh* therefore represents the inexperienced soul, whose development is helped by the Yazatas Sarosh, Rashne and Ashtad. Similar explanations are given for the other watches, each of which represents a higher stage of evolution. Birth in human form is the highest and last stage of evolution (after existences as waters, mountains, plants and animals); after many births as a human the soul becomes perfect.

Mrs Nusservanjee is strongly opposed to Baba cults, and has in fact lost pupils because of her condemnation of those who follow Sai Baba. The cult of Kookadaru, on the other hand, she regards with approval. She tells the story of Kookadaru in her classes: how, as a poor and simple priest, Kookadaru was under pressure to contribute a large amount towards the building of the Anjuman Atash Behram; how he prayed for help and found the required sum in his fire temple.[84] Formerly Mrs Nusservanjee believed that one of Kookadaru's friends knew of his plight and put the money there, but now she is inclined to attribute the miracle to Kookadaru's knowledge of alchemy, which he shared with Zarathustra. Mrs Nusservanjee is a staunch believer in the existence of Zoroastrian saints, including Kookadaru and Homaji, and has a book about such saints.

Story-telling has always played an important role in Mrs Nusservanjee's methods of teaching the religion. Most of her stories come from the *Shahname*; they include tales which go back to the Avestan tradition and some that do not, such as the romance of Bizhan and Manizhe.[85] She also tells stories to illustrate the power of prayer. One of these describes an incident which Mrs Nusservanjee says she found reported in a newspaper. Two Parsis were living in an isolated house in the Bombay suburb of Andheri. One day seven Pathan robbers came to the house, but the Parsis prayed the *Sarosh Yasht Vadi* and the Pathans were forced to leave as they could not see the entrance to the house. Another story is about a baby that cried all the time. When it was laid on one particular carpet the crying stopped, and the five-month-old child began to babble in a foreign tongue. Eventually it was discovered that the carpet had been woven in Iran by very pious women, the vibrations of whose prayers had been woven into the carpet. The baby could perceive these vibrations because it was pure and innocent.

ERVAD YAZDI NADARSHA AIBARA

Ervad Yazdi Nadarsha Aibara was born in 1969 as a son of the well-known Ervad Nadarsha Aibara, who received messages from the spirit of Dastur Kookadaru. Ervad Aibara holds a degree in Commerce and has worked as a full-time priest since 1989. His views on religion are clearly influenced by those of his father. The interview is reproduced here almost *verbatim*.

Nadarsha Navroji Aibara, my father, when he was very small, at the age of seven, his inner voice was speaking from within and he never used to tell anybody about it. The first words of the inner voice – inner voice means, voice from the soul, which only he himself could hear, nobody else – the first voice he heard was in Surat (my father was born in Surat). The first voice which he heard was *Ya Ahu*, which means Dadar [Creator] Ahura Mazda ... Can I speak about my father a little bit, because it all started with him?

Of course, please do.
My father was born in Surat, his father's name was Navroji Kawasji Aibara. At a very small age my father became *Navar* and *Martab* also.[86] He had not much interest in studies, but he was very fond of learning more about religion, religious studies and prayers. So after becoming *Navar* and *Martab*, of course he went to school and did studies up to S.S.C. level. After becoming *Martab* he practised priesthood in Surat. His father was alive up to seven years of age only, when my father was seven years of age my grandfather expired. His elder brother was twenty years older than he, so he looked after my father. Then after becoming a priest he practised priesthood in Surat, and at the age of thirteen my father came to Bombay. The first thing he did there was a *Nirangdin* ceremony at the age of thirteen, in Mithaiwalla Agiary in

Sleater Road. Nobody does such a big ceremony at such a young age.[87] Then he practised priesthood in many of the Agiaries in Bombay. Then he became a religious teacher in the Cama Athornan Institute in Andheri.[88] He was there for nineteen years, he used to teach the prayers to the students and he taught religious knowledge, that is why he was called religious teacher. Over there he read more than four to five hundred religious books, and he got much knowledge from that. But apart from that, his inner voice constantly used to be telling him ... That spiritual knowledge was more than the religious knowledge he got from books. He was nineteen years in Andheri, and of course in the meantime he got married also. And my father had no house to stay; he was staying at his mother-in-law's place. So because of housing problems, he left there and he took a *panthak* [parish] in Sodawaterwalla Agiary. He did that just because of housing problems, otherwise he had no interest in this *panthak* line as such.[89] He had interest in teaching the students more about religious knowledge, prayers and everything. Otherwise he would have taken a *panthak* a long time back. So his housing problem was solved. We were very happy there, of course the salary was extremely low but still we were happy because the main problem was housing.

In 1969 my father took a *panthak* in Sodawaterwalla Agiary and he wanted to know about Kookadaru Saheb. That started from that Agiary only. In Sodawaterwalla Agiary there is Kookadaru's frame [picture], near the Atash Padshah *qibla* [fire chamber].[90] That frame, the picture inside, had tremendous power in it. If you or myself, if we see the picture, if we see the frame, we just say, 'Oh, it is a picture.' But the inner voice of Aibara Saheb told him that this picture had tremendous power inside, and whenever he used to go and bow down near the frame, he used to get some replies from that frame. And from that it started, little little.

His work was as usual in the *panthak* line, and some Zoroastrians used to come to him, saying, 'Dasturji, my problem is this, my problem is that ... ,' sickness problems, business problems, anything. Anyone can come and say, please give me some prayers so that I can get relief. So he used to give certain lines, 'You pray this.' Those lines were given from the reply which he was getting from inside, from the inner voice, but nobody knew about this. They thought, this is a priest, so he knows the prayers which he is giving, from the *Khordeh Avesta* or the religious books.

Was that frame talking to him, and then did he give the prayer?
No, the voice which he used to hear was from within his soul. So that is how it started. But in Sodawaterwalla Agiary it was becoming more and more. One day – he used to give Atash Padshah *boy* 5 times a day;

259

every day he used to give it, because no Mobed was kept over there,[91] because the salary was so low and there was hardly any work in the Agiary, so he used to perform all the ceremonies, and even to give Atash Padshah's *boy* every day for ten years, until we, myself and my brother, became *Navar* and *Martab*, then we started helping him; till then he was all alone. One day he was about to perform Ushahin *geh* at 3 o'clock in the night. In Ushahin *geh*, the last watch, he was about to perform and pray the *faraziyat* before giving the *boy* in Atash Padshah's *qibla*, at that time he saw a light, we say *prakash*,[92] a divine light that was so bright that you cannot see even. He was surprised to see all this, he could not speak, he could not say his prayers, he was just surprised. And we [Ervad Yazdi Aibara and his brother] were just sleeping at that time, we were sleeping in the hall of the Agiary only. We had a place to stay nearby, but we were sleeping there.[93] So on seeing this great light he asked, 'Who are you, what is all this?' And he got a reply from the light, 'I am Kookadaru Saheb.' First he could not believe, for throughout his lifetime he had never seen anything, he had never heard anything, only the inner voice. But the voice which came from that light was similar to the voice which my father was hearing throughout his life from his soul. So his mind struck that this is something which is very familiar. So he asked, and got a reply from that light, 'Yes what is in you is myself, and I am giving the replies to you all the time when you need it.' So from that it started. But the light was so powerful – light means, not only ordinary ... it means a great force, which was so bright, so bright, like when there is a sunrise, you cannot see the sun when the sun is rising.

And he told you about this?
Yes. He spoke about in public lectures also. And he got the reply from that light, the light of Kookadaru Saheb. And he was asked to do the work of Kookadaru Saheb from the very next day. At that time my father was forty years old. Then he was asked to do Kookadaru Saheb's work, to help the people by giving prayers. So he got a reply from that light, 'You tell the people, the Zoroastrians who come to the Agiary, from tomorrow onwards, "I am giving the prayers of Kookadaru Saheb."' So my father said, 'How can I tell anyone? I cannot just hold anyone and tell them, "I am giving Kookadaru Saheb's prayers, take it," it cannot happen like that.' The light said, 'You have to do it, this is your job, and this is my *farman* [command].' So my father said, 'OK, if this is your *farman* I'll do it, but I am quite scared, I cannot just step forward.' Then the great force of light started coming nearer and nearer to him, and it immersed inside the body of my father, the whole light. At that time my father felt so much power in his body that he felt that another person was entering his body. He

felt so heavy! Then after some time, everything was finished and he went to his Ushahin *geh*'s prayers and he gave the *boy*. After that he went to sleep. In the morning he forgot everything that had happened. He gave Havan *geh*'s *boy* to Atash Padshah, and then after coming out from the *qibla* room, early morning, seven o'clock, he saw seven Zoroastrians sitting on the bench of the Agiary. In those days there was hardly any work, [i.e.] the ceremonies for which Zoroastrians come. So he was just wondering, 'Why have seven people come today? There is work for only one or two.' That Agiary was such that hardly anyone used to come, only a few people used to come, and that at ten o'clock, eleven o'clock – perhaps one would come at eight o'clock, but seven![94] He was quite surprised. But he did not bother, thinking that maybe they had come to pray. Then after half an hour, one hour, he saw that they are not praying either, and they are waiting for someone to come, they were just sitting idle on the first bench. So my father went to ask them, 'What have you come for? Have you come to pray in the Agiary? You are just sitting idle, I don't understand what you want.'

He had forgotten about what had happened in the night. So all seven of them said together, 'We have come to take Kookadaru Saheb's prayers from you.' Then he realised what had happened in the night, that the light of Kookadaru Saheb had said, 'From tomorrow morning you have to start my work, and you have to say, "I am giving Kookadaru's prayers."' When those seven Zoroastrians said together, 'We want Kookadaru Saheb's prayers,' at once he heard from his inner voice, 'Are you satisfied now, about what happened in the night? Now you have to start.' From that time onward Kookadaru Saheb's work began. He had to start, because there was force from the other side, [saying] that 'We want Kookadaru Saheb's prayers.' Then it went on, he did not have to tell anybody he was giving the prayers.

Then he started, so the seven people, ladies and gentlemen, they had different problems. First a gentleman came who had problems in his business, then a lady came who for many years was not carrying a child. Another came about sickness, a cancer patient, the doctors had said, 'There is no hope, you can live for two months, two years, we cannot say.' So all those seven Zoroastrians, for all of them he gave the prayers which he got from his soul, from what Kookadaru Saheb had told him. But what happened is that Kookadaru Saheb gave the same prayers to all those Zoroastrians, the same prayers! Now for example if you go to a doctor and you have different problems, the medicine always changes according to the sickness. But for them, Kookadaru Saheb gave the same prayers for all of them! So my father was quite shocked, thinking, 'What will happen? All of them have got different problems and all have got the same prayers.' He was very much frightened – what to do, this was just starting and somebody might come and fight with him. So that is how his life started on Kookadaru Saheb's job.

And there was a *farman* of praying these prayers for forty days, and on the 41st day come again, to say what had happened. And according to that, he would give another prayer, if he gets one from the soul. So all those Zoroastrians went and after forty days they came. My father was very much frightened on that day, thinking 'What will happen today, everybody will burst out on me!' But you believe it, all of them came with a smile on their face! First, the gentleman came about the cancer: 'Now my doctor is saying, "I cannot find any cancer germs in your body. I don't understand what has happened to you. I was getting medicine for you from America, Canada and all, now you have no need of it."' Then that doctor also came afterwards, and met my father. He said, 'If you can heal all those things then there is no need for doctors like me.' Then the other lady came who was not carrying a child; she came with a smile on her face, 'I am carrying a baby.' All of them were happy about the prayers, and that was his starting point.

It went on and on. He started in 1974. Every day my father used to sit at ten o'clock in the morning – before that he had to see to the Agiary's work. Ten to twelve in the morning, and 4.30–6.30 in the evening he used to sit, for so many years. And as the years passed so many Zoroastrians came, because only Parsis can come to our Agiary.

Also maybe because the prayers were Zoroastrian?
Zoroastrian prayers only! From our Dadar Ahura Mazda, prayers from *Gathas* and *Khordeh Avesta*.[95] But he was guided by Kookadaru Saheb's voice, saying, 'You give this line from this book, from this *Gatha* book, from this *Vendidad* book.' Like that, and he did not have to refer to books either, because he knew them all by heart. After all, a boy who can do the *Nirangdin* ceremony at the age of thirteen does not need any book. So at once he could make out which line Kookadaru Saheb was saying, and he used to write it. At first he used to write on the paper, everything, the whole *nirang*. But so many people were coming, he was getting tired; two hours he had to write in the morning, two hours in the evening, plus all this Agiary work, plus five *gehs' boy* and everything ... He was getting very tired. So he requested Kookadaru Saheb: 'This is a very tiring job for me. Please, I totally reject it. I don't want to do this job and I am getting very tired. How can I live my life like this?' So Kookadaru Saheb said, 'We will make a solution.' He told my father to make cyclostyle prayers, which Kookadaru Saheb was giving. But at that time he was not earning so much, so he said, 'Where will I get the money from?' 'Don't worry, everything will be fine.' Then, one day, when he went to give *geh boy* at three o'clock in the night, as soon as he entered the *qibla* room he saw

three 100-rupee notes on the *khvan* [table] of the *qibla*, the white stone on which the fire *afarganiyu* [fire vase] is kept. He saw three 100-rupee notes, but so new that you would think that someone had taken them straight from the Reserve Bank. First he thought somebody must have brought the money from outside. Then he got the reply from Kookadaru Saheb, 'This is for you, you have to use this money for the cyclostyling which you have to do for my work.' Then he started cyclostyling the prayers with this money. Then, when the money was finished he used to get 300 rupees again, and again ... He never worried about what would happen afterwards. He was getting only 300 rupees, and that he was using for so many years.

Then, people were getting so much benefit from his prayers and many people used to come carrying boxes of sweets and what not for him. But my father did not accept anything. Because Kookadaru Saheb's *farman* was: 'Do not take a single *paisa* [penny] of money, nor sweets or anything!' Nothing! Only he used to tell everybody, 'Keep one rose near Kookadaru Saheb's frame, and then go. But don't put anything on the table!' But some people were benefiting so much that one day a gentleman came with a lawyer and he said, 'I have made a will, all sorts of contracts sort of, that I am giving you one *lakh* [100,000] of rupees' – 1975/6 I am talking of – 'one *lakh* rupees everything in your name, plus a two-room kitchen flat on Marine Drive.[96] I want you to live nicely.' But my father said no. That gentleman was so much annoyed, 'You are refusing just? Who would refuse it?' He said, 'No, I don't want a single *paisa*, forget about one *lakh*. Don't even put one rupee on my table!' So that gentleman was very much depressed, and he went away. But still he used to come for getting prayers from Kookadaru Saheb.

One day a lady came, she had benefited so much in her business due to the prayers and all, she came with a cheque for 35,000 rupees. 'You take it, it is not even crossed. If you want you can take the amount from the bank.' He said, 'No, I cannot take it.' That lady was forcing us so much that my father said, 'Now you take the cheque or I'll tear it up!' Still she forced my father and my father tore up the cheque and threw it in the waste-paper basket. There were many such cases in his life.

Then Kookadaru Saheb told my father, 'The people are so eager to give something because they are benefiting so much. So you open a Trust in my (Kookadaru Saheb's) name. The Dasturji Jamshedji Sohrabji Kookadaru Trust. And you can take money and put in the Trust. You accumulate the amount and after some years, when you get a lump sum amount, you can build a Hall in my name (Kookadaru Saheb's name), so that people can remember for ages to come.' So he said, 'OK, I'll do it.'

And in no time he had to leave Sodawaterwalla Agiary because the Trustees who were over there, they had stopped his work of giving prayers. They said, 'Why are so many people coming to the Agiary? We don't want so many people to come. You stop this work, do your normal Agiary work.' So he said, 'Whatever you say, you are my Trustees. I will stop it, I don't mind.' Then he stopped, and as soon as he stopped many Parsi Zoroastrians came from Cusrow Baug, Colaba [saying], 'There is a place in our Agiary also, Karani Agiary, there is a vacancy for a *panthaki*. Why don't you come to our Agiary? We will ask our Trustees to let Ervad Aibara come over here, so that his work will start again.' So, many people from Cusrow Baug went to the Trustees and they accepted. 'He is a nice man and he is doing a nice job also, beside his Agiary work he is doing a great job benefiting others.' So within two months only, my father was called and appointed as a *panthaki* in the Karani Agiary in Cusrow Baug ... My father came there in 1979, and he started the work of Kookadaru Saheb with the permission of the Trustees of the Karani Agiary. Then I have told you about the Trust ... He explained [to the Trustees] that people want to give money to me but I cannot accept. Even if Saheb's *farman* had not been there I would not have accepted. Saheb's *farman* is this: 'Open a Trust in the name of Kookadaru Saheb.' He explained all these things. Then our Trustees agreed, they allowed him to open a registered Trust in Karani Agiary. They allowed us to put a box also, in the Karani Agiary, so that people put a little contribution if they want. Not more. Then he chose the Chairman [of the Trust], Mr Jehangirji Shroff. He said, 'Saheb Kookadaru Saheb is saying that you have to become the Chairman. Will you accept?' So Mr Shroff, our senior-most Trustee, he at once said, 'Yes, I accept,' and he became the Chairman. Other Trustees also were there. All the Trustees were made by the *farman* of Kookadaru Saheb. Jehangirji Shroff, Mr Homi Ranina, Mr Faramroze Madan, who expired a few years back, and other Trustees. Then he started taking money, and putting it in the Trust. After so many years his wish is fulfilled, but by that time he was not alive. He had tried so much in his life about building a Kookadaru Hall. First he had seen a place on Marine Drive – that was also shown by Kookadaru Saheb, from inside: 'See here, there is empty space, just opposite to the two pillars at Marine Drive where all Zoroastrians go and pray, near Taraporewalla Aquarium ...' There was an empty space, twenty, fifteen years back there was empty space over there. So he had gone, and urged Mrs Indira Gandhi also, but at that time there was no reply and some time later a reply came that they were building a Nehru Bhavan[97] there. But there is still some space left even now. Then he tried at Bandra,[98] and then ten years back he tried in the [Karani] Agiary also, he wanted to extend the Agiary, some part of the gardens was to be taken. All plans were put before the Trustees, but some residents of Cusrow Baug said, 'No, we won't allow you to do this and that ...' So he did not succeed.

But Kookadaru Dar-e Meher[99] in Sanjan was built during his lifetime.
Yes that is right, and he was happy. But the main purpose of the Trust was to build a Hall in the name of Kookadaru. An Agiary was not so important because there are so many Agiaries, and many Agiaries today are closing down because they cannot get priests. So Kookadaru's *farman* was to build a Hall, and a *Dadgah* in it, that is a 24 hours' fire in which priests can go and look after the fire, and even other Zoroastrians who are not priests, ladies as well as gentlemen, can look after the fire.[100] So it was a *farman* to build a Kookadaru Hall with a *Dadgah* only, not an Agiary, so that even after many years there would not be any problem about priests. In Sanjan unfortunately an Agiary was built, but he was happy that in the name of Kookadaru Saheb at least something is there! But times are very bad nowadays, everywhere you don't find priests. In Sanjan there is one priest at present. But you cannot say what will happen after one year, two years if you cannot get priests. There were two Agiaries in Sanjan, then they were closed down, one was closed down ...

They are both still there, you know ...
But there are so many problems. That is why my father said not to build an Agiary. But they built it, the Trustees said we will build an Agiary. He said, 'I have no problem as such, no objection as such, but then you have to look after it. You have to get the priests to look after Atash Padshah fire, that is the job of priests.' But at least he was happy that something was done in his lifetime. But still he was searching somewhere in Bombay. And his intention was [to have it] in this Agiary, so that he himself could look after it.

Just two days before he expired – my father expired on Govad *roj*, yesterday was the sixth anniversary of his death, he expired in 1989, that is why I told you to come today, yesterday I was extremely busy the whole day.

Do you do special prayers? What did you do?
Yes, morning, evening, both times. In the morning the *Jashan* ceremony and other prayers also, with other Mobeds. In the evening there was the prayer by *Hama Anjuman*;[101] every year all the people come together, they contribute and they have the prayers done the whole evening. And they give the Mobeds [money] afterwards.

So you were saying, two days before he expired ...
Yes, two days before he expired, on Behram *roj* 1989, 10th January (it was 12th January when he expired), he called my mother and me and

said, 'If something happens to me, you keep in mind that the prayers I am giving throughout my life, for sixteen years, if something happens to me this should not discontinue.' And he told my mother, 'You have to continue my work.' And my mother started laughing, 'What is happening to you?' At that time he was not sick, nothing was wrong, but he had inspiration from inside. And he was just telling me, in a kind of joke. Then he said again, 'I am just saying it'[102] (*hū to khālī kahūchh*). He was hearing from his inner voice, but every time he used to say '*hū to khālī kahūchh*' – those who can understand will understand in one shot, those who cannot will never understand in their life. So he said, 'You have to continue the prayers.' But he used to get those from his inner voice and my Mummy, Nergish Banu, she started laughing and said, 'How can I do your work, it is not my business, forgive me, I cannot do it.' So he got a little bit angry also, 'No, you have to do it, you have to continue it. You will get blessings, and you'll get all the help from Kookadaru Saheb. You'll get it, believe me! And the second thing is, you have to keep in mind that Kookadaru Hall is to be built in Bombay! If not in this Agiary, then in Bombay. Even if I am not there, keep that in mind.' Those things he told us.

Here follows a slight digression. Both sons were initiated as priests at an early age. Ervad Yazdi Aibara works as a full time priest, whereas his brother has secular job but also helps at the Agiary whenever required.

We were talking about your father's death.
Yes, those things he told us. He was having tea, it was four o'clock in the evening, we had had our tea and he called us. We did not bother much, but it was hurting from inside, for me and for my mother also. In the night we could not sleep properly. But we never said anything to anyone. I got a dream on that day and on the next day also, that my father had expired and was taken to *Doongerwadi* [the Towers of Silence], and so many people have come, there is no place to walk at *Doongerwadi*. Two days I saw such a dream. I was so frightened, but my father was hale and hearty. I did not say anything to anybody, I kept it in my heart only. I thought I was imagining things because my father had talked like that. But my mother saw the same dream, she saw that her husband had expired and she was going for a ceremony, and there were so many people. The other days she dreamt that she herself had expired, and her husband was crying, there were so many people. But she also did not say anything to anybody.

Then on Govad *roj* we had tea and breakfast together, then he came down, and sat near our Paigambar Saheb's [Prophet's] frame [picture], a big frame. I was inside the *qibla* room, I was praying. As soon as I finished my prayers I took off my *jamo* [prayer clothes]. He told me, 'You take me near the *Ava* [Waters], near the sea, I would like to bow near the sea.' So I said OK – it was in the early morning, not early but 10, 10.30. I said, 'OK, I'll take you in your car, as you wish.' We went near the sea and he bowed down and prayed. Then we came back in our car. As soon as we came home he started feeling unwell. He said, 'I want to sleep, I am not feeling well.' I said OK. Then, fortunately, my brother came in the afternoon. He said, 'I'd like to eat with you.' My father said, 'I am not feeling well, I want you all to eat in front of my eyes, right now.' I had to go soon afterwards, for Rapithvin *geh boy*,[103] so I said, 'There is hardly any time, I will eat after my *boy* ceremony.' So he pressurised me, 'No, you have to eat now, in front of my eyes!' He made us sit together, and then he went to sleep. Afterwards he got up and said he wanted to go to the toilet. As soon as he came back, he said to my mother, *'Nergiś, Nergiś, mane śū thāy chhe?'* [Nergish, Nergish, what is happening to me?] So my mother went and held him, and as soon as she held him my father put his head on her and he expired. She was so shocked, she started screaming, 'Yazdi, Homyar, come here! I don't understand what has happened.' She could not even believe that her husband has expired, she thought he must have fainted. But he was gone. I was so shocked I forgot to go for my Rapithvin ceremony also, and the doctors came ... Then at 1.15 my mother realised, 'Yazdi, you have to go for Rapithvin *boy*, you have not gone yet.' We were so much in pain, crying and all. Then my brother took a half day off and said, 'I'll go for the Rapithvin *geh boy*.' And we took him to *Doongerwadi*.

But his words were true, his words were true! On Behram *roj* he said that Kookadaru Saheb's job should be continued and Kookadaru Hall should be built in Bombay. And on Behram *roj* in the evening, on the terrace, he told my mother, 'I have two days left.' My mother said, 'What is that you say, I don't like it!' He said, 'I just say it', he was just joking, but it came true. Two days later he was dead.

It is a fascinating story. What I would really like to know, did your father ever tell you whether he had studied Kookadaru's life before all this happened, before he saw the light?
No. He never knew that the voice he was hearing was Kookadaru's voice. He was studying all the religious knowledge at the Cama Athornan Institute.

Apart from Kookadaru Saheb, who obviously plays a central role in the religious life of your family, what other aspects of the religion do you focus on? Say the parabs, do you do any special ceremonies for those days in the fire temple? On your own behalf, do you do anything special for the fire. Also, how do you follow the rules of purity in your house? And what prompted you to become a priest?

Here Ervad Aibara explains what a *parab* is. The family does nothing special in the house; anything special (not specified) is done in the Agiary.[104]

Ervad Aibara then refers with approbation to what he sees as a new interest among Zoroastrians in the feast of Mehragan:[105]

> But nowadays [see] what is happening at Mehragan *parab*, Meher *mahino* Meher *roj*. Mehragan is for Shah-e Faridun, Afsun-e Shah-e Faridun Saheb.[106] These, Shah-e Faridun, Shah-e Lohraspa, Shah-e Jamshed,[107] these were ....

[SM points to a picture frame containing a number of images of obviously venerable men.]

Who is that other one?

The first is Shah Lohraspa, then Jarthostra [Zarathustra] Saheb, then this is Kookadaru Saheb, then Shah-e Jamshid, Shah-e Kaikhusrow, and Shah-e Faridun. Shah-e Jamshid, there on the left, he was on the throne for 716 years, can you believe it? They lived for more than 1000 years; these are not people like us, they are born from, we say *nūrmāthī nūr* [light from light].[108] But they are in the form of human beings, so that normal people can see that he is a man, he is a powerful man, but actually speaking they have not been born as such: *nūrmāthī nūr*.

And Jarthostra also... we say that Dogdov Mata[109] and Porush-aspa, they were Jarthostra's father and mother. But not in reality! They were shown to the public [as such], because how can anybody accept a child without a father and a mother. So when Jarthostra Saheb was about to be born, many, many years ago, Dogdov was only seven years and Porushaspa was only three years older. They were brought by our *Manvant Dastur Sahebs* [Venerable High Priests], because they knew that Paigambar Saheb was going to be born. And this Dogdov Mata and Porushaspa were so powerful, and all *ruvani* [spiritual power] and *nur* – *nur* means *prakash* [light] – was coming from all over their body. They had been kept on Demavand mountain[110] for so many years, and they had been kept in prayers for so many years. After some time Dadar Ahura Mazda said, 'Now it is the time for *Paigambar Saheb* to take a birth in this world.' So Dogdov Mata was brought near a tree of Hom, you know, Hom Yazad, in our ceremonies also we have *hom kriya*,[111] in the *Ijeshne,Vendidad, Nirangdin.* So she was put near the Hom tree, and Porushaspa sat near there, and he did an *Ijeshne* and *Vendidad* ceremony according to the *roj* they were given by Ahura Mazda. So he was to take *hom sali* [Haoma twigs] to do the Hom ceremony. From those twigs he had to make Hom water [i.e. extract Haoma juice]. That was given to Dogdov, and from that water which went inside she got her baby. And then Ahura Mazda sent the soul of

Asho Jarthostra Paigambar Saheb [the righteous Prophet Zarathustra] through the clouds, the rain and everything. And that soul came into the Hom tree first, and before that ceremony was done by Porushaspa, the soul of Asho Jarthostra Paigambar Saheb came into that Hom tree first, near where Dogdov Mata was sitting. And from that tree *hom sali* was taken and the ceremony was done; then the water of the ceremony was given to Dogdov Mata, and through that water and through that ceremony the soul entered.

That is what my father used to tell me, and he explained it in lectures also. And I can say that what my father was saying was, not just from his heart but from the voice, Kookadaru Saheb's voice that he was hearing. I don't know whether it is in the Book or not,[112] but my father used to say it in lectures also. In the same way all these Prophets were born: *nūrmāthī nūr*. Except Kookadaru Saheb, Kookadaru Saheb's soul was so high, he was on the fourth stage. We have stages in our life [along] which our soul progresses. Reincarnation, we take birth and death, and our soul progresses. And his soul was in fourth generation, that is why my father has put his photograph with all these others [i.e. Zarathustra, Shah Lohrasp *etc.*][113] Because after the fourth generation [i.e. incarnation as a human], you have to live in astral body, you don't take the form of a human being ... From that fourth generation your spiritual life as a soul begins, with all the Yazatas, Amesha Spentas. But the soul does not take the form of a human being as such, in this world, there is no connection with a human.

Mrs Munshi returns to the question of observances in the home, and asks whether a fire is kept burning for 24 hours during the *parab* for the fire. This is not the case; not even a *divo* is kept in the house for, Ervad Aibara says, it would have the status of a *Dadgah* fire and have to be kept burning always, whereas the family might have to leave Bombay from time to time. So any special prayers are done in the Agiary. About Adar *mahino* Adar *roj*, Ervad Aibara has this to say:

Adar *mahino* Adar *roj*, it is a most powerful Yazad.[114] Our calendar, you see, from Hormazd *roj* to Aneran *roj*,[115] they are Yazatas, Amesha Spentas and *Minoi Shaktis* [spiritual powers], the whole world progresses because of them.[116] And on top of that these Sahebs are there.[117] In the early morning, even before sunrise, these Sahebs – Shah Lohraspa, Jarthostra Saheb, Kookadaru Saheb, Jamshed Saheb, Kaikhusrow Saheb and Faridun Saheb – their souls come to the world before sunrise every day, to start it.

There follows a discussion of the precarious financial position of Parsi priests and the problems surrounding the Muktads: there is a shortage of priests, but people have ceremonies done for their departed for increasing numbers of years so that there is a greater need for services each year. This in turn leads to increased demands on the part of the priests, and some hardship for the laity.[118] Ervad Aibara deplores this, but admits that he himself would be emotionally incapable of giving up the Muktad ceremonies for his father. Ervad Aibara is training his own son for the priesthood, and stresses the need for sacrifice in a priest's life, which cannot be compared to that of a businessman.

Do you have any of the prayers that your father gave?
Yes, my mother is now continuing the work. She was so hesitant at first, 'How can I start, I just cannot do it.' She could not put a step on the *chaharom* day,[119] after we finished the four days' ceremony at *Doongerwadi*. On *chaharom* day she sat for prayers, and when my father was still alive she used to say after praying, *'Mane sohvāsaṇ rākhjo'* ['allow me to stay a married woman,' do not make me a widow]. Since so many years she had worshipped like that, and then on the *chaharom* she said the same things, and she realised, 'What am I saying, my husband is no more.' And then she heard the voice from Kookadaru Saheb's frame, 'Daughter, you are not a widow, you husband is immortal.' She heard the voice within her soul, and at that time she realised what the inner voice of the soul is. It was the first time she heard the inner voice from her soul, her first experience. And after that many Zoroastrians came to her [saying], 'Now you have to start Kookadaru's work.' But she was quite reluctant, saying, 'No, it is not my capability to take my husband's seat. His soul was great and I respect his soul. I cannot sit in his place.' Then after one year she got inspiration from within: 'On such-and-such a day you have to start Ervad Aibara Saheb's work, the work he was doing from Kookadaru.' Then she started, she told the people, 'Such a thing has happened to me.' And the people were so happy. She realised, 'What my husband said was true, "You will be helped by these Sahebs."'

Have you ever used any of these prayers for your personal use?
Yes, many times since I was a child. In Sodawaterwalla Agiary I was praying, and my brother also.

There follows a discussion on the importance of ritual purity. Ervad Aibara says that the purity laws have to do with the invisible *khoreh*,[120] which comes out of the body all the time. Observing the rules of menstruation is of paramount importance in this respect.

The world is going to *kalyug*,[121] to its end, for that reason only. Because of *menses* .... at that time the *khoreh* which comes out of the woman is so bad all the time that even if you stand one foot away from that lady your *khoreh* is disturbed, forget about touching. But in this world, nothing can be done, that is why you find all the problems in

270

everyone's life. At least in our house we provide full *chokkhai* [purity], my wife also, eight days in a month she stays separate, on a steel bed. It is a sacrifice for everyone in the house, to maintain purity in the house. It is not just that you cannot come to the Agiary, the purity should be maintained fully. Nobody can do it,[122] but still, they would come to my father and he would explain to them, 'You cannot just sit still, but for these eight days you keep your clothes separate, you keep your *sudreh* and *kusti* separate, you keep everything separate.[123] You go to your work, but when you come home, just sit separate for eight days. Then you will find a tremendous change in your life. Even if you cannot sit separately, then see to it that at least some pure parts of your house are not touched, don't go in that area. At least you should maintain that. Then at least fifty per cent should get some relief.'

People don't realise that … you cannot see it, but our life depends on the stars. When there are good stars,[124] at certain times, it is well and good. But when weak stars come in, in someone's life, then it is horrible. At that time you'll think that you'd better find the doors of the Agiary. 'What to do, I'd better go into the Agiary and sit near the fire.'[125]

The interview ends with a statement to the effect that evil is not an independent principle that is active in the world, but more like a lapse from right which is man's fault, not God's: 'What is good or bad is within you, within ourselves only. That is called Ahriman.'

————

Notes

1 From Pahlavi *rayenidar*, 'one who orders, arranges, restores'.
2 i.e. Avestan prayers and texts.
3 Taraporewala 1951.
4 On Behramshah N. Shroff see, apart from Dr Moos's own works, Chiniwalla n.d., Mama 1944, Mistree 1990: 238ff., Hinnells 1988, and above, p. 49f.
5 An idea perhaps connected with a *Vendidad* passage (*Vend.* 13.51) claiming that, when a dog dies, its consciousness 'passes to the water springs, and from these come together two *udras*, from a thousand female dogs and a thousand male dogs one pair, female and male.'
6 i.e. the ceremonies which must be performed in a consecrated place, see above, p. 9.
7 The implication being that this was due to the mystical power of the ceremony.
8 Dr Moos clearly attributes this sequence of events to divine guidance.
9 *Dahyu* is an Avestan word meaning 'land, region'. Dr Moos, it seems, uses the term to refer to 'regions' outside this world. Compare the interview with Mr Doctor, above, p. 244.
10 In other words, the better prepared the soul is through its own deeds and the

rituals performed for it after death, the sooner it reaches the Bridge (on which see above, p. 6).

11 The word *fravashi* is most often used for the eternal aspect of the human soul (see the interview with Mrs X above, p. 210 with n. 20). However, there are references in the Avesta to the *fravashis* of Ahura Mazda and other divine beings.

12 Western scholars generally take this term to refer to marriages between close relatives. That interpretation is hotly contested by many Parsis, who do not believe that their ancestors accepted a practice which seems abhorrent to them.

13 'King Fire', a way of alluding to an Atash Behram.

14 Another term for *Sahebdelan*, see above.

15 Ervad Nadarsha N. Aibara, the leader and initiator of the Kookadaru cult. For further references see Index.

16 A technique for photographing auras.

17 Another way of photographing auras.

18 Another form of the word *fravashi*, on which see above, n. 11.

19 For further references to both teachers see Index.

20 Behram Yazad is usually invoked for success.

21 This is a Kadmi Atash Behram, Mr Doctor's mother being a Kadmi (on this group see above, p. 47).

22 A prayer for good health.

23 Hindu festivals, for further references see Index.

24 cf. the interview with Mr K with n. 101.

25 The importance of the vibrations engendered by the Avestan prayers plays an important role in Khshnoomist teaching.

26 On this controversy, which goes back to the 18th century, see Boyce 1979: 189.

27 This suggests that Mr Doctor's sense of dissatisfaction with his religion was such that he wished to make a clean break.

28 Two brothers who played a central role in promoting Ilm-e Khshnoom, cf. the interview with Dr Master-Moos.

29 The reference is to a passage from the *Gathas* (Y. 46.1).

30 The well-known Theosophist Dastur, cf. the interview with Dr Bharucha, above, p. 149 with n. 19, and below, n. 80; for further references see Index.

31 A mountain in Iran where B. N. Shroff is said to have been instructed by the Masters.

32 In other words, since the study of Avestan is based upon knowledge of a different (if closely cognate) language, Mr Doctor feels it is less than authoritative. Many Khshnoomists argue that Western-based Avestan studies are unreliable (cf. the interview with Dr Master-Moos).

33 See also the interview with Mr Pithavala.

34 The reference, it seems, is mainly to matters of ritual and observance.

35 In other words, evil is not seen as an independent cosmic force but rather as the result of a lack of spiritual perfection, which can be remedied through reincarnation.

36 cf. above, n. 9.

37 On the Chinvad Bridge see above, n. 10. Classical Zoroastrianism teaches that every soul crosses the Bridge on the fourth morning after death, and that the judgement takes place at that time. Khshoomists, on the other hand, believe that the pace of the progress of the soul towards the Bridge depends on the quality of its religious life.

38 Very similar views are found in the interview with Dr Master-Moos.

39 See also above, p. 6.

40 The *Patet Pashimani*.

41 See also the interview with Mr Pithavala.

42 Some Khshnoomists believe that reincarnation is not explicitly taught in the classical Zoroastrian tradition because Zoroastrians are spiritually so advanced that they do not need to be reborn at all (cf. p. 170 n. 21, p. 230 n. 69, and see Index). Opinions on this question evidently vary.

43 The family thus followed the father's tradition, Mr Doctor's mother being a Kadmi (see above, n. 21); on the various calendars see above, p. 47.

44 See the interview with Mrs Nusservanjee.

45 At the time of writing Rs. 50/- approximately equals one Pound Sterling.

46 Presumably a Theosophist lodge.

47 The son-in-law of the Prophet Mohammad, who is greatly revered in Shi'ite Islam. Ali has no obvious connection with Zoroastrianism.

48 The word is usually understood to mean 'evil, wicked'. The remark implies that interpretations claiming that dualism is a central part of classical Zoroastrian teaching are mistaken.

49 See Appendix.

50 *Bazm* is Persian for 'feast, assembly', *dunya* means 'world'. Why such a meeting was called a 'world-assembly' is not clear.

51 For a similar belief see the interview with Dr Bharucha, above, p. 149 with n. 18.

52 A people living mainly in Afghanistan and the North-West Frontier Province of what is now Pakistan, whose capital is Peshawar. The Pathans have a reputation for bravery and intractability.

53 Khurshedji R. Cama, the founder of the K.R. Cama Oriental Institute in Bombay.

54 A fire temple where the Fasli calendar (see above, p. 47) would be observed.

55 In classical Zoroastrian teaching these are the divinities of the Judgement of the soul after death.

56 Y. 12.2.

57 A Pazand formula meaning, 'May the Zoroastrian religion be happy.'

58 Mrs Munshi uses this word in the sense of 'non-orthodox, of non-Zoroastrian origin'.

59 i.e it has been passed on by example rather than formal teaching.

60 For a more elaborate account of these events see above.

61 A confession of sins, which at present is not generally taught to children.

62 One of the few leading Zoroastrian priests who offered religious instruction. For further references see Index.

63 See above, p. 57 n. 55.

64 For further references to Dastur Mirza see Index.

65 A Theosophist group.

66 In other words, Mrs Nusservanjee's knowledge of grammar enabled her to understand the literal meaning of the Avestan texts, but only Theosophy offered some insight into their deeper significance.

67 It is interesting to note that a man whose nickname was 'the Protestant Dastur' because of the profound influence of Western thought on his theology (see Hinnells 1997: 70-1), attended such classes.

68 The word *yasht* means 'hymn', *yazad*, 'divine being'. Mrs Nusservanjee is about to speak of the hymn, and indicates that it is devoted to the Yazad Tir.

69 See also the interview with Mr Pithavala.

70 i.e. the divine beings are both immanent and transcendent.

71 In other words, good and non-good were both created by God in order to bring the world into being. Evil is a different matter, it has nothing to do with God and exists only in men.

72 See above, n. 54.

73 The 'Birthday of the Waters'.

74 An Avestan prayer.

75 Another prayer formula.

76 In other words, Mrs Nusservanjee is aware that the *Ardibehesht Yasht* is often recited for purposes of healing, but she herself perfers *Ahmai raeshca*.

77 On these ceremonies for babies see above, p. 36.

78 Charles W. Leadbeater (1847–1934) was an influential member of the Theosophist movement. Information I owe to Dr A.F. de Jong.

79 The well-known Theosophist leader.

80 On Dastur Khurshed S. Dabu and Dastur Framroze A. Bode see Hinnells 1997: 76, 78–9.

81 Mrs Nusservanjee presumably means 'physical life' here, as opposed to continued existence in the hereafter.

82 i.e. 'purgatory', a place between heaven and hell.

83 Most Iranists would understand the word *ushahina* as an adjective deriving from Av. *ushah*, 'dawn'.

84 cf. Y. Aibara's account of this event (above, p. 257).

85 A romantic tale about two lovers.

86 i.e. he became a fully qualified priest.

87 It is indeed exceptional for a young and inexperienced priest to be chosen to officiate at a *Nirangdin*. On the ceremony see above, p. 10.

88 A Madressa, see above, n. 63.

89 i.e. he did not much care for the day-to-day, practical activities demanded of such a priest.

90 The word *qibla* is of Arabic origin and in Islamic contexts refers to Mecca, to which Muslims turn when praying; here it is used for the fire chamber in the Agiary.

91 i.e. there were no other priests to feed the fire, so that the demanding task of offering fuel to the fire five times every twenty-four hours devolved on Ervad Aibara alone, on top of his other duties as a 'parish priest'.

92 An Indian word for 'light, lustre'.

93 Priests who have to feed the fire during the night often sleep in the fire temple.

94 The number seven has special significance as there are seven Amesha Spentas.

95 See above, pp. 6, 7.

96 An expensive and prestigious location.

97 A building dedicated to Nehru.

98 A Bombay suburb.

99 The term *Dar-e Meher* is generally used for an area in which high rituals are performed; here it is apparently used as a synonym of Agiary (see also the interview with Mr Ranina, above, p. 89f.).

100 An *Atash Adaran* requires qualified priests (of whom there is a shortage) to tend it, whereas even lay people who are in a state of purity may look after a *Dadgah* fire. See also above, p. 9.

101 lit. 'the entire community', i.e. a ceremony to whose cost members of the community have contributed.

102 This was said in Gujarati.

103 The ceremony of feeding the fire in the early afternoon.

104 This appears often to be the case in the families of practising priests, possibly because the family is too busy on such days to organise festivities in the home.

105 See above, p. 22.

106 *Afsun-e Shah-e Faridun* is the name of a popular prayer formula connected with Faridun, an ancient Iranian hero (but, in classical Zoroastrianism, not a Yazata), on which see also above, p. 41 n. 19. Ervad Aibara, it seems, uses the whole phrase as a proper name.

107 All these are ancient Iranian figures, best known from the *Shahname*, who play a much more prominent role in the beliefs of the Kookadaru cult than in classical Zoroastrianism.

108 i.e., they have emanated form a source of light and light is their essence.

109 *Mata*, 'mother' is a title generally used by Hindus.

110 A mountain in Iran which plays a role in the teachings of several 'esoteric' Zoroastrian groups, cf. above, p. 49, and the interviews with Mr Doctor and Mr Pithavala.

111 i.e. the Haoma ritual. The word *haoma* or *hom* refers to the juice of the plant of that name, which is extracted and consecrated as part of high rituals.

112 i.e. I do not know if there is scriptural confirmation.

113 In other words, pictures of Kookadaru and the ancient Iranian heroes are venerated by followers of Kookadaru because these figures are held to have reached at the highest stage of spiritual development a soul can achieve by means of incarnations as a human being before moving on to another mode of existence.

114 Note the absence of a clear distinction between a *roj*, a day dedicated to a divine being, and the being itself.

115 i.e. all the days of the month.

116 The last phrase was said in Gujarati: *te lokothī ākhī dunyā chālechh.*

117 *viz.* the group consisting mostly of ancient Iranian heroes but also including Zarathustra and Kookadaru.

118 See also above, p. 25.

119 The fourth day after death.

120 i.e. *khvarnah*, an ancient Iranian concept connected with light and fortune. Here it is apparently understood as an aura emanating from the body and affecting the environment. The importance of the aura is also stressed by Dr Master-Moos.

121 A Hindu term, meaning the worst part of a cycle of history, a time of death and destruction.

122 i.e. in practice it is impossible to keep all the rules of purity in modern life.

123 i.e. use special items instead of the normal ones.

124 This remark suggests that, like many Parsis, Ervad Aibara takes it for granted that the stars direct one's life to a certain extent.

125 i.e. when times are bad only religion can help.

Chapter Nine

Religion as Cultural Heritage

MR B

Mr B was born in 1955. He is a well-known Parsi journalist and is also active in the World Zoroastrian Organisation (W.Z.O.).

Mr B belongs to the priestly class. Both his parents were religious and he had a religious upbringing. When the children were young their mother taught them prayers, while their father gave them further religious education, discussing among other topics, 'how one has to relate to circumstances, how one relates to other people.' About prayers, Mr B says:

> My father laid a lot of emphasis on the *Yatha Ahu Vairyo* prayer – somehow that is very fortifying for the soul of the Parsis when they utter it. But even later on, when I went abroad for my studies, he gave me a special prayer which I learnt by heart; I have said it ever since that time – I was about 21 then, and now I am twice that age. So for the last two decades I have been saying that prayer almost on a daily basis ... [Here Mr B recites the prayer.] It is a prayer asking for strength in our everyday actions and in our everyday dealings with people and situations.

> *Did your father explain the meaning of the prayer?*
> Yes, he gave me the prayer together with an English translation, so basically I knew what I was uttering.

Although Mr B belongs to the priestly class, neither he nor his father underwent priestly training (*Navar*). As a child he felt it was all too remote from ordinary reality, but later in life this has become one of Mr B's major regrets.

Mrs Munshi then asks if there was a perpetual fire in Mr B's parents' household.

276

Yes, we lived in a very old building in an old Parsi area. The building is now almost a hundred years old and the flats are designed in the old-fashioned way. In the kitchen we had a fire-place, with ash. Every year we used to celebrate the birthday of the kitchen fire, which is part of our community traditions. We had this fire-place with ash, on which my father put sandalwood every day. Every evening my sisters and I would pray together with my father in front of the fire, before he put the fire to sleep for the night, so to speak, by covering the embers with ash. These are our early memories. Unfortunately, since the building was old, that portion of the kitchen collapsed – the portion which my father had religiously sanctified with prayers for almost a generation.

Did your father have an explanation for this?
If an explanation is necessary – there was one remarkable thing: the kitchen went down with my father in it. It was strange, one ascribes certain religious [powers] to certain things we do – even if it is only ritualistically – there are some very important and serious elements which are created when we pray. And these forces, one would imagine, are forces of security, of safeguarding and so on. And in a way it was also an elemental force which saved my father from certain death, because when he fell down he fell on a narrow ledge in the kitchen and that probably held him up so that he did not get buried under soft debris.

So you feel that it was the force of prayers that saved his life.
Undoubtedly! These are things which are inexplicable, they are beyond our mortal comprehension, but these are the workings of the world beyond.

Mr B and his family have always had a strong emotional bond with Udwada and, as a leading figure in the Youth Wing of the World Zoroastrian Organisation (W.Z.O.), he is now hoping to be able to do something to restore Udwada to its former more prosperous state. Mrs Munshi asks how this bond with Udwada originated. Mr B says:

I have always felt very much at home with our community, even as a child I felt at home with the older members of the community, I related quite naturally to them. It may be something that carried over from a previous incarnation, I would not be able to say. I found some kind of connection with Udwada even as a child, I had a sense of well-being when I was in Udwada: the houses there – at that time Udwada was very alive, when you went through the streets, the small charming alleyways and winding lanes, you always heard prayers being chanted and muttered by priests on the verandahs. There was always the fragrance of sandalwood and incense, because most of the houses were occupied by the priestly class. These are the memories I have of

277

my early connections with Udwada. Unfortunately that is all in the past. It is something that pricks my mind, which is why I am so keen that something should be done about Udwada. Udwada is really the last bastion of our community, the last stronghold of the Zoroastrian religion as such. Because after all the Holy Iranshah [Fire] is there.

So for you the Udwada fire is the best and holiest of fires? Do you relate more strongly to it than to other fires?
No, I would not want to compare fires or belittle other fires in any way. But of course the Iranshah has always had a very special place for us as a family, and we do venerate it. It is just the entire atmosphere of Udwada as a village – it is not that I keep the fire in my mind as something exceptional, but this whole village has had a strong influence on us. And the Iranshah is the ultimate fire, of course, and the priests there are the highest among the priesthood.

Returning to the topic of his religious education, Mr B says:

Basically my parents gave us quite a sound training – to be honest in our dealings, you know, the basic things, but those played a very prominent role and influenced us very much in our lives. And it really did help, later, to confront various people and situations.

Mr B says that his mother was very particular about cleanliness, and that he and his elder sister have inherited this. Even today Mr B is sometimes laughed at because he has 'this very, very strong thing about cleanliness', and insists on having a bath even abroad in sub-zero temperatures.

Mrs Munshi goes on to ask about the doctrinal side of Mr B's religious upbringing. Mr B answers:

My sisters, who are older than I and played an important role in my life, and also, particularly, my father, are very academically oriented. They have done an immense amount of studies, of comparative religion for example. And although I did not have any religious instruction by way of courses or classes, I have had this exposure to many aspects of our religion through them. And of course I was taught Persian mythology, which has a connection with our religion.

So which aspect of religion has had the greatest impact on you?
I would say the history of the community as a whole, the status of the Parsis of the past. They have been identified very strongly as people of integrity, that is one element; another was honesty; another, accountability and trustworthiness. These basic attributes, those were the things about our past that struck me very deeply, more than anything else, more than stories. I just felt that we were a breed apart in the past.

When Mr B was studying abroad he gave up wearing the *sudreh* and *kusti* for a time, feeling that it was 'too much of an encumbrance'. When he returned to India his mother was upset when she discovered this, and he went back to wearing the 'sacred' garments. Although he does not regard it as very important, he quite likes wearing the *sudreh* and *kusti*. Furthermore, 'It gives you an identity as a member of the Parsi community, it gives you a religious identity, which is quite important to me.'

Mr B has no beliefs that are of non-Zoroastrian origin; Baba-worship was always strongly condemned in his family. He has a great respect for other religions, especially Christianity, but nothing more. His father is convinced that the Fasli calendar should be adopted, not just by the Parsi community but by the whole world but Mr B himself is not very familiar even with the Shehenshahi calendar.[1]

When discussing his wife, Mr B says:

> She is religious in a very secular sort of way, not in terms of institutionalised religion. She is deeply religious, as a Parsi – she comes with me to Atash Behrams, and often to Udwada, but I must say she has been influenced by me. She tells me she had never been so often to Atash Behrams in her entire life as she has in the few years since we married. But she has a deep concern for the well-being of the community and of course for the religion as well.

> *Could you describe a typical day in your life, what role does religion play?*
> Well, in the morning – we have a table with [religious objects] and an *afarganiyu* with a burning fire, and I take the *loban* around the house. I pray a little as soon as I get up, then after my bath I pray [again], and then I worship the photo-frames [on the table] and do *loban*. Then at night, just before going to sleep I say a few prayers, and that is all.

Mr B would ideally like to visit Agiaries frequently, the more so since he works in an area where many fire temples are to be found, but in practice he does not go there very often. He mentions a special link with one Agiary, which he explains a follows:

> I have a deep veneration, a deep nostalgia for things past and this happens to be [a very old Agiary]. Also I have done a lot of study on Agiaries in Bombay, I've written a lot of articles and things like that. And this Agiary has a long history behind it, it is 280-odd years old – not the structure as such, but the location.

Mrs Munshi goes on to ask about Mr B's views on the afterlife.

> I think one cannot explain anything in life without having a deep realisation that reincarnation is true. One cannot really explain many mysteries of existence without truly knowing that there is reincarnation – that we are products of past incarnations and precursors of future ones.

Did you come to this belief on the basis of personal study, or did your father tell you about it?
My sisters and I have read things, we have been exposed to literature which was very comprehensive, and our beliefs are based on that.

Was that Zoroastrian literature?
No, non-Zoroastrian.

About disposal of the dead in the Towers, Mr B says that he thinks that it is an excellent system in itself but that modern circumstances have created problems so that things have deteriorated. He mentions the building of high-rise flats in the area, the decline in the number of vultures, and he talks at some length about the pitiful social conditions of the corpse-bearers and *nasesalars*. These, he says, are not only very poor but are regarded by many Parsis almost as social outcasts. As a result it is getting more and more difficult to get people to do these necessary jobs, and he expects that those who are there now may take the first available opportunity to find other work.

When we [W.Z.O.] started dealing with the *khandiyas* they used to sit at our feet, at a considerable distance. We had to somehow reorient their thinking, and [make them realise] that they are human, that they are part of the community, that they are Zoroastrians themselves. It was only later that they actually felt that they were needed. People have been talking a lot about their habits – that they are alcoholics and if you give them any kind of dole they will just spend it on drinks – but they said, 'If we did not drink we would not be able to set foot in the *dakhme*.' They have to drink, they have to be intoxicated in order to bear the burden of their occupation.

Mrs Munshi then comes back to what Mr B said about his love of the past, and asks what he feels about the future.

I think the basic problem lies in our loss of religious identity. We no longer have that strong identity we had in the past

What is the reason for that, do you think?
I think that the entire Parsi culture is being eroded to a large extent. It may have something to do with late marriages or with intermarriage, which Parsis are now so often open to. Or it might be the growing element of secularism – a negative kind of secularism. Secularism is becoming so strong that we are almost getting away from the roots of our religion. Also, many Parsis have gone abroad and our numerical strength has dwindled alarmingly. There used to be entire localities that were predominantly inhabited by Parsis, there used to be many such areas and they were strongholds of Zoroastrianism. That really held our identity together. Now there is a kind of diaspora even within

Bombay. We have migrated to suburbs and other places, where we have become more individualised.

Do you think other factors have had a negative influence on our identity, apart from these social changes?
I would not be able to put my finger on one particular aspect. But Parsis, because of their education and affluence, have always had a strong concern for their own well-being. Parsis would never move smilingly to suburbs from which they had to commute for two hours each way, as members of other communities do. In one way of course it is good that we have set standards, but on the other hand such constraints are preventing Parsis from marrying – they would rather stay where they are than having to face such hardships.

Do you think it may have something to do with lack of religious awareness and education?
Of course it has all gone side by side. As far as India is concerned I think that to a large extent the role of the Parsis is over. Everything has its cycle and the Parsis have had their zenith in the past. As far as present-day circumstances go we are almost inundated by other cultures which go against the grain of our culture and community, which is why we have such difficulties in surmounting obstacles and coming to grips with the present situation. I think the glorious days of the Parsis are well and truly over.

————

MR N

Mr N, the son of Mrs N (see above, pp. 107–12), was born in Nagpur in 1942, but has lived in Bombay all his life. He studied Physics and Electrical Engineering but became a partner in the family business, a shop supplying articles for religious use such as sandalwood and *kustis*.

Mr N had no formal religious education at school, just an hour of 'moral instruction'. At home his mother told tales from the *Shahname*, and he was taught the basic prayers before his Navjote. Otherwise Mr N has no recollection of being instructed in any way; he had no clear idea what would happen at his Navjote. When Mrs Munshi remarks that, to outsiders visiting the shop, Mr N's parents always appeared to be strictly religious, Mr N says:

That was just a tradition of covering the head in the shop. In fact when I started working in the shop they more or less insisted I do that, and I said I would not. In the past several customers, elderly customers, on a big day like Navroz, would say, 'What, you are selling sandalwood and you have not got your head covered?' But at home none of us do this. Dad was not, as I recall it, a very religious person. I never remember him praying till his mother died. Then all of a sudden he became very religious, began to pray for long hours. And he wanted to know what he was saying, he is the one person I know who taught himself Avesta-Pehlevi. And he began to collect – at times when books were available – a considerable number of our religious books .... He knows exactly what he is saying when he prays. I did read all the other books in English, like Darmesteter[2] and so on, but unfortunately many of the books were in Gujarati and unfortunately I am semi-literate in Gujarati even today.

About his grandmother's death, Mr N says:

My grandmother was the matriarch of our family, and she passed away. I had never experienced death in a personal sense, except when a pet or two died. So this was the first time I saw the *sachkar* and all the other ceremonies. And at that time *Doongerwadi* was so isolated from the rest of Bombay, you could not even hear the traffic noises on the crown of the hill. You did not see any skyscrapers as you do today. So you were absolutely in a world of your own, in communion with the next world you might say. And that had an impact on me, probably because I was young and it was the first time ... Naturally Dad and Mum would answer all my questions as to what was going on, and what all the ceremonies meant, and what was supposed to happen to Granny's soul on the *chaharom* day:[3] on the fourth day Granny would be crossing the *Chinvad Pul*,[4] and she would be questioned by her deeds,[5] and so on. And the significance of the Towers of Silence as a scientific means of the disposal of the dead, without causing any pollution to any of the elements of the universe.

Mr N has travelled widely and has seen several forms of disposal of the dead. He feels that for a small community like the Parsis exposure is ideal:[6]

I am sure it would not work if we had a population, say, the size of Bombay. Can you imagine how many Towers and how many birds would be needed? This was ideally suited to the pastoral communities who lived in Iran. The irony is that we are practising it in the midst of one of the largest cities in the world. When talking to non-Zoroastrians I often find that they express a resentment at our method of disposal. They have never been able to prove it to me, but they say that the vultures pick up pieces and then drop them on the neighbouring homes. It is utter rubbish! Because the vulture does not have the claws to be able to carry off any ... The vulture cannot take off for quite a period of time! But this is the attitude of the neighbours, so ultimately

I fear the time might come when we will be compelled to move the premises outside the city of Bombay. Normally these places are always outside the city. Here also it was well outside what was then Bombay. In fact as recently as 1830 the last tiger was shot on Malabar Hill, precisely where the Towers of Silence are today. But today you are in the most prime location, and there is some resentment.

Mr N's shop is at its busiest on festive days, which makes it impossible for him to observe such occasions himself. The family pays daily visits to the Atash Behrams in the neighbourhood, since Parsis who cannot go themselves pay the shop to take sandalwood there. However, it is usually Mr N's father who goes; Mr N confesses that he is not 'a regular praying Johnny.'

In the last ten, fifteen years there have not been many occasions where I have been able to sit with a book and pray. And frankly, you see, all my training has been as a scientist, physics and electrical engineering. So I have always found it quite anachronistic that I should be mumbling some words in a language I do not know ... I have seen Buddhists in monasteries turn over leaf after leaf and mumble away in the expectation that they are accumulating merit for the hereafter. That is not something I, as a trained scientist, find acceptable. It is about your deeds, not your mumblings. What I live by is just Good Thoughts, Good Words, Good Deeds. That is common to every religion, isn't it? Can you show me one prophet who has not said this? It is a central part of every religion, just as there is a conscience in every human being.

Now Dad has developed cataracts so he is no longer able to read fine print, but formerly he did pray. Among the conservative and orthodox Parsis it is a necessary ritual that you should sit with a prayer book for maybe at least half an hour or an hour every day, and pray! Most of my cousins do it. Of course you are really supposed to pray five times a day, but apart from the priests I don't think that any of the lay people are able to do it today. For example Dad still observes the custom that every time he goes to the toilet and comes back, he will do his *kusti* as a purification measure, but none of us do it any more.

Sadly most of my young friends no longer wear the *sudreh* and *kusti*. Oddly I was never much aware of this, although I sell them. I thought that as they were not buying them from me they were buying them from someone else. And I came face to face with this fact two years ago, when I went to the Caves of Bahrot, which is a minor place of pilgrimage, because that is the place where the Zoroastrians took the Fire after the fall of Sanjan [here follows a detailed account of the history of the first Parsi Atash Behram] ... So I went to Bahrot with some friends and we stayed as guests with a very devout family at the village below, and the old man was insistent that the day before we set out for the climb, we should have a ritual bath.[7] Which I gladly did. And I found that my friends did not have a *sudreh* and *kusti* on, which was an extremely embarrassing situation, and we had to cover up so that the old gent did not realise the sacrilege.[8]

From the pressures of the shop, the interview goes on to discuss its history. At one time it was run by Mr N's father and two of his brothers. In the course of time both his brothers died and his mother had to come and help in the shop.

Since we consider a menstruating woman to be unclean, Mum obviously could not have come to the shop at such times. Mum underwent a hysterectomy which was otherwise not necessary.[9] No Parsi male will ask his wife to undergo this, but Mum did it. Most other ladies including my sister will not come to the shop when they are menstruating. At home we have never followed segregation at all. I can tell you that apart from a very few very orthodox lay families and the families of practising priests, segregation is no longer observed and has not been observed for the last fifty years – I cannot tell you about before that.

Mr N follows the rules of purity concerning hair and nails. He does not object to non-Parsis coming into his shop, since this seems to him a natural part of living in India.

Nirangdin ceremonies, *Gahambars* and initiation ceremonies for priests were performed in the name of both his grandmothers on their death.[10] The latter ceremony, which took place in Udwada, was attended by the entire family except Mr N himself, who could not get away from Bombay. The *Nirangdin* ceremonies made a great impression on Mr N, who attended throughout the night and was given an explanation of the meaning of the ritual by the late Dastur K.S. Dabu. When asked about his feelings about the ritual consecration of a bull's urine Mr N says:

I remember a mental observation at the time of my grandmother's funeral – there were these white-robed priests and they were chanting in a language I knew nothing about – the observation that came to me is that we have been doing exactly this for a few thousands of years, so the weight of tradition ... The continuity – this was done in Iran for more than a thousand years, and now for more than a thousand years we have been doing it here!

Dabuji [Dastur Dabu] explained that the figure of eight with which the priest stirs the water is exactly like the coil windings in a motor or a magneto.[11] I remember these words from Dabuji, because I was studying physics at the time.

One day a kitten walked into the shop and there have been cats – which in classical Zoroastrianism were regarded as evil – in the shop for thirty years. Most customers reacted positively to this, but a few traditional people objected or indeed refused to buy sandalwood from the shop. When a customer advised him to keep a dog instead, Mr N drily replied, 'Dogs are of great use at *Doongerwadi*, not here.'[12] Asked about his opinion of Parsis who worship at non-Zoroastrian shrines, Mr N says:

> Well, this is probably because we have had to come to live in another land. As a community we have developed a great respect and tolerance for other people's religious observance. I remember in my time, on the feast of Mount Mary,[13] on a Sunday we would drive up in our old Austin and offer a candle. Not as a religious observance particularly, but as a mark of respect. When I have been to a Hindu temple or a mosque, I have behaved in a deferential manner. It is something ingrained in most Indians, except the rabid lot!

With amusement Mr N recalls infuriating an American Seventh Day Adventist preacher, by asking a question about evolution.

> I found it astounding that a learned man had come from America to tell us that Darwin's theory was, according to him, a load of rubbish. ... There is no way you can marshal facts against it ... And yet there are people today in so-called progressive nations who believe that God created the world on a particular day, in a particular time, and so on.

Mr N then describes another incident that seemed significant to him:

> You probably are aware that little more than a month ago a Navjote was performed which is going to create, presumably, a minor storm in the community. Mr Neville Wadia was born a Christian because his father had converted to Christianity and married an English lady.[14] They are the industrial family who founded Bombay Dyeing and all these *Baugs* where Parsis live. So at the fag-end of his life Neville Wadia felt the need to return to the faith ... Naturally since [the father] had voluntarily converted to another religion his son was brought up as a member of the Church of England. And on a number of occasions at Cusrow Baug, Neville Wadia had said that he had been brought up in the Church of England and was perfectly happy there, but that he did feel nostalgic for the faith of his forefathers. Now at this stage, when he was over eighty, he had his Navjote ceremony performed and announced it in the Press. Before he had his Navjote done he wrote and asked for the opinion of seven High Priests – he has not given the names of those High Priests. And five of the seven said he could have it done. That seems to be going to cause a tremendous storm in the

Parsi community. Already in the Press various articles are being written for and against. Now the almost amusing experience I had at the shop two weeks ago was: an elderly customer, well over seventy himself, bought something from me and then almost started to give me a sermon. He brought out a *Jam-e-Jamshed*[15] of many years ago where Neville Wadia's remarks at Cusrow Baug were published. And then this man made derogatory remarks about Neville Wadia, and what amused me most was that he started telling me: 'We belong to the ninth plane.' They have levels of spiritual excellence, or whatever.[16] 'We Zoroastrians belong to the ninth plane,' he says, 'the Christians belong on the fifth rung, and the Moslems belong to the third.' The intellectual arrogance of that man! Unfortunately many Parsis have such attitudes.

Mr N puts such attitudes down to the 'siege mentality' which the Parsi minority developed in order to survive in an alien land. He condemns all forms of arrogance and intolerance on the part of religious leaders and communities.

Asked about spiritual or mystical experiences Mr N says:

I have never had a mystical experience. I don't think what I am now going to relate could be called a mystical experience. On two or three occasions I have had a feeling of suffused pleasure and pride. One was when I saw a slide of the Fire of Gushnasp.[17] And I wanted tremendously to see those places in Iran. And also when I stood in the Caves at Bahrot, the nearest to what you could call a mystical experience I had there. I was in communion you might say with a piece of the history of my forefathers.

————

MRS M

Mrs M was born in Bombay in 1947 but grew up in Pune (Poona), where she was educated up to BA level. She later studied music in London. She is married with two children, and belongs to one of the 'first' Parsi families of Bombay. She is actively involved in organising concerts of Western classical music in Bombay. Besides their Bombay residence the family has a house in London and Mrs M regularly travels back and forth.

Mrs M received her early religious education from her mother; she feels that living in Pune, with its relatively large and active Parsi community, helped to strengthen her sense of Parsi identity. At home chalk designs were made every day, and there were garlands and 'festive trays' (*ses*) on auspicious occasions. The laws of purity were not followed in her parents' house; the *loban* was done in the evening but no fire was kept burning. The *parabs* were not observed, except that Mrs M's mother did not eat meat on Bahman *mahino* Bahman *roj*. No beef was eaten at all, Mrs M does not know whether that had any religious significance. She is aware of having eaten *dalni poris*, but has never connected this with the 'birthday of the Waters'. Mrs M used to visit the Agiary with her mother, but did not ask many questions about the religion; similarly, when she was taught the Navjote prayers by a priest there were no explanations. She has vivid memories of her Navjote which felt like 'an extended birthday party'. She did not go to Udwada immediately afterwards, but was taken there at a later time. She mostly remembers the lovely beach of Udwada, but also calls the visits to the Atash Behram 'very important'. After her Navjote Mrs M said her prayers regularly at first, but gradually gave up doing so. Asked for the reason, she says:

> Well, I see it now with my own children. Anything that is inflicted as something you have to do categorically, you start resenting. I mean in religion you should be given the freedom to pray whenever you want. I must say, I did not inflict it on my children either. They [just] had their Navjotes and learnt their prayers. My daughter was very much under the influence of her grandmother who kept repeating the prayers to her, and she still knows them all perfectly. But my son, who was not under such a strong influence, he tended to forget them ... I think the children like to identify themselves as Parsis, as members of the community, but religious identification they don't have. You see, my children have never been given any kind of religious instruction, and neither was I. The identification as a race, as a people, we very much have, in our eating habits and such things it affects us more, on a daily basis, but not in the religion ... I think that the religion is not rigid at all in its demands, so one takes it or leaves it. And it is easier to leave it, if you know what I mean.

Mrs M has never observed special days of the Parsi calendar, and does not know when her *roj* birthday is. The only annual religious occasions she remembers are the Muktad days, when the family went to the fire temple in Pune, where prayers were said for her grandparents. She cannot say that this was a very spiritual experience for her, but she liked the atmosphere.

Mrs M's wedding was a traditional one. About the *madav saro* she says that she realised it was a fertility rite; she thought it was a Hindu custom but had no objection to doing it. During pregnancy the *agharni* ceremony was done for her, but when her children were born she did not have a *nahn* after the first forty days:

You see, we were not living in a joint family or anything like that; it is usually the older generation that observes these things, and when you are not in touch with them ...

She had the *pagladu* done for both children because her mother-in-law insisted, and because she felt that 'it is nice to have these traditions; it does not hurt you, and it is a opportunity for the family to draw together.' For much the same reasons, she has a *Jashan* performed at home every two years or so:

I think that our prayers, even though one may not follow them word by word, the way they are said does create an atmosphere of vibrations – it must be good vibrations, and I think everybody needs good vibrations. We all have our share of problems, health and this and that, so I feel that if you can create an atmosphere of good vibrations in your own home, why not do it? I am not convinced that it is connected [with positive benefit], but I see no harm in it.

Mrs M and her children visit the fire temple occasionally, on New Year's day and sometimes for birthdays and for Muktad. A *divo* is lit on birthdays; *loban* used to be done every day, but the custom was given up because there were no servants left who knew how to do it. When either grandmother comes to stay with the family the children see them pray, which Mrs M thinks is the best way to familiarise them with the religion.

Mrs M is aware that many people are against the traditional Parsi way of disposing of the dead but she herself has no such objections. She likes the simplicity of the ceremony which 'is very clean and there is nothing gruesome about it.' As far as the rituals for the dead are concerned, Mrs M says:

Yes, I think it is something nice. Again I think it is this belief of having good vibrations, of having the soul leave in peace – you know, with the satisfaction that whoever is departed has had the final rituals done as they should be.

Asked about any supernatural or inexplicable experiences she may have had, Mrs M says:

On one or two occasions there have been occurrences which cannot be explained, but I do not want to give it too much importance, because I think that to a large degree we are in control of our lives. There may be a larger design or plan, but I think you can direct your life quite a bit.

That is a very Zoroastrian way of thinking.
Oh, really, is it? I believe that you are in control, you are in the driving seat and you can direct your life. Even when you have some kind of accident or fatal illness and you think, 'Well this is my fate,' or

something, I don't believe in that totally. I believe one has a very very strong consciousness and will, and it pervades your whole life and being . . . . We all have a certain power within us, it is how we use that power. That is what I feel. And I don't think that is from the religion, it is just from my own life the way I have lived it so far.

And where does God feature in all this?
I think religion, if it is mixed up with a lot of rites and rituals, creates a lot of confusion. Because religion is one thing – I think it is very important because you may follow different principles of religion, [but] basically what you learn is a basic morality – to be able to tell right from wrong, truth, justice, honesty, all these basic moral values. I think religion teaches you those, and that is very important. [But] not somebody who does a lot of rituals but on the other hand is doing something totally immoral in his life. The two don't go together. So a religious person for me is not a person who prays and follows the rituals and does everything correctly from that point of view, but [one] who leads his life according to certain principles.

About family traditions, Mrs M says that she always tells her children that they have to live up to the family name, since the family has done so much for the community and for Bombay generally. This leads to general observations about the decline of the social, moral and intellectual standing of the modern Parsis. 'I think we are going to be left behind, because we have no ambition and no work ethic left in our community.' She puts this down to a lack of motivation, since the younger generations are financially secure because of the drive and enterprise of their ancestors. About the dwindling numbers of the community, Mrs M says:

Girls who marry outside the community and who do have the option, *should* have the option of raising their children as Zoroastrians,[18] because you can always be more sure of the mother than of the father . . . I don't believe that the Parsis who came for Persia, I am sure they all mixed. I am positive that we are not such a pure race, I am sure there was a mixture. I am sure these are not rules which were laid down by religion, they are more man-made . . . The alternative is that we will all disappear.

As to her ideas about her own daughter's marriage, Mrs M says that the important thing is that her daughter should find a nice man and that they are happy; religious and ethnic background do not seem to her to be overly important considerations.

What Mrs M would really like to see happening is the foundation in Bombay of a good museum of Parsi history and culture, recapturing some of the ancient glories of Parsi life in India.

———

289

Notes

1 On these calendars see above, p. 47.
2 Among other works, the 19th century French Iranist J. Darmesteter published a translation of the Avesta, which was later translated into English.
3 i.e. the fourth day after death.
4 The Chinvad Bridge, which the soul must cross on its way to the hereafter; see above, p. 6.
5 The remark refers to the idea that, on the Chinvad Bridge, one meets a beautiful girl or an unpleasant old woman, who represents one's thoughts, words and acts in the world.
6 A good example, it would seem, of the pragmatism of many Parsis. There is no suggestion that Mr N thinks that only this custom pleases God; he merely feels that it works well for his community.
7 It is not clear what type of bath is referred to here.
8 The 'sacrilege' being the fact that Zoroastrians who had come on such a pilgrimage did not wear the emblems of the faith.
9 See the interview with Mrs N (above, p. 109).
10 Mr N's mother only mentioned that two *Vendidads* were performed at Udwada for the soul of her mother.
11 As a Theosophist, the late Dastur K.S. Dabu (on whom see above, Ch. 8, nn. 30, 80) would stress the significance of such similarities.
12 The reference is to the *sagdid*, when a dead body is shown to a dog (see also above, p. 37f.). To some traditional Parsis this remark may well have seemed shocking.
13 A Christian festival in Bombay.
14 Mr Neville Wadia, a scion of a prominent Parsi family, decided to come back to the religion of his forefathers and his return to the fold was welcomed by most of the Dasturs of India; shortly afterwards his son also became a Zoroastrian. Some Parsis felt that this proved that there was one rule for the rich and another for the poor, and there was an uproar in the Press.
15 A Parsi paper, see above, p. 55.
16 The remark probably refers to the belief that Zoroastrians have reached the highest level of human potential in a chain of incarnations. For further references see the Index, under Reincarnation.
17 One of the three great 'national Fires' of ancient Iran.
18 On the current tendency in the community to accept children of mixed marriages whose father is a Parsi but not those of Parsi mothers see above, p. 58 n. 67.

Part Three

Conclusions

Chapter Ten

Parsi Religion in the Light of the Interviews

Perhaps the most important conclusion to be drawn from the accounts published here is that the core of a tradition apparently survives which enables Parsis to lead religious lives that are mutually recognisable as Zoroastrian. Clearly the mere fact of ethnicity plays a role there, as do such outward aspects of Parsi culture as feasts, Navjotes and weddings, which may or may not have strong religious connotations for individuals. Still, when Parsis discussed their religion with their coreligionist, Mrs Munshi, mutual recognition went beyond the purely external. A wide range of practices and observances, mind-sets and attitudes, religious symbols and allusions – however different their role and significance in the life of each individual – were obviously familiar enough as expressions of Parsi religious life to allow the interviews to proceed without the need for clarification.

The interviews further show that significant differences exist between classical Zoroastrianism as it has been described by scholars on the basis of the ancient scriptural tradition, and the realities accepted by modern Indian Parsis as part of the religious life of the community. While academic descriptions tend to focus on the coherence and lucidity of ancient Zoroastrian teaching, with some reference to the high rituals which are the exclusive province of priests, the modern community appears to be more strongly characterised by a staunch faith in prayer and personal observance on the one hand, and by its heated debates on doctrine on the other.

On the basis of the evidence of the interviews it can be argued that the latter features – a non-reasoning faith in prayer and observance, and the various attempts to rediscover the true teachings of Zoroastrianism – represent two profoundly different ways of understanding religion which coexist in the community, and in many cases in the mind of a single believer. These mind-sets will here be called, respectively, the 'faith paradigm' and the 'belief paradigm'. The community is of course aware that some of its members are more traditional in their thinking than others, but relatively few Parsis may think of these two paradigms as equally valid but essentially different conceptions of the nature and function of religion, which engender different views and attitudes and thus contribute to the pluriformity and complexity of Parsi religious life.

The history of the community, which presumably evolved (or perhaps preserved) a predominantly 'faith-oriented', orthopractic form of religion over the centuries and was then confronted with Western, 'belief-oriented' definitions of religion, probably helps to account for the co-existence of these paradigms. Other historical developments, such as the loss of prestige of the priesthood, urbanisation and the increasing influence of 'modernity', probably contributed to make the authority of religious laws and commands seem less absolute to almost all Parsis. As a strong sense of the menacing reality of the powers of evil disappeared, moreover, it seems that many Parsis came to think of religion predominantly as a source of good things (ranging from a sense of well-being to supernatural boons). This may further have strengthened a tendency to shape one's religious life according to individual needs, views and preferences. While many Parsis still seek to exercise such choices within the bounds set by tradition, others now regard their personal judgement, reason and understanding as the main criteria for accepting or rejecting elements of religious life. Besides the opposition between the faith and belief paradigms, this difference in attitude towards religious authority and individual judgement can be seen as another important factor to add to the diversity reflected by the interviews.

PRAYER AND THE FAITH PARADIGM

It is clear that informants have different views as to the aspects of religion they find most meaningful. For some, as we saw, an intellectual understanding of religious teaching is crucial (see further below). For others, good works in the practical sphere are an essential, or indeed the most essential, part of religious life.[1] Several informants value Zoroastrianism first and foremost as the source of the system of morals which had guided and motivated the community throughout its proud history.[2] In other cases a sense of nostalgia appears to play an important role in the subject's feelings about religion.[3]

For a significant number of our interviewees, however, religion seems to be predominantly a matter of faith. While classical Zoroastrianism tends to be described in terms of doctrine and rational belief, for many Parsis today the essential elements of their religious life are clearly faith and tradition. Khojeste Mistree,[4] who is critical of current attitudes but has an excellent knowledge of them, says that most Parsis grow up with 'a faith-based paradigm, which is belief in terms of what you emotionally experience without in any way polishing your mind.' The University Professor here called Dr F says:

> Not that we were given much detailed education about the religion, but what we were basically taught was faith. And even today I don't go in so much for theology, or what I am supposed to believe, but I believe with faith.

'Faith' of course means slightly different things to different people. It can manifest itself primarily as strong sense of divine guidance[5] or of communication with God[6] or a fire;[7] very often it is connected with a belief in the beneficent effects of prayer and ritual.

Perceptions of prayer

Prayer, sometimes in combination with ritual, can be seen as a source of strength or a sense of well-being,[8] of beneficent vibrations,[9] protection against danger,[10] healing,[11] or miracles.[12] The view that one should pray in order to thank God, rather than for the sake of obtaining personal benefit, was stressed in one interview and mentioned in another.[13]

The term 'prayer', however, needs to be defined. In Parsi English the word can be used for purely verbal prayer but also for what Westerners would call 'rituals', either domestic or priestly (e.g. for a daily *Satum* ceremony performed at home, or for a complex priestly ritual like a *Vendidad*).[14] In the interviews, however, informants most often used the word to refer to their verbal prayers, i.e. the recitation of traditional Avestan or Pazand prayer formulas either at home or in the fire temple. In some cases such prayers are accompanied by personal requests (*dua*) in the speaker's own language. Individual prayer sequences can take a few minutes or over an hour to perform, and may consist of a few repetitions of one of the basic prayers, or of lengthy combinations of texts, including less well-known ones.

Some informants spoke of a special affinity with certain prayers rather than others, although they did not understand exactly what the texts meant.[15] For such purposes as healing or solving problems, particular texts are widely held to be effective. Many Parsis choose some of their prayers according to the day of the month, often reciting a text dedicated to the Yazad whose *roj* it is; in some cases the number of recitations of a prayer is held to be important.[16] Some Parsis consider the task of prescribing appropriate prayers to be the province of qualified priests,[17] but it is clearly not unusual to pass on advice about 'effective' prayers or ritual acts to friends or neighbours.[18]

Prayer, in short, is widely held to be effective, and it seems that this effectiveness is generally felt to be unrelated to the intellectual understanding of the one who prays. Some informants in fact reported that a better grasp of the meaning of a text had had an adverse effect on their sense of well-being when praying.[19] Only a minority of the interviewees showed a clear grasp of what might be called the 'doctrinal context' of prayer – the way in which it relates to the wider context of Zoroastrian teaching.

Some interviewees made it clear that their prayers were mainly directed to God (Hormazd),[20] while in several cases prayers to other Yazads were also recited.[21] Other informants' religious feelings seemed to be strongly focused on one or more Yazads other than Hormazd,[22] who were often closely associated with their day of the month (*roj*). Several of those who stressed the importance of prayer in their lives did not specify to whom they felt their prayers were addressed, and in some cases their words suggest that they think of prayers as having a power of their own.[23]

Mrs O, for instance, feels that the Bhika Behram Well in Bombay has helped her during a difficult time. For her the Well obviously represents the power of the Waters, which can be invoked by means of the hymn addressed to them. In another part of the interview, however, the same informant ascribes satisfactory results to certain prayer sequences without implying that a particular Yazad was instrumental in bringing these about. This suggests that, like many other Parsis, Mrs O assumes that prayers are connected with divine powers in some way but that they are effective in their own right, and not merely as a means to address a Yazad. Another interviewee describes the effect of prayer, which he associates with vibrations, as follows:[24]

> ... one must always recite *Yatha* and *Ashem*, they are very powerful and vibrant prayers. And when you want to succeed you must always go with the recitation of these words, [in order] not to get harmed in any way. Another very powerful prayer, we have been told, is the *Yenghe Hatam* prayer. I was told this as a child. Our prayers are very vibrant ... I always feel the power, vigour, the vibrations from any such activities appertaining to our Zoroastrian religion. I feel it when I pray before the sea, even when I pray before the *kuva* [well], and at the Banaji Atash Behram well I have always felt it. I feel I am getting some power from outside and going within; it clarifies, it signifies, it ignites my soul, and also the brain.

A number of informants said that some of their prayers were primarily connected with (i.e. either directed to or prescribed in the name of) such figures as Kookadaru, Homaji or Jal Baba.[25] Observances with non-Zoroastrian associations, such as prayers to the Virgin Mary, singing 'The Lord is my Shepherd' as a protective *mantra*, Hindu prayers, or expressions of devotion to Sai Baba or other *gurus*,[26] were mentioned by some of those we interviewed.[27]

It should perhaps be stressed that many interviews indicating a less than perfect grasp of classical Zoroastrian doctrine also suggest a strong sense of spirituality, a firm faith, or a deep commitment to the religion expressed by means of good works. Indications that articulate views on Zoroastrian theology do not feature prominently in a subject's thoughts naturally tell us nothing about other aspects of his or her religious life.

On traditional religious education

A certain vagueness about doctrinal questions surrounding the theme of prayer is hardly surprising in view of the nature of religious education in the Parsi community. Many informants stated that they had received no religious education at all, either at home or in school.[28] Most of those who did receive some instruction – whether from parents, schoolteachers, from a priest in preparation for their Navjote, or from a combination of all three – say that they were mostly taught to memorise a number of prayers, and learned the accompanying actions from the example of adults in their family. Prayer and other daily observances, it seems, are what children in traditional households first experience as 'religion'. In many cases this seems to have led to an understanding of religion primarily as a tradition involving a complex of words and actions rather than articulate beliefs, i.e. to a view of religion that stresses orthopraxy more than 'orthodoxy' in the Western sense of the word.[29]

As far as Zoroastrian doctrine was concerned, some interviewees were taught elementary maxims, such as 'a Zoroastrian never lies', or 'Good Thoughts, Good Words, Good Deeds'. Several informants associated religious teaching with stories from the *Shahname* – a work whose contents, though of ancient Iranian origin, are not principally concerned with questions of belief. Only one informant remembered discussions on morals as part of religious education at school.[30]

Until recently, therefore, the only form of religion most Parsis encountered during their formative years seems to have been a faith-based one.[31] Insofar as they were influenced by discussions on Zoroastrian teaching this generally occurred later in life, which means that the belief paradigm was superimposed on a faith-oriented understanding of religion.[32]

Conclusion

It is clear from all this that the religious lives of many Parsis reflect a conception of Zoroastrianism which is not primarily based on an intellectual understanding of a system of teachings, but on a view of religion as mainly consisting in a divinely-given set of prayers, observances and rules, the deeper significance of which neither can nor need be understood by the human mind. A strong reliance on the effectiveness of prayer and ritual may always have been a characteristic feature of Zoroastrianism but it is widely assumed by scholars that in ancient times, when a Zoroastrian world-view informed all of Iranian culture, this orthopractic side was complemented and underpinned by a greater understanding of teaching and doctrine. The almost exclusive emphasis on the devotional, non-rational, and mysterious side of religion may have developed as a result of the community's later history. In the course of the period between the Parsis' arrival in India and the 19th century, when the influence of Western culture became powerful, the doctrinal knowledge of the priesthood seems to have declined[33] whereas its authority did not. Such a development is likely to have affected the community's understanding of the very nature of the religion; since neither the meaning of prayers, rituals and *tarikats* nor their original doctrinal context could be explained, lay Parsis presumably came to think of religion as an essentially mysterious phenomenon which could, with the help of priests, be used for their personal benefit. The model of the Indian caste, moreover, which combines elements of religious and communal identity, may have contributed to a view of religion largely as part of community culture. Thus, priestly authority and community tradition together probably fostered an orthopractic form of Zoroastrianism which stressed the mysterious and the miraculous, as well as the importance of obedience to priestly instruction.

THE QUESTION OF DUALISM, THE UNDERSTANDING OF OBSERVANCE, AND THE INDIVIDUALISATION OF RELIGION

Another factor which may have played a considerable role in the development of Parsi religion is the apparent change in most Parsis' perception of matters connected with dualism.[34] A community's ideas and beliefs with regard to the power of evil may obviously have profound implications for its understanding of the nature and function of religion generally, and of ritual and observance in particular. According to the scriptural tradition of classical Zoroastrianism, ritual and devotional acts had the dual purpose of furthering good and defeating evil. If it is accepted that the concept of evil has little meaning for many modern Parsis, the question arises how this affects their understanding of the ritual aspects of their religion.

The question of dualism in the interviews

A belief in the existence of the Devil, a strong sense of sin, and a fear of hell are found in some forms of monotheistic religions, such as

Christianity and Islam, as well as in dualist ones. The only formal element to define classical Zoroastrianism as a dualist system is the doctrine that the powers of evil are wholly separate from, rather than subordinate to, God. In any case, since classical Zoroastrian teaching is thus defined as dualist, for the purpose of the present discussion other elements of the tradition which reflect a strong awareness of the opposition between good and evil – such as a pronounced sense of merit and sin or purity and impurity – will be regarded as expressions of a dualist world-view.

Plainly, such a way of understanding reality is not prominently reflected in the accounts published here. The word 'sin', for example, is twice used in light-hearted comments,[35] but never in a serious sense; none of our informants indicated that they were afraid of going to hell; the belief in an independently powerful devil[36] is rarely mentioned. Only Dr Bharucha's remark about 'this damned Ahriman' in connection with the death of her husband, shows that the Evil One represents an emotional reality for her. (Perhaps significantly, Dr Bharucha is one of the two informants who mention a real fear of Ahriman when speaking of her childhood.[37]) Mr Mistree and Ms Khurody refer to their dualist beliefs in intellectual terms.[38] A few other interviews contain remarks which could be regarded as traces of a dualist world-view, although the central beliefs of the speakers cannot be defined a dualist.[39]

It is clear, in any case, that most of our informants did not see the world in dualist terms, and some explicitly rejected such ideas. If the evidence of the interviews is representative of wider trends, followers of 'esoteric' movements[40] are among the most articulate opponents of the notion of dualism. Mr Doctor explained an Avestan expression normally understood to refer to hell as denoting our terrestrial existence; Mr Pithavala stated that *'durvand'* (Phl. *druwand*, 'evil person') is merely a term for non-Zoroastrians, from whom Zoroastrians should stay aloof. Ervad Yazdi Aibara and Mrs Nusservanjee believe that evil exists 'in men only'. Mrs Nusservanjee, moreover, distinguishes between 'evil' and 'Ahriman', the latter being one of two opposite forces created by God. Dr Master-Moos refers to Ahriman and the demons as 'souls created by Ahura Mazda'.

Parsis whose views on religion have not been shaped by years of study tend to ignore Ahriman altogether. Mrs E had difficulty in recalling his name and associated the notion of evil powers with superstition. Others did not refer to the question of evil at all, which suggests that their thoughts were not much preoccupied with such questions. Several informants unequivocally explained good and evil as the effect of previous lives.[41]

The concepts of sin and pollution

It seems clear that large sections of the Parsi community have made the transition from a dualist to a non-dualist paradigm as far as their ideas and beliefs are concerned. The question remains, though, how deeply this change has affected other aspects of religious life. Some Parsis – and scholars – assert that in essence nothing has changed on the ritual level, where good and evil, purity and impurity, are still felt to be stark and absolute opposites. If this were true – i.e. if modern Parsi attitudes in matters of ritual and observance were essentially similar to those associated with classical Zoroastrianism – then failure to observe the traditional religious rules and observances could still be expected to be strongly associated with evil and sin.

Such views do not seem characteristic of the Parsi community in modern India. Far from defining her religion as one that emphasises the objective importance of orthopraxy, Mrs V described Zoroastrianism as 'a very wise and simple religion ... [which has] nothing like Ten Commandments or millions of laws to follow.' Mrs V's opinion may owe something to the fact that she spent part of her life away from traditional Zoroastrian circles, but many other Parsis view their religion in much the same light. Mrs Q, who would probably describe herself as orthodox, said that Zoroastrians 'have no enforced rituals, like the Catholics have to go to church every Sunday and during Lent they have to abstain.'

The rules of menstruation

Of all forms of observance, those which figure most prominently in the interviews are the 'laws of purity' surrounding menstruation. It is probably significant that many informants say that these were strictly observed in their grandparents' houses, less so by their parents or in-laws, and at best perfunctorily in their present life.[42] Statistical evidence would be needed to weigh the relative importance of the various factors contributing to this trend; in the interviews frequent mention is made of the cramped housing of many families in modern Bombay (which makes it impossible for a menstruating woman to 'sit separately'),[43] and of the fact that the younger generation tends to reject these customs.[44] One informant implicitly referred to the adverse effect the nuclear, as opposed to the extended, family has on such traditions.[45]

An aspect that was perhaps too obvious to mention explicitly but which can be inferred from the interviews, is the effect of modern education. One interviewee said that her grandmother thought that disease could be caused by the shadow of a menstruating woman; another grandmother was certain that pickles would spoil if such a woman was allowed into the kitchen.[46] It may be significant that such a world-view, implying that the taboos surrounding menstruation are based on the laws of nature and infringements may do objective harm, is reported most often in connection with grandparents.[47] In the 1990s Ervad Yazdi Aibara still maintained that a disregard of the rules of menstruation is the prime cause of the decline of the world, but most Parsis now view these precepts in a different light: that of obedience to human rather than divine authority, man-made custom rather than eternal law.

Several informants said they found the laws of purity unimportant.[48] Four women described their transition from a 'strict' household to a 'liberal' one, where such laws were not strictly enforced.[49] Although they had obviously been taught to regard the Zoroastrian purity laws as important, these women clearly accepted the relaxed ways of their new homes without wondering if they would turn them into sinners. The highly traditional Mrs O described her youthful peccadilloes in this respect as pranks born of ignorance; the thought that they might be offences against God, it seems, did not occur to her. Mrs N, who had a hysterectomy in order to be able to serve in her shop throughout the month, talked about this as a practical decision outside the sphere of religious merit or sin. Mrs L's father, who bought two adjoining flats because his traditional mother and his non-observant wife could not live in the same apartment, presumably regarded both life-styles as valid.

Other Tarikats

About other religious laws, customs and observances, a range of opinions and attitudes is again attested in the interviews. To judge by this evidence (which is of course not statistically significant), Khshnoo-mists and traditionalists tend to hold strongly that these laws are meaningful and should be followed. The former have their own, esoteric explanations for the reasons behind these customs. The traditionalist Mr Antia is also convinced that the *tarikats* have a scientific foundation and recounts instances from his personal experience where strict observance brought a positive result, or negligence led to illness. (It is interesting to note however, that in Mr Antia's view one's conduct in such matters has consequences for oneself rather than for the world at large; this may reflect a more general tendency to think of the role of religion chiefly in personal and individual terms, on which see further below.) Mrs Nusservanjee, a Theosophist, holds no such views and is inclined to follow only those rules she regards as sensible; several informants who do not belong to a particular movement do the same thing.[50] Others, particularly those who have had Western-type education, either dismiss such rules as archaic[51] or observe some of them, partly from a sense of nostalgia.[52]

Apart from some strong traditionalists and Khshnoomists, in other words, few people would regard it as compulsory even in theory to observe all *tarikats*. Dr Bharucha's development in this respect may be illuminating: as a child, she was told never to walk barefoot for fear that Ahriman would enter her body through her feet.[53] In a later conversation with the present writer, she said:[54]

> As a child I thought it unfair that only Parsis were forbidden ever to walk barefoot, when all other religions could do it freely. I thought it was unfair and I knew that God was never unfair, so I could not understand it. Later I understood that God won't mind about such things! It is our tradition that we must always wear shoes. God won't mind, you do it because it is your tradition.

In other words, from a childhood belief that the taboo on walking barefoot was based on real, objective danger connected with the power of Ahriman, Dr Bharucha has come to see it as a matter of tradition. Tradition offers an explanatory context for Dr Bharucha's profound spiritual life and she scrupulously observes its directions, but her remark implies that she does not think of these as being objectively important in the eyes of God. Thus an element of the complex system of Zoroastrian laws, rules and prohibitions continues to be observed, but has come to be understood in a different way. Once perceived as an absolute law, it is now held to be part of a wise and ancient tradition but no longer as the only way of fighting Ahriman or obeying God's Will.

Perceptions of priestly rituals

While such ceremonies as Navjotes and *Jashans* continue to have meaning for many, the 'inner' rituals[55] no longer seem to play an important role in most Parsis' religious lives, except perhaps in connection with death and the afterlife. The *Ijeshne* ceremony, which in earlier times was regularly performed, is now celebrated much less frequently;[56] such high rituals as the *Vendidad* and the *Nirangdin* are sometimes commissioned, often as part of the rites for a departed soul.[57] Some Traditionalists, Neo-traditionalists and 'Esotericists' believe deeply in the efficacy of high rituals,[58] but to most Parsis such rites probably seem too remote. The fact that one can now commission high rituals at Udwada via the Internet without any need for further personal involvement,[59] may seem strange to outsiders, but in effect the practice continues an ancient custom by modern means.[60] The crucial difference with the past may lie in the fact that the importance of such rituals was formerly stressed by an authoritative priesthood, whereas the modern layman must be guided by his own lights in such matters.

To sum up, the interviews suggest that choices in the sphere of religious practice and observance are now rarely motivated by a mental association between Zoroastrian observance and a cosmic battle between good and evil.[61] Contrary to what is sometimes asserted, this suggests that attitudes inspired by dualism have virtually disappeared from the ritual sphere as well as the doctrinal one. The transition to a non-dualist world-view, in other words, appears to have been as profound as it was widespread.

The tendency towards individualism

It may be significant in this context that all informants who expressed themselves on the subject were of the opinion that all religions were equally valid, or essentially similar.[62] Given the sense of the relativity of religious teaching implied by this and by some of the views discussed earlier, together with the decline of priestly authority, the virtual disappearance of a fear of the powers of evil, and the resulting tendency to regard religion predominantly as a source of pleasant things,[63] it seems natural that most Parsis feel free to adapt to the pressures of modern life by adhering to part of the religious tradition only,[64] and generally shape their religious lives to suit their personal needs and wants. Together with such factors as the decline of communal aspects of religion,[65] this seems to have led to a different understanding of the very function of religion; from being at least partly a community matter concerned with the objective welfare of the world, in the mind of modern Parsis religion seems to be more exclusively associated with the well-being of the individual or the family.

THE BELIEF PARADIGM AND THE RECEPTION
OF MODERN TEACHING

As was said earlier, the interviews suggest that, in the community and indeed in the minds of many individual informants, mental categories deriving from the faith paradigm coexist with others which are inspired by a very different understanding of the nature of religion, which is here called the 'belief paradigm'. Historically this state of affairs can be accounted for by assuming that a 'mental map' of religion which was shared by most Parsis before the community was exposed to strong Western influences, now interacts with another set of concepts, values and ideas which may largely have been inspired by Western, Protestant culture.

Pre-modern definitions of religion

Just as a strong sense of community probably did much to preserve the religious tradition of the Parsis in the past, it also helped to shape it. As was suggested earlier, the Hindu concept of caste probably played an important role in the way the Parsi community understood itself.[66] This presumably implied that no clear distinctions were drawn between religious and ethnic or communal identity, so that whatever was felt to be distinctively 'Parsi' was associated equally with the group's cultural heritage and with its religion. Such characteristic features of Parsi life probably had more to do with orthopraxy than orthodoxy;[67] the community demanded – and implicitly guaranteed the validity of[68] – the observance of rules and forms of behaviour which were felt to belong to Zoroastrianism, but personal views and intellectual beliefs may have been considered largely irrelevant to a person's status as a Parsi Zoroastrian.[69]

The impact of Western definitions

One can only speculate as to how, or indeed if, the average 18th century Parsi layman would have defined Zoroastrian religious beliefs. The 19th century, however, saw a profound change in the realities of Parsi religious life. Priestly authority declined sharply, as did the general confidence in priestly knowledge, which must until then have underpinned the structure of Parsi religious life.[70] At the same time, European ideas and values had an increasing impact on the world-view of leading sections of the Parsi community. Educated Parsis must have learned that 'religion' needed to be defined as a separate category, distinct from other components of Parsi identity. Furthermore, their views on the essential nature and function of religion came to be largely based on Western, Protestant ideas, emphasising the importance of personal belief in, and awareness of rationally formulated religious teachings.

In addition to these general concepts, the Parsi community was faced with a range of Western academic opinions on their religion. These scholarly views differed from each other on many points but unanimously regarded doctrine as the essence of Zoroastrianism, and it was often implied that the living tradition was corrupt.[71] For whatever reason,[72] the increasing knowledge of the Zoroastrian scriptures appeared to show that 'original' Zoroastrianism had more in common with European views on what a religion ought to be than with current Parsi realities. In other words, instead of the form of religion they had grown up with, cultural pressure was brought to bear on the Parsis to accept as their own a concept of religion that stressed the importance of religious knowledge and personal conviction.

This development deeply affected the community without, however, eradicating old customs, beliefs and attitudes. The interviews show that the faith paradigm, based on a non-intellectual understanding of religion, continues to determine the religious lives of a significant section of the community, but it seems equally clear that many people's confidence in the validity of that paradigm is shaken. Questions as to the true meaning of religion now preoccupy many Parsis to some extent. Mrs V says that she has become interested in 'the Zoroastrian religion as a religion, rather than as the Parsis were actually practising it.' Dr Y probably means much the same thing when she says that 'ritual and religion are two different things.' Several of our informants had sought more religious knowledge at some stage in their lives or felt they ought to do so in future.[73]

The ideal of 'True Zoroastrianism'

The impact of Western concepts, it seems, prompted Parsis to search for the original, 'true' form of Zoroastrianism. Based on God's revelation to Zarathustra, this ideal religion was presumably held to consist essentially in a system of rational, wise and humane teachings. Its validity, as we saw, was held to be supported by the evidence of Western academic publications, and probably also by its perceived similarity to other religions such as Christianity and Islam. It was clearly believed to have little in common with contemporary Parsi reality, which was felt to be inadequate and which it was intended to replace.

In the course of time, it seems, the notion that an ideal if unfamiliar form of Zoroastrianism existed, was accepted by important sections of the community and affected their thoughts on religion. It seems unlikely that the concept of pluriformity, implying that various forms of Zoroastrianism could be equally valid, played a part in this ideal. Different belief-oriented approaches to religious truth therefore led to the emergence of several movements (notably the Reformists, Theosophy, Ilm-e Khshnoom, and the Neo-traditionalists), which were in a sense competing in the quest for the one true form of Zoroastrianism. As teaching and doctrine were felt to be essential elements of religion, these movements presented Zoroastrianism in terms of objective, more or less rational tenets. In doing so they further enhanced the importance of the belief paradigm in the minds of those equipped to take an interest in such things, whose opinions and definitions of religion inevitably influenced the rest of the community. More faith-oriented forms of Zoroastrianism gradually came to be perceived by many as old-fashioned and intellectually inferior.

The religious movements:[74] teachings and reception

The history of Parsi religious movements suggests that those who sought to rediscover the teachings of the faith and to promote the re-emergence of the true form of Zoroastrianism, encountered several problems. Apart from the fact that the community, whose understanding of religion had long been based on the faith paradigm, did not readily accept any system of teachings as a foundation of its religious life, the process of defining true Zoroastrian teaching itself proved to be fraught with difficulties.

One of the chief problems the early Reformists must have encountered was that the implicit offer of Western recognition of Zoroastrianism as a respectable faith came with the *proviso* that no acceptable religion could be dualist.[75] Initially this may not have seemed insurmountable. Such factors as the decline of the intellectual tradition of the priesthood (with the resulting loss of the connection between ancient teaching and modern views) and earlier influences from the surrounding Indian culture, may have caused Ahriman to become a shadowy figure even before Wilson attacked dualist beliefs.[76] Initially, therefore, ordinary believers and modernist intellectuals may have had little difficulty in agreeing that dualism was alien to their religion. In the long run, however, this discrepancy was to cause grave problems. Clearly the most obvious way to rediscover true Zoroastrianism was the study of the Scriptures, but to the unbiased eye most of these[77] undoubtedly reflect a dualist world-view. Such factors must have suggested at an early stage that more than a simple translation of the Scriptures was needed to ensure a valid interpretation of the Prophet's message. The discovery by the German Iranist, M. Haug, that the *Gathas* were the only Avestan texts to be ascribed to Zarathustra, together with Haug's assertion that these texts represented a pure monotheism, led many Reformists to regard only the *Gathas* as authoritative.[78] From that time onward, there was no longer a consensus even on the status of the Avesta as an authoritative source of religious truth.

Of the religious movements of the last two centuries, the Reformists now seem to be least influential among Indian Parsis. In several communities outside India, on the other hand, ideas originating with this group continue to play a major role.[79] This suggests that this very rational movement, which made few concessions to traditional devotional life and implicitly rejected 'faith' as superstitious, seemed intellectually attractive for a time but ultimately failed to bring about the profound change of paradigm which would have been needed for it to gain ascendancy in India. Such a change of fundamental assumptions is of course often caused by a move to a different cultural environment, which may explain the popularity of 'reformist' ideas among Parsis living in the West.

Theosophy, another movement that has long been influential, also seems to have lost ground among Parsis. Although ultimately based on a system of teachings and 'beliefs', Theosophist thought contained elements that might appeal to faith-oriented Parsis: it stressed the validity of the mysterious, while at the same time presenting elements of Zoroastrian observance as being capable of scientific explanation. Theosophy may thus have seemed to provide a link between the faith and belief paradigms. Essentially, however, Theosophist ideas are cerebral, and complex; they explain elements of Zoroastrian observance in a way that seems both lucid and mysterious, but offer little outlet for devotional feelings. The fact that Theosophy can inform views on Zoroastrianism but is not an exclusively Zoroastrian movement, may have been a contributory factor to its decline in the Parsi community.

Like Theosophy, Ilm-e Khshnoom is essentially a system of occult teachings. In different ways both movements attach great importance to Zoroastrian observance. Significant distinctions are that Khshnoomist interest in observance and ritual is more strongly rooted in practice, and that the movement is Zoroastrian in origin. As in the case of Theosophy, several aspects of Khshnoomist teachings may attract 'faith-based' Parsis, who could perceive its complex teachings essentially as an expression of divine wisdom which passes human understanding. The same is probably true of the Pundol movement.

One can only speculate, at the time of writing, about the eventual impact of the major modern non-esoteric movement, the Neo-tradition-alist group around 'Zoroastrian Studies'. After a period of spectacular popularity and success in the late 1970s and early 1980s, when Khojeste Mistree first began teaching,[80] the movement has now reached a more stable stage. Several of our informants said that they had learned much from Mr Mistree or other members of 'Zoroastrian Studies',[81] but the group as such remains limited in size. As far as the contents of Neo-traditionalist teachings are concerned, their uncompromising adherence to unpopular elements of classical Zoroastrianism, such as dualism, may prove an obstacle to wider acceptance. Moreover, as we saw earlier, although many Parsis express the wish to learn more about the doctrinal background of their religion, the community's recent history suggests that relatively few are prepared to accept any version of such intellectual knowledge as the main foundation of their religious lives. 'Zoroastrian Studies' is not exclusively belief-oriented, however. Mr Mistree says that he regards intellectual 'belief' and 'faith' as complementary aspects of religion, and devotional practices play an important part in the life of the group. During meetings intellectual debate alternates with the chanting of Zoroastrian prayers, and visits to Zoroastrian shrines in Iran, led by Mr Mistree, often engender strong devotional or spiritual feelings in participants.[82]

All of the 'religious movements' discussed here essentially regard teaching as the foundation of religion, and thus presuppose and inculcate the belief paradigm to some extent at least. The above survey indicates, however, that the Neo-traditionalist movement and Ilm-e Khshnoom, which are both more recent in origin and apparently more successful in the community, acknowledge the significance of the devotional side of religion more strongly than the other movements. This could point to a trend away from a predominant concern with intellectual 'belief'. It may be that an increasing number of those who recognise the importance of an intellectual basis for their religious life are now prepared also to admit the validity of their emotional needs in the sphere of religion, and to integrate devotion and observance into their fundamentally belief-based view of religion.

RELIGIOUS AUTHORITY VS. PERSONAL JUDGMENT

A more spectacular instance of the tendency to adapt one's religious life to fit one's emotional needs can be found in the recent popularity of 'Baba cults'. Most Babas are non-Parsis, but such newly emerging 'home-grown' cults as that of Jal Baba and the Nagrani clearly form part of the same trend.[83] The widespread popularity of these cults is generally spoken of as a recent phenomenon in the Parsi community,[84] and it seems likely that their influence is increasing.

Typologically, the progressive integration of devotional elements into some of the religious movements and the growing popularity of Baba cults represent very different developments. The former are essentially belief-based and accept the authority of the Zoroastrian tradition. The nature of the Baba cults, on the other hand, suggests a profoundly different approach to religion. The fundamental attraction of such cults may lie in the fact that they define religion as something mysterious and beneficial, and thus fit in with the faith paradigm. However, while other faith-oriented Parsis (such as Traditionalists) combine the faith paradigm with a strong reliance on religious authority, those who venerate Babas are clearly prepared to follow their personal judgement in defiance of the condemnation of those who represent or uphold religious authority.

This suggests that, in addition to the faith and belief paradigms, another contributory factor to the pluriformity of Parsi religion can be found in differences in attitude to religious authority and personal judgement. As was said earlier, choice and individual discretion in religious matters inevitably play a role in modern Parsis' lives. The interviews suggest, however, that there is a perceptible difference between the views of those who exercise that judgement within the boundaries of traditional Zoroastrianism as they understand it,[85] and those who rate the weight of their personal conscience and under-standing higher than that of authority.[86]

The tendency to rely on either 'obedience' or 'personal judgment', it seems, can be combined with both the faith and the belief paradigm. It could be argued that each combination predisposes Parsis towards a particular type of religious life, and thus to a degree of affinity with one of the main trends in modern Parsi religion. These trends can in fact be regarded as exponents of different combinations.

1 Traditionalists represent the combination 'faith + obedience'. Their religious lives are largely based on devotion and orthopraxy, and they understand religion as an ancient and God-given system whose component elements work and interact in ways that are beyond human understanding. The tradition, therefore, is to be accepted and obeyed without question.

2 The religious movements which are still influential at the time of writing represent 'belief + obedience'. Both 'Zoroastrian Studies' and the Ilm-e Khshnoom movement seek to understand the true meaning of Zoroastrianism, and both groups accept that the basis for such understanding is the authority of the Zoroastrian tradition. The profound dissimilarities between the groups arise from their very different definitions of the sources of that authority, and from their respective attitudes to the occult.[87] Zoroastrian Theosophists, while not confining their legitimate sources of knowledge to the Zoroastrian tradition, accept a well-defined body of teachings in order to elucidate the truth of Zoroastrianism, and could thus also be said to represent the combination 'belief + obedience'.

3 The tendency to integrate Baba cults and other eclectic elements into a life-style which is defined as Zoroastrian can, as we saw, be explained as deriving from the combination 'faith + personal judgment'. Like Traditionalists, these believers understand religion as an essentially non-intellectual system of observance, which is expected to produce benefits. However, while Traditionalists regard their life-style as valid primarily because it is based on the authority of tradition, the 'eclecticist' obviously feels that the validity of religion can best be judged by one's personal experience of its beneficial results. Thus if eclectic practices are seen or believed to be effective, it follows that they must be regarded as valid in spite of the disapproval of Zoroastrian authority.

4 The combination 'belief + personal judgment' is perhaps most strikingly typified by the mentality of the early Reformists, who were looking for true Zoroastrianism, took it for granted that what they held to be true must form part of that religion, and were prepared to reform and reinterpret the tradition to fit their views. In modern days,

this combination is found in those Parsis who incorporate elements of the tradition into their lives but are ultimately guided by rational judgments deriving from a modern world-view. Generally speaking, the views of these 'modernists' are too much in line with the spirit of the times to necessitate the foundation or continuation of a movement.

It is interesting to note that the groups generally labelled 'orthodox' by the community itself (Traditionalists, Neo-traditionalists and esoteric movements) belong to groups 1 and 2. However different these groups may seem to an outsider, in the eyes of the community 'orthodoxy' largely seems to consist in a fundamental acceptance of religious authority.

In a book on Parsi religion, the voices of those who do not regard themselves as practising Zoroastrians is of course not strongly heard, nor can it be assumed that these Parsis form a homogeneous group. It may be relevant nevertheless to suggest that the absence of both faith and belief paradigm (resulting in some cases from the fact that neither observance nor religious teaching played a role in childhood), together with a predominant reliance on personal judgment,[88] may lead to a world-view in which there is little place for religion. Mrs M's testimony may not be untypical in this respect; brought up virtually without observance or doctrine, she thinks of religion mostly as a basis for private morality (which is of course ultimately determined by personal judgment); she values Zoroastrianism because it has inspired her illustrious ancestors but otherwise seems to have little affinity with it. Her remark, 'I think that religion is not rigid at all in its demands, so one takes it or leaves it – and it is easier to leave it!' illustrates a remoteness from traditional Zoroastrianism which may be shared by many who are born into the Parsi community.[89]

DEBATES ON RELIGIOUS ISSUES: A COMMUNITY AT CROSS-PURPOSES

On the individual level, the interviews show that – in spite of inevitable uncertainties and confusions[90] – most Parsis have found solutions to the problems and perplexities resulting from the factors mentioned above, and have arrived at an understanding adequate to serve as a framework for their religious lives. Also, as was pointed out at the beginning of this chapter, the interviews indicate that enough survives of a common tradition to make different forms of Zoroastrianism mutually intelligible as such. As far as the community as a whole is concerned, however, the frequent discussions about religion – particularly about questions involving definitions of religious identity – show that the views and arguments of the various groups are too different to admit of constructive debate. (Ironically, given this diversity of views, such arguments are generally based on the assumption that only one form of Zoroastrianism can be valid.) Arguments about the question of 'marrying out' and conversion which are based consistently on either the faith or belief paradigm may be coherent enough to impress those who are of like mind, yet utterly fail to convince those who have a different view of the nature of religion. The reasoning of those who are unconsciously influenced by both paradigms naturally tends to be less logical, and generally does little more than to make clear their personal views.

Rather than 'faith *vs.* belief', however, the principal factor dividing the community on these issues seems to be 'obedience *vs.* personal judgment'. Traditionalists (group 1),[91] Neo-traditionalists (group 2)[92] and members of esoteric movements (group 2)[93] all tend to be opposed to a departure from tradition in this respect. On this issue, as on many others, what unites the 'orthodox' groups is clearly their acceptance of the authority of tradition. Those who advocate a more open policy often base their views on a rational interpretation of religion and on the validity of personal judgment (group 4).[94] Neither the interviews nor community consensus suggests that 'eclecticists' (group 3) have characteristic views on this issue.[95]

The way in which incompatible unconscious assumptions and attitudes can lead to complexities of reasoning in the case of individuals, and to mutual incomprehension between opponents in a debate, is illustrated by several passages in the interviews. For instance, Mrs E says:

> It is just common sense to me that Zoroaster wanted to convert the people to good, what he felt was the best for everybody. So why would he want to exclude some people, 'No, you are not fit for my religion, you are not fit for my thoughts!' I don't think that anyone with any intelligence or goodness in him could do that, and I really don't see that it should be even an issue. We are supposed to be the charitable religion, and we are being so exclusive and stupid. It makes no sense to me, I am sorry!

The concept of 'religion' implied here – a belief-oriented form of Zoroastrianism whose teachings may prompt outsiders to convert[96] – is clearly distinct in Mrs E's mind from that of 'tradition', by which she means Parsi observance:

> I feel tradition is important. If we have no tradition, slowly nothing will matter, everything will disappear into 'Why do this, why do that?' So I feel these few things are like hooks for you to identify what you are.

Although Mrs E has no doubts that she would prefer a Parsi daughter in law, she finds it difficult to decide how important this would be to her:

What I am trying to see is ... . what is more important? I feel that eventually the soul has to be pure and good, the other things are extras in a way. How do I know that if he [her son] married a wonderful girl who loved the religion, why should she not want to follow our religion? And supposing he married a very sophisticated money-grubbing Parsi woman who did not care for any of this? You cannot be really sure.

As far as religion generally is concerned Mrs E predominantly thinks in terms of the belief paradigm, and what clinches the argument for her is the force of reason rather than the weight of authority and tradition. When it comes to her own family, however, aspects of a more traditional set of assumptions and values come to the fore and make her more doubtful.

We find similar complexities in the views of Mrs H, who makes it clear that the faith paradigm of her youth now has little meaning in her life. Religion is essentially a personal matter for her, but her discovery of a literature explaining the meaning of Zoroastrianism has caused her to take a lively interest in these matters. The belief paradigm, in other words, has proved a more acceptable model than the faith paradigm. The question of marrying out is an important issue for Mrs H because some of her in-laws have married non-Zoroastrians. Part of the debate on the subject between Mrs H and the Neo-traditionalist Mrs Munshi[97] goes as follows:

Since there is this in your family, how is it reconciled? On the one hand one has given up part of the religion ...
[Politely, but with some vehemence.] I don't think my sister-in-law has given up her religion at all!

Not in the sense of practising it, of course, but one forsakes something of the religion when one takes that step, and yet everything about the religion ...
I don't think so! That may be the difference between what you are saying and what I am thinking. I don't believe my sister-in-law has forsaken anything. As a matter of fact both my nieces have had their Navjote done, together with my children. And there was a Zoroastrian priest who taught them their prayers. All the children go to the Agiaries. I don't think my sister-in-law has forsaken her religion at all! She has just married out of the community.

The dilemma is going to come if these girls ... [do not marry Zoroastrians]. I don't know what sort of Zoroastrianism they [would] be handing over to their children. Because even though they see their mother practise the religion at home and they take part in all Zoroastrian activities and festivities, and they have this great anchor of Zoroastrian grandparents, uncles, aunts, nieces ... If they marry a non-Zoroastrian, I don't know. It is that generation we should think about. In India, at least in Bombay, they'll still see it, we have a strong presence here. But what about those places where there are just four Zoroastrian families, or even forty? Those kids are being reared in a totally different environment ...

In other words, in spite of her definition of religion mainly in terms of belief and her reference to some aspects of observance as 'hocus-pocus', Mrs H doubts if future generations could practise a valid form of the religion without the example of the living tradition, which in practice is largely based on tradition and observance.

Mrs H, who is interested in and generally supportive of the activities of 'Zoroastrian Studies', would agree with Mrs Munshi on many issues. However, mutual incomprehension could hardly be more complete than at the point where Mrs H says, 'That may be the difference between what you are saying and what I am thinking.' Mrs Munshi regards marrying out as wrong because she holds that the Zoroastrian tradition forbids it. Mrs H has made a rational appraisal of what she personally knows about the subject, and drawn her own conclusions.

If Mrs H's reasoning could thus be called inductive, Mrs E's is deductive; her argument is based on the general premise that Zarathustra must have converted others, from which she concludes that conversion cannot be forbidden in Zoroastrianism, and that non-Parsis may therefore convert. Using different types of logic, both women (group 4) arrive at very similar conclusions. Mrs Munshi (group 2), who shares many of their belief-based assumptions but for whom the weight of authority is greater than that of personal judgment, is unlikely to see the force of arguments of either type, and *vice versa*.

As we have seen, profoundly different sets of assumptions about the essential nature of religion, together with dissimilar views on the role of personal judgement, have caused Parsis to shape their religious lives in a variety of ways, and thus contributed to the emergence of the range of religious views, trends and movements that characterises the community today. Since it is widely felt at the same time that only one form of Zoroastrianism can be right and valid, most Parsis presumably see the current pluriform state of affairs in a negative light.

Differences of this kind are of course not peculiar to Parsis, but the impact of such divisions may prove to be particularly strong in their case. The community is small and relatively well educated, which means that religious debates and disagreements affect the average Parsi more directly than they might do in other religions. Secondly, since religion is an important component of Parsi identity, a general feeling of pessimism and a belief that the great days of the Parsis are over[98] are presumably reinforced by the perception of modern religious life as muddled and possibly corrupt.

Against this, it might be pointed out that the interviews show that a tradition which is recognisably Parsi continues to inspire strong devotional feelings and a great deal of thought on religion. Furthermore, however striking the dissimilarities between the various forms of Zoroastrianism that are currently in evidence, an analysis of those differences suggests that they result from divergent interpretations of what is essentially a shared tradition. This would seem to imply that modern Parsi Zoroastrianism is no more corrupt – if also no less complex – than the religion of most other communities today.

It is curious and perhaps ironic that, whilst many Parsis hold that all religions are equally valid, no such acceptance of religious pluriformity informs their views on Zoroastrianism. If the different groups in the community were viewed as valid or at least acceptable parts of a greater whole, rather than as exponents of inadequate and therefore fallacious attempts to achieve a monolithic ideal, the community might be able to celebrate its contemporary, pluriform reality as another phase in the long and varied history of Zoroastrianism in India.

Notes

1 Mr Ranina, Dr Y, Mr Tamboly, Mrs H, and several others.
2 Mrs M, Mr B, Mr N.
3 Mrs V, Mrs E, in a sense Mr B.
4 See above, p. 144.
5 Mr Mistree, Mr Ranina, Dr Master-Moos, Mr Dadrawala.
6 Dr Bharucha, Mr S, Mrs Q.
7 Mr Mistree, Mr Dadrawala, Dr Master-Moos, Mr T.
8 Mrs O, Mrs V, Mrs U.
9 Mr Antia, Mr Doctor.
10 Mrs O, Mrs E.
11 Mrs O, Mr K, Mrs U, Dr Y.
12 Ervad Yazdi Aibara.
13 Mr T and Dr Y respectively.
14 For examples of this usage see e.g. the interview with Ms Khurody (pp. 156, 160).
15 e.g. Mrs N.
16 See Mrs Munshi's account above, p. 41 n. 19.
17 Mrs O.
18 See the interview with Mrs U. In its publication *Ushta Te*, the Neo-traditionalist organisation 'Zoroastrian Studies' now publishes short prayer formulas (*nirang*) as potential remedies for various problems. Although these are generally chosen on the basis of their meaning, it is not felt to be essential that recipients should understand the text.
19 Notably Mr Doctor and Mrs E. Mrs E's remarks on the subject at the time of the recorded interview were brief, but she expressed herself more fully in a conversation with the present writer before the recorded interview began.

20 Mr Mistree, Mrs Q, Mr S.

21 See e.g. the interview with Dr Bharucha, whose worship of God is clearly the core of her existence; when a patient's life was in danger, however, she called on the Yazad Sarosh. In the cases of both Mrs Q and Mrs X a devotion to the Waters seems to act as a focus for their worship of God; as far as personal prayers are concerned, Mrs Q said that these were 'between my God and myself'.

22 e.g. Mrs E, Mrs L, Mr T.

23 Interviews where prayer plays an important role but no doctrinal context is mentioned include those with Mrs N, Mrs L, Mrs U and Dr Y.

24 Mr Antia, see above, pp. 76–7.

25 On these figures see above, p. 50. For an example of devotion to Kookadaru see the interview with Mrs U. On the prayers prescribed by the late Ervad Aibara see the interview with Mrs L.

26 Or 'Babas', i.e. living people who are believed to have great spiritual powers. On Baba cults see further below.

27 e.g. Mrs E, Mrs U, Mrs X.

28 e.g. Mr Mistree, Mrs V, Mrs E.

29 In Parsi usage 'orthodox' is practically synonymous with 'traditional', and appears to be associated primarily with obedience to authority in matters of religion (see e.g. the interview with Ms Khurody, above, p. 153, and see further below).

30 Dr Y.

31 In recent years 'Zoroastrian Studies' has taken the initiative of teaching in primary schools in Bombay, which means that significant numbers of children are now confronted with belief-oriented teaching at an early age.

32 Examples are Mrs H, Ms Khurody, Dr Bharucha, and several others.

33 For exceptions to this general trend see above, p. 55 n. 6.

34 On historical aspects of this change see Maneck 1994, Stausberg 1997.

35 Mrs H says of something she considers justifiable, 'if it is a sin, it is between her and her Maker' (p. 174); Ms Khurody remarks that it is no 'sin or crime' to read Avestan texts from a book (p. 160).

36 Mrs E, for example, had considerable difficulty in remembering the name of Ahriman.

37 See above, p. 147; the other is Mr Pithavala (p. 248), cf. n. 39, below.

38 This does not mean, of course, that these beliefs have no emotional reality for these informants. Soon after the interview with Mr Mistree was recorded, Mrs Munshi was diagnosed with a very serious illness. Reports to the present writer on the long process of recovery, in which the members of 'Zoroastrian Studies' shared to an extent not normally known in the West, indicated that the existence of evil was, or came to be, perceived by many group members as far more than an intellectual idea. In a letter to the author (June 1996), Mrs Munshi wrote about the emotional comfort of knowing it was not God who did this to her.

39 Dr Master-Moos explains, for example, that the machinations of her adversaries were inspired by Ahriman; the rest of the interview suggests, however, that the concept of evolution to ever higher stages of development plays a far greater role in her metaphysics than dualism. Mr T's wife's remarks about the power of some ceremonies to ward off evil spirits can hardly be taken as evidence of a fundamentally dualist world-view, but these ideas obviously originated in a dualist tradition. Mr Pithavala, who does not otherwise appear to hold dualist views, stated that prayer is particularly

effective at noon because the sun is at its zenith and 'the strength of evil is somewhat lessened' (p. 252); like Dr Bharucha, Mr Pithavala further mentioned a childhood belief that Ahriman might enter the body if one failed to follow certain rules (p. 248). The fact that two somewhat older informants reported such beliefs suggests that such ideas were not unusual in the earlier decades of the 20th century.

40 This term is used here for those groups whose ideas are based on a system of occult teachings, such as the Theosophists, Khshnoomists and Pundolites. In its earlier stages, Ervad Aibara's campaign to promote Kookadaru seems to have had some of the characteristics of such movements (e.g. some teachings of an esoteric nature and the beginnings of an organisation), but in its present form the phenomenon is probably best described as a cult (see also above, p. 50f).

41 Mrs Q, Mr B, and two 'esotericists' (Dr Master-Moos, Mr Pithavala). The belief in reincarnation (on which see also above, p. 54), is in fact so widespread among Parsis that the magazine *Parsiana* sent questionnaires to Western scholars in the 1980s, asking whether they regarded reincarnation as part of Zoroastrian teaching. The debate still continues in Parsi circles.

42 e.g. Dr Y, Mrs L, Ms Khurody.

43 e.g. Mr T.

44 cf. the interview with Mrs A, whose daughters said, 'Are we *harijans* that you are trying to tell us not to touch ... '

45 Mrs M.

46 See the interviews with Mrs O and Dr Y respectively. Mr Pithavala also mentioned the effect of menstruating women on pickles.

47 Mr Pithavala, who was 96 years old at the time of the interview, may safely be included in this category (see previous note).

48 Mrs X, Mrs V; Mrs M implies a similar attitude.

49 Mrs O, Mrs A, Mrs L, Mrs X.

50 Dr Y, Mrs X.

51 See e.g. Ms Khurody's remarks about her father; the same view can be found in the interviews with Mrs V and Mrs M.

52 Mrs E, Mr N, Mr B.

53 cf. Mr Pithavala's remarks discussed in n. 39, above.

54 This conversation, which was not recorded but whose main points were written down by the present writer immediately afterwards, took place in Bombay on 6 March 1996. The theme of the Zoroastrian ban on walking barefoot also occurs in the published interview with Dr Bharucha (p. 147).

55 i.e. the high ceremonies that can only be performed in a fire temple or an especially consecrated area (see above, p. 9).

56 Information I owe to Dastur Kotwal; see also the interview with Ms Khurody.

57 e.g. Mrs A, Mrs N, Dr Master-Moos, Mr Doctor, Mr Ranina, Mr Tamboly. In a communication dated 3 March 1999, Mrs Munshi informs me that in her opinion the demand for high rituals is increasing significantly.

58 See e.g. the interview with Dr Master-Moos. The increased interest in high rituals noted by Mrs Munshi (see previous note) is presumably to be found mainly among these groups.

59 See Internet, http://www.weareindia.com/parsibazaar/praycer.html.

60 In the 9th century CE it was not unusual for priests to visit outlying areas in order to solicit commissions (and payment) from the locals for rituals which were to be performed in their absence in far-away fire temples, see Kreyenbroek 1987b.

61 The Neo-traditionalists, who believe in dualism, are presumably exceptions to this rule.

62 Mrs V, Mr S, Mr Ranina, Mr N, Mrs U, Dr Y, Mrs Q, Mrs X. Such statements are almost a commonplace in Parsi discourse; some followers of esoteric teachings hold that the various religions are 'assigned' to individuals of different degrees of spiritual development (see above, p. 238).

63 Some informants (e.g. Mr Antia, Dr Master-Moos, Ervad Aibara, Mr K) seemed to imply that the validity of a person's religion can be demonstrated by the power of their prayers to bring about positive results.

64 But see further below, under 'Religious authority *vs.* personal judgment'.

65 See e.g. the interviews with Mrs O, Mrs A, Mrs N, and Mrs U.

66 See Writer 1996, and compare Mr Pithavala's references to the Parsis as a 'caste' (p. 247). For elements of Hindu origin which are mentioned in the interviews see Index, s.v. Hindu.

67 Hence probably the widespread view that wedding customs and celebrations marking stages of pregnancy and early childhood are as much part of the Zoroastrian religious tradition as Navjotes or funerals (see above, p. 27).

68 Even in our time several informants (Mrs O, Mrs A, Mrs L, Mr Tamboly) said that they had not questioned the validity of religious observances in their youth because these were followed by all community members.

69 That some traditional Parsis do not strongly associate religious identity with personal beliefs even now was illustrated by a conversation I had with Dastur Dr F.M. Kotwal (Bombay, August 1995), in which the latter inquired about my religion. The reply that I had none led to further questioning, which ended with a query as to my parents' religion. On learning that they had been Christians, Dastur Kotwal simply concluded, 'Ah, so you are a Christian.'

70 See above, p. 45f.

71 For a brief survey of early Orientalists' views see Boyce's remarks on Hyde, Anquetil du Perron, Haug, and West (Boyce 1979: 194–204).

72 The priestly character of the Zoroastrian scriptures probably played a role here, and may have reinforced a tendency on the part of Western Iranists to describe Zoroastrianism in terms deriving from their knowledge of Christian or Islamic doctrine.

73 Mr Mistree, Mr Dadrawala, Dr Bharucha, Dr Master-Moos, Mr Doctor, Mrs Nusservanjee, Mrs V, Mr T, Dr Y; to some extent Mrs Q (who calls for a 'revival'), and Mrs E.

74 On Baba cults, which are not defined here as 'movements', see below.

75 On the role of the Rev. John Wilson in this process see above, p. 46.

76 See Maneck 1994.

77 On the Reformists' use of M. Haug's conclusions on the *Gathas* see Boyce 1979: 203, and below.

78 See Boyce 1979: 202–3.

79 See above, p. 48 with n. 22.

80 See the interview with Mr Mistree.

81 e.g. Ms Khurody, Mrs X, Mr Tamboly.

82 See the interview with Mr Dadrawala.

83 On the ambiguous status of the Kookadaru-Aibara cult in this respect see above, n. 40.

84 See the interview with Dr F (p. 103), and Mrs Munshi's remarks in the interview with Mr Tamboly (p. 189).

85 Mrs A, Mr S, and Mr T, for example, believe in the validity of the Purity Laws but accept that it is not always possible to comply with all of them.

86 Members of the latter group often mention their independence of judgement with a certain pride, e.g. Dr Y, Mrs H, Mrs E, and Mrs V.

87 Neo-traditionalists regard Scripture and tradition as the exclusive basis of religious knowledge and are not looking for esoteric explanations, whereas Khshnoom recognises Behramshah Shroff's occult teachings as another legitimate source of authority. The same is true, *mutatis mutandis,* of the Pundolites.

88 The combination 'no paradigm + obedience' is unlikely to exist, or in any case to persist for any length of time, as it would logically develop into 'belief + obedience' (the life histories of Mr Mistree and Ms Khurody show elements of such a development).

89 Dr F's husband indicates that he often, though not always, thinks along the same lines.

90 Mrs X, for example, uses belief-type arguments to justify her eclectic but clearly faith-based religion; Dr Y clearly has faith in the power of prayer, but in other matters she attaches great importance to understanding.

91 Mr Antia, Mr Ranina.

92 Mr Dadrawala, 'Zoroastrian Studies'.

93 Mr Doctor, Mr Pithavala, Mrs E's mother.

94 Mrs V, Mrs E, Mrs H, see further p. 312f.

95 Mrs X, whose views and assumptions largely correspond to those of group 3, is strongly against marrying out, but there is not enough evidence to suggest that her views are characteristic of the group as a whole.

96 After the interview, Mrs E emphatically asked the present writer whether he would wish to convert to Zoroastrianism if this were possible.

97 One of the reasons for Mrs Munshi's uncharacteristic openness during the interview with Mrs H may have been that the two women are acquainted and know each other's point of view, which could have made a more reticent approach seem unnatural.

98 Mr N, Mr B. See also Luhrman 1996.

Appendices

1 Divisions of Time in Zoroastrianism

MONTHS, DAYS, WATCHES

[These are given in the form generally used by Parsis.]

MONTHS

1. Fravardin, Farvardin	7. Meher
2. Ardibehesht	8. Ava(n)
3. Khordad	9. Adar
4. Tir	10. Dae
5. Amardad	11. Bahman
6. Shehrevar	12. Aspandad, Aspandarmad

DAYS

1. Hormazd (Lord Wisdom, God the Creator)	5. Aspandad, Aspandarmad (Beneficent Devotion)	9. Adar (Fire)	14. Gosh (Soul of the Ox)
2. Bahman (Good Thought)	6. Khordad (Wholeness)	10. Ava(n) (Waters)	15. Dae-pa-Meher, Dep-Meher (Creator's day before Meher)
3. Ardibehesht (Best Righteousness)	7. Amardad (Immortality)	11. Khurshed (Sun)	
4. Shehrevar (The Power which must be chosen)	8. Daepadar, Dep-Adar (Creator's day before Adar)	12. Mohor (Moon)	16. Meher (Mithra, Guardian of Order)
		13. Tir (Planet Mercury)	17. Sarosh (Hearkening, between God and Man)

18. Rashne (The Judge)	22. Govad (Wind)	25. Ashishvang (Recompense)	28. Zamyad (Earth)
19. Fravardin, Farvardin (All Souls)	23. Dae-pa-Din, Dep-Din (Creator's day before Din)	26. Ashtad (Justice) 27. Asman	29. Mahraspand (Holy Word) 30. Aneran
20. Behram (Victory, Success)	24. Din (Religion)	(Sky)	(Endless Light)
21. Ram (Peace)			

The last five days of the year are known by the names of the five *Gathas*: Ahunavad, Ushtavad, Spentomad, Vohukhshathra, and Vahishtoisht.

THE WATCHES OF THE DAY (GEH)

HAVAN *geh*: from daybreak to mid-morning.

RAPITHVIN *geh* (in spring and summer): from mid-morning to mid-afternoon.

SECOND HAVAN (in autumn and winter, when the spirit of Rapithvin is thought to be underground): from mid-morning to mid-afternoon.

UZIRAN *geh*: from mid-afternoon to sunset.

AIWISRUTHRIM *geh*: from sunset to midnight.

USHAHIN *geh*: from midnight to dawn.

2 Word List

The aim of this word list is to explain common Gujarati and Iranian terms which occur in the interviews. For terms which are not found here (such as the names of divinities or prayers), the reader is referred to the Index.

Achu Michu	a welcoming or celebratory ceremony
Adar	Fire
Adaran Fire, Atash Adaran	sacred fire of the second grade
Adravanu,	the first day of the wedding ceremonies, often also regarded as the engagement day
Afarganiyu	fire vase
Afrinagan	a ceremony. See also *Jashan*
Agar batti	incense stick
Agharni	a ceremony held during pregnancy
Agiary	fire temple
Amesha Spentas, Amshaspands, Ameshaspands, Amahraspandan	great divine or angelic beings
Anjuman	assembly, community, local council
Annaroja	the five days of each month when some Parsis abstain from eating meat
Aramgah	cemetery
Ardibeheshtni Chavi	a divining ritual
Arti, aarti	Hindu act of worship
Ashirvad	'benediction', part of the wedding service
Ashodad	cash gift to a priest
Atash	Fire
Atash Behram	fire temple of highest grade
Atashkade	fire temple (Iranian usage)
Atash Niyayesh	the prayer to Fire
Atashnu Git	a long song with religious connotations
Athornan	priestly caste, member of priestly family
Ava(n)	the Waters, water
Ava(n) Ardvisur Niyayesh	the prayer to the Waters
Avesta	the Sacred Book of the Zoroastrians
Baba	'holy man'

Baj	(1) silence kept on certain occasions; (2) anniversary of a death; (3) a religious ceremony
Bangli	a building for funerary purposes, in the precincts of the Towers of Silence
Bareshnum	purificatory ritual
Baug	(1) Parsi housing estate or 'colony'; (2) area where Navjotes and weddings take place
Behdin	member of a non-priestly family
Besna	ceremony held when a baby learns to sit
Boy	fuel to be offered to a temple fire (by priests)
Boyvala	priest serving a sacred fire
Chaharom	(observances of) the fourth day after death
Chana	chickpeas
Chashni	(1) ritual tasting of consecrated food; (2) the food itself
Chatthi	observance of the sixth day after birth
Chavi ceremony	see under *Ardibeheshtni Chavi*
Cheragno Namaskar	a prayer
Chok	chalk pattern
Chokkhai	purity
Dadar(ji)	Creator, God
Dadgah Fire, Atash-e Dadgah	sacred fire of the third grade
Dahi machli	a tray with yoghurt and fish, exchanged between families as part of the wedding ceremonies
Dahyu	(1) spiritual region; (2) plane of nature
Dakhme, dakhma, dokhme	Tower of Silence
Dakhme-nashini, dokhme-nashini	exposure of the dead in the Towers of Silence
Dal	id., lentils, pulse
Dalni pori	round flat cakes with sweet dal filling
Dar-e Meher	place for performance of high rituals
Dargah	Sufi-type shrine
Darun, dron	'sacred bread', consecrated and partaken of by priests during some rituals
Dasmu	(observances of) the tenth day after death
Dastur(ji)	(1) a High Priest; (2) a priest
Dasturi	formula recited by *nasesalars* before laying out a body
Dhan Teras	13th day of the second half of the Hindu month of Aso, when some Parsis wash their jewellery in milk
Dhandar patyo	rice with sweet dal and a savoury fish dish
Dhobi	washerman, laundry

322

Diso	day; death anniversary
Divo	oil lamp, often kept burning as a religious symbol
Divo adarni rit	a ceremonial exchange of gifts during the wedding rituals
Doongerwadi	Towers of Silence
Dron,	see *Darun*
Druj, drug	personification of Evil
Drujo Demana	'House of Evil', Hell
Dua, doa	prayer
Dua magvi	offering personal prayers for blessings
Dudh phul	milk and flowers rubbed over a child before its bath on festive occasions
Dussera	a Hindu festival
Ek-so-ek nam	'the 101 Names of God', a prayer
Faraziyat	the obligatory prayers
Fareshta	(1) angel; (2) a ceremony
Farman	command
Farohar, Asho Farohar	*fravashi* (q.v.)
Farokhshi	a ritual for the soul of the dead
Farvardiyan, Fravardiyan	*fravashis* (q.v.)
Fravashi	an aspect or part of the soul
Fui	paternal aunt
Gah	see *Geh*
Gahambar	a gathering of religious and social importance, centred around a communal meal
Garbo, garba	(1) dance with singing; (2) the song
Garo Demana	'House of Song', Heaven
Gatha days	the last five days of the year, named after the five *Gathas*
Gathas	the most sacred texts of the Avesta, probably composed by Zarathustra
Geh, gah	watch (of day or night)
Geh-sarnu, geh-sarna	recitation of the *Gathas* by priest during funeral
Gomez	unconsecrated bull's urine, see also *Taro*
Gor	jaggery (brown sugar)
Gorani	woman who specialises in tasks of a religious nature, such as preparing *daruns* (q.v.)
Gorni bharvani rit	ceremony held when a baby begins to eat solids (mostly in villages)
Goyan	professional singer

323

Gulabdan	container for rose-water
Guru	spiritual teacher
Haldi	turmeric (powder or paste)
Hamajor, Hamazor	ceremonial way of greeting each other
Hambandagi	communal prayers
Hamkara	(in Parsi usage) an important divine being
Hamkara day	the day of the month devoted to a *hamkara* (q.v.)
Havan *geh*	watch of the day, from daybreak till mid-morning
Hamayasht	a sequence of rituals
Hoshbam	(1) dawn; (2) a prayer recited at dawn
Ijashne, Ijeshne	see *Yasna*
Iranshah	the Atash Behram at Udwada
Jamo, jama	white overcoat worn by priests
Jamshedi Navroz	the New Year festival celebrated on 21 March
Jarthoshtno Diso	(1) the 11th day of the month of Dae, the death anniversary of the Prophet Zarathustra; (2) a prayer for this occasion
Jashan	a ceremony. See also *Afrinagan*
Jashn-e Sadeh	an ancient Iranian festival, not generally observed by Parsis
Jhabhlu	loose smock, with Chinese embroidery, worn by children on some solemn occasions
Jorani Kriya	ceremonies for surviving spouse, which are performed together with those of deceased
Jori pori	ceremonial gift of a cradle and other things when mother and baby leave mother's parents' house
Kali Chowdas	14th day of the second half of the Hindu month of Aso, when some people engage in black magic
Karma	id., a Hindu concept
Khandiyo, khandiya	professional who takes corpse into the Tower, corpse-bearer
Kharaptu	yellow paste made with turmeric and wheat flour
Kharek	areca nut
Khariyu	trotters
Khichri	'yellow rice'
Khichrini rit	a ceremony forming part of the wedding celebrations
Khordadsal	the 6th day of the month of Fravardin, celebrated as Zarathustra's birthday

Khoreh, khorre	(in Parsi usage) an aura emanating from the body (Old Iranian *khvarnah*)
Khorshed	sun
Khvan	table for ritual purposes
Kriya	ceremony, ritual
Kumkum	a red powder or paste
Kusti	'sacred girdle'
Larvo	a sweet
Lengha	loose trousers
Loban	incense
Lobandan	incense burner
Machi	(1) a 'throne' of nine pieces of sandalwood to be offered to a sacred fire; (2) the ritual offering of this wood
Madav saro	ceremony in which a plant is sown or planted, part of the wedding celebrations
Mah Bokhtar Niyayesh	a prayer addressed to the Moon
Mahino	month
Malmal	thin muslin cloth from which the *shyav* (q.v.) is made
Manthra	Sacred Word, prayer or sacred formula
Martab, Maratib	(1) the second initiation ceremony for the priesthood; (2) (the priest holding) the degree thus obtained
Masiso	(observances performed) one month after a death
Mathabanu	scarf-like headcover
Matku, matlu, matla	earthenware pot
Misvanem Gatu	purgatory
Mohalla, mahalla	quarter, area, part of town
Monajat	devotional song
Moridar	plain dal without spices
Muktad	festival dedicated to the spirits of the dead, beginning on the 10th day before Navroz and traditionally lasting for 18 days
Mushkil Asan	(1) 'problem-solver', epithet of Behram; (2) a popular ceremony in honour of Behram
Nahn, nahan	a purification ritual
Najar	evil eye
Nasesalar	professional who lays out a dead body and places it on the bier, pall bearer
Navar	(1) the first initiation ceremony for the priesthood; (2) (the priest holding) the degree thus obtained

Word List

Navjote	initiation as a member of the community
Navroz	New Year
Nirang	(1) consecrated bull's urine
	(2) a short prayer formula
Nirangdin	a ritual to consecrate bull's urine
Niyayesh	prayer
Ovarna	rite to remove evil
Pachli ratnu uthamnu	the *Uthamna* of the fourth morning after death
Padan	piece of cloth covering the mouth, generally worn by priests during rituals
Padyab	ablution of hands and face, usually preceding the untying and retying of the *kusti*
Paghri, pugree	Parsi cap, see also *pheta*
Pagladu	ceremony held when a baby begins to walk
Pahlavi, Pehelvi	Middle Persian, the language of many Zoroastrian religious works
Paidast	(Parsi) funeral
Paigambar	prophet
Paivand	'contact', made by two people during funeral by holding one end of a cord each
Pallu, pallav	loose front part of the sari
Panchmasyu	ceremony held during fifth month of pregnancy
Panthak	'parish'
Panthaki	'parish priest'
Papeti	last *Gatha* day, originally known as *Pateti*
Parab	feast day, observed when day and month devoted to a prominent *Yazata* coincide
Parsipanu	Parsi culture and identity
Pateti	see *Papeti*
Patlo	a small platform
Patyo	a thick curry with fish (see *dhandar patyo*)
Pavi	space for ritual purposes
Pazand	late Middle Persian written in Avestan script
Peheramni	gift of cash made on special occasions
Penda	a sweet
Pheta	Parsi cap, see also *paghri*
Pichi	a healing ritual
Pichori	piece of cloth which a child wears over the shoulder during Navjote (q.v.) before investiture with the *sudreh* (q.v.)
Pijama	baggy trousers
Pithi	a yellow powder which is mixed with turmeric and used at weddings

Pithi chorvani rit	'*pithi*-rubbing ceremony', part of the wedding ceremonies
Prakash	(divine) light
Qibla	(1) direction of prayer (Muslim usage); (2) fire chamber (Zoroastrian usage)
Randel, rander, randel bharvani rit	a ceremony performed some time after a wedding
Rangoli	chalk pattern (on thresholds)
Rapithvin *geh*	(in spring and summer) watch of mid-morning till mid-afternoon
Rasi	astrological calculations to identify the letters with which a child's name may begin
Ravo	semolina
Roj	day of the month, each *roj* being devoted to a divine being
Rupiya pehervani kriya	solemn exchange of gifts of money to signify an engagement
Sabi	portrait (of Prophet, etc.)
Sachkar	the ceremony of laying out a body
Sagan	a short ceremony to greet and honour s.o.
Sagdid	the rite of exposing a corpse to the gaze of a dog
Sagri	a small fire kept in the precinct of the Towers of Silence
Saheb	Master, lord
Salgireh	anniversary of the enthronement of a sacred fire
Saoshyant	Saviour
Sapat	slipper
Satum	a ceremony for the dead in which prayers are said over food and drink
Ses	silver tray used on ceremonial occasions
Sev	sweet vermicelli
Sezdo	the ceremony of paying the last respects to the dead
Sheri	Gahambar (q.v.) for women
Shyav	set of muslin clothes, which is ritually consecrated during some ceremonies for the dead
Sohvasan	a woman whose husband is alive
Sopari	betel nut
Soparo	a hollow silver or metal cone, representing the mythical Mt Hara
Sudreh, sadro	'sacred' shirt

327

Word List

Sukhad	sandalwood
Suprani rit	the 'winnowing ceremony', part of the wedding celebrations
Suraj vadhavani rit	a ceremony to greet the sun
Swastik	Indian *swastika* symbol
Tandorosti	(a prayer for) well-being
Taro	unconsecrated bull's urine
Tavil	exegesis
Toran	garland, usually of flowers
Ukardi lutvani rit	a game played during the wedding days
Ushahin *geh*	the dawn watch
Uthamna, Uthamnu	a funerary ceremony
Uthyanu	synomym of *Uthamna*, q.v.
Uziran *geh*	the late afternoon watch, 3.40 p.m. till sunset
Vadhavo	ceremony to welcome a new baby to the father's house
Val	a pulse, bean
Val ne rotli	dish of *val* (q.v.) and bread
Valavo	day of bidding farewell to the *fravashis* (q.v.)
Varadhni rit	part of the wedding celebrations
Varovar	the rites of the eighth day after a celebration, which in a sense complete it
Vendidad	(1) an Avestan text; (2) a ritual
Yasna, Ijeshne, Ijashne	(1) the central priestly ritual of Zoroastrianism; (2) the liturgy of this ritual
Yazata, Yazad, Yajad	divine being

Bibliography

Bose, S. and R. Kullara (1978), *A Socio-economic Survey of the Parsis of Delhi*, Delhi

Boyce, M. (1975, 1982), *A History of Zoroastrianism*, vols. I, II, Leiden and Cologne

Boyce, M. (1977), *A Persian Stronghold of Zoroastrianism*, Oxford

Boyce, M. (1979), *Zoroastrians: their Religious Beliefs and Practices*, London etc.

Boyce, M. (1984), *Textual Sources for the Study of Zoroastrianism*, Manchester

Boyce M. and F.M. Kotwal (1971), 'Zoroastrian *bāj* and *drōn*', *Bulletin of the School of Oriental and African Studies* XXXIV, pp. 56–73, 298–313

Chiniwalla, F. (n.d.), *The Essential Origins of Zoroastrianism*, Bombay

Choksy, J.K. (1997), *Conflict and Cooperation: Zoroastrian Subalterns and Muslim Elites in Medieval Iranian Society*, New York

Corbin, H. (1989), 'Āzar (Ādar) Kayvān' in: E. Yarshater (ed.), *Encyclopaedia Iranica*, London and New York, vol. III, pp. 183–7

Desai, Sh.F. (1977), *History of the Bombay Parsi Panchayat 1860–1960*, Bombay

Dhalla, M.N. (1914), *Zoroastrian Theology from the Earliest Times to the Present Day*, New York

Dhalla, M.N. (1975), *An Autobiography*, trsl. by G. and B.H.J. Rustomji, Karachi

Duchesne-Guillemin, J. (1962), *La religion de l'Iran ancien*, Paris

Geldner, K.F. (1896), *The Sacred Books of the Parsis*, 3 vols., Stuttgart

Eduljee, H.E. (1991), *Kisseh-i Sanjan*, Bombay

Firby, N. (1988), *European Travellers and their Perceptions of Zoroastrians in the 17th and 18th Centuries*, Berlin

Hinnells, J.R. (1988), 'Behramshah Shroff' in: E. Yarshater (ed.), *Encyclopaedia Iranica*, London and New York, vol. III, p. 109f.

Hinnells, J.R. (1996), *Zoroastrians in Britain*, Oxford

Hinnells, J.R. (1997), 'Contemporary Zoroastrian philosophy', in: B. Carr and I. Mahalingam (eds.), *Companion Encyclopaedia of Asian Philosophy*, London and New York, pp. 64–92

Karaka, D.F. (1884), *History of the Parsis*, 2 vols., London

Kotwal, F.M. and J.W. Boyd (1982), *A Guide to the Zoroastrian Religion: a Nineteenth Century Catechism with Modern Commentary*, Chico, California

Kotwal, F.M. and J.W. Boyd (1991), *A Persian Offering. The Yasna: a Zoroastrian High Liturgy*, Paris

Kotwal, F.M. and P.G. Kreyenbroek (1992, 1995), *The Hērbedestān and Nērangestān*, vol. I: the Hērbedestān; vol. II: Nērangestān, Fragard 1, Paris

Kreyenbroek, [P.] G. (1985), *Sraoša in the Zoroastrian Tradition*, Leiden

Kreyenbroek, P.G. (1987a), 'The Zoroastrian priesthood after the fall of the Sasanian empire' in: Ph. Gignoux (ed.), *Transition Periods in Iranian History*, (Actes du Symposium de Fribourg-en-Brisgau), Louvain, pp. 151–166

Kreyenbroek, P.G. (1987b), 'The *Dādestān ī Dēnīg* on priests', *Indo-Iranian Journal* 30, pp. 185–208

Kreyenbroek, P.G. (1993), 'On Spenta Mainyu's role in the Zoroastrian cosmogony' in: C. Altman Bromberg (ed.), *Bulletin of the Asia Institute* 7, pp. 97–103

Kreyenbroek, P.G. (1994), 'Mithra and Ahreman in Iranian cosmogonies' in: J.R. Hinnells (ed.), *Studies in Mithraism*, Rome, pp. 173–82

Kulke, E. (1974), *The Parsees in India*, Munich; repr. New Dehli, 1993

Luhrman, T.M. (1996), *The Good Parsi: the Fate of a Colonial Elite in a Postcolonial Society*, Cambridge, Massachusetts and London

Mama, N.F. (1944), *A Mazdaznan Mystic: Life of the Late Behramshah Navroji Shroff*, Bombay

Maneck, S. Stiles (1994), *The Death of Ahriman: Culture, Identity and Theological Change among the Parsis of India*, unpubl. thesis, University of Arizona, UMI order no. 9426587

Menant, D. (1898), *Les Parsis: histoire des communautés zoroastriennes de l'Inde*, Paris; repr. Osnabrück 1975

Mistree, K.P. (1982), *Zoroastrianism: an Ethnic Perspective*, Bombay

Mistree, K.[P.] (1990), 'The breakdown of the Zoroastrian tradition as viewed from a contemporary perspective', in: S. Shaked and A. Netzer (eds.), *Irano-Judaica* II, Jerusalem, pp. 227–54

Modi, J.J. (1922), *The Religious Ceremonies and Customs of the Parsees*, Bombay

Russell, J. (1989), 'Parsi Zoroastrian *garbās* and *monājāts*', *Journal of the Royal Asiatic Society*, pp. 51–63

Smith, G. (1878), *The Life of John Wilson, D.D., F.R.S: For Fifty Years Philanthropist and Scholar in the East*, London

Stausberg, M. (1997), 'John Wilson und der Zoroastrismus in Indien: Eine Fallstudie zur interreligiösen Kritik', *Zeitschrift für Religionswissenschaft* 5, pp. 87–114

Stausberg, M. (1998), *Faszination Zarathustra*, 2 vols., Berlin and New York

Taraporewala, I.J.S. (1951), *The Divine Songs of Zarathushtra*, Bombay

Wadia, K.J.B. (1931), *Fifty Years of Theosophy in Bombay, 1880–1930*, Madras

Writer, R. (1994), *Contemporary Zoroastrians: an Unstructured Nation*, Lanham, New York and London

Writer, R. (1996), 'Hindu caste: custodian of Parsi survival in India', in: H.J.M. Desai and H.N. Modi (eds.), *K.R. Cama Oriental Institute, Second International Congress Proceedings*, Bombay, pp. 185–94

Index

331

BASIC
English
Grammar

FIFTH EDITION

VOLUME A

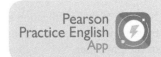

Betty S. Azar
Stacy A. Hagen

Basic English Grammar, Fifth Edition
with Pearson Practice English App
Volume A

Copyright © 2022, 2014, 2006, 1996, 1984 by Betty Schrampfer Azar
All rights reserved.

Pearson Education, 221 River Street, Hoboken, NJ 07030

Staff credits: The people who made up the *Basic English Grammar Fifth Edition* team, representing content development, design, multimedia, project management, publishing, and rights management, are Jennifer Castro, Tracey Cataldo, Dave Dickey, Warren Fischbach, Gosia Jaros-White, Amy McCormick, Mary Perrotta Rich, Robert Ruvo, Katarzyna Starzynska-Kosciuszko, Joseph Vella, Ian Wood, and Marcin Wozniak.

Contributing Editors: Barbara Lyons, Janice L. Baillie
Text composition: Page Designs International

Disclaimer: This work is produced by Pearson Education and is not endorsed by any trademark owner referenced in this publication.

Printed in the United States of America
ISBN 13: 978-0-13-672619-7

12 2024

To Larry Harris

1930–2020

Contents

Preface to the Fifth Edition

Basic English Grammar is a beginning skills text for English language learners. It functions principally as a classroom teaching text but also serves as an introductory reference for students and teachers.

Using a time-tested approach that has helped millions of students around the world, *Basic English Grammar* blends direct grammar instruction with carefully sequenced practice to develop speaking, writing, listening, and reading skills. Rather than presenting grammar as a mere collection of rules, it provides a foundation for organizing English. Students have a natural, logical framework to help make sense of the language they see and hear.

The Fifth Edition has been extensively revised to keep pace with advances in theory and practice, particularly from cognitive science. We are pleased to introduce new features and updates.

Reorganization of the Fifth Edition

- **Chapter 2:** The chapter now begins with *this*/*that*/*these*/*those* so that students can learn classroom and other everyday vocabulary right away.

- **Chapter 4:** The imperative is now in Chapter 4 instead of Chapter 13 since it is so commonly used.

- **Chapters 5–7:** Based on user feedback, we felt it was important to introduce nouns earlier. Former Chapter 6 is now Chapter 5; former Chapter 7 is now Chapter 6; and former Chapter 5 is now Chapter 7.

- **Chapters 8 and 9:** Previously, irregular verbs in the simple past tense were spread out over these two chapters. Now, for greater clarity and simplicity, the verb forms are introduced in Chapter 8, grouped according to patterns, as research shows that the adult brain is wired to look for patterns.

  In Chapter 9, questions with *whom* have been deleted. They are difficult for this level and are covered in the next book in the series, *Fundamentals of English Grammar*.

- **Chapter 10:** More information is given about the differences between *be going to* and *will*.

- **Chapter 12:** Expressing permission with the modal *can* has been added to Chapter 12, including permission questions that were previously in Chapter 13.

- **Chapter 13:** With the move of permission questions to Chapter 12, *Polite Questions* (formerly two charts) now focuses on modals used in requests and has become one chart: *Polite Requests with Modals*.

Features

- **Chapter Pretests:** Pretests at the start of every chapter allow learners to assess what they already know and orient themselves to the chapter material. Research indicates that taking a pretest may enhance learning even if students get every answer wrong.

- **Jump-Start Your English:** Recognizing that within the beginning level there is a range of proficiency levels and needs, we have created a new section, *Jump-start your English*. This feature, highlighted by its distinctive design, uses the chapter grammar as a jumping-off point to provide more functional language early on, particularly for students who need an additional challenge. It focuses on practical, colloquial language and may include structures that students will study in greater depth later. This content is optional and is not tied to the pretests or review exercises.

- **Life-Skills Vocabulary:** Many exercises have been created or revised to include everyday vocabulary that beginning students need. Authentic language use has been incorporated into a wide range of themes relevant to students' daily lives.

- **Practice:** Practice, spaced out over time, helps students learn better. Longer exercises have been shortened, and additional practice has been created to give students more incremental practice.

  This edition features additional oral exercises to encourage automaticity (the ability to speak more naturally and fluidly), an important marker of fluency.

- **Updated Grammar Charts:** Based on corpus research, grammar content has been added, deleted, or modified to reflect current usage suitable for a beginning level.

- **Listening Practice:** Research has highlighted the importance of helping students at all levels understand authentic spoken English. New as well as revised exercises include a focus on relaxed, reduced speech. The audio is available on the Pearson Practice English App and in MyEnglishLab through the Pearson English Portal.★ A listening script can be found at the back of the Student Book.

- **Reading and Writing Tasks:** Reading and writing tasks have been fine-tuned as needed to better reflect student needs.

- **Learning Checks:** End-of-chapter learning checks that help students assess their knowledge can be found on the Pearson Practice English App and in MyEnglishLab through the Pearson English Portal.★

- **PowerPoint Lessons:** Online PowerPoint lessons are available in two versions: one for teachers with presentations to teach from, interactive practice, and games; and another for students for review and self-study. The teacher version is available in the Teacher Resource folder in MyEnglishLab through the Pearson English Portal.★ The student version is available on the Pearson Practice English App and in MyEnglishLab.

Components of *Basic English Grammar*, Fifth Edition

- **Student Book with Pearson Practice English App** (access code included★) for online audio, video, review, and assessments.

- **Student Book with MyEnglishLab** and **Pearson Practice English App** (access code included★). With an easy-to-use online learning management system for teachers, MyEnglishLab provides a range of learning options:
  - Rich online practice for all skill areas: grammar, reading, writing, speaking, and listening
  - Instant feedback on incorrect answers
  - Remediation activities
  - Grammar Coach videos
  - PowerPoint video lessons

★See inside front cover.

- Assessments
- Student Book audio
- A comprehensive **Workbook**, consisting of self-study exercises for independent work
- An expanded **Test Bank**, with additional quizzes, chapter tests, mid-terms, and final exams
- An updated **Teacher's Guide**, with step-by-step teaching suggestions for each chart, notes to the teacher on key grammar structures, vocabulary lists, expansion activities, and answer key
- An Instructor Access code provides (please contact your rep for Instructor Access)
  - Robust assessments that include diagnostic tests, chapter review tests, mid- and end-of-term review tests, and final exams
  - Gradebook and diagnostic tools to monitor student progress and analyze data for remediation and support
  - A Teacher Resource Folder with a downloadable GSE Booklet, Teacher's Guide, and Student Book Answer Key (Teachers can choose to make the answer key available to their students.)
  - PowerPoint presentations for instructors to teach from
  - Videos for students
  - Student Book audio
- Print components for Instructor Support include
  - An expanded Test Bank, with additional quizzes, chapter tests, mid-terms, and final exams
  - An updated Teacher's Guide, with step-by-step teaching suggestions for each chart, notes to the teacher on key grammar structures, vocabulary lists, expansion activities, and answer key

The Azar-Hagen Grammar Series consists of

- *Understanding and Using English Grammar* (blue cover), for upper-level students
- *Fundamentals of English Grammar* (black cover), for mid-level students
- *Basic English Grammar* (red cover), for lower- or beginning-level students

Tips for Using the Fifth Edition

Pretests

The **Pretest** allows teachers to assess their students' knowledge of the topics covered in the chapter. Teachers can provide the answers after students take the test, but it works best if *explanations* for the answers are not given until each section is completed. Another option is to have students take a second look at their test answers after they have completed the chapter. Working in groups, they can give explanations for the correct answers as a way to review key points.

Warm-ups

The **Warm-up** exercises are a brief pre-teaching tool for the charts. They highlight the key point(s) that will be introduced in the chart that follows. Before beginning the task, teachers will want to familiarize themselves with the material in the chart. Then, with the teacher's guidance, students can discover many or all of the new patterns while completing the **Warm-up** activity. After students finish the exercise, teachers may find that no further explanation is necessary, and the charts* can then serve as a useful reference.

Jump-start your English

The optional **Jump-start** lessons often begin with a listening task. Teachers can play the audio a few times, and students can follow along in their books the first time and then with books closed. Depending on how advanced the class is, the teacher may want to have students role-play the conversations.

The listening is followed by varied types of interactive practice that lead up to a short presentation, usually by pairs of students. It's important that students not read from their papers. They can look at their paper before they speak, but when they speak, they should look at their partner.

Listening

The **Listening** exercises have been designed to help students understand American English as it is actually spoken. They include reductions and other phenomena that are part of the natural, relaxed speech of everyday English. Because the pace of speech in the audio may be faster than what students are used to, they may need to hear sentences two or three times as they complete a task.

These exercises do not encourage active practice of pronunciation (unless they are linked to a specific pronunciation task). Receptive skills precede productive ones, and it is essential that students gain familiarity with the speech patterns before they begin using them in their own speech.

Students are encouraged to listen to conversations the first time without looking at their text. Teachers can explain any vocabulary that has not already been clarified. During the second listening, students complete the assigned task. Teachers will want to pause the audio appropriately. Depending on the level of the class, pauses may be needed after every sentence or even within a sentence.

It is inevitable that sound representations in the text will at times differ from the instructor's speech, whether due to register or regional variation. A general guideline is that if the instructor expects students will *hear* a variation, or if students themselves raise questions, alternate representations can be presented.

A listening script is included in the back of the Student Book.

---

*Note: The charts were designed so that the example sentences on the left are for students, and the explanations on the right help teachers present the grammar points. Students are not expected to understand the language in the explanations.

Readings

The readings give students an opportunity to work with the grammar structures in extended contexts. Vocabulary that may be new to students is presented on yellow notes for teachers to introduce. One approach to the reading is to have students read the passage independently the first time through. Then they can work in small groups or as a class to clarify vocabulary questions that didn't come up in the yellow notes. A second reading may be necessary. Varied reading tasks allow students to check their comprehension, use the target structures, and expand upon the topic in speaking or writing.

Writing

As students gain confidence in using the target structures, they are encouraged to express their ideas by writing sentences and short paragraphs. They are given models to follow, and prompts help them develop their ideas.

Editing checklists, focused on the grammar in each chapter, help with proofreading. They provide guidance for either self- or peer-editing. One suggested technique is to pair students, have them exchange papers, and then have the *partner* read the paragraph aloud. The writer can *hear* if the content is what he or she intended. This also keeps the writer from automatically self-correcting while reading aloud. The partner can then offer comments and complete the checklist.

For classes that have not had much experience with writing, the teacher may want students to complete the task in small groups. The group composes a paragraph together, which the teacher then collects and marks by calling attention to beginning-level errors, but not correcting them. The teacher makes a copy for each group member, and each student makes the corrections *individually*.

Let's Talk

Each **Let's Talk** activity is set up as one of the following: pairwork, small group, class activity, interview, or game. Language learning is a social activity, and these tasks encourage students to speak with others about their ideas, their everyday lives, and the world around them. Students speak more easily and freely when they can connect language to their own needs and experiences.

Check Your Knowledge

Toward the end of each chapter, students can practice sentence-level editing skills by correcting errors common to this level. They can work on the sentences for homework or in small groups in class.

This task can easily be set up as a game. The teacher calls out an item number at random. Students work in teams to correct the sentence, and the first team to correctly edit it wins a point.

Please see the **Teacher's Guide** for detailed information about teaching from this book, including expansion activities and step-by-step instructions.

Acknowledgments

We are grateful to the teachers and students who use *Basic English Grammar* and have provided critical feedback. They let us know what works best for them and how we can better suit their educational needs in a changing market. We are indebted as well to the following reviewers and focus group participants for their invaluable observations: Luke Anh, Houston Community College; Roseanna Bird, Approach International Student Center; David Crooks, Houston Community College; Liza Daily, Houston Community College; Jeffrey Kamm, Houston Community College; Jill Lynch, Houston Community College; Sirje Russell, Tidewater Community College; Andrea Silva; English Language Center; Cynthia Schuemann, Miami Dade Community College; Geneva Tesh, Houston Community College; Joy Tesh, Houston Community College; and Melissa Villamil, Houston Community College.

The Fifth Edition of *Basic English Grammar* reflects the talented assistance of three dedicated individuals. Janice Baillie, who has been the production editor for the Azar-Hagen Grammar Series since 2005, drew upon her encyclopedic knowledge to meticulously edit thousands of manuscript pages and deftly track a mind-boggling number of details. We have benefited from the expertise of Barbara Lyons, development editor, since 2014. Her gifted editing, creativity, and sense of style can be seen in every chart and exercise. Mary Rich, Content Owner, recently joined our project and has brought a wealth of experience to the oversight of the Student Book and ancillaries.

The series would not be complete without the expertise of our supplement writers: Geneva Tesh, Houston Community College, for the Workbook, MyEnglishLab, and PowerPoint lessons; Scott Tesh, for the design, development, and narration of the PowerPoints; Kelly Roberts Weibel, Edmonds Community College, for the Test Bank; and Martha Hall, New England School of English, for the Teacher's Guide. They each bring years of teaching and writing experience to their respective projects.

We would like to thank Sue Van Etten, our business manager, who skillfully oversaw a multitude of complex issues related to the creation of the Fifth edition.

We are indebted to Don Williams at Page Designs International for the fresh, stylish design and layout of the Fifth Edition. He has our enthusiastic thanks. We are also grateful to Warren Fischbach, Senior Visual Designer at Pearson, for his valuable insights and suggestions. Our appreciation goes to Aptara for the new art that brightens our pages and to Don Martinetti and Chris Pavely for illustrations from previous editions.

We once again had our extraordinary team at Pearson Education to oversee the entire revision: Amy McCormick, Product Manager, and Robert Ruvo, Senior Content Producer. We treasure Amy's incomparable vision, attention to detail, and passion for the series. We thank Rob for masterfully juggling the schedule, production, and delivery of this edition with precision and unfailing professionalism.

We are, as always, grateful for the encouragement and support from our families. How fortunate we are!

Stacy Hagen
Betty Azar

CHAPTER 1

Using *Be*

For App resources,
scan the QR code.

PRETEST: What do I already know?

Check (✓) the correct sentences.

1. _____ Bus 7 is here. (Chart 1-1)

2. _____ Jack he is late. (Chart 1-1)

3. _____ Ella and Sophie is absent. (Chart 1-2)

4. _____ You and I are ready. (Chart 1-2)

5. _____ Beijing is city. (Chart 1-3)

6. _____ Hawaii is a island. (Chart 1-3)

7. _____ Kuwait and Syria are country. (Chart 1-4)

8. _____ They,re hungry. (Chart 1-5)

9. _____ He no a doctor. (Chart 1-6)

10. _____ It is expensive. (Chart 1-7)

11. _____ Rika is in the classroom. (Chart 1-8)

12. _____ Josh is not upstairs. (Chart 1-9)

EXERCISE 1 ▸ Warm-up. (Chart 1-1)
Read the sentences. Choose *yes* or *no*.

happy

tired

1. She is happy.   yes   no

2. He is tired.   yes   no

3. I am happy.   yes   no

1-1 Singular Pronouns + Be

	PRONOUN + BE				Singular means "one."
(a)	I	am	late.		
(b)	You	are	late.		I, you, she, he, and it in (a)–(e) refer to one person.
(c)	She	is	late.		
(d)	He	is	late.		am, are, is = forms of be
(e)	It	is	late.		

(f) Maria is late. ↓ She is late.	Pronouns refer to nouns. In (f): **She** (feminine) = Maria *INCORRECT:* Maria she is late. Maria late.
(g) Tom is late. ↓ He is late.	In (g): **He** (masculine) = Tom
(h) Bus 10 is late. ↓ It is late.	In (h): **It** = Bus 10

EXERCISE 2 ▸ Looking at grammar. (Chart 1-1)

Write the correct pronoun: *he, she,* or *it.* Some items have two answers.

1. Maria ____she____

2. Daniel _____

3. Mr. Smith _____

4. Canada _____

5. Dr. Wong _____

6. Ms. Silva _____

7. Professor Lee _____

8. English _____

9. Robert _____

10. Miss Allen _____

EXERCISE 3 ▸ Looking at grammar. (Chart 1-1)

Write *am, is,* or *are.*

1. He ____is____ here.

2. You _____ late.

3. I _____ ready.

4. She _____ early.

5. He _____ hot.

6. It _____ cold.

EXERCISE 4 ▶ Vocabulary and speaking. (Chart 1-1)
Part I. Check (✓) all the words that are true for you right now.

I am ...

1. a. _____ happy.   b. _____ sad.
2. a. _____ hot.   b. _____ cold.
3. a. _____ nervous.   b. _____ relaxed.
4. a. _____ hungry.   b. _____ not hungry.
5. a. _____ tired.   b. _____ not tired.

sick

nervous

relaxed

hungry

Part II. Share some sentences with a partner: *I am _____.*

Part III. Tell the class a few things about your partner: *He is _____.* OR *She is _____.*

Jump-start your English

Introductions

Part I. Listen to the conversation.

A: Hi, my name is **Ali**.
B: Hi, I am **Kofi**.
A: I am from **Lebanon**.
B: I am from **Ethiopia**.
A: It is nice to meet you.
B: Nice to meet you too.

Part II. Practice the conversation with a partner. Use your own names and information. Practice until you can do both parts without your book. Say the conversation for the class.

EXERCISE 5 ▸ Warm-up. (Chart 1-2)
Choose the correct answer. One sentence has two answers.

How many people?

1. **We** are ready.   one   two, three, or more

2. **You** are ready.   one   two, three, or more

3. **They** are ready.   one   two, three, or more

1-2	Plural Pronouns + *Be*	
	PRONOUN + BE	*Plural* means "two, three, or more."
(a)	*We* *are* here.	***We, you,*** and ***they*** in (a)–(c) refer to two, three, or more persons.
(b)	*You* *are* here.	
(c)	*They* *are* here.	
(d)	Sam and I are here. ↓ *We* are here.	In (d): ***We*** = Sam and I
(e)	Sam and you are here. ↓ *You* are here.	In (e): ***You*** = Sam and you NOTE: ***You*** can be singular or plural.
(f)	Sam and Lisa are here. ↓ *They* are here.	In (f): ***They*** = Sam and Lisa

EXERCISE 6 ▸ Looking at grammar. (Chart 1-2)
Circle the correct pronoun.

1. Lee and Bill   (they)   we

2. Alice and I   they   we

3. Mr. and Mrs. Martin and I   they   we

4. you and Dr. Taher   they   you

5. she and Tony   they   we

6. you and Tony   they   you

EXERCISE 7 ▸ Looking at grammar. (Charts 1-1 and 1-2)
Write *am*, *is*, or *are*.

Opposites

1. a. We ___are___ late.

   b. You (one person) _____ early.

2. a. He _____ sad.

   b. You and I _____ happy.

3. a. They _____ late.

   b. It _____ early.

4. a. She _____ nervous.

   b. Sara and I _____ relaxed.

5. a. Abdul and Taka _____ absent.

   b. You and Emily _____ here.

EXERCISE 8 ▸ Looking at grammar. (Charts 1-1 and 1-2)
Write complete sentences.

1. He \ here ___He is here.___

2. They \ absent _____

3. She \ friendly _____

4. I \ homesick _____

5. You and I \ homesick _____

6. We \ late _____

7. Jack \ hungry _____

8. You (one person) \ busy _____

9. You (two persons) \ busy _____

10. Mr. and Mrs. Nelson \ late _____

11. Amy and I \ late _____

EXERCISE 9 ▸ Warm-up. (Chart 1-3)
Read the sentences. Choose *yes* or *no*.

1. Canada is a country.   yes   no

2. Toronto is a city.   yes   no

3. Vancouver is an island.   yes   no

1-3 Singular Nouns + Be

NOUN + *IS* + NOUN (a) *Canada* *is* *a country.* INCORRECT: *Canada is country.*	In (a): **Canada** = a singular noun **is** = a singular verb **country** = a singular noun **A** often comes in front of singular nouns. In (a): **a** comes in front of the singular noun **country**. **A** is called an "article."

(b) Bali is *an* island.
 	
INCORRECT: *Bali is island.*
	A and **an** have the same meaning. They are both articles.
	A is used in front of words that begin with consonants:
	b, c, d, f, g, etc.
	    Examples: a **bed**, a **cat**, a **dog**, a **friend**, a **girl**
	
	An is used in front of words that begin with the vowels:
	a, e, i, and *o.**
	    Examples: an **animal**, an **ear**, an **island**, an **office**

*__An__ is sometimes used in front of words that begin with *u*. See Chart 6-2, p. 169.
  Vowels = a, e, i, o, u
  Consonants = b, c, d, f, g, h, j, k, l, m, n, p, q, r, s, t, v, w, x, y, z

EXERCISE 10 ▶ Grammar and vocabulary. (Chart 1-3)
Part I. Write *a* or *an*.

Places

building

1. __a__ town

2. _____ city

3. _____ island

4. _____ street

5. _____ avenue

6. _____ building

7. _____ bank

8. _____ hospital

9. _____ airport

Part II. Find a picture for each word in Part I (except *building*).

EXERCISE 11 ▸ Vocabulary and grammar. (Chart 1-3)

Part I. Put the words from the box in the correct column. Two words go in two places.

✓ Arabic	Cuba	Hawaii	Mexico	Paris	Saudi Arabia
✓ Beijing	France	Japanese	Moscow	Russia	Spanish
Chinese	French	Lima	New Zealand	Russian	Tokyo

COUNTRY	LANGUAGE	CITY	ISLAND
	Arabic	*Beijing*	

Part II. Work in small groups. Check your answers for Part I. Then make sentences. Take turns. Share some of your sentences with the class.

Example: France/Japanese

STUDENT A: France is a country.
STUDENT B: Japanese is a language.

EXERCISE 12 ▸ Warm-up. (Chart 1-4)

Write ***an animal*** or ***animals***. What do you notice about the verbs in red?

1. A dog is _____ .

2. Dogs are _____ .

3. Dogs and cats are _____ .

a cat

a dog

1-4 Plural Nouns + *Be*

NOUN + *ARE* + NOUN (a) *Cats* *are* *animals.*	*Cats* = a plural noun *are* = a plural verb *animals* = a plural noun
(b) SINGULAR: a cat, an animal PLURAL: cats, animals	Plural nouns end in *-s*. *A* and *an* are used only with singular nouns.
(c) SINGULAR: a ci*t*y, a coun*t*ry PLURAL: ci*ties*, coun*tries*	Some singular nouns that end in *-y* have a special plural form: They omit the *-y* and add *-ies*.*
NOUN AND NOUN + *ARE* + NOUN (d) *Canada* *and* *China* *are* *countries.* (e) *Dogs* *and* *cats* *are* *animals.*	Two nouns connected by *and* are followed by *are*. In (d): *Canada* is a singular noun. *China* is a singular noun. They are connected by *and*. Together they are plural, i.e., "more than one."

*See Chart 3-5, p. 66, for more information about adding *-s/-es* to words that end in *-y*.

EXERCISE 13 ▶ Listening, vocabulary, and grammar. (Charts 1-3 and 1-4)

Part I. Listen to the names of the food. Write *a* or *an*.

1. _____ apple

2. _____ egg

3. _____ hamburger

4. _____ orange

5. _____ peanut

6. _____ sandwich

Part II. Is the noun singular or plural? Circle the correct answer.

1. an egg   (one)   two or more

2. hamburgers   one   two or more

3. apples   one   two or more

4. a peanut   one   two or more

5. a sandwich   one   two or more

6. oranges   one   two or more

EXERCISE 14 ▸ Listening, vocabulary, and grammar. (Charts 1-3 and 1-4)

Part I. Listen to the words. Write the plural form.

1. a pea → _____

2. a pretzel → _____

3. a carrot → _____

4. a strawberry → _____

5. a blueberry → _____

Part II. Change the singular sentences to plural.

SINGULAR		PLURAL
1. A soda is a drink.	→	*Sodas are drinks.*
2. A pea is a vegetable.	→	
3. A pretzel is a snack.	→	
4. A pea is a vegetable. A carrot is a vegetable.	→	
5. A pretzel is a snack. A peanut is a snack.	→	
6. A strawberry is a berry. A blueberry is a berry.	→	

EXERCISE 15 ▸ Game. (Charts 1-3 and 1-4)

Work in teams. Your teacher says the beginning of a sentence. As a team, finish the sentence and write it down. The team with the most correct sentences wins the game. Close your book for this activity.

Example:

TEACHER: Spanish …
TEAM A: Spanish is a language.

1. Vietnam …
2. Arabic …
3. London …
4. Sodas …
5. A hospital …

6. Mexico and Canada …
7. A dog …
8. Tokyo and Bangkok …
9. Carrots …
10. Chinese …

EXERCISE 16 ▸ Let's talk: pairwork. (Charts 1-3 and 1-4)

Work with a partner. Partner A asks Partner B to name something. Partner B answers in a complete sentence. You can look at your book before you speak. When you speak, look at your partner.

Example: a country

PARTNER A: Name a country.
PARTNER B: Brazil is a country.
PARTNER A: Good. Your turn now.

Partner A	Partner B
1. a language	1. two cities
2. two languages	2. an island
3. a street in this city	3. two countries in Asia
4. two berries	4. a snack
5. a drink	5. a vegetable

EXERCISE 17 ▸ Warm-up: listening. (Chart 1-5)

Listen to the conversation. Note the words in red. Do you know the long form for them?

A: Hi. My name is Mrs. Smith. I'm the substitute teacher.
B: Hi. I'm Franco.
C: Hi. I'm Lisa. We're in your class.
A: It's nice to meet you.
B: We're glad to meet you too.

1-5 Contractions with *Be*

	PRONOUN	+	*BE*	→	CONTRACTION		
AM	*I*	+	*am*	→	*I'm*	(a)	*I'm* a student.
IS	*she*	+	*is*	→	*she's*	(b)	*She's* a student.
	he	+	*is*	→	*he's*	(c)	*He's* a student.
	it	+	*is*	→	*it's*	(d)	*It's* a city.
ARE	*you*	+	*are*	→	*you're*	(e)	*You're* a student.
	we	+	*are*	→	*we're*	(f)	*We're* students.
	they	+	*are*	→	*they're*	(g)	*They're* students.

When people speak, they often push two words together. A *contraction* = two words that are pushed together

Contractions of a *subject pronoun* + ***be*** are used in both speaking and writing.

PUNCTUATION: The mark in the middle of a contraction is called an "apostrophe" (').*

★NOTE: Write an apostrophe above the line. Do not write an apostrophe on the line.

CORRECT: <u>I'm a student</u> .

INCORRECT: <u>I,m a student</u> .

EXERCISE 18 ▸ Looking at grammar. (Chart 1-5)

Write the contractions.

1. I am ___*I'm*___

2. she is _____

3. you are _____

4. we are _____

5. it is _____

6. they are _____

7. he is _____

EXERCISE 19 ▸ Looking at grammar. (Chart 1-5)

Write the long form for each contraction.

1. They're sick. ___*They are*___ sick.

2. He's absent. _____ absent.

3. It's hot. _____ hot.

4. I'm late. _____ late.

5. She's busy. _____ busy.

6. We're students. _____ students.

7. You're here. _____ here.

EXERCISE 20 ▸ Looking at grammar. (Chart 1-5)
Write the pronouns for the words in red. Use contractions.

At School

1. Sara is a student. _____*She's*_____ in my class.

2. James is a student. _____ in my class.

3. I am at school. _____ in the cafeteria.

4. Yuri and Anna are absent. _____ at home.

5. Anna is from Russia. _____ nice.

6. Ali and I are in the same class. _____ friends.

7. Yuri, Ali, and Anna are friends. _____ nice.

EXERCISE 21 ▸ Listening. (Chart 1-5)

Part I. Listen to the conversation. Write the contractions.

Do you know these words?
- *substitute teacher*
- *take a seat*

A: Hello. ___*I'm*___ Mrs. Brown. _____ the
   ⏤1⏤   ⏤2⏤
   substitute teacher.

B: Hi. _____ Paulo, and this is Marie. _____ in your class.
        ⏤3⏤   ⏤4⏤

A: _____ nice to meet you.
   ⏤5⏤

B: _____ happy to meet you too.
          ⏤6⏤

A: _____ time for class. Please take a seat.
   ⏤7⏤

Part II. Listen to the conversation again and check your answers.

EXERCISE 22 ▸ Warm-up: pairwork. (Chart 1-6)
Work with a partner. Make true sentences with the words in the box. Share a few of your answers with the class.

an adult	a husband	a teacher
a baby	a student	a wife

1. I'm not _____.

2. You're not _____.

1-6 Negative with *Be*

		CONTRACTIONS	
(a)	I *am not* a teacher.	I'*m not*	
(b)	You *are not* a teacher.	you'*re not* / you *aren't*	
(c)	She *is not* a teacher.	she'*s not* / she *isn't*	
(d)	He *is not* a teacher.	he'*s not* / he *isn't*	
(e)	It *is not* a city.	it'*s not* / it *isn't*	
(f)	We *are not* teachers.	we'*re not* / we *aren't*	
(g)	You *are not* teachers.	you'*re not* / you *aren't*	
(h)	They *are not* teachers.	they'*re not* / they *aren't*	

Not makes a sentence negative.

CONTRACTIONS
Be and ***not*** can be contracted.

Note that *I am* has only one contraction with ***be***, as in (a), but there are two contractions with ***be*** for (b)–(h).

EXERCISE 23 ▸ Looking at grammar. (Chart 1-6)

Complete the sentences with the negative form of ***be***.

FULL FORM

1. I ___am not___ an astronaut.

2. He _____ an astronaut.

3. They _____ astronauts.

4. You _____ an astronaut.

5. She _____ an astronaut.

6. We _____ astronauts.

CONTRACTION

I ___'m not___ an astronaut.

He _____ an astronaut. OR
He _____ an astronaut.

They _____ astronauts. OR
They _____ astronauts.

You _____ an astronaut. OR
You _____ an astronaut.

She _____ an astronaut. OR
She _____ an astronaut.

We _____ astronauts. OR
We _____ astronauts.

EXERCISE 24 ▶ Looking at grammar. (Charts 1-5 and 1-6)
Write sentences with *is*, *isn't*, *are*, and *aren't*.

Examples: Africa \ city ... It \ continent
  Africa isn't a city. It's a continent.

  Baghdad and Miami \ city ... They \ continent
  Baghdad and Miami are cities. They aren't continents.

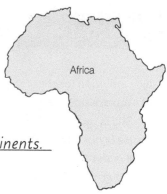

1. Canada \ country ... It \ city

   _____

2. Argentina \ city ... It \ country

   _____

3. Beijing and London \ city ... They \ country

   _____

4. Asia \ country ... It \ continent

   _____

5. Asia and South America \ continent ... They \ country

   _____

EXERCISE 25 ▶ Grammar, vocabulary, and listening. (Charts 1-3 and 1-6)
Part I. Write *a* or *an*.

Peterson Family Tree

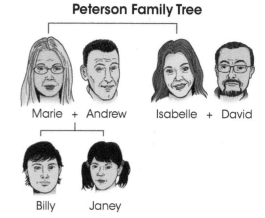

Marie + Andrew   Isabelle + David

Billy   Janey

1. _*a*_ mother   8. ____ son

2. ____ mom   9. ____ aunt

3. ____ father   10. ____ uncle

4. ____ dad   11. ____ parent

5. ____ sister   12. ____ adult

6. ____ brother   13. ____ child

7. ____ daughter

 Part II. Listen to the sentences. Choose the verb that you hear. NOTE: In spoken English, the "t" in negative contractions may be hard to hear.

1. is   isn't   3. is   isn't   5. are   aren't   7. are   aren't

2. is   isn't   4. is   isn't   6. are   aren't   8. are   aren't

EXERCISE 26 ▶ Vocabulary and grammar. (Charts 1-5 and 1-6)

Part I. Write the name of the person next to the job.

Antonio Callas

Rachel Costa

Nurse Michael Torres

Karl Sanders

Kristin Anderson

Dr. Amita Sharma

Rudy Heinz

Lisa Goh

1. bus driver _____*Antonio*_____

2. auto mechanic _____

3. nurse _____

4. gardener _____

5. plumber _____

6. doctor _____

7. construction worker _____

8. police officer _____

Part II. Complete the sentences. Answers may vary in items 4–7.

1. Lisa _____*isn't*_____ a gardener. She _*'s a police officer*_____.

2. Michael _____*is*_____ a nurse. He _____ a doctor.

3. Antonio _____ a construction worker. He's _____.

4. Rachel _____ an auto mechanic. She isn't _____.

5. Karl _____. _____.

6. Amita _____. _____.

7. I'm not a _____. I'm _____.

EXERCISE 27 ▸ Warm-up. (Chart 1-7)

Complete each sentence with a word in the box.

happy	old	small	young

1. Victor is _____.

2. Victor is also _____.

3. Billy is _____ and _____.

Victor   Billy

1-7 Be + Adjective

NOUN	+	BE	+	ADJECTIVE		
(a) The baby		is		*small.*	*small*	
(b) The babies		are		*small.*	*smart*	
(c) Lulu		is		*smart.*	*happy*	
(d) Maria and Tom		are		*happy.*	*tired*	⎫ = adjectives
					old	
PRONOUN	+	BE	+	ADJECTIVE	*comfortable*	⎭
(e) I		am		*tired.*		
(f) It		is		*old.*		
(g) They		are		*comfortable.*		

Adjectives often follow a form of **be** (*am, is, are*).

In (a)–(g), the adjectives give information about a noun or pronoun at the beginning of a sentence.*

*The noun or pronoun at the beginning of a sentence is called a "subject." See Chart 1-9.

EXERCISE 28 ▸ Grammar and vocabulary. (Charts 1-5 → 1-7)

Underline the adjective in the first sentence. Then complete the second sentence with **be** + *an adjective* with an opposite meaning. Use the words in the box. Use contractions.

beautiful	easy	✓ happy	poor
clean	expensive	noisy	short
cold	fast	old	tall

Opposites

1. I'm not <u>sad</u>. I _'m happy_____.

2. The weather isn't hot. It _____.

3. Mr. Thomas isn't rich. He _____.

4. My hair isn't long. It _____.

5. My clothes aren't dirty. They _____.

6. Flowers aren't ugly. They _____.

7. Cars aren't cheap. They _____.

8. Airplanes aren't slow. They _____.

9. Grammar isn't difficult. It _____.

10. My sister isn't short. She _____.

11. My grandparents aren't young. They _____.

12. The classroom isn't quiet. It _____.

EXERCISE 29 ▸ Vocabulary, grammar, and speaking. (Chart 1-7)
Work as a class or in small groups. Look at the colors. Your teacher will say a color. Point to
things in the classroom or outside with that color. Make sentences with **is** or **are**. Your teacher
can help you with new vocabulary.

| red | yellow | green | blue | brown | purple | pink | orange |

Example: brown
TEACHER: Point to something brown.
STUDENT: (*Student points to a backpack.*) The backpack is brown.

EXERCISE 30 ▸ Grammar and vocabulary. (Charts 1-5 → 1-7)
Write **is** or **are** and the correct pronoun. Use contractions if possible. Some sentences
are negative.

Colors

1. A pea ____is____ green. ____It isn't____ red.

2. Carrots ___aren't___ blue. ____They're____ orange.

3. Bananas _____ yellow. _____ white.

4. A banana _____ yellow. _____ white.

5. A strawberry _____ black. _____ red.

6. An orange _____ orange. _____ brown.

7. An onion _____ orange. _____ brown, white, or green.

8. Apples _____ red, green, or yellow. _____ purple.

9. A tomato _____ blue. _____ red or green.

Work with a partner. Take turns. Make two sentences for each picture. Use contractions and the given adjectives. You can look at your book before you speak. When you speak, look at your partner.

Example: The garden ... beautiful/ugly

PARTNER A: The garden is beautiful. It isn't ugly.

Example: The flowers ... beautiful/ugly

PARTNER B: The flowers aren't beautiful. They're ugly.

Partner A	Partner B
 1. The table ... clean/dirty.	 1. The man ... friendly/unfriendly.
 2. The woman ... sick/well.	 2. The coffee ... cold/hot.
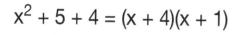$$x^2 + 5 + 4 = (x + 4)(x + 1)$$ 3. The algebra problem ... easy/difficult.	 3. The trees ... tall/short.

Partner A	Partner B
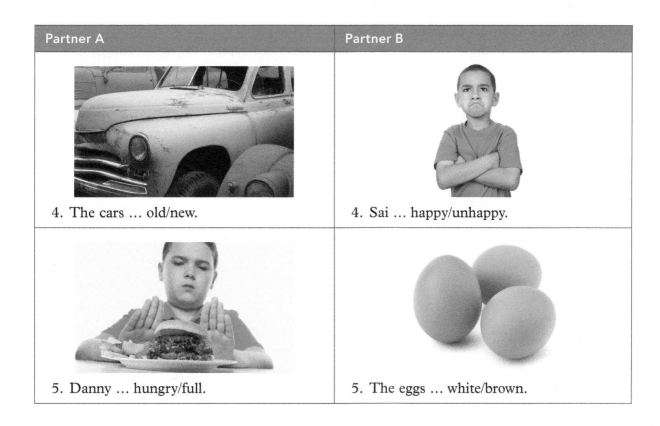4. The cars ... old/new.	4. Sai ... happy/unhappy.
5. Danny ... hungry/full.	5. The eggs ... white/brown.

Jump-start your English

How are you?

Part I. Listen to the conversation.

Responses

fine	pretty good	OK	not so good
great			
good			

Hi, Nadia. How are you?

Hi, Sofia. I'm pretty good. How about you?

I'm fine, thanks.

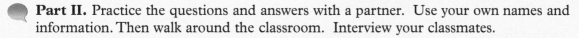**Part II.** Practice the questions and answers with a partner. Use your own names and information. Then walk around the classroom. Interview your classmates.

EXERCISE 32 ▶ Game. (Charts 1-5 → 1-7)

Part I. Check (✓) all the words you know. Your teacher will explain the new words to you.

1. _____ hungry   11. _____ angry

2. _____ thirsty   12. _____ nervous

3. _____ sleepy   13. _____ friendly

4. _____ tired   14. _____ lazy

5. _____ talkative   15. _____ hard-working

6. _____ young   16. _____ famous

7. _____ happy   17. _____ sick

8. _____ homesick   18. _____ healthy

9. _____ married   19. _____ nice

10. _____ single   20. _____ shy

Part II. Sit in a circle. Student A makes a sentence with "I" and the first word. Student B repeats the information about Student A and makes a new sentence using the second word. Continue around the circle until everyone in class speaks. The teacher is the last person to speak and repeat the information about everyone in the class.

Example:

STUDENT A: I'm not hungry.
STUDENT B: He's not hungry. I'm thirsty.
STUDENT C: He's not hungry. She's thirsty. I'm sleepy.

EXERCISE 33 ▶ Let's talk: pairwork. (Charts 1-5 → 1-7)

Work with a partner. Check (✓) each adjective that describes your city/town (the city or town where you are studying now). When you finish, compare your answers with a partner. Do you and your partner have the same answers? Tell the class about some of your differences.

1. _____ big   11. _____ noisy

2. _____ small   12. _____ quiet

3. _____ clean   13. _____ crowded

4. _____ dirty   14. _____ not crowded

5. _____ friendly   15. _____ hot

6. _____ unfriendly   16. _____ cold

7. _____ safe   17. _____ warm

8. _____ dangerous   18. _____ cool

9. _____ beautiful   19. _____ expensive

10. _____ ugly   20. _____ inexpensive/cheap

Read the sentences. Choose *yes* or *no*.

1. The cat is on the dog.   yes   no

2. The dog is on the cat.   yes   no

3. The cat is under the dog.   yes   no

1-8 *Be* + a Place

(a) Maria is *here*. (b) Bob is *at the library*.		In (a): **here** = a place In (b): **at the library** = a place **Be** is often followed by *a place*.
(c) Maria is {	*here.* *there.* *downstairs.* *upstairs.* *inside.* *outside.* *downtown.*	A place may be one word, as in the examples in (c).

	PREPOSITION +	NOUN	A place may be a prepositional phrase (*preposition* + *noun*), as in (d).
(d) Bob is {	*at* *on* *in* *at* *next to*	*the library.* *the bus.* *his room.* *work.* *Maria.*	

on

in

next to

above

under

behind

SOME COMMON PREPOSITIONS

above	behind	from	in front of	next to	under
at	between	in	in back of	on	

EXERCISE 35 ▸ Looking at grammar. (Chart 1-8)
Write the letter of the picture next to the sentence. Use each letter one time.

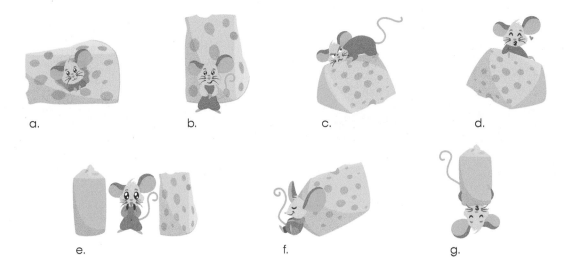

a.   b.   c.   d.

e.   f.   g.

1. The mouse is under the cheese. _____

2. The mouse is between the cheese. _____

3. The mouse is in front of the cheese. _____

4. The mouse is behind the cheese. _____

5. The mouse is in the cheese. _____

6. The mouse is on the cheese. _____

7. The mouse is next to the cheese. _____

EXERCISE 36 ▸ Let's talk: pairwork. (Chart 1-8)
Work with a partner. Make sentences about the animals. Use the prepositions in the box.
Take turns.

Animals

behind	next to
between	on
in back of	under
in front of	

Example:
The bird is on the dog.

EXERCISE 37 ▸ Let's talk: pairwork. (Chart 1-8)

Work with a partner. Follow your partner's instructions.

Example:

PARTNER A: Put your hand under your chair.
PARTNER B: (*Partner B does the action.*)

Partner A	Partner B
Put your pen ...	*Put an eraser ...*
1. on your book.	1. behind your back.
2. in your hand.	2. between two fingers.
3. next to your thumb.	3. next to your thumb.
4. under your desk.	4. in the air.

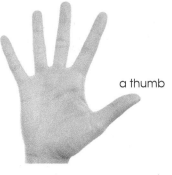

a thumb

a hand

EXERCISE 38 ▸ Listening. (Charts 1-1 → 1-8)

Listen to the sentences. Write the words you hear. Some answers have contractions.

The First Day of Class

Paulo ___*is a student*___ from Brazil. Marie _____ student from France.
                    1   2

_____ the classroom. Today _____ exciting day. _____
        3   4   5

the first day of school. They _____ nervous. _____ to
                                    6   7

be here. Mrs. Brown _____ the teacher. She _____ in the classroom
                            8   9

right now. _____ late today.
            10

EXERCISE 39 ▸ Reading and writing. (Charts 1-1 → 1-8)

Read the paragraph. Then complete the sentences with true answers. More than one answer is possible.

A Substitute Teacher

Today is Monday. It is the first day of English class. Mr. Anderson is an English teacher, but he isn't in class today. He is at home in bed. Mrs. Anderson is in the classroom today. Mrs. and Mr. Anderson are husband and wife. Mrs. Anderson is a good teacher. The students are a little nervous, but they're happy. Mrs. Anderson is very funny, and her explanations are clear. It's a good class.

1. Mr. Anderson is ___*an English teacher, sick, etc.*_____.

2. Mrs. Anderson is not _____.

3. Mr. and Mrs. Anderson are _____.

4. The students are _____ .

5. The English class is _____ .

1-9 Summary: Basic Sentence Patterns with *Be*

(a)	SUBJECT + *BE* VERB + NOUN I am *a student*.	The noun or pronoun at the beginning of a sentence is called the "subject."
(b)	SUBJECT + *BE* VERB + ADJECTIVE He is *smart*.	***Be*** is a "verb." Almost all English sentences have a subject and a verb.
(c) (d)	SUBJECT + *BE* VERB + A PLACE We are *in class*. Amy is *upstairs*.	Note the words in red: There are three basic completions for sentences that begin with a *subject* + *the verb **be***: • *a noun*, as in (a) • *an adjective*, as in (b) • *an expression of place*,* as in (c) and (d)

*An expression of place can be a *preposition* + *noun*, or it can be one word: *upstairs*.

EXERCISE 40 ▶ Looking at grammar. (Chart 1-9)

Write the form of ***be*** (***am***, ***is***, or ***are***) for each sentence. Then write the grammar structure after ***be***.

	BE	+	COMPLETION
1. We're friends.	*are*	+	*noun*
2. Anna is in Rome.	*is*	+	*place*
3. I'm hungry.	*am*	+	*adjective*
4. Dogs are animals.	_____	+	_____
5. Jack is at home.	_____	+	_____
6. He's sick.	_____	+	_____
7. They're in class.	_____	+	_____
8. I'm a plumber.	_____	+	_____
9. Gina is upstairs.	_____	+	_____
10. Two students are absent.	_____	+	_____
11. Dan and I are nurses.	_____	+	_____
12. Nora is downstairs.	_____	+	_____
13. We aren't homesick.	_____	+	_____
14. They are doctors.	_____	+	_____

Jump-start your English

Saying Good-bye

 Part I. Listen to the conversations.

1. A: Oh, no! I'm late for class. Bye.
   B: Bye. Have a good day.

2. A: It's time to go. See you tomorrow.
   B: OK. Have a good evening.
   A: You too.

3. A: It's time for work.
   B: See you later.
   A: Good-bye.

 Part II. Practice the conversations with a partner. Practice until you can do both parts without your book. Say the conversations for the class.

 EXERCISE 41 ▸ Listening. (Chart 1-9)

Contractions with nouns + *is* and *are* are common in spoken English. Listen to the sentences. Practice saying them yourself. NOTE: *'s* and *'re* can be hard to hear.

1. Grammar is easy. → *Grammar's easy.*
2. My name is Josh.
3. The books are on the table.
4. My brother is 21 years old.
5. The weather is cold today.
6. The dogs are hungry.
7. The students are homesick.
8. Mr. Smith is a teacher.
9. My parents are at work now.
10. The bed is comfortable.
11. Tom is sick today.
12. My mom and dad are from Montreal.
13. My sister is a student in high school.

EXERCISE 42 ▸ Check your knowledge. (Chapter 1 Review)

Choose the correct answer.

Example: My friend _____ from South Korea.
  a. he   (b.) 's   c. he is   d. Ø*

1. The test _____ easy.
   a. are   b. is   c. it is   d. Ø

2. The table _____ clean.
   a. is   b. are   c. it is   d. Ø

★Ø = nothing

3. My grandparents _____ downstairs.

    a. is   b. are   c. they are   d. Ø

4. Kim _____ a student.

    a. is   b. she   c. he is   d. Ø

5. The weather _____ warm today.

    a. is   b. it   c. it is   d. Ø

6. My friends _____ from Cuba.

    a. are   b. is   c. they are   d. Ø

7. Japan _____ a country.

    a. it   b. is   c. it is   d. Ø

8. The teachers _____ in class.

    a. is   b. are   c. they are   d. Ø

9. The teacher _____ kind.

    a. 's   b. are   c. she is   d. Ø

10. Dinner _____ ready.

    a. it   b. is   c. it   d. Ø

EXERCISE 43 ▸ Reading and writing. (Chapter 1)

Part I. Read the paragraph. Look at new vocabulary with your teacher first.

> Do you know these words?
> - bright
> - at night
> - rocky
> - dusty
> - temperature

Venus

    Venus is the second planet from the sun. It isn't big and it isn't small. It is between Earth and Mercury. It is an interesting planet. It is very bright at night. It is rocky and dusty. It is also hot. The temperature on Venus is 464 degrees Celsius, or 867 degrees Fahrenheit.

Part II. Write a paragraph about Mars. Use the following information. Use the paragraph about Venus as a model.

Facts:
- 4th (fourth) planet from the sun
- small
- between Earth and Jupiter
- red
- very rocky
- very dusty
- very cold (–55°C / –67°F)

Before you begin, look at the paragraph format.

Paragraph Format

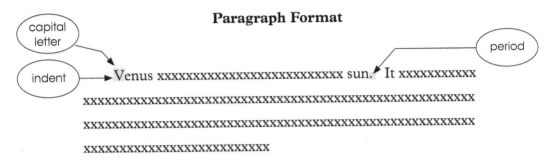

Part III. Edit your writing. Work individually or change papers with a partner. Check (✓) for the following:

1. ☐ a capital letter at the beginning of each sentence
2. ☐ a period at the end of each sentence
3. ☐ a paragraph indent
4. ☐ a verb (for example, *is* or *are*) in every sentence
5. ☐ correct spelling (use a dictionary or spell-check)

■■■■■ For digital resources, go to MyEnglishLab on the Pearson English Portal. You can also go to the Pearson Practice English App for mobile practice.

CHAPTER 2

Using *Be* and *Have*

PRETEST: What do I already know?

For App resources, scan the QR code.

Check (✓) the correct sentences.

1. _____ This car is old. That car is new. (Chart 2-1)

2. _____ Those pillow are comfortable. (Chart 2-2)

3. _____ Are you a new student? (Chart 2-3)

4. _____ A: Is outside Simone? (Chart 2-4)

   _____ B: Yes, she's.

5. _____ Where is the hospital? (Chart 2-5)

6. _____ Alana have a son and a daughter. (Chart 2-6)

7. _____ His cell phone is on the table. (Chart 2-7)

8. _____ What that? (Chart 2-8)

EXERCISE 1 ▸ Warm-up. (Chart 2-1)
Match the sentence to the picture.

Picture A

1. This cell phone is old. _____

2. That cell phone is new. _____

Picture B

2-1 Using *This* and *That*

(a) **This book** is red.	*this* book = The book is near me.
(b) **That book** is blue.	*that* book = The book is not near me.
(c) **That's** an old book.	CONTRACTION: **that is** = **that's**
(d) **This is** ("This's") a new book.	In spoken English, *this is* is usually pronounced as "this's." It is not used in writing.

EXERCISE 2 ▸ Grammar and vocabulary. (Chart 2-1)

Write **this** or **that**.

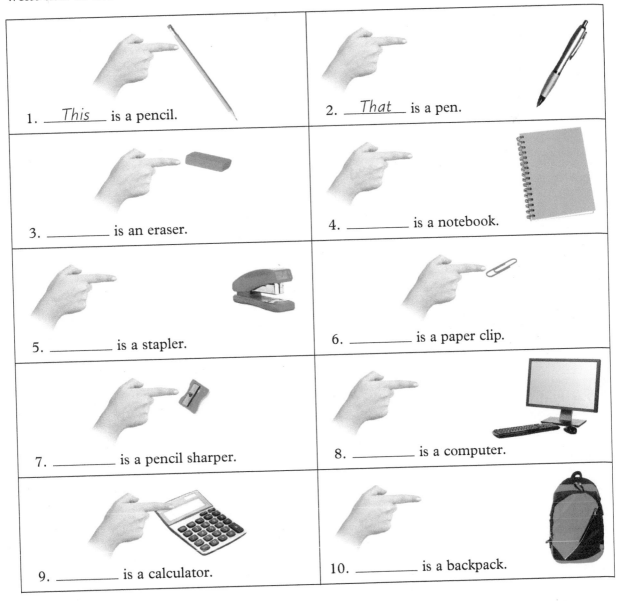

1. ___This___ is a pencil.

2. ___That___ is a pen.

3. _____ is an eraser.

4. _____ is a notebook.

5. _____ is a stapler.

6. _____ is a paper clip.

7. _____ is a pencil sharper.

8. _____ is a computer.

9. _____ is a calculator.

10. _____ is a backpack.

Work with a partner. Look at the words in the box. Find the objects in the classroom. Point and make sentences. Use **this** or **that**.

a backpack	a desk	a pencil sharpener
a board or a whiteboard	a door	a piece of paper
a chair	an eraser	✓ a ruler
a clock	✓ a keyboard	a window
a computer	a light	

Examples:

PARTNER A: This is a keyboard.
Your turn now.

PARTNER B: That is a ruler.
Your turn now.

EXERCISE 4 ▸ Warm-up. (Chart 2-2)

Check (✓) the sentence that describes the picture.

1. Those are keys. _____

2. These are keys. _____

2-2	Using *These* and *Those*		
(a) *These* are new books.		SINGULAR	PLURAL
(b) *Those* are old books.		this → these	
		that → those	

EXERCISE 5 ▸ Grammar and vocabulary. (Chart 2-2)
Write *these* or *those*.

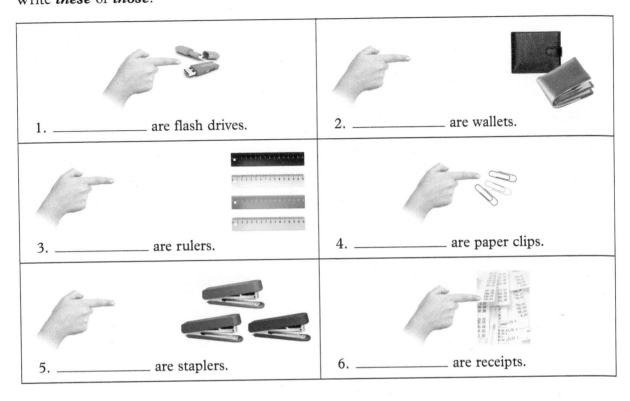

1. _____ are flash drives.

2. _____ are wallets.

3. _____ are rulers.

4. _____ are paper clips.

5. _____ are staplers.

6. _____ are receipts.

EXERCISE 6 ▸ Looking at grammar. (Chart 2-2)
Make plural sentences.

1. This is a pencil.   →   *These are pencils.* _____

2. That is a book.   →   _____

3. That is a pen.   →   _____

4. This is a notebook.   →   _____

5. This is a computer.   →   _____

6. That is a laptop.   →   _____

7. That is a backpack.   →   _____

8. This is a light.   →   _____

9. That is a desk.   →   _____

10. This is a chair.   →   _____

EXERCISE 7 ▶ Vocabulary and grammar. (Charts 2-1 and 2-2)
Choose the correct verb.

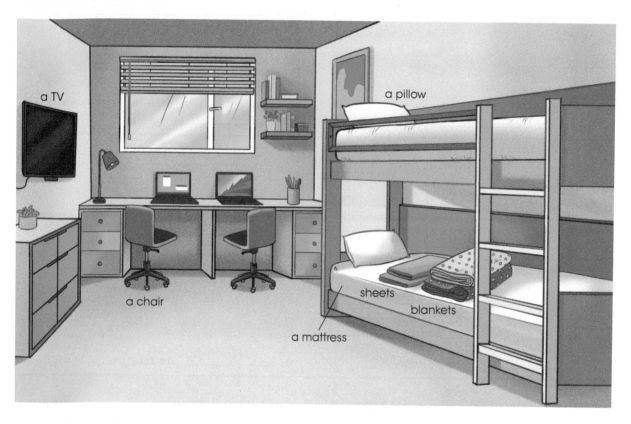

a TV

a pillow

a chair

a mattress

sheets

blankets

In Our Dorm Room

1. This (is)/ are a soft pillow.

2. That is / are a hard pillow.

3. Those sheets is / are for you.

4. These blankets is / are for me.

5. That TV is / are a smart TV.

6. This chair is / are new.

7. Those mattresses is / are soft.

8. This mattress is / are uncomfortable.

EXERCISE 8 ▶ Let's talk: pairwork. (Chart 2-2)
Work with a partner. Walk around the classroom. Point to objects. Make sentences with *these* and *those*.

Examples: PARTNER A: Those are chairs.
PARTNER B: These are desks.

EXERCISE 9 ▶ Warm-up. (Chart 2-3)
Answer the questions.

1. Are you in the cafeteria?   Yes.   No.

2. Is the library open?   Yes.   No.

2-3 Yes/No Questions with Be

QUESTION			STATEMENT			In a question, **be** comes in front of the subject.
BE	+	SUBJECT	SUBJECT	+	BE	**PUNCTUATION**
(a) *Am*	*I*	early?	*I*	*am*	early.	A question ends with a question mark (?).
(b) *Is*	*Ana*	a student?	*Ana*	*is*	a student.	A statement ends with a period (.).
(c) *Are*	*they*	at home?	*They*	*are*	at home.	

EXERCISE 10 ▶ Looking at grammar. (Chart 2-3)

Write *am*, *is*, or *are*.

At School

1. _____ you ready?

2. _____ he absent?

3. _____ I late?

4. _____ we early?

5. _____ she tired?

6. _____ he a new student?

7. _____ they new students?

8. _____ you and Bill ready?

9. _____ it lunchtime?

10. _____ Mr. and Mrs. Chu sick?

EXERCISE 11 ▶ Looking at grammar. (Chart 2-3)

Make questions.

1. A: ____*Is the homework easy?*_____

   B: Yes, the homework is easy.

2. A: _____

   B: Yes, Stefan is absent.

3. A: _____

   B: Yes, I am OK.

4. A: _____

   B: Yes, Lucca and Danny are late.

5. A: _____

   B: Yes, she is the teacher.

6. A: _____

   B: Yes, I am ready for the next exercise.

7. A: _____

   B: Yes, it is time to go home.

EXERCISE 12 ▸ Let's talk: pairwork. (Chart 2-3)
Make questions. Ask and answer with a partner.

Example: you \ in the classroom
          A: Are you in the classroom?
          B: Yes, I am.

Partner A	Partner B
1. you \ a teacher	1. you \ a new student
2. this classroom \ big	2. this classroom \ nice
3. the homework \ hard	3. English \ difficult
4. it \ break time	4. the teacher \ absent
5. the desks \ comfortable	5. the students \ at their desks

Jump-start your English

Classroom Questions

Part I. Listen to the conversations.

1. A: Is this sentence correct?
   B: Yes, it's fine.

2. A: Is this spelling OK?
   B: No, it's incorrect.

Part II. Work with a partner. Ask and answer questions with the words in the boxes.

QUESTIONS			ANSWERS	
Is this	word sentence spelling	correct? OK?	Yes, it's	fine. good.
			No, it's	not OK. wrong. incorrect.

EXERCISE 13 ▸ Warm-up. (Chart 2-4)
Answer the questions. In b., both answers are possible. Which negative contraction do you prefer?

1. Is the classroom new?

   a. Yes, it is.   b. No, it isn't. / No, it's not.

2. Are the desks in the classroom comfortable?

   a. Yes, they are.   b. No, they aren't. / No, they're not.

2-4 Short Answers to Yes/No Questions

	QUESTION		SHORT ANSWER	Spoken contractions are not used in short answers that begin with *yes*.
(a)	*Is Kari* a student?	→	Yes, *she is.*	In (a): INCORRECT: *Yes, she's.*
		→	No, *she's not.*	
		→	No, *she isn't.*	
(b)	*Are they* at home?	→	Yes, *they are.*	In (b): INCORRECT: *Yes, they're.*
		→	No, *they aren't.*	
			No, *they're not.*	
(c)	*Are you* ready?	→	Yes, *I am.*	In (c): INCORRECT: *Yes, I'm.*
		→	No, *I'm not.**	

*Am and not are not contracted.

EXERCISE 14 ▶ Looking at grammar. (Charts 2-3 and 2-4)
Make questions and give short answers.

Questions at School

1. A: _Are Lia and Nobu in the cafeteria?_
   B: _No, they aren't._ (They aren't in the cafeteria.)

2. A: _Is Ali in the library?_
   B: _Yes, he is._ (Ali is in the library.)

3. A: _____
   B: _____ (It isn't lunchtime.)

4. A: _____
   B: _____ (It is break time.)

5. A: _____
   B: _____ (I am not hungry.)

6. A: _____
   B: _____ (We are tired.)

7. A: _____
   B: _____ (Julia is absent.)

8. A: _____
   B: _____ (She isn't sick.)

9. A: _____
   B: _____ (The homework is difficult.)

10. A: _____
    B: _____ (The test isn't today.)

EXERCISE 15 ▸ Grammar and speaking. (Charts 2-3 and 2-4)

Part I. Work with a partner. Complete the conversations with your own words.

At School

1. A: _____*Are*_____ you a student at this school?

   B: Yes, ____*I am*____.

   A: _____ you from _____?

   B: No, _____ from _____.

2. A: Are you a/an _____?

   B: No, _____ not. I'm a/an _____.

3. A: Is _____ in the library?

   B: No, _____.

   A: Is _____?

   B: Yes, _____.

4. A: _____ the computer lab open?

   B: Yes, _____ is.

   A: _____ the library open?

   B: Yes, _____ is.

   A: _____ in the library?

   B: No, _____ not. They're in the _____.

Part II. Choose one conversation to say in front of the class. You can look at your book before you speak. When you speak, look at your partner.

Jump-start your English

Questions with Days of the Week

Part I. Listen to the days of the week: *Sunday, Monday, Tuesday, Wednesday, Thursday, Friday, Saturday.* Repeat each day after the speaker.

JANUARY

Sunday	Monday	Tuesday	Wednesday	Thursday	Friday	Saturday
		1	2	3	4	5
6	7	8	9	10	11	12
13	14	15	16	17	18	19
20	21	22	23	24	25	26
27	28	29	30	31		

Part II. Listen to the conversations.

  1. A: Is it Monday?
     B: Yes, it is.

  2. A: Is the library open late on Saturday?
     B: No, it isn't.

  3. A: Is the homework due on Friday?
     B: Yes, it is.

💬 **Part III.** Work with a partner. Practice the conversations. Then make one new conversation.
Practice it and say it for another pair of classmates.

EXERCISE 16 ▸ Warm-up. (Chart 2-5)
Choose the correct answer for each question.

On your head!	No, they aren't.

A: Are my glasses in the kitchen?

B: _____
   1

A: Where are they?

B: _____
   2

glasses

2-5 Questions with *Be:* Using *Where*

Where asks about place. *Where* comes at the beginning of the question, in front of *be*.

	QUESTION			SHORT ANSWER	(LONG ANSWER)
	BE	+	SUBJECT		
(a)	*Is*		*the book* on the table? →	Yes, *it is*.	(The book is on the table.)
(b)	*Are*		*the books* on the table? →	Yes, *they are*.	(The books are on the table.)
	WHERE +	*BE* +	SUBJECT		
(c) *Where*	*is*		*the book?* →	*On the table.*	(The book is on the table.)
(d) *Where*	*are*		*the books?* →	*On the table.*	(The books are on the table.)

EXERCISE 17 ▸ Looking at grammar. (Chart 2-5)
Choose the correct question for each response.

QUESTION	RESPONSE
1. a. Is Adam absent? b. Where is Adam?	At home.
2. a. Where are the boxes? b. Are the boxes in the classroom?	Yes, they are.
3. a. Are you in the cafeteria? b. Where are you?	No, I'm not.
4. a. Is the homework on the desk? b. Where is the homework?	On the desk.

EXERCISE 18 ▸ Looking at grammar. (Chart 2-5)
Make questions.

Around Town

1. A: _____*Is the train station near school?*_____
   B: Yes, it is. (The train station is near school.)

2. A: _____*Where is the train station?*_____
   B: Near school. (The train station is near school.)

3. A: _____
   B: Yes, it is. (The bank is across the street.)

4. A: _____
   B: Across the street. (The bank is across the street.)

5. A: _____
   B: Yes, it is. (The ATM* is nearby.)

6. A: _____
   B: Over there. (The bus stop is over there.)

7. A: _____
   B: On Broadway. (The post office is on Broadway.)

8. A: _____
   B: Yes, they are. (The restrooms are down the street.)

---

*ATM = automatic teller machine. We also say *cash machine*.

Work with a partner. Make questions with **where**. Use the words in the box or your own words for answers. If necessary, you can look at a city/town map. Look at your book before you speak. When you speak, look at your partner.

nearby	down the street	at the mall
far away	across the street	on _____ Street/Avenue, etc.

Examples: bus stop
PARTNER A: Where is the bus stop?
PARTNER B: It's on 6th Street.

           computer store
PARTNER B: Where is the computer store?
PARTNER A: It's at the mall.

Partner A	Partner B
1. bank	1. train station
2. library	2. grocery store
3. restroom	3. gas station
4. movie theater	4. park
5. hospital	5. pharmacy

EXERCISE 20 ▶ Warm-up. (Chart 2-6)

Check (✓) the true sentences.

a headache

a cold

a cough

1. _____ I have a headache.

2. _____ Some teachers have colds.

3. _____ Everyone in this class has a cough.

2-6 Using *Have* and *Has*

	SINGULAR				PLURAL					
(a)	*I*	have	a problem.	(f)	*We*	have	problems.	I you we they	} +	**have**
(b)	*You*	have	a problem.	(g)	*You*	have	problems.			
(c)	*She*	has	a problem.	(h)	*They*	have	problems.	she he it	} +	**has**
(d)	*He*	has	a problem.							
(e)	*It*	has	a problem.							

EXERCISE 21 ▸ Looking at grammar. (Chart 2-6)
Write **have** or **has**.

1. You _____ a toothache.

2. I _____ a toothache.

3. She _____ a headache.

4. They _____ headaches.

5. We _____ medicine.

6. The doctor _____ medicine.

7. You and I _____ colds.

8. The Molinas _____ colds.

EXERCISE 22 ▸ Vocabulary and grammar. (Chart 2-6)
Complete each sentence with **have** or **has** and words in the box.

a backache	a fever	a sore throat
the chills	high blood pressure	✓ a stomachache

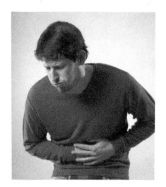

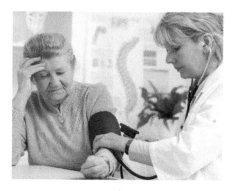

1. He ___*has a stomachache*___ .

2. She _____ .

3. He ———————————————.

4. They ———————————————.

5. He ———————————————.

6. He ———————————————.

EXERCISE 23 ▶ Let's talk: pairwork. (Chart 2-6)

Complete the conversations with a partner. Take turns. You can look at your book before you speak. When you speak, look at your partner.

Example: Jamal? … a toothache.

PARTNER A: How is Jamal?
PARTNER B: Not so good. He has a toothache.
PARTNER A: That's too bad.

1. you? … a headache.
2. you? … the chills.
3. your mother? … a sore back.
4. Mr. Park? … a backache.
5. your parents? … colds.
6. the tourists? … stomachaches.
7. your little brother? … a sore throat.
8. Mrs. Luna? … a fever.
9. your sister? … an earache.
10. Grandma? … high blood pressure.

Jump-start your English

Talking About Food Allergies

 Part I. Listen to the conversations.

1. A: Do you have food allergies?
   B: Yes, I do. I'm allergic to eggs.

2. A: Do you have food allergies?
   B: No, I don't.

Part II. Work with a partner. Ask and answer questions with the words in the boxes.

QUESTION	ANSWERS	
Do you have food allergies?	Yes, I do. I'm allergic to	nuts. peanuts. eggs. wheat. dairy. shellfish.
	No, I don't.	

EXERCISE 24 ▸ Looking at grammar. (Chapter 1 and Chart 2-6)

Rewrite the paragraph. Change **I** to **he**. You also need to change the verbs in red.

Dr. Tran

I am a doctor. I am 70 years old. I have many patients. Some patients are very sick. I have a clinic downtown. I also have patients at the hospital. It is hard work. I am often very tired. But I am also happy. I help many people.

He is a doctor.

_____

_____

_____

_____

_____ _He helps many people._

EXERCISE 25 ▸ Warm-up. (Chart 2-7)
Complete each sentence with a word in the box. Use each word one time.

Her	His	My	Their

1. _____ name is Evita.

2. _____ name is Paulo.

3. _____ name is Nadia.

4. _____ names are Hugo and Kristin.

2-7 Using *My, Your, Her, His, Our, Their*

SINGULAR	PLURAL	SUBJECT FORM		POSSESIVE FORM
(a) *I* have a book. **My** book is red.	(e) *We* have books. **Our** books are red.	I	→	my
(b) *You* have a book. **Your** book is red.	(f) *You* have books. **Your** books are red.	you	→	your
(c) *She* has a book. **Her** book is red.	(g) *They* have books. **Their** books are red.	she	→	her
(d) *He* has a book. **His** book is red.		he	→	his
		we	→	our
		they	→	their

I *possess* a book. = I *have* a book. = It is *my* book.

My, your, her, his, our, and *their* are called "possessive adjectives." They come in front of nouns.

EXERCISE 26 ▸ Looking at grammar. (Chart 2-7)
Complete each sentence with a word in the box.

her	his	my	our	their	your

1. You are next. It's _____ *your* _____ turn.

2. Susana's next. It's _____ turn.

3. Bruno and Maria are next. It's _____ turn.

4. My aunt is next. It's _____ turn.

5. I'm next. It's _____ turn.

6. The children are next. It's _____ turn.

7. You and Mohamed are next. It's _____ turn.

8. Marcos and I are next. It's _____ turn.

9. Bill's next. It's _____ turn.

10. Mrs. Sung is next. It's _____ turn.

EXERCISE 27 ▸ Vocabulary and grammar. (Chart 2-7)
Part I. Complete the sentences with the information on the ID and business cards. Use *his*, *her*, and *their*.

Derek

1. _____ last name is _____ .

2. _____ first name is _____ .

3. _____ middle initial is _____ .

Ellen and Daniel

4. _____ zip code is _____ .

5. _____ area code is _____ .

Medco Employee ID

Derek C. Williams

13684 Park Lane
Vista, CA 98301

09/25/2000

TechLearn

Ellen Ryan
Sales Associate
14 Center St.
Silicon, CA 98203
cell: 888-555-2589
email: ertechlearn@tech.com
website: www.techlearn.intl

TechLearn

Daniel Ryan
Sales Associate
14 Center St.
Silicon, CA 98203
cell: 888-555-2588
email: drtechlearn@tech.com
website: www.techlearn.intl

Vivian

6. _____ birthdate is _____ .

7. _____ birthday is _____ .

8. _____ middle name is _____ .

Part II. Write about yourself.

Medco Employee ID

Vivian Grace Marr

1340 State Ave. #7
Vista, CA 98301

04/12/1980

1. _____ first name is _____ .

2. _____ last name is _____ .

3. _____ middle name is _____ .

4. _____ middle initial is _____ .

5. _____ area code is _____ .

6. _____ phone number is _____ .

7. _____ zip code is _____ .

8. _____ birthday is _____ .

APRIL

Sunday	Monday	Tuesday	Wednesday	Thursday	Friday	Saturday
		1	2	3	4	5
6	7	8	9	10	11	(12)
13	14	15	16	17	18	19
20	21	22	23		25	26

EXERCISE 28 ▸ Looking at grammar. (Chart 2-7)

Choose the correct answer.

My Family

1. (We)/ Our have a daughter.

2. Our / We daughter is in college.

3. She / Her major is business.

4. My / I son is an engineer.

5. He / His has a wife and two children.

6. Their / They children are young.

7. I / My have a big family.

8. I / My family is friendly.

EXERCISE 29 ▸ Looking at grammar. (Charts 2-6 and 2-7)

Complete the sentences. Use *have* or *has* and *my, your, her, his, our,* or *their*.

Families

1. You ____*have*____ a big family. ____*Your*____ family is nice.

2. You and Tina _____ many cousins. _____ cousins are friendly.

3. I _____ a brother. _____ brother is a high school student.

4. William _____ a sister. _____ sister is a doctor.

5. Lisa _____ a twin sister. _____ sister is disabled.

6. Iman and Amir are married. They _____ a baby. _____ baby is six months old.

7. Anton and I _____ a son. _____ son is seven years old.

8. Pietro and Julieta _____ a daughter. _____ daughter is ten years old.

9. I _____ two brothers. _____ brothers are twenty-five and thirty.

10. Lidia is single. She _____ three sisters. _____ sisters are single too.

EXERCISE 30 ▸ Reading and grammar. (Chapter 1 and Charts 2-6 and 2-7)

Part I. Read about Kanai and her family and answer the questions. Look at new vocabulary with your teacher first.

One Big Happy Family

Kanai is thirteen years old. She has a big family. She has four sisters and five brothers. Kanai and her siblings are adopted. They are from several different countries. Kanai and her brothers and sisters are close. They have fun. They are always busy. Kanai's parents are busy too. Her mother is an airline pilot. She is away overnight fifteen days a month. Kanai's dad is a stay-at-home father. He has a lot of work, but the older kids are helpful. Kanai's parents love children. They are one big happy family.

Do you know these words?
- *sibling*
- *adopted*
- *pilot*
- *overnight*
- *stay-at-home father*

1. Kanai is a girl.   yes   no

2. Only the girls are adopted.   yes   no

3. Kanai's father is home a lot.   yes   no

4. Her mother is home every night.   yes   no

Part II. Complete the sentences with *her*, *his*, or *their*. One sentence has two possible answers.

1. Kanai is adopted. _____ brothers and sisters are adopted too.

2. Her parents are busy. _____ mother is an airline pilot. _____ father is a stay-at-home dad.

3. She has nine siblings. _____ family is very large.

4. Kanai's dad is very busy. _____ children are helpful.

Part III. Complete the paragraph with *is*, *are*, *has*, or *have*. Do not look at Part I.

One Big Happy Family

Kanai _____ thirteen years old. She _____ a big family. She
⎯⎯⎯⎯⎯⎯ 1 ⎯⎯⎯⎯⎯⎯⎯ 2 ⎯⎯⎯⎯

_____ four sisters and five brothers. Kanai and her siblings are adopted. They
⎯⎯⎯⎯ 3 ⎯⎯

_____ from several different countries. Kanai and her brothers and sisters are close.
⎯⎯⎯⎯ 4 ⎯⎯

They _____ fun. They _____ always busy. Kanai's parents _____
⎯⎯⎯ 5 ⎯⎯ ⎯⎯⎯ 6 ⎯⎯ ⎯⎯⎯ 7 ⎯⎯

busy too. Her mother _____ an airline pilot. She _____ away overnight
⎯⎯⎯ 8 ⎯⎯ ⎯⎯⎯ 9 ⎯⎯

fifteen days a month. Kanai's dad _____ a stay-at-home father. He _____ a
⎯⎯⎯ 10 ⎯⎯ ⎯⎯⎯ 11 ⎯⎯

lot of work, but the older kids are helpful. Kanai's parents love children. They are one big

happy family.

EXERCISE 31 ▸ Vocabulary and grammar: pairwork. (Chart 2-7)

Part I. Work with a partner. Look at the vocabulary. Check (✓) the words you know. Ask your partner about new words. Your teacher can help you.

_____ belt	_____ sandals	
_____ blouse	_____ shirt	
_____ boots	_____ shoes	
_____ coat	_____ skirt	
_____ dress	_____ socks	
_____ gloves	_____ suit	
_____ hat	_____ sweater	
_____ jacket	_____ tie, necktie	
_____ jeans	_____ T-shirt	
_____ pants		

Part II. Complete the sentences with *my, your, her, his, our,* or *their.*

1. Malena has on* a blouse. _____*Her*_____ blouse is light blue.

2. Tom has on a shirt. _____ shirt is yellow and brown.

3. I have on jeans. _____ jeans are blue.

4. Kiril and Oleg have on boots. _____ boots are brown.

5. Diana and you have on dresses. _____ dresses are red.

6. Salma and I have on sweaters. _____ sweaters are green.

7. You have on shoes. _____ shoes are dark brown.

8. Nora has on a skirt. _____ skirt is black.

9. Leo has on a belt. _____ belt is white.

10. Sashi and Akira have on socks. _____ socks are gray.

11. Arturo has on pants. _____ pants are dark blue.

EXERCISE 32 ▸ Warm-up. (Chart 2-8)
Answer the questions.

1. What is that? _____

2. Who is that? _____

a bee

Sami

---

* *has on* and *have on* = wear (clothes)

2-8 Asking Questions with *What* and *Who* + *Be*

(a) *What is* this (thing)?	It's a pen.	***What*** asks about things. ***Who*** asks about people. Note: In questions with ***what*** and ***who***, • ***is*** is followed by a singular word. • ***are*** is followed by a plural word.
(b) *Who is* that (man)?	That's Mr. Lee.	
(c) *What are* those (things)?	They're pens.	
(d) *Who are* they?	They're Mr. and Mrs. Lee.	

(e) *What's* this?
(f) *Who's* that man?
		CONTRACTIONS:
		  what is = ***what's***
		  who is = ***who's***

EXERCISE 33 ▸ Looking at grammar. (Chart 2-8)

Choose the correct responses. More than one answer may be correct.

1. A: Who is that?
   B: a. That is my cousin.   b. That is an island.

2. A: What is that?
   B: a. That is a flower.   b. That is Mr. Michelli.

3. A: Who are they?
   B: a. My friends.   b. Anita and Thomas.

4. A: What are those?
   B: a. Snacks.   b. Peanuts.

5. A: Who is that?
   B: a. My apartment.   b. My brother.

EXERCISE 34 ▸ Looking at grammar. (Chart 2-8)

Complete the questions with ***what*** or ***who*** and ***is*** or ***are***.

1. A: _____*Who is*_____ that woman?
   B: She's my sister. Her name is Sonya.

2. A: _____ those things?
   B: They're erasers.

3. A: _____ that?
   B: That's Ms. Walenski.

4. A: _____ this?
   B: It's a vegetable.

5. A: _____ those?
   B: They're vegetables.

6. A: _____ those people?
   B: They're new students from Thailand.

EXERCISE 35 ▸ Vocabulary and speaking: pairwork. (Charts 2-1, 2-2, and 2-8)

Part I. Work with a partner. Write the names of the parts of the body on the picture below. Use the words in the box.

arm
back
chest
ear
elbow
eye
fingers
foot
hand
hair
head
knee
leg
mouth
neck
nose
shoulder
thigh

Part II. With your partner, ask questions about the parts of the body with **this** and **these**.

Example:

PARTNER A: What is this?
PARTNER B: This is his leg. (*to Partner A*) What are these?
PARTNER A: These are his fingers.

EXERCISE 36 ▸ Let's talk: class activity. (Charts 2-1, 2-2, and 2-8)

Your teacher will ask questions. Answer with **this, that, these**, and **those**. Close your book for this activity.

Example: hand

TEACHER: What is this? (*The teacher indicates her or his hand.*)
STUDENT: That is your hand.

            OR

TEACHER: What is that? (*The teacher indicates a student's hand.*)
STUDENT: This is my hand.

1. nose	3. arm	5. legs	7. foot	9. fingers
2. eyes	4. elbow	6. knee	8. shoulder	10. ears

EXERCISE 37 ▸ Looking at grammar. (Chapters 1 and 2 Review)
Part I. Write *is* or *has*.

I have a college roommate, Tia. She ...

1. ___is___ from a small town.

2. _____ nice.

3. _____ a motorcycle.

4. _____ a smartphone.

5. _____ smart.

6. _____ homework every night.

7. _____ homesick.

8. _____ a large family.

9. _____ quiet.

10. _____ a boyfriend.

11. _____ a pet bird at home.

12. _____ serious.

Part II. Write *are* or *have*.

The two students in the room next to us ...

1. _____ a TV.

2. _____ two computers.

3. _____ noisy.

4. _____ messy.

5. _____ from a big city.

6. _____ busy.

7. _____ a lot of friends.

8. _____ friendly.

9. _____ parties on weekends.

10. _____ low grades.

EXERCISE 38 ▸ Listening. (Chapter 2 Review)
Part I. Listen to the conversations. Listen again and write the words you hear.

1. A: Where _____ your book?

   B: Hiroko _____ it.

   A: Where _____ your notebooks?

   B: Nasir and Angela _____ them.

2. A: _____ this?

   B: _____ a picture of my family.

   A: _____ this?

   B: _____ father.

   A: _____ they?

   B: _____ brother and sister.

3. A: What's _____?

   B: I don't know. Ask the teacher.

   A: What's _____?

   C: It's _____ for tonight.

4. A: _____ the teacher?

   B: _____ the library.

   A: _____ the students?

   B: _____ the cafeteria.

Part II. Work with a partner. Make a short conversation. Practice it and then say it in front of the class. You can look at your book before you speak. When you speak, look at your partner.

EXERCISE 39 ▸ Check your knowledge. (Chapter 2 Review)
Correct the mistakes.

 1. She ~~have~~ a headache.
    has

 2. What are that?

 3. Roberto he is a student in your class?

 4. I am have a backache.

 5. This is you dictionary. I my dictionary is at home.

 6. Where my keys?

 7. I am a sore throat.

 8. He's father is from Cuba.

 9. This books are expensive.

10. Where is the teachers?

11. My cousin she is a new student.

12. Where is my shoes?

13. Who that person in the office?

14. He laptop is on the desk.

15. A: Are you tired?

    B: Yes, I'm.

EXERCISE 40 ▶ Grammar and writing. (Chapter 2)

Part I. Complete the sentences in the composition by Carlos.

Do you know these words?
- *businessman*   - *engineer*
- *accountant*   - *married*

An Introduction

My name _____is_____ Carlos. __I am OR I'm__ from Mexico.
      1   2

_____ a student. _____ twenty years old.
     3   4

My family lives in Mexico City. _____ father _____
                                    5   6

a businessman. _____ fifty-one years old. _____ mother
                7   8

_____ an accountant. _____ forty-nine years old.
     9   10

I _____ two sisters. Their names _____ Rosa and Patricia. Rosa
   11   12

_____ a teacher. _____ twenty-eight years old. Patricia _____ a
   13   14   15

student. _____ eighteen years old. I also have a brother. My brother
          16

_____ an engineer. His name _____ Pedro. He is married. He
   17   18

_____ two children.
   19

I live in a dorm. _____ a tall building on Pine Street. My address
             20

_____ 3225 Pine St. I live with my roommate. _____ name is Bob.
   21   22

_____ from Chicago. _____ nineteen years old.
   23   24

I like my classes. They _____ interesting. I like _____ classmates.
                    25   26

_____ friendly.
   27

Part II. Write about yourself. Follow the format below. Use complete sentences.

Paragraph I: *Information about you*:
                        your name, hometown, age (optional)

Paragraph II: *Information about your parents (if they are alive)*:
                        their ages, jobs

Paragraph III: *Information about other people in your life*:
                        your siblings: names, ages, jobs OR
                        your husband/wife: name, job OR
                        your roommate/partner/friend: name, job

Paragraph IV: *Additional information*:
                        your home (apartment/dormitory/house): I live in a/an _____.
                        your classes
                        your classmates

Part III. Edit your writing. Work individually or change papers with a partner. Check (✓) for the following:

1. ☐ a capital letter at the beginning of each sentence
2. ☐ a capital letter at the beginning of a person's name
3. ☐ a period at the end of each sentence
4. ☐ paragraph indents
5. ☐ a verb in every sentence
6. ☐ correct use of *be* and *have*
7. ☐ correct spelling (use a dictionary or computer spell-check)

▪▪▪▪▪ For digital resources, go to MyEnglishLab on the Pearson English Portal. You can also go to the Pearson Practice English App for mobile practice.

CHAPTER 3

Using the Simple Present

PRETEST: What do I already know?

Check (✓) the correct sentences.

1. _____ Ivan he speak Russian. (Chart 3-1)

2. _____ Always my father cooks breakfast. (Chart 3-2)

3. _____ Len and Sam are often late for work. (Chart 3-3)

4. _____ Hans teachs math. (Chart 3-4)

5. _____ My grandma enjoyes sports. (Chart 3-5)

6. _____ Professor Lee have a big class. (Chart 3-6)

7. _____ I need leave early today. (Chart 3-7)

8. _____ It no snow in my country. (Chart 3-8)

9. _____ Do you do your homework every day? (Chart 3-9)

10. _____ Where do Emma and George live? (Chart 3-10)

11. _____ What time you usually eat dinner? (Chart 3-11)

EXERCISE 1 ▶ Warm-up. (Chart 3-1)

Read the paragraph. Write the verb forms for **take, post,** and **share**.

    I often take videos on vacation. I post them online. I share them with my family and friends. My brother Mario is a photographer. He takes pictures of famous places like Iguazu Falls. He posts them online. He shares them with followers on social media.

Iguazu Falls (Brazil and Argentina)

TAKE	*POST*	*SHARE*
1. I _____	3. I _____	5. I _____
2. Mario _____	4. He _____	6. He _____

3-1 Form and Basic Meaning of the Simple Present Tense

I *talk*. You *talk*. He *talks*. She *talks*. It *rains*. We *talk*. They *talk*.	The verb after 3rd person singular (***she, he, it***) has a final ***-s: talks***.

	SINGULAR	PLURAL
1st person:	I talk	we talk
2nd person:	you talk	you talk
3rd person:	she talks	they talk
	he talks	
	it rains	

(a) I *eat* breakfast *every morning*. (b) Olga *speaks* English *every day*. (c) We *sleep* *every night*. (d) They *go* to the beach *every weekend*.	The simple present tense expresses (talks about) habits. In (a): Eating breakfast is a habit, a usual activity. *Every morning* = Monday morning, Tuesday morning, Wednesday morning, Thursday morning, Friday morning, Saturday morning, and Sunday morning.

EXERCISE 2 ▶ Looking at grammar. (Chart 3-1)
Write ***speak*** or ***speaks***.

1. Noor _____ English.

2. I _____ German.

3. Suki _____ several languages.

4. Her husband _____ Thai and Vietnamese.

5. My friends and I _____ a little Chinese.

6. My friends _____ Arabic.

7. They _____ Arabic fluently.

8. You _____ Spanish well.

9. You and I _____ Spanish well.

10. We _____ it well.

11. You and Peter _____ it well.

EXERCISE 3 ▸ Let's talk: pairwork. (Chart 3-1)

Part I. Look at the list of habits. Check (✓) your habits every morning. Put them in order. Write them on the lines.

HABITS	MY HABITS EVERY MORNING

HABITS

_____ eat breakfast

_____ go to class

_____ put on my clothes

_____ drink a cup of coffee/tea

_____ shave

_____ put on my makeup

_____ take a shower/bath

_____ get up

_____ check social media

_____ watch TV

_____ make breakfast

__✓__ turn off the alarm clock

_____ check my email

_____ brush/comb my hair

_____ say good-bye to (someone)

_____ brush my teeth

_____ exercise

_____ wash my face

MY HABITS EVERY MORNING

1. _____ _I turn off the alarm clock._ _____

2. _____

3. _____

4. _____

5. _____

6. _____

7. _____

8. _____

9. _____

10. _____

11. _____

12. _____

13. _____

14. _____

15. _____

16. _____

17. _____

18. _____

Part II. Work with a partner. Talk about your morning habits. Close your book for this activity.

Examples: I shave.
I say good-bye to my kids.
Etc.

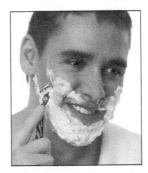

EXERCISE 4 ▸ Listening. (Chart 3-1)
Listen to the sentences. Choose the verbs you hear.

Beginning the Day

   1. (wake)   wakes

   2. wake   wakes

   3. get   gets

   4. go   goes

   5. do   does

   6. watch   watches

   7. take   takes

   8. take   takes

   9. take   takes

  10. talk   talks

EXERCISE 5 ▸ Looking at grammar. (Chart 3-1)
Choose the correct answer.

Daily Habits

   1. My mother and father (eat)/ eats breakfast at 7:00 every day.

   2. My mother drink / drinks tea with her breakfast.

   3. I take / takes a bath every morning.

   4. My sister take / takes a shower.

   5. I study / studies English with my friends.

   6. We walk / walks to school together every morning.

   7. Class begin / begins at 9:00 every day.

   8. It stop / stops at 12:00 for lunch.

   9. We eat / eats in the cafeteria.

  10. You bring / brings your lunch from home every day.

  11. My friends and I go / goes home at 3:00 every afternoon.

  12. You and Jamal go / goes to the library after school every day.

EXERCISE 6 ▸ Warm-up. (Chart 3-2)
Which sentence is true for you?

1. I always do my homework.
2. I usually do my homework.
3. I sometimes do my homework.
4. I never do my homework.

3-2 Frequency Adverbs

100%	*always*	(a)	Ivan *always* eats breakfast.
	usually	(b)	Maria *usually* eats breakfast.
	often	(c)	They *often* watch TV.
50%	*sometimes*	(d)	We *sometimes* watch TV.
	seldom	(e)	Sam *seldom* drinks milk.
	rarely	(f)	Rita *rarely* drinks milk.
0%	*never*	(g)	I *never* drink milk.

subject + { *always* / *usually* / *often* / *sometimes* / *seldom* / *rarely* / *never* } + verb

The words in this list are called "frequency adverbs." They usually come between the subject and the simple present verb.*

OTHER FREQUENCY EXPRESSIONS

(h) I drink tea {
once a day.
two times / twice a day.
three times a day.
four times a day.
etc.
}

We can express frequency by saying how many times something happens
 a day.
 a week.
 a month.
 a year.

(i) I see my grandparents *three times a week*.

(j) I see my aunt *once a month*.

(k) I see my cousin Sam *twice a year*.

(l) I see my doctor *every year*.

Every is singular. The noun that follows (e.g., *morning*) must be singular.

INCORRECT: every mornings

*Some frequency adverbs can also come at the beginning or at the end of a sentence. For example:
 Sometimes *I get up at seven.* *I* ***sometimes*** *get up at seven. I get up at seven* ***sometimes***.
 See also Chart 3-3 for the use of frequency adverbs with **be**.

EXERCISE 7 ▸ Looking at grammar. (Chart 3-2)

Complete each sentence with a word from the box.

always	often	never	rarely	sometimes	usually

SLEEP HABITS	SUN.	MON.	TUES.	WED.	THURS.	FRI.	SAT.
1. Ana _____ wakes up early.	🕐	🕐	🕐	🕐	🕐	🕐	🕐
2. Kenji _____ wakes up early.		🕐	🕐	🕐	🕐	🕐	🕐
3. Clara _____ wakes up early.			🕐	🕐	🕐	🕐	🕐
4. Igor _____ wakes up early.					🕐	🕐	🕐
5. Sonya _____ wakes up early.							🕐
6. Sami _____ wakes up early.							

EXERCISE 8 ▸ Looking at grammar. (Chart 3-2)

Write "S" over the subject and "V" over the verb in each sentence. Rewrite the sentences. Add the frequency adverbs.

Habits

1. always   S V
   I eat lunch with my friends.

   _____*I always eat lunch*_____ with my friends.

2. never   I eat carrots for breakfast.

   _____ for breakfast.

3. seldom   I watch TV during the day.

   _____ during the day.

4. sometimes   Luis has dessert after dinner.

   _____ after dinner.

5. usually   Kiri texts her friends at lunch.

   _____ at lunch.

6. often   We stream movies after dinner.

   _____ after dinner.

7. always   The students speak English in class.

_____ in class.

EXERCISE 9 ▸ Let's talk: class activity. (Chart 3-2)

Your teacher will ask you to talk about your morning, afternoon, and evening activities. Close your book for this activity.

Tell me something you …

1. always do in the morning.
2. never do in the morning.
3. sometimes do in the morning.
4. usually do in the afternoon.
5. seldom do in the afternoon.
6. never do in the afternoon.
7. often do in the evening.
8. sometimes do in the evening.
9. rarely do in the evening.
10. sometimes do on weekends.

EXERCISE 10 ▸ Warm-up. (Chart 3-3)

Agree or disagree with the statements. What do you notice about the placement of the verb and the frequency adverb?

1. It often rains here.   yes   no

2. It sometimes snows.   yes   no

3. It is usually cold here.   yes   no

4. It is sometimes very hot.   yes   no

It often rains in London.

It is usually hot in Malaysia.

It sometimes snows in Tokyo.

It is often cold in Alaska.

3-3 Position of Frequency Adverbs

SUBJECT + BE +	FREQUENCY ADVERB	Frequency adverbs usually come after the simple present tense forms of *be*: *am*, *is*, and *are*.
I am You are He is She is + { It is We are They are	*always* *usually* *often* *sometimes* } + late. *seldom* *rarely* *never*	

SUBJECT +	FREQUENCY ADVERB	+ OTHER SIMPLE PRESENT VERBS	Frequency adverbs usually come before all simple present verbs except *be*.
Tom +	{ *always* *usually* *often* *sometimes* } + *seldom* *rarely* *never*	*comes* late.	

🗨 **EXERCISE 11 ▸ Grammar and speaking.** (Chart 3-3)
Work with a partner. Add frequency adverbs to the sentences. Take turns.

Work Habits

1. always	Anita is on time for work.	→ *Anita is always on time for work.*
2. always	Anita comes to work on time.	→ *Anita always comes to work on time.*
3. often	Liliana is late for work.	
4. often	Liliana comes to work late.	
5. never	Ian leaves early.	
6. never	Ian is lazy.	
7. usually	Hiroshi goes home at 6:00.	
8. usually	Hiroshi is in the office on weekends.	
9. seldom	Willy takes a vacation.	
10. seldom	Willy is at home.	
11. sometimes	I eat breakfast at work.	
12. rarely	I have time for lunch.	

EXERCISE 12 ▶ Let's talk. (Chart 3-3)

Part I. Check (✓) the boxes to describe your evening activities.

MY EVENING	ALWAYS	USUALLY	OFTEN	SOMETIMES	RARELY	NEVER
1. eat dinner						
2. go to a movie						
3. go shopping						
4. check social media						
5. spend time with friends						
6. go to class						
7. be at home						
8. watch videos or DVDs						
9. study English						
10. send emails						
11. surf the internet						
12. drink coffee after 9:00 P.M.						
13. be in bed at 10:00						
14. go to bed late						

Part II. Exchange books with a partner. Your partner will tell the class two things about your evening.

Examples: Carlos is usually at home. He sometimes sends emails.

Olga sometimes drinks coffee after 9:00 P.M. She usually goes to bed late.

EXERCISE 13 ▶ Writing. (Chart 3-3)

Write about a usual day in your life, from morning to night. Use the following words to show the order of your activities: **then, next, at** (+ time), **after that, later**.

Example:

My Day

I usually get up at 7:30. I shave, brush my teeth, and take a shower. Then I put on my clothes. I go to the student cafeteria for breakfast. After that, I go back to my room. I sometimes check the news on my phone. At 8:15, I leave the dorm. I go to class. My class begins at 8:30. I'm in class from 8:30 to 11:30. After that, I eat lunch. I usually have a sandwich and a cup of tea for lunch …

EXERCISE 14 ▸ Warm-up: listening. (Chart 3-4)
Listen to the words. Decide if they have one syllable or two.

1. eat   one   two   4. pushes   one   two

2. eats   one   two   5. sleeps   one   two

3. push   one   two   6. fixes   one   two

3-4 Spelling and Pronunciation of Final -es

		SPELLING	PRONUNCIATION	
-sh (a) push →		*pushes*	push/əz/	ENDING OF VERB: **-sh, -ch, -ss, -x**
-ch (b) teach →		*teaches*	teach/əz/	SPELLING: add **-es**
-ss (c) kiss →		*kisses*	kiss/əz/	PRONUNCIATION: /əz/
-x (d) fix →		*fixes*	fix/əz/	The **-es** ending forms a new syllable.

EXERCISE 15 ▸ Looking at grammar. (Chart 3-4)
Write the correct form of the verbs. Remember to add **-es** for the third person singular forms if necessary.

Chores

1. wash   Eric usually _____ the dishes.

2. vacuum   Mika _____ the carpets once a week.

3. fix*   Pedro _____ the school lunches for his children.

4. watch**   Silvia sometimes _____ her brother and sister on weekends.

5. brush   Arianna often _____ her dog.

6. sweep   Robert _____ the kitchen floor after dinner.

7. finish   Carlita _____ her chores in the evening.

8. wax   Jamal _____ his car every month.

9. change   My sister _____ her sheets every Monday.

10. pay   Mr. Rovero _____ the bills twice a month.

11. catch   The family cat _____ mice.

---

*fix = make (with food)

**watch = take care of

EXERCISE 16 ▸ Listening. (Chart 3-4)

Listen to the sentences and choose the verbs you hear.

1. teach   (teaches)
2. teach   teaches
3. fix   fixes
4. fix   fixes
5. watch   watches

6. watch   watches
7. brush   brushes
8. brush   brushes
9. wash   washes
10. wash   washes

EXERCISE 17 ▸ Looking at grammar. (Charts 3-1 and 3-4)

Complete the sentences. Use the words in the box and add **-s** or **-es**. Practice reading the information about Laura aloud. Work with a partner or in small groups.

brush	✓ leave	sit	wash
cook	read	stream	
fall	ride	take	

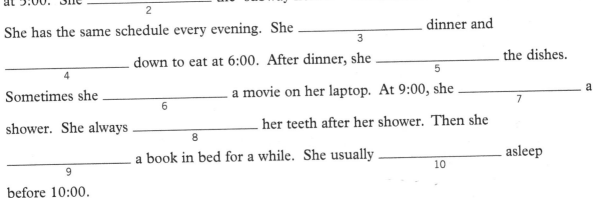

Laura's Evening

Laura _____*leaves*_____ her office every night
         1

at 5:00. She _____ the subway home.
              2

She has the same schedule every evening. She _____ dinner and
                                            3

_____ down to eat at 6:00. After dinner, she _____ the dishes.
      4   5

Sometimes she _____ a movie on her laptop. At 9:00, she _____ a
                 6   7

shower. She always _____ her teeth after her shower. Then she
                        8

_____ a book in bed for a while. She usually _____ asleep
      9   10

before 10:00.

EXERCISE 18 ▸ Warm-up. (Chart 3-5)

What ending does each verb have? Write the verbs from the box in the correct column.

buy	fly	play	study

CONSONANT + -**y**   VOWEL + -**y**

_____   _____

_____   _____

3-5 Adding Final -s/-es to Words That End in -y

(a) *cry*	→	*cries*	ENDING OF VERB:	consonant + **-y**
try	→	*tries*	SPELLING:	change **y** to **i**, add **-es**
(b) **pay**	→	**pays**	ENDING OF VERB:	vowel + **-y**
enjoy	→	*enjoys*	SPELLING:	add **-s**

EXERCISE 19 ▸ Looking at grammar. (Chart 3-5)
Write the correct form of each verb.

1. I try.   He _____*tries*_____.

2. We study.   She _____.

3. They say.   It _____.

4. I enjoy video games.   Ann _____ video games.

5. You worry a lot.   My mother _____ a lot.

6. We pay bills.   Gina _____ bills.

7. You stay awake.   Paul _____ awake.

8. We fly.   A bird _____.

9. Students buy books.   My brother _____ books.

10. I play music. ♪♪   My friend _____ music.

EXERCISE 20 ▸ Looking at grammar. (Chart 3-5)
Complete each sentence. Use the simple present form of a verb in the box.

buy	cry	pay	stay
carry	employ	✓ play	study

Campus Friends

1. Monique likes sports. She _____*plays*_____ tennis and soccer for her school.

2. Professor Li travels around the country in the summer. He _____ with university friends.

3. The college library has student workers. It _____ some of my friends.

4. Elizabeth is always tired in class. Her new baby _____ during the night.

5. The meals at the school cafeteria are cheap. Chen _____ lunch there every day.

6. Laila _____ her books in a backpack.

7. I pay my tuition with a check. My girlfriend _____ with a credit card.

8. Zara is a medical student. She _____ every night and on weekends.

EXERCISE 21 ▸ Let's talk: pairwork. (Charts 3-1 → 3-5)
Work with a partner. Make sentences with words from each column in the box. Make some sentences singular and some sentences plural. Add **-s** to the singular verbs. Some words may be used more than one time.

Jobs

Examples: An auto mechanic fixes cars. OR An auto mechanic takes care of cars.
Auto mechanics fix cars. OR Auto mechanics take care of cars.

	auto mechanic	build	teeth
	cashier	clean	food
	construction worker	cook	people
	cook	fix	in an office
(A)	dentist	help	rooms
(An)	doctor	serve	in a restaurant
	hotel housekeeper	take	cars
	janitor	take care of	money from store customers
	office assistant	vacuum	buildings
	restaurant server	work	sick people

Read the information about Milos. Complete the chart.

Milos is a college student. He **has** a part-time job. He **does** the breakfast dishes at his dorm. Then he **goes** to class.

HAVE	DO	GO
I **have**	I **do**	I **go**
you **have**	you **do**	you **go**
he _____	he _____	he _____
she _____	she _____	she _____
it _____	it _____	it _____
we **have**	we **do**	we **go**
they **have**	they **do**	they **go**

3-6 Irregular Singular Verbs: *Has, Does, Goes*

(a) I *have* a book. (b) He *has* a book.	she he } + *has* /hæz/ it	**Have**, **do**, and **go** have irregular forms for 3rd person singular: have → has do → does go → goes	
(c) I *do* my work. (d) She *does* her work.	she he } + *does* /dəz/ it	Note that final **-s** is pronounced /z/ in these verbs.	
(e) They *go* to school. (f) She *goes* to school.	she he } + *goes* /gowz/ it		

EXERCISE 23 ▸ Looking at grammar. (Chart 3-6)
Write the correct form of the verbs.

At School

1. do   Pierre always _____*does*_____ his homework.

2. do   We always _____*do*_____ our homework.

3. have   Yoko and Hamid _____ a lot of homework.

4. have   Mrs. Chang _____ a test today.

5. go   Andy _____ to the cafeteria every day for coffee.

6. go   Roberto and his wife _____ to the library during lunch.

7. do   Sara seldom _____ her homework.

8. do   We _____ some homework in class every day.

EXERCISE 24 ▸ **Listening and grammar.** (Chart 3-6)
Listen to the information about Marco. Listen again and write *is*, *has*, *does*, or *goes*.

An Unusual Schedule

Marco _____*is*_____ a student. He _____*has*_____
                 1   2

an unusual schedule. All of his classes are at night. His

first class _____ at 6:00 P.M. every day. He takes
                 3

a break from 7:30 to 8:00. Then he _____ classes from 8:00 to 10:00.
                                      4

He _____ home at 10:00. He _____ dinner and watches TV. Then
       5   6

he _____ his homework from midnight to 3:00 or 4:00 in the morning.
     7

Marco _____ a new computer. He finishes his homework, and he goes on the
               8

internet. He often stays at his computer until morning. Then he _____ some
                                           9

exercises. He _____ breakfast and _____ to bed. He sleeps all day.
               10   11

Marco likes his schedule. His friends think it _____ strange.
                                      12

EXERCISE 25 ▸ **Looking at grammar.** (Charts 3-1 and 3-6)
Choose the correct verb.

Work

1. Ivan   works / work   part-time.

2. Henry and Jason   works / work   full-time.

3. Mr. and Ms. Jolson   goes / go   to work early.

4. Mrs. Jolson   goes / go   home late.

5. The workers   has / have   two breaks in the morning.

6. The manager has / have one break.

7. Nadia arrives / arrive early every morning.

8. The manager always stays / stay late.

EXERCISE 26 ▸ Let's talk: game. (Charts 3-1 → 3-6)
Part I. Your teacher will give you a verb from the list below. Make a sentence with that verb. Walk around the room. Say your sentence to other students. Listen to other students say their sentences.

1. eat
2. go
3. drink
4. brush
5. have
6. study
7. get up
8. watch

9. speak
10. do
11. listen to
12. wash
13. put on
14. carry
15. miss

Part II. Work in teams of 5–8 students. Write as many sentences as you can remember. Use the speaker's name. Each team has one paper. The team with the most correct sentences wins.

Example: brush
STUDENT: (*says*) I brush my teeth every day.
TEAMS: (*write*) *(Student) brushes her teeth every day.*

EXERCISE 27 ▸ Let's talk: pairwork. (Charts 3-1 → 3-6)
Use frequency adverbs like *sometimes, rarely, etc.*, to make sentences.

Part I. Nadia, Levi, and Peter do many things in the evening. How often do they do the things in the chart? Pay attention to final *-s*. Work with a partner.

Example: Nadia rarely/seldom does homework.

IN THE EVENING	NADIA	LEVI	PETER
DO HOMEWORK	once a week	6 days a week	every day
SURF THE INTERNET	every day	once a week	0 days
WATCH TV	3–4 days a week	3–4 days a week	3–4 days a week
READ FOR FUN	5 days a week	5 days a week	5 days a week
GO TO BED EARLY	once a week	5–6 nights a week	6–7 nights a week

Part II. For homework, write ten sentences about the activities of Nadia, Levi, and Peter.

Jump-start your English

Expressions with *Do* and *Make*

Part I. Look at the expressions with **do** and **make**.

COMMON EXPRESSIONS WITH **DO**	COMMON EXPRESSIONS WITH **MAKE**
do homework	make breakfast/lunch/dinner
do the housework	make coffee/tea
do the dishes	make a sandwich/salad
do the laundry	make a reservation (restaurant, plane, hotel)
do the shopping	make plans
do a good/bad job	make a mistake
	make the bed

Part II. Work with a partner. Make sentences with words from each column in the box. You can also add frequency words (**often**, **sometimes**, etc.).

I You He She We They	do does make makes	dinner. the shopping. tea. a reservation. a good job. the dishes. homework. the laundry. plans. the bed. housework. a sandwich. a mistake.

EXERCISE 28 ▸ Looking at grammar. (Charts 3-1 → 3-6)
Add **-s**, **-es**, or **Ø** to the verbs.

Abdul and Pablo

My friend Abdul live_s___ in an apartment near school. He walk____ to school almost
              1   2

every day. Sometimes he catch____ a bus, especially if it's cold and rainy outside. Abdul
                                3

share____ the apartment with Pablo. Pablo come____ from Venezuela. Abdul and Pablo
       4   5

go____ to the same school. They take____ English classes. Abdul speak____ Arabic as his
   6   7   8

first language, and Pablo speak_____ Spanish. They

communicate_____ in English. Sometimes Abdul teach_____

Pablo to speak a little Arabic, and Pablo give_____ Abdul Spanish

lessons. They laugh_____ a lot during the Arabic and Spanish

lessons. Abdul enjoy_____ his roommate, but he miss_____ his

family back home.

(9, 10, 11, 12, 13, 14, 15 numbered blanks)

🗨 **EXERCISE 29 ▸ Speaking and writing: pairwork. (Charts 3-1 → 3-6)**
Work with a partner. Tell your partner 5–10 things you do every morning. Use the list you made in Exercise 3. Your partner will also give you information about his/her morning. Take notes. Then write a paragraph about your partner's morning activities. Pay special attention to the use of final **-s/-es**. Ask your partner to read your paragraph and to check your use of final **-s/-es**.

EXERCISE 30 ▸ Warm-up. (Chart 3-7)
Which sentences are true for you?

1. I like to speak English.   yes   no

2. I need to learn English.   yes   no

3. I want to speak English fluently.   yes   no

3-7	*Like To, Want To, Need To, Would Like*

VERB + INFINITIVE	***Like**, **want**, and **need** can be followed by an infinitive.*
(a) I *like* *to travel* by train.	infinitive = **to** + *the base form of the verb.**
(b) I *want* *to travel* by high-speed train.	**Need to** is stronger than **want to**.
(c) I *need* *to travel* for my job. I have no choice.	**Need to** = necessary, important.
(d) I *would like* to travel by high-speed train.	**Would like**** is a more polite way to say **want**.
(e) He *would like* to travel by high-speed train.	Note in (e): There is no final **-s** on **would** or **like**.
(f) *He'd like* to travel by high-speed train.	Contractions may be used, as in (f) and (g):
(g) *I'd like* to travel by high-speed train.	*pronoun* + **'d** + **like**.

*The base form of a verb = a verb without *-s, -ed,* or *-ing*. Examples of the base form of a verb: *come, help, answer, write*. Examples of infinitives: *to come, to help, to answer, to write*. The base form is also called the simple form of a verb.

See Chart 7-9, p. 223, for more information about ***would like*.

EXERCISE 31 ▸ Looking at grammar. (Chart 3-7)

Write sentences. Pay attention to the final **-s** ending on singular verbs.

Likes, Wants, and Needs

1. Maya \ need \ study _____ *Maya needs to study.* _____

2. We \ want \ go home _____

3. Bill and I \ like \ eat sweets _____

4. You \ need \ speak more quietly _____

5. She \ like \ talk on the phone _____

6. Sonya \ would like \ have pizza for lunch _____

7. Elian \ need \ save money _____

8. He \ want \ buy a car _____

9. Mia \ would like \ order dessert _____

10. Dr. Devi and Dr. Karo \ want \ retire next year _____

EXERCISE 32 ▸ Reading and grammar. (Charts 3-1 → 3-7)

Part I. Read about Roberto. Look at new vocabulary with your teacher first.

A Wonderful Cook

    Roberto is a wonderful cook. He often tries new recipes. He likes to cook for friends. He frequently invites my girlfriend and me to dinner. We sit in the kitchen. He usually has three or four pots on the stove. He makes a big mess! We like to watch him. He wants to tell us about each recipe. His dinners are delicious. After dinner, he needs to clean the kitchen. We want to help him. We would like him to invite us back soon.

Do you know these words?
- recipe
- invite
- pot
- a mess
- delicious

Part II. Complete each sentence with a word in the box.

help	invite	is	like	likes to	wash

1. Roberto _____ a great cook.

2. He _____ try new recipes.

3. He likes to _____ friends to dinner.

4. After dinner, he needs to _____ the pots. His friends

   _____ him.

5. His friends _____ his food.

EXERCISE 33 ▸ Game. (Chart 3-7)

Work in teams. What do you know about mosquitoes? Choose the correct answer. The team with the most correct answers wins.*

Mosquitoes

1. They like to look for food during the day.	yes	no
2. They like to look for food at night.	yes	no
3. They need to lay their eggs in water.	yes	no
4. They like to travel.	yes	no
5. They need to sleep in water.	yes	no
6. Male mosquitoes need to bite.	yes	no
7. Female mosquitoes need to bite.	yes	no

EXERCISE 34 ▸ Warm-up. (Chart 3-8)

Which sentences are true for you?

1. a. I like vegetables.
   b. I don't like vegetables.

2. a. I eat meat.
   b. I don't eat meat.

3. a. I drink tea.
   b. I don't drink tea.

---

*See *Let's Talk: Answers,* p. 280.

3-8 Simple Present Tense: Negative

					SINGULAR	PLURAL
(a)	I	*do not*	drink coffee.	1st person:	I do not	we do not
(b)	You	*do not*	drink coffee.	2nd person:	you do not	you do not
(c)	He	*does not*	drink coffee.	3rd person:	she does not	they do not
(d)	She	*does not*	drink coffee.		he does not	
(e)	It	*does not*	drink coffee.		it does not	
(f)	We	*do not*	drink coffee.			
(g)	They	*do not*	drink coffee.			

Do and *does* are called "helping verbs."

Note that in the 3rd person singular, there is no *-s* on the main verb, *drink*. The final *-s* is part of the helping verb, *does*.
INCORRECT: *She does not drinks coffee.*

(h) I *am not* thirsty.	When the main verb is a form of *be*, *do* is NOT used.
(i) He *is not* thirsty.	See Chart 1-6, p. 13, for negative forms with *be*.
(j) We *are not* thirsty.	

(k) I *don't* drink coffee.	CONTRACTIONS: **do not = don't**
(l) He *doesn't* drink coffee.	**does not = doesn't**

People usually use contractions when they speak.
People often use contractions when they write.

EXERCISE 35 ▶ Looking at grammar. (Chart 3-8)
Choose the correct verb.

1. I   does not / (do not)   understand.

2. She   does not / do not   speak English.

3. He   does not / do not   need help.

4. You   does not / do not   have time.

5. We   does not / do not   do homework.

6. They   does not / do not   work hard.

EXERCISE 36 ▶ Looking at grammar. (Charts 3-6 and 3-8)
Choose the correct verb: **has** or **have**. Then write **doesn't have** or **don't have** to make negative sentences.

1. I has / (have) a big family.   I ___*don't have*___ a small family.

2. My parents has / have sons.   They _____ daughters.

3. My sister has / have an apartment.   She _____ a house.

4. It has / have stairs.   It _____ an elevator.

5. My brother has / have a quiet apartment.   He _____ a noisy apartment.

6. We has / have a dog.   We _____ a cat.

7. You has / have a cat.   You _____ a dog.

EXERCISE 37 ▸ Let's talk: pairwork. (Charts 3-1 and 3-8)
Work with a partner. Make two sentences about each picture.

Examples:

   (Isabel \ take)
shower
baths

   (Omar \ have)
a cat
a dog

PARTNER A: Isabel takes showers. She doesn't take baths.
PARTNER B: Omar doesn't have a cat. He has a dog.

   1. (I \ drink)
tea
coffee

   2. (Rob and Ed \ live)
an apartment
a house

   3. (Julia \ drive)
a car
a truck

 4. (I \ play)
soccer
tennis

 5. (Ms. Ortiz \ teach)
Spanish
English

 6. (We \ use)
typewriters
computers

 7. (Nina \ have)
an umbrella
a raincoat

 8. (Marco \ study)
chemistry
physics

EXERCISE 38 ▶ Game. (Chart 3-8)

Sit in a circle. Use any of the verbs in the box. Make sentences with **not**.

| have | like | need | play | read | speak |

Example: like

STUDENT A: I don't like bananas.
STUDENT B: (*Student A*) doesn't like bananas. I don't have a dog.
STUDENT C: (*Student A*) doesn't like bananas. (*Student B*) doesn't have a dog. I don't
play baseball.

Continue around the circle. Each time, repeat the information of your classmates before you say your sentence. If you have trouble, your classmates can help you. Your teacher will be the last one to speak.

EXERCISE 39 ▸ Looking at grammar. (Chart 3-8)

Complete the sentences with the verbs in the box. Make all of the sentences negative with **does not** or **do not**. You can use contractions (**doesn't/don't**). Some verbs may be used more than one time.

do	eat	make	smoke	wear
drink	✓ go	shave	speak	

1. Ricardo _____*doesn't go*_____ to school every day.

2. My roommates are from Japan. They _____ Spanish.

3. Roberto has a beard. He _____ in the morning.

4. We _____ to class on Sunday.

5. Camilla is healthy. She _____ cigarettes.

6. Nadia and Anton always have lunch at home. They _____ in the cafeteria.

7. Sometimes I _____ my homework after school. I watch TV instead.

8. My sister likes tea. She _____ coffee.

9. Hamid is a careful writer. He _____ spelling mistakes in his work.

10. Sometimes Julianna _____ her shoes outside. She likes to go barefoot.

EXERCISE 40 ▸ Looking at grammar. (Charts 1-6, 1-7, and 3-8)

Write the correct negative forms of the verbs **be** and **eat**.

SIMPLE PRESENT: *BE*

1. I _____*am not*_____ hungry.
2. You _____ hungry.
3. She _____ hungry.
4. We _____ hungry.
5. It _____ hungry.
6. They _____ hungry.
7. He _____ hungry.
8. Raj _____ hungry.
9. You and I _____ hungry.

SIMPLE PRESENT: *EAT*

1. I _____*do not eat*_____ meat.
2. You _____ meat.
3. She _____ meat.
4. We _____ meat.
5. It _____ meat.
6. They _____ meat.
7. He _____ meat.
8. Raj _____ meat.
9. You and I _____ meat.

EXERCISE 41 ▶ Looking at grammar. (Charts 1-6, 1-9, and 3-8)
Choose the correct verb.

At Home

1. Joseph   (is not)/ does not   awake.

2. He   is not / does not   wake up early.

3. His parents   are not / do not   sleep a long time.

4. They   are not / do not   get up late.

5. Maya and Ken   are not / do not   do the dishes.

6. They   are not / do not   helpful.

7. The house key   is not / does not   here.

8. It   is not / does not   in the kitchen.

9. The refrigerator   is not / does not   work.

10. The refrigerator   is not / does not   cold.

EXERCISE 42 ▶ Let's talk. (Charts 1-6, 1-9, and 3-8)
Part I. Work in small groups or as a class. Make true sentences for each pair.

Example: a. Bananas \ be pink
            b. Bananas \ be yellow
STUDENT A: Bananas aren't pink.
STUDENT B: Bananas are yellow.

Example: a. We \ eat soup with spoons
            b. We \ eat soup with knives
STUDENT C: We eat soup with spoons.
STUDENT D: We don't eat soup with knives.

1. a. A restaurant \ sell shoes
   b. A restaurant \ serve food

2. a. People★ \ wear clothes
   b. Birds \ wear clothes

3. a. A child \ need love, food, and care
   b. A child \ need a driver's license

4. a. Potato chips \ be healthy
   b. Vegetables \ be healthy

5. a. Fire \ be hot
   b. Ice \ be warm

6. a. Mountains \ have snow
   b. Hot deserts \ have snow

★*People* is a plural noun. It takes a plural verb.

Part II. Make true sentences.

7. Doctors in my country \ be expensive
8. A bus \ carry people from one place to another
9. It \ be cold today
10. English \ be an easy language to learn
11. People in this city \ be friendly
12. It \ rain a lot in this city

EXERCISE 43 ▶ Warm-up. (Chart 3-9)

What do you notice about the questions with *have* and *need*?

1. Are you OK?   Do you have a stomachache?
2. Are you sick?   Do you need a doctor?

3-9 Simple Present Tense: *Yes/No Questions*

DO/DOES + SUBJECT + MAIN VERB	QUESTION FORMS, SIMPLE PRESENT
(a) *Do* *I* *work?* (b) *Do* *you* *work?* (c) *Does* *he* *work?* (d) *Does* *she* *work?* (e) *Does* *it* *work?* (f) *Do* *we* *work?* (g) *Do* *they* *work?*	*Do I* *Do you* *Does he* *Does she* } + *main verb* (base form) *Does it* *Do we* *Do they*

	Note in (c), (d), and (e): The main verb in the question does not have a final *-s*. The final *-s* is part of *does*. INCORRECT: *Does she works?*

(h) *Am I* late? (i) *Are you* ready? (j) *Is he* a teacher? (k) *Are we* early? (l) *Are they* at home? (m) *Are you* a student? INCORRECT: *Do you be a student?*	When the main verb is a form of *be, do* is NOT used. See Chart 2-3, p. 33, for question forms with *be*.

QUESTION	SHORT ANSWER	
(n) *Do* you *like* fish? →	Yes, I *do.* No, I *don't.*	*Do, don't, does,* and *doesn't* are used in the short answers to *yes/no* questions in the simple present.
(o) *Does* Liam *like* fish? →	Yes, he *does.* No, he *doesn't.*	

(p) Brad *does* his homework every day. (q) *Does* Brad *do* his homework every day?	Note that *do* can also be a main verb, as in (p) and (q).

EXERCISE 44 ▶ Looking at grammar. (Chart 3-9)

Make *yes/no* questions. Choose the correct answer.

Common Questions

1. A: speak \ you \ English _____Do you speak English?_____
   B: (a.) Yes, I do.
      b. Yes, I speak.

2. A: want \ you \ help _____
   B: a. Yes, I do.
      b. Yes, I want.

3. A: have \ the teacher \ time _____
   B: a. No, she doesn't.
      b. No, she doesn't have.

4. A: need \ you \ money _____
   B: a. Yes, I do.
      b. Yes, I need.

5. A: like \ they \ it here _____
   B: a. No, they don't.
      b. No, they don't like.

6. A: have \ the café \ Wi-Fi _____
   B: a. No, it doesn't.
      b. No, it doesn't have.

EXERCISE 45 ▶ Speaking and grammar: pairwork. (Chart 3-9)

Part I. Work with a partner. Take turns making questions and giving short answers. Use the names of your classmates in the questions. NOTE: Part I is speaking practice. Do not write the answers until **Part II**.

Example:
PARTNER A: _____Is Ali in class today?_____
PARTNER B: _____Yes, he is._____ (He is in class today.)

Example:
PARTNER B: _____Does Akiko speak Spanish?_____
PARTNER A: _____No, she doesn't._____ (She doesn't speak Spanish.)

1. PARTNER A: _____
   PARTNER B: _____ (He speaks English in class every day.)

2. PARTNER B: _____
   PARTNER A: _____ (She comes to class every day.)

3. PARTNER A: _____

   PARTNER B: _____ (They're in class today.)

4. PARTNER B: _____

   PARTNER A: _____ (He wears jeans every day.)

5. PARTNER A: _____

   PARTNER B: _____ (They aren't from Australia.)

6. PARTNER B: _____

   PARTNER A: _____ (They don't have their laptops on their desks.)

7. PARTNER A: _____

   PARTNER B: _____ (They speak English.)

Part II. Now write the questions and answers in your book.

EXERCISE 46 ▸ Vocabulary and speaking. (Chart 3-9)
Part I. Check (✓) the activities you do at least once a week.

1. _____ have a nap

2. _____ take a break

3. _____ take a shower

4. _____ ride a bus

5. _____ take a bus/train/taxi

6. _____ make breakfast

7. _____ fix lunch

8. _____ cook dinner

9. _____ have a snack

10. _____ make your bed

11. _____ do homework

12. _____ wash the dishes

13. _____ fold the laundry

Part II. Walk around the room. Ask questions with the phrases in **Part I.** For each question, find someone who can answer *yes*.

Example:

To STUDENT A: Do you have a nap in the afternoon?
   STUDENT A: No.
To STUDENT B: Do you have a nap in the afternoon?
   STUDENT B: Yes.
To STUDENT C: Do you make your bed every day?
   STUDENT C: Yes.

EXERCISE 47 ▸ Looking at grammar. (Chart 3-9)
Write *do*, *does*, or *is*.

Weather Questions

1. _____ it hot outside?

2. _____ it raining?

3. _____ it rain often?

4. _____ it warm today?

5. _____ it snowing?

6. _____ it snow in the winter?

7. _____ you like the snow?

8. _____ it nice outside?

EXERCISE 48 ▸ Looking at grammar. (Charts 3-1, 3-8, and 3-9)
Write the correct form of the verb. Use the full form or contractions for the negative.

Part I. Statement Forms

LIVE	*BE*
1. I _____*live*_____ here.	I _____*am*_____ here.
2. They _____ here.	They _____ here.
3. He _____ here.	He _____ here.
4. You _____ here.	You _____ here.
5. She _____ here.	She _____ here.
6. We _____ here.	We _____ here.

Part II. Negative Forms

LIVE	*BE*
7. They __*do not / don't live*__ here.	They __*are not / aren't*__ here.
8. I _____ here.	I _____ here.
9. She _____ here.	She _____ here.
10. You _____ here.	You _____ here.
11. He _____ here.	He _____ here.
12. We _____ here.	We _____ here.

Part III. Question Forms

	LIVE			BE
13.	_Do_ you _live_ here?		_Are_ you here?
14.	_____ they _____ here?		_____ they here?
15.	_____ he _____ here?		_____ he here?
16.	_____ we _____ here?		_____ we here?
17.	_____ she _____ here?		_____ she here?

EXERCISE 49 ▸ Game: trivia. (Chart 3-9)
Work in teams. Complete the sentences with *is, are, do,* or *does*. Answer the questions with *yes* or *no*. The team with the most correct answers wins.

1. ___Does___ February always have 28 days?   Yes.   (No.)

2. _____ September and April have 31 days?   Yes.   No.

3. _____ Australia hot in December?   Yes.   No.

4. _____ Canada have seven time zones?   Yes.   No.

5. _____ Canada big?   Yes.   No.

6. _____ Russia and Canada big?   Yes.   No.

7. _____ the moon hot?   Yes.   No.

8. _____ the sun go around the planets?   Yes.   No.

9. _____ the sun a planet ?   Yes.   No.

EXERCISE 50 ▸ Warm-up. (Chart 3-10)
Match the questions with the correct answers.

1. Where is the lost-and-found? _____   a. The lost-and-found.

2. Is the lost-and-found office in this building? _____   b. Yes, it is.

3. What is in this building? _____   c. Down the hall.

3-10 Simple Present Tense: Yes/No Questions and Information Questions with Where and What

(WHERE/ WHAT)	+ DO/ DOES	+ SUBJECT	+ MAIN VERB		SHORT ANSWER	
(a)	Do	they	live	in Miami? →	Yes, they do. No, they don't.	(a) = a yes/no question (b) = an information question
(b) Where	do	they	live?	→	In Miami.	**Where** asks for information about a place.
(c)	Does	Gina	live	in Rome? →	Yes, she does. No, she doesn't.	The form of yes/no questions and information questions is the same:
(d) Where	does	Gina	live?	→	In Rome.	**Do/Does** + subject + main verb
(e)	Do	they	need	help? →	Yes, they do. No, they don't.	**What** asks for information about a thing.
(f) What	do	they	need?	→	Help.	
(g)	Does	Lee	need	help? →	Yes, he does. No, he doesn't.	
(h) What	does	Lee	need?	→	Help.	

EXERCISE 51 ▶ Let's talk: pairwork. (Chart 3-10)

Work with a partner. Ask and answer questions with **where**.

Examples:

eat breakfast
PARTNER A: Where do you eat breakfast?
PARTNER B: At home.

keep your student ID
PARTNER B: Where do you keep your student ID?
PARTNER A: In my wallet.

Partner A	Partner B
1. live	1. buy groceries
2. eat lunch every day	2. go on weekends
3. go after class	3. sit during class
4. study at night	4. eat dinner
5. go to school	5. do your homework
6. buy school supplies	6. see your friends

EXERCISE 52 ▸ Looking at grammar. (Chart 3-10)
Make questions.

1. A: _____*Does Hana eat lunch in the cafeteria every day?*_____
   B: Yes, she does. (Hana eats lunch in the cafeteria every day.)

2. A: _____*Where does Hana eat lunch every day?*_____
   B: In the cafeteria. (Hana eats lunch in the cafeteria every day.)

3. A: _____
   B: Rice. (She eats rice for lunch every day.)

4. A: _____
   B: At the post office. (Alfonso works at the post office.)

5. A: _____
   B: Yes, he does. (Alfonso works at the post office.)

6. A: _____
   B: Yes, I do. (I live in an apartment.)

7. A: _____
   B: In an apartment. (I live in an apartment.)

8. A: _____
   B: Popcorn. (Hector and Eliza like popcorn for a snack.)

9. A: _____
   B: At the University of Toronto. (Ming goes to school at the University of Toronto.)

10. A: _____
    B: Biology. (Her major is biology.)

11. A: _____
    B: To class. (I go to class every morning.)

12. A: _____
    B: In class. (The students are in class right now.)

EXERCISE 53 ▸ Reading. (Chart 3-10)
Read the paragraph and answer the questions, orally or in writing.

Opposite Roommates

    I have two roommates, Fernando and Matt.
Fernando is always neat and clean. He washes his clothes
once or twice a week. Matt is the opposite of Fernando.
For example, Matt doesn't change the sheets on his
bed. He keeps the same sheets week after week. He
rarely washes his clothes. He wears the same dirty jeans
every day. His clothes smell bad, but he doesn't care.

Do you know these words?
- *opposite*
- *neat*
- *change the sheets*
- *hang up*
- *put everything away*

Fernando's side of the room is always neat. He makes his bed, hangs up his clothes, and puts everything away. Matt's side of the room is always a mess. He doesn't make his bed. He doesn't hang up his clothes. He doesn't put things away. What habits do you think I prefer?

1. What are some of Fernando's habits?
2. What are some of Matt's habits?
3. Are you more similar to Fernando or Matt?

EXERCISE 54 ▶ Let's talk: class activity. (Chart 3-10)
Ask your teacher questions to get more information about each person's life.* Decide who has the best life and why.

Example:

STUDENT A: Where does Antonio live?
   TEACHER: On a boat.
STUDENT B: What does Lena do?
   TEACHER: She teaches skiing.
STUDENT C: Where does Kane work?
   TEACHER: He works at a jewelry store.

Continue asking questions until your chart is complete.

	Where does she/he live?	What does he/she do?	Where does she/he work?	What pets does he/she have?
ANTONIO	on a boat			
LENA		teaches skiing		
KANE			at a jewelry store	
LISA				
JACK				

*Teacher: See *Let's Talk: Answers*, p. 280.

Jump-start your English

Common Questions at a Café

 Part I. Listen to the conversations.

1. A: Are you ready to order?
   B: Yes, we're ready.

2. A: Do you want coffee or tea?
   B: I'd like coffee, please.
   A: Cream and sugar?
   B: No, thank you. Black, please.

3. A: Do you want something else?
   B: No, thanks. I'm full.

4. A: Do you take credit cards?
   B: Yes, we do.

5. A: Where is the restroom?
   B: It's down the hall on your left.

 Part II. Work with a partner. Create a short conversation at a café. Perform it for the class.

EXERCISE 55 ▸ Warm-up. (Chart 3-11)
Answer the questions. Write the time.

1. What time does your first class of the day begin? _____

2. When does your last class of the day end? _____

3-11	Simple Present Tense: Asking Information Questions with *When* and *What Time*					

	QUESTION* WORD	+ DO/ DOES	+ SUBJECT	+ MAIN VERB		SHORT ANSWER	*When* and *what time* ask for information about time.
(a)	*When*	do	you	go	to class? →	*At nine o'clock.*	
(b)	*What time*	do	you	go	to class? →	*At nine o'clock.*	
(c)	*When*	does	Anna	eat	dinner? →	*At six P.M.*	
(d)	*What time*	does	Anna	eat	dinner? →	*At six P.M.*	
(e)	*What time* do you *usually* go to class?					The frequency adverb *usually* comes immediately after the subject in a question: *Question word* + *does/do* + *subject* + *usually* + *main verb*	

* *Where, when, what, what time, who,* and *why* are examples of question words.

EXERCISE 56 ▶ Looking at grammar. (Chart 3-11)

Make questions.

 1. A: ___*When/What time do you usually eat lunch?*___
     B: At 1:00. (I eat usually lunch at 1:00.)

 2. A: _____
     B: At 6:00. (I get up at 6:00.)

3. A: _____
   B: At 6:00. (Maria usually gets up at 6:00.)

 4. A: _____
     B: At 6:15. (The movie starts at 6:15.)

5. A: _____
   B: At a quarter after six. (Classes end at a quarter after six.)

 6. A: _____
     B: At 8:30. (They usually eat breakfast at 8:30.)

7. A: _____
   B: Around 10:00. (I usually go to bed around 10:00.)

 8. A: _____
     B: Between 10:00 and 10:30. (The restaurant closes between 10:00 and 10:30.)

Jump-start your English

Saying the Time

 Part I. Listen to the questions and answers.

What time is it?

6:00   It's six o'clock.★
       It's six.

6:05   It's six-oh-five.
       It's five after six.

6:10   It's six-ten.
       It's ten after six.

6:50   It's six-fifty.
       It's ten to seven.

6:55   It's six-fifty-five.
       It's five to seven.

★See Appendix 3 for more information about saying the time.

What time is it?
9:30   It's nine-thirty.

What time is it?
11:15   It's eleven-fifteen.
        It's a quarter after eleven.

11:45   It's eleven forty-five.
        It's a quarter to twelve.

What time is it?
12:00   It's twelve.
        It's noon. (12 P.M.**)
        It's midnight. (12 A.M.***)

 **p.m. = afternoon/evening/night
***a.m. = morning

Part II. Work with a partner. Say the time. Begin with **It's**. NOTE: You only need to say the time one way. You can check *Let's Talk: Answers*, page 280, when your partner states the times.

Partner A	Partner B
1. 5:50	1. 9:15
2. 3:05	2. 10:10
3. 11:30	3. 6:55
4. 7:40	4. 8:20
5. 2:15	5. 11:00
6. 4:00	6. 12:45
	Change roles.

Part III. Write the times you hear. Use numbers.

1. _____   3. _____   5. _____   7. _____   9. _____

2. _____   4. _____   6. _____   8. _____   10. _____

EXERCISE 57 ▸ Let's talk: interview. (Chart 3-11)
Walk around the room. Ask a question beginning with **when** or **what time**. Write the answer and your classmate's name. Then ask another classmate a different question with **when** or **what time**. Share a few of your answers with the class.

Example: eat breakfast

STUDENT A: When/What time do you eat breakfast?
STUDENT B: I usually eat breakfast around seven o'clock.

ACTIVITY	NAME	ANSWER
1. wake up		
2. usually get up		
3. eat breakfast		
4. leave home in the morning		
5. usually get to class		
6. eat lunch		
7. get home from school		
8. have dinner		
9. usually study in the evening		
10. go to bed		

EXERCISE 58 ▸ Grammar and speaking. (Chapter 3 Review)
Work with a partner. Use the information about Professor Vega to make questions and answers. Take turns.

Professor Vega

Office hours:
Tuesday and Thursday
3:00 – 4:00

Classes:
Psychology 101, Room 213
9:00 – 10:00 daily

Child Psychology 205, Room 201
11:00 – 12:50
Tuesday and Thursday

Partner A	Partner B
1. be \ Professor Vega \ a physics teacher	1. be \ he \ a professor
2. what \ teach \ he	2. teach \ he \ at 7:00 A.M.
3. teach \ he \ Psychology 102	3. be \ he \ in his office \ at 9:00
4. where \ teach \ he \ Child Psychology 205	4. what time \ leave \ he \ the office on Tuesdays and Thursdays
5. be \ he \ in his office \ every day	5. teach \ he \ every day
	Change roles.

EXERCISE 59 ▸ Grammar and speaking. (Chapter 3 Review)

Part I. Complete the conversations with *is, are, does,* or *do*.

Conversation 1:

A: What time ____does____ the movie start?
            1

B: Seven-fifteen. _____ you want to go with us?
                      2

A: Yes. What time _____ it now?
                       3

B: Almost seven o'clock. _____ you ready to leave?
                              4

A: Yes, let's go.

Conversation 2:

A: Where _____ my keys to the car?
              5

B: I don't know. Where _____ you usually keep them?
                            6

A: On the kitchen counter. But they're not there.

B: Are you sure?

A: Yes. _____ you see them?
            7

B: No. _____ they in your coat pocket?
           8

A: I don't think so.

B: _____ your husband have them?
       9

A: No. He has a different set of car keys.

B: Well, good luck!

A: Thanks.

Conversation 3:

A: _____ you go to school?
        10

B: Yes.

A: _____ your brother go to school too?
        11

B: No, he works full-time.

A: Where _____ he work?
            12

B: At a hotel.

A: _____ he happy?
      13

B: Yes, he loves his job.

Part II. Work with a partner. Practice one conversation. Say it for the class. You can look at your book before you speak. When you speak, look at your partner.

EXERCISE 60 ▶ Check your knowledge. (Chapter 3 Review)

Correct the mistakes.

   lives
1. Niko ~~live~~ in Greece.

2. Lisa comes usually to class on time.

3. Diego use his cell phone often.

4. Amira carry a laptop to work every day.

5. She enjoy her job.

6. Miguel don't like milk. He never drink it.

7. Tina doesn't speaks Chinese. She speakes Spanish.

8. You a student?

9. Does your roommate sleeps with the window open?

10. Where your parents live?

11. What time is your English class begins?

12. Olga isn't need a car. She have a bike.

13. I no speak English.

14. Omar speak English every day.

15. A: Do you like strong coffee?

  B: Yes, I like.

EXERCISE 61 ▸ Speaking and writing. (Chapter 3)

Part I. Work with a partner. Take turns asking about things you have and don't have (for example, a car, a computer, a pet, children, a TV set, a briefcase, etc.). Take notes.

Example:

PARTNER A: Do you have a car?
PARTNER B: No.
PARTNER A: Do you have a computer?
PARTNER B: Yes, but it's not here. It's in my country.
Etc.

Part II. Take turns asking about things you like and don't like.

Example:

PARTNER B: Do you like pizza?
PARTNER A: Yes.
PARTNER B: Do you like the music of (*name of a group or singer*)?
PARTNER A: No, I don't.
Etc.

Part III. Write about your partner.

- Give a physical description.
- Write about things this person has and doesn't have.
- Write about things this person likes and doesn't like.

Here is some helpful vocabulary for the physical description:

HAIR TYPE	HAIR COLOR		EYE COLOR
straight	brown	blond	brown
curly	black	dark	blue
wavy	red	light	green
bald			gray

straight hair   curly hair   wavy hair   bald

Example:

My Partner Jin

My partner is Jin. He is very tall. He has brown eyes and black hair. He has a nice smile. He is very friendly.

Jin has an apartment near school. He doesn't have a car. He has a bike. He rides his bike to school. He has a laptop computer.

His family doesn't live here. He talks to them by video a few times a week. He is often homesick.

Jin likes to watch movies from his country in the evening. He enjoys comedy and drama. He likes many kinds of music. He listens to music on his cell phone. He doesn't really like the food here. He likes spicy food. The food here is not spicy. Unfortunately, he is not a good cook. He doesn't cook much. He likes to eat with his friends. They are good cooks.

Part IV. Edit your writing. Work individually or change papers with a partner. Check (✓) for the following:

1. ☐ a capital letter at the beginning of each sentence
2. ☐ a capital letter at the beginning of a person's name
3. ☐ a period at the end of each sentence
4. ☐ paragraph indents
5. ☐ a verb in every sentence
6. ☐ correct use of *doesn't* or *isn't* in negative sentences
7. ☐ correct spelling (use a dictionary or spell-check)

▪▪▪▪▪ For digital resources, go to MyEnglishLab on the Pearson English Portal. You can also go to the Pearson Practice English App for mobile practice.

CHAPTER 4

Using the Present Progressive and the Imperative

For App resources, scan the QR code.

PRETEST: What do I already know?

Choose the correct answer.

1. They _____ TV right now. (Chart 4-1)
   a. watching
   b. is watching
   c. are watching

2. It _____ today. (Chart 4-2)
   a. is rainning
   b. is raining
   c. rainying

3. The printer _____ right now. (Chart 4-3)
   a. no work
   b. doesn't working
   c. isn't working

4. Why _____ now? (Chart 4-4)
   a. is Khalifa sleeping
   b. Khalifa is sleeping
   c. Khalifa sleeping

5. My brother _____ my breakfast every day. (Chart 4-5)
   a. make
   b. is making
   c. makes

6. The flowers _____ wonderful. (Chart 4-6)
   a. smell
   b. are smelling
   c. smells

7. Shhh. I _____ to music. (Chart 4-7)
   a. am listen
   b. listen
   c. am listening

8. I _____ Professor Casey explains biology well. (Chart 4-8)
   a. am think
   b. think
   c. thinking that

9. Please _____ your books. (Chart 4-9)
   a. open
   b. you open
   c. opening

EXERCISE 1 ▶ Warm-up. (Chart 4-1)

Choose the correct words to complete the sentences.

1. The baby is happy / sad. He is laughing / crying.

2. The boy is happy / sad. He is laughing / crying.

4-1 Be + -ing: The Present Progressive

am + -ing	(a) I *am sitting* in class right now.	In (a): When I say this sentence, I am in class. I am sitting. I am not standing. The action (sitting) is happening right now, and I am saying the sentence at the same time.
is + -ing	(b) Rita *is sitting* in class right now.	
are + -ing	(c) You *are sitting* in class right now.	
		am, **is**, **are** = helping verbs **sitting** = the main verb
		am, **is**, **are** + **-ing** = the present progressive*

*The present progressive is also called the "present continuous."

EXERCISE 2 ▶ Looking at grammar. (Chart 4-1)
Complete the sentences with the present progressive form of **talk**.

1. I _____am_____ _____talking_____.

2. You _____ _____.

3. She _____ _____.

4. He _____ _____.

5. It _____ _____.

6. We _____ _____.

7. They _____ _____.

8. The students _____ _____.

9. My friend _____ _____.

10. Mr. Caras _____ _____.

EXERCISE 3 ▶ Looking at grammar. (Chart 4-1)
Write the correct form of **be** (**am, is,** or **are**).

Right now ...

1. it ____is____ raining outside.

2. we _____ sitting in the college library.

3. you _____ writing.

4. some students _____ studying.

5. I _____ looking out the window.

6. two women _____ waiting for a bus.

7. they _____ talking.

8. a bus _____ coming.

EXERCISE 4 ▸ Let's talk: pairwork. (Chart 4-1)
Work with a partner. Describe the pictures. Use the present progressive form of the verbs in the box. Take turns.

What is everyone doing?

Example:

PARTNER A: He is painting.

drive	swim
fish	take a selfie
fix a car	talk on the phone
✓ paint	wait for the bus
shop for clothes	walk on the beach

EXERCISE 5 ▸ Looking at grammar. (Chart 4-1)
Write the present progressive form of the verbs.

Grocery Shopping

Lynn and David are at the grocery store. They (*pick*) _____
1
up food for dinner. Lynn (*stand*) _____ in the fruit and
2
vegetable department. David (*look*) _____ at chicken and fish.
3
He (*cook*) _____ dinner tonight. Their son and daughter
4
(*ask*) _____ for chocolate ice cream. Many people
5
(*buy*) _____ groceries right now. The store is crowded.
6

EXERCISE 6 ▸ Let's talk: pairwork. (Chart 4-1)
Work with a partner. One partner acts out a verb. The other partner says the action.
Take turns.

Example: read
PARTNER A: (*acts out reading*)
PARTNER B: You are reading.

Partner A (*Partner B: book closed*)	Partner B (*Partner A: book closed*)
1. write	1. sit
2. stand	2. count
3. speak your language	3. walk
4. laugh	4. open your book
5. wave with your left hand	5. wave with your right hand
6. pick up a book	6. erase a word on a piece of paper

EXERCISE 7 ▸ Looking at grammar. (Chart 4-1)
Write the present progressive form of the verbs.

At the Airport

An airplane ...

1. land _____*is landing*_____ at the airport.

2. park _____ at the gate.

3. wait _____ for passengers.

A pilot ...

4. enter _____ the plane.

5. talk _____ to flight attendants.

Some people ...

6. stand _____ in line.

7. carry _____ suitcases.

8. eat _____ snacks.

9. watch _____ airplanes.

10. read _____ books.

EXERCISE 8 ▸ Game. (Chart 4-1)
Work with a partner. Answer the questions orally. Then write your sentences on a piece of
paper. Your teacher will give you a time limit. The pair with the most correct sentences wins.

1. What is happening in your classroom right now?

   _____*A student is talking. Students are writing.*_____

2. What are you and your partner doing?

3. What is the teacher doing?

4. What is happening in the school library? (*Use your imagination.*)

5. What is happening in the school cafeteria? (*Use your imagination.*)

6. What is happening in the computer lab? (*Use your imagination.*)

EXERCISE 9 ▸ Listening. (Chart 4-1)
Read about Kumar. Then listen to each sentence.
Choose the correct answer.

A Hard-Working Student

    Kumar is a business major. On Mondays,
he is very busy. He has classes from 9:00 A.M.
to 2:00 P.M. Then he stays in the classroom. He
studies until 5:00. He always studies alone. He
turns off his phone. He doesn't check the internet.
    Today is Monday. It is 3:00.

Example:

You will hear: Kumar is talking on his cell phone.
You will choose: yes   (no)

1. yes   no

2. yes   no

3. yes   no

4. yes   no

5. yes   no

6. yes   no

7. yes   no

8. yes   no

EXERCISE 10 ▸ Warm-up. (Chart 4-2)
Answer the questions about the verbs in the box.

count	ride	sleep	stop

1. Which verb ends in a consonant + *-e?*

    _____

2. Which verb ends in two consonants?

    _____

3. Which verb ends in one vowel + one consonant?

    _____

4. Which verb ends in two vowels + one consonant?

    _____

4-2 Spelling of -ing Verbs

	END OF VERB	→	-ING FORM
RULE 1	A CONSONANT* + -e	→	DROP THE -e AND ADD -ing
	smile	→	smiling
	write	→	writing
RULE 2	ONE VOWEL* + ONE CONSONANT	→	DOUBLE THE CONSONANT AND ADD -ing**
	sit	→	sitting
	run	→	running
RULE 3	TWO VOWELS + ONE CONSONANT	→	ADD -ing; DO NOT DOUBLE THE CONSONANT
	read	→	reading
	rain	→	raining
RULE 4	TWO CONSONANTS	→	ADD -ing; DO NOT DOUBLE THE CONSONANT
	stand	→	standing
	push	→	pushing

*Vowels = *a, e, i, o, u*. Consonants = *b, c, d, f, g, h, j, k, l, m, n, p, q, r, s, t, v, w, x, y, z*.
**Exception to Rule 2: Do not double *w, x,* and *y*. *snow* → *snowing; fix* → *fixing; say* → *saying*

EXERCISE 11 ▶ Spelling. (Chart 4-2)
Write the **-ing** form of the verbs.

1. take _____*taking*_____
2. come _____
3. make _____
4. do _____
5. hit _____
6. rain _____

7. hurt _____
8. plan _____
9. bake _____
10. snow _____
11. study _____
12. stop _____

EXERCISE 12 ▶ Spelling. (Chart 4-2)
Your teacher will act out a verb and say a sentence. Write the **-ing** verb on a separate piece of paper. Close your book for this activity.

Example: wave

TEACHER: (*waves and says*) I'm waving.

STUDENTS: (*write*) _____*waving*_____

1. smile
2. read
3. drink

4. sit
5. eat
6. clap

7. write
8. fly
9. wait

10. sneeze
11. cut a piece of paper
12. cry

EXERCISE 13 ▸ Looking at grammar. (Chart 4-2)

Complete the sentences. Use the present progressive form of the verbs in the box.

call	charge	eat	search	send	✓ wait

At Work

1. People are standing in the lobby. They ____*are waiting*____ for the elevator.

2. An office assistant _____ an email to the staff.

3. A customer is using his phone. He _____ his office.

4. Several people are in the lunchroom. They _____ lunch.

5. A manager has his cell phone on his desk. He _____ the battery.

6. An employee needs information. She _____ the internet.

EXERCISE 14 ▸ Warm-up. (Chart 4-3)

Choose the correct verbs.

1. The birds are / aren't flying.

2. They are / aren't sitting on a telephone wire.

3. An airplane is / isn't flying near the birds.

4-3 Present Progressive: Negative Forms

(a) I *am not* (*I'm not*) *sleeping*. I am awake.	Present progressive negative:
(b) Ben *is not* (*isn't*) *listening*. He's daydreaming.	am is } + *not* + *-ing* are
(c) Mr. and Mrs. Silva *are not* (*aren't*) *watching* TV. They're reading.	Contractions may also be used.

EXERCISE 15 ▸ Grammar and speaking. (Chart 4-3)

Part I. Work with a partner. Say two sentences about each situation, one negative and one affirmative. Use the present progressive.

Example: cooking / eating a sandwich
→ *She isn't cooking. She's eating a sandwich.*

1. working / relaxing

2. working / relaxing

3. dancing / listening to music

4. swimming / riding bikes

5. sitting at his desk / fixing the printer

6. sleeping / dancing

Part II. Write the sentences.

1. He _____ . He _____ .

2. He _____ . He _____ .

3. She _____ . She _____ .

4. They _____ . They _____ .

5. He _____ . He _____ .

6. They _____ . They _____ .

EXERCISE 16 ▸ Looking at grammar. (Chart 4-3)
Part I. Read about Pavel.

Pavel is a car mechanic. He owns a car repair business. He is very serious and works very hard. Right now Pavel is at work. What is he doing? Check (✓) the possible actions.

1. __✓__ talk to customers
2. _____ play soccer in a park
3. _____ change the oil in a car
4. _____ watch a movie in a theater
5. _____ put on a new tire

6. _____ spend time with friends
7. _____ give a customer a bill
8. _____ repair an engine
9. _____ eat at a restaurant
10. _____ replace a battery

Part II. Use your answers in Part I to make true sentences about Pavel.

1. ___*He is talking to customers.*___
2. ___*He isn't playing soccer in a park.*___
3. _____
4. _____
5. _____
6. _____
7. _____
8. _____
9. _____
10. _____

EXERCISE 17 ▸ Let's talk. (Chart 4-3)
Work in small groups. Make sentences about the people in the list. What are they doing now? What are they not doing now? Take turns.

Example: a neighbor
→ *Mrs. Martinez is working in her office right now.*
→ *She is not working in her garden.*

1. someone in your family
2. your favorite actor, writer, or sports star
3. a friend from childhood

4. a classmate
5. your teacher
6. the leader of a country

EXERCISE 18 ▸ Warm-up. (Chart 4-4)
Choose the correct answer.

What is Siri doing?   a. She is sleeping.   b. Yes, she is.

4-4 Present Progressive: Question Forms

	QUESTION				SHORT ANSWER (LONG ANSWER)	
	BE + SUBJECT + *-ING*					
(a)	*Is*	Marta	*sleeping?*	→	Yes, *she is.*	(She's sleeping.)
				→	No, *she's not.*	(She's not sleeping.)
				→	No, *she isn't.*	(She isn't sleeping.)
(b)	*Are*	you	*watching* TV?	→	Yes, *I am.*	(I'm watching TV.)
				→	No, *I'm not.*	(I'm not watching TV.)
	QUESTION WORD + *BE* + SUBJECT + *-ING*					
(c)	*Where*	*is*	Marta	*sleeping?*	→	*In bed.*	(She's sleeping in bed.)
(d)	*What*	*is*	Ted	*watching?*	→	*A movie.*	(Ted is watching a movie).
(e)	*Why*	*are*	you	*watching* TV?	→	*Because it's the championship game.* (I'm watching TV because it's the championship game.)

EXERCISE 19 ▸ Looking at grammar. (Chart 4-4)
Make questions.

Waiting for the Doctor

1. A: _____*Is someone checking in*_____?
   B: Yes, someone is. (Someone is checking in.)

2. A: _____?
   B: No, I'm not. (I'm not waiting for the nurse.)

3. A: _____?
   B: Yes, he is. (Ivan is sneezing and coughing.)

4. A: _____?
   B: Yes, they are. (The children are playing in the waiting room.)

5. A: _____?

   B: Yes, she is. (Yolanda is looking for her insurance card.)

6. A: _____?

   B: No, we're not. (We're not getting prescriptions.)

7. A: _____?

   B: Yes, I am. (I'm filling out my medical history.)

EXERCISE 20 ▸ Vocabulary and speaking: pairwork. (Chart 4-4)

Part I. Work with a partner. Check (✓) the expressions you know. Your teacher will explain the ones you don't know.

DO	*MAKE*	*TAKE*
_____ do the dishes	_____ make a mess	_____ take a nap
_____ do the laundry	_____ make a bed	_____ take a shower
_____ do homework	_____ make a phone call	_____ take a bath
_____ do the ironing	_____ make breakfast/ lunch/dinner	_____ take a test
		_____ take a break
		_____ take medicine

Part II. With your partner, ask and answer questions about the pictures. Use phrases from Part I, and find the differences. You can look at your book before you speak. When you speak, look at your partner. Take turns. Partner A: Use the pictures on page 108. Partner B: Use the pictures in *Let's Talk: Answers*, page 281.

Example:

Partner A

Partner B

PARTNER A: Is the person in your picture taking a test?
PARTNER B: No, she isn't.
PARTNER A: What is she doing?
PARTNER B: She's taking a break.

Partner A

EXERCISE 21 ▶ Looking at grammar. (Chart 4-4)
Make questions with *where*, *why*, and *what*.

In the Classroom

1. A: _____*What are you reading?*_____
   B: My grammar book. (I'm reading my grammar book.)

2. A: _____
   B: Because we're doing an exercise. (I'm reading my grammar book because we're doing an exercise.)

3. A: _____
   B: A sentence. (I'm writing a sentence.)

4. A: _____
   B: In the back of the room. (Yoshi is sitting in the back of the room.)

5. A: _____
   B: To the cafeteria. (I'm going to the cafeteria.)

6. A: _____
   B: Jeans and a sweatshirt. (Jonas is wearing jeans and a sweatshirt today.)

7. A: _____
   B: Because I'm happy. (I'm smiling because I'm happy.)

EXERCISE 22 ▸ Looking at grammar. (Chart 4-4)

Make questions. For the *yes/no* questions, give short answers.

In a Café

1. A: Where ___*is Ingrid sitting?*___
   B: By the window. (Ingrid is sitting by the window.)

2. A: ___*Is Ingrid having dinner?*___
   B: No, ___*she isn't / she's not.*___ (Ingrid isn't having dinner.)

3. A: What _____
   B: Coffee. (She's having coffee.)

4. A: _____
   B: Yes, _____ (Anna is eating lunch.)

5. A: What _____
   B: A glass of lemonade. (Sam is drinking a glass of lemonade.)

6. A: _____
   B: No, _____ (Angela isn't drinking a glass of lemonade.)

7. A: What _____
   B: Takeout. (I'm ordering takeout.)

8. A: _____
   B: Yes, _____ (Elaine is ordering takeout.)

9. A: Where _____
   B: Back to the office. (They're going back to the office.)

10. A: Why _____
    B: Because they have a lot of work. (They're going back to the office because they have a lot of work.)

Jump-start your English

Questions at Passport Control

 Part I. Listen to the conversations.

1. A: Where are you coming from?
   B: I'm coming from Canada.

2. A: Where are you going?
   B: I'm going to Munich.

3. A: Where are you staying?
   B: I'm staying with relatives.

4. A: Are you traveling alone?
   B: Yes, I am.

5. A: How long are you staying there?
   B: I'm staying two weeks.

6. A: What is the purpose* of your visit?
   B: I'm on vacation.

*purpose = reason

 Part II. Work with a partner. Ask and answer questions with the words in the boxes.

QUESTIONS			ANSWERS
Where	are you	coming from? going? staying?	I'm coming from … I'm going to … I'm staying at the … hotel. I'm staying with … (friends/family/ relatives).
	Are you	traveling alone? with a group?	Yes. / No.
How long	are you	staying?	… weeks. … months.
What	is	the purpose of your visit?	I'm here on business. I'm on vacation. I'm a student. I'm studying at …

EXERCISE 23 ▶ Warm-up. (Chart 4-5)
Answer the questions with *yes* or *no*.

1. Do you eat breakfast every day?
2. Are you eating breakfast right now?
3. Do you text every day?
4. Are you texting right now?

4-5 The Simple Present Tense vs. the Present Progressive Tense

	SIMPLE PRESENT	PRESENT PROGRESSIVE
	The simple present expresses habits or usual activities. Common time words are *every day*, *every year*, *every month*, *often*, *sometimes*, and *never*. The simple present uses *do* and *does* in negative sentences and questions.	The present progressive expresses actions that are happening right now, while the speaker is speaking. Common time words are *now*, *right now*, and *today*. The present progressive uses *am*, *is*, and *are* in negative sentences and questions.
STATEMENT	I *talk* You *talk* He, She, It *talks* } *every day.* We *talk* They *talk*	I *am* *talking* You *are* *talking* He, She, It *is* *talking* } *now.* We *are* *talking* They *are* *talking*
NEGATIVE	I *don't* *talk.* You *don't* *talk.* He, She, It *doesn't* *talk.* We *don't* *talk.* They *don't* *talk.*	I *am* *not* *talking.* You *are* *not* *talking.* He, She, It *is* *not* *talking.* We *are* *not* *talking.* They *are* *not* *talking.*
QUESTION	*Do* I *talk?* *Do* you *talk?* *Does* he, she, it *talk?* *Do* we *talk?* *Do* they *talk?*	*Am* I *talking?* *Are* you *talking?* *Is* he, she, it *talking?* *Are* we *talking?* *Are* they *talking?*

EXERCISE 24 ▸ Looking at grammar. (Chart 4-5)

Choose the correct time words.

At a Pharmacy

1. Mari is working   (now.)   every day.

2. Mari works at a pharmacy   now.   every day.

3. A customer is getting a prescription   right now.   every day.

4. The pharmacist answers questions   now.   every day.

5. An assistant is answering questions   right now.   every day.

6. You take medication   right now.   every day.

7. The medication helps you   right now.   every day.

8. I am feeling sick   today.   every day.

9. Customers are waiting for their prescriptions   right now.   every day.

EXERCISE 25 ▶ Looking at grammar. (Chart 4-5)
Write the correct form of the words in parentheses.

The Weather

1. Right now it (*be*) _____*is*_____ cold outside. The sun (*shine, not*)
   _____*isn't shining*_____. It (*snow*) _____. We
   (*stay*) _____ inside. We often (*stay*) _____
   inside in the winter.

2. (*snow, it*) _____ in your city very often? (*snow, it*) _____
   _____ right now?

3. What a beautiful day! The sky (*be*) _____ clear. It (*be, not*)
   _____ cloudy. The sun (*shine*) _____.

4. Oh, no, it (*rain*) _____. I (*wear, not*) _____
   _____ my boots. My feet (*get*) _____ wet.
   I (*get*) _____ cold.

EXERCISE 26 ▶ Listening. (Chart 4-5)
Listen to each sentence. Choose the correct completion.

Example: You will hear: Pedro is sleeping late …
            You will choose: (now)   every day

1. now   every day   5. now   every day

2. now   every day   6. now   every day

3. now   every day   7. now   every day

4. now   every day   8. now   every day

EXERCISE 27 ▸ Let's talk: pairwork. (Chart 4-5)

Work with a partner. Ask and answer questions about the pictures. Use the verbs in the box. Take turns. Use the present progressive and the simple present.

Example: exercise

PARTNER A: Is he exercising?
PARTNER B: Yes, he is.
PARTNER A: Does he exercise every day?
PARTNER B: Yes, he does.

check for phone messages	drink water	ride bikes
daydream	drive	run
do homework	play in the park	shave

EXERCISE 28 ▸ Looking at grammar. (Chart 4-5)

Complete each question with all the correct answers. Use the words in the boxes.

a teacher	at school	early	sick	study	studying	work

1. a. Are you ___a teacher / early / studying / at school / sick___ ?

   b. Do you ___work / study___ ?

angry	a dancer	cook	dance	driving	ready	understand

2. a. Do you _____ ?

   b. Are you _____ ?

a problem	help	here	new	raining	ready	true	work

3. a. Is it _____ ?

   b. Does it _____ ?

EXERCISE 29 ▸ Looking at grammar. (Chart 4-5)

Write *do*, *does*, *is*, or *are*.

On the Subway

1. ___Do___ you have your ticket?

2. ___Is___ your ticket in your wallet?

3. _____ the train usually leave on time?

4. _____ the train on time?

5. _____ the tickets cheap?

6. _____ you looking at a map?

7. _____ you have enough money?

8. _____ the train here?

9. _____ we have extra time?

10. _____ the train leaving?

11. _____ someone check for tickets?

EXERCISE 30 ▶ Listening. (Chart 4-5)

Listen to the conversation with your book closed. Then listen again and write the words you hear.

Example: You will hear: Are you doing an exercise?

You will write: _Are you doing_ an exercise?

What are you doing?

A: _____ on your English paper?
     ¹

B: No. _____. _____ an email to my sister.
          ²   ³

A: _____ to her often?
          ⁴

B: Yes, but I _____ a lot of emails to anyone else.
                    ⁵

A: _____ to you often?
          ⁶

B: No, but she _____ me a lot.
                    ⁷

EXERCISE 31 ▶ Looking at grammar. (Chart 4-5)

Write the correct form of the words in parentheses.

1. A: Tom is on the phone.

   B: (*he, talk*) _____ *Is he talking* _____ to his wife?

   A: Yes.

   B: (*he, talk*) _____ *Does he talk* _____ to her often?

   A: Yes, he (*talk*) _____ *talks* _____ to her every day during his lunch break.

2. A: I (*walk*) _____ to school every day. I (*take, not*) _____ the

      bus. (*you, take*) _____ the bus?

   B: No, I don't.

3. A: Selena is in the hallway.

   B: (*she, talk*) _____ to her friends?

   A: No, she isn't. She (*run*) _____ to her next class.

4. A: I (*read*) _____ the newspaper every day.

   B: (*you, read*) _____ it online?

   A: Yes, I do. I (*read*) _____ it on my phone.

5. A: What (*you, read*) _____ right now?

   B: I (*read*) _____ my grammar book.

6. A: (*you, want*) _____ your coat?

B: Yes.

A: (*be, this*) _____ your coat?

B: No, my coat (*hang*) _____ in the closet right now.

EXERCISE 32 ▸ Reading, grammar, and speaking. (Chart 4-5)

Part I. Read the paragraph. Look at new vocabulary with your teacher first.

Do you know these words?
- server   - tips   - shift
- earn   - average - co-worker
- minimum wage

Kaya's Job

Kaya is a server at a restaurant. She works long hours, and she earns minimum wage. She earns extra money from tips. Kaya is an excellent server. She is friendly and fast. Customers leave her good tips. Fifteen percent is average. Kaya often gets twenty percent. Today Kaya is working an extra shift. A co-worker is sick. Kaya is feeling tired at the moment. But she is also happy because the tips are good. She is earning a lot of extra money today.

Part II. Write *is*, *do*, or *does*.

1. _____Is_____ Kaya a good server?

2. _____ the restaurant pay Kaya a lot of money?

3. _____ customers leave her good tips?

4. _____ Kaya work extra hours every day?

5. _____ Kaya working extra hours today?

6. _____ she happy today?

7. _____ she earning extra money?

8. _____ she usually get good tips?

9. _____ servers earn a lot of money from tips?

Part III. In small groups, discuss the questions.

1. In your opinion, what are some important qualities for a restaurant server? Check (✓) the items.

   _____ fast   _____ formal

   _____ friendly   _____ speaks other languages

   _____ talkative   _____ smiles a lot

   _____ polite   _____ has a good memory

2. Do customers leave tips at restaurants in your country? If so, what percentage is an average tip? Do you like to leave tips?

3. What is more important for you at a restaurant: the food or the service?

4. In some countries, a usual workday is eight hours, and a usual workweek is 40 hours. What is the usual workday and workweek in your country?

EXERCISE 33 ▸ Warm-up. (Chart 4-6)
Read the sentences. What do you notice about the verbs in red?

Right now, I am waiting at a bus stop. I see an ambulance. I hear a siren. A car and a motorcycle are stopping. The ambulance is going fast.

4-6 Non-Action Verbs Not Used in the Present Progressive

	Some verbs are usually NOT used in the present progressive. They are called "non-action verbs."
(a) I'm hungry *right now*. I *want* an apple.	In (a): ***Want*** is a non-action verb. *Want* expresses a physical or emotional need, not an action.
(b) I *hear* a siren. *Do* you *hear* it too? INCORRECT: *I'm hearing a siren.* *Are you hearing it too?*	In (b): ***Hear*** is a non-action verb. *Hear* expresses a sensory experience, not an action.

NON-ACTION VERBS*

dislike	need	hear	believe
hate	want	see	know
like		smell	think (*meaning* believe)**
love		taste	understand

*Some verbs can be both action and non-action. This is discussed in the intermediate and advanced books of this series: *Fundamentals of English Grammar* and *Understanding and Using English Grammar*.

**See Chart 4-8 for a discussion of *think about* and *think that*.

EXERCISE 34 ▸ Looking at grammar. (Chart 4-6)
Write the simple present or the present progressive form of the verbs in parentheses.

1. Alicia is in her room right now. She (*listen*) _____*is listening*_____ to a podcast. She
   (*like*) _____*likes*_____ the podcast.

2. It (*snow*) _____ right now. It's beautiful! I (*like*) _____
   _____ this weather.

3. I (*know*) _____ Jessica Santos. She's in my class.

4. The teacher (*talk*) _____ to us right now. I (*understand*)
   _____ everything she's saying.

5. Emilio is at a restaurant right now. He (*eat*) _____ dinner. He
   (*like*) _____ the food. It (*taste*) _____ good.

6. Sniff-sniff. I (*smell*) _____ gas. (*you, smell*) _____ it?

7. Taro (*tell*) _____ us a story right now. I (*believe*) _____
   his story.

8. Ugh! Someone (*smoke*) _____ a cigar. It (*smell*) _____
   terrible! I (*hate*) _____ cigars.

9. Look at Alek. He (*look*) _____ at his new baby daughter. He
   (*love*) _____ her. He (*smile*) _____.

EXERCISE 35 ▸ Let's talk: interview. (Chart 4-6)
Ask two students each question. Use **do** or **does**. Write their answers in the chart. Share
some of their answers with the class.

QUESTION	STUDENT A	STUDENT B
1. What \ you \ like?		
2. What \ a baby \ like?		
3. What \ you \ want?		
4. What \ children \ want?		
5. What \ you \ love?		

QUESTION	STUDENT A	STUDENT B
6. What \ a teenager \ love?		
7. What \ you \ dislike or hate?		
8. What \ you \ not \ understand?		
9. What \ you \ need?		
10. What \ you \ not \ need?		

EXERCISE 36 ▶ Looking at grammar. (Chart 4-6)

Choose the usual sentence in each pair.

1. a. Look! I am seeing a cat in the tree.
   b. Look! I see a cat in the tree.

2. a. Our teacher is knowing many languages.
   b. Our teacher knows many languages.

3. a. Yuck. The milk tastes sour.
   b. Yuck. The milk is tasting sour.

4. a. Look! It is snowing outside.
   b. Look! It snows outside.

5. a. I hear you. You can lower your voice.
   b. I am hearing you. You can lower you voice.

6. a. My parents are not believing me.
   b. My parents don't believe me.

7. a. Do you like vegetables?
   b. Are you liking vegetables?

8. a. Shhh! Someone comes.
   b. Shhh! Someone is coming.

Jump-start your English

A Job Interview

 Part I. Listen to the conversation.

A: What job are you applying for?
B: I'm applying for the server position.
A: Are you looking for full-time or part-time work?
B: I'm looking for full-time. But part-time is OK for now.
A: What shift do you want to work?
B: I want to work nights.
A: Can you work weekends?
B: Yes, I can.
A: When can you start?
B: Immediately.

Part II. Work with a partner. Ask and answer questions with the words in the boxes. Share one of your conversations with the class.

QUESTIONS	ANSWERS		
What job are you applying for?	I'm applying for the	server salesclerk gardener cashier janitor lab assistant etc.	position.
Are you looking for full- or part-time work?	Full-time. Part-time.		
What shift do you want to work?	Day. Night.		
Can you work weekends?	Yes, I can. No, I can't.		
When can you start?	Immediately. Tomorrow. Next week. Next month.		

EXERCISE 37 ▶ Warm-up. (Chart 4-7)
Write the correct verb for each sentence.

1. *am looking at / am watching*

    a. I _____ my cell phone. It is 10:00 P.M.

    b. I _____ a movie. It is very funny.

2. *hear / am listening to*

    a. I _____ the teacher carefully. She is explaining grammar
    to me.

    b. Shhh! I _____ a noise. Maybe someone is downstairs!

4-7 See, Look At, Watch, Hear, and Listen To

SEE, LOOK AT, AND WATCH	
(a) I *see* many things in this room.	In (a): *see* = a non-action verb. Seeing happens because my eyes are open. Seeing is a physical reaction, not a planned action.
(b) I'*m looking at* my watch. I want to know the time.	In (b): *look at* = an action verb. Looking is a planned or purposeful action. Looking happens for a reason.
(c) Bob *is watching* TV.	In (c): *watch* = an action verb. I *watch* something for a long time, but I *look at* something for a short time.
HEAR AND LISTEN TO	
(d) I'm in my apartment. I'm trying to study. I *hear* music from the next apartment. The music is loud.	In (d): *hear* = a non-action verb. Hearing is an unplanned act. It expresses a physical reaction.
(e) I'm in my apartment. I'm studying. I'*m listening to* music on my phone. I like to listen to music when I study.	In (e): *listen* (*to*) = an action verb. Listening happens for a purpose.

EXERCISE 38 ▶ Let's talk: class activity. (Chart 4-7)
Your teacher will ask you questions. Close your book for this activity.

Example:
TEACHER: Look at the floor. What do you see?
STUDENT: I see shoes/dirt/etc.

1. What do you see in this room? Now look at something. What are you looking at?
2. Turn to page 108 of this book. What do you see? Now look at one thing on that page. What are you looking at?
3. Look at the board. What do you see?
4. What programs do you like to watch on TV?

5. What sports do you like to watch?

6. What do you hear at night at home?

7. Who has headphones? What do you listen to?

EXERCISE 39 ▸ Looking at grammar. (Chart 4-7)
Choose the correct verb.

1. Listen. _____ that noise? What is it?
   a. Do you hear   b. Do you listen to

2. I _____ music. It helps me study.
   a. am listening to   b. hear

3. The teacher _____ us. Why? What does she want?
   a. sees   b. is watching

4. My parents _____ TV after dinner.
   a. see   b. watch

5. Help! I _____ a snake.
   a. see   b. am watching

EXERCISE 40 ▸ Looking at grammar. (Charts 4-5 → 4-7)
Complete the sentences. Use the simple present or the present progressive form of the verbs in parentheses.

In Class

I (sit) _____*am sitting*_____ in class right now. I (sit, always)
                    1

_____*always sit*_____ in the same seat every day in the middle of the room. We (do)
            2

_____ homework. Some students (help) _____
            3   4

me. Right now we (speak) _____ English. Sometimes we (speak)
                                    5

_____ our language. But our teacher (want) _____
            6   7

us to speak English.

I (see) _____ Sandro in the corner. He (work, not)
                    8

_____. He (look) _____
            9   10

around the room. Kim (check) _____ the
                                        11

answer key in his grammar book. Francisco (watch)

_____ the clock. Abdullah
            12

(*smile*) _____ . Lidia (*get*) _____ things out of
                        13   14

her backpack. Hans (*chew*) _____ gum.
                                        15

EXERCISE 41 ▶ Warm-up. (Chart 4-8)

Do you agree or disagree with each sentence? Circle *yes* or *no*.

1. I think about my parents every day.   yes   no

2. I am thinking about my parents right now.   yes   no

3. I think that it is difficult to be a good parent.   yes   no

4-8	*Think About* and *Think That*	
	THINK + ABOUT + A NOUN	In (a): Ideas about my family are in my mind every day.
(a) I	**think about *my family*** every day.	
(b) I	**am thinking about *grammar*** right now.	In (b): My mind is busy now. Ideas about grammar are in my mind right now.
	THINK + THAT + A STATEMENT	In (c): In my opinion, Emma is lazy. I believe that Emma is lazy. People use ***think that*** when they want to say (to state) their beliefs.
(c) I	**think that *Emma is lazy.***	
(d) Ed	**thinks that *I am lazy.***	The present progressive is often used with ***think about***. The present progressive is almost never used with ***think that***.
(e) I	**think that *the weather is nice.***	
(f)	I ***think that*** Marco is a nice person.	Examples (f) and (g) have the same meaning. People often omit ***that*** after ***think***, especially in speaking.
(g)	I ***think*** Marco is a nice person.	

EXERCISE 42 ▶ Grammar and speaking. (Chart 4-8)

Use ***I think that*** to give your opinion. Share a few of your opinions with the class.

1. English grammar is easy / hard / fun / interesting.

   I think that English grammar is interesting.

2. People in this city are friendly / unfriendly / kind / cold.

   _____

3. The food at (*name of a place*) is delicious / terrible / good / excellent / awful.

   _____

4. Baseball / football / soccer / golf is interesting / boring / confusing / etc.

   _____

EXERCISE 43 ▸ Writing and speaking. (Chart 4-8)

Complete the sentences with your own words. Share a few of your ideas with the class.

1. I think that the weather today is _____

2. In my opinion, the weather here is _____

3. I think my classmates are _____

4. Right now I'm thinking about _____

5. In my opinion, English grammar is _____

6. I think that my parents are _____

7. I think this school is _____

8. I think about _____ often.

9. I think that _____

10. In my opinion, _____

EXERCISE 44 ▸ Let's talk: game. (Charts 4-5 → 4-8)

Work in small groups. One person thinks about an animal or a food. The other students ask questions and try to guess the answer.

Example: food

STUDENT A: I'm thinking about a food.
STUDENT B: Does it taste sweet?
STUDENT A: Yes.
STUDENT C: Is it brown?
STUDENT A: Yes.
STUDENT D: Is it chocolate?
STUDENT A: Yes!

Another student chooses an animal or a food.

EXERCISE 45 ▸ Warm-up. (Chart 4-9)

What does your teacher say every day? Check (✓) the sentences.

1. ____ Put your phones away.

2. ____ Take out a piece of paper.

3. ____ Open your books.

4. ____ Raise your hand.

5. ____ Work with a partner.

6. ____ Turn in your homework.

4-9 Imperative Sentences

(a) *Put your phones away.*	In (a): ***Put your phones away*** is a command or an IMPERATIVE SENTENCE. The sentence means "I am telling you to put your phones away."
(b) *Sit* down. (c) *Stand* up. (d) *Be* quiet. (e) *Stop* talking.*	An imperative sentence uses the base form of a verb (*sit, stand, be,* etc.). The subject is *you*. Sit down. = (You) sit down.
(f) *Don't open* the window. (g) *Don't be* late.	NEGATIVE IMPERATIVE ***don't*** + *the base form of a verb*
(h) *Please* put your phones away.	***Please*** makes an imperative sound more polite.

*For an imperative with *stop*, use the base form of a *verb* + *-ing*.

EXERCISE 46 ▶ Looking at grammar. (Chart 4-9)

Underline the imperative verbs in the conversations.

1. TOM: What's the matter?

   JIM: I have the hiccups.

   TOM: Hold your breath.

   BOB: Drink some water.

   JOE: Breathe into a paper bag.

   KEN: Bite on a lemon.

   JIM: I'm OK now, thanks.

2. ANDY: Bye, Mom. I'm going over to Billy's house.

   MOM: Wait a minute. Did you clean your room?

   ANDY: Uh …

   MOM: Do it now. Hang up your clothes. Make your bed. Put your books away. Empty
   the wastepaper basket. OK?

   ANDY: OK.

3. ANYA: I'm leaving now.

   IVAN: Wait for me.

   ANYA: Don't forget your keys.

   IVAN: I have them.

EXERCISE 47 ▸ Looking at grammar. (Chart 4-9)
Write the correct command for each picture.

| Don't let go! | Go! Go! | March! | Relax! | Wait for me! |

1. _____   2. _____   3. _____

4. _____   5. _____

EXERCISE 48 ▸ Speaking and writing. (Chart 4-9)
Work with a partner or in small groups. Make suggestions for each situation. Write them down.

1. You are the teacher. Your students are very noisy. You want to begin class.
   a. _____Sit down._____
   b. _____
   c. Don't _____

2. Your friend has a headache.
   a. _____
   b. _____
   c. Don't _____

3. A college friend is using a washing machine in the dorm for the first time.
   a. _____
   b. _____
   c. _____
   d. _____

EXERCISE 49 ▶ Reading. (Chapter 4 Review)
Read the paragraph and the statements. Circle "T" for true and "F" for false.

SLEEP: HOW MUCH DO PEOPLE NEED?

Adults need about eight hours of sleep a night. Some need more and some need less. Newborn babies need the most sleep, about 14 to 16 hours every 24 hours. They sleep for about four hours. Then they wake up, eat, and sleep again. As babies grow, they need a little less sleep, about 10 to 14 hours. Here is an interesting fact. Teenagers also need about 10 to 14 hours of sleep a night. Some people think teenagers sleep a lot because they are lazy. Actually, their bodies are changing, They need a lot of rest. Think about your sleep. How much do you get every night? Is it enough?

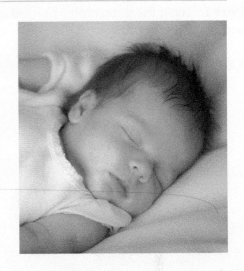

1. Everyone needs eight hours of sleep a night.   T   F

2. Newborn babies sleep all day.   T   F

3. Teenagers need a lot of sleep.   T   F

4. Teenagers and adults need the same amount of sleep.   T   F

EXERCISE 50 ▶ Check your knowledge. (Chapter 4 Review)
Correct the mistakes.

1. It's ~~rainning~~ *raining* today. I ~~no~~ *don't* like the rain.

2. I like New York City. I am thinking that it is a wonderful city.

3. Does Abdul be sleeping right now?

4. Why you are going downtown today?

5. I am liking flowers. They are smelling good.

6. Bill at a restaurant right now. He usually eat at home, but today he eating dinner at a restaurant.

7. Please you turn in your homework now.

8. Alex is siting at his desk. He writting a letter.

9. Where do they are staying right now?

EXERCISE 51 ▸ Reading and writing. (Chapter 4)
Part I. Read the paragraph. Look at new vocabulary with your teacher first.

Do you know these words?
- *medical school* - *toss and turn*
- *final exams* - *wide-awake*
- *pass*

A Sleepless Night

Mika is in bed. It is 3:00 A.M. She is very tired, but she isn't sleeping. She is thinking about medical school. She is worrying about her final exams tomorrow. She needs to pass because she wants to be a doctor. She is tossing and turning in bed. She wants a few more days to study. She is thinking about possible test questions. She is wide-awake. This is a sleepless night for Mika.

Part II. Imagine it is 3:00 A.M. You are in bed, and you are wide-awake. You are having a sleepless night. What are you thinking about? Write a paragraph. Use both simple present and present progressive verbs.

Part III. Edit your writing. Work individually or change papers with a partner. Check (✓) for the following:

1. ☐ a paragraph indent
2. ☐ a capital letter at the beginning of each sentence
3. ☐ a period at the end of each sentence
4. ☐ a verb in every sentence
5. ☐ use of present progressive for activities right now
6. ☐ correct spelling (use a dictionary or spell-check)

▪▪▪▪▪ For digital resources, go to MyEnglishLab on the Pearson English Portal. You can also go to the Pearson Practice English App for mobile practice.

PRETEST: What do I already know?
Check (✓) the correct sentences.

1. _____ Lilly and Thomas have seven boy. (Chart 5-1)

2. _____ Do you have one children or two? (Chart 5-2)

3. _____ This is a city safe. (Chart 5-3)

4. _____ Indian food is very hot. (Chart 5-3)

5. _____ The kids are playing games. (Chart 5-4)

6. _____ Mark and Julie are coming. Do you see them? (Chart 5-5)

7. _____ The teacher is helping my friend and I. (Chart 5-6)

8. _____ This is my coffee cup. That is yours. (Chart 5-7)

9. _____ The students' are here. (Chart 5-8)

10. _____ Whose is this coat? (Chart 5-9)

11. _____ The children's bedrooms are upstairs. (Chart 5-10)

EXERCISE 1 ▸ Warm-up. (Chart 5-1)
Check (✓) each noun (person, place, or thing).

1. ✓ places

2. _____ interesting

3. _____ London

4. _____ near

5. _____ there

6. _____ famous

7. _____ write

8. _____ tourist

9. _____ outside

10. _____ Japan

5-1 Nouns: Singular and Plural Forms

	SINGULAR	PLURAL	
(a)	one pen one apple one cup one elephant	two pens three apples four cups five elephants	To make the plural form of most nouns, add **-s**.
(b)	baby city	babies cities	END OF NOUN: consonant + **-y** PLURAL FORM: change **y** to **i**, add **-es**
(c)	boy key	boys keys	END OF NOUN: vowel + **-y** PLURAL FORM: add **-s**
(d)	wife thief	wives thieves	END OF NOUN: **-fe** or **-f** PLURAL FORM: change **f** to **v**, add **-s** or **-es**
(e)	dish match class box	dishes matches classes boxes	END OF NOUN: **-sh**, **-ch**, **-ss**, **-x** PLURAL FORM: add **-es** PRONUNCIATION: /əz/
(f)	tomato potato	tomatoes potatoes	END OF NOUN: consonant + **-o** PLURAL FORM: add **-es**
	zoo radio	zoos radios	END OF NOUN: vowel + **-o** PLURAL FORM: add **-s**

EXERCISE 2 ▸ Looking at grammar. (Chart 5-1)

How many? Choose the correct number.

On the Table

1. fork   one   two or more
2. spoons   one   two or more
3. knives   one   two or more
4. plate   one   two or more
5. dishes   one   two or more

EXERCISE 3 ▸ Looking at grammar. (Chart 5-1)
Choose the correct noun.

1. It is fall. The leaf / leaves are falling from the trees.

2. Klara and Astrid have husbands. They are wife / wives.

3. My parents are visiting three city / cities in Canada: Montreal, Toronto, and Calgary.

4. Do cats have nine life / lives?

5. Police officers catch thief / thieves.

6. Where are my key / keys?

7. I need four knife / knives for the table.

EXERCISE 4 ▸ Grammar and speaking. (Chart 5-1)
Interview your classmates. Ask one student each question. Use the plural form for the word in parentheses.

1. Are (*tax*) in your country high or low?

2. What do you prefer for dinner: rice, noodles, or (*potato*)?

3. Do (*leaf*) change color in your country? What season?

4. What (*class*) do you have in the morning?

5. Do you like (*sandwich*)? What kind?

6. Are (*zoo*) a good idea or bad idea? Why?

7. Name some famous (*college*) or (*university*).

8. Are the speaking (*exercise*) in this book easy or difficult?

9. What (*country*) are near your country?

10. Do you use online (*dictionary*)?

EXERCISE 5 ▸ Looking at grammar. (Chart 5-1)
Write the plural form of the words in parentheses.

1. The Hans have one daughter and two sons. They have one girl and two
   (*boy*) ———————————————— .

2. Women give birth to (*child*) ———————————————— .

3. I like to go to (*party*) ———————————————— because I like to meet and talk to people.

4. People carry their food on (*tray*) ———————————————— in a cafeteria.

5. Good evening, (*lady*) ———————————————— and gentlemen.

6. (*Cowboy*) ———————————————— ride horses.

Complete the sentences. Write the plural form of the words in the box.

class	match	tax
dish	potato	tomato
glass	sandwich	zoo

1. Steve drinks eight _____ of water every day.

2. Please put the _____ and the silverware on the table.

3. All citizens pay money to the government every year. They pay their _____.

4. I want to light some candles. I need some _____.

5. When I make a salad, I use lettuce and _____.

6. Sometimes Pam has a hamburger and French-fried _____ for dinner.

7. Some animals live all of their lives in _____.

8. Mehmet is a student. He likes his _____.

9. We often eat _____ for lunch.

EXERCISE 7 ▶ Listening. (Chart 5-1)
Choose the word you hear.

1. toy   (toys)   6. box   boxes

2. table   tables   7. package   packages

3. face   faces   8. chair   chairs

4. hat   hats   9. edge   edges

5. office   offices   10. top   tops

EXERCISE 8 ▶ Listening. (Chart 5-1)
Listen to each sentence. Choose the word you hear.

1. desk   (desks)   6. exercise   exercises

2. place   places   7. glass   glasses

3. sandwich   sandwiches   8. box   boxes

4. sentence   sentences   9. box   boxes

5. snack   snacks   10. college   colleges

EXERCISE 9 ▸ Grammar and speaking. (Chart 5-1)

Write the correct ending. Write **Ø** if no ending is necessary. Do you agree or disagree with each statement? Share some of your answers. Remember: **a/an = one**.

1. I like banana _s_, strawberry _ies_, and peach _es_.   yes   no

2. I eat a banana_____ every day.   yes   no

3. My favorite animals are elephant_____.   yes   no

4. A baby elephant_____ is cute.   yes   no

5. Baby_____ are cute.   yes   no

6. The grammar exercise_____ in this book are easy.   yes   no

7. A ride on a motorcycle_____ is fun.   yes   no

8. A ride on an airplane_____ is comfortable.   yes   no

9. This exercise_____ is easy.   yes   no

10. The measurements inch_____ and feet confuse me.   yes   no

Jump-start your English

Shopping: At a Shoe Store

Part I. Listen to the conversations.

1. A: Can I help you?
   B: Yes, I'm looking for running shoes.
   A: Here are our running shoes.
   B: Thanks.

2. A: How can I help you?
   B: I'd like to try on these shoes. Do you have them in size 8?
   A: Let me check.

3. A: May I help you?
   B: I'd like to try on these shoes.
   A: What size are you?
   B: I'm a 12 1/2.
   A: I'm sorry. They don't come in half sizes. Just whole sizes.
   B: OK, I'll try a 13.

(*continues*)

4. A: How do they feel?
   B: They're too small. I'd like to try the next size.
   A: OK.

5. A: How do they fit?
   B: They're too big.
   A: OK. Let me get you the next size down.

Part II. Work with a partner. Ask and answer questions with the words in the boxes. Say your conversation in small groups. (For students not in your home country: Shoes sizes may be different from your country. You can find your shoe size online. Type "shoe size (*name of home country*) to (*name of new country*)." For example: "shoe size Japan to US.")

QUESTIONS	ANSWERS	
May I help you? Can I help you? How can I help you?	I'd like to try on	these shoes. some boots. running shoes. comfortable shoes. Etc.
What size are you? What size do you need?	I'm a … I need a …	
How do they feel? How do they fit?	They're	good. too big. too small. too tight.

EXERCISE 10 ▸ Warm-up. (Chart 5-2)
Write *a* before the singular nouns.

1. a. _____ child

   b. _____ children

2. a. _____ men

   b. _____ man

3. a. _____ teeth

   b. _____ tooth

4. a. _____ foot

   b. _____ feet

5-2 Nouns: Irregular Plural Forms

	SINGULAR	PLURAL	EXAMPLES
(a)	child	children	Mr. Smith has one *child*. Mr. Cook has two **children**.
(b)	foot	feet	I have a right *foot* and a left *foot*. I have two **feet**.
(c)	man	men	I see a *man* on the street. I see two **men** on the street.
(d)	mouse	mice	My cat sees a *mouse*. Cats like to catch **mice**.
(e)	tooth	teeth	My *tooth* hurts. My **teeth** are white.
(f)	woman	women*	One *woman* is in our class. Ten **women** are in your class.
(g)	sheep	sheep	Annie drew a picture of one *sheep*. Tommy drew a picture of two **sheep**.
(h)	fish	fish	Nancy has one *fish*. Katie has three **fish**.
(i)	(none)**	people	Fifteen **people** are in this room. (Note: **People** does not have a final **-s**.)

*Pronunciation: "wih-muhn"
**People is always plural. It has no singular form.

EXERCISE 11 ▸ Looking at grammar. (Chart 5-2)

Complete the sentences with the correct form of the noun in each picture.

1. The dentist is checking the patient's _____. One _____ has a problem.

2. It's 3:00 A.M. I can't sleep. I'm counting _____. One _____, two _____, ... one hundred _____. Oh, no, I'm still awake!

3. The dancer is standing on one _____. After a dance, her _____ are sore.

4. Janine has two _____. I have one _____.

5. Look at the two _____ . One _____ is jumping.

6. One _____ is talking on the phone. One _____ is
thinking about something.

7. These _____ are having a conversation.

8. I see a _____ in the garage. Oh, no! Now I see three

_____ .

EXERCISE 12 ▸ Reading, grammar, and speaking. (Charts 5-1 and 5-2)
Part I. Read the paragraph. Look at new vocabulary with your teacher first.

An Online Shopper

Tara likes to buy clothes online. She lives far away
from stores and shopping malls. She knows many good
online sites. She frequently checks for sales. She finds
shirts, pants, and jackets for her husband and children.
She buys skirts, dresses, warm coats, and hats for herself.
But she doesn't get shoes online. She has big feet, and
often shoes don't fit. Sometimes she returns her purchases.
For Tara, the best websites have free shipping for returns.

Do you know these words?
- malls
- sales
- purchases
- free shipping

Part II. Make the nouns plural. Write Ø for "no ending."

1. Tara shops at online site_____.

2. She lives far away from mall_____.

3. She checks website_____ for sale_____.

4. She likes to buy clothes for her husband and child_____.

5. She buys jacket_____, skirt_____, shirt_____, dress_____, and coat_____.

6. She doesn't buy shoe_____ online because she has big _____, and the shoe_____ often don't fit.

7. Tara likes website_____ with free shipping for return_____.

Part III. Work in small groups. Answer the questions.

1. Here are some ways to shop for clothes. What words are new for you? How do you like to shop for clothes?

_____ a. online

_____ b. department stores

_____ c. discount stores

_____ d. secondhand stores

_____ e. social media (e.g., Facebook Marketplace)

_____ f. garage sales/yard sales

2. What websites are good for shopping? What websites are not good?

_____

_____

3. What advice do you have for your classmates about shopping in this area? What are some good stores? Bad stores? Cheap stores? Expensive stores?

_____

_____

_____

EXERCISE 13 ▶ Warm-up. (Chart 5-3)

Do you agree or disagree with each sentence? Choose *yes* or *no*.

1. I cook delicious meals.   yes   no

2. I like raw vegetables.   yes   no

3. Fresh fruit is expensive.   yes   no

5-3 Adjectives with Nouns

(a) I don't like **cold** *weather*. adj. + noun	An ADJECTIVE (adj.) describes a noun. In grammar, we say that adjectives modify nouns. The word *modify* means "change a little." Adjectives give a little different meaning to a noun: *cold weather, hot weather, nice weather, bad weather.*
(b) Alex is a **happy** *child*. adj. + noun	
(c) The **hungry** *boy* has a **fresh** *apple*. adj. + noun adj. + noun	Adjectives come in front of nouns.
(d) The *weather* is **cold**. noun + *be* + adj.	Reminder: An adjective can also follow ***be***; the adjective describes the subject of the sentence. (See Chart 1-7, p. 16.)

COMMON ADJECTIVES

beautiful – ugly	good – bad	angry	hungry
big – little	happy – sad	bright	important
big – small	large – small	busy	intelligent
boring – interesting	long – short	delicious	interesting
cheap – expensive	noisy – quiet	exciting	kind
clean – dirty	old – new	famous	lazy
cold – hot	old – young	favorite	nervous
dangerous – safe	poor – rich	free	nice
dry – wet	sour – sweet	fresh	raw
easy – hard	strong – weak	healthy	serious
easy – difficult		honest	wonderful

● **EXERCISE 14 ▸ Grammar and vocabulary.** (Chart 5-3)

Work with a partner. Write the words from the box in the correct columns on page 139. Then look at the picture and add three more words to each column. Share some of your new nouns and adjectives with the class.

In the City

big
buildings
buses
busy
cars
fast
green
noisy
people
street
tall
trees

NOUNS	**ADJECTIVES**
_____	_____
_____	_____
_____	_____
_____	_____
_____	_____
_____	_____
_____	_____
_____	_____

EXERCISE 15 ▸ Looking at grammar. (Chart 5-3)

Circle the nouns about food. <u>Underline</u> the adjectives. Draw an arrow from each adjective to the noun it describes.

1. Jake is a <u>wonderful</u> (cook.)

2. My sister makes delicious soups.

3. We often eat at an Italian restaurant.

4. Valentina buys expensive ice cream.

5. Max likes American hamburgers.

EXERCISE 16 ▸ Let's talk. (Chart 5-3)

Work in small groups. Add adjectives to the sentences. Use any adjectives that make sense. Take turns. Think of at least three possible adjectives for each sentence.

1. I don't like ____*cold / hot / wet / rainy / bad / etc.*____ weather.

2. Do you like _____ food?

3. I admire _____ people.

4. _____ people make me angry.

5. Pollution is a/an _____ problem.

6. I had a/an _____ experience yesterday.

7. I don't like _____ cities.

8. I had a/an _____ dinner last night.

EXERCISE 17 ▸ Let's talk. (Chart 5-3)

Part I. Work in small groups. Complete each sentence with the name of a country and the adjective form of it.

1. Food from _____ *China* _____ is _____ *Chinese* _____ food.

2. Food from _____ *Mexico* _____ is _____ food.

3. Food from _____ is _____ food.

4. Food from _____ is _____ food.

5. Food from _____ is _____ food.

6. Food from _____ is _____ food.

7. Food from _____ is _____ food.

8. Food from _____ is _____ food.

Part II. What is the favorite international food in your group? Give an example of this kind of food. Share your information. Find out the most popular international food in other groups.

Example: What is your favorite international food?
GROUP: Italian.

Example: Give an example of Italian food.
GROUP: Spaghetti.

Favorite international food in our group: _____

An example of this kind of food: _____

Part III. Work as a class. Make a list of adjectives for nationality.

Example: Mexico → *Mexican*

EXERCISE 18 ▸ Warm-up. (Chart 5-4)
Underline the nouns in the sentences.

1. Children play games.

2. Athletes play sports.

3. Kids play music.

5-4 Nouns: Subjects and Objects

(a)	NOUN Karl	is washing NOUN dishes.
	subject verb object	
(b)	NOUN The *dishes*	are drying.
	subject verb	

In (a): A NOUN is used as the SUBJECT of a sentence. A NOUN can also be used as the OBJECT of a verb.*

Dishes is a NOUN. *Dishes* is the object of the verb *is washing*. Objects come after the verb.

In (b): *Dishes* is a NOUN. It is used as the subject of the sentence. There is no object.

*Some verbs can be followed by an object. These verbs are called "transitive verbs" (*v.t.* in a dictionary). Some verbs cannot be followed by an object. These verbs are called "intransitive verbs" (*v.i.* in a dictionary).

EXERCISE 19 ▸ Looking at grammar. (Chart 5-4)
For each sentence, write the object or write Ø for no object.

Cats and Mice

NOUN

1. Cats catch mice.   object = _____*mice*_____

2. Cats purr sometimes.   object = _____Ø_____

3. Mice like cheese.   object = _____

4. Mice don't like people.   object = _____

5. Cats sleep a lot.   object = _____

6. Cats chase mice.   object = _____

7. Cats scratch furniture.   object = _____

8. Mice run around.   object = _____

EXERCISE 20 ▸ Grammar and speaking. (Chart 5-4)

Part I. Complete each diagram with the correct subject, verb, and object.

A Weekend Afternoon

1. Emily is washing her clothes today.

Emily	is washing	clothes
subject	verb	object of verb

2. Her roommate is sleeping right now.

Her roommate	is sleeping	∅
subject	verb	object of verb

3. Sonya is watching a video.

subject	verb	object of verb

4. Leo is studying.

subject	verb	object of verb

5. He is reading a textbook.

subject	verb	object of verb

6. Veronica is checking Twitter.

subject	verb	object of verb

7. Eddie is making some popcorn.

subject	verb	object of verb

Part II. Work in small groups or with a partner. Answer this question: *What do you do on weekends?* Give several answers. Use this form: *subject + verb + object.*

EXERCISE 21 ▸ Warm-up. (Chart 5-5)

Choose <u>all</u> the correct completions for each sentence.

he	him	it
she	her	

1. I understand _____.

2. You don't understand _____.

3. _____ understands us.

5-5 Subject Pronouns and Object Pronouns

SUBJECT PRONOUNS	OBJECT PRONOUNS	SUBJECT — OBJECT
(a) *I* speak English.	Bob knows *me*.	I — me
(b) *You* speak English.	Bob knows *you*.	you — you
(c) *She* speaks English.	Bob knows *her*.	she — her
(d) *He* speaks English.	Bob knows *him*.	he — him
(e) *It* starts at 8:00.	Bob knows *it*.	it — it
(f) *We* speak English.	Bob knows *us*.	we — us
(g) *You* speak English.	Bob knows *you*.	you — you
(h) *They* speak English.	Bob knows *them*.	they — them
(i) I know *Tony*. *He* is a friendly person.		A pronoun has the same meaning as a noun. In (i): *He* has the same meaning as *Tony*. In (j): *Him* has the same meaning as *Tony*. In grammar, we say that a pronoun "refers to" a noun. The pronouns *he* and *him* refer to the noun *Tony*. The pronoun is necessary. *INCORRECT: I know well.*
(j) I like *Tony*. I know *him* well.		
(k) I have *a red book*. *It* is on my desk.		Sometimes a pronoun refers to a *noun phrase*. In (k): *It* refers to the phrase *a red book*.

EXERCISE 22 ▸ Looking at grammar. (Chart 5-5)

Write the correct subject and object pronouns.

1. Jack loves Janey. _____*He*_____ loves _____*her*_____ very much.

2. Janey loves Jack. _____ loves _____ very much.

3. Janey and Jack love their daughter, Mia. _____ love _____ very much.

4. Janey and Jack love their son, Todd. _____ love _____ very much.

5. Todd loves his little sister, Mia. _____ loves _____ very much.

6. Janey loves her children. _____ loves _____ very much.

7. Jack loves his children. _____ loves _____ very much.

8. Janey and Jack love Todd and Mia. _____ love _____ very much.

EXERCISE 23 ▸ Looking at grammar. (Chart 5-5)
Choose the correct answers.

1. Rita has a book. (She)/ It bought her /(it) last week.

2. I know the new students. Franco doesn't know him / them yet.

3. Where are my keys? Are they / them in your purse?

4. Ary is in Canada. She / Her is studying at a university.

5. I have two pictures on my bedroom wall. I like it / them.   It / They are beautiful.

6. Zola and I / me have a dinner invitation. Mr. and Mrs. Soto want we / us to come to dinner at their house.

7. Min has a new car. He / It is a convertible.

8. My husband and I have a new car. We / Us got it / him last month.

EXERCISE 24 ▸ Let's talk: interview. (Chart 5-5)
Interview your classmates. Find someone who can answer *yes* to a question. Then ask the follow-up question. Use the appropriate object pronoun.

Example:

STUDENT A: Do you send emails?
STUDENT B: No, I don't.
STUDENT A: (*Ask another student.*) Do you send emails?
STUDENT C: Yes, I do.

Follow-up question:

STUDENT A: When do you send **them**?
STUDENT C: I send **them** all day.

1. Do you do your homework?
   When do you ... ?

2. Do you visit friends?
   When do you ... ?

3. Do you check your phone?
   When do you ... ?

4. Do you talk to (*name of classmate*)?
When do you ... ?

5. Do you watch TV?
When do you ... ?

6. Do you buy groceries?
When do you ... ?

7. Do you wear boots?
When do you ... ?

8. Do you use a laptop computer?
When do you ... ?

EXERCISE 25 ▸ Looking at grammar. (Chart 5-5)
Choose the correct answer.

1. When do you take your medicine?
    a. I take in the morning.   b. I take it in the morning.

2. When do you feed your cat?
    a. I feed at noon.   b. I feed her at noon.

3. When do you see your advisor?
    a. I see him on Friday.   b. I see on Friday.

4. Where do you take the kids on weekends?
    a. I take to the park.   b. I take them to the park.

5. Where do you do your homework?
    a. I do it in the library.   b. I do in the library.

EXERCISE 26 ▸ Warm-up. (Chart 5-6)
Check (✓) the sentences with correct grammar.

1. _____ He is talking to her.

2. _____ He is talking to she.

3. _____ She is talking to he.

4. _____ She is talking to him.

5-6 Prepositions + Object Pronouns

	OBJECT PRONOUNS	
(a)	The teacher is talking *to me*.	In (a), *to* is a preposition; *me* is an object pronoun.
(b)	The teacher is talking *to you*.	In (a)–(f), object pronouns, not subject pronouns (*I, he, she, etc.*), follow prepositions.
(c)	The teacher is talking *to him*.	
(d)	The teacher is talking *to her*.	Note the pronouns in (g) and (h).
(e)	The teacher is talking *to us*.	
(f)	The teacher is talking *to them*.	*INCORRECT:* The teacher is talking to Marta and I.
(g)	The teacher is talking *to* Marta and *me*.	The teacher is talking to Ron and she.
(h)	The teacher is talking *to* Ron and *her*.	

SOME COMMON PREPOSITIONS

about	between	for	near	to
across	by	from	of	under
at	during	in	on	with

EXERCISE 27 ▸ Looking at grammar. (Chart 5-6)
<u>Underline</u> the prepositions.

1. Miguel is giving graduation presents <u>to</u> us.

2. Lesley sits by me during class.

3. This package is for you.

4. Ramona sits between Samuel and her.

5. Who is going to the store with you?

6. Ali is walking home with Norm and Kelly. She lives near them.

EXERCISE 28 ▸ Looking at grammar. (Chart 5-6)
Choose the correct answers.

People I Know

1. Bert lives in my dorm. I eat breakfast with he / him every morning.

2. The Johnsons walk their dog in the park. I talk to they / them several times a week.

3. My dad lives nearby. He eats out with my sister and I / me once a week.

4. Professor Jones is my advisor. I meet with she / her once a month.

5. Aunt Ellen rents an apartment near my husband and I / me .

6. My boss has twin boys. He takes care of they / them when his wife travels.

7. Sandra is my neighbor. I speak with she / her every day. She / Her and I / me have interesting conversations.

8. A: Is Paul Peterson in your class?

   B: Yes, he / him and I / me sit next to Katherine.

EXERCISE 29 ▸ Listening. (Charts 5-5 and 5-6)

Listen to the sentences. Notice that the "h" in *her* and *him* is often dropped in spoken English. The "th" in *them* can also be dropped. *Him* and *them* may sound the same.

1. Renata knows Oscar. She knows him very well.
2. Where does Shelley live? Do you have her address?
3. I see Vince. Let's go talk to him.
4. I see Dave and Lois. Let's go talk to them.
5. I'm looking online for JoAnne's phone number. What's her last name again?
6. I need to see our airline tickets. Do you have them?

EXERCISE 30 ▸ Looking at grammar. (Charts 5-5 and 5-6)

Complete the short conversations with the correct pronouns.

Going to a Movie

1. A: Does the movie start at 7:00?

   B: No, _____*it*_____ doesn't.

      _____*It*_____ starts at 8:00.

2. A: Are Maggie and Omar coming with us?

   B: _____ am not sure. I need to

      ask _____ .

3. A: Do Julia and you want to leave for the theater early?

   B: Yes, _____ do. Julia and _____ want to leave early.

4. A: Where does Julia like to sit?

   B: _____ likes to sit in the center. But I like to sit near the aisle.

   A: Do you want to sit with _____?

   B: Yes. But maybe the aisle is OK with _____ . Maybe she wants to sit near the aisle with _____ .

   A: Maybe!

5. A: I'm on the theater website. _____ isn't working.

   B: Let me look at _____ .

EXERCISE 31 ▸ Looking at grammar. (Charts 5-5 and 5-6)
Choose the correct answer.

Updates

1. Katie is graduating today. We're having a party for _____ .
   a. them   b. it   c. she   d. her

2. Jared is working at the office with my husband and _____ .
   a. I   b. me   c. he   d. she

3. Maya and Leo are expecting a new baby. _____ are very excited.
   a. They   b. You   c. We   d. She

4. Our grandkids have a one-week vacation. We are planning a trip with _____ .
   a. it   b. they   c. them   d. him

5. Grandma isn't driving now. Her car is old. She wants to sell _____ .
   a. her   b. them   c. him   d. it

6. My husband and _____ are traveling a lot for our jobs.
   a. I   b. me   c. us   d. them

7. Dan is really sick. His wife is taking care of _____ .
   a. he   b. him   c. them   d. it

8. My brother and I share an apartment now. You are welcome to visit _____ .
   a. us   b. them   c. we   d. they

EXERCISE 32 ▸ Warm-up. (Chart 5-7)
Complete the sentences.

Who does this book belong to?

1. Student A: It's his book.   OR   It's his.

2. Student B: It's her book.   OR   It's hers.

3. Student C: It's your book.   OR   It's yours.

4. Student D: It's our book.   OR   It's _____ .

5. Student E: It's their book.   OR   It's _____ .

Do you know this exception?

6. It's my book.   OR   It's _____ .

5-7 Possessive Adjectives and Possessive Pronouns

	POSSESSIVE ADJECTIVE	POSSESSIVE PRONOUN	
(a) This book belongs to me. It is *my* book. It is *mine*.	my your her	mine yours hers	A POSSESSIVE ADJECTIVE is used in front of a noun: *my* book.
(b) That book belongs to you. It is *your* book. It is *yours*.	his	his	
(c) That book is *mine*. INCORRECT: *That is mine book.*	our their	ours theirs	A POSSESSIVE PRONOUN is used alone, without a noun after it, as in (c).

EXERCISE 33 ▸ Looking at grammar. (Chart 5-7)
Write or say the correct possessive pronoun.

1. It's your money. It's _____.

2. It's our money. It's _____.

3. It's her money. It's _____.

4. It's their money. It's _____.

5. It's his money. It's _____.

6. It's my money. It's _____.

7. The money belongs to Matt. It's _____.

8. The money belongs to Elena. It's _____.

9. The money belongs to Matt and Elena. It's _____.

10. The money belongs to Stuart and me. It's _____.

EXERCISE 34 ▸ Looking at grammar. (Charts 2-7, 5-5 → 5-7)
Complete the sentences. Use object pronouns, possessive adjectives, and possessive pronouns.

1. **I** own this book.
   a. This book belongs to ____*me*____.
   b. This is ____*my*____ book.
   c. This book is ____*mine*____.

2. **They** own these books.
   a. These books belong to _____.
   b. These are _____ books.
   c. These books are _____.

3. **You** own that book.

  a. That book belongs to _____.

  b. That is _____ book.

  c. That book is _____.

4. **She** owns this pen.

  a. This pen belongs to _____.

  b. This is _____ pen.

  c. This pen is _____.

5. **He** owns that pen.

  a. That pen belongs to _____.

  b. That is _____ pen.

  c. That pen is _____.

6. **We** own those books.

  a. Those books belong to _____.

  b. Those are _____ books.

  c. Those books are _____.

EXERCISE 35 ▶ Let's talk: pairwork. (Charts 2-7 and 5-7)
Work with a partner. Point to objects in the classroom. Ask and answer *yes/no* questions. Use possessive adjectives in questions. Answer with possessive pronouns.

Examples: PARTNER A: (*pointing to phone*) Is that your phone?
  PARTNER B: Yes, it's mine.

  PARTNER B: (*pointing to desk*) Is this your desk?
  PARTNER A: No, it's his.

EXERCISE 36 ▶ Looking at grammar. (Charts 2-7 and 5-7)
Choose the correct completion.

1. Is this your / yours pen?

2. Please give this dictionary to Oksana. It's her / hers.

3. A: Don't forget your / yours hat. Here.

  B: No, that's not my / mine hat. My / Mine is a baseball cap.

4. A: Please take this bouquet of flowers as a gift from me. Here. They're your / yours.

  B: Thank you. You're very thoughtful.

5. A: That car belongs to Mr. and Mrs. Townsend.

  B: No, that's not their / theirs.   Their / Theirs car is new.

6. A: Malik and I really like our / ours new apartment. It has lots of space. How do you
      like your / yours?

   B: Our / Ours is small, but it's comfortable.

7. A: Excuse me. Is this your / yours umbrella?

   B: I don't have an umbrella. Ask Jay. Maybe it's he / his.

8. A: This isn't my / mine phone.

   B: Are you sure?

   A: Yes, I have a blue case. This one belongs to Carla. Her / Hers has a red case.

Jump-start your English

Useful Idioms

Part I. Look at the idioms in the box. Then listen to the short conversations. Note the words
in boldface.

> *take my time* = do something slowly; not hurry
> *do my best* = do very well; try hard
> *change my mind* = change my decision
> *make plans with* = plan
> *get along with* = have a good relationship with

1. A: We're late for the train. We need to hurry.
   B: No, you're OK. Take **your** time.

2. A: Why are you studying so much?
   B: I want to do **my** best.

3. A: Thomas always changes **his** mind.
   B: I know. First he says "yes." Then he
      says "no." Or, first he says "no," and
      then he says "yes." It's frustrating.

4. A: Do you want to make plans with Joe
      and **me** for the weekend?
   B: Thanks, but I just want to stay home
      and relax.

5. A: Do you know Joe and Lisa?
   B: Yes, I get along with **them** well.

Part II. Choose the best answers for you.

1. a. I get ready slowly in the morning. I take my time.
   b. I hurry in the morning. I don't take my time.

2. a. On weekends, I like to make plans with friends.
   b. On weekends, I don't like to make plans with anyone.

3. a. I usually do my homework carefully. I want to do my best.
   b. I usually do my homework quickly. I don't check for mistakes. I don't do my best.

4. a. I often change my mind.
   b. I sometimes change my mind.
   c. I rarely change my mind.

5. a. I get along with everyone.
   b. I don't get along with some people.

Part III. Share your answers with a partner. Then, in small groups, tell about your partner.

Example: Josef likes to take his time in the morning. OR Suzanne doesn't like to make plans for weekends.

EXERCISE 37 ▶ Warm-up. (Chart 5-8)
Check (✓) the sentences with correct grammar.

1. _____ His bedroom is messy.

2. _____ The boy his bedroom is messy.

3. _____ The boy bedroom is messy.

4. _____ The boy's bedroom is messy.

5-8 Possessive Nouns

		SINGULAR NOUN	POSSESSIVE FORM	To show that a person possesses something, add an apostrophe (') and -s to a singular noun.
(a)	My *friend* has a car. My *friend's* car is blue.	**friend**	**friend's**	POSSESSIVE NOUN, SINGULAR: *noun + apostrophe (') + -s*
(b)	The *student* has a book. The *student's* book is red.	**student**	**student's**	

		PLURAL NOUN	POSSESSIVE FORM	Add an apostrophe (') at the end of a plural noun (after the -s).
(c)	The *students* have books. The *students'* books are red.	**students**	**students'**	POSSESSIVE NOUN, PLURAL: *noun + -s + apostrophe (')*
(d)	My *friends* have a car. My *friends'* car is blue.	**friends**	**friends'**	Do not use an apostrophe when the noun is not possessive. *INCORRECT: My friends' have a car.*

(e) *Eva's* car is new.	Names of people can also take the possessive form.
(f) That car is *Joe's*.	In (e): The car belongs to Eva. In (f): The car belongs to Joe.

EXERCISE 38 ▸ Looking at grammar. (Chart 5-8)
Complete the sentences with the correct words.

1. My friend's house is in the city.

   The _____*house*_____ belongs to _____*my friend*_____.

2. The manager's schedule is on her desk.

   The _____ belongs to _____.

3. Dave's car is expensive.

   The _____ belongs to _____.

4. Where is Samir's room?

   The _____ belongs to _____.

5. Is the doctor's office crowded?

   The _____ belongs to _____.

EXERCISE 39 ▸ Looking at grammar. (Chart 5-8)
Choose the correct answer for each noun in red.

1. My teacher's office is large.   one teacher   more than one

2. My teachers' office is large.   one teacher   more than one

3. The nurses' uniform is green.   one nurse   more than one

4. The nurse's uniform is green.   one nurse   more than one

5. My friends' work is interesting.   one friend   more than one

6. The dentist's schedule is busy.   one dentist   more than one

EXERCISE 40 ▸ Looking at grammar. (Chart 5-8)
Work in small groups. Complete the sentences with your classmates' names.

1. _____ hair is short and straight.

2. _____ grammar book is on her desk.

3. _____ last name is _____.

4. I don't know _____ address.

5. _____ eyes are brown.

6. _____ shirt is blue.

7. _____ backpack is on the floor.

8. I need to borrow _____ pen.

EXERCISE 41 ▸ Game. (Chart 5-8)
Work in teams. Complete the sentences with words in the box. You may use a word more than one time. The team with the most correct answers wins.

| brother | daughter | mother | son |
| children | father | sister | wife |

Family Relationships

1. My uncle is my father's _____.

2. My grandmother is my mother's _____.

3. My brother-in-law is my husband's _____.

4. My sister's _____ are my nieces and nephews.

5. My niece is my brother's _____.

6. My nephew is my sister's _____.

7. My aunt's _____ is my mother.

8. My wife's _____ is my mother-in-law.

9. My brother's _____ is my sister-in-law.

10. My father's _____ and _____ are my grandparents.

EXERCISE 42 ▶ Looking at grammar. (Charts 2-7, 5-7, and 5-8)
Write the correct possessive form of the given words.

1. I   a. This bookbag is _____*mine*_____.

   Ava   b. That bookbag is _____*Ava's*_____.

   I   c. _____*My*_____ bookbag is red.

   she   d. _____*Hers*_____ is green.

2. we   a. These books are _____.

   they   b. Those books are _____.

   we   c. _____ books are on the table.

   they   d. _____ are on the desk.

3. Don   a. This raincoat is _____.

   Kate   b. That raincoat is _____.

   he   c. _____ is light brown.

   she   d. _____ is light blue.

4. I   a. This notebook is _____.

   you   b. That one is _____.

   I   c. _____ has _____ name on it.

   you   d. _____ has _____ name on it.

5. Ray   a. _____ apartment is on Pine Street.

   we   b. _____ is on Main Street.

   he   c. _____ apartment has three rooms.

   we   d. _____ has four rooms.

6. I   a. This is _____ pen.

   you   b. That one is _____.

   I   c. _____ is in _____ pocket.

   you   d. _____ is on _____ desk.

7. we   a. _____ car is big.

   they   b. _____ is small.

   we   c. _____ gets poor gas mileage.

   they   d. _____ car gets good gas mileage.

8. Gabi   a. These books are _____ .

Evan   b. Those are _____ .

she   c. _____ are on _____ desk.

he   d. _____ are on _____ desk.

EXERCISE 43 ▸ Listening. (Chart 5-8)

Listen to each sentence. Choose the word you hear.

Example: You will hear: Your dad's job sounds interesting.

          You will choose: dad   (dad's)

1. Mack	Mack's		5. friend	friend's
2. Mack	Mack's		6. friend	friend's
3. teacher	teacher's		7. manager	manager's
4. teacher	teacher's		8. cousin	cousin's

EXERCISE 44 ▸ Grammar and listening. (Chart 5-8)

Part I. Choose the correct meaning: possessive or *is*.

1. The doctor's coming.	possessive	is
2. The doctor's office is nearby.	possessive	is
3. Ben's wife is planning a birthday party for him.	possessive	is
4. Ben's planning a trip for his family.	possessive	is
5. The teacher's speaking slowly.	possessive	is
6. The teacher's speech is easy to understand.	possessive	is

Part II. Listen to the sentences. Practice pronouncing them.

EXERCISE 45 ▸ Looking at grammar. (Chart 5-8)

Add apostrophes where necessary.

    Brian's
1. ~~Brians~~ last name is Wolf.

2. Stefan likes to work late at night. → *(no change)*

3. My teachers give a lot of homework.

4. My teachers names are Ms. Cordova and Mr. Durisova.

5. My teachers first name is Ellen.

6. The teacher collected all the students test papers at the end of the class.

7. Nicole is a girls name.

8. Erica and Natalie are girls names.

9. Do you know Monicas brother?

10. Ryans friends visited him last night.

EXERCISE 46 ▶ Warm-up. (Chart 5-9)
Choose the correct answer.

1. Who is that?
   a. It's Tom.
   b. It's Tom's.

2. Whose is that?
   a. It's Tom.
   b. It's Tom's.

5-9 Questions with *Whose*

(a)	*Whose book* is this?	→ *Mine.* → It's *mine*. → It's *my* book.	*Whose* asks about possession. *Whose* is often used with a noun (e.g., *whose book*), as in (a) and (b).
(b)	*Whose books* are these?	→ *Rita's.* → They're *Rita's*. → They're *Rita's* books.	
(c)	*Whose* is this? (*The speaker is pointing to one book.*)		*Whose* can be used without a noun if the meaning is clear, as in (c) and (d).
(d)	*Whose* are these? (*The speaker is pointing to some books*.)		
(e)	*Who's* your teacher?		In (e): *Who's* = *who is* *Whose* and *who's* have the same pronunciation.

Whose is this? I don't see a name on it. Who's the artist?

EXERCISE 47 ▸ Looking at grammar. (Chart 5-9)
Choose the correct answer.

1. Whose birthday is today?
   a. Audrey's.
   b. Audrey.

2. Who is on the phone?
   a. Audrey's.
   b. Audrey.

3. Who is working at the bakery?
   a. Allen.
   b. Allen's.

4. Whose bakery is the best?
   a. Allen.
   b. Allen's.

5. Who's joining us for lunch?
   a. Toshi's.
   b. Toshi.

6. Whose dirty socks are on the floor?
   a. Julian's.
   b. Julian.

EXERCISE 48 ▸ Looking at grammar. (Chart 5-9)
Write **Whose** or **Who's**.

1. _____ your roommate this year?

2. _____ pen is this?

3. _____ on the phone?

4. _____ that?

5. _____ is that?

6. _____ making so much noise?

EXERCISE 49 ▸ Listening. (Chart 5-9)
Listen to each sentence. Do you hear **Whose** or **Who's**?

In Class

1. Whose   Who's
2. Whose   Who's
3. Whose   Who's
4. Whose   Who's

5. Whose   Who's
6. Whose   Who's
7. Whose   Who's
8. Whose   Who's

EXERCISE 50 ▸ Looking at grammar. (Charts 2-1, 2-2, and 5-9)
Choose the correct answers.

1. Whose watch (is)/ are   (this)/ these?

2. Whose glasses is / are   that / those?

3. Whose hat   is / are   that / those?

4. Whose shoe   is / are   this / these?

5. Whose keys   is / are   this / these?

6. Whose phone charger   is / are   that / those?

EXERCISE 51 ▸ Let's talk: pairwork. (Chart 5-9)
Work with a partner. Touch or point to something in the classroom that belongs to someone.
Ask a question with **Whose**. Take turns.

Example:
PARTNER A: (*points to a book*) Whose book is this?
PARTNER B: It's mine. / Mine. / It's my book.

EXERCISE 52 ▸ Warm-up. (Chart 5-10)
What phrase describes the picture: a., b., or c.?

a. Woman's and Man's Restrooms

b. Women's and Men's Restrooms

c. Men and Women Restrooms

5-10 Possessive: Irregular Plural Nouns

(a) The ***children's** toys* are on the floor.	Irregular plural nouns (***children, men, women, people***) have an irregular plural possessive form. The apostrophe (') comes <u>before</u> the final **-s**.
(b) That store sells ***men's** clothing*.	REGULAR PLURAL POSSESSIVE NOUN: the ***students'** books*
(c) That store sells ***women's** clothing*.	
(d) I like to know about other ***people's** lives*.	IRREGULAR PLURAL POSSESSIVE NOUN: the ***women's** books*

EXERCISE 53 ▶ Looking at grammar. (Charts 5-8 and 5-10)
Write the possessive form of the noun.

These books belong to ...

1. Maggie.   They're ___*Maggie's*___ books.

2. my friend.   They're _____ books.

3. my friends.   They're _____ books.

4. the child.   They're _____ books.

5. the children. They're _____ books.

6. the woman.   They're _____ books.

7. the women.   They're _____ books.

EXERCISE 54 ▶ Looking at grammar. (Charts 5-8 and 5-10)
Choose the correct answers.

Names

1. My dog's / dogs' name is Fido.

2. My dog's / dogs' names are Fido and Rover.

3. Ivan and Peter are men's / mens' names.

4. Chris can be a man's / men's nickname or a woman's / women's nickname.

5. Some people's / peoples' nicknames are funny.

6. What is your brother's / brothers' name?

7. What are your brother's / brothers' names?

8. Our doctor's / doctors' last name is Doctor.

EXERCISE 55 ▶ Looking at grammar. (Charts 5-8 and 5-10)
Write the possessive form of the noun.

1. children   That store sells ___*children's*___ books.

2. wife   Antonio fixed his _____ car.

3. person   A biography is the story of a _____ life.

4. people   Biographies are the stories of _____ lives.

5. students   _____ lives are busy.

6. sister   Do you know my _____ husband?

7. children   Our _____ school is near our house.

EXERCISE 56 ▶ Listening. (Chapters 1–5 Review)

Listen to each conversation. Write the missing words.

Examples: You will hear: How is Mr. Park doing?
You will write: How _____*is*_____ Mr. Park doing?

You will hear: Great! I see him every week at the office.
You will write: Great! I see _____*him*_____ every week at the office.

1. A: Mika and _____ downtown this afternoon. Do you want to

    come _____?

    B: I don't think so, but thanks anyway. Chris and _____ to the library.

    _____ study for our test.

2. A: Hi, Abby. How do you like your new apartment?

    B: _____ great. I have a new roommate too. She's very nice.

    A: What's _____ name?

    B: Rita Lopez. Do you _____?

    A: No, but I know _____ brother. He's in my math class.

3. A: Do you see Mike and George very much?

    B: Yes, I see _____ often. We play video games at my house.

    A: Who usually wins?

    B: Mike. We never beat _____!

EXERCISE 57 ▶ Check your knowledge. (Chapter 5 Review)

Correct the mistakes.

1. Jamil a car has. → *Jamil has a car.*

2. Babys cry.

3. Kurt helps Justin and I.

4. Our teacher gives tests difficult.

5. Charlie is cutting with a lawnmower the grass.

6. Do you know Yuko roommate?

7. My roommate desk is always a mess.

8. Nineteen peoples are in my class.

9. Veronica and Victor have three childrens.

10. Excuse me. Where is the men room?

11. This building has twenty classroom.

12. Mr. Torro is our teacher. Me like he very much.

13. Does that store sell children toys?

14. Whose is book on the chair?

15. It is mine book.

EXERCISE 58 ▸ Grammar, reading, and writing. (Chapter 5)

Part I. Read the paragraph. Look at the words in red. Write "S" if the word is singular and "P" if it is plural.

My Favorite Store

My favorite store is City Market. It is a grocery store. I like this store because it has many kinds of groceries. I can buy interesting ingredients there. I often cook dishes from my country. City Market has a big selection of rice and fresh vegetables. I like to buy fresh, not frozen, vegetables and meat, but the meat at City Market is expensive, so I don't buy much. The store is near my house, and I can walk to it. The people are friendly and helpful.

Part II. Where do you like to shop? It can be a grocery store, clothes store, online store, etc. Complete the sentences. Combine the sentences into a paragraph. Add a few extra details to make your writing more interesting. Use the reading in Part I as an example. Begin with *My favorite store is*.

1. My favorite store is _____ .

2. I like this store because it _____ .

3. I often/sometimes buy _____ .

4. I don't like to buy _____ .

5. The store is _____ .

Part III. Edit your writing. Work individually or change papers with a partner. Check (✓) for the following:

1. ☐ an indented paragraph

2. ☐ a capital letter at the beginning of each sentence

3. ☐ a period at the end of each sentence

4. ☐ a verb in every sentence

5. ☐ correct use of *-s*/*-es*/*-ies* endings for plural nouns

6. ☐ correct use of irregular plural forms

7. ☐ correct spelling (use a dictionary or spell-check)

▪▪▪▪▪ For digital resources, go to MyEnglishLab on the Pearson English Portal. You can also go to the Pearson Practice English App for mobile practice.

CHAPTER 6

Count and Noncount Nouns

PRETEST: What do I already know?

Choose the correct answer.

1. Do you have some advice / suggestion for me? (Chart 6-1)

2. My brother has a lot of information / informations about that school. (Chart 6-1)

3. Joan is applying to an / a university nearby. (Chart 6-2)

4. I need an / a hour for my homework tonight. (Chart 6-2)

5. Would you like an / some eggs for breakfast? (Chart 6-3)

6. Here is a cup / bottle of soup for you. (Chart 6-4)

7. Do you have a little / a few sugar for the coffee? (Chart 6-5)

8. It's a beautiful day.   A / The sun is out.   A / The sky is blue. (Chart 6-6)

9. Everyone needs the / Ø love in life. (Chart 6-7)

10. I have some / any time for you right now. (Chart 6-8)

EXERCISE 1 ▶ Warm-up. (Chart 6-1)

Which can you count (1, 2, 3, …): sugar cubes or sugar? Check (✓) the correct answer.

1. _____ sugar

2. _____ sugar cubes

6-1 Nouns: Count and Noncount

	SINGULAR	PLURAL	
COUNT NOUN	*a book* *one book*	*books* *two books* *some books* *a lot of books*	**A COUNT NOUN**
NONCOUNT NOUN	*mail* *some mail* *a lot of mail*	(no plural form)	**A NONCOUNT NOUN**

A COUNT NOUN

SINGULAR ***a*** + *noun* ***one*** + *noun*	PLURAL *noun* + ***-s***

A NONCOUNT NOUN

SINGULAR Do not use ***a***. Do not use ***one***.	PLURAL A noncount noun does not have a plural form.

COMMON NONCOUNT NOUNS

advice	mail	bread	pepper
furniture	money	cheese	rice
help	music	coffee	salt
homework	traffic	food	soup
information	vocabulary	fruit	sugar
jewelry	weather	meat	tea
luck	work	milk	water

EXERCISE 2 ▸ Looking at grammar. (Chart 6-1)

Look at the words in *italics*. <u>Underline</u> the noun. Is it count or noncount?

1. She has *a coin*.   count   noncount

2. She has *some money*.   count   noncount

3. The street is full of *heavy traffic*.   count   noncount

4. *A lot of cars* are on the street.   count   noncount

5. Our school has *a big library*.   count   noncount

6. Would you like *some coffee?*   count   noncount

7. I need *some advice*.   count   noncount

8. Margo wears *a lot of bracelets*.   count   noncount

EXERCISE 3 ▸ Let's talk. (Chart 6-1)

Work with a partner. Answer one of the questions. Use nouns in your answers. Begin with **one** or **some**.

What do you have in your bag or backpack?

What is on your teacher's desk?

EXERCISE 4 ▶ Vocabulary and grammar. (Chart 6-1)

Add -**s** to the ends of the words if necessary or write **Ø** (no ending).

1. one earring____

2. two earring____

3. some jewelry____

4. one desk____

5. some chair____

6. some furniture____

7. one card____

8. a lot of postcard____

9. some mail____

10. a. a lot of car____

    b. a lot of traffic____

11. a. a lot of money____

    b. a lot of coin____

EXERCISE 5 ▸ Looking at grammar. (Chart 6-1)
Write *a* or *Ø*.

Homework

1. Peter is sitting at _____ desk.

2. He has _____ new chair.

3. He has _____ comfortable furniture.

4. He is working on _____ big assignment.

5. His teacher gives _____ homework every day.

6. He is looking for _____ information about _____ sugar.

7. He is writing down _____ fact.

EXERCISE 6 ▸ Looking at grammar. (Chart 6-1)
Choose <u>all</u> the words that can come in front of each noun in red.

1.	a	one	four	(some)	(a lot of)	music
2.	a	one	four	some	a lot of	song
3.	a	one	four	some	a lot of	songs
4.	a	one	four	some	a lot of	work
5.	a	one	four	some	a lot of	homework
6.	a	one	four	some	a lot of	jobs
7.	a	one	four	some	a lot of	job
8.	a	one	four	some	a lot of	assignments

EXERCISE 7 ▸ Let's talk: game. (Chart 6-1)
Work in small groups. Complete the list with nouns close in meaning. Use *a* with the count nouns. The group that finishes first and has the most correct answers wins.

	COUNT	NONCOUNT
1.	a suggestion	advice
2.		furniture
3.		money
4.	a job	
5.	a cloud	

	COUNT	NONCOUNT
6.		*music*
7.	*a fact*	
8.		*jewelry*
9.		*mail*

EXERCISE 8 ▸ Looking at grammar. (Chart 6-1)
Write **-s** or **Ø**.

1. a house_____, one house_____, two house_____, a lot of house_____, some house_____

2. a car_____, one car_____, four car_____, a lot of car_____

3. water_____, some water_____, a lot of water_____

4. a computer_____, three computer_____, some computer_____, a lot of computer_____

EXERCISE 9 ▸ Grammar and speaking. (Chart 6-1)
Work in small groups. Complete the sentences with as many nouns as possible. Write the names of things you see in the photo. Share some of your answers with the class.

I see ...

1. a
2. one
3. two
4. some
5. a lot of
6. many

EXERCISE 10 ▸ Warm-up (Chart 6-2)

Are the words in red correct or incorrect?

1. I work in an office.
2. It is in a hotel.
3. I take an elevator to the top floor.
4. I have an amazing view.

6-2 Using A vs. An

(a) *A dog* is *an animal*.	*A* and *an* are used in front of singular count nouns. In (a): *dog* and *animal* are singular count nouns.
(b) I work in *an office*.	Use *an* in front of words that begin with the vowels *a, e, i,* and *o: an apartment, an elephant, an idea, an ocean.*
(c) Mr. Tang is *an old man*.	In (c): Note that *an* is used because the adjective (*old*) begins with a vowel and comes in front of a singular count noun (*man*).
(d) I have *an uncle*.	Use *an* if a word that begins with "u" has a vowel sound: *an uncle, an ugly picture.*
COMPARE (e) He works at *a university*.	Use *a* if a word that begins with "u" has a /yu/ sound: *a university, a usual event.*
(f) I need *an hour* to finish my work.	In some words that begin with "h," the "h" is not pronounced. Instead, the word begins with a vowel sound and *an* is used: *an hour, an honor.*
COMPARE (g) I live in *a house*. He lives in *a hotel*.	In most words that begin with "h," the "h" is pronounced. Use *a* if the "h" is pronounced.

EXERCISE 11 ▸ Grammar and speaking. (Chart 6-2)

Part I. Work with a partner. Write *a* or *an*. Your teacher can help with new vocabulary.

1. _____ refrigerator
2. _____ oven
3. _____ stove
4. _____ electric stove
5. _____ fan
6. _____ microwave
7. _____ dishwasher
8. _____ espresso maker
9. _____ toaster
10. _____ freezer

KITCHEN APPLIANCES

Part II. Work with a partner. What is in your kitchen? Make sentences. Take turns. Begin with *My kitchen has a/an*.

EXERCISE 12 ▸ Looking at grammar. (Chart 6-2)
Write *a* or *an*.

Working at the Airport

1. a. Bashir has _____ exciting job.
   b. He is _____ pilot.
   c. He flies _____ airplane.
   d. Sometimes he flies _____ helicopter.

2. a. Alice works at _____ airport.
   b. She is at _____ meeting.
   c. She is talking about _____ idea.
   d. It is _____ good idea.

3. a. Mira works at _____ café in the airport.
   b. Right now she is helping _____ customer.
   c. He is ordering _____ snack.
   d. He wants _____ healthy snack.
   e. He is asking for _____ apple or _____ banana.

Listen to each sentence. Choose the word you hear.

Tell me some things about you and your family.

Example: You will hear: I come from a small town.
You will choose: (a)   an

1.	a	an		6.	a	an
2.	a	an		7.	a	an
3.	a	an		8.	a	an
4.	a	an		9.	a	an
5.	a	an		10.	a	an

EXERCISE 14 ▸ Warm-up (Chart 6-3)

Answer the questions about the nouns in the box. Can you make a rule about when to use **some**?

✓ a bike	some cars	some motorcycles
some pollution	some traffic	a truck

1. Which nouns are count?

   ___bike,_____

2. Which nouns are noncount?

   _____

3. Which nouns are singular count?

   _____

4. Which nouns are plural count?

   _____

6-3 Using A/An vs. Some

(a) I have *a pen*.	**A/An** is used in front of SINGULAR COUNT nouns. In (a): The word **pen** is a singular count noun.
(b) I have **some** *pens*.	**Some** is used in front of PLURAL COUNT nouns. In (b): The word **pens** is a plural count noun.
(c) I have **some** *rice*.	**Some** is used in front of NONCOUNT nouns.* In (c): The word **rice** is a noncount noun.

*Reminder: Noncount nouns do not have a plural form. Noncount nouns are grammatically singular.

EXERCISE 15 ▸ Looking at grammar. (Chart 6-3)

Look at each noun and circle the correct word: **a, an,** or **some.** Is the noun singular count, plural count, or noncount?

						SINGULAR COUNT	PLURAL COUNT	NONCOUNT
1.	a	an	(some)	letters			✓	
2.	a	an	(some)	mail				✓
3.	(a)	an	some	letter		✓		
4.	a	an	some	table				
5.	a	an	some	tables				
6.	a	an	some	furniture				
7.	a	an	some	car				
8.	a	an	some	motorcycles				
9.	a	an	some	buses				
10.	a	an	some	traffic				
11.	a	an	some	egg				
12.	a	an	some	eggs				
13.	a	an	some	hour				
14.	a	an	some	minutes				

EXERCISE 16 ▸ Looking at grammar. (Chart 6-3)

Write each word from the box in the correct column.

✓ answer	computer	evening	ideas	uncle	word
✓ boy	day	idea	mail	vocabulary	words

A	*AN*	*SOME*
boy	answer	

EXERCISE 17 ▸ Let's talk: pairwork. (Chart 6-3)
Work with a partner. Ask questions with *Do you want,* and answer with *Yes.*
Use *a, an,* or *some* in your questions and answers.

What's for lunch?

Partner A	Partner B
1. fruit	1. bread
2. apple	2. sandwich
3. potato	3. potatoes
4. soup	4. eggs
5. cheese	5. orange
6. cookie	6. ice cream
	Change roles.

EXERCISE 18 ▸ Let's talk. (Chart 6-3)
Work in small groups. Complete the lists with nouns. You may use adjectives with the nouns.
Share some of your answers with the class.

What do you usually see …

1. in an apartment?

   a. a _____

   b. an _____

   c. some _____ (*plural noun*)

   d. some _____ (*noncount noun*)

2. at a zoo?

   a. a _____

   b. an _____

   c. some _____ (*plural noun*)

   d. some _____ (*noncount noun*)

3. outdoors?

   a. a _____

   b. an _____

   c. some _____ (*plural noun*)

   d. some _____ (*noncount noun*)

EXERCISE 19 ▸ Looking at grammar. (Chart 6-3)
Write *a, an,* or *some*.

1. Marisol is wearing _____ silver jewelry. She's wearing _____ necklace
   and _____ earrings.

2. Amir and I are busy. I have _____ homework to do. He has _____ work
   to do.

3. Asha has _____ job. She is _____ teacher.

4. We have _____ table, _____ couch, and _____ chairs in our
   living room.

5. We have _____ furniture in our living room.

6. Natalie is listening to _____ music.

EXERCISE 20 ▸ Grammar and speaking. (Chart 6-3)
Work with a partner. Complete the sentences orally. Add *-s* to a count noun (or give the
irregular plural form). Do not add *-s* to a noncount noun. Take turns.

1. I need some _____.
   a. money
   b. euro
   c. information
   d. advice
   e. suggestion
   f. help

2. Do you want some _____ for lunch?
   a. sandwich
   b. coffee
   c. rice
   d. bean
   e. banana
   f. hamburger

3. I see some _____.
   a. key
   b. flower
   c. jewelry
   d. picture
   e. animal
   f. child

EXERCISE 21 ▸ Reading, grammar, and speaking. (Chart 6-3)

Part I. Read the paragraph. Look at new vocabulary with your teacher first.

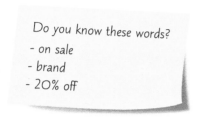

some ice cream

a coupon

A Coupon Shopper

Beth likes to shop with coupons. Coupons save her **some** money. She usually gets coupons from newspapers, online, or in **some** stores. Today she is shopping for paper products like toilet paper and tissues. She has **a** coupon for free toilet paper. It says, "Buy one package — get one free." She also wants **some** rice and butter. She doesn't have **a** coupon for rice, but her favorite rice is on sale. She has **a** coupon for butter, but it is still expensive with the coupon. She is looking for a cheaper brand. She also has **some** "20% off" coupons for frozen food. Ice cream sounds good. She loves ice cream, and she thinks **a** 20% coupon is good. Beth is happy because she is saving **some** money today.

Part II. Look at the words in **bold** in the paragraph. Write the noun after each bold word. Can you explain the use of *a* or *some* for each noun?

1. some ___money___

2. some _____

3. a _____

4. some _____

5. a _____

6. a _____

7. some _____

8. a _____

9. some _____

Part III. Work in small groups. Discuss the questions.

1. What do people generally buy with coupons?

2. Do people buy unnecessary things with coupons?

3. Do you use coupons? Why or why not?

EXERCISE 22 ▸ Looking at grammar. (Chart 6-3)
Choose <u>all</u> the correct sentences.

1. a. I'm hungry. I want a orange.
   b. I'm hungry. I want an orange.
   c. I'm hungry. I want some fruit.

2. a. I need an information about the bus schedule.
   b. I need some information about the bus schedule.
   c. I need a information about the bus schedule.

3. a. We have problem.
   b. We have a problem.
   c. We have some problem.
   d. We have some problems.

4. a. I have a suggestion for you.
   b. I have an advice for you.
   c. I have some advice for you.
   d. I have some suggestions for you.

EXERCISE 23 ▸ Warm-up. (Chart 6-4)
Which answers are true for you? Check (✓) them.

1. What do you drink every day?

   a. _____ coffee

   b. _____ milk

   c. _____ tea

   d. _____ water

   e. _____ juice

2. What do you put your drink(s) in?

   a. _____ a cup

   b. _____ a glass

3. Which phrases sound OK to you?

   a. _____ a cup of coffee

   b. _____ a glass of water

   c. _____ a glass of coffee

   d. _____ a glass of tea

   e. _____ a cup of water

   f. _____ a cup of juice

6-4 Measurements with Noncount Nouns

(a) I'd like **some** water.	Units of measure are used with noncount nouns to express a specific quantity. Examples: *a glass of, a cup of, a piece of*
(b) I'd like **a glass of** water.	In (a): **some water** = an unspecific quantity
(c) I'd like **a cup of** coffee.	In (b): **a glass of water** = a specific quantity
(d) I'd like **a piece of** fruit.	

COMMON EXPRESSIONS OF MEASURE

a bag of rice   a bunch of bananas   a jar of pickles
a bar of soap   a can of corn*   a loaf of bread
a bottle of olive oil   a carton of milk   a piece of cheese
a bowl of cereal   a cube of butter   a sheet of paper
a box of candy   a head of lettuce   a tube of toothpaste

bag   bar   bottle   box

can   carton   jar   tube   bunch

*In British English: *a tin of corn*

EXERCISE 24 ▶ Vocabulary and grammar. (Chart 6-4)
Complete the sentences. Use *a piece of, a cup of, a glass of, a bowl of*.

I'm hungry and thirsty. I'd like …

1. _____*a cup of*_____ coffee.

2. _____ bread.

3. _____ water.

4. _____ tea.

5. _____ cheese.

6. _____ soup.

7. _____ meat.

8. _____ wine.

9. _____ fruit.

10. _____ rice.

EXERCISE 25 ▸ Let's talk: pairwork. (Chart 6-4)

Part I. Work with a partner. What do you eat and drink every day? Check (✓) the items. Add your own words to the list. Then make sentences.

Example:

___✓___ egg   ___✓___ fruit

_____ banana   _____ ice cream

___✓___ coffee   _____ orange juice

PARTNER A: I have one egg every day.
              I usually eat two pieces of fruit.
              I drink two cups of coffee.

_____ egg   _____ rice

_____ soup   _____ ice cream

_____ fruit   _____ water

_____ bread   _____ chicken

_____ banana   _____ cheese

_____ apples   _____ tea

_____   _____

_____   _____

_____   _____

Part II. Tell your partner the usual quantity you have every day. Use *a piece of, two pieces of, a cup of, three cups of, a glass of, a bowl of,* or *one, two, a, some, etc.,* in your answers. Share a few of your partner's answers with the class.

EXERCISE 26 ▸ Grammar and speaking. (Chart 6-4)

Complete the sentences with nouns. Tell another student about your shopping list.

Shopping List

1. I'm going to the store. I need to buy a carton of ____*orange juice / milk / etc.*____

2. I also need a tube of _____ and two bars of _____.

3. I need to find a can of _____ and a jar of _____.

4. I need to get a loaf of _____ and a box of _____.

5. I want a head of _____ if it looks fresh.

6. Finally, I want a bottle of _____ and a jar of _____.

EXERCISE 27 ▶ Let's talk: pairwork. (Charts 6-1 → 6-4)

Work with a partner. Imagine that you are moving into a new apartment. What do you need? First, make a list. Then write the things you need and indicate quantity (*two, some, a lot of, etc.*). List fifteen to twenty things. Begin with *We need*.

A New Apartment

Example:

PARTNER A: a couch and two beds
PARTNER B: a can opener
PARTNER A: pots and pans
PARTNER B: bookcases
PARTNER A: paint (etc.)

Possible answer: We need one couch and two beds, one can opener, some pots and pans, a lot of bookcases, one can of paint, etc.

EXERCISE 28 ▶ Let's talk: pairwork. (Charts 6-1 → 6-4)

Work with a partner. Complete the sentences with *a*, *an*, or *some* and the nouns.
Partner A: Your book is open to this page. Partner B: Your book is open to *Let's Talk: Answers*, page 281. Help your partner with the correct responses if necessary.

1. I'm hungry. I'd like …
   a. food.
   b. apple.
   c. hamburger.
   d. bowl of soup.

2. I'm thirsty. I'd like …
   a. glass of milk.
   b. water.
   c. cup of tea.

3. I'm sick. I need …
   a. medicine.
   b. ambulance.

4. I'm cold. I need …
   a. coat.
   b. hat.
   c. warm clothes.*
   d. heat.

5. I'm tired. I need …
   a. sleep.
   b. break.
   c. relaxing vacation.

---

*Clothes is always plural. The word *clothes* does not have a singular form.

Change roles.
Partner B: Your book is open to this page. Partner A: Your book is open to page 281.

6. I'm hungry. I'd like …
   a. snack.
   b. fruit.
   c. orange.
   d. piece of chicken.

7. I'm thirsty. I'd like …
   a. juice.
   b. bottle of water.
   c. glass of iced tea.

8. I'm sick. I need …
   a. doctor.
   b. help.

9. I'm cold. I need …
   a. boots.
   b. blanket.
   c. hot bath.
   d. gloves.

10. I'm tired. I need …
   a. strong coffee.
   b. strong cup of coffee.
   c. vacation.
   d. nap.

Jump-start your English

Ordering from a Menu

 **Part I.** Listen to the conversations.

1. A: Hi, what can I get you?
   B: I'd like a chicken sandwich, please.
   A: Is that all?
   B: I'd like a glass of water, please.

2. A: What would you like?
   B: I'd like a tuna salad.
   A: Anything else?
   B: No, thanks. I'm not very hungry.

3. A: Are you ready to order?
   B: Yes, I'd like a hamburger.
   A: Do you want anything else?
   B: Some iced tea, please.

4. A: What is the soup today?
   B: It's vegetable.
   A: OK. That sounds good.
   B: A cup or a bowl?
   A: A cup, please.

5. A: Would you like dessert?
   B: I don't think so. I'm pretty full.
   A: OK.

LUNCH MENU

Soup of the Day

Green Salad
Tuna Salad

Cheese Sandwich
Chicken Sandwich
Hamburger

Coffee
Tea
Iced Tea
Milk

Homemade Ice Cream

Part II. Work with a partner. Ask and answer these questions. Take turns.

What's your favorite ...

1. drink /beverage?
2. entrée/main dish (chicken, fish, steak, etc.)?
3. sandwich?
4. pizza?
5. dessert?
6. snack?

Part III. With your partner, create a short menu with some of your favorite foods. Then make a conversation. Order from your menu. One person is the server and one person is the customer. Say it for the class. Remember, you can look at your paper before you speak. When you speak, look at your partner.

EXERCISE 29 ▸ Warm-up. (Chart 6-5)
Which answers are true for you?

1. Do you eat much fruit?

    a. Yes, I eat a lot.   b. I eat a little.   c. No, I don't like fruit.

2. Do you eat many bananas?

    a. Yes, I eat a lot.   b. I eat a few.   c. No, I don't like bananas.

6-5 Using *Many, Much, A Few, A Little*

(a)	I don't get *many* letters.	*Many* is used with PLURAL COUNT nouns.
(b)	I don't get *much* mail.	*Much* is used with NONCOUNT nouns.
(c)	Jan gets *a few* letters.	*A few* is used with PLURAL COUNT nouns.
(d)	Ken gets *a little* mail.	*A little* is used with NONCOUNT nouns.

EXERCISE 30 ▸ Grammar and speaking. (Chart 6-5)
Work with a partner. Complete the questions with *many* or *much*. Then give true answers. (If the answer is "zero," use "any" in the response.) Take turns. Share a few of your answers with the class.

Example: How _____*much*_____ tea do you drink in a day?

Possible answers: I drink three cups. I drink one cup. I drink a lot of tea. I drink a little tea. I don't drink any tea. Etc.

1. How _____*much*_____ fruit do you eat every day?

2. How _____*many*_____ roommates do you have?

3. How _____ languages do you speak?

4. How _____ homework does your teacher usually assign?

5. How _____ water do you drink in a day?

6. How _____ coffee do you drink in a day?

7. How _____ sentences are in this exercise?

8. How _____ pages are in this chapter?

EXERCISE 31 ▸ Grammar and speaking. (Chart 6-5)
Complete the sentences with **many** or **much**. Then work with a partner. Ask about each item.
Circle the answer your partner gives. Who has more items?

In your kitchen, do you have …

1. _____*much*_____ sugar?   Yes, I do.   No, I don't.

2. _____ paper bags?   Yes, I do.   No, I don't.

3. _____ flour?   Yes, I do.   No, I don't.

4. _____ salt?   Yes, I do.   No, I don't.

5. _____ spices?   Yes, I do.   No, I don't.

6. _____ olive oil?   Yes, I do.   No, I don't.

7. _____ butter?   Yes, I do.   No, I don't.

8. _____ honey?   Yes, I do.   No, I don't.

EXERCISE 32 ▸ Looking at grammar. (Chart 6-5)
Read the paragraph. Write **a little** or **a few** before each noun.

Andrew's Problem

     Andrew is having a party, but he has
a problem. He doesn't like to cook. His
cabinets and refrigerator are almost empty.
He has only …

1. _____ eggs.

2. _____ juice.

3. _____ potatoes.

4. _____ fruit.

5. _____ meat.

6. _____ vegetables.

7. _____ butter.

8. _____ ketchup.

9. _____ pieces of chicken.

10. _____ cans of soup.

EXERCISE 33 ▶ Looking at grammar. (Chart 6-5)

Change *a lot of* to *many* or *much*.

1. Daniel has a lot of problems.

   → *Daniel has many problems.*

2. I don't have a lot of money.

3. I don't put a lot of sugar in my coffee.

4. I have a lot of questions to ask you.

5. Pietro and Mia have a small apartment. They don't have a lot of furniture.

6. Lara is lazy. She doesn't do a lot of work.

7. I don't drink a lot of coffee.

8. Do you send a lot of text messages?

EXERCISE 34 ▶ Looking at grammar. (Chart 6-5)

Change *some* to *a few* or *a little*.

1. I need some soap.

   → *I need a little soap.*

2. I usually add some salt to my food.

3. I have some questions to ask you.

4. Robert needs some help. He has some problems. He needs some advice.

5. I need to wash some shirts.

6. I have some homework to do tonight.

7. When I'm hungry in the evening, I usually eat some dark chocolate.

8. We usually do some speaking exercises in class each day.

Work with a partner. Ask questions with **much** or **many**. Answer with *a little* or *a few*. Take turns. Remember, you can look at your book before you speak. When you speak, look at your partner.

Examples: chicken

PARTNER A: How **much chicken** would you like?
PARTNER B: I'd like **a little**, please. Thanks.

                    pencil

PARTNER B: How **many pencils** would you like?
PARTNER A: I'd like **a few**, please.

Partner A	Partner B
1. pen	1. salt
2. tea	2. banana
3. book	3. soup
4. apple	4. coffee
5. money	5. toy
6. help	6. cheese

EXERCISE 36 ▸ Let's talk. (Charts 6-1, 6-3, and 6-5)

Work in small groups. Imagine you are famous chefs. Create a dessert with some of the ingredients below. Check (✓) them. Give your recipe a name (it can be funny or strange). Tell the class about your dessert. Begin with *We need a little / a few / a lot of / some / two / three / etc.* OR *We don't need any*.

1. _____ salt
2. _____ flour
3. _____ honey
4. _____ sugar
5. _____ nuts
6. _____ coconut
7. _____ pieces of chocolate
8. _____ baking soda
9. _____ baking powder
10. _____ eggs
11. _____ cream
12. _____ butter

other ingredients:

_____

Jump-start your English

Talking About Email and Emails

Part I. Look at the difference in meaning between *email* and *emails*. Both are correct, but they have different meanings. Then listen to the conversations. Practice them with a partner.

> *email* = email in general (noncount)
>
> *an email* OR *emails* = single email message(s) (count)

1. A: Do you get much email?
   B: Yes, I do.

2. A: Do you get many emails?
   B: No, I don't.

3. A: What are you doing?
   B: I'm reading an email.

4: A: Do you get much junk email?
   B: Yes, I get a lot of junk email.

5. A: Do you get many junk emails?
   B: Yes, I get a lot of junk emails.

Part II. Which sentences are true for you? Check (✓) them. Which sentences are talking about single email messages? Which sentences are talking about email in general?

		single messages	email in general
1.	_____ I use email.	single messages	email in general
2.	_____ I don't use email.	single messages	email in general
3.	_____ I check email every day.	single messages	email in general
4.	_____ I send 5–10 emails every day.	single messages	email in general
5.	_____ My friends send me many emails.	single messages	email in general
6.	_____ I get an email from my family every week.	single messages	email in general
7.	_____ I don't get many junk emails.	single messages	email in general
8.	_____ I don't get much junk email.	single messages	email in general

Part III. Make a short conversation with your partner about your use of email. Say your conversations in small groups.

Read the two conversations. In which conversation are Speaker A and Speaker B thinking about the same bedroom?

1. A: Where are the kids?
   B: They're probably hiding in a bedroom.

2. A: Where's Raymond?
   B: He's in the bedroom.

6-6 Using *The*

(a) A: Where's Max? B: He's in *the* kitchen.	A speaker uses *the* when the speaker and the listener are thinking of the same thing or person. *The* shows that a noun is specific (not general).
(b) A: I have two pieces of fruit for us, an apple and a banana. What would you like? B: I'd like *the* apple, please.	In (a): Both A and B are thinking of the same kitchen. In (b): When B says "the apple," both A and B are thinking of the same apple.
(c) A: *The* sky is blue. *The* sun is hot. It's a nice summer day today. B: Yes, it's perfect.	In (c): Both A and B are thinking of the same sky (there is only one sky for them to think of) and the same sun (there is only one sun for them to think of).
(d) Nick has *a pen* and *a pencil*. *The* pen is blue. *The* pencil is yellow.	*The* is used with • singular count nouns, as in (d). • plural count nouns, as in (e). • noncount nouns, as in (f).
(e) Nick has *some* pens and pencils. *The* pens are blue. *The* pencils are yellow.	Note in the examples: The speaker is using *the* for the <u>second</u> mention of a noun. When the speaker mentions a noun for a second time, both the speaker and listener are now thinking about the same thing.
(f) Nick has *some* rice and *some* cheese. *The* rice is white. *The* cheese is yellow.	First mention: I have *a pen*. Second mention: *The* pen is blue.

Complete the sentences with *the* where necessary.

1. Elizabeth is standing outside. It is midnight.

   a. She's looking up at _____ sky.

   b. She sees _____ moon.

   c. She doesn't see _____ sun.

   d. _____ stars are very bright.

2. Frank and Louise are looking for an apartment to rent. Right now they are standing in a new apartment. They like it.

a. _____ kitchen is modern.

b. _____ appliances are nice.

c. _____ bedrooms are big.

d. _____ living room has a view of the park.

e. _____ apartment is near the subway.

EXERCISE 39 ▸ Looking at grammar. (Chart 6-6)
Complete the sentences with *a, an,* or *the*.

1. I have _____*a*_____ notebook and _____ grammar book. _____ notebook is brown. _____ grammar book is red.

2. Right now Maurice is sitting in class. He's sitting between _____ woman and _____ man. _____ woman is Graciela. _____ man is Mustafa.

3. Hana is wearing _____ ring and _____ necklace. _____ ring is on her left hand.

4. Brad and Angela are waiting for their plane to leave. Brad is looking at _____ magazine. Angela is reading _____ newspaper online. _____ newspaper has many interesting articles. Brad doesn't like _____ magazine.

5. I see four figures below: _____ circle, _____ triangle, _____ square, and _____ rectangle. _____ circle is next to _____ triangle. _____ square is between _____ triangle and _____ rectangle.

circle   triangle   square   rectangle

6. I gave my friend _____ card and _____ flower for her birthday. _____ card wished her "Happy Birthday." She liked both _____ card and _____ flower.

Work with a partner. Read the conversation aloud. Add *a*, *an*, or *the*. After you finish, write the answers.

A: Look at the picture. What do you see?

B: I see _____ TV, _____ remote, _____ couch, and _____ plant.
$\quad\quad\quad\quad$ 1 $\quad\quad\quad\quad$ 2 $\quad\quad\quad\quad$ 3 $\quad\quad\quad\quad$ 4

A: Where is _____ TV?
$\quad\quad\quad\quad$ 5

B: _____ TV is on a TV stand.
$\quad\quad$ 6

A: Where is _____ plant?
$\quad\quad\quad\quad$ 7

B: _____ plant is beside _____ couch.
$\quad\quad$ 8 $\quad\quad\quad\quad\quad\quad$ 9

Change roles.

A: Do you see any people?

B: Yes. I see _____ man and _____ little boy. _____ man is sitting on _____
$\quad\quad\quad\quad\quad$ 10 $\quad\quad\quad\quad\quad$ 11 $\quad\quad\quad\quad\quad$ 12 $\quad\quad\quad\quad\quad\quad$ 13

$\quad$ couch. _____ little boy is sitting on the floor.
$\quad\quad\quad\quad$ 14

A: What is _____ man doing?
$\quad\quad\quad\quad$ 15

B: He is holding _____ TV remote.
$\quad\quad\quad\quad\quad$ 16

A: What is _____ little boy doing?
$\quad\quad\quad\quad$ 17

B: He's playing with _____ airplane.
$\quad\quad\quad\quad\quad\quad$ 18

A: Where is _____ airplane?
$\quad\quad\quad\quad$ 19

B: It's in his hand.

EXERCISE 41 ▸ Grammar and speaking. (Chart 6-6)
Work with a partner. The sentences below make a story. Put them in order. The articles (*a*
and *the*) can help you with the answers. Answers may vary.

A Happy Cat

_____ It's not the fish.

_____ A cat jumps out of the water.

_____ The boy is young.

__1__ A man and a boy are at a lake.

_____ The lake has many fish.

_____ Suddenly, they hear a loud noise.

_____ A fish is swimming near them.

_____ Something big is in the water.

_____ The cat isn't hungry now.

_____ The man is old.

_____ The boy wants to catch the fish.

EXERCISE 42 ▸ Looking at grammar. (Chart 6-6)
Complete the conversations with *a, an,* or *the*.

1. A: I need to go to the mall. I need to buy _____ coat.

   B: I'll go with you. I need to get _____ jacket.

2. A: Look. It's raining. Do you have _____ umbrella?

   B: Yes, it's in _____ kitchen.

3. A: Gloria has _____ interesting job. She eats in _____ new restaurant every week.

   B: Why?

   A: She reviews restaurants.

4. A: How much longer do you need to use _____ computer?

   B: Just five more minutes, and then you can have it.

5. A: I need _____ stamp for this letter. Do you have one?

   B: Right here.

6. A: Would you like _____ egg for breakfast?

   B: No, thanks. I'll just have _____ glass of juice and some toast.

7. A: Do you see my pen? I can't find it.

   B: There it is. It's on _____ floor.

   A: Oh. I see it. Thanks.

8. A: Could you answer _____ phone? Thanks.

   B: Hello?

EXERCISE 43 ▸ Let's talk: game. (Chart 6-6)

Work in teams. Answer the questions. One person on each team writes the answers. You have five minutes. The team with the most grammatically correct answers wins.

1. What's on the floor? → *Some desks, a piece of gum, some dirt, the garbage can, etc.*
2. What's on the ceiling?
3. What's out in the hallway?
4. What's outside the window?
5. What's on the board (chalkboard, whiteboard, or bulletin board)?

EXERCISE 44 ▸ Warm-up. (Chart 6-7)

Which sentence (a. or b.) is true for each statement?

1. Oranges are expensive right now.
   a. Only some oranges are expensive.
   b. Oranges in general are expensive.

2. The oranges are sweet.
   a. A specific group of oranges is sweet.
   b. Oranges in general are sweet.

6-7 Using Ø (No Article) to Make Generalizations

(a) Ø *Apples* are good for you.	No article (Ø) is used to make generalizations with
(b) Ø *Students* use Ø *pens* and Ø *pencils*.	• plural count nouns, as in (a) and (b), and
(c) I like to listen to Ø *music*.	• noncount nouns, as in (c) and (d).
(d) Ø *Rice* is good for you.	
(e) Tim and Jan ate some fruit. *The apples* were very good, but *the bananas* were old.	COMPARE: In (a), the word ***apples*** is general. It refers to all apples, any apples. No article (Ø) is used.
	In (e), the word ***apples*** is specific, so ***the*** is used in front of it. It refers to the specific apples that Tim and Jan ate.
(f) We went to a concert last night. *The music* was very good.	COMPARE: In (c), ***music*** is general. In (f), ***the music*** is specific.

EXERCISE 45 ▸ Looking at grammar. (Chart 6-7)
Decide if the words in red are general or specific.

1. The eggs are delicious.	general	specific
2. Are eggs healthy?	general	specific
3. Please pass the salt.	general	specific
4. I love salt!	general	specific
5. Apples have vitamin C.	general	specific
6. The apples have brown spots.	general	specific

EXERCISE 46 ▸ Grammar and speaking. (Chart 6-7)
Part I. Complete the sentences with *the* or **Ø** (no article).

Food

1. Everybody needs ___Ø___ food to live.

2. _____ food in the fridge doesn't look very fresh.

3. We ate at a good restaurant last night.

   _____ food was excellent.

4. Is _____ chicken healthy?

5. _____ chicken in my sandwich is salty.

6. _____ coffee has caffeine.

7. _____ coffee in the pot is fresh.

8. I love _____ salads!

9. Thank you for _____ salad. It's delicious!

Part II. Work with a partner. Answer the questions.

1. What do you like to eat for breakfast?
2. What do you like to have for a snack during the day?
3. What do you like to drink during the day?
4. What do you eat in the evening?
5. What do you never eat?

EXERCISE 47 ▸ Listening. (Charts 6-6 and 6-7)
Listen to each sentence. Does the noun have a general or a specific meaning?

1. vegetables	(general)	specific
2. cats	general	specific
3. teacher	general	specific
4. bananas	general	specific
5. cars	general	specific
6. car	general	specific
7. computers	general	specific
8. park	general	specific

EXERCISE 48 ▸ Looking at grammar. (Charts 6-6 and 6-7)
Choose the meaning of the given sentence.

1. The dog is waiting by the door.
   a. We know the dog.
   b. We don't know the dog.

2. A cat is waiting by the door.
   a. We know the cat.
   b. We don't know the cat.

3. I need to call the library.
   a. You know the library.
   b. You don't know the library.

4. Where is the TV remote?
   a. I'm asking about a specific remote.
   b. I'm asking about a remote in general.

5. Vegetables are healthy.
   a. I'm talking about specific vegetables.
   b. I'm talking about vegetables in general.

EXERCISE 49 ▸ Grammar and speaking. (Charts 6-3, 6-6, and 6-7)
Work in small groups or as a class. Which sentence is closest in meaning to each situation?
Discuss the differences.

1. Mark is at a computer store. Five tablets are on the shelf. He buys one.
   a. He buys a tablet.
   b. He buys the tablet.

2. Pat is at a music store. The store has one guitar. She buys it.
   a. She buys a guitar.
   b. She buys the guitar.

3. Martha is at the library. It has five books about Nelson Mandela.
   a. She checks out the book about Nelson Mandela.
   b. She checks out a book about Nelson Mandela.

4. Misako walks outside and looks up at the sky.
   a. She sees the sun.
   b. She sees a sun.

5. Horses are my favorite animals.
   a. I love the horses.
   b. I love horses.

6. Fifty cars are in a parking lot. Ten cars are white.
   a. The cars in the parking lot are white.
   b. Some cars in the parking lot are white.

EXERCISE 50 ▸ Listening. (Charts 6-1, 6-2, 6-6, and 6-7)
Listen to the sentences and write the words you hear: *a*, *an*, or *the*.

1. A: Do you have ____*an*____ eraser?

   B: I see one on _____ desk.

2. A: Where are _____ keys to _____ car?

   B: I'm not sure. You can use mine.

3. A: Shhh. I hear _____ noise.

   B: It's just _____ bird outside. Don't worry.

4. A: Henry Jackson teaches at _____ university.

   B: I know. He's _____ English professor.

   A: He's also the head of _____ department.

5. A: We need to leave for _____ train station.

   B: We have _____ hour.

   A: That's not enough. Traffic is very heavy.

EXERCISE 51 ▸ Warm-up. (Chart 6-8)
Which words can complete each sentence?

1. I have some fruit / some oranges / any oranges.

2. I don't have some fruit / any fruit / any oranges.

3. Do you have some fruit / some oranges / any fruit / any oranges?

6-8	Using *Some* and *Any*		
AFFIRMATIVE	(a) Vera has **some** money.		Use **some** in affirmative statements.
NEGATIVE	(b) Vera doesn't have **any** money.		Use **any** in negative statements.
QUESTION	(c) Does Vera have **any** money?		Use either **some** or **any** in a question.
	(d) Does Vera have **some** money?		
(e) I don't have **any** money. (noncount noun)			**Any** is used with noncount nouns and plural count nouns.
(f) Do you have **any** coins? (plural count noun)			

EXERCISE 52 ▸ Looking at grammar. (Chart 6-8)
Write **some** or **any**.

1. Harry has ___*some*___ money.

2. I don't have ___*any*___ money.

3. Do you have _*some / any*_ money?

4. Do you need _____ help?

5. No, thank you. I don't need _____ help.

6. Kalil needs _____ help.

7. Diana usually doesn't get _____ mail.

8. We don't have _____ fruit in the apartment. We don't have _____
   apples, _____ bananas, or _____ oranges.

9. I need _____ paper. Do you have _____ paper?

10. Sasha is doing well. He doesn't have _____ problems.

11. I need to go to the grocery store. I need to buy _____ food. Do you need to
    buy _____ groceries?

12. I'm not busy tonight. I don't have _____ homework to do.

13. I don't have _____ money in my wallet.

14. Lynn's garden has _____ beautiful flowers this year.

EXERCISE 53 ▸ Let's talk: pairwork. (Chart 6-8)
Work with a partner. Make questions and answers with **some** and **any**.

Example: gum
PARTNER A: Do you have some gum? OR Do you have any gum?
PARTNER B: Yes, I have some gum. OR No, I don't have any gum.

Partner A	Partner B
1. notebook paper	1. chocolate
2. snacks	2. pets
3. money in your pocket	3. worries
4. suggestions for me	4. advice for me
5. time	5. water
	Change roles.

EXERCISE 54 ▸ Looking at grammar. (Chapters 5 and 6)
Complete the sentences with the words in the box. If necessary, use the plural form.

knife	piece
✓ match	woman
page	work
paper	

1. I want to light a candle. I need some _____ *matches* _____.

2. This puzzle has 200 _____.

3. The restroom downstairs is for men. This restroom is for _____.

4. Ron is studying. He has a lot of _____ to do.

5. Some _____, forks, and spoons are on the table.

6. My dictionary has 437 _____.

7. I need to write a note. I have a pen. I need some _____.

glass	size	thief
side	strawberry	weather

8. A piece of paper has four _____.

9. When the temperature is around 35°C (77°F), I'm comfortable. But I don't like very

   hot _____.

10. _____ take things from people: money, jewelry, cars, etc.

11. _____ are small, red, sweet, and delicious.

12. This sweater comes in three _____: small, medium, and large.

13. In some countries, people usually use cups for their tea. In other countries, they serve tea

    in _____.

EXERCISE 55 ▸ Let's talk. (Chart 6-8)
Work in small groups. Your group has a gift card for online shopping. Choose the site. The amount of the card is equal to the cost of a new laptop. What do you want to buy for your group? What don't you want to buy?

1. We want to buy some / a lot of / two …
2. We don't want to buy any …

EXERCISE 56 ▸ Check your knowledge. (Chapter 6 Review)
Correct the mistakes.

     some
1. I need ~~an~~ advice from you.

2. I don't like hot weathers.

3. I usually have a egg for breakfast.

4. Sun rises every morning.

5. The students in this class do a lot of homeworks every day.

6. How many language do you know?

7. I don't have many money.

8. Alexander and Carmen don't have some children.

9. A pictures are beautiful. You're a good photographer.

10. I can't find any bowl for my soup.

EXERCISE 57 ▸ Reading, grammar, and writing. (Chapter 6)

Part I. Read the paragraph about the photo. <u>Underline</u> the articles (*a/an/the*) and *some*. With a partner, explain their usage.

On a Hike

It's a beautiful summer day. The sky is very blue. A father, daughter, and mother are hiking together. They are holding hands. Some mountains and snow are behind them. The mom is reading some signs. She has a backpack on her back. It has their lunch. The family is having a nice time. They are enjoying the hike.

Part II. Write a paragraph. Describe the photo. Add details. You can use your imagination. Use articles (*a/an/the*) and *some*. Begin with *It is a busy day at the office*.

Part III. Edit your writing. Work individually or change papers with a partner. Check (✓) for the following:

1. ☐ a paragraph indent
2. ☐ a capital letter at the beginning of each sentence
3. ☐ a period at the end of each sentence
4. ☐ a verb in every sentence
5. ☐ correct use of *a, an, the, some*
6. ☐ *-s/-es* endings for plural nouns
7. ☐ correct spelling (use a dictionary or spell-check)

▪▪▪▪▪ For digital resources, go to MyEnglishLab on the Pearson English Portal. You can also go to the Pearson Practice English App for mobile practice.

Count and Noncount Nouns   **197**

CHAPTER 7

More About the Present Tense

PRETEST: What do I already know?
Write "C" if the sentence is correct and "I" if it is incorrect.

1. _____ What the date today? (Chart 7-1)

2. _____ We have class at Tuesdays and Thursdays. (Chart 7-2)

3. _____ How the weather in Hong Kong? (Chart 7-3)

4. _____ There is a mouse in the kitchen! (Chart 7-4)

5. _____ Are there any new students in your class? (Chart 7-5)

6. _____ How many eggs are there in the refrigerator? (Chart 7-6)

7. _____ Simon is in bed. He's not feeling well. (Chart 7-7)

8. _____ Please sit next me. (Chart 7-8)

9. _____ We live far away school. (Chart 7-8)

10. _____ What would you like for dinner? (Chart 7-9)

11. _____ I am like some chicken for dinner. (Chart 7-10)

EXERCISE 1 ▶ Warm-up. (Chart 7-1)
Match the questions to the pictures.

A. It's 5:00.

B. It's April.

C. It's Sunday.

1. What month is it? _____   2. What day is it? _____   3. What time is it? _____

7-1 Using *It* to Talk About Dates and Time

QUESTION		ANSWER	In English, people use *it* to express (to talk about) time.
(a) What day is it?	→	*It's* Monday.	
(b) What month is it?	→	*It's* September.	
(c) What year is it?	→	*It's* 2021.	
(d) What's the date today?	→	*It's* September 15.	
	→	*It's* September 15th.	
	→	*It's* the 15th of September.	
(e) What time is it?	→	*It's* 9:00.*	
	→	*It's* nine.	
	→	*It's* nine o'clock.	
	→	*It's* 9:00 A.M.	

*American English uses a colon (two dots) between the hour and the minutes: 9:00 A.M. British English uses one dot: 9.00 A.M.

EXERCISE 2 ▸ Looking at grammar. (Chart 7-1)
Make questions. Begin with ***What***.

1. A: _____*What day is it?*_____
   B: It's Tuesday.

2. A: _____
   B: It's March 14th.

3. A: _____
   B: (It's) ten-thirty.

4. A: _____
   B: (It's) March.

5. A: _____
   B: (It's) six-fifteen.

6. A: _____
   B: (It's) Wednesday.

7. A: _____
   B: (It's) the 1st of April.

8. A: _____
   B: (It's) 2021.

9. A: _____
   B: It's 7:00 A.M.

EXERCISE 3 ▸ Listening, grammar, and speaking. (Chart 7-1)

Part I. Listen and repeat after the speaker.

THE MONTHS OF THE YEAR

January	May	September
February	June	October
March	July	November
April	August	December

Part II. Complete the questions. Then work with a partner. Ask and answer the questions. Take turns.

1. A: What month _____?
   a. is   b. is it

   B: It's _____.

2. A: What _____ the date today?
   a. is   b. is it

   B: It's _____.

3. A: What day _____?
   a. is   b. is it

   B: It's _____.

4. A: What time _____?
   a. is   b. is it

   B: It's _____.

5. A: What year _____?
   a. is   b. is it

   B: It's _____.

6. A: What _____ the date of New Year's Day?
   a. is   b. is it

   B: It's _____.

7. A: What _____ the date of your favorite holiday?
   a. is   b. is it

   B: It's _____.

Change roles.

Jump-start your English

Using Calendar Expressions for Days and Weeks

Part I. Work with a partner. Do you know the meaning of the time expressions? Today is the 17th. Find the dates on the calendar, and write the number.

1. tomorrow __18__

2. the day after tomorrow _____

3. the day after next _____

4. two days from now _____

5. a week from now _____

6. a week from tomorrow _____

7. yesterday _____

8. one day ago _____

9. two days ago _____

10. one week ago today _____

11. two weeks ago today _____

12. a week from Wednesday _____

MAY						
Sunday	Monday	Tuesday	Wednesday	Thursday	Friday	Saturday
1	2	3	4	5	6	7
8	9	10	11	12	13	14
15	16	(17)	18	19	20	21
22	23	24	25	26	27	28
29	30	31				

Part II. Work with a partner. Choose a different date in the third week of the month. Ask your partner to give the date for the expressions. Say both the day and date in your answer, for example: *It's Wednesday, May 25.*

Partner A	Partner B *(Choose a new date.)*
What is ... ?	*What is ... ?*
1. the day after tomorrow	1. five days ago
2. three days ago	2. three days from now
3. one week ago yesterday	3. a week ago today
4. a week from tomorrow	4. the day after next
5. a week from now	5. a day ago

More About the Present Tense   **201**

EXERCISE 4 ▸ Warm-up. (Chart 7-2)
Check (✓) the true answers. For item 3, write about your English class.

1. I go to school

_____ on Monday.

_____ on Tuesday.

_____ on Wednesday.

_____ on Thursday.

_____ on Friday.

_____ on Saturday.

_____ on Sunday.

2. I have class

_____ in the morning.

_____ in the evening.

_____ at night.

3. I have class from _____ to _____.
  (time)   (time)

7-2	Prepositions of Time	
AT	(a) We have class *at* one o'clock.	
	(b) I have an appointment with the doctor *at* 3:00.	*at* + a specific time on the clock
	(c) We sleep *at* night.	*at* + *night*
IN	(d) My birthday is *in* October.	*in* + a specific month
	(e) I was born *in* 1999.	*in* + a specific year
	(f) We have class *in* the morning.	*in* + *the morning*
	(g) Bob has class *in* the afternoon.	*in* + *the afternoon*
	(h) I study *in* the evening.	*in* + *the evening*
ON	(i) I have class *on* Monday(s).	*on* + a specific day of the week
	(j) I was born *on* October 31.	*on* + a specific date
	(k) I was born *on* October 31, 2005.	
FROM ... TO	(l) We have class *from* 1:00 *to* 2:00.	*from* (a specific time) *to* (a specific time)

EXERCISE 5 ▸ Looking at grammar. (Chart 7-2)
Complete the sentences with prepositions of time.

1. We have class ...

a. ___*at*___ ten o'clock.

b. _____ ten _____ eleven.

c. _____ the morning and _____ the afternoon.

2. I study …

    a. _____ the evening.

    b. _____ night.

3. I was born …

    a. _____ May.

    b. _____ 1990.

    c. _____ May 21.

    d. _____ May 21, 1990.

4. a. The post office isn't open _____ Sundays.

    b. It's open _____ 8:00 A.M. _____ 5:00 P.M., Monday through Saturday.

    c. The post office closes _____ 5:00 P.M.

EXERCISE 6 ▸ Let's talk: pairwork. (Chart 7-2)
Interview a partner. Complete the sentences with time expressions. Share some of your partner's answers with the class.

1. When do you eat breakfast?

    a. I eat breakfast in ___*the morning*___.

    b. I eat breakfast at _____.

    c. I eat breakfast from _____ to _____.

2. When do you study?

    a. I study at _____.

    b. I study in _____.

    c. I study on _____.

    d. I study from _____ to _____.

3. Tell about the time of your birth.

    a. I was born in _____.

    b. I was born on _____.

    c. I was born at _____.

EXERCISE 7 ▶ Listening and grammar. (Chart 7-2)

Part I. Listen to each description. Write the name of the person.

Who am I?

Example: You will hear: I was born in June. I was born in the morning.
My name is …

You will write: _____*Nia*_____

Nia
June 2, 2000,
7:00 A.M.

Marisol
June 24, 1995,
11:00 P.M.

Min
July 7, 2000,
7:00 P.M.

Yusuf
July 24, 1993,
11:00 A.M.

1. _____   3. _____

2. _____   4. _____

Part II. Complete the sentences with the information in the pictures.

1. I was born _____ July. I was born _____ July 7. I was

   born _____ the evening. My name is _____.

2. I was born _____ 1995. I was born _____ June 24, 1995. I was

   born _____ night. My name is _____.

3. I was born _____ June 2. I was born _____ 2000. My name

   is _____.

4. Hi, my name is _____. I was born _____ July.

   I was born _____ the morning.

EXERCISE 8 ▶ Warm-up. (Chart 7-3)
Which answers are true for you?

1. In your hometown, how's the weather in June?
   It's sunny / cloudy / rainy / cold / hot / windy.

2. What's the weather like in January?
   It's sunny / cloudy / rainy / cold / hot / windy.

7-3 Using *It*, *What*, and *How* to Talk About the Weather

(a) *It's* sunny today. (b) *It's* hot and humid today. (c) *It's* a nice day today.	In English, people usually use *it* when they talk about the weather.
(d) *What's the weather like* in Istanbul in January? (e) *How's the weather* in Moscow in the summer? (f) *What's the temperature* in Bangkok today?	People commonly ask about the weather by saying, *What's the weather like?* OR *How's the weather?* *What* is also used to ask about the temperature.

EXERCISE 9 ▸ Let's talk: pairwork. (Chart 7-3)

How's the weather today? Choose *yes* or *no*. Share your answers with a partner. Do you and your partner agree?

1. hot	yes	no
2. warm	yes	no
3. cool	yes	no
4. cold	yes	no
5. sunny	yes	no

6. nice	yes	no
7. clear	yes	no
8. cloudy	yes	no
9. windy	yes	no
10. stormy	yes	no

EXERCISE 10 ▸ Let's talk. (Chart 7-3)

Work in small groups. Change the Fahrenheit (F) temperatures to Celsius* (C) by choosing temperatures in the box. Then describe the temperature in words.

38°C	24°C	✓10°C	0°C	−18°C

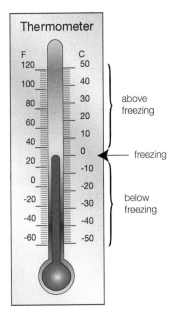

FAHRENHEIT	CELSIUS	DESCRIPTION
1. 50°F	*10°C*	*cool*
2. 32°F	_____	_____
3. 100°F	_____	_____
4. 75°F	_____	_____
5. 0°F	_____	_____

*Celsius is also called "Centigrade."

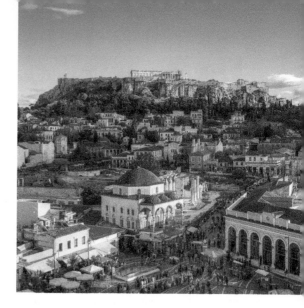

EXERCISE 11 ▶ Let's talk: interview. (Chart 7-3)
Interview your classmates about their hometowns.
Follow the example, and write down their information
in the chart. Share some of their answers with the class.

Example:

STUDENT A: What's your hometown, Sophia?
STUDENT B: Athens.
STUDENT A: Where is it?
STUDENT B: In southeastern Greece near the Aegean Sea.
STUDENT A: What's the population of Athens?
STUDENT B: Almost four million.
STUDENT A: What's the weather like in Athens in May?
STUDENT B: It's mild. Sometimes it's a little rainy.
STUDENT A: What's the average temperature in May?
STUDENT B: The average temperature is around 21° Celsius.

NAME	Sophia			
HOMETOWN	Athens			
LOCATION	SE Greece			
POPULATION	almost 4 million			
WEATHER	mild in May, around 21°C, in the mid-seventies Fahrenheit			

EXERCISE 12 ▶ Let's talk: pairwork. (Chart 7-3)
Work with a partner. Ask and answer the questions. For items 3 and 4, you can choose
the place.

1. A: _____ the weather today?
   a. How   b. How's

   B: It's _____.

2. A: What's the weather _____ today?
   a. is   b. like

   B: It's _____.

3. A: What's the weather _____ in _____?
     a. is   b. like

   B: It's _____.

4. A: _____ the weather in _____?
     a. How's   b. How

   B: It's _____.

5. A: What's the weather _____ in your hometown today?
     a. like   b. does

   B: It's _____.

Jump-start your English

Talking About the Seasons

Part I. What happens in each season? Write the letter of the photo next to the correct sentence.

THE SEASONS (IN THE NORTHERN HEMISPHERE)
fall: September to December
winter: December to March
spring: March to June
summer: June to September

1. _____ In the spring, the trees and the flowers bloom.

2. _____ In the winter, it snows.

3. _____ In the fall, the leaves change color.

4. _____ In the summer, it is very green.

Part II. Listen to the conversations.

1. A: How's the weather here in the spring?
   B: It's cool.
   A: Does it snow?
   B: No, it never snows.

2. A: What's the weather like in the summer?
   B: It's really nice.
   A: Is it hot?
   B: Sometimes, but mostly it's warm.

Part III. Work with a partner. Ask and answer questions about the weather in your hometown in different seasons.

QUESTIONS		ANSWERS		
How's the weather What's the weather like	in the summer? in the winter? in the spring? in the fall?	It's	hot. cold. warm. cool. sunny. cloudy. rainy. humid.	windy. chilly. below freezing. stormy. foggy. nice. beautiful.
		It	rains. / doesn't rain. snows. / doesn't snow.	
		The sky is	clear. cloudy. hazy.	

QUESTIONS		ANSWERS
Is it	hot? cold? warm? cool? sunny? Etc.	Yes, it is. No, it isn't.
Does it	rain? snow?	Yes, it does. No, it doesn't.

EXERCISE 13 ▶ Warm-up. (Chart 7-4)
Complete the sentences.

1. There is / isn't a whiteboard in this room.

2. There are / aren't computers in this room.

3. There are _____ students in this room.
               (number)

7-4 There + Be

THERE	+	BE	+	SUBJECT	+	PLACE	*There + be* is used to say that something exists in a particular place.
(a) *There*		*is*		*an apple*		on the tree.	
(b) *There*		*are*		*many apples*		on the tree.	

There + be is used to say that something exists in a particular place.

Note: The subject follows *be:*
   there + ***is*** + *singular noun*
   there + ***are*** + *plural noun*

CONTRACTIONS:
   there + ***is*** = ***there's***
   there + ***are*** = ***there're***

(c) ***There's*** an apple on the tree.

(d) ***There're*** many apples on the tree.

EXERCISE 14 ▶ Looking at grammar. (Chart 7-4)

Write ***is*** or ***are***. Then choose *yes* or *no*. Share a few of your answers with the class.

1. There _____*is*_____ a grammar book on my desk.   yes   no

2. There _____*are*_____ many grammar books in this room.   yes   no

3. There _____ comfortable chairs in this classroom.   yes   no

4. There _____ a nice view from the classroom window.   yes   no

5. There _____ interesting places in this area.   yes   no

6. There _____ a good café near school.   yes   no

7. There _____ fun activities for the weekends in this area.   yes   no

8. There _____ difficult words in this exercise.   yes   no

EXERCISE 15 ▸ Let's talk. (Chart 7-4)

Work in small groups. Everyone puts two or three objects (e.g., a coin, some keys, a pen, a dictionary) on a table in the classroom. Then take turns describing the items on the table. Begin with *There is* and *There are*.

Example:

STUDENT A: There are three dictionaries on the table.
STUDENT B: There are some keys on the table.
STUDENT C: There is a pencil sharpener on the table.

EXERCISE 16 ▸ Let's talk: pairwork. (Chart 7-4)

Work with a partner. Complete each sentence with words in the box or your own words. You can look at your book before you speak. When you speak, look at your partner.

What do you see?

a book/books	a light switch/light switches	a post office
a bulletin board	a mall	restaurants
a chair/chairs	a notebook/notebooks	a sink
a chalkboard	a park	a store/stores
a clock	a pen/pens	a whiteboard
a café	a pencil sharpener	a window/windows
desks	a picture/pictures	

Partner A	Partner B
1. There is / isn't ... on this desk.	1. There are / aren't ... on that desk.
2. There are / aren't ... on that wall.	2. There is / isn't ... on this wall.
3. There are / aren't ... in this room.	3. There is / isn't ... in this room.
4. There is / isn't ... near our school.	4. There are / aren't ... near our school.
	Change roles.

EXERCISE 17 ▸ Listening. (Chart 7-4)

Listen to each sentence. Choose the word you hear. NOTE: You will hear contractions for *There is* and *There are*.

Example: You will hear: There're several windows in this room.
           You will choose: There's   (There're)

1. There's   There're

2. There's   There're

3. There's   There're

4. There's   There're

5. There's	There're
6. There's	There're
7. There's	There're
8. There's	There're

EXERCISE 18 ▸ Warm-up. (Chart 7-5)

Answer the questions.

1. Is there an elevator in this building?　　　yes　　no

2. Are there stairs in this building?　　　yes　　no

7-5 There + Be: Yes/No Questions

QUESTION				SHORT ANSWER
BE + *THERE* + SUBJECT				
(a) *Is* *there* *an apple* in the refrigerator?			→	Yes, *there is*.
			→	No, *there isn't*.
(b) *Are* *there* *eggs* in the refrigerator?			→	Yes, *there are*.
			→	No, *there aren't*.

EXERCISE 19 ▸ Looking at grammar. (Chart 7-5)

Choose *Is* or *Are*. Then answer the questions.

What's around here?

1. (Is)　Are　there a zoo in this town? ___*Yes, there is. / No, there isn't.*___

2. Is　Are　there an airport nearby? _____

3. Is　Are　there lakes near this area? _____

4. Is　Are　there good restaurants near here? _____

5. Is　Are　there an urgent care clinic in this town? _____

6. Is　Are　there an aquarium in this town? _____

7. Is　Are　there a subway stop near school? _____

8. Is　Are　there a good public transportation system in this town? _____

9. Is　Are　there movie theaters nearby? _____

EXERCISE 20 ▶ Let's talk: pairwork. (Chart 7-5)

Work with a partner. Ask questions about the refrigerator in the picture. Begin with **Is there** or **Are there**.

Examples: bottles of milk
PARTNER A: Are there bottles of milk in the refrigerator?
PARTNER B: Yes, there are.

        sandwich
PARTNER B: Is there a sandwich in the refrigerator?
PARTNER A: No, there isn't.

Partner A	Partner B
1. two eggs	1. a carton of eggs
2. a loaf of bread	2. oranges
3. apples	3. juice
4. tomatoes	4. a bowl of rice
5. a cube of butter	5. bowls
6. vegetables	6. broccoli
7. a bottle of juice	7. milk
	Change roles.

EXERCISE 21 ▶ Let's talk: class activity. (Chart 7-5)

Solve the puzzle. Ask your teacher questions to decide which hotel is the best for the Romero family and why.★

    The Romero family needs to choose a hotel for their summer vacation. They want a hotel with everything listed in the box below. Your teacher has information about several hotels. Ask her/him questions with the words in the box. Then write *yes* or *no* in the correct column of the chart on page 213. Which hotel is perfect for the Romero family?

hiking trails	a swimming pool
a beach	ocean-view rooms
horses to ride	

★Teacher: See *Let's Talk: Answers,* p. 281.

Example:

STUDENT A: Is there a swimming pool at Hotel 1?
  TEACHER: Yes, there is.
STUDENT B: Are there hiking trails at Hotel 3?
  TEACHER: Yes, there are.

Continue asking questions until your chart is complete.

	A SWIMMING POOL	A BEACH	HIKING TRAILS	HORSES	OCEAN-VIEW ROOMS
HOTEL 1	*yes*				
HOTEL 2					
HOTEL 3			*yes*		
HOTEL 4					
HOTEL 5					

EXERCISE 22 ▶ Warm-up. (Chart 7-6)

Answer the questions.

1. How many students are there at this school?

   _____

2. How many people are there in your country?

   _____

3. How many people are there in this town?

   _____

7-6 *There + Be: Asking Questions with How Many*

QUESTION						SHORT ANSWER
	HOW MANY +	SUBJECT +	*ARE* +	*THERE* +	PLACE	
(a)	*How many*	*chapters*	*are*	*there*	in this book?	→ *Fifteen.* (There are 15 chapters in this book.)
(b)	*How many*	*provinces*	*are*	*there*	in Canada?	→ *Ten.* (There are ten provinces in Canada.)
(c)	How many *words* do you see? INCORRECT: *How many word do you see?*					Note: The noun that follows *how many* is plural.

EXERCISE 23 ▸ Grammar and speaking. (Chart 7-6)

Part I. Choose the correct subject in red for each question.

1. How many	cup	cups	are there?
2. How many	chair	chairs	are there?
3. How many	phone	phones	are there?
4. How many	desk	desks	are there?
5. How many	computer	computers	are there?
6. How many	wastebasket	wastebaskets	are there?
7. How many	book	books	are there?
8. How many	printer	printers	are there?
9. How many	calendar	calendars	are there?
10. How many	window	windows	are there?

Part II. Work with a partner. Ask and answer the questions about the office picture. Take turns.

Example: A: How many cups are there?
B: There is one cup.

EXERCISE 24 ▸ Let's talk: trivia game. (Chart 7-6)

Work in teams. Answer the questions. Your teacher will give you a time limit. The team with the most correct answers wins.

1. How many letters are there in the English alphabet?
2. How many vowels are there in English?

3. How many syllables are there in the word *take?*

4. How many days are there in September?

5. How many kilometers are there in a mile?

6. How many countries are there in North America?

7. How many continents are there in the world?

EXERCISE 25 ▸ Warm-up. (Chart 7-7)
Guess the person. Note the prepositions in red.

Who am I?

1. I live in London.

2. I live on Downing Street.

3. I live at 10 Downing Street.

7-7	Prepositions of Place	
(a)	My book is **on** *my desk*.	In (a): *on* = a preposition *my desk* = object of the preposition *on my desk* = a prepositional phrase
(b)	Ned lives **in** *Miami*. **in** *Florida*. **in** *the United States*. **in** *North America*.	A person lives **in** a city. **in** a state. **in** a country. **in** a continent.
(c)	Meg lives **on** *Hill Street*.	**on** a street, avenue, road, etc.
(d)	She lives **at** *4472 Hill Street*.	**at** a street address.
(e)	My father is **in** *the kitchen*.	In (e): *in* is used with rooms: **in** *the kitchen*, **in** *the classroom*, **in** *the hall*, **in** *my bedroom*, etc.
(f)	Ivan is **at** *work*.	**At** + *work, school, home* expresses activity:
(g)	Yoko is **at** *school*.	In (f): Ivan is working at his office (or other place of work).
(h)	Olga is **at** *home*.	In (g): Yoko is a student. She is studying. (Or, if she is a teacher, she is teaching.) In (h): Olga is doing things at her home.
(i)	Siri is **in** *bed*.	**In** + *bed, class, hospital, jail* has these special meanings:
(j)	Tim is **in** *class*.	In (i): Siri is resting or sleeping *under* the covers.
(k)	Mr. Lee is **in** *the hospital*.	In (j): Tim is studying (or teaching).
(l)	Paul is **in** *jail/prison*.	In (k): Mr. Lee is sick. He is a patient. In (l): Paul is a prisoner. He cannot leave. Note: American English = *in the hospital* British English = *in hospital*

EXERCISE 26 ▸ Looking at grammar. (Chart 7-7)
Write *in, on,* or *at.*

Write about Alonso.

Alonso Sales
5541 Lake Street
Toronto, Canada

1. Alonso lives _____ Canada.

2. He lives _____ Toronto.

3. He lives _____ Lake Street.

4. He lives _____ 5541 Lake Street

_____ Toronto, Canada.

Dr. John Eng
342 First Street
Miami, Florida

Write about Dr. Eng.

5. Dr. Eng lives on _____.

6. He lives in _____.

7. He lives at _____.

Write about yourself.

8. I live _____.
    (name of country)

9. I live _____.
    (name of city)

10. I live _____.
    (name of street)

11. I live _____.
    (street address)

EXERCISE 27 ▸ Let's talk: game. (Chart 7-7)
Work in teams. Write *in, on,* or *at.* Then guess the person, building, or company. Use the words in the box. The team with the most correct answers wins.

Alexandria Pyramids	Facebook Inc.	Nike Inc.
Apple Inc.	Giza Pyramids	president of the United States
Boeing Co.	Louvre Museum	prime minister of Canada
Eiffel Tower	Microsoft Corp.	vice president of the United States

1. I am a building.

   a. I am _____ Paris.

   b. I am _____ Anatole Avenue.

   c. I am _____ 5 Anatole Avenue.

   ANSWER: _____

2. I am a person.

   a. I live _____ Ottawa.

   b. I live _____ 24 Sussex Drive.

   c. I live _____ Sussex Drive.

   ANSWER: _____

3. I am a building.

   a. I am _____ Pyramid Street.

   b. I am _____ 124 Pyramid Street.

   c. I am _____ Egypt.

   ANSWER: _____

4. I am a company.

   a. I am _____ Oregon.

   b. I am _____ Bowerman Drive.

   c. I am _____ One Bowerman Drive.

   ANSWER: _____

5. I am a person.

   a. I live _____ Pennsylvania Avenue.

   b. I live _____ 1600 Pennsylvania Avenue N.W.

   c. I live _____ the United States.

   ANSWER: _____

6. I am a company.

   a. I am _____ Illinois.

   b. I am _____ 100 North Riverside Plaza.

   c. I am _____ Chicago.

   ANSWER: _____

EXERCISE 28 ▸ Looking at grammar. (Chart 7-7)
Write *at* or *in*.

Rachel isn't …

1. _____ her bedroom.

2. _____ bed.

3. _____ work.

4. _____ prison.

5. _____ home.

6. _____ jail.

7. _____ class.

8. _____ Africa.

9. _____ the hall.

10. _____ the hospital. She's well now.

EXERCISE 29 ▸ Looking at grammar. (Chart 7-7)
Write *at* or *in*.

What's new?

1. Last year at this time, Eric was _____ Vietnam. This year he's _____ Spain.

2. Professor Gomez isn't _____ school this week. He's very sick and is now _____ the hospital.

3. There are thirty-seven students but thirty desks _____ our classroom.

4. Rob is _____ jail. He's going to be _____ prison for a long time.

5. Our dorm rooms are next to each other! I'm _____ 301 and you're _____ 302.

6. Leo is traveling _____ Asia this year.

7. The kids are _____ the kitchen. They're making dinner for us!

8. Lexie is _____ home? She's never _____ home!

9. A: When I was _____ work yesterday, I had a call from an old boyfriend.

   B: Tell me more!

10. A: Where's Jack?

    B: He's _____ his room.

    A: What's he doing?

    B: He's _____ bed. He has a headache.

EXERCISE 30 ▸ Warm-up. (Chart 7-8)
Look around the classroom and answer the questions.

Where is everyone?

1. Who is in front of you?
2. Who is behind you?
3. Who is beside you?
4. Who is far away from the teacher?
5. Who is in the middle of the room?
6. Who is near the door?
7. Who is in the back of the room?
8. Who is next to the door?

7-8 More Prepositions of Place: A List

above	beside	in back of	in the middle of	on
around	between	in the back of	inside	on top of
at	far (away) from	in front of	near	outside
behind	in	in the front of	next to	under
below				

(a) The book is *beside* the cup.
(b) The book is *next to* the cup.
(c) The book is *near* the cup.

(d) The book is *between* two cups.

(e) The book is *far away from* the cup.

(f) The cup is *on* the book.
(g) The cup is *on top of* the book.

(h) The cup is *under* the book.

(i) The cup is *above* the book.

(j) The hand is *around* the cup.

(k) The man is *in back of* the bus.
(l) The man is *behind* the bus.

(m) The man is *in the back of* the bus.

(n) The man is *in front of* the bus.
   In (k), (l), and (n): the man is *outside* the bus.

(o) The man is *in the front of* the bus.

(p) The man is *in the middle of* the bus.
   In (m), (o), and (p): the man is *inside* the bus.

EXERCISE 31 ▸ Looking at grammar. (Chart 7-8)
Describe the pictures. Write the correct prepositions of place.

1. The apple is _____on / on top of_____ the plate.

2. The apple is _____ the plate.

3. The apple is _____ the plate.

4. The apple is _____ the glass.

5. The apple isn't near the glass. It is _____ the glass.

6. The apple is _____ the glass.

7. The apple is _____ two glasses.

8. The hand is _____ the glass.

9. The dog isn't inside the car. The dog is _____ the car.

10. The dog is in _____ the car.

11. The dog is in _____ the car.

12. The dog is in _____ the car.

13. The dog is in _____ the car.

EXERCISE 32 ▸ Listening. (Chart 7-8)

Look at the picture and listen to the statements. Choose "T" for true and "F" for false.

A New Apartment

Example: You will hear: There's a carpet on the floor.

You will choose: (T)   F

1. T F	4. T F	7. T F
2. T F	5. T F	8. T F
3. T F	6. T F	9. T F

EXERCISE 33 ▸ Let's talk: pairwork. (Chart 7-8)

Work with a partner. Choose a small object (a pen, pencil, coin, etc.). Give and follow directions. You can look at your book before you speak. When you speak, look at your partner.

Example: (*a small object such as a coin*)

PARTNER A (*book open*):   Put it on top of the desk.
PARTNER B (*book closed*):   (*Partner B puts the coin on top of the desk.*)

Partner A	Partner B
1. Put it on your head.	1. Put it inside your grammar book.
2. Put it above your head.	2. Put it next to your grammar book.
3. Put it between your fingers.	3. Put it on top of your grammar book.
4. Put it near me.	4. Put it in front of me.
5. Put it far away from me.	5. Put it behind me.
6. Put it under your book.	6. Put it in back of your back.
7. Put it below your knee.	7. Put it in the back of your grammar book.
8. Put it in the middle of your grammar book.	8. Put your hand around it.
	Change roles.

EXERCISE 34 ▸ Vocabulary and grammar. (Chapters 1→5 and 7)

Part I. Work with a partner. Answer the questions.

Partner A	Partner B
1. Where is Max?	1. What is Max looking at?
2. What is he sitting on?	2. What is he wearing on his head?
3. What is he doing?	3. Is there a librarian in the room?
4. What is behind him?	4. What is next to him?
5. What is there on the table?	5. Is there an open book on the table?

Part II. Complete the sentences.

1. Max is studying _____ the library.

2. He is sitting _____ a table.

3. He is sitting _____ a chair.

4. His legs are _____ the table.

5. There are books _____ the shelves.

6. Max is not writing _____ a piece of paper.

7. He _____ not reading a book.

8. He _____ looking at his laptop.

9. He has headphones _____ his head.

EXERCISE 35 ▸ Warm-up. (Chart 7-9)
Work with a partner. Answer the questions.

Kristin is hungry. She would like something sweet. What about you? Are you hungry? What would you like to eat? What would your partner like?

7-9 Would Like

(a) I'm thirsty. I *want* a glass of water. (b) I'm thirsty. I *would like* a glass of water.	Examples (a) and (b) have the same meaning, but *would like* is usually more polite than *want*. *I would like* is a nice way of saying *I want*.	
(c) *I would like* *You would like* *She would like* *He would like* — a glass of water. *We would like* *They would like*	Note in (c): There is no final *-s* on *would*. There is no final *-s* on *like*.	
(d) CONTRACTIONS *I'd* = *I would* *you'd* = *you would* *she'd* = *she would* *he'd* = *he would* *we'd* = *we would* *they'd* = *they would*	*Would* is often contracted with pronouns in both speaking and writing. In speaking, *would* is usually contracted with nouns too. WRITTEN: Ray would like to come. SPOKEN: "Ray'd like to come."	
WOULD LIKE + INFINITIVE (e) I *would like* *to eat* a sandwich.	Note in (e): *would like* can be followed by an infinitive.	
WOULD + SUBJECT + *LIKE* (f) *Would* you *like* some tea?	In a question, *would* comes before the subject.	
(g) Yes, I *would*. (I would like some tea.)	In (g): *Would* is used alone in short answers to questions with *would like*. It is not contracted in short answers.	

EXERCISE 36 ▸ Looking at grammar. (Chart 7-9)
Restate the sentences with *would like*.

1. **Dan wants** a cup of coffee.

    _____Dan would like_____ a cup of coffee.

2. **He wants** some sugar in his coffee.

    _____He would like_____ some sugar in his coffee.

3. **Hassan and Eva want** some coffee too.

    _____ some coffee too.

4. **They want** some sugar in their coffee too.

    _____ some sugar in their coffee too.

5. **I want to thank** you for your help.

    _____ you for your help.

6. **My friend wants to thank** you too.

    _____ you too.

7. **My friends want to thank** you too.

    _____ you too.

EXERCISE 37 ▸ Let's talk. (Chart 7-9)
Work in small groups. Ask another student a question. Take turns.

1. What would you like to do this weekend?
2. What would you like to do after class today?
3. What would you like to have for dinner tonight?
4. (_____), are you hungry? What would you like?
5. (_____), are you thirsty? What would you like?
6. (_____), are you sleepy? What would you like to do?
7. Pretend that you are the host at a party at your home. Your classmates are your guests. Ask them what they would like to eat or drink.
8. Think of something fun to do tonight or this weekend. Use *would you like* and invite a classmate.

EXERCISE 38 ▶ Warm-up. (Chart 7-10)

Which statement best matches the picture?

a. I would like some coffee.
b. I like coffee.

7-10 *Would Like* vs. *Like*

(a) I *would like to go* to the zoo.	In (a): **I would like to go to the zoo** means *I want to go to the zoo.* **Would like** indicates that I want to do something now or in the future.
(b) I *like to go* to the zoo.	In (b): **I like to go to the zoo** means *I enjoy the zoo.* **Like** indicates that I always, usually, or often enjoy something.

EXERCISE 39 ▶ Let's talk: pairwork. (Charts 7-9 and 7-10)

Work in pairs. Ask and answer questions. You can look at your book before you speak. When you speak, look at your partner.

Example:

PARTNER A: Do you like oranges?
PARTNER B: Yes, I do. OR No, I don't.
PARTNER A: Would you like an orange right now?
PARTNER B: Yes, I would. OR Yes, thank you. OR No, but thank you for asking.
PARTNER A: Your turn now.

Partner A	Partner B
1. Do you like coffee? Would you like a cup of coffee?	1. Do you like chocolate? Would you like some chocolate right now?
2. Do you like to watch movies? Would you like to go to a movie with me later today?	2. Do you like to shop? Would you like to go to the mall later today?
3. What do you like to do on weekends? What would you like to do this weekend?	3. What do you like to do in your free time? What would you like to do in your free time tomorrow?
4. What do you need to do this evening? What would you like to do this evening?	4. Do you like to travel? What countries would you like to visit?

EXERCISE 40 ▶ Listening. (Chart 7-10)

Listen to the sentences. Choose the verbs you hear. Some sentences have contractions.

Example: You will hear: I'd like some tea.
            You will choose: like   ('d like)

1. like	'd like		6. likes	'd like
2. like	'd like		7. like	'd like
3. like	'd like		8. like	'd like
4. likes	'd like		9. like	'd like
5. like	'd like		10. like	'd like

EXERCISE 41 ▶ Let's talk: pairwork. (Charts 7-4, 7-5, 7-9, and 7-10)

Work with a partner. Imagine you are at a farmers' market. Complete the sentences with your own words. Take turns.

Partner A	Partner B
1. I would like … .	1. Would you like … ?
2. Do you like … ?	2. Do you want … ?
3. There are … .	3. There is … .
4. Is there … ?	4. Are there … ?
5. Would you like to … ?	5. Do you like to … ?
	Change roles.

EXERCISE 42 ▶ Verb review. (Chapters 1 → 5 and 7)

Complete the sentences with the correct form of the verbs in parentheses.

A Ride Home

Every day Alana (*take*) _____ the
1
subway to work. She (*leave*) _____
2
her apartment at 5:30 A.M. She usually (*come*)

_____ home at 7:00 P.M. Usually, she
3
(*do*) _____ more work on the subway.
4
Today she (*be*) _____ very tired. It
5
(*be*) _____ the end of her work week. Right now she (*work, not*)
6
_____. She (*sleep*) _____ on the subway.
7   8

EXERCISE 43 ▶ Verb review. (Chapters 1 → 5 and 7)

Complete the sentences with the correct form of the verbs in parentheses.

Two Jobs

Three days a week, Daniel (*work*) _____ from home. He and his wife
1
(*have*) _____ a young daughter. He (*take*) _____ care of their
2   3
daughter, and his wife (*go*) _____ to the office. Right now he (*feed*)
4

_____ their daughter lunch. At
5
the same time, he (*look*) _____
6
at his laptop. Every day after lunch, their daughter

(*take*) _____ a nap. She (*sleep*)
7

_____ for a few hours, and Daniel
8
(*do*) _____ more work.
9

EXERCISE 44 ▸ Verb review. (Chapters 1 → 5 and 7)
Complete the sentences with the correct form of the verbs in parentheses.

A Sore Back

Susanne (*have*) _____ an office

1

job. She (*sit*) _____ at her desk for

2

several hours every day. She (*exercise, not*)

_____ much. Her back

3

(*get*) _____ very sore. Susanne's

4

doctor (*want*) _____ her to exercise more. She (*leave*) _____

5 6

work right now. There (*be*) _____ a gym nearby. She (*go*)

7

_____ to a yoga class.

8

EXERCISE 45 ▸ Check your knowledge. (Chapter 7 Review)
Correct the mistakes.

1. Samuel is not at school. He is at the work.

2. There's many problems in big cities today.

3. I'd like see a movie tonight.

4. Mr. Rice woulds likes to change jobs.

5. How many students there are in your class?

6. What day it is today?

7. We like to find a new apartment soon.

8. What time is now?

9. The teacher would like to checking our homework now.

10. How the weather in Kenya?

11. I am like to leave right now.

12. What does the weather like in your hometown?

EXERCISE 46 ▸ Reading and writing. (Chapter 7)

Part I. Read the paragraph. <u>Underline</u> the verbs.

Do you know these words?
- ocean   - calm
- park   - peaceful
- paths   - waves
- hikers   - crash

A Favorite Place

A favorite place for me is near the ocean. There is a park, and there are many paths for hikers. The ocean views are beautiful. In the summer, I often walk for one or two hours. It is very calm and peaceful. I like to think about things. Sometimes I listen to music. In the winter, the weather is often windy. Sometimes there are storms. The waves are very high. They crash onto the rocks again and again. The sound makes me relax. I would like to fall asleep, with the sound of the waves, in a house near the ocean.

Part II. Write about a favorite outdoor place. You can describe a photo. Use present verbs. The paragraph in Part I can be a model. Include answers to these questions:

- What do you see there?
- What do you do there?
- What is the weather like?
- What are your thoughts or feelings about this place?

Part III. Edit your writing. Work individually or change papers with a partner. Check (✓) for the following:

1. ☐ a paragraph indent
2. ☐ a capital letter at the beginning of each sentence
3. ☐ a period at the end of each sentence
4. ☐ a verb in every sentence
5. ☐ correct use of prepositions of place
6. ☐ use of present progressive for activities right now
7. ☐ *there is* + singular noun
8. ☐ *there are* + plural noun
9. ☐ correct spelling (use a dictionary or spell-check)

▪▪▪▪▪ For digital resources, go to MyEnglishLab on the Pearson English Portal. You can also go to the Pearson Practice English App for mobile practice.

PRETEST: What do I already know?

Are the words in **bold** correct or incorrect? Write "C" for correct and "I" for incorrect.

1. _____ I **am** sick yesterday. (Chart 8-1)

2. _____ They **was** absent last week. (Chart 8-1)

3. _____ Sylvia **wasn't** at home last weekend. (Chart 8-2)

4. _____ **Were** you at home last weekend? (Chart 8-3)

5. _____ It **rain** a lot yesterday. (Chart 8-4)

6. _____ I **was cook** dinner for my friends last night. (Chart 8-4)

7. _____ **Three day ago**, my parents visited me. (Chart 8-5)

8. _____ Were you in class **last evening**? (Chart 8-5)

9. _____ We **were see** a movie last night. (Chart 8-6)

10. _____ Antony **pay** for his tuition with a credit card yesterday. (Chart 8-6)

11. _____ They **no walked** to school yesterday. (Chart 8-7)

12. _____ **Did you come** to school early today? (Chart 8-8)

13. _____ Samuel **hurt** his back at work. (Chart 8-9)

14. _____ The cat **brung** a mouse to the door. (Chart 8-9)

EXERCISE 1 ▶ Warm-up. (Chart 8-1)

Read the statements and choose the answers.

1. I am tired now.   yes   no

2. I was tired two hours ago.   yes   no

3. Many students are absent today.   yes   no

4. Many students were absent yesterday.   yes   no

8-1 Simple Past Tense: Be

PRESENT TIME	PAST TIME
(a) I *am* in class *today*.	(d) I *was* in class *yesterday*.
(b) Alison *is* sick *today*.	(e) Alison *was* sick *yesterday*.
(c) My friends *are* at home *today*.	(f) My friends *were* at home *yesterday*.

SIMPLE PAST TENSE OF *BE*		
SINGULAR	PLURAL	I
		she
I *was*	we *were*	he } + *was*
you *were* (one person)	you *were* (more than one person)	it
she *was*	they *were*	we
he *was*		you } + *were*
it *was*		they

EXERCISE 2 ▸ Looking at grammar. (Chart 8-1)
Write *was* or *were*.

TODAY	YESTERDAY
1. You are at school.	You ___*were*___ at home.
2. We are at school.	We _____ at home.
3. He is at school.	He _____ at home.
4. You and I are at school.	You and I _____ at home.
5. She is at school.	She _____ at home.
6. They are at school.	They _____ at home.
7. Brian and James are at school.	Brian and James _____ at home.
8. My parents are at school.	My parents _____ at home.
9. I am at school.	I _____ at home.
10. The teacher is at school.	The teacher _____ at home.
11. You and your roommate are at home.	You and your roommate _____ at home.

EXERCISE 3 ▸ Let's talk: pairwork. (Chart 8-1)

Work with a partner. Change the sentences to past time. Use **yesterday**. You can look at your book before you speak. When you speak, look at your partner.

At School

Partner A	Partner B
1. Bashar is in class today.	1. I'm happy today.
2. They are in class today.	2. The classrooms are hot today.
3. Martina is at the library today.	3. Professor Devon is in her office today.
4. I'm in the library today.	4. Our teaching assistants are in their offices today.
5. You're busy today.	5. Ms. Jackson is in her classroom today.
	Change roles.

EXERCISE 4 ▸ Let's talk: pairwork. (Chart 8-1)

Part I. Think about yourself as a three-year-old child. Check (✓) the words that describe you best.

_____ quiet   _____ curious

_____ shy   _____ afraid

_____ funny   _____ friendly

_____ loud   _____ talkative

_____ smart   _____ a troublemaker

Part II. Work with a partner. Tell your partner about yourself. Use the information in Part I. Begin with **I was**.

EXERCISE 5 ▸ Warm-up. (Chart 8-2)

Choose the correct verb. Make true sentences.

The Weather

1. Last month, it   was / was not   nice.

2. The weekends   were / were not   sunny.

3. Yesterday, it   was / was not   hot.

8-2 Simple Past Tense of *Be*: Negative

(a) I *was not* in class yesterday.
 	
(b) I *wasn't* in class yesterday.
	NEGATIVE CONTRACTIONS
	  was + *not* = *wasn't*
	  were + *not* = *weren't*

(c) They *were not* at home last night. (d) They *weren't* at home last night.	I she ⎫ he ⎬ + *wasn't* we it ⎭ you ⎫ they ⎬ + *weren't* we ⎭

EXERCISE 6 ▶ Looking at grammar. (Chart 8-2)
Write *wasn't* or *weren't*.

Joe and JoAnn were on a trip. They were very happy because …

1. the flight _____*wasn't*_____ long.

2. the trains _____ slow.

3. the hotel _____ expensive.

4. the restaurants _____ expensive.

5. the tourist areas _____ crowded.

6. the language _____ difficult.

7. the weather _____ too cold.

EXERCISE 7 ▶ Let's talk: pairwork. (Chart 8-2)
Work with a partner. Make true sentences with the given words. You can look at your book before you speak. When you speak, look at your partner.

Yesterday at noon, I was/wasn't …

Partner A	Partner B
1. hungry. 2. tired. 3. at home. 4. at school. 5. with my family.	1. sick. 2. in the hospital. 3. on an airplane. 4. outdoors. 5. at the movies. *Change roles.*

EXERCISE 8 ▸ Listening. (Charts 8-1 and 8-2)
Listen to the sentences. Choose the verbs you hear.

Example: You will hear: I was at school all day yesterday.
You will choose: (was) wasn't

1. was   wasn't

2. was   wasn't

3. was   wasn't

4. was   wasn't

5. was   wasn't

6. was   wasn't

7. were   weren't

8. were   weren't

9. were   weren't

10. were   weren't

 EXERCISE 9 ▸ Warm-up. (Chart 8-3)
Work with a partner. Ask and answer these questions.

Last night at midnight,

1. were you asleep?
2. were you on the phone?
3. was it quiet at your home?

8-3 Simple Past Tense of *Be*: Questions

YES/NO QUESTIONS	SHORT ANSWER	(LONG ANSWER)
(a) **Were you** in class yesterday? (*be*) + (subject)	→ **Yes, I was.** → **No, I wasn't.**	(I was in class yesterday.) (I wasn't in class yesterday.)
(b) **Was Carlos** tired last night? (*be*) + (subject)	→ **Yes, he was.** → **No, he wasn't.**	(He was tired last night.) (He wasn't tired last night.)
INFORMATION QUESTIONS	SHORT ANSWER	(LONG ANSWER)
(c) **Where were you** yesterday? *Where* + (*be*) + (subject)	→ **In class.**	(I was in class yesterday.)
(d) **When was Emily** sick? *When* + (*be*) + (subject)	→ **Last week.**	(She was sick last week.)

EXERCISE 10 ▸ Looking at grammar. (Chart 8-3)
Make questions and give short answers. Use the words in the box.

at the train station	in Iceland
at the dentist	in the hospital
✓ at the library	

Where was everyone?

1. (Diego \ at home \ last night)

    A: _____Was Diego at home last night?_____

    B: No, _____he wasn't._____

    A: Where _____was he?_____

    B: He _____was at the library._____

2. (you \ at work \ last week)

    A: _____

    B: No, _____

    A: Where _____

    B: I _____

3. (you and your family \ in Canada \ last year)

    A: _____

    B: No, _____

    A: Where _____

    B: We _____

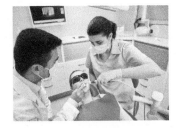

4. (Gabriella \ at the gym \ yesterday afternoon)

    A: _____

    B: No, _____

    A: Where _____

    B: She _____

5. (Emily and Anya \ at the airport \ last night)

A: _____

B: No, _____

A: Where _____

B: They _____

EXERCISE 11 ▸ Let's talk: class activity. (Chart 8-3)
Think about your first day in this class. Check (✓) the words that describe your feelings that day. Then answer your teacher's questions.

Example: happy

TEACHER: Were you happy the first day of class?
STUDENT A: Yes, I was happy.
STUDENT B: No, I wasn't happy.
TEACHER: (*to Student C*) Tell me about (*Student A*) and (*Student B*).
STUDENT C: (*Student A*) was happy. (*Student B*) wasn't happy.

1. _____ excited   3. _____ nervous   5. _____ quiet

2. _____ scared/afraid   4. _____ relaxed (not nervous)   6. _____ talkative

EXERCISE 12 ▸ Let's talk: pairwork. (Chart 8-3)
Work with a partner. Make questions orally. Take turns. After you finish, write the verbs.

SITUATION: You were at an amusement park yesterday. A friend is asking you about a ride.

1. _____*Was*_____ it fun?

2. _____ it scary?

3. _____ you afraid?

4. _____ the ride long?

5. _____ you sick afterwards?

6. _____ your friend sick?

7. _____ you nervous?

8. _____ your friend nervous?

9. _____ the ride safe?

10. _____ you dizzy?

EXERCISE 13 ▸ Let's talk: Find someone who ... . (Charts 8-2 and 8-3)
Interview your classmates about their days in elementary school. Make questions with
was/were. Who can answer *yes* to your questions? Write down the first names.

In Elementary School

Example: you \ shy
STUDENT A: Were you shy?
STUDENT B: No, I wasn't.
STUDENT A: (*to Student C*) Were you shy?
STUDENT C: Yes, I was.

	FIRST NAME			FIRST NAME
1. you \ shy			7. you \ noisy	
2. you \ outgoing★			8. you \ athletic	
3. you \ talkative			9. you \ active	
4. you \ happy			10. you \ well-behaved	
5. you \ hard-working			11. you \ a serious student	
6. you \ quiet			12. you \ artistic	

EXERCISE 14 ▸ Warm-up. (Chart 8-4)
Check (✓) your activities this morning. What do you notice about the verb endings?

Earlier today, I ...

1. _____ washed my face.

2. _____ brushed my teeth.

3. _____ combed my hair.

4. _____ skipped breakfast.

5. _____ checked social media.

6. _____ called a friend.

7. _____ asked someone for help.

8. _____ sneezed.

★*outgoing* = not shy

8-4 Simple Past Tense: Regular Verbs

SIMPLE PRESENT	(a)	I	*walk*	to school	*every day*.	*verb + -ed* = simple past tense of regular verbs
SIMPLE PAST*	(b)	I	*walked*	to school	*yesterday*.	
SIMPLE PRESENT	(c)	Ann	*walks*	to school	*every day*.	I you she he } + ***walked*** (verb + ***-ed***) it we they
SIMPLE PAST	(d)	Ann	*walked*	to school	*yesterday*.	

*For pronunciation of the simple past tense, see Appendix 6.

EXERCISE 15 ▸ Grammar and speaking. (Chart 8-4)
Work with a partner. Complete the sentences orally with the simple past. Take turns. Then write the answers.

Using Technology

1. Every day I use my computer. Yesterday I _____*used*_____ my computer.

2. Every day Samuel uses his computer. Yesterday he _____ his computer.

3. Every day you turn off your laptop. Last night you _____ off your laptop.

4. Every day I talk on my cell phone. Yesterday I _____ on my cell phone.

5. Every day Hiro listens to podcasts. Yesterday he _____ to podcasts.

6. Every day we text people. Yesterday we _____ people.

7. Every day people stream movies. Yesterday they _____ movies.

8. Every day I look for information on the internet. Yesterday I _____ for information on the internet.

EXERCISE 16 ▸ Let's talk: pairwork. (Chart 8-4)
Work with a partner. Check (✓) all your activities yesterday. Tell your partner about them. Share a few of your partner's answers with the class.

Yesterday I …

1. ____ ask the teacher a question
2. ____ cook dinner
3. ____ wash some clothes
4. ____ listen to music
5. ____ use a computer
6. ____ stay home in the evening
7. ____ walk in a park

8. ____ watch TV
9. ____ work at my desk
10. ____ wait for a bus
11. ____ smile at several people
12. ____ talk on a cell phone
13. ____ dream in English
14. ____ dream in my language

EXERCISE 17 ▸ Looking at grammar. (Chart 8-4)
Complete the sentences. Use the simple present or the simple past of the verbs in the box.

ask	erase	smile	wait	watch
cook	✓ rain	stay	walk	work

1. It often _____ *rains* _____ in the morning. It _____ *rained* _____ yesterday.

2. I _____ to school every morning. I _____ to school yesterday morning.

3. Sara often _____ questions. She _____ a question in class yesterday.

4. I _____ a movie on television last night. I usually _____ TV in the evening. I want to improve my English.

5. Mario _____ his own dinner yesterday evening. He _____ his own dinner every evening.

6. I usually _____ home at night because I have to study.

   I _____ home last night.

7. I have a job at the library. I _____ at the library every evening. I

   _____ there yesterday evening.

8. Linda usually _____ for the bus at a bus stop in front of her apartment

   building. She _____ for the bus there yesterday morning.

9. The teacher _____ some words from the board a couple of minutes ago.

   He used his hand instead of an eraser.

10. Our teacher is a warm, friendly person. She often _____ when she talks

   to us.

 EXERCISE 18 ▸ Vocabulary and listening. (Chapter 3 and Chart 8-4)
The simple past tense ending can be difficult to hear. Listen to each sentence and choose the
verb you hear. Look at new vocabulary with your teacher first.

A Soccer Coach

Example: You will hear: Jeremy loves soccer.
              You will choose: love   (loves)   loved

> *Do you know these words?*
> - coach
> - tournament
> - score
> - goals

1.	work	works	worked
2.	play	plays	played
3.	play	plays	played
4.	score	scores	scored
5.	help	helps	helped
6.	learn	learns	learned
7.	watch	watches	watched
8.	like	likes	liked
9.	work	works	worked
10.	work	works	worked

EXERCISE 19 ▸ Warm-up. (Chart 8-5)

Make true sentences with the correct time words.

1. I was at home yesterday morning / one hour ago / last night.

2. I watched a movie last weekend / yesterday afternoon / yesterday evening.

3. I talked to a friend last month / last week / an hour ago.

8-5 Past Time Words: *Yesterday, Last,* and *Ago*

PRESENT		PAST	Note the changes in time expressions from present to past.
today	→	yesterday	
this morning	→	yesterday morning	
this afternoon	→	yesterday afternoon	
this evening	→	yesterday evening	
tonight	→	last night	
this week	→	last week	
this year	→	last year	
this semester	→	last semester	

REFERENCE LIST: TIME EXPRESSIONS

YESTERDAY	LAST	AGO

(a) Bob was here ...
     yesterday.
     yesterday morning.
     yesterday afternoon.
     yesterday evening.
	(b) Sue was here ...
	     last night.
	     last week.
	     last weekend.
	     last month.
	     last year.
	
	     last spring.
	     last summer.
	     last fall.
	     last winter.
	
	     last Monday.
	     last Tuesday.
	     last Wednesday.
		(c) Tom was here ...
		     five minutes ago.
		     a few minutes ago.
		     two hours ago.
		     three days ago.
		     six months ago.
		     a/one year ago.

NOTE

In (a): **yesterday** is used with *morning, afternoon,* and *evening.*

In (b): **last** is used with *night,* with long periods of time (*week, month, year*), with seasons (*spring, summer, etc.*), and with days of the week.

In (c): **ago** means "in the past." It follows specific lengths of time (e.g., *two minutes* + *ago, five years* + *ago*).

EXERCISE 20 ▸ Looking at grammar. (Chart 8-5)
Complete the sentences with *yesterday* or *last*.

1. *I applied for a job …*

   a. _____ *last* _____ Friday.

   b. _____ week.

   c. _____ fall.

   d. _____ morning.

   e. _____ year.

   f. _____ summer.

2. *I interviewed for the job …*

   a. _____ night.

   b. _____ evening.

   c. _____ month.

   d. _____ afternoon.

   e. _____ Monday.

   f. _____ spring.

EXERCISE 21 ▸ Looking at grammar. (Chart 8-5)
Complete the sentences. Use *wasn't* or *weren't* and a past time expression.

1. I'm at home tonight, but _____ *I wasn't at home last night.* _____

2. I am here today, but _____

3. Kaya is busy today, but _____

4. Mia and Bo are at work tonight, but _____

5. Ben is at the library this afternoon, but _____

6. You're here today, but _____

7. Dr. Ruckman is in her office this morning, but _____

8. It's cold this week, but _____

9. We're tired this evening, but _____

EXERCISE 22 ▶ Grammar and speaking. (Chart 8-5)

Part I. Ava is a college student. Use the information in the calendar to complete the sentences about her activities. Begin with a time expression from Chart 8-5.

✕ DAY WEEK **MONTH**						SEARCH
MARCH						
Sunday	Monday	Tuesday	Wednesday	Thursday	Friday	Saturday
						1
2	**3**	**4**	**5**	**6** take Kate to dr. appointment 9 AM	**7**	**8** overnight ski trip
9	**10**	**11**	**12**	**13** health sciences lecture 7 PM	**14**	**15** outdoor campus concert
16 baseball game	**17** volunteer at food bank	**18** dorm meeting 5 PM	**19** 10 AM dentist movie/Sam	**20**	**21**	**22**
23 spring dance	**24**	**25**	**26**	**27**	**28** biology test	**29**
30	**31**					

Today is Thursday, March 20th.

1. _____*Three days ago*_____, Ava _____*was*_____ at the food bank.

2. _____, she _____ at a baseball game.

3. _____, she _____ at a lecture.

4. _____, she _____ at the dentist.

5. _____, Ava and Kate _____ at the doctor.

6. _____, Ava _____ at a dorm meeting.

7. _____, Ava and Sam _____ at a movie.

Part II. Think about six events from your calendar in the past month. Tell a classmate about your activities. Use time expressions.

EXERCISE 23. Grammar and speaking. (Chart 8-5)
Complete the sentences with your own words. Use ***ago***. Tell another classmate your answers.

1. I'm in class now, but I was at home ___*ten minutes ago / two hours ago / etc.*___

2. I'm in class today, but I was absent from class _____

3. I was in elementary school _____

4. I arrived in this city/area _____

5. We finished Exercise 16 _____

6. I was home in bed _____

EXERCISE 24 ▸ Listening. (Chart 8-5)
Part I. Write the date.

Today's date is _____ .

Answer the questions.

1. _____   5. _____

2. _____   6. _____

3. _____   7. _____

4. _____

Part II. Write the time.

Right now the time is _____ .

Listen to the questions. Write the times.

1. _____   3. _____

2. _____

EXERCISE 25 ▸ Warm-up. (Chart 8-6)
Read the information about Jerry. Change the verbs in red to present time.

Last Night

Last night, Jerry made dinner at 7:00. Then he did his homework for two hours. At 10:00, he had some ice cream.

Every Night

Every night, Jerry _____ dinner at 7:00. Then he _____ his
                              1   2
homework for two hours. At 10:00, he _____ some ice cream.
                                              3

8-6 Simple Past Tense: Irregular Verbs, Part I

Some verbs do not have **-ed** forms. Their past forms are irregular.

PRESENT	SIMPLE PAST	
do	– did	(a) I *do* my homework *every day*.
get	– got	(b) I *did* my homework *yesterday*.
go	– went	(c) I *go* to class *every day*.
have	– had	(d) I *went** to class *yesterday*.
see	– saw	(e) Meg *has* eggs for breakfast *every morning*.
write	– wrote	(f) Meg *had* eggs for breakfast *yesterday morning*.

*Unlike the other verbs in this chart, **go** does not follow a pattern when it changes to the past tense.

1. THE FINAL SOUND CHANGES TO *D*.

PRESENT	SIMPLE PAST	PRESENT	SIMPLE PAST
do	did*	hear	heard**
have	had	make	made
hide	hid	pay	paid*
		say	said*

*Note the vowel changes. Also, the vowel sound in *said* rhymes with *red*.

**"ea" is pronounced like the vowel in *her*.

2. VOWELS CHANGE TO *A*.

PRESENT	SIMPLE PAST	PRESENT	SIMPLE PAST
become	became	ring	rang
begin	began	run	ran
come	came	see	saw
drink	drank	sing	sang
eat	ate	sit	sat
give	gave	swim	swam

3. VOWELS CHANGE TO *O*.

PRESENT	SIMPLE PAST	PRESENT	SIMPLE PAST
break	broke	sell	sold*
choose	chose	tell	told*
drive	drove	wake	woke
get	got	wear	wore
forget	forgot	win	won
ride	rode	write	wrote
speak	spoke		

*The final sound changes to /d/.

4. THE VOWEL CHANGES TO *OO*.

PRESENT	SIMPLE PAST
take	took
stand	stood
understand	understood

EXERCISE 26 ▶ Looking at grammar. (Chart 8-6)

Write the correct verb.

SIMPLE PRESENT	SIMPLE PAST
1. _____*run*_____	ran
2. wear	_____
3. choose	_____
4. _____	paid
5. begin	_____
6. forget	_____
7. _____	stood
8. _____	told
9. say	_____
10. understand	_____
11. hide	_____

EXERCISE 27 ▶ Looking at grammar. (Chart 8-6)

Check (✓) the true sentences. Share a few of your checked sentences with the class.

1. _____ I had a sandwich for lunch yesterday.

2. _____ I wore jeans to class last week.

3. _____ I drank tea for breakfast today.

4. _____ I sold something online last month.

5. _____ I swam in the ocean last year.

6. _____ I gave a birthday present to someone last month.

7. _____ I forgot a friend's birthday last year.

8. _____ I won something last year.

9. _____ I got a headache last week.

10. _____ I spoke English with a native speaker yesterday.

11. _____ I told my friends a funny story yesterday.

12. _____ I heard a funny story yesterday.

13. _____ I saw some cousins last month.

14. _____ I took the bus to school last week.

EXERCISE 28 ▸ Looking at grammar. (Chart 8-6)
Write the simple past form.

Exercise

EVERY DAY	YESTERDAY
1. Ivan runs after work for exercise.	Ivan _____ after work for exercise.
2. They run after work for exercise.	They _____ after work for exercise.
3. We run after work for exercise.	We _____ after work for exercise.
4. I ride a bike.	I _____ a bike.
5. You ride a bike.	You _____ a bike.
6. She rides a bike.	She _____ a bike.
7. My alarm rings at 6:00 A.M.	My alarm _____ at 6:00 A.M.
8. I go to the gym at 6:30.	I _____ to the gym at 6:30.
9. My exercise class begins at 7:00.	My exercise class _____ at 7:00.

EXERCISE 29 ▸ Let's talk: pairwork. (Chart 8-6)
Work with a partner. Change the sentences from the present to the past. Take turns. You can look at your book before you speak. When you speak, look at your partner.

Example: I have class every day.
PARTNER A (*book open*): I have class every day.
PARTNER B (*book closed*): I have class every day. I had class yesterday.

Partner A (*Partner B: book closed*)	Partner B (*Partner A: book closed*)
1. I get text messages every day.	1. We have lunch every day.
2. They take the bus every day.	2. I write work emails every week.
3. The students choose their meals at the cafeteria every day.	3. Jin comes to class late every day.
4. You see your friends every day.	4. I do my homework every day.
5. Hamid sits in the front row every day.	5. I make breakfast every morning.
6. Mari does her homework every evening.	6. Carlos wakes up early every day.
	Change roles.

EXERCISE 30 ▸ Looking at grammar. (Chart 8-6)

Complete the sentences with the verbs in the box. Use the simple past.

break	drink	forget	make	sing
do	drive	go	pay	wake

Yesterday ...

1. Leo _____ several cups of coffee.

2. Alex stepped on his glasses. He _____ them.

3. I _____ my homework after school.

4. my dad _____ breakfast.

5. Vanessa _____ her computer password.

6. Elaine _____ up at 5:00 A.M.

7. Tony _____ his car to the beach.

8. my parents _____ their bill for their rent.

9. Nina _____ a song in the shower.

10. Roger and his girlfriend _____ to a wedding.

EXERCISE 31 ▸ Warm-up. (Chart 8-7)

Which sentences are true for you? Check (✓) them. Share your answers with a classmate.

1. _____ I eat a big breakfast every morning.

   _____ I ate a big breakfast this morning.

   _____ I didn't eat a big breakfast this morning.

2. _____ I listen to podcasts every week.

   _____ I listened to podcasts last week.

   _____ I didn't listen to podcasts last week.

3. _____ I am hungry right now.

   _____ I was hungry at this time yesterday.

   _____ I wasn't hungry at this time yesterday.

8-7 Simple Past Tense: Negative

	SUBJECT +	DID +	NOT +	MAIN VERB	
(a)	I	did	not	walk	to school yesterday.
(b)	You	did	not	walk	to school yesterday.
(c)	Tim	did	not	have	lunch yesterday.
(d)	They	did	not	come	to class yesterday.

INCORRECT: *I did not walked to school yesterday.*
INCORRECT: *Tim did not had lunch yesterday.*

I
you
she
he
it
we
they
} + **did not** + *main verb**

Note: The base form of the main verb is used with **did not**.

(e) I **didn't walk** to school yesterday.

(f) Tim **didn't have** lunch yesterday.

NEGATIVE CONTRACTION
did + **not** = **didn't**

*EXCEPTION: **did** is NOT used when the main verb is **be**. See Charts 8-2 and 8-3.
CORRECT: Dan *wasn't* here yesterday.
INCORRECT: *Dan didn't be here yesterday.*

EXERCISE 32 ▶ Looking at grammar. (Chart 8-7)
Complete the sentences. Use **not**.

TWO DAYS AGO

1. I got to school late.

2. You got to school late.

3. She got to school late.

4. They stayed home.

5. We stayed home.

6. She did her homework.

7. You did your homework.

8. We did our homework.

9. I was sick.

10. They were sick.

11. She was here.

12. We were here.

YESTERDAY

1. I _did not get OR didn't get_ to school late.

2. You _____ school late.

3. She _____ to school late.

4. They _____ home.

5. We _____ home.

6. She _____ her homework.

7. You _____ your homework.

8. We _____ our homework.

9. I _____ sick.

10. They _____ sick.

11. She _____ here.

12. We _____ here.

EXERCISE 33 ▶ Let's talk: pairwork. (Chart 8-7)

Work with a partner. Use **I don't … every day** and **I didn't … yesterday**. Take turns. You can look at your book before you speak. When you speak, look at your partner.

Example: walk to school
PARTNER A: I don't walk to school every day. I didn't walk to school yesterday.

Example: shop for groceries
PARTNER B: I don't shop for groceries every day. I didn't shop for groceries yesterday.

Partner A	Partner B
1. eat chocolate	1. drink tea
2. watch TV	2. visit my friends
3. wake up early	3. see my parents every day
4. make dinner	4. do my homework
5. study at midnight	5. stream a movie
	Change roles.

EXERCISE 34 ▶ Let's talk: game. (Chart 8-7)

Work in groups of 6–8 students. Tell your group things you didn't do yesterday. Use the suggestions in the box. Repeat the information from the other students in your group. The last person in the group repeats all the sentences.

Example: go
STUDENT A: I didn't go to the zoo yesterday.
STUDENT B: (*Student A*) didn't go to the zoo yesterday. I didn't have lunch in Beijing yesterday.
STUDENT C: (*Student A*) didn't go to the zoo yesterday. (*Student B*) didn't have lunch in Beijing yesterday. I didn't swim in the Pacific Ocean yesterday.

break	have	study	wake up
drink	make	swim	walk to
drive to	sing	use	wear

EXERCISE 35 ▶ Warm-up. (Chart 8-8)

Answer the questions.

1. a. Do you wake up early every day?   Yes, I do.   No, I don't.

   b. Did you wake up early this morning?   Yes, I did.   No, I didn't.

2. a. Do you eat lunch every day?   Yes, I do.   No, I don't.

   b. Did you eat lunch yesterday?   Yes, I did.   No, I didn't.

8-8 Simple Past Tense: Yes/No Questions

DID + SUBJECT + MAIN VERB					SHORT ANSWER	(LONG ANSWER)
(a) *Did*	*Tess*	*walk*	to school?	→	*Yes, she did.*	(She walked to school.)
				→	*No, she didn't.*	(She didn't walk to school.)
(b) *Did*	*you*	*come*	to class?	→	*Yes, I did.*	(I came to class.)
				→	*No, I didn't.*	(I didn't come to class.)

EXERCISE 36 ▸ Let's talk. (Chart 8-8)

Work in small groups. Ask and answer the simple past tense questions. Take turns. Ask a new question after 3–5 students have answered.

Example:

STUDENT A: Did you work late last night?
STUDENT B: No, I didn't. (*to Student C*) Did you work late last night?
STUDENT C: Yes, I did. (*to Student D*) Did you work late last night?
Etc.

1. Did you walk home yesterday?

2. Did you come to class late today?

3. Did you get up early today?

4. Did you play soccer yesterday?

5. Did you drink coffee this morning?

6. Did you go online today?

7. Did you play video games yesterday?

8. Did you text someone before 7:00 A.M.?

9. Did you make your bed this morning?

10. Did you wash the dishes this morning?

EXERCISE 37 ▸ Looking at grammar. (Chart 8-8)

Make questions and give short answers.

1. A: _____ *Did you walk downtown yesterday?* _____

   B: _____ *Yes, I did.* _____ (I walked downtown yesterday.)

2. A: _____ *Did it rain last week?* _____

   B: _____ *No, it didn't.* _____ (It didn't rain last week.)

3. A: _____

   B: _____ (I had lunch at the cafeteria.)

4. A: _____

   B: _____ (Mr. Kwan didn't travel last month.)

5. A: _____

   B: _____ (Ivan chose his major last week.)

6. A: _____

   B: _____ (Ricardo and I spoke English yesterday.)

7. A: _____

   B: _____ (Galina studied English in high school.)

8. A: _____

   B: _____ (Kirsten and Ali didn't do their homework yesterday.)

9. A: _____

   B: _____ (I saw Gina at dinner last night.)

10. A: _____

   B: _____ (I didn't dream in English last night.)

EXERCISE 38 ▸ Let's talk: Find someone who … . (Chart 8-8)

Interview your classmates. Make simple past questions with the given words. Find people who can answer *yes* and write their names in the chart on page 253. Share a few of their responses with the class.

Example: have dessert \ yesterday?

STUDENT A: Did you have dessert after dinner yesterday?

STUDENT B: No, I didn't. I didn't have dessert after dinner yesterday.

STUDENT A: (*to Student C*) Did you have dessert after dinner yesterday?

STUDENT C: Yes, I did. I had dessert after dinner yesterday. (*Write Student C's name.*)

ACTIVITY	FIRST NAME
1. have rice for lunch \ yesterday?	
2. do homework \ last night?	
3. get an email \ yesterday?	
4. drive with someone to a mall \ yesterday?	
5. make dinner \ last night?	
6. drink coffee for breakfast \ this morning?	
7. see a good movie \ last week?	
8. write in English \ today?	
9. sit on the floor \ yesterday?	
10. run outside \ last week?	

EXERCISE 39 ▸ Reading and grammar. (Charts 8-7 and 8-8)

Part I. Read about Kevin's visits with the doctor.

Unhealthy Habits

Kevin didn't feel well. He saw Dr. Benson. Dr. Benson checked him and asked him about his lifestyle. Kevin had some unhealthy habits: he didn't sleep much, he didn't exercise, he ate unhealthy foods, and he smoked. He needed to change these habits. Kevin listened to the doctor, but he didn't change any habits. He continued to feel bad. He went back to the doctor a month later. The doctor asked him some questions.

Part II. Now write the questions the doctor asked Kevin and give Kevin's answers.

1. Dr. Benson: you \ continue

   _____*Did you continue*_____ to smoke last month? Kevin: _____*Yes, I did.*_____

2. Dr. Benson: you \ change

   _____ your eating habits? Kevin: _____

3. Dr. Benson: you \ exercise

   _____? Kevin: _____

4. Dr. Benson: you \ sleep

   _____ more? Kevin: _____

5. Dr. Benson: you \ follow

   _____ my advice? Kevin: _____

EXERCISE 40 ▸ Listening. (Chart 8-8)

Listen to the questions. Write the words you hear.

English Class

Example: You will hear: Did you have your test already?
             You will write: ___*Did you*___ have your test already?

1. _____ do well on the test?

2. _____ finish the assignment?

3. _____ make sense?

4. _____ answer your question?

5. _____ need more help?

6. _____ understand the homework?

7. _____ explain the project?

8. _____ complete the project?

9. _____ do well?

10. _____ pass the class?

EXERCISE 41 ▸ Looking at grammar. (Charts 8-3 and 8-8)
You went to a birthday party last night. A friend is asking you about it. Complete the questions with *did*, *was*, or *were*.

1. _____ you go with a friend?

2. _____ your friends at the party?

3. _____ the party fun?

4. _____ many people there?

5. _____ you have a good time?

6. _____ there a birthday cake?

7. _____ you eat a piece of birthday cake?

8. _____ everyone sing "Happy Birthday"?

9. _____ you hungry?

10. _____ you take a present?

EXERCISE 42 ▸ Warm-up. (Chart 8-9)
Which sentences are true for you? Check (✓) them.

1. _____ I sleep eight hours a night.

2. _____ I slept eight hours last night.

3. _____ I spend time online every morning.

4. _____ I spent time online yesterday morning.

8-9 Simple Past Tense: Irregular Verbs, Part II

1. THE VERB FORM DOESN'T CHANGE.

PRESENT	SIMPLE PAST		PRESENT	SIMPLE PAST
cost	cost		put	put
cut	cut		read	read*
hit	hit		shut	shut
hurt	hurt			

*The pronunciation is the same as the word *red*.

2. THE VOWELS CHANGE TO *E*.

PRESENT	SIMPLE PAST
fall	fell
meet	met

3. THE FINAL SOUND IS /t/. SOME VOWELS AND CONSONANTS MAY ALSO CHANGE.

PRESENT	SIMPLE PAST		PRESENT	SIMPLE PAST
build	built		send	sent
feel	felt		sleep	slept
leave	left		spend	spent
lose	lost*			

*Note the vowel <u>sound</u> change.

4. THE VERB ENDS IN *EW*.

PRESENT	SIMPLE PAST		PRESENT	SIMPLE PAST
fly	flew		know	knew
grow	grew		throw	threw

5. THE VOWEL CHANGES TO *OU*.

PRESENT	SIMPLE PAST
find	found

6. THE VERB ENDS IN *OUGHT*.

PRESENT	SIMPLE PAST		PRESENT	SIMPLE PAST
buy	bought		fight	fought
bring	brought		think	thought

7. THE VERB ENDS IN *AUGHT*.

PRESENT	SIMPLE PAST
catch	caught
teach	taught

EXERCISE 43 ▸ Looking at grammar. (Chart 8-9)
Write the correct verb.

SIMPLE PRESENT	SIMPLE PAST
1. hit	*hit*
2. bring	_____
3. feel	_____
4. _____	grew
5. find	_____
6. meet	_____
7. _____	knew
8. teach	_____
9. _____	built
10. send	_____

EXERCISE 44 ▸ Looking at grammar. (Chart 8-9)
Check (✓) the true sentences. Share a few of your checked sentences with the class.

1. _____ I spent money on food yesterday.

2. _____ I bought a present for a friend last week.

3. _____ I grew vegetables in a garden last year.

4. _____ I read an online newspaper yesterday.

5. _____ I met a friend for dinner last month.

6. _____ I threw a ball yesterday.

7. _____ I spent two hours on my homework last night.

8. _____ I built a website last year.

9. _____ I shut a window during the night.

10. _____ I slept ten hours last night.

11. _____ I brought my lunch to school every day last week.

12. _____ I fought with someone a few days ago.

13. _____ I caught a cold last month.

14. _____ I hurt my back last year.

EXERCISE 45 ▸ Looking at grammar. (Charts 8-6 and 8-9)
Complete the sentences with the correct form of the verbs in the box. There are two extra verbs.

✓catch	cut	hurt	meet	sell
cost	eat	leave	put	think

1. A: What does your cat have in his mouth?

   B: He _____*caught*_____ a mouse, I think!

2. A: Do you still have your bike?

   B: No. I _____ it. I needed some extra money.

3. A: What did you have for lunch?

   B: I didn't have much time, so I just _____ a few snacks.

4. A: Did you buy a new car?

   B: No, it _____ too much. I bought a used one.

5. A: When did Jessica leave for Egypt?

   B: She _____ for Egypt five days ago.

6. A: Do you know Meg Adams?

   B: Yes. I _____ her a couple of weeks ago.

7. A: Are you changing schools?

   B: No. I _____ about it, but I decided to stay here.

8. A: I really like your hair!

   B: Thanks. A friend _____ it for me.

EXERCISE 46 ▸ Listening. (Charts 8-6 and 8-9)
Listen to the beginning of each sentence. Choose the correct completion(s). There may be more than one correct answer.

Example: You will hear: He drank ...
   You will choose: (a.) some tea.   b. bread.   (c.) water.

1. a. last week.   b. a fish.   c. happy.

2. a. very fast.   b. a house.   c. to the store.

3. a. books.   b. the kids.   c. the newspaper.

4. a. a story.   b. a bike.   c. a horse.

5. a. good.   b. some food.   c. a doctor.

6. a. people.   b. into town.   c. home.

EXERCISE 47 ▸ Looking at grammar. (Charts 8-4 and 8-6 → 8-9)
Complete each sentence with the correct form of the words in parentheses.

Talking with a Classmate

1. A: (*you, find*) _____ your T-shirt at the campus bookstore?

   B: No. I (*buy*) _____ it online.

2. A: (*you, study*) _____ last night?

   B: Not really. I was tired. I (*read*) _____ a few pages and then

      (*fall*) _____ asleep.

3. A: (*you, leave*) _____ your calculator at home?

   B: No. I (*bring*) _____ it to class with me.

4. A: (*you, enjoy*) _____ the field trip yesterday?

   B: Not really. I (*catch*) _____ a cold a few days ago and

      (*feel*) _____ very tired.

5. A: (*you, do*) _____ much in music class yesterday?

   B: Professor Neal (*teach*) _____ us a new song. We also

      (*review*) _____ for the test.

EXERCISE 48 ▸ Let's talk: pairwork. (Charts 8-6 → 8-9)
Work with a partner. Take turns asking and answering simple past tense questions. You can look at your book before you speak. When you speak, look at your partner.

Example: think about your family
PARTNER A: Did you think about your family last night/yesterday/last week, etc.?
PARTNER B: Yes, I did. I thought about my family last night. OR
            No, I didn't. I didn't think about my family last night.

Partner A	Partner B
1. lose a key	1. send an email to your teacher
2. ride a bike	2. shut a window
3. catch a cold	3. sleep outdoors
4. teach someone	4. fight with anyone
5. go on social media	5. run in a park
	Change roles.

EXERCISE 49 ▶ Listening. (Charts 8-6 and 8-9)

Listen to the beginning of each sentence. Choose the correct completion(s). There may be more than one correct answer.

Example: You will hear: He did …
       You will choose: (a.) his homework.   (b.) a good job.   c. absent.

1. a. a chair.   b. some rice.   c. some numbers.

2. a. on the floor.   b. a man.   c. together.

3. a. late.   b. yesterday.   c. car.

4. a. an answer.   b. hungry.   c. a book.

5. a. a good grade.   b. last month.   c. a new truck.

6. a. the floor.   b. next to my parents. c. at the bus stop.

Jump-start your English

At the Lost-and-Found

Part I. Listen to the conversations.

1. A: Did someone turn in a wallet?
   B: What does it look like?
   A: It's black.
   B: Let me check.
      Is this it?
   A: Yes! Thank you!

2. A: I lost my backpack.
   B: What color is it?
   A: Blue.
   B: What size?
   A: Small.
   B: Hold on a minute. Let me look.
      Sorry. We don't have it.

3. A: I lost my sweater.
   B: Where did you lose it?
   A: In the cafeteria.
   B: Sorry. No one turned in a sweater from the cafeteria.

Part II. Work with a partner. Practice sentences with the words in the box. Take turns.

I lost	my glasses. a sweater. a baseball cap. some gloves.
Did someone turn in	a package? some sunglasses? a wallet? a backpack? two coats?
What does it look like? What do they look like? What color is it? What color are they? What size is it? What size are they?	It's big. They're small. It's blue and white. They're brown. Large. Size 7.

Part III. Work in small groups. Create a lost-and-found office with items from your group. Create conversations about the items for your group to practice. Share a few with the class.

EXERCISE 50 ▶ Looking at grammar. (Chapter 8 Review)
Choose the correct verbs.

1. Jasmin didn't come / came / comes to the meeting yesterday. She stays / stayed / stay in her office.

2. Kay is reading / reads / read a book right now. She isn't watching / doesn't watch / didn't watch TV. She isn't liking / doesn't like / didn't like to watch TV during the day.

3. Toshi is a busy student. Sometimes he doesn't eat / didn't eat / isn't eating lunch because he doesn't have / isn't having / didn't have enough time.

4. Yesterday Karim isn't having / doesn't have / didn't have time for lunch. He gets / is getting / got hungry during his afternoon class. He is eating / eats / ate an early dinner later.

EXERCISE 51 ▸ Looking at grammar. (Chapter 8 Review)

Complete each sentence with a verb in the box. You will not use all of them.

is coming	finish	is putting	see	is standing
comes	finishes	puts	saw	stands
came	finished	put		stood

1. Our teacher usually _____ in the middle of the room.

2. She _____ in the front of the room yesterday.

3. Right now she _____ in the back of the room.

4. Hanna _____ her homework at 11:00 last night.

5. Yesterday I _____ Lisa at the library.

6. My wife _____ home around five every day.

7. Yesterday, she _____ home at 5:45.

8. Kevin was tired yesterday. He _____ the ice cream in the refrigerator!

9. Look! Jeremy _____ on one blue sock and one brown sock!

10. Before we get to class every day, the teacher _____ the desks in a circle.

EXERCISE 52 ▸ Looking at grammar. (Chapter 8 Review)

Complete the sentences. Change the verbs in parentheses to the simple present, the present progressive, or the simple past. Pay attention to the spelling.

1. I (get) _____ got _____ up at eight o'clock yesterday morning.

2. Ellie (talk) _____ to Barack on the phone right now.

3. Ellie (talk, not) _____ to Barack on the phone last night.

4. Ellie (talk) _____ to Barack on the phone every day.

5. Jim and I (eat) _____ lunch in the cafeteria two hours ago.

6. We (eat, not) _____ lunch in the cafeteria every day.

7. I (go) _____ to bed early last night.

8. My roommate (study) _____ Spanish last year.

9. Kate (send, not) _____ an email to her parents right now.

10. Kate (send) _____ an email to her parents every week. They enjoy her messages.

EXERCISE 53 ▸ Reading and grammar. (Chapter 8 Review)

Read about Matthew's morning. Then read the sentences that follow. If a sentence is true, do not change it. If it is not true, write a correct negative statement.

My Early Morning

Yesterday, my alarm clock didn't go off. I jumped out of bed and looked at the clock. I was late for work. I hurried to the kitchen and quickly prepared breakfast. I had some juice and toast. After breakfast, I put the dishes in the sink. I didn't have time to wash them. Then I quickly got dressed. Soon, I was ready. I walked to the bus. At the bus stop, I didn't recognize anyone. Then I looked at my watch. I was two hours early! I was half asleep when I jumped out of bed earlier and misread* the time on my clock.

1. Matthew's alarm clock went off. ___*Matthew's alarm clock didn't go off.*___

2. He got out of bed quickly. ___*(no change)*___

3. He cooked a big breakfast. _____

4. He washed the dishes. _____

5. He got ready in a hurry. _____

6. He saw his friends at the bus stop. _____

7. He was late for work. _____

8. It was time for work. _____

9. He didn't read the time on the clock correctly. _____

EXERCISE 54 ▸ Listening. (Chapter 8 Review)

Listen to the story. Then read each sentence and choose the correct answer.

A Doctor's Appointment?

1. The man was at the doctor's office.	yes	no
2. He took some medicine.	yes	no
3. He was in bed for a short time.	yes	no
4. The man spoke to the nurse.	yes	no
5. He is feeling OK now.	yes	no

---

misread = read incorrectly

EXERCISE 55 ▸ Writing. (Chapter 8 Review)

Use the expressions from the list to write sentences about yourself. When did you do these things in the past? Use the simple past tense and past time expressions (***yesterday, two days ago, last week,*** *etc.*) in all of your sentences. Use your own paper.

Example: go downtown with (*someone*)

Possible sentence: I went downtown with Marco two days ago.

1. arrive in (*this city*)
2. eat at a restaurant
3. buy (*something*)
4. have a cold
5. be in elementary school
6. drink a cup of coffee
7. talk to (*someone*) on the phone
8. study arithmetic
9. read a newspaper
10. play (soccer, a video game, etc.)
11. see (*someone* or *something*)
12. think about (*someone* or *something*)

EXERCISE 56 ▸ Looking at grammar. (Chapter 8 Review)

Write ***did, was,*** or ***were***.

1. I _____*did*_____ not go to work yesterday. I _____*was*_____ sick, so I stayed home.

2. Ray _____ not in his office yesterday. He _____ not go to work.

3. A: _____ Mr. Chan in his office yesterday?

   B: Yes.

   A: _____ you see him about your problem?

   B: Yes. He answered all my questions. He _____ very helpful.

4. A: _____ you at the meeting yesterday?

   B: Yes.

   A: _____ I miss anything?

   B: No. It _____ really short. The fire alarm went off. We _____ outside for a long time.

5. A: Where _____ you yesterday?

   B: I _____ at the zoo.

   A: _____ you enjoy it?

   B: Yes, but the weather _____ very hot. I tried to stay out of the sun. Most of the animals _____ in their houses or in the shade. The sun _____ too hot for them too. They _____ not want to be outside.

EXERCISE 57 ▶ Let's talk. (Chapter 8 Review)

Work in pairs or small groups. Read the facts about four people: Lara, Josh, Max, and Kira. They live in an apartment building on the same floor. Which apartment does each person live in? Use the clues to find out.

Clues:

1. Lara painted her door yellow.
2. Josh and Lara lived in the same neighborhood when they were children. Now they are next-door neighbors.
3. Max loves music. He works at a music store. His parents were musicians in a band.
4. Kira isn't very social. She didn't want neighbors on both sides. She rented an end unit.
5. Lara moved into her apartment last year.
6. The first time Max played loud music, both Kira and Josh knocked on the walls. They told him to turn it down.

APARTMENT NUMBER	1	2	3	4
NAME				

EXERCISE 58 ▶ Looking at grammar. (Chapter 8 Review)

Make questions.

A Bad Experience

1. A: _Do you live in an apartment?_
   B: Yes, I do. (I live in an apartment.)
2. A: _Do you have a roommate?_
   B: No, I don't. (I don't have a roommate.)

3. A: _____

   B: No, I don't. (I don't want a roommate.)

4. A: _____

   B: Yes, I did. (I had a roommate last year.)

5. A: _____

   B: No, it wasn't. (It wasn't a good experience.)

6. A: _____

   B: Yes, he was. (He was messy.) For example, he never picked up his dirty clothes. He
   never washed his dirty dishes. He was always late with his part of the rent.

7. A: _____

   B: No, he didn't. (He didn't help me clean.)

8. A: _____ when he left?

   B: Yes, I was. (I was glad when he left.)

EXERCISE 59 ▶ Listening. (Chapter 8 Review)
Listen to Lara's story about her wedding ring. Then read each sentence and choose the
correct answer.

A Wedding Ring

1. The woman lost her mother's ring.	yes	no
2. Someone took the ring.	yes	no
3. Her dog found the ring in the garden.	yes	no
4. Her mother wore the ring for a while.	yes	no
5. The woman was happy at the end of the story.	yes	no

EXERCISE 60 ▶ Check your knowledge. (Chapter 8 Review)
Correct the mistakes.

1. Someone ~~was take~~ *took* my bike two days ago.

2. Did you went to the party last weekend?

3. I hear an interesting story yesterday.

4. The teacher not ready for class yesterday.

5. Did came Dennis to work last week?

6. Yesterday night I staied home.

7. Several students wasn't on time for the final exam yesterday.

8. Your phone rang before a few minutes.

9. Did you the movie watch?

10. The store no have yellow bananas. I get some green ones.

11. Did you nervous about your test last week?

12. I didn't saw you at the party. Did was you there?

EXERCISE 61 ▶ Reading and writing. (Chapter 8)

Part I. Read about Andy's week.

An Embarrassing Week

Do you know these words?
- *embarrassing* - *boss*
- *slippers* - *salad*
- *stupid* - *lettuce*
- *hide* - *mirror*

Andy did some embarrassing things last week. For example, on Monday, he wore his slippers to work. He got on the bus and looked down at his feet. He felt very stupid and wanted to hide his feet.

That night, he typed an email to his girlfriend. He told her he loved her. But he hit the wrong button, and he sent the message to his boss. His girlfriend and his boss have the same first name. He didn't know about his mistake until the next morning at work. His boss didn't look very happy.

On Friday, he went to a nice restaurant with co-workers for lunch and ate a salad. After lunch he had a meeting. He talked a lot at the meeting. People gave him strange looks, but Andy didn't know why. Later he found out the reason. He had lettuce on his front teeth.

Andy is hoping for a better week this week. He hid his slippers under the bed and put a mirror in his desk drawer. But he didn't tell his girlfriend about the email because he is still very embarrassed.

Part II. Write about something embarrassing that you did or something embarrassing that happened to you. Your title can be "An Embarrassing Week," "An Embarrassing Day," "An Embarrassing Night," "An Embarrassing Experience," etc. If you prefer, write about a family member or a friend. Follow the steps on page 268.

1. First, write single sentences about one or more embarrassing things you or someone else did. Use simple past tense verbs.

2. Add details to make the story interesting. Answer these questions:
   - Where and/or when did it happen?
   - What did you think?
   - How did you feel?
   - What did you do next?
   - Did you need to find a solution?

3. Put this information into one or more paragraphs.

Part III. Edit your writing. Work individually or change papers with a partner. Check (✓) for the following:

1. ☐ paragraph indents
2. ☐ a capital letter at the beginning of each sentence
3. ☐ a period at the end of each sentence
4. ☐ correct use of the simple past for a completed activity
5. ☐ correct use of *didn't* and *wasn't* for simple past negatives
6. ☐ correct spelling (use a dictionary or computer spell-check)

■■■■■ For digital resources, go to MyEnglishLab on the Pearson English Portal. You can also go to the Pearson Practice English App for mobile practice.

Appendix

Appendix 1

English Handwriting

PRINTING			CURSIVE		
Aa	Jj	Ss	Aa	Jj	Ss
Bb	Kk	Tt	Bb	Kk	Tt
Cc	Ll	Uu	Cc	Ll	Uu
Dd	Mm	Vv	Dd	Mm	Vv
Ee	Nn	Ww	Ee	Nn	Ww
Ff	Oo	Xx	Ff	Oo	Xx
Gg	Pp	Yy	Gg	Pp	Yy
Hh	Qq	Zz	Hh	Qq	Zz
Ii	Rr		Ii	Rr	

Vowels = a, e, i, o, u
Consonants = $b, c, d, f, g, h, j, k, l, m, n, p, q, r, s, t, v, w, x, y, z$★

★The letter ***z*** is pronounced "zee" in American English and "zed" in British English.

Appendix 2

Numbers

CARDINAL NUMBERS		ORDINAL NUMBERS	
1	one	1st	first
2	two	2nd	second
3	three	3rd	third
4	four	4th	fourth
5	five	5th	fifth
6	six	6th	sixth
7	seven	7th	seventh
8	eight	8th	eighth
9	nine	9th	ninth
10	ten	10th	tenth
11	eleven	11th	eleventh
12	twelve	12th	twelfth
13	thirteen	13th	thirteenth
14	fourteen	14th	fourteenth
15	fifteen	15th	fifteenth
16	sixteen	16th	sixteenth
17	seventeen	17th	seventeenth
18	eighteen	18th	eighteenth
19	nineteen	19th	nineteenth
20	twenty	20th	twentieth
21	twenty-one	21st	twenty-first
22	twenty-two	22nd	twenty-second
23	twenty-three	23rd	twenty-third
24	twenty-four	24th	twenty-fourth
25	twenty-five	25th	twenty-fifth
26	twenty-six	26th	twenty-sixth
27	twenty-seven	27th	twenty-seventh
28	twenty-eight	28th	twenty-eighth
29	twenty-nine	29th	twenty-ninth
30	thirty	30th	thirtieth
40	forty	40th	fortieth
50	fifty	50th	fiftieth
60	sixty	60th	sixtieth
70	seventy	70th	seventieth
80	eighty	80th	eightieth
90	ninety	90th	ninetieth
100	one hundred	100th	one hundredth
200	two hundred	200th	two hundredth
1,000	one thousand	1,000th	one thousandth
10,000	ten thousand	10,000th	ten thousandth
100,000	one hundred thousand	100,000th	one hundred thousandth
1,000,000	one million	1,000,000th	one millionth

Ways of Saying the Time

9:00   It's nine o'clock.
        It's nine.

9:05   It's nine-oh-five.
        It's five (minutes) after nine.
        It's five (minutes) past nine.

9:10   It's nine-ten.
        It's ten (minutes) after nine.
        It's ten (minutes) past nine.

9:15   It's nine-fifteen.
        It's a quarter after nine.
        It's a quarter past nine.

9:30   It's nine-thirty.
        It's half past nine.

9:45   It's nine-forty-five.
        It's a quarter to ten.
        It's a quarter of ten.

9:50   It's nine-fifty.
        It's ten (minutes) to ten.
        It's ten (minutes) of ten.

12:00 It's noon.
        It's midnight.

A.M. = morning: It's 9:00 A.M.
P.M. = afternoon/evening/night: It's 9:00 P.M.

Days/Months/Seasons

DAYS	ABBREVIATION	MONTHS	ABBREVIATION	SEASONS*
Monday	Mon.	January	Jan.	winter
Tuesday	Tues.	February	Feb.	spring
Wednesday	Wed.	March	Mar.	summer
Thursday	Thurs.	April	Apr.	fall or autumn
Friday	Fri.	May	May	
Saturday	Sat.	June	Jun.	
Sunday	Sun.	July	Jul.	
		August	Aug.	
		September	Sept.	
		October	Oct.	
		November	Nov.	
		December	Dec.	

*Seasons of the year are only capitalized when they begin a sentence.

Writing Dates

MONTH/DAY/YEAR

10/31/41 = October 31, 1941
4/15/98 = April 15, 1998
7/4/1906 = July 4, 1906
7/4/09 = July 4, 2009
3/21/30 = March 21, 2030

Saying Dates

USUAL WRITTEN FORM	USUAL SPOKEN FORM
January 1	January first / the first of January
March 2	March second / the second of March
May 3	May third / the third of May
June 4	June fourth / the fourth of June
August 5	August fifth / the fifth of August
October 10	October tenth / the tenth of October
November 27	November twenty-seventh / the twenty-seventh of November

Basic Capitalization Rules

	Use a capital letter for:
(a) Joan and I are friends.	the pronoun "I"
(b) They are late.	the first word of a sentence
(c) Sam Bond and Tom Adams are here.	names of people
(d) Mrs. Peterson Professor Jones Dr. Costa	titles of people*
(e) Monday, Tuesday, Wednesday	the days of the week
(f) April, May, June	the months of the year
(g) New Year's Day	holidays
(h) Los Angeles Florida, Ontario Germany Lake Baikal Amazon River Pacific Ocean Mount Everest Broadway, Fifth Avenue	names of places: cities, states and provinces, countries, lakes, rivers, oceans, mountains, streets
(i) German, Chinese, Swedish	languages and nationalities
(j) Pirates of the Caribbean Romeo and Juliet	the first word of a title, for example, in a book or movie. Capitalize the other words, but not: articles (*the, a, an*), short prepositions (*with, in, at,* etc.), and these words: *and, but, or.*
(k) Buddhism, Christianity, Hinduism, Islam, Judaism	religions

*Mrs. = woman: married   Miss = woman: unmarried
Ms. = woman: married or unmarried   Mr. = man: married or unmarried

Pronunciation for Verb Endings -*s* and -*ed*

Voiceless and Voiced Sounds for -*s* Endings on Verbs

VOICELESS	VOICED	

(a) /p/   sleep
    /t/   write
    /f/   laugh
	(b) /b/ rub
	    /d/ ride
	    /v/ drive
	
	I can feel my voice box. It vibrates.
		Some sounds are "voiceless." You don't use your voice box. You push air through your teeth and lips. For example, the sound /p/ comes from air through your lips. The final sounds in (a) are voiceless.
		
		Common voiceless sounds are *f, k, p, t, sh, ch,* and voiceless *th*.

		Some sounds are "voiced." You use your voice box to make voiced sounds. For example, the sound /b/ comes from your voice box. The final sounds in (b) are voiced. Common voiced sounds are *b, d, g, j, l, m, n, r, v,* and voiced *th*.

(c)   sleeps   =   sleep/s/
      writes   =   write/s/
      laughs   =   laugh/s/
	(d) rubs = rub/z/
	      rides = ride/z/
	      drives = drive/z/
		Final -*s* is pronounced /s/ after voiceless sounds, as in (c).
		
		Final -*s* is pronounced /z/ after voiced sounds, as in (d).

Final -*ed* Pronunciation for Simple Past Verbs

Final -*ed* has three pronunciations: /t/, /d/, and /əd/.

END OF VERB	BASE FORM	SIMPLE PAST	PRONUNCIATION	

VOICELESS	(a) help
	      laugh
	      wash
		helped
		laughed
		washed
			help/t/
			laugh/t/
			wash/t/
				Final -*ed* is pronounced /t/ if a verb ends in a voiceless sound, as in (a).

VOICED	(b) rub
	      live
	      smile
		rubbed
		lived
		smiled
			rub/d/
			live/d/
			smile/d/
				Final -*ed* is pronounced /d/ if a verb ends in a voiced sound, as in (b).

-d OR *-t*	(c) need want	needed wanted	need/əd/ want/əd/	Final -*ed* is pronounced /əd/ if a verb ends in the letters *d* or *t*, as in (c).

Appendix 7

Common Irregular Verbs: A Reference List

SIMPLE FORM	SIMPLE PAST	SIMPLE FORM	SIMPLE PAST
be	was, were	leave	left
become	became	lose	lost
begin	began	make	made
break	broke	meet	met
bring	brought	pay	paid
build	built	put	put
buy	bought	read	read
catch	caught	ride	rode
choose	chose	ring	rang
come	came	run	ran
cost	cost	say	said
cut	cut	see	saw
do	did	sell	sold
drink	drank	send	sent
drive	drove	shut	shut
eat	ate	sing	sang
fall	fell	sit	sat
feel	felt	sleep	slept
fight	fought	speak	spoke
find	found	spend	spent
fly	flew	stand	stood
forget	forgot	swim	swam
get	got	take	took
give	gave	teach	taught
go	went	tell	told
grow	grew	think	thought
have	had	throw	threw
hear	heard	understand	understood
hide	hid	wake	woke
hit	hit	wear	wore
hurt	hurt	win	won
know	knew	write	wrote

Listening Script

NOTE: You may want to pause the audio during written tasks so that there is enough time to complete each item.

Chapter 1: Using *Be*

Exercise 13 ▶ p. 8
1. apple
2. egg
3. hamburger
4. orange
5. peanut
6. sandwich

Exercise 14 ▶ p. 9
1. a pea
2. a pretzel
3. a carrot
4. a strawberry
5. a blueberry

Exercise 21 ▶ p. 12
A: Hello. I'm Mrs. Brown. I'm the substitute teacher.
B: Hi. I'm Paulo, and this is Marie. We're in your class.
A: It's nice to meet you.
B: We're happy to meet you too.
A: It's time for class. Please take a seat.

Exercise 25 ▶ p. 14
Part II
1. Andrew isn't a child.
2. Isabelle is an aunt.
3. Marie is a mom.
4. David isn't a dad.
5. Billy and Janey are brother and sister.
6. Marie and Andrew are adults.
7. Billy and Janey aren't parents.
8. David and Andrew aren't daughters.

Exercise 38 ▶ p. 23
The First Day of Class

Paulo is a student from Brazil. Marie is a student from France. They're in the classroom. Today is an exciting day. It's the first day of school. They aren't nervous. They're happy to be here. Mrs. Brown is the teacher. She isn't in the classroom right now. She's late today.

Exercise 41 ▶ p. 25
1. Grammar's easy.
2. My name's Josh.
3. My books're on the table.
4. My brother's 21 years old.
5. The weather's cold today.
6. The dogs're hungry.
7. The students're homesick.
8. Mr. Smith's a teacher.
9. My parents're at work now.
10. The bed's comfortable.
11. Tom's sick today.
12. My mom and dad're from Montreal.
13. My sister's a student in high school.

Chapter 2: Using *Be* and *Have*

Exercise 38 ▶ p. 51
Part I
1. A: Where is your book?
   B: Hiroko has it.
   A: Where are your notebooks?
   B: Nasir and Angela have them.

2. A: What's this?
   B: It's a picture of my family.
   A: Who's this?
   B: That's my father.
   A: Who are they?
   B: They're my brother and sister.

3. A: What's this?
   B: I don't know. Ask the teacher.
   A: What's this?
   C: It's your homework for tonight.

4. A: Where is the teacher?
   B: He's in the library.
   A: Where are the students?
   B: They're in the cafeteria.

Chapter 3: Using the Simple Present

Exercise 4 ▶ p. 58

Beginning the Day

1. I wake up early every day.
2. My brother wakes up late.
3. He gets up at 11:00.
4. I go to school at 8:00.
5. My mother does exercises every morning.
6. My little sister watches TV in the morning.
7. I take the bus to school.
8. My brother takes the bus to school.
9. My friends take the bus too.
10. We talk about our day.

Exercise 14 ▶ p. 64

1. eat
2. eats
3. push
4. pushes
5. sleeps
6. fixes

Exercise 16 ▶ p. 65

1. Mrs. Miller teaches English on Saturdays.
2. Mr. and Mrs. Hanson teach English in the evenings.
3. Chang fixes cars.
4. His son fixes cars too.
5. Carlos and Chris watch movies on weekends.
6. Their daughter watches TV shows on her computer.
7. I brush my hair every morning.
8. Jimmy seldom brushes his hair.
9. The Nelsons wash their car every weekend.
10. Jada rarely washes her car.

Exercise 24 ▶ p. 69

An Unusual Schedule

Marco is a student. He has an unusual schedule. All of his classes are at night. His first class is at 6:00 P.M. every day. He takes a break from 7:30 to 8:00. Then he has classes from 8:00 to 10:00.

He goes home at 10:00. He has dinner and watches TV. Then he does his homework from midnight to 3:00 or 4:00 in the morning.

Marco has a new computer. He finishes his homework, and he goes on the internet. He often stays at his computer until morning. Then he does some exercises. He has breakfast and goes to bed. He sleeps all day. Marco likes his schedule. His friends think it is strange.

Jump-start your English ▶ p. 90

Saying the Time

Part III

1. It's ten after two.
2. It's two-ten.
3. It's nine-oh-five.
4. It's six-fifty-five.
5. It's eleven o'clock.
6. It's midnight.
7. It's three-fifteen.
8. It's a quarter after three.
9. It's a quarter to four.
10. It's three-forty-five.

Chapter 4: Using the Present Progressive and the Imperative

Exercise 9 ▶ p. 101

1. Kumar is sitting in the library.
2. He is eating lunch.
3. He is studying alone.
4. He is working on homework.
5. He is checking social media.
6. He is studying hard.
7. He is talking to friends.
8. He is sending text messages.

Exercise 26 ▶ p. 112

1. I write in my grammar book …
2. I am writing in my grammar book …
3. It is raining outside …
4. It doesn't rain …
5. My cell phone rings …
6. My cell phone isn't ringing …
7. My friends and I listen to music in the car …
8. We're not listening to music …

Exercise 30 ▶ p. 115

What are you doing?

A: Are you working on your English paper?
B: No, I'm not. I'm writing an email to my sister.
A: Do you write to her often?
B: Yes, but I don't write a lot of emails to anyone else.
A: Does she write to you often?
B: No, but she texts me a lot.

Chapter 5: Nouns and Pronouns

Exercise 7 ▶ p. 132

1. toys
2. table
3. face
4. hats
5. offices
6. boxes
7. package
8. chairs
9. edge
10. tops

Exercise 8 ▶ p. 132

1. The desks in the classroom are new.
2. I like to visit new places.
3. Luke wants a sandwich for lunch.
4. The teacher is correcting sentences.
5. The snack is in the refrigerator.
6. We are doing an exercise in class.
7. Here is a glass of milk.
8. The box is for you.
9. The boxes are heavy.
10. This college is very good.

Exercise 43 ▶ p. 156

1. Mack's parents live in Singapore.
2. Mack has two brothers and one sister.
3. My teacher's apartment is near mine.
4. My teacher is very funny.
5. What is your friend saying?
6. My friend's birthday is today.
7. The store manager's name is Dean.
8. My cousin studies engineering.

Exercise 49 ▶ p. 158

In Class

1. Who's that?
2. Whose homework is this?
3. Who's sitting next to you?
4. Who's next?
5. Whose turn is it?
6. Who's ready?
7. Whose work is ready?
8. Who's absent?

Exercise 56 ▶ p. 161

1. A: Mika and I are going downtown this afternoon. Do you want to come with us?
   B: I don't think so, but thanks anyway. Chris and I are going to the library. We need to study for our test.

2. A: Hi, Abby. How do you like your new apartment?
   B: It's great. I have a new roommate too. She's very nice.
   A: What's her name?
   B: Rita Lopez. Do you know her?
   A: No, but I know her brother. He's in my math class.

3. A: Do you see Mike and George very much?
   B: Yes, I see them often. We play video games at my house.
   A: Who usually wins?
   B: Mike. We never beat him!

Chapter 6: Count and Noncount Nouns

Exercise 13 ▶ p. 171

Tell me some things about you and your family.

1. I live in an apartment.
2. It's a small apartment.
3. I study at an English school.
4. I have an interesting class.
5. We have a fun teacher.
6. My mom has an office downtown.
7. It's an insurance office.
8. My dad is a nurse.
9. He works at a hospital.
10. He has a busy job.

Exercise 47 ▶ p. 192

1. Vegetables have vitamins.
2. Cats make nice pets.
3. The teacher is absent.
4. I love bananas.
5. Cars are expensive.
6. I need the keys to the car.
7. Are the computers in your office working?
8. I want to go for a walk in the park.

Exercise 50 ▶ p. 193

1. A: Do you have an eraser?
   B: I see one on the desk.

2. A: Where are the keys to the car?
   B: I'm not sure. You can use mine.

3. A: Shhh. I hear a noise.
   B: It's just a bird outside. Don't worry.

4. A: Henry Jackson teaches at the university.
   B: I know. He's an English professor.
   A: He's also the head of the department.

5. A: We need to leave for the train station.
   B: We have an hour.
   A: That's not enough. Traffic is very heavy.

Chapter 7: More About the Present Tense

Exercise 7 ▶ p. 204

Part I

1. My birthday is in July. I was born in the morning. I was born in 1993. My name is …
2. I was born at 11:00 at night. My birthday is in June. I was born on June 24th. My name is …
3. I was born in 2000. My birthday is July 7th. I was born in the evening. My name is …
4. My birthday is in June. I was born at 7:00 o'clock. I was born in 2000. My name is …

Exercise 17 ▶ p. 210

1. There're ten students in the classroom.
2. There's a new teacher today.
3. There're two new math teachers this year.
4. There's a piece of gum on the floor.
5. There's some information on the bulletin board.
6. There're some spelling mistakes on this paper.
7. There's a grammar mistake in this sentence.
8. There're two writing assignments for tonight.

Exercise 32 ▶ p. 221

A New Apartment

1. There's a big couch.
2. There's a TV.
3. There are some windows.
4. There are chairs around the TV.
5. There's a lamp near the window.
6. There is a picture on the wall.
7. There are pillows on the couch.
8. There's a view of the city.
9. There's a big table on the carpet.

Exercise 40 ▶ p. 226

1. I'd like a hamburger for dinner.
2. We like to eat at fast-food restaurants.
3. Bob'd like to go to the gym now.
4. He likes to exercise after work.
5. The teacher'd like to speak with you.
6. The teacher likes your work.
7. We like to ride our bikes on weekends.
8. We'd like to ride in a race.
9. Bill and Kay like jazz music.
10. They'd like to go to a concert next week.

Chapter 8: Expressing Past Time, Part 1

Exercise 8 ▶ p. 234

1. I wasn't at home last night.
2. I was at the library.
3. Our teacher was sick yesterday.
4. He wasn't at school.
5. There was a substitute teacher.
6. She was friendly and funny.
7. Many students were absent.
8. They weren't at school for several days.
9. My friends and I were nervous on the first day of school.
10. You weren't nervous.

Exercise 18 ▶ p. 240

A Soccer Coach

1. Jeremy works as a soccer coach.
2. His team plays many games.
3. His team played in a tournament.
4. Yesterday, they scored five goals.
5. Jeremy helped the players a lot.
6. They learned about the other team.
7. They watched movies of the other team.
8. The players like Jeremy.
9. All year, they worked very hard.
10. Every practice, each player works very hard.

Exercise 24 ▶ p. 244

Part I

1. What was the date two days ago?
2. What was the date five days ago?
3. What was the date yesterday?
4. What month was it last month?
5. What year was it ten years ago?
6. What year was it last year?
7. What year was it one year ago?

Part II

1. What time was it one hour ago?
2. What time was it five minutes ago?
3. What time was it one minute ago?

Exercise 40 ▶ p. 254

English Class

1. Did we do well on the test?
2. Did you finish the assignment?
3. Did it make sense?
4. Did I answer your question?
5. Did they need more help?
6. Did he understand the homework?
7. Did she explain the project?
8. Did they complete the project?
9. Did you do well?
10. Did she pass the class?

Exercise 46 ▶ p. 258

1. She caught ...
2. They drove ...
3. We read ...
4. I rode ...
5. He bought ...
6. We ran ...

Exercise 49 ▶ p. 260

1. I ate ...
2. We sat ...
3. They came ...
4. She had ...
5. He got ...
6. I stood ...

Exercise 54 ▶ p. 263

A Doctor's Appointment?

I woke up with a headache this morning. I took some medicine and went back to bed. I slept all day. The phone rang. I heard it, but I was very tired. I didn't answer it. I listened to the voicemail. It was the doctor's office. The nurse said I missed my appointment. Now my headache is really bad!

Exercise 59 ▶ p. 266

A Wedding Ring

My mother called me early this morning. She had wonderful news for me. She had my wedding ring. I lost it last year during a party at her house. She told me she was outside in her vegetable garden with her dog. The dog found my ring under some vegetables. My mom said she immediately put it on her finger and wore it. She didn't want to lose it. I was so happy. I hung up the phone and began to laugh and cry at the same time.

Let's Talk: Answers

Chapter 3, Exercise 33, p. 74

1. no   [They like to look for food at night.]
2. yes
3. yes
4. yes
5. yes
6. no   [Only female mosquitoes bite.]
7. yes

Chapter 3, Exercise 54, p. 87

Name	Where does she/he live?	What does he/she do?	Where does she/he work?	What pets does he/she have?
ANTONIO	(on a boat)	catches fish	on his boat	a turtle
LENA	in a cabin in the mountains	(teaches skiing)	at a ski school	ten fish
KANE	in an apartment in the city	makes jewelry	(at a jewelry store)	three cats
LISA	in a beach cabin on an island	surfs and swims	has no job	a snake
JACK	in a house in the country	designs web pages	at home	a horse

Jump-start your English: Saying the Time, p. 90

Part II

Partner A:

1. It's five-fifty. / It's ten to six.
2. It's three-oh-five. / It's five after three.
3. It's eleven-thirty. / It's half past eleven.
4. It's seven-forty. / It's twenty to eight.
5. It's two-fifteen. / It's a quarter after two.
6. It's four o'clock. / It's four.

Partner B:

1. It's nine-fifteen. / It's a quarter after nine.
2. It's ten-ten. / It's ten after ten.
3. It's six-fifty-five. / It's five to seven.
4. It's eight-twenty. / It's twenty after eight.
5. It's eleven o'clock. / It's eleven.
6. It's twelve-forty-five. / It's a quarter to one.

Chapter 4, Exercise 20, pp. 107–108
Part II
Partner B

Chapter 6, Exercise 28, pp. 179–180

Partner B's answers:

1. a. some food.
    b. an apple.
    c. a hamburger.
    d. a bowl of soup.

2. a. a glass of milk.
    b. some water.
    c. a cup of tea.

3. a. some medicine.
    b. an ambulance.

4. a. a coat.
    b. a hat.
    c. some warm clothes.
    d. some heat.

5. a. some sleep.
    b. a break.
    c. a relaxing vacation.

Partner A's answers:

6. a. a snack.
    b. some fruit.
    c. an orange.
    d. a piece of chicken.

7. a. some juice.
    b. a bottle of water.
    c. a glass of iced tea.

8. a. a doctor.
    b. some help.

9. a. some boots.
    b. a blanket.
    c. a hot bath.
    d. some gloves.

10. a. some strong coffee.
    b. a strong cup of coffee.
    c. a vacation.
    d. a nap.

Chapter 7, Exercise 21, p. 213

	A SWIMMING POOL	A BEACH	HIKING TRAILS	HORSES	OCEAN-VIEW ROOMS
HOTEL 1	(yes)	yes	yes	no	yes
HOTEL 2	yes	yes	yes	yes	no
HOTEL 3	yes	yes	(yes)	yes	yes
HOTEL 4	yes	yes	no	yes	yes
HOTEL 5	no	yes	yes	yes	yes

Answer: Hotel 3

Index

Always, 59, 62 (*Look at pages 59 and 62.*)	The numbers following the words listed in the index refer to page numbers in the text.
a.m., 90*fn.* (*Look at the footnote on page 90.*)	The letters *fn.* mean "footnote." Footnotes are at the bottom of a chart, at the bottom of a page, or within *Jump-start your English*.

A

A/an, 169
  a vs. *an*, 6, 6*fn.*, 169
  with count/noncount nouns, 165, 169, 171, 177
  with singular nouns, 6, 8
  vs. *some*, 171
Abbreviations, for days and months, 272
About, in *think about*, 123
Action verbs in present progressive, 121
Adjectives (*good, beautiful*), 138
  after *be* (*are beautiful*), 16, 24, 138
  defined, 138
  lists of, 16, 138
  before nouns (*happy child*), 138
  possessive (*my, our*), 43, 149
  this and *that* as (*this book*), 29
Adverbs (*quickly*):
  of frequency (*always, sometimes*), 59
    with *be* (*am always*), 62
    position of, 59, 59*fn.*, 62
A few, 181
Ago, 241
A little, 181
A lot of, 165
Always, 59, 62
Am, is, are + -ing (*am sitting*), 97 (SEE ALSO Present progressive)
a.m., 90*fn.*
An (SEE *A/an*)
And, connecting nouns with, 8
Answers, short, 35

Any, 194
Apostrophes:
  defined, 11
  placement of, 11*fn.*
  in possessive nouns (*Eva's, students', men's*), 153, 159 (SEE ALSO Contractions)
Articles (*the, a, an*) (SEE ALSO *individual articles*)
  defined, 6
  making generalizations using no articles, 190
At:
  in *look at*, 121
  as preposition of place, 215
  as preposition of time, 202
Auxiliary (helping) verbs, 75, 97

B

Base form of verbs:
  defined, 72*fn.*
  after *did not*, 249
  in imperative sentences, 125
  in infinitives, 72
  in *yes/no* questions in simple present, 80
Be:
  adjectives after (*are beautiful*), 16, 24, 138
  in contractions:
    with *not* (*isn't*), 13, 103
    with pronouns (*she's*), 11, 13, 35
    with question words (*who's*), 49
    with *that* (*that's*), 29
  frequency adverbs after (*am always*), 62
  with nouns (*is a country*), 6, 8, 24
  places after (*is here*), 21, 24

CREDITS

Photo Credits: Page 1 (L): Ariwasabi/Shutterstock; **1** (R): Photomak/Shutterstock; **3** (sick): Iatsenko Olga/Shutterstock; **3** (nervous): WAYHOME studio/Shutterstock; **3** (relaxed): Antonio Guillem/123RF; **3** (hungry): Rohappy/Shutterstock; **3** (B): Wavebreakmedia/Shutterstock; **6**: Leonello calvetti/Shutterstock; **7** (dog): Ferli/123RF; **7** (cat): Eric Isselee/Shutterstock; **8** (1): Topseller/Shutterstock; **8** (2): Elena Elisseeva/Shutterstock; **8** (3): PMN PHOTO/Shutterstock; **8** (4): Samokhin/Shutterstock; **8** (5): Gresei/Shutterstock; **8** (6): 3445128471/Shutterstock; **9** (1): Dionisvera/Shutterstock; **9** (2): Jiri Hera/Shutterstock; **9** (3): Africa Studio/Shutterstock; **9** (4): Elena Schweitzer/Shutterstock; **9** (5): Matin/Shutterstock; **13**: Dima Zel/Shutterstock; **15** (bus driver): Minerva Studio/Shutterstock; **15** (mechanic): Wavebreak Media Ltd/123RF; **15** (nurse): Kzenon/123RF; **15** (gardener): Welcomia/123RF; **15** (plumber): Phovoir/Shutterstock; **15** (doctor): Godsandkings/123RF; **15** (construction workers): Vadim Ratnikov/Shutterstock; **15** (police officer): John Roman Images/Shutterstock; **16** (L): Aastock/Shutterstock; **16** (R) Andresr/Shutterstock; **17** (balloons): Minur/Shutterstock; **17** (banana): Maks Narodenko/Shutterstock; **17** (onion): Hong Vo/Shutterstock; **17** (tomato): Tim UR/Shutterstock; **18** (tulips): BESTWEB/Shutterstock; **18** (dead flowers): Malcolm Harris/Pearson Education Ltd; **18** (1L): PhotosIndia.com LLC/123RF; **18** (1R): Flashon Studio/Shutterstock; **18** (2L): Irina Bg/Shutterstock; **18** (2R): Stefanie Mohr Photography/Shutterstock; **18** (3L): Tilborg Jean-Pierre/Shutterstock; **19** (3R): Vicspacewalker/Shutterstock; **19** (4R): 3445128471/Shutterstock; **19** (5L): Fh Photo/Shutterstock; **19** (5R): Nattika/Shutterstock; **19** (B): Olesia Bilkei/Shutterstock; **21**: Ermolaev Alexandr Alexandrovich/123RF; **22** (mouse and cheese): VikiVector/Shutterstock; **22** (pets): Photodeti/123RF; **23**: Antonio Guillem/Shutterstock; **25**: Antonio Guillem/Shutterstock; **26**: Aaron Rutten/Shutterstock; **28** (hand): Stylephotographs/123RF; **28** (modern cell phone): Shtanzman/123RF; **28** (hand): Stylephotographs/123RF; **28** (old cell phone): Anna Chelnokova/Shutterstock; **29** (hand): Stylephotographs/123RF; **29** (pencil): Vitaly Zorkin/Shutterstock; **29** (hand): Stylephotographs/123RF; **29** (pen): Vastram/Shutterstock; **29** (hand): Stylephotographs/123RF; **29** (eraser): Joe Belanger/Shutterstock; **29** (hand): Stylephotographs/123RF; **29** (notebook): Akekoksomshutter/Shutterstock; **29** (hand): Stylephotographs/123RF; **29** (stapler): Nordling/Shutterstock; **29** (hand): Stylephotographs/123RF; **29** (paperclip): Zerbor/123RF; **29** (hand): Stylephotographs/123RF; **29** (pencil sharpener): Seregam/Shutterstock; **29** (hand): Stylephotographs/123RF; **29** (monitor): Valeriy Lebedev/Shutterstock; **29** (hand): Stylephotographs/123RF; **29** (calculator): Karandaev/123RF; **29** (hand): Stylephotographs/123RF; **29** (backpack): Srapulsar38/123RF; **30** (ruler): Tatiana Popova/Shutterstock; **30** (keyboard): GreenLandStudio/Shutterstock; **30** (hand): Stylephotographs/123RF; **30** (keys): Odua Images/Shutterstock; **31** (hand): Stylephotographs/123RF; **31** (USB drives): Andre Nitsievsky/Shutterstock; **31** (hand): Stylephotographs/123RF; **31** (red wallet): Jiggo_Putter Studio/Shutterstock; **31** (brown wallet): Morganka/Shutterstock; **31** (hand): Stylephotographs/123RF; **31** (rulers): Iunewind/Shutterstock; **31** (hand): Stylephotographs/123RF; **31** (paperclips): Martin Damen/123RF; **31** (hand): Stylephotographs/123RF; **31** (staplers): Sergei Vidineev/123RF; **31** (hand): Stylephotographs/123RF; **31** (receipts): Vesna cvorovic/Shutterstock; **34**: AVAVA/Shutterstock; **38**: Stuart Monk/Shutterstock; **39** (headache): Theerapol Pongkangsananan/Shutterstock; **39** (cold): Dora Zett/Shutterstock; **39** (cough): New Africa/Shutterstock; **40** (toothache): G-stockstudio/Shutterstock; **40** (1): Photographee.eu/Shutterstock; **40** (2): Alexander Raths/123RF; **41** (3): Dragon_fang/Shutterstock; **41** (4L): Nico Traut/Shutterstock; **41** (4R): Slasny/123RF; **41** (5): Kleber Cordeiro Costa/123RF; **41** (6): Tom Wang/Shutterstock; **42** (T): Jimena Catalina Gayo/Shutterstock; **42** (B): Dragon Images/Shutterstock; **43** (1): Ken Hurst/Shutterstock; **43** (2): Aaron Amat/Shutterstock; **43** (3): Dkovalenko/Shutterstock; **43** (4): Stockfour/Shutterstock; **44** (Derek C. Williams): Kurhan/123RF; **44** (Ellen Ryan): 663268/Shutterstock; **44** (Daniel Ryan): Antonio Guillem/123RF; **45** (Vivian Grace Marr): Akiyoko/123RF; **45** (cake): Damedeeso/123RF; **46**: Gerain0812/Shutterstock; **47**: View Apart/Shutterstock; **48** (T): Djomas/Shutterstock; **48** (bee): Alekss/123RF; **48** (Sami): Viorel Sima/Shutterstock; **53**: Daniel Ernst/123RF; **55**: R.M/Nunes/Shutterstock; **56**: Szefei/Shutterstock; **57**: Pindyurin Vasily/Shutterstock; **59**: Jasminko Ibrakovic/Shutterstock; **60** (wall clock, multiple uses): Arvind Singh Negi/Red Reef Design Studio/Pearson India Education Services Pvt.Ltd; **61** (umbrella): Basheera Designs/Shutterstock; **61** (sun): Basheera Designs/Shutterstock; **61** (snowman): Basheera Designs/Shutterstock; **61** (snowflakes): Basheera Designs/Shutterstock; **65**: Fizkes/Shutterstock; **67**: Odua Images/Shutterstock; **69**: DavideAngelini/Shutterstock; **71**: Elnur Amikishiyev/123RF; **72**: Mimagephotography/Shutterstock; **73**: Rommel Canlas/Shutterstock; **74**: Refluo/Shutterstock; **76** (shower): Dmitry Bruskov/Shutterstock; **76** (tub): Morphart Creation/Shutterstock; **76** (dog): Billion Photos/Shutterstock; **76** (cat): Haru/Shutterstock; **76** (coffee): Valentyn Volkov/Shutterstock; **76** (tea): Sergey Rusakov/123RF; **76** (apartment building): NAAN/Shutterstock; **76** (house): Ratthaphong Ekariyasap/Shutterstock; **76** (blue SUV): Svitac/123RF; **76** (red pickup): Artem Konovalov/Shutterstock; **77** (tennis): Zimmytws/123RF; **77** (soccer): Grafner/123RF; **77** (Spanish): Maridav/Shutterstock; **77** (English): Woaiss/Shutterstock; **77** (computer): KitchBain/Shutterstock; **77** (typewriter): Nito500/123RF; **77** (umbrella): Luisa Leal Photography/Shutterstock; **77** (raincoat):